LEVANT SUPPLEMENTARY SERIES
VOLUME 12

THE MEDIEVAL AND OTTOMAN HAJJ ROUTE IN JORDAN

An Archaeological and Historical Study

Andrew Petersen

with contributions by

Michael Diboll, Dennis Genequand, Tony Grey,
St John Simpson and Mehmet Tütüncü

OXBOW BOOKS
Oxford and Oakville

Published jointly by
the Council for British Research in the Levant
and
Oxbow Books, Oxford, UK

ISBN 978-1-84217-502-6

Cover image: View of 18th century Ottoman fort at Mudawwara, southern Jordan. Photograph by the author.

This book is available direct from:

Oxbow Books, Oxford, UK
(Phone: 01865-241249; Fax: 01865-794449)

and

The David Brown Book Company
PO Box 511, Oakville, CT 06779, USA
(Phone: 860-945-9329; Fax: 860-945-9468)

or from our website

www.oxbowbooks.com

A CIP record for this book is available from the British Library

Library of Congress Cataloging-in-Publication Data

Petersen, Andrew.
The medieval and Ottoman hajj route in Jordan : an archaeological and historical study / Andrew Petersen ; with contributions by Michael Diboll ... [et al.].
    p. cm. -- (Levant supplementary series ; v. 12)
  Includes bibliographical references and index.
  ISBN 978-1-84217-502-6
  1. Muslim pilgrims and pilgrimages--Jordan--History. 2. Jordan--Antiquities. 3. Fortification--Jordan--History. 4. Excavations (Archaeology)--Jordan. I. Council for British Research in the Levant. II. Title.
  DS153.3.P47 2012
  933'.5--dc23
                    2012012271

Printed and bound in Great Britain by
Short Run Press, Exeter

This book is for Heather, Jamie and Rowan,
who kept me going on this journey

Contents

List of maps   vii
List of figures   viii
List of plates   ix
List of tables   xiii
Acknowledgements   xiv
Preface   xv

PART I: INTRODUCTION

1   Introduction   1

2   Principal Written Sources   4

3   The Medieval Hajj Route through Syria and Jordan   9

4   Early Ottoman Arabia and the Syrian Hajj Route   17

5   The Ottoman Hajj Route: Motivation and Ideology   20

6   Travelling on the Darb al-Hajj   29

7   Ottoman Fortification in Palestine and Transjordan   38

8   The Hajj Route in Syria   51

PART II: THE FORTS

9   Catalogue of Hajj Forts in Jordan   57

10 Catalogue of Forts in Saudi Arabia   130

PART III: THE ARCHAEOLOGY – EXCAVATION, FINDS AND INSCRIPTIONS

11 Arabic and Turkish Inscriptions on the Darb al-Hajj al-Shami   155
    Mehmet Tütüncü and Andrew Petersen with a contribution by Gotfried Hagen

12 Excavations at Qal'at 'Unaiza   164

13 Ceramics from Qal'at 'Unaiza and other Hajj Forts in Jordan   174
    Tony Grey and Andrew Petersen

14 Finds from Qal'at 'Unaiza and other Ottoman Forts on the Darb al-Hajj   190
    St John Simpson

PART IV: CONCLUSION

15   Conclusions   209

APPENDIX 1 – Report Presented to His Highness Muhammad Ali Pasha, Viceroy of Egypt, 1828   214
        Translated by Michael V. Diboll

APPENDIX 2 – The Early Islamic Lintel from Qal'at al-Dab'a   223
        Denis Genequand

Bibliography   227
Index   237

List of maps

Map 1. Pilgrimage routes of Arabia.

Map 2. The Medieval Hajj route through Jordan based on the account of Ibn Battuta.

Map 3. Ottoman Arabia.

Map 4. Hajj route showing locations of forts in the 16th century.

Map 5. Hajj route showing locations of forts in the 18th century.

Map 6. Sixteenth century fortress network in Palestine and Trans-Jordan.

Map 7. Map of Syrian Hajj route with areas of basalt.

Map 8. Schematic plan of Hajj route to show relationship of forts to tribal migrations.

List of figures

Fig. 1. Plan of fortress at Muzayrib in southern Syria. After Schumacher 1886 and Meinicke 1996.

Fig. 2. Plan of Qasr Doshaq, near Shawbak, southern Jordan. Plan after Brünnow and Domaszewski 1905.

Fig. 3. Plan of Qal'at Ras al-'Ayn, Palestine.

Fig. 4. Plan of Qal'at Burak near Bethlehem. After Hawari *et al.* 2000.

Fig. 5. Plan of Qal'at al-'Aqaba in Jordan, before recent restorations and excavations.

Fig. 6. Plan of Ottoman fortress at Quseir on the Red Sea coast of Egypt. After Le Quesne 2004.

Fig. 7. Plan of Qal'at al-Sai in northern Sudan. After Alexander 1997.

Fig. 8. Ground floor plan of Qasr Shebib at Zerka in northern Jordan.

Fig. 9. Ground floor plan of Medieval fort at Zizia in Jordan.

Fig. 10. First floor plan of Medieval fort at Zizia, in Jordan, with modern additions.

Fig. 11. Plan of fort and reservoir at Zizia in Jordan.

Fig. 12. Plan of fort and cisterns at Qal'at Dab'a in Jordan.

Fig. 13. Ground floor plan of Qal'at Dab'a in Jordan.

Fig. 14. First floor plan of Qal'at Dab'a in Jordan.

Fig. 15. Detail of rainspout from Qal'at Dab'a in Jordan.

Fig. 16. Ground floor plan of Qal'at Qatrana in Jordan.

Fig. 17. First floor plan of Qal'at Qatrana in Jordan.

Fig. 18. Upper floor plan of Qal'at Qatrana in Jordan.

Fig. 19. Location plan of fort, cistern and wadi at Qal'at Qatrana in Jordan.

Fig. 20. Location plan of fort, cistern, bridge and wadi at Qal'at al-Hasa in Jordan.

Fig. 21. Ground floor plan of Qal'at al-Hasa in Jordan.

Fig. 22. First floor plan of Qal'at al-Hasa in Jordan.

Fig. 23. Plan of cistern at Qal'at al-Hasa in Jordan.

Fig. 24. Elevation drawing of bridge over Wadi al-Hasa in Jordan.

Fig. 25. Plan of bridge over Wadi al-Hasa in Jordan.

Fig. 26. Location plan of Ottoman fort and early building at 'Unaiza in Jordan.

Fig. 27. Plan of Ottoman building in relation to early building at 'Unaiza in Jordan.

Fig. 28. Reconstruction of early building at 'Unaiza in Jordan.

Fig. 29. 'Unaiza, Jordan. Ottoman fort plan of ground floor with phases of construction indicated.

Fig. 30. 'Unaiza, Jordan. Ottoman fort plan of first floor with phases indicated.

Fig. 31. Ma'an, Jordan. Location plan of fort and cistern.

Fig. 32. Ma'an, Jordan. Plan of ground floor of Ottoman fort.

Fig. 33. Ma'an, Jordan. Plan of first floor of Ottoman fort.

Fig. 34. Ma'an, Jordan. Plan and section of cistern.

Fig. 35. Fassu'a, Jordan. Location plan of fort and cisterns.

Fig. 36. Fassu'a, Jordan. Plan of ground floor of Ottoman fort.

Fig. 37. Fasuu'a, Jordan. Plan of first floor of Ottoman fort.

Fig. 38. Mudawwara, Jordan. Plan of ground floor of Ottoman fort.

Fig. 39. Mudawwara, Jordan. Plan of first floor.

Fig. 40. Plan of cisterns at Mudawwara, Jordan.

Fig. 41. Plan of setlement at Tabuk, Saudi Arabia. After Jaussen and Savignac 1997.

Fig. 42. Plan of cisterns at Tabuk. After Jaussen and Savignac 1997.

Fig. 43. Plan of fort and cisterns at al-Ukhaydhir. After Jaussen and Savignac 1997.

Fig. 44. Plan of ground floor of fort at Medain Saleh. After Jaussen and Savignac 1997.

Fig. 45. Plan of first floor of fort at Medain Saleh. After Jaussen and Savignac 1997.

Fig. 46. 'Unaiza site plan showing location of trenches.

Fig. 47. 'Unaiza, Area A, section and elevation.

Fig. 48. 'Unaiza, Area B elevation and sections.

Fig. 49. 'Unaiza, Area B plan.

Fig. 50. 'Unaiza, Area E, plan and section.

Fig. 51. 'Unaiza, Area F sections.

Fig. 52. Fineware ceramics.

Fig. 53. Coarseware ceramics.

Fig. 54. Tobacco pipes from 'Unaiza F2 and F3.

Fig. 55. Tobacco pipes 'Unaiza.

Fig. 56. Tobacco pipes from al-Hasa, Mudawwara and Dab'a.

Fig. 57. Glass bangles from 'Unaiza F2 and F4.

Fig. 58. Glass bangles and beads.

Fig. 59. Metalwork.

List of plates

Plate 1. Doshaq southern Jordan near Shawbak 1898 (courtesy of the University of Princeton).

Plate 2. Bridge on Hajj route near Muzayrib, built during reign of Mamluk Sultan Baybars in mid-13th century (Creswell Archive EA.CA.5383).

Plate 3. Qal'at Ras al-'Ayn, Ottoman fortress (1988).

Plate 4. Qal'at Ras al-'Ayn, Ottoman fortress, detail of south-west tower (1988).

Plate 5. Qal'at al-'Aqaba, interior of courtyard looking north towards entrance (1985).

Plate 6. Qal'at al-'Aqaba, interior looking south-east (1985).

Plate 7. Qal'at al-'Aqaba, south-west tower (1985).

Plate 8. Qal'at al-'Aqaba, gateway exterior, with Hashemite arms above entrance (1985).

Plate 9. Qal'at al-'Aqaba, gateway, exterior detail showing 16th century Ottoman inscription (1985).

Plate 10. Qal'at al-'Aqaba, interior of courtyard west range with south-west tower in background (1985).

Plate 11. Sulayman I mosque in Damascus (1554–60) (Tony Grey 1998).

Plate 12. Takiyya complex, Damascus, viewed from north (Photograph B_083 courtesy of the Gertrude Bell Archive, University of Newcastle-Upon-Tyne).

Plate 13. Interior of Takiyya complex, Damascus (Photograph B_081 courtesy of the Gertrude Bell Archive, University of Newcastle-Upon-Tyne).

Plate 14. Sinaniyya Mosque (1591 AD), located 300 m south of the citadel in Damascus (Photograph courtesy of Stefan Weber).

Plate 15. Darwishiyya mosque (1574–75 AD), located 100 m south of the citadel in Damascus (Photograph courtesy of Stefan Weber).

Plate 16. Khan Assad Pasha (1751–53 AD), nine-domed khan located in the Suq al Buzuriyya, Damascus (Photograph courtesy of Stefan Weber).

Plate 17. Mafraq fort, distant view (courtesy of the Israel Antiquities Authority).

Plate 18. Mafraq fort, exterior with entrance to right. Note entrance with box machicolation above (courtesy of the Israel Antiquities Authority).

Plate 19. Mafraq fort, interior (courtesy of the Israel Antiquities Authority).

Plate 20. Mafraq fort, interior with gateway in centre (courtesy of the Israel Antiquities Authority).

Plate 21. Qasr Shebib, Zerka, north face with entrance in foreground (1986).

Plate 22. Qasr Shebib, Zerka, west face of fort (1986).

Plate 23. Zizia fort from the south-east (1986).

Plate 24. Zizia fort from the east (1986).

Plate 25. Zizia fort from the north (1986)

Plate 26. Zizia fort, interior upper floor showing arches leading to stairs up and down (1986).

Plate 27. Zizia fort, interior upper floor detail of arch and lintel over doorway (1986).

Plate 28. Zizia, interior of upper floor showing doorways and niches (1986).

Plate 29. Zizia reservoir from fort, showing Desert highway in background (1986).

Plate 30. Zizia fort, Desert Police camp (1986).

Plate 31. Qal'at Dab'a, exterior from West in 1898, by Rudolf-Ernst Brünnow (courtesy of Princeton University).

Plate 32. Qal'at Dab'a, interior of courtyard in 1898, by Rudolf-Ernst Brünnow (courtesy of Princeton University).

Plate 33. Qal'at Dab'a, interior of courtyard in 1898, by Rudolf-Ernst Brünnow (courtesy of Princeton University).

Plate 34. Qal'at Dab'a, from north-east in 1907, by Jaussen and Savignac (courtesy of the École Biblique).

Plate 35. Qal'at Dab'a, from the south in 1907, with graves in foreground, by Jaussen and Savignac (courtesy of the École Biblique).

Plate 36. Qal'at Dab'a, east face with entrance (2006).

Plate 37. Qal'at Dab'a, west face with buttress (2006).

Plate 38. Qal'at Dab'a, cistern to north of fort (2006).

Plate 39. Qal'at Dab'a, gateway interior north side with doorway and paving visible (2006).

Plate 40. Qal'at Dab'a, interior of courtyard with stairs to first floor and arch over the gateway (2006).

Plate 41. Qal'at Dab'a, interior with roofless room in foreground and gateway visible to left (2006).

Plate 42. Qal'at Dab'a, interior of roofless room on south side of courtyard with remains of curve vault visible to left (2006).

Plate 43. Qal'at Dab'a, interior of vaulted room to north of gateway (2006).

Plate 44. Qal'at Qatrana, fort and cistern from east in 1898, by Rudolf-Ernst Brünnow (courtesy of Princeton University).

Plate 45. Qal'at Qatrana, cistern in 1898, by Rudolf-Ernst Brünnow (courtesy of Princeton University).

Plate 46. Qal'at Qatrana, south façade with entrance (1986).

Plate 47. Qal'at Qatrana, detail of entrance, note slight horseshoe profile of arch (1986).

Plate 48. Qal'at Qatrana, interior entrance passage with roof of corbelled stone beams (1986).

Plate 49. Qal'at Qatrana, interior with *iwans* on north side of courtyard (1986).

Plate 50. Qal'at Qatrana, interior courtyard from upper floor looking west (1986).

Plate 51. Qal'at Qatrana, interior north-east corner (1986).

Plate 52. Qal'at Qatrana, interior looking west (1986).

Plate 53. Qalʻat Qatrana, interior looking south towards entrance (1986).

Plate 54. Qalʻat Qatrana, water inlet from wadi (1986).

Plate 55. Qalʻat Qatrana, settling tank next to large cistern (1986).

Plate 56. Qalʻat al-Hasa, bridge from west in 1898, by Rudolf-Ernst Brünnow (courtesy of Princeton University).

Plate 57. Qalʻat al-Hasa, road surface on bridge in 1898, by Rudolf-Ernst Brünnow (courtesy of Princeton University).

Plate 58. Qalʻat al-Hasa, bridge from east in 1898, by Rudolf-Ernst Brünnow (courtesy of Princeton University).

Plate 59. Qalʻat al-Hasa, interior of fort in 1898 looking south, by Rudolf-Ernst Brünnow (courtesy of Princeton University).

Plate 60. Qalʻat al-Hasa, interior in 1898 looking north by Rudolf-Ernst Brünnow (courtesy of Princeton University).

Plate 61. Qalʻat al-Hasa, interior looking north-east in 1907, by Jaussen and Savignac (courtesy of the École Biblique).

Plate 62. Qalʻat al-Hasa, bridge from west in 1907, by Jaussen and Savignac (courtesy of the École Biblique).

Plate 63. Qalʻat al-Hasa, exterior with entrance and collapsed north wall (1986).

Plate 64. Qalʻat al-Hasa, exterior south wall (1986).

Plate 65. Qalʻat al-Hasa, exterior east wall (1986).

Plate 66. Qalʻat al-Hasa, exterior west wall (1986).

Plate 67. Qalʻat al-Hasa, interior north wall with remains of upper floor (1986).

Plate 68. Qalʻat al-Hasa, exterior with south wall with remains of projecting casement (1986).

Plate 69. Qalʻat al-Hasa, exterior with west wall with projecting casement (1986).

Plate 70. Qalʻat al-Hasa, interior looking south with *mihrab* visible in centre of first floor (1986).

Plate 71. Qalʻat al-Hasa, detail of *mihrab* (1986).

Plate 72. Qalʻat al-Hasa, door jamb with scroll shaped corbel (1986).

Plate 73. Qalʻat al-Hasa, bridge from west (1986).

Plate 74. Qalʻat al-Hasa, bridge, detail of west face of north arch (1986).

Plate 75. Qalʻat al-Hasa, interior looking north (2006).

Plate 76. Qalʻat al-Hasa, exterior from north-west (2006).

Plate 77. Qalʻat al-Hasa, interior long gallery on south side of courtyard looking west (2006).

Plate 78. Qalʻat al-Hasa, bridge from east (2006).

Plate 79. Qalʻat al-Hasa, interior courtyard after restoration looking south (2006).

Plate 80. Qalʻat ʻUnaiza, with entrance from east (1986).

Plate 81. Qalʻat ʻUnaiza, from west with remains of early building in foreground (1986).

Plate 82. Qalʻat ʻUnaiza, north side (1986).

Plate 83. Qalʻat ʻUnaiza, south side (1986).

Plate 84. Qalʻat ʻUnaiza, detail of projecting opening on exterior of south wall (1986).

Plate 85. Qalʻat ʻUnaiza, interior with entrance looking east (1986).

Plate 86. Qalʻat ʻUnaiza, north side of entrance with plaster decoration visible (1986).

Plate 87. Qalʻat ʻUnaiza, interior looking west (1986).

Plate 88. Qalʻat ʻUnaiza, interior looking south (1986).

Plate 89. Qalʻat Maʻan, interior of courtyard looking south (1986).

Plate 90. Qalʻat Maʻan, interior looking north. Note prison bars (1986).

Plate 91. Qalʻat Maʻan, detail of decoration above doorway (2006).

Plate 92. Qalʻat Maʻan, decoration above doorway (2006).

Plate 93. Qalʻat Maʻan, south face with machicolation and original entrance below (2006).

Plate 94. Qalʻat Maʻan, interior of courtyard looking east (2006).

Plate 95. Qalʻat Maʻan, exterior of fort from north (2006).

Plate 96. Qalʻat Maʻan, exterior from east (2006).

Plate 97. Qalʻat Maʻan, detail of Turkish inscription above entrance (2006).

Plate 98. Qalʻat Fassuʻa, north façade with entrance (1986).

Plate 99. Qalʻat Fassuʻa, corner tower detail (1986).

Plate 100. Qalʻat Fassuʻa, entrance (1986).

Plate 101. Qalʻat Fassuʻa, remains of inscription above entrance (1986).

Plate 102. Qalʻat Fassuʻa, detail of door jamb with beam slot for securing door visible behind (1986).

Plate 103. Qalʻat Fassuʻa, view of cisterns from within entrance (1986).

Plate 104. Qalʻat Fassuʻa, interior looking north with gateway below (1986).

Plate 105. Qalʻat Fassuʻa, interior looking south with prayer room and *mihrab* in centre (1986).

Plate 106. Qalʻat Fassuʻa, interior looking east (1986).

Plate 107. Qalʻat Fassuʻa, interior looking west (1986).

Plate 108. Qalʻat Fassuʻa, detail of *mihrab* on first floor (1986).

Plate 109. Qalʻat Fassuʻa, detail of gun slit (1986).

Plate 110. Qalʻat Fassuʻa, interior west staircase (1986).

Plate 111. Qalʻat Fassuʻa, fort and cisterns from north (1986).

Plate 112. Qalʻat Fassuʻa, cisterns outside fort (1986).

Plate 113. Qalʻat Fassuʻa, detail of cistern (1986).

Plate 114. Qalʻat Fassuʻa, from east (2006).

Plate 115. Qalʻat Fassuʻa, from west with location marker in foreground (2006).

Plate 116. Qalʻat Fassuʻa, view from south (2006).

Plate 117. Qalʻat Fassuʻa, view from south (2006).

Plate 118. Qalʻat Fassuʻa, illegal excavation of foundations (2006).

Plate 119. Qalʻat Fassuʻa, prayer room on ground floor (2006).

Plate 120. Qalʻat Fassuʻa, wall above entrance after removal of inscription panels (2006).

Plate 121. Qalʻat Fassuʻa, *mihrab* in middle of prayer room on upper floor (2006).

Plate 122. Qalʻat Mudawwara, north side with entrance (1986).

Plate 123. Qalʻat Mudawwara, west wall (1986).

Plate 124. Qalʻat Mudawwara, south side (1986).

Plate 125. Qalʻat Mudawwara, east side (1986).

Plate 126. Qalʻat Mudawwara, detail of projecting corner tower at north-east corner (1986).

Plate 127. Qalʻat Mudawwara, machicolation on north side above entrance (1986).

Plate 128. Qalʻat Mudawwara, interior looking north (1986).

Plate 129. Qalʻat Mudawwara, interior with domed chamber from east (1986).

Plate 130. Qalʻat Mudawwara (2006).

Plate 131. Qalʻat Mudawwara, foundations (2006).

Plate 132. Qalʻat Mudawwara, east side after collapse (2006).

Plate 133. Qalʻat Mudawwara, interior with entrance (2006).

Plate 134. Dhat al-Hajj, interior of fort in 1907, by Jaussen and Savignac (courtesy of the École Biblique).

Plate 135. Dhat al-Hajj fort, from railway station in 1907, by Jaussen and Savignac (courtesy of the École Biblique).

Plate 136. Dhat al-Hajj, from south-west in 1907, by Jaussen and Savignac (courtesy of the École Biblique).

Plate 137. Tabuk, exterior of fort with entrance in 1907, by Jaussen and Savignac (courtesy of the École Biblique).

Plate 138. Tabuk, exterior, west face with cisterns in 1907, by Jaussen and Savignac (courtesy of the École Biblique).

Plate 139. Tabuk, interior of fort in 1907, by Jaussen and Savignac (courtesy of the École Biblique).

Plate 140. Tabuk, south-east corner of fort in 1907, by Jaussen and Savignac (courtesy of the École Biblique).

Plate 141. Qal'at al-Ukhaydhir, from north in 1907, by Jaussen and Savignac (courtesy of the École Biblique).

Plate 142. Qal'at al-Ukhaydhir, from south-west in 1907, by Jaussen and Savignac (courtesy of the École Biblique).

Plate 143. Qal'at al-Mu'azzam, in 1907, by Jaussen and Savignac (courtesy of the École Biblique).

Plate 144. Dar al-Hamra, in 1907, by Jaussen and Savignac (courtesy of the École Biblique).

Plate 145. Medain Saleh, exterior in 1907, by Jaussen and Savignac (courtesy of the École Biblique).

Plate 146. Qal'at 'Unaiza from the Desert Highway with Jabal 'Unaiza behind (2002).

Plate 147. Qal'at 'Unaiza from the north with modern Bedouin cemetery in foreground (2002).

Plate 148. Excavations in progress at Qal'at 'Unaiza (2002).

Plate 149. Excavations at Qal'at 'Unaiza. Trench A (2002).

Plate 150. Excavations at Qal'at 'Unaiza. Trench B (2002).

Plate 151. Excavations at Qal'at 'Unaiza. Trench B showing wall (B2) projecting from wall of Ottoman fort (2002).

Plate 152. Excavations at Qal'at 'Unaiza. Trench B from west (2002).

Plate 153. Excavations at Qal'at 'Unaiza. Trench C (2002).

Plate 154. Excavations at Qal'at 'Unaiza. Trench D (2002).

Plate 155. Excavations at Qal'at 'Unaiza. Trench E (2002).

Plate 156. Excavations at Qal'at 'Unaiza. Trench F (2002).

Plate 157. 'Unaiza, F1 ceramics. A = Batavian rim sherd; B = Pearl ware, English?; C = Chinese Imari body sherd.

Plate 158. 'Unaiza F2, ceramics. A = rim sherd with green glaze; B = square cut foot ring with patchy green glaze; C = body sherd of Batavian bowl; D–E = body sherds of Chinese Imari bowl; F = ring base of Kutahya frit ware bowl with makers mark; G = buff ware body sherd with transparent glaze; H = body sherd olive green glaze with buff fabric; I = buff ware bowl body sherd with incised line.

Plate 159. 'Unaiza F3. A = body sherd Chinese blue-on-white with irridesence; B = Chinese blue-on-white base of bowl; C = Chinese blue-on-white body sherd; D = Kutahya ware bowl fragment with white glaze over frit body; E–F = Chinese Imari body sherds; G–H = body sherds Chinese blue-on white.

Plate 160. 'Unaiza F4, ceramics. A–E = Chinese cup fragments with powder blue ground and gilding (for detail see Plate 161); F = blue-on-white Chinese porcelain bowl rim sherd; G = Kutahya blue-on-white bowl fragment; H = Chinese celadon sherd; I = Batavian ware base sherd; J = Chinese blue-on-white; K–M = 3 Kutahya ware blue-on-white frit body; N–P three body sherds alkaline blue glaze on red fabric; Q = body sherd of red ware with alkaline green glaze.

Plate 161. 'Unaiza F4. Rim of Chinese cup with powder blue ground and gilding.

Plate 162. 'Unaiza F5. A = rim sherd dark green glaze on reddish body; B = body sherd of buff ware jug with pale green glaze; C–F laminating red ware with dark green glaze; G = Chinese blue-on-white bowl fragment; H = body sherd Kutahya ware with decorative band; I = rim of Chinese porcelain cup with powder blue ground; J–K two body sherds of Kutahya ware blue-on-white bowl; L= Batavain ware cup base with *famille rose* design.

Plate 163. 'Unaiza, B4 ceramics. Rim sherd, Chinese blue-on-white.

Plate 164. 'Unaiza, F1 ceramics. A = foot stand of reduced ware bowl; B = flat base of hand made cooking pot; C = foot stand of large bowl with glaze over white slip; D = foot stand of reduced ware bowl.

Plate 165. 'Unaiza F1, ceramics. A = jar handle orange/red ware; B = broken tubular spout orange/red ware; C = handle stump orange/red ware.

Plate 166. 'Unaiza F1. Various jar body sherds in reduced buff ware.

Plate 167. 'Unaiza F1. Body sherd of jar buff ware with black exterior and ridged decoration (Fig. 52, No. 11).

Plate 168. 'Unaiza Trench F2. A = base of amphora buff ware; B = body sherd pale yellow glaze on hard buff fabric; C = coarse reddish ware body sherd; D = coarse reddish ware body sherd; E–K = body sherds buff or cream fabric.

Plate 169. 'Unaiza F3, ceramics. A–L = assorted body sherds in reduced coarse ware; M = base of amphora in buff coarse ware; N–P = coarse ware jar sherds.

Plate 170. 'Unaiza, B1 ceramics. A = tubular handle; B = buff ware reduced fired body sherd; C = buff ware reduced fired body sherd; D = buff ware reduced fired body sherd; E = buff ware reduced fired body sherd; F = buff ware reduced fired body sherd.

Plate 171. 'Unaiza, B4 ceramics. A = base of buff ware jar; B = wheel made body sherd, reduced ware; C = body sherd, reduced ware; D = rim of possible jar buff ware; E = body sherd reduced ware; F = body sherd reduced ware.

Plate 172. 'Unaiza, C1 ceramics. A = ridged orange/red ware body sherd; B = plain orange/red ware body sherd; C = lid rim sherd orange/red ware; D = coarse ware buff body sherd.

Plate 173. 'Unaiza. Rim of storage Jar from Trench F context 002 (*c.f.* Fig. 53 no. 1).

Plate 174. Qal'at Mudawwara. A = blue-on-white Kutahya ware body sherd; B = rim sherd Kutahya blue-on-white; C = alkaline blue-green glaze on reddish fabric.

Plate 175. Qal'at Mudawwara. A = rim of collared jar in red/orange ware; B = rim sherd of necked jar in pale reddish ware with traces of green glaze; C = body sherd of cooking pot in coarse red ware; D = rim of bowl with incurving rim and traces clear glaze over red ware body; E–F = rim and body sherd of coarse red ware bowl with flat rim; G = fine red-orange ware body sherd; H = body sherd buff ware over fired to green; I–J two body sherds with traces of green painted decoration; K = body sherd reduced grey ware with combed decoration; L = body sherd red fabric with green glaze over white slip.

Plate 176. Dab'a. A = Body sherd of green lead glaze on red body; B = handle stem alkaline turquoise glaze; C = rim sherd Chinese blue-on-white.

Plate 177. Qal'at al-Hasa. A = foot stand base blue-on-white Kutahya frit body; B = cup base Imari style porcelain south-east Asia; C = moulded ware imitation Meissen.

Plate 178. Qal'at al-Hasa. A = ring base fragment orange/red ware; B = orange slip painted ware body sherd; C = bowl rim in coarse wheel made buff ware; D = buff ware with incised decoration; E = body sherd with ridges red/orange ware; F = buff ware fragment of jar neck; G = reduced ware body sherd with handle stump; H–J light buff body sherds covered with turquoise alkaline glaze.

Plate 179. 'Unaiza F2, glass bangles and beads. A = glass bangle in two parts (Table 16, Cat No. 35); B = glass bangle (Table 16, Cat No. 37); C= glass bangle (Table 16, Cat No. 48); D = clear glass bead (Table 15, Cat No. 29); E = square blue glass bead (Table 15, Cat No. 32); F = blue glass bangle (Table 16, Cat No. 42); G = orange glass bangle (Table 16, Cat No. 33).

Plate 180. 'Unaiza F5, glass bangles. A = glass bangle black (Table 16, Cat No. 39); B = blue glass bangle (Table 16, Cat No. 43); C = glass bangle, black with marvered decoration (Table 16, Cat No. 49); D = green glass bangle (Table 16, Cat No. 46); E = black glass bangle (Table 16, Cat No. 41); F = black glass bangle (Table 16, Cat No. 40).

Plate 181. 'Uniaza F4, glass beads and bangles. A = fragment of black glass bangle (Table 16, Cat No. 38); B = glass bead (Table 15, Cat No. 35); C = glass bead (Table 15, Cat No. 31); D = green glass bangle (Table 16, Cat No. 47).

Plate 182. 'Uniaza F4, metalwork. A = copper alloy tweezers (Table 20, Cat No. 55); B = copper alloy sheet (Table 20, Cat No. 58); C = copper alloy sheet (Table 20, Cat No. 59); D = copper alloy sheet (Table 20, Cat No. 60); E = copper alloy bell (Table 20, Cat No. 54).

Plate 183. Metalwork from 'Unaiza F2. A = copper alloy sheet fragment (Table 20, Cat No. 62); B = lead musket ball (Table 17, Cat No. 50); C = copper alloy band with attached coarse khaki canvas (Table 17, Cat No. 56); D = copper coin (Table 18, Cat No. 51); E = copper alloy sheet (Table 20, Cat No. 61).

Plate 184. 'Unaiza, F1 metalwork. Iron hoop fragment (Table 20; Cat No. 63).

Plate 185. A = Textile probably hemp with traces of red dye, possibly part of storage sack; B = matted piece of fabric made of vegetable fibre, possibly used as padding.

Plate 186. Udruh, Ottoman period fort with entrance (1986).

Plate 187. Udruh, Ottoman period fort detail of box machicolation above entrance (1986).

Plate 188. Udruh, Ottoman period fort rear (1986).

Plate 189. Udruh, Ottoman period fort interior with gun slots (1986).

Plate 190. Udruh, Ottoman period fort first floor interior (1986).

Plate 191. The lintel over the gateway of Qal'at al-Daba'a (Photo: Denis Genequand).

Plate 192. Dab'a Lintel. Detail of the right part of the lintel (Photo: Denis Genequand).

Plate 193. Fragment of a carved lintel from Zizia (Photo: Denis Genequand).

List of tables

Table 1. Syrian Hajj caravanserais north of Damascus based on Sauvaget (1937).

Table 2. Sequence of openings in the walls of Qatrana Fort.

Table 3. Hajj Fort inscriptions.

Table 4. Trench B contexts.

Table 5. Trench C contexts.

Table 6. Trench D contexts.

Table 7. Trench E contexts.

Table 8. Trench F contexts.

Table 9. Catalogue of ceramic smoking pipes from 'Unaiza.

Table 10. Catalogue of ceramic smoking pipes from Qal'at al-Hasa.

Table 11. Catalogue of ceramic smoking pipes from Qal'at Dab'a.

Table 12. Catalogue of ceramic smoking pipes from Qal'at al-Mudawwarra.

Table 13. Gaming piece from 'Unaiza.

Table 14. Glassware from 'Unaiza.

Table 15. Glass beads from 'Unaiza.

Table 16. Glass bangles from 'Unaiza.

Table 17. Military equipment from 'Unaiza.

Table 18. Coins from 'Unaiza.

Table 19. Metalwork from 'Unaiza.

Table 20. Environmental finds from 'Unaiza.

Table 21. Charcoal fragments from 'Unaiza.

Acknowledgements

The fieldwork and research on which this book is based would not have been possible without the assistance of a number of organizations and people. I would like to express my deep appreciation to all and hope that the resulting publication does some justice to their efforts.

Organizations

None of this work would have been possible without the continuing institutional support of the Department of Antiquities, Jordan. The major sponsors of the project were the Council for British Research in the Levant and the Barakat Trust Oxford, both of whom not only provided financial support, but considerable encouragement. In addition, the United Arab Emirates University supported fieldwork in 2006 through an Individual Research Grant. In the early stages of the project I was assisted by travel grants from the British Institute at 'Amman, the British School of Archaeology in Jerusalem and the Palestine Exploration Fund. Further research was supported by the Skilliter Award for Ottoman Studies; Clare Hall, Cambridge; Pembroke College, Oxford; and the Vaughn Cornish Bequest Oxford University. A Turkish Government Scholarship introduced me to Ottoman Turkish and the splendour of Ottoman architecture in the Imperial capital. HSBC (formerly British Bank of the Middle East) sponsored an exhibition on the Hajj forts which was shown at the Oriental Museum in Durham and the School of Oriental and African Studies in London. A number of institutions were generous with their archives giving access and permission to publish photographs including, the Gertrude Bell Photographic Archive at the University of Newcastle-Upon-Tyne; Princeton University; the Israel Antiquities Authority; and the École Biblique. The Staatsbibliothek zu Berlin gave me a copy of their manuscript of Murtada ibn 'Alawan and the British Library sent me a copy of Bianchi's translation of Mehmed Edib. In the final stages of the preparation of this book The British Museum enabled me to revisit some of the forts.

People

This project was carried out entirely with the help of volunteers who gave their time to help record and research this unique aspect of Jordan's heritage. The fieldwork was carried out with the help of the following people, Matthew Thompson (1986), Ifan Edwards (2006), Pierre Brun (2002), Cherry Pickles (1986), Ahmad Shurma (2002), Ahmad al-Shami (2006), Heather Nixon (2006), Rowan Petersen (2006) and Marinus Petersen (2006). In December 2010 I was fortunate to revisit Jordan in the company of Venetia Porter and Dudley Hubbard, both of whom developed considerable enthusiasm for the forts. Other people who provided assistance in Jordan include, Rauf Abu Jaber, Andrew Garrard, Stephen Hart, Nadia al-Qaisi and David Kennedy. In the early stages of report writing I benefited from the advice and assistance of a number of people including, Michael Meinicke, Alastair Northedge, John Ruffle, John Healey, Rex Smith and Bob Petersen. The preparation of this report was made possible with the support of St John Simpson, Mehmet Tütüncü, Denis Genequand, Gotfried Hagen, Tony Grey and Mike Diboll, all of whom took the time to lend their expertise to the project. I am particularly grateful to Gotfried Hagen for collaborating with Mehmet Tütüncü on deciphering the inscription at Ma'an. I would like to thank all those who helped with the procurement of photographs and other images, in particular Mark Jackson and Stefan Weber. At very short notice Mark Jackson provided photographs from the Gertude Bell Archive and Stefan Weber generously allowed me to use his own photographs of Damascus. In the final stages leading to the production of this volume I benefited from the advice and encouragement of Hamida Abdullah Alireza, Alan Walmsley and Timothy Insoll, and the editorial expertise of Hilary Meeks and Caroline Middleton.

Preface

The principal aim of this work is to provide an architectural and archaeological documentation of the forts and associated facilities on the Syrian Hajj route.

The volume is comprised of four parts. Part I discusses the historical development of the Syrian Hajj from the Medieval to the Ottoman period, as well as aspects of the social and political context of the Hajj. Part II is a catalogue of the forts along the Hajj route in both Jordan and Saudi Arabia, as well as a chapter on the inscriptions. Part III discusses the archaeological excavations undertaken at Qal'at 'Unaiza, as well as surface finds from the other forts. Part IV comprises the conclusion as well as two appendices; Appendix 1 is a translation of a previously unpublished early 19th century survey of the Syrian Hajj route, whilst Appendix 2 is a discussion of an important early Islamic lintel incorporated into the Ottoman fort of Dab'a.

Parts of some of the chapters have previously been published in a different form. Chapter 3 incorporates part of a paper published in the *Festschrift* for Professor Urban Vermeulen (Petersen 2008a). Chapter 4 is based on a paper given at a British Academy workshop on *Ottoman Frontiers* which took place in London in 2006 (Petersen 2008c). Chapter 5 is based on a paper given at a workshop on *Power in the Age of the Sultanates* held in Amman in 2005 (Petersen 2008b). Chapter 6 is based on an unpublished paper given at a workshop on *Theoretical Archaeology Group* in York in 2006. Chapter 7 is a based on a paper given at the Archaeology of Jordan Conference held in Irbid in 1992 (Petersen 1995).

To facilitate reading the text no diacritical marks have been used. Arabic terms are generally written in italics and their meanings explained within the text. In some cases Arabic text is used to show the exact wording used in an original source, though the English equivalent is also given. Transcriptions of Ottoman Turkish are given in the Latin alphabet using the transcription system employed in modern Turkish.

1. Introduction

This study began as a survey of Hajj forts in Jordan, carried out in 1986, for an M.Phil Thesis at the Oriental Institute in Oxford. The idea of working on the Hajj forts was suggested to me by Professor Ghazi Bishe, then Director of the Department of Antiquities in Jordan and Dr Andrew Garrard, Director of the British Institute at 'Amman for Archaeology and History. They pointed out that a study of the Hajj forts would be both more important and more interesting than my chosen field of research, Umayyad Desert Castles. Whilst there are still major questions to be addressed in relation to the Umayyad period in Jordan and Syria (see, for example, Walmsley 2007) a considerable amount of investigation had, by 1986, already taken place, whereas very little was known about the archaeology of the region during the Ottoman period. It was also pointed out that the Hajj forts were threatened with destruction, both through neglect and also by wanton acts of destruction by people searching for buried treasure or antiquities. There was also the problem that many people regarded the Hajj forts as Ottoman and Turkish, and therefore not part of Jordan's Arab heritage. Hopefully, the research contained within this volume will answer all three of these points by providing an historical and archaeological context for the forts, an added incentive for conservation, and showing that, far from being foreign, they are an integral part of Jordan's historical archaeology.

Having completed the M.Phil Thesis (Petersen 1986) a number of articles, based on the survey work, were published (Petersen 1989; 1991; 1994; 1995). However, it became clear that more survey, excavation and historical investigation were needed before the forts could be published as a monograph. Unfortunately no further work was possible until 2002, when a small excavation was carried out at Qal'at 'Unaiza in order to investigate the material culture and structural history of one fort in greater detail (Petersen, Brun and Shurma 2003; Petersen 2003).

The 2002 season showed that the other forts were also in need of more detailed survey. In 2006 a final season of fieldwork, consisting of a detailed photographic survey and the collection of samples of ceramics from each site, was undertaken. The results of these three seasons (1986, 2002 and 2006) are at the heart of this monograph, whilst further chapters set the forts within their historical, geographical and archaeological context. One of the by-products of conducting fieldwork over such an extended period is the capacity to monitor the changing condition of the forts over time. The remaining part of this short introduction will provide a brief review of existing archaeological studies of the Hajj routes and then show how the study of Hajj routes fits into the wider discipline of archaeology.

Other Studies of Hajj Routes (Map 1)

In addition to the present work a number of Hajj route related archaeological projects have been published. Probably the earliest archaeological survey of a Hajj route was that of Sauvaget, a study of the Syrian Hajj route from the Turkish Syrian border to Damascus (Sauvaget 1937). This pioneering study focused on the Ottoman khans and caravanserais utilized by pilgrims on their journey from Anatolia to Damascus, and is one of the first studies to treat the Ottoman architecture of Syria seriously. In one sense the present work is a continuation of that project, tracing the remains of the Hajj from Damascus southwards towards Medina. Here it should be stressed that the fundamental difference between the route north of Damascus and the Hajj route to the south, is that the latter had no caravanserais and the facilities were intended to support pilgrims, not house them.

The first large scale archaeological project concerned with Hajj routes was the Darb Zubayda project, initiated by

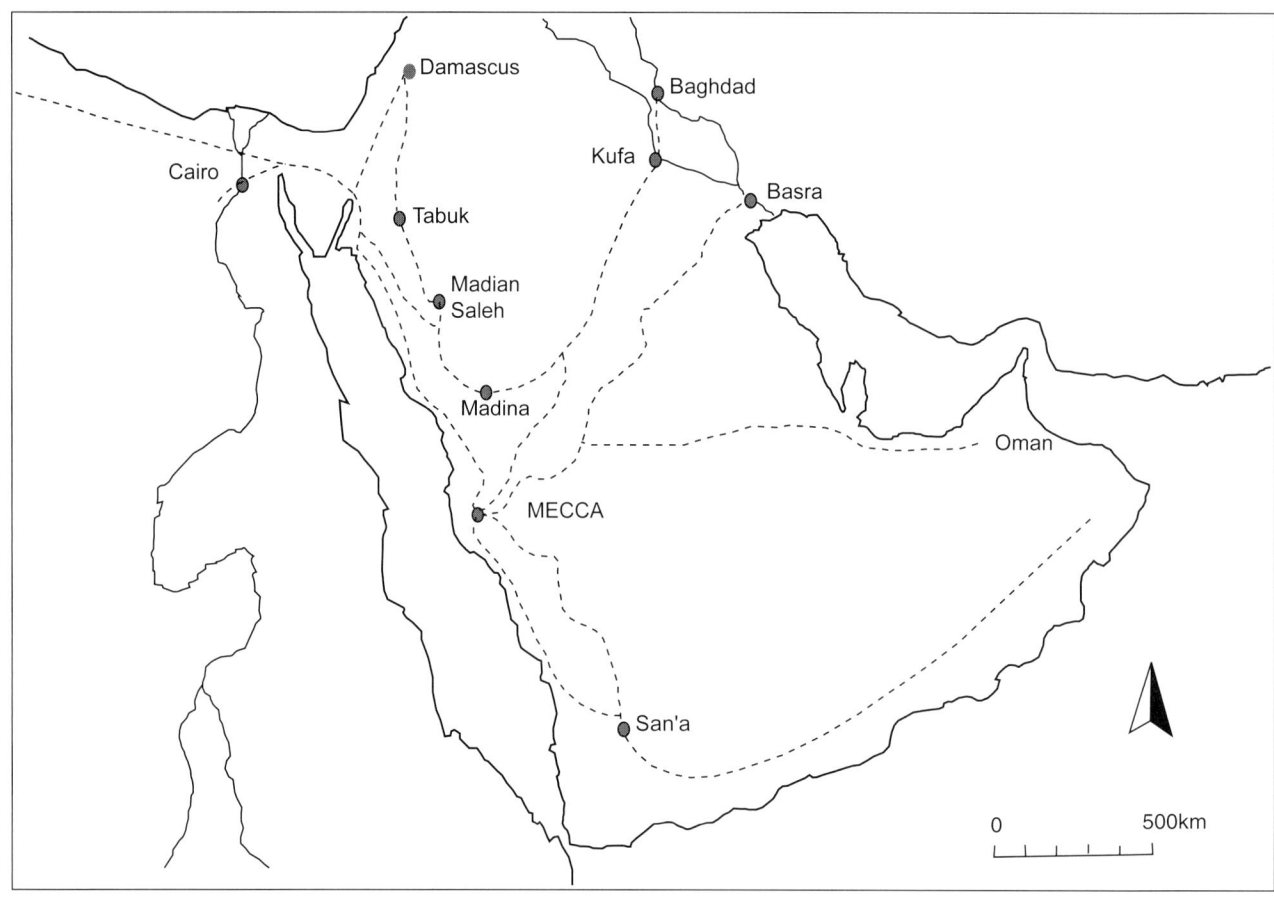

Map 1. Pilgrimage routes of Arabia.

Saad al-Rashid of the Saudi Antiquities Department, during the 1970s (al-Rashid 1978). This project documented the 1,140 km long pilgrim route, between Kufa and Mecca, established by the Abbasids in the 9th century. The route was provided with a wide variety of facilities, including 100 reservoirs, more than 1,300 wells and 54 way stations. The primary historical research for this project was published as a monograph in 1980 (al-Rashid 1980) although archaeological investigation continued into the 1980s. This project also led to the discovery of al-Rabadah, an urban settlement (850 × 500 m) with two mosques, built as part of the development of the pilgrimage route (al-Rashid 1986). From this time the study of the pilgrim routes became one of the priorities of the Saudi Antiquities Department, a number of articles were published in *Atlal*: the Journal of Saudi Arabian Antiquities (al-Dayel and al-Helwa 1978; Gilmore, al-Hiwah and Resseeni 1982, 1984 and 1985; Knudstad 1977; Morgan and Helwa 1981; al-Rashid 1979). Several monographs relating to the archaeology of the Hajj routes in Arabia have been published, including Mohammed al-Thenayian's study of the Yemeni highland pilgrim route between San'a and Mecca (al-Thenayian 2000). Ghabbani's two volume study of the northern Hijaz (Ghabbani 1993, I and II) and, most recently, there has been an exhibition and catalogue of pilgrimage routes and related antiquities in Saudi Arabia (Andre-Salvani *et al.* 2010). There were two main Hajj routes from Yemen, one which ran along the coastal plain and another which connected the capital San'a with Mecca via a mountainous route. Mohammed al-Thenayian's study, documents a series of facilities including reservoirs, wells, mosques and milestones. However, the most intersting aspect of the Yemeni route is the construction of the road, in a number of places the road was not only paved but was also levelled and had built up shoulders or kerbs. Ghabbani's research has focused on the Egyptian and Syrian pilgrimage routes in the northen part of Saudi Arabia, with particular attention given to inscriptions by pilgrims. The exhibition, *Roads of Arabia*, held at the Louvre in Paris, demonstrates the extent to which the Hajj routes have become a defining feature of Saudi Arabia's archaeology and image of itself (Andre-Salvani *et al.* 2010).

A number of archaeological studies related to the Egyptian pilgrimage route have also been published, most notably Tamari's study of the Sinai section of the overland Hajj (Tamari 1982; see also Tate 2007) as well as a number of studies by Saudi scholars (see, for example, Ghabbani 1998). Charles Le Quesne has recently published an account of the Ottoman fortress at Quseir, which, as well as servicing the route from Lower Egypt, provided a base for grain exports to Mecca and Medina (Le Quesne 2004). Further south, the port of Aidhab in the Sudan, formed an important entreport for Egyptian pilgrims from the 12th century onwards. Archaeological survey of Aidhab has revealed extensive pilgrim cemeteries, as well as wells and cisterns (Paul 1955; Elisséeff and el-Hakim 1981). The port of Suakin, further south in the Sudan, was primarily used by African pilgrims, some of whom had travelled overland through the Sahara from Africa. Recent archaeological excavations at the site have revealed that the port may have fulfilled this function in the Medieval period (Breen *et al.* 2011). It is also worth pointing out that there is considerable scope for investigating the maritime dimension of pilgrimage from India and South East Asia. So far studies have been primarily historical (see, for example, Pearson 1995) though investigation of wreck sites in the Red Sea shows how archaeology can increase our knowledge of the maritime routes (Ward 2000).

Pilgrimage and Archaeology

Pilgrimage is an activity of interest to a number of academic disciplines outside archaeology, most notably religious studies, anthropology, psychology, geography, history and ethnology. Amongst a number of theoretical studies the most influential work is probably a series of articles and books by Victor and Edith Turner based on a comparison of Medieval Christian pilgrimage with contemporary tribal initiation rituals (Turner and Turner 1978). Amongst the ideas formulated by the Turners were those of *communitas* (a temporary community of pilgrims), liminality, egalitarianism and transition. For archaeologists the Turners' conceptualization is particularly interesting because it emphasizes temporal change as one of the products of pilgrimage and therefore marks pilgrimage as a key component of historical change. There has been considerable criticism of the Turners' theoretical approach, most recently by the archaeologist Joy McCorriston (2011, 22–28) who instead sees pilgrimage as socially conservative, preserving social continuity over millennia.

Archaeological studies of pilgrimage have generally been less theoretical, with more emphasis on description and analysis of sites and routes. In general, archaeological studies have focused on World Religions, with many studies of Hindu, Buddhist, Jewish, Christian and Muslim pilgrimage (for an overview see Insoll 2001). The archaeology of Christian pilgrimage is particularly well developed, with studies of pilgrim routes and shrines in Europe (*e.g.* Stopford 1994) as well as Jerusalem and the Middle East (see, for example, Bangert 2010; Pringle 1987). It should also be pointed out that whilst pilgrimage to Mecca is the main form of pilgrimage within Islam, there are other forms of local, regional and sectarian pilgrimages, some of which have been studied through archaeology. Of particular importance are the Shi'a pilgrim routes to Najaf and other sacred cities within Iraq and Iran, these were provided with caravanserais and other facilities.

There are a number of studies of the archaeology of local, often Sufi shrines, which have survived the modernizing, reformist tendencies within Sunni Islam that disapprove of the veneration of shaykhs and saints. Palestine has a particularly rich network of local shrines that have been studied through both ethnology and archaeology (see for example Petersen 1999).

Hajj routes to Mecca relate to a number of research areas within archaeology that may be characterized as Islamic Archaeology, Historical Archaeology, the Archaeology of Travel and the Archaeology of Religion. Certainly the study of Hajj routes lies at the heart of Islamic archaeology, however this sub discipline is defined, because of the centrality of the Hajj to Muslim life (for a discussion of Islamic archaeology, see, Petersen 2011; Insoll 1999). Historical archaeology developed in North America to investigate the colonial (post 1492) archaeology of the region and by extension its contacts with Europe and the wider world. The Ottoman phase of the Hajj forts (16th–19th centuries) relates directly to historical archaeology, both because of the time period and because of the global significance of the Ottoman Empire. The Hajj routes also fit into historical archaeology in the sense that there are numerous historical documents against which the archaeology can provide an alternative reading and secondly because of the large distances involved making it relevant to global history. However, there has been little attempt to set the Hajj routes within the context of historical archaeology, this is partly because most of the studies have been carried out by scholars specializing in Islamic historical studies and therefore disconnected from the wider world of historical archaeology. Similarly, there has been little attempt to set the Hajj routes within the wider context of archaeology and travel, particularly in relation to road systems, migrations, or, through the perspective of phenomenology. Certainly the Hajj routes would be good material for such studies; one calls to mind Tim Ingold's study of lines, where the concern with destination is replaced with an emphasis on the lines, or route itself, that has been travelled (Ingold 2007). An example of how this can be applied to archaeology can be seen in Candy's study of the pilgrimage route to Santiago di Compostella in Spain (Candy 2003). Recently there have been some attempts to look at the Hajj routes from a landscape and travel perspective, most notably Wilkinson's study of the Darb Zubayda (Wilkinson 2003, 165–68) and Tate's study of the Egyptian Hajj route in Sinai (Tate 2007).

Finally, it is worth considering the Hajj routes within the context of the Archaeology of Religion. In this case the emphasis would be on how the archaeology informs perceptions of Islam as a religion. Although this perspective may overlap with that of Islamic archaeology its emphasis is on variations from a monolithic view of Islam to a more nuanced study looking at the plurality of beliefs within Islam (*c.f.* Insoll 1999).

2. Principal Written Sources

The centrality of the Hajj to Islamic civilization means that there is plentiful documentation about the rituals and events that took place in connection with this annual undertaking. Predictably, the number and quality of the reports increase as we move closer to our own era, so that, for the Ottoman period there are reports in a number of languages (European and Islamic) allowing an insight into the workings of the Hajj route. In 1828 the water resources on the Hajj route were surveyed by engineers working for Muhammad 'Ali Pasha, ruler of Egypt (1805–48). A translation of this account by Michael Diboll is included as Appendix 1 of this volume.

Arabic and Turkish Primary Sources

Because it functioned as one of the principal routes between the birthplace of Islam and the capital of the first ruling dynasty (the Umayyads), the Syrian Hajj road features in the work of many early Arabic authors. A convenient summary of early Arabic writing relating to this route can be found in al-Wohaibi (1973) *The Northern Hijaz in the writings of the Arab geographers 800–1150*. Another summary of early Islamic sources for the Hajj can be found in Musil (1926, appendix XV, 326–31). The majority of these early accounts simply give a sequence of place names, with no further information about the nature of the settlement.

There are no descriptions of the Syrian Hajj route from the period of the Crusades (1099–1250). This is because the northern part of the route was within striking distance of Crusader strongholds such as Karak, Montreal (Shawbak established 1115) and 'Ayla (established 1116). Even the Egyptian pilgrimage route was effected by the Crusader occupation, thus the Spanish pilgrim Ibn Jubayr made his way to Mecca via southern Egypt avoiding 'Aqabat al-

'Ayla (modern 'Aqaba) and crossing instead from Aydhab to Jedda (Ibn Jubayr trans. Broadhurst 1952).

The earliest description of the Syrian Hajj following the expulsion of the Crusaders is the account of Ibn Battuta, one of the world's most famous travellers. Ibn Battuta (Shams al-Din Abu 'Abd Allah Muhammad b. 'Abd Allah b. Muhammad b. Ibrahim b. Muhammad b. Ibrahim b. Yusuf al-Lawti al Tanji) was born in Tangier on 25th February 1304 (17th Rajab 703) and died in Morocco either in 1368–69 or 1377. Ibn Battuta's travels were written down by the scholar Ibn Juzay under commission from Abu 'Inan, the Marinid ruler of Morocco (Ibn Battuta 1958, 1). The dictation of the text by Ibn Battuta was completed in December 1357 and the final edited version was presented to the Sultan in early 1358. The narrative, beginning with the departure from Tangier for Mecca in 1325, follows a series of journeys to Iraq, Iran, Arabia, Egypt, Anatolia, Central Asia, India, China, South-East Asia, North Africa and sub Saharan West Africa. Scholars investigating the text have noticed borrowings from earlier writers, such as Ibn Jubayr, as well as fantastic embellishments of an otherwise sober narrative. It is has been convincingly argued that these departures, from an otherwise faithful account, were embellishments added by Ibn Juzayy to improve the style of the text in accordance with the norms of literary composition (*adab*) (Miquel, 735–36). The first part of the text, which describes the Hajj route, conforms to the standard literary form of a *rihala* (travelogue) centred on the Holy Places of Arabia, though the later parts of the text diverge markedly from this literary form. This brings into question the reliability of the text in relation to the Syrian Hajj route, firstly because this journey took place more than 20 years before it was dictated to Ibn Juzayy and secondly, because the narrative of this part of the journey may have been altered to conform to the literary style of the *rihala*. However, examination of the text and comparisons with similar works indicates that only those parts of the work specifically related to Mecca and Medina may have been influenced by other accounts and that the places and events described in relation to the Hajj route largely reflect the experience of a specific journey. Although the description of the journey from Damascus to Mecca is fairly short, it remains the fullest Medieval account of the route.

One of the first descriptions of the Syrian Hajj route after the Ottoman conquest is a work entitled, *Manazil al-Hajj min al-Sham ila Makka* (منازل الحج من الشام إلى مكة), which is preserved in two manuscripts (nos 286 and 287) in the library of 'Arif Hikmat in Medina, Saudi Arabia (Bilge 1979, 213). The account is written in Turkish, though it was probably based on an Arabic original, as manuscript no. 286 states that it was ordered by Mustapha Pasha and translated by Husayn b. Mullah Shams (Jasir 1969, 174). The account is useful because it gives a large number of place names as well as the main stopping places. The manuscript is dated to the year 971 AH (1562/1563 AD).

Evliya Çelebi is one of the best known Muslim travellers and, like Ibn Battuta, he has achieved a legendary status for his travels to diverse parts of the Islamic world, described in his 10 volume work the *Seyhatnâme*. Evliya is a pen name, unfortunately the real name of the author, who spent more than 40 years travelling through the Balkans, North Africa, the Middle East and Arabia, is unknown. Despite this, Evliya's accounts include plentiful personal information, including his date of birth (March 1611) and the name of his father, Derwish Mehemed Efendi, a royal goldsmith whose commissions included fixing a golden gutter for the Ka'ba (Bilge 1979, 214; Kortepeter 1979, 232). It is also clear from Evliya's accounts that he was wealthy and well connected, often travelling with a group of friends. Evliya's description of the Hajj route from Damascus to Mecca is contained in the 9th volume of the *Seyhatnâme*, which also contains details of his travels in Anatolia, Syria and Egypt. Volume 9 has been reprinted in a scholarly edition, in modern Turkish, based on three original manuscripts held in libraries in Istanbul (Kortpeter 1979, 232; Evliya Çelebi *Seyhatnâme* IX).

Evliya's description of the road from Damascus to Medina occupies 21 pages of the modern printed edition and includes details of the conversations, speeches and events which took place on the Hajj, as well as descriptions of people, halting places and buildings. Evliya undertook the Hajj in 1672 (1082 AH) when it was under the leadership of Husayn Pasha, the newly appointed governor of Damascus. Earlier in 1672 (1081 AH) the Ottoman governor of Jedda, Hasan Pasha, had been killed by the troops of the Sharif of Mecca, Sa'd b. Zayd. This was an affront to the dignity of the Ottoman Sultan as Guardian of the Two Holy Shrines (*Khadhim al-Haramayn*). One of the tasks of the commander of the 1672 pilgrimage was to avenge the insult and re-enforce Ottoman authority in the Hijaz. In consequence, the 1672 pilgrimage was accompanied by 5,000 troops, with an additional 3,000 being sent via Egypt. Once Husayn Pasha arrived in Mecca he mounted a display of force that forced Sharif Sa'd to flee Mecca for Taif and ultimately Constantinople. Husayn Pasha then organized the appointment of Barakat as Sharif of Mecca in return for an oath of allegiance to the Ottoman Sultan. Evliya's in depth description of these events gives us a unique insight into the high level politics involved in the Hajj (Kortepeter 1979, 239–42).

One of the less well known descriptions of the Syrian Hajj is the account of a pilgrim from Damascus, Murtada b. 'Ali b. 'Alawan, who went on the Hajj in 1709 (1120–21 AH). The account (*rihala*) is written in Arabic and occupies 28 pages of a manuscript compilation in Berlin (Haarman 1979). Little is known of Murtada beyond the information contained in this manuscript, which states that he had previously made the Hajj as a young man in 1677–78 (1088 AH). Murtada was a Sufi and appears to have been of some significance in religious circles. He was on close terms with the amir al-Hajj Nasuh Muhammad Pasha, as well as the Sharif of Mecca and his family from whom he enjoyed some hospitality. Only part of the account (*rihala*) discusses the Hajj from Damascus to Mecca; the remainder is a description of his travels to various Sufi and Shi'a shrines in Arabia, Syria and Iraq. One of the more interesting parts of his narrative is the description of how he was robbed on his return journey from Mecca to Medina. Murtada and his companions were accosted at night by members of the Banu Hudhayl who left them naked in the desert. The incident was reported to the Sharif, who imprisoned the Shaykh of the Bani Hudhayl, pending the return of their belongings. Although some sandals and skull caps were soon recovered, Murtada had to continue his journey before anything of significance could be returned (Haarman 1979, 250).

The most comprehensive description of the Syrian Hajj route was written by Mehmed Edib (al-Hajj Muhammad Adib-efendi b. Muhamad Darvish), an Ottoman judge from Candia in Crete, who travelled from Constantinople to Mecca in 1779. His work contains a detailed description of the journey, from its beginnings in July 1779 (Rajab 1193) to the return in April 1780 (Rabi' 2 1194). Mehmed Edib's account is significant because he gives construction dates for forts and other buildings, and facilities found on the Hajj route; he is the main source used for reconstructing the Syrian Hajj route. The earliest surviving manuscript containing this account is an autograph copy in the Chester Beatty Library in Dublin, dated 31 August 1790 (Dhul-qa'da 1204). Although the majority of the text is written/copied by an anonymous scribe, this manuscript contains an index and appendix written in red ink by Mehmed Edib himself, as well as having the author's seal on the final page (*f.*239b) (for a full discussion of this manuscript, which also contains miniature paintings of Mecca, Medina and Jerusalem, see Minorsky 1958, 98–99). This work was clearly regarded as important by contemporaries and in 1816–17 (1232 AH) a printed version of the work was published in Constantinople under the title *Menasik-i hacc-ı şerif.* Eight years later part of the work was translated into French by M. Bianchi and published by la Société de Géographie de Paris, under the title *Itinéraire de Constantinople à la Mecque* (Bianchi 1825). This translation has been criticized by Max van Berchem (1978, 621) and Karl Barbir (1980, 109), both of whom point out that it contains many inaccuracies, including the date Mehmed Edib made the Hajj, which Bianchi wrongly gives as 1682 (1093 AH). Despite these reservations Bianchi's translation remains the only version of this report in a European language.

European Primary Sources

Possibly the earliest European Christians to have visited Mecca were remnants of the Crusader force sent by Renauld de Chatillion to attack the Holy Cities in 1183 (Pearson 1995, 14; Leiser 1977, 90). Other early visitors include the Portuguese explorer Pedro Covilham, who claimed to have visited Mecca in the 1490s (Ficalho 1898) and Arnold von Harff who may also have reached the city in the late 1400s (Harff, ed. Letts 1946). In each of these examples there is some doubt as to whether they actually visited Mecca and in any case the accounts do not give any useful descriptions of either the Hajj, or the Holy Cities.

The earliest useful European account of the Syrian Hajj is contained in the writings of Ludivico di Varthema (*c.* 1465–*c.* 1517), a native of Bologna, who enlisted as a mercenary and accompanied the Hajj, as a guard, during the last years of Mamluk rule in Egypt and Syria, between April and June 1503 (Varthema, ed. Temple 1928). Little is known about Ludovico di Varthema, except what is contained in the account of his travels published in Rome in 1510. He left Italy in 1502, reaching Alexandria in early 1503, from where he travelled to Damascus and subsequently accompanied the Syrian Hajj to Mecca. From Mecca he travelled first to India and Sri Lanka before visiting South East Asia and the islands of Java, Sumatra and Borneo. Ludovico returned to Italy via Africa and the Cape of Good Hope. In the present context, the chief value of Ludivico di Varthema's account is that although a number of European (Christian) travellers visited Mecca during the early modern period (16th–18th century), the majority travelled via Egypt and the Red Sea and there are very few accounts of the Syrian Hajj. The descriptions of Damascus and Mecca are invaluable, although the description of the actual route taken by the Hajj is of limited use for identifying particular locations.

The first detailed description of the Syrian Hajj route is provided by the Swiss traveller Johan Luis (Eng. John Lewis) Burckhardt (1784–1817) generally remembered for the re-discovery of Petra in August 1812. Burckhardt travelled under the name of Shaykh Ibrahim ibn 'Abdalla and used the excuse of making a sacrifice at Aaron's tomb, as a means of entering Petra at a time when foreigners were excluded. It is unclear whether Burckhardt actually converted to Islam, or whether he was merely acting the part, though the fact that he was given a Muslim funeral and was buried in Cairo suggests a genuine conversion (Adams 1973, 221). Burckhardt has been described as the '..first Arabian traveller to realize fully the explorer's obligation to serve all sorts of enquiry' (Hogarth 1905, 88–91). Burckhardt's explorations were sponsored by the African Association of London, which charged him with the task of discovering the source of the Niger river (Adams 1973, 215). A combination of factors meant that Burckhardt never reached the Niger, though he did manage to make a series of journeys within Syria, Arabia and the Sudan, the accounts of which were published posthumously by the African Society in five volumes (Burckhardt 1819, 1822, 1829, 1830 and 1831). The main books of relevance to the Hajj are *Travels in Syria and the Holy Land* (1822) and *Travels in Arabia* (1829). Appendix III of *Travels in Syria and the Holy Land* provides a detailed list of stations on the Syrian Hajj route, the earliest description of the route in a European language. However, Burckhardt only followed the Hajj route from Damascus to Ma'an; his visit to Mecca and Medina was made later (in 1814) via Egypt and the Red Sea, arriving by ship at Jedda. Therefore, it seems likely that his account of the Syrian Hajj route was, at least in part, based on the accounts of pilgrims who had made the complete journey overland. In terms of reliability, this means that his account is at its most reliable in the descriptions of the northern part of the route, the descriptions of the southern part are rather sketchy and less reliable. *Travels in Arabia* contains a detailed first hand description of the cities of Mecca and Medina where he stayed from July1814 until June 1815.

Probably the most detailed European account of the Syrian Hajj was written by Charles Doughty, who accompanied the Hajj as far as Medain Saleh, staying in the Hajj fort there for two months (for a biography of Doughty see Hogarth 1929). Doughty's main interest was in Nabatean antiquities, in this case the 'Petra-like sculptured cliff-monuments of Medain Saleh [*Hejr*]' (Doughty 1979, 31). However, the only way that Doughty was able to gain access to these monuments was by joining the Hajj caravan from Damascus and travelling with it as far as Medain Saleh. Whilst staying at Medain Saleh Doughty was able to make a thorough investigation of the monuments, the inscriptions he recorded were subsequently published by the Académie in Paris, with translations by M. Renan (Renan 1891). Doughty did not return with the Hajj caravan to Damascus, instead he made a trip into 'the high deserts of Arabia' (Nafud, Nejd and Taif) returning to England via boat from Jedda. Doughty travelled with a large amount of equipment, which caused problems at the beginning of his journey when his camel became ill and died as a result of carrying his 'over-heavy load' (Doughty 1979, 106–7). The equipment included an altimeter for recoding elevations and a large chest of medicine that he used for treating the Bedouin who came to him with various ailments. Unlike Burckhardt, Doughty never pretended to be Muslim and always presented himself as a *Nasrany* (Christian) (Lawrence in Doughty 1979, 19; Doughty 1979, 40–41). Doughty's academic training was as a geologist and a poet, though he justified his interest in Arabia in terms of his Christianity. In the preface to the third edition of his book he wrote that from the account of his experiences 'we are better able to read the bulk of the Old Testament books, with the further insight and understanding, which comes of a living experience' (Doughty 1979, 35).

From the perspective of the Syrian Hajj route, Doughty's work has three unique advantages. Firstly, his account is the only description of the Syrian route to describe the process of travelling on the Hajj, including the different modes of transport, landmarks and their significance, the condition and form of the actual road, or surface of the Hajj road, as well as the interaction between the Bedouin and the Ottoman authorities. Secondly, Doughty's account is invaluable because he actually stayed in the Hajj fort at Medain Saleh and he provides us with an intimate portrait of life in the *kella* where he resided for over two months. Thirdly, Doughty's work included the first detailed maps and drawings. Despite not having the advantage of a camera, Doughty's drawings are highly accurate and provide the first visual records of the route, including geological features, buildings, plants and people. The only part of the Hajj route not described by Doughty in detail, is the southern portion of the route between Medain Saleh and Medina, for which the only first hand descriptions are those of Muslim pilgrims and travellers. The accuracy of Doughty's work can be gauged from the comments of T. E. Lawrence, who stated that 'the great picture-book of nomad life, became a military text book, and helped guide us to victory in the East' (Lawrence's Introduction in Doughty 1979, 27).

The earliest photographic record of the Hajj forts was made in the 1890s, by Rudolf-Ernst Brünnow and Alfred von Domaszewski as part of their extensive survey of the former Roman provinces that today comprise parts of Syria, Jordan and Lebanon. Brünnow was Professor of Semitic Philology and Languages at the University of Heidelberg, whilst von Domaszewski's interests were in Roman antiquities. The survey was firmly focused on Roman antiquities and was subsequently published as *Die Provincia Arabia* (Brünnow and Domaszewski 1905). The photographs taken by Brünnow were some of the earliest photographic images of important sites such as 'Amman, Bosra and Petra. Of particular importance are the photographs of the façade of the Umayyad palace at Mshatta before it was dismantled and moved to Berlin in 1903. Ottoman forts investigated by Brünnow and Domaszewski include, Qal'at Dab'a, Qal'at al-Hasa, Qal'at Qatrana and Ma'an. They interpreted many of the features on the Hajj route to be of Roman origin, despite evidence to the contrary, thus they attributed the paved road and bridge at al-Hasa to the Roman period.

Less than ten years later, between 1907 and 1909, the northern part of the Hajj route was explored by the Dominican fathers, Raphaël Savignac (1874–1951) and Antonin Jaussen (1871–1962) from the recently established École Biblique et Archéologique Française, in Jeruslaem. Using the newly built Hijaz railway line as their primary means of transport, Jaussen and Savignac made an intensive archaeological investigation of the Hejaz and southern Syria, which was published in three volumes between 1907 and 1922 (all three volumes were reprinted in 1997 by L'Institut Français d'Archéologie Orientale; for a review see Farès-Drappeau 2004). Like Doughty their primary interest was the Nabatean monuments at Medain Saleh, although they also recorded other aspects of archaeological and historical interest they encountered on the way. One of the more important aspects of their work is the record of the Hajj forts in the Hijaz as far as Medain Saleh, including a discussion of inscriptions, some of which have subsequently disappeared (for a review of this aspect of their work see van Berchem 1978). In addition to written descriptions Jaussen and Savignac took a large number of photographs, which can be compared with those of Brünnow, to monitor changes in the appearance of the forts. There is particular emphasis on the fort at Medain Saleh, including a measured plan and section of the building.

A few years later, in 1910, the northern part of the route was investigated by the Czech anthropologist, Alois Musil (1868–1944) who was famous for the discovery of the Umayyad bath complex of Qusayr 'Amra (Musil 1907). Musil's work was made available in English through an association with the American philanthropist, Charles Crane, who paid for the publication of Musil's work in 6 volumes. Musil's visit to the Hijaz was part of a project investigating the evasion of quarantine regulations by pilgrims and others. This work was being carried out for the Ottoman government and in return Musil was allowed to carry out anthropological investigations in the area. Musil and his assistants travelled by means of the Hijaz railway and investigated the area around each station using camels (for a discussion of Musil's methodology and fieldwork techniques see Wright 1927). The most useful part of Musil's work, in relation to the Hajj route, is contained in an appendix to *The Northern Heĝâz* (Musil 1926, appendix XV, 326–31) which contains a detailed discussion of historical sources relating to the Damascus pilgrimage route. Although he mentions many of the Ottoman forts, Musil only discusses one, Qal'at Fassu'a, in any detail including photographs in his description (Musil 1926, 38–39).

From this brief review it can be seen that European sources have mostly been concerned with the northern part of the route and there are few that give any information for the area south of Medain Saleh.

Secondary Sources based on Archival Material

The primary sources cited above are narrative accounts,

which provide, sometimes highly personalized, accounts of the Hajj route. In addition to these narrative sources there are a number of administrative documentary sources from the Ottoman period, which give definitive information on the development of the facilities and the use of the Hajj route. These sources have been studied in detail by a number of Ottoman historians including, Abdul Karim Rafeq (1966), Muhammad Adnan Bakhit (1982), Karl Barbir (1980) and Suraya Faroqhi (1994). The earliest archival research in relation to the Hajj was carried out by Rafeq, who based his research on the 18th century *shari'a* court records (*kadi sijils)* housed in Damascus (for a discussion of these records see Rafeq 1976). The archives contain copies of orders to the provincial governor from Constantinople, as well as details of disputes brought before the provincial judge (*kadi*) who applied both religious law (*shari'a*) and Ottoman regulations (*kanun*). Bakhit also made use of the *Shari'a* records of Syria (Damascus, Aleppo and Hama) and the *Awqaf* records of Damascus. In addition, Bakhit made extensive use of the Başbakanlik Arşivi (archives of the Prime Minister's Office) in Istanbul, focusing on material in the *Mühimme Defteri* (series of outgoing orders)*, Tapu Defteri* (tax registers) and the *Maliyeden müdevver defteri* (assorted financial registers). Karl Barbir's study was also based on material from these registers in the Başbakanlik Arşivi, although he also used the Ali Emiri, Ibnülemin and Cevdet collections as well as the *Kamil Kepeci defteri* (assorted registers). Faroqhi's work was based on the registers in the Başbakanlik Arşivi, using the *Mühimme Zeyli* in addition to the *Mühimme Defteri* and the *Maliyeden müdevver*. Each of these historians emphasized that considerably more archive material was available which, in the future, would give more information about this period (16th–18th centuries).

Oral History

In addition to the written sources noted above, some mention should be made of the oral history recorded by a number of authors including, Musil (1926 and 1927), Doughty (1979) and Peake Pasha (1958). Whilst Musil and Doughty used oral history to provide information on points of topography, or local tradition, Peake Pasha's work stands out as an attempt to write a tribal history of Jordan. Fredrick Peake (1886–1970) joined the British Army in 1906 and served in the Imperial Camel Corps in Egypt during the First World War. During this time he learnt Arabic and became experienced in Bedouin culture. In 1920, following the end of the war, he was posted to Transjordan to assess the state of security in the fledgling state. As a result of this visit, Peake Pasha, as he was known by the Arabs, was asked to set up two small police forces which became the nucleus of the Arab Legion which he commanded until his retirement in 1939. In 1935 Peake published *A History of Jordan and its Tribes* based on the spoken traditions of the Balqa tribes of Jordan, many of whom served in the Arab legion. This was later translated into English and published by the University of Miami Press in 1958.

For many years Peake Pasha's history was 'the only authoritative history of tribal Jordan' (Shryock 1997, 32). More recently Peake's work was neglected by anthropologists and other academics, who regarded him as part of the colonial power structure and therefore unreliable as an historical source (Scham 2006). However, native Jordanian historians regarded his work with respect, primarily because, it was written by somebody from outside the tribal system (Shryock 1995, 346). The main benefits of Peake's work for studying the Hajj are firstly, that he provides an alternative historical source for the Ottoman period, which is otherwise dominated by the narrative of the Ottoman sources and secondly, that his work displays an intimate knowledge of the topography of Jordan. In the future it is likely that more oral history will become available, through the efforts of local Jordanian historians of Bedouin origin.

3. The Medieval Hajj Route through Syria and Jordan

The history of the Syrian Hajj route and its pre-Islamic predecessors is, in many ways, the history of the relationship between Bilad al-Sham (Greater Syria) and Arabia. During the 1st and 2nd centuries BC the Nabateans traded along this route and in the 1st century AD it was formalized as the Via Nova Traiana, by the Roman Emperor Trajan (Bowerstock 1981; see also Borstad 2008). Later, the route was used by pre-Islamic Arabs trading with the Byzantine cities of Syria (Groom 1981), while in the 7th century, after the death of Muhammad it was the main route for the Arab invasion of Syria and Palestine.

During the early Islamic period the route can be seen as the direct connection between Damascus, the developed form of Islamic urban civilization, and the Holy Cities of Mecca and Medina, repositories of original Islam. In this connection it is worth noting that the prophet Muhammad is known to have travelled, as a merchant, to Bosra in Syria and probably followed the route later used by the pilgrimage and known as the *Darb al-Hajj al-Shami*. Syria's close connection with the early years of Islam is further demonstrated by the fact that it was the first region outside the Arabian Peninsula to become incorporated into the Islamic world (*Dar al-Islam*). Under the Umayyads the route grew to be one of the major arteries of Islamic civilization, conveying both politics and culture. Examples of Islamic culture can be seen in the Umayyad palaces located along the route, including Qasr Mashatta, Khan al-Zebib and Qastal (Creswell 1969; Genequand 2003). Whilst the precise functions of these palaces may be in dispute, it is clear that they played a role in the politics of the time, the most famous example being the palace at Humeima that acted as a crucible for the later Abbasid revolution (Foote 1999; Oleson 2001; Oleson *et al.* 1999). The cultural significance of this route in early Islamic times can be seen from the numerous nationalities using the route, this is exemplified by the finding of Persian/ Sassanian coins in Umayyad levels at Humeima and by the way the route was used for the rapid transmission of designs. Without doubt the Abbasid revolution and the shifting of the centre of power to Baghdad, significantly reduced the importance of the Syrian route. The Abbasids renovated a pre-existing route from Iraq to Mecca in the 9th century AD, this became known as the Darb Zubayda after the wife of Harun al-Rashid (al-Rashid 1978). Despite this the Syrian route continued to be used throughout the 9th, 10th and 11th centuries, and it is possible that the number of pilgrims may even have increased (see, for example, al-Wohaibi 1973, 426–30).

The first major setback to the Syrian Hajj route came with the Crusader conquest and subsequent occupation of Palestine and parts of modern Jordan and Syria during the 12th and 13th centuries. The Hajj route was particularly vulnerable to harassment when it passed within striking distance of the Crusader strongholds at Karak, Shawbak and Ayla ('Aqaba); there are examples of the Syrian Hajj being suspended for several years whilst pilgrims took alternative routes. However, this disruption was not confined to the Syrian route, we known from Ibn Jubayr's account that the Egyptian pilgrimage caravan was obliged to travel into the south of Egypt, where it crossed by boat from 'Aydhab directly to Jedda, in order to avoid the whole area around 'Ayla (Aqaba) which, at that time, was controlled by the Franks (Ibn Jubayr 1949–51, 81–83/Ar. 71–73).

From the mid-13th century the situation began to improve with the expulsion of the Crusaders from much of Palestine and the accession of the Mamluk Sultan Baybars, who provided unified rule over much of the area. Another factor, which improved the position of the Syrian Hajj route, was the final collapse of the Abbasid caliphate in 1258 when the Mongols sacked Baghdad. There were two main advantages to this situation. Firstly, the fall of the Abbasid dynasty meant that the Mamluk Sultanate had more power within the Holy cities. Secondly, there were no longer official pilgrimage caravans leaving from Baghdad, which meant that Iraqi, Persian and Khurasani pilgrims were now obliged to travel via Damascus along with pilgrims from Syria and Anatolia. The improvement in security also benefited the Egyptian overland route via 'Ayla ('Aqabah) which was resumed in 1266 under the leadership of the Mamluk Sultan Baybars (Peeters 1994, 93–94).

Under Mamluk rule both Cairo and Damascus became nodal points for pilgrims from all over the Islamic world: those from North and West Africa and Andalusia travelling via Cairo and those from the eastern Islamic world travelling via Damascus. Both the Egyptian and Syrian caravans were official, in the sense that each had an *Amir al-Hajj* appointed either by the Mamluk ruler or his deputy (in the case of the Syrian caravan the *Amir al-Hajj* was usually appointed by the Mamluk governor though occasionally he was appointed directly by the Sultan himself). In addition to the Damascus caravan there were a number of semi-official caravans from other Syrian cities, such as Karak and Aleppo. In Fatimid times these caravans had received official decrees, though this practice was discontinued under the Mamluks (Qalqashandi *Subh* XI, 422 and XII 435–6, cited in 'Ankawi 1974, 154). Interestingly, when one of the Mamluk rulers performed the Hajj it was the *Amir al-Hajj* who presided over the ceremonies rather than the ruler ('Ankawi 1974, 154).

Because of its closer connection to the Mamluk regime the Egyptian caravan had some priority over the Syrian caravan, thus on a number of occasions the Egyptian *Amir al-Hajj* was charged with removing the Sharif of Mecca, or Medina, and replacing him with another Sharif nominated by the Sultan (for example this happened twice in 1386). The Egyptian *Amir al-Hajj* also had precedence in the ceremonial rites of the Hajj, this is witnessed by the fact that this caravan carried the *Kiswah*, or covering, for the Ka'ba, which was made in Egypt and replaced annually (Lawrie 2005; Tezcan 1966). One other respect in which the Egyptian caravan had priority over the Syrian and other caravans was with regard to the taxation of merchants. Between 1422 and 1438 the Mamluk Sultan Barsbay, wished to make all merchants travel with the Egyptian caravan in an attempt to monopolize the Indian trade (Ibn Taghribirdi *al-Najum al-zahirah*, VI, II, 624, and Ibn Fahd *Ithaf al-Wara'*, MS, II, 202 cited in 'Ankawi 1974, 150 n. 30). In general, however, both the Syrian and Egyptian caravans had similar status and similar administrative structures.

One of the innovations of the Mamluk period was the *mahmal*, a camel litter covered with heavy cloth, decorated with coloured silk embroidery. The interior of the *mahmal* was empty, except for a copy of the Quran and a carpet, which was intended to cover the tomb of the prophet in Medina. The precise significance, or symbolism, of the *mahmal* is unknown, though it is generally supposed to indicate the presence of some important personage (*i.e.* a ruler or a religious figure) temporarily absent (Jomier 1953). According to Jomier the first recorded appearance of the *mahmal* was during the pilgrimage of the Mamluk Sultan Baybars in 1266 (Maqrizi *Suluk* 1.544 cited in Jomier 1953, 27). However, an illustration of al-Harriri's *Maqamat* by al-Wasiti, dated 1237, shows what appears to be a *mahmal*, with a small domed top, being carried on a riderless camel and accompanying the Syrian Hajj caravan (Guthrie 1995, 40–47 and colour plate 1). There is also evidence that the practice was adopted by the semi-official caravans originating in Aleppo and Karak during the Mamluk period, although it was stopped after the Ottoman conquest in 1515 (Bakhit 1982, 107).

Details of the Route (Map 2)

Whilst we know a lot about the organization of the Mamluk Hajj, including its rituals administration and finance, we know less about the actual routes followed. What is certain is that the route changed depending on the time of year, the security situation and the availability of water resources. The main historical sources for the Hajj route are the Moroccan traveller Ibn Battuta and the Venetian traveller Ludico di Varthema. Unfortunately neither account provides much detail about the precise course of the route, probably because this was not their primary concern and because they will have had little, or no, knowledge of the local place names through which they travelled. In addition to these narrative descriptions we also have details from other authors such as Abu al-Fida, al-Muqaddasi and al-Idrissi, though again they provide few details about the actual route taken.

In the 13th century, the departure date from Damascus was fixed at a date around the 10th of Shawwal, with pilgrims assembling in Damascus about a week earlier. Later, during the 15th and 16th centuries, the departure date was shifted to the 18th or 20th of Shawwal, with the assembly at Damascus beginning around the 10th of Shawwal. This change meant that the caravan either travelled faster (*i.e.* fewer and shorter stops) or, that it took a faster route ('Ankawi 1974).

After leaving Damascus the first stop was at al-Kiswa, 15 km south of Damascus, where the caravan would halt and await the arrival of latecomers and caravans from other Syrian cities. From Kiswa the caravan travelled a further 30 km to Sanamayn, which Ibn Battuta described as a large settlement, as opposed to al-Kiswa, which he described as a village (Ibn Battuta 1958, 158–59). After Sanamayn the caravan would travel via Zur'a (Ezra) to Bosra, on the west side of Jabal al-'Arab, where it would remain for four days awaiting latecomers from Damascus. Bosra derived some sanctity from its association with Muhummad and Ibn Battuta took note of the mosque, built over the place where his camel stopped while working as a merchant for Khadija. Bosra evidently did well out of the pilgrimage

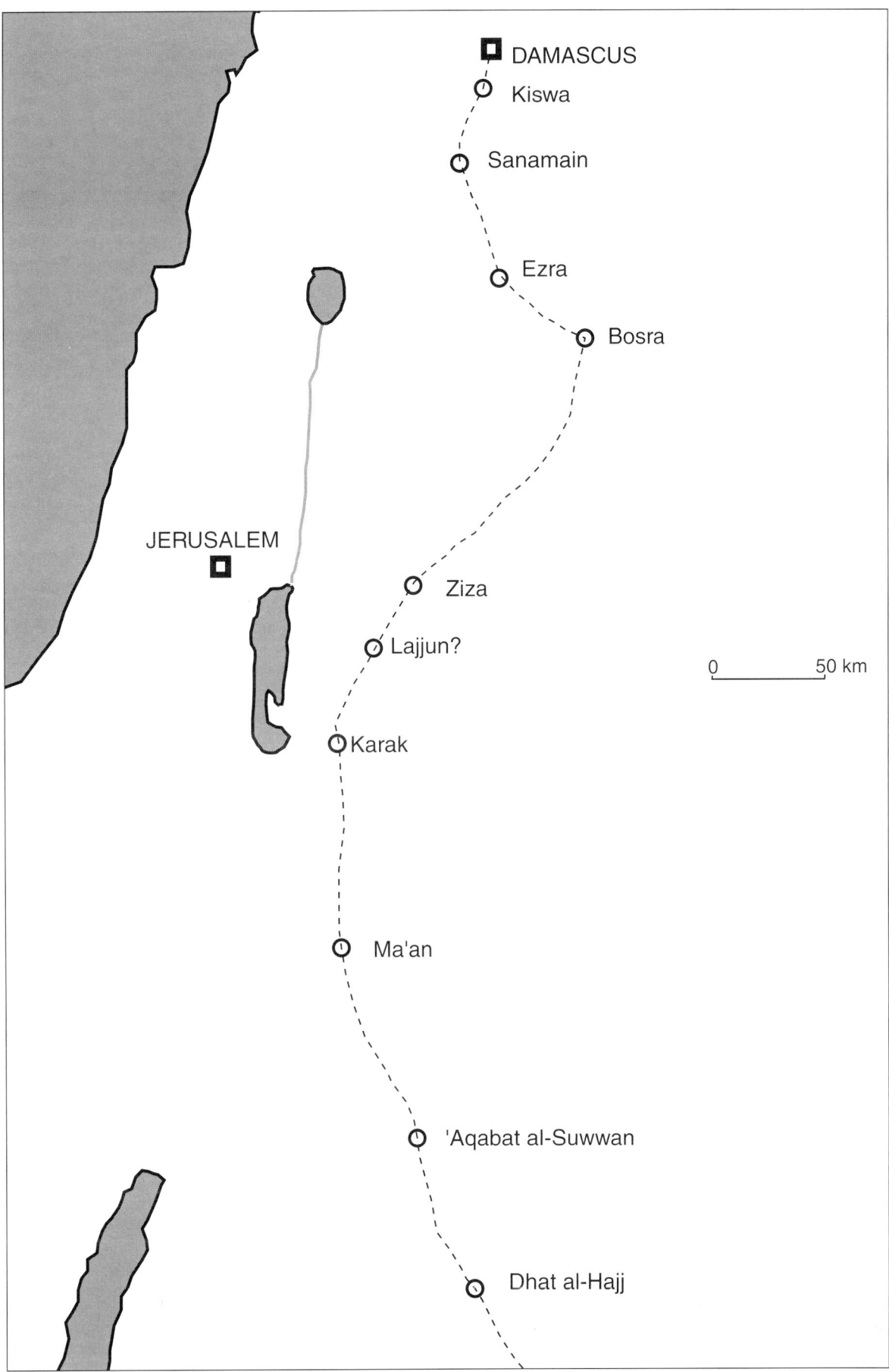

Map 2. The Medieval Hajj route through Jordan based on the account of Ibn Battuta.

caravan and it is surprising that by the end of the 15th century it had been abandoned in favour of Muzayrib (Varthema 1863, 16). The decline of Bosra may largely be attributed to the Timurid occupation of Damascus in 1400. Although Damascus later recovered, Bosra appears to have sunk into obscurity and did not recover until the 19th century, largely because it had been bypassed by the Hajj caravan. The route via Muzayrib may have been favoured because it was quicker and more direct than the Bosra route; it is noticeable that the Hijaz railway also follows this more westerly route. Although the caravan waited at Muzayrib for three days (one day less than Bosra) it was clearly a better stop, both because of the availability of water (from Lake Muzayrib) and because it did not involve an eastwards diversion into the desert. By the time of the Ottoman conquest in 1516 the western route via Muzayrib was well established and remained the preferred route up until modern times.

The precise route which the Hajj caravan took through Jordan is not certain and appears to have varied depending on circumstances. The only place within modern Jordan mentioned by Abu al-Fida' (al-Fida' 1960, 73) on his high speed journey between Mecca and Hama in 1313, is Birka Ziyza (modern Jize, located 30 km south of 'Amman) which appears to have remained an important stop throughout the Medieval period. We know for example that Ibn Battuta travelled directly from Bosra to Birka Ziyza (بركة زيزى), a total distance of nearly 100 km, apparently without a stop. Ibn Battuta's caravan stayed at Ziyza for one day before departing for Lajjun where there was running water (الماء الجارى). Ibn Battuta (1958, 159, n. 12) identifies Lajjun as a site 12 miles (20 km) north-west of Kerak, though it is more likely to be the site of Lahun (see below for discussion). From Lajjun the caravan travelled to Karak where it camped outside the walls, at a place known as al-Thaniyya (the name suggests 'part of a mountain which a road crosses over' (Groom 1983, 290)). Karak appears to have been the first major stop after Bosra and it is notable that the caravan remained there for a similar amount of time (*i.e.* four days). After leaving Karak, Ibn Battuta's caravan headed south-east via Ma'an. Unfortunately Ibn Battuta does not give a description of Ma'an, or state how long the caravan rested there, though it is interesting that he described it as the last town in Syria (هو آجر بلاد الشام). Ibn Battuta's caravan took the inland route from Ma'an via Tabuk and Medina to Mecca. The last identifiable place which he describes in modern Jordan is 'Aqabat al-Suwwan (The Flint Pass) which is the steep escarpment at the edge of the Jordanian plateau before it descends into the sand desert. Ludivico di Varthema also mentions this place, which he referred to as 'the steps of 'Aqaba' (Varthema 1863, 19). Beyond this place, which can be identified as modern 'Aqabat al-Hijaziyya, the only place mentioned by Medieval accounts which may be in modern Jordan is Sorar, which Musil (1926, 327) identifies with the site currently known as Mudawwara (see discussion under Ottoman sites).

While it is difficult to generalize from these accounts it is notable that neither caravan travelled via 'Aqabat 'Ayla (modern 'Aqaba), which appears to have been used exclusively by Egyptian pilgrims (despite the fact that 'Aqaba was generally regarded as part of Syria rather than Egypt or the Hijaz). It is also notable that both caravans appear to have avoided places such as Hesban, Salt and Ajlun, known to be large settlements at this time. The reason for avoiding these larger settlements may have been a desire to prevent unnecessary delays, which could have occurred at a major stop, and also to avoid the damage to crops, livestock and property which would, inevitably, have occurred when thousands of camels passed through a settled agricultural environment.

Archaeological Evidence

Kiswa is located 15 km south of Damascus, on the south side of the Nahr al-A'waj and is thought to have been the home of the pre-Islamic Ghassanid dynasty (Ibn Battuta 1958, 158 n. 1). Al-Idrissi, writing in 1154, describes Kiswa as a settlement on a hill with a large khan for travellers to the east (Musil 1926, 328). Today Kiswa contains the remains of a *zawiya*, built on the orders of Manjak al-Yusuf, the governor of Damascus during the 1370s (Meinecke 1992, II, 247). Five km further to the south there is a large caravanserai, Khan Dannun, built by Yusuf al-Manjak in 1376 as part of a programme for improving the pilgrim facilities in the area under his control (Sauvaget 1935–45, 41–48; Meinecke 1992, II, 257; Meinecke 1996, 46) (for Kiswa in the Ottoman period, see Chapter 8).

Bosra was the capital of the Roman Provincia Arabia and as such contains many remains from the Nabatean, Roman and Byzantine periods. During the early Islamic period it functioned as the capital of the Hauran, though the majority of Islamic remains are from the Medieval period (12th–14th centuries). Probably the most famous building activity was the conversion of the Roman theatre into a citadel, beginning in the 11th century. Other Medieval remains include six mosques (al-'Umari (1112–13), al-Mabrak (1136), al-Fatima, al-Khidr (1134), al-Dabbangan and Masjid Yaqut (1257–58)), two madrassas (Madrassa of Sunquuur al-Hakimi (1225–6) and a Dar al-Quran of 'Abd al-Wahid al-Shafi'i (1254)) and two bath-houses (the North bath house and Hamman al Manjak 1372). Although much of the infrastructure was inherited from the Roman period important restoration work was carried out, in particular the renovation of the south reservoir, currently known as Birkat al-Hajj.

Although some of this building activity was associated with Bosra's role as a regional capital, much of it was as a result of the town's position on the Hajj route. The Birkat al-Hajj is the most obvious example of a structure servicing the Hajj caravan, a huge (160 × 125 m) pre-Islamic open-air cistern, located to the south-east of the city. The cistern was restored under the orders of the Ayyubid governor of

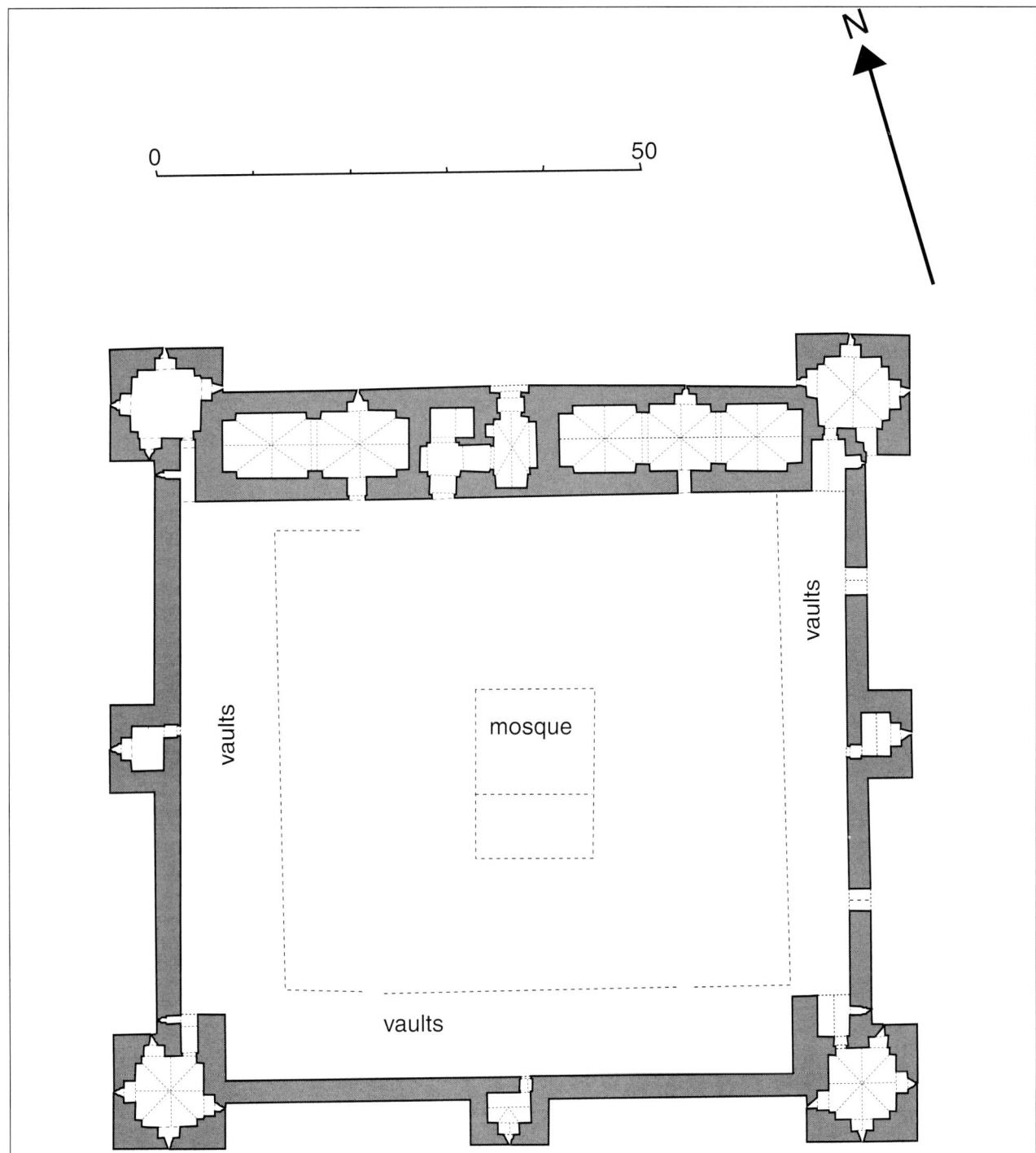

Fig. 1. Plan of fortress at Muzayrib in southern Syria. After Schumacher 1886 and Meinicke 1996.

Damascus, al-Mu'azzam 'Issa (1218–27) and included the renovation of the water conduits which supplied the city (Ibn Shaddad II 2 in ad-Dahan (ed.) 1963, 64, 8–10). In addition to the renovation of the water system, a small madrassa (later enlarged) was built at the north-east corner of the cistern, providing both a visual and spiritual focus for the pilgrims using the water.

Another Medieval building, which can be specifically linked to the Hajj caravan, is the bathhouse Hammam al-Manjak, its unusually large dimensions (45 × 14 m)

suggest that it was built as a facility for the pilgrims (Meinecke 1996, 46). One further building with a direct association with the pilgrimage is the Mabraq mosque and madrassa, which includes an ancient shrine containing the imprints of a camel's knees. The mosque was described by Ibn Battuta (see above) and evidently re-enforced the religious historical associations of Bosra with Muhammad and Mecca.

Muzayrib (Fig. 1) is not mentioned before the end of the 15th century, after which it replaces Bosra as the meeting place for Syrian pilgrims. It is possible that the Mamluks built some facilities for pilgrims, though the large, fortified caravanserai was built by the Ottoman Sultan, Selim (Bakhit 1982, 98–99; Meinecke 1996, 47–48) (for Muzayrib in the Ottoman period, see Chapter 8).

Zerka (Fig. 8 and Plates 21–22) (Zarka, Zerqa, Zarqa') is first mentioned in connection with the Hajj route by the 9th century writer al-Harbi (al-Harbi 1969, 653) who describes it as a stop between Adhra'at (أذرعات) and Qastal (القسطل). The place is also mentioned in several Medieval pilgrimage accounts, which describe it as a place where there was plentiful water, although there is no suggestion of a permanent settlement (Bakhit 2008; Majali and Mas'ad 1987, 314).

There are two sites of archaeological relevance to the Medieval Hajj route: Qasr Shebib and Khirbat Makhloul. Whilst Qasr Shebib is dealt with in detail, elsewhere in this volume (Chapter 9), there are other locations and buildings in the vicinity of Zerka, which may be associated with the Medieval Hajj. One of these other sites is Khirbat al-Makhul (36.03E 32.05N) located on a hilltop between the modern settlements of al-Sukhna and Zarqa. The site was first noted by Glueck (1951, 209–12), who identified it as Khirbet al-Breitawi, more recently it has been surveyed by Wilson and Peruzzetto as part of the Wadi Zarqa survey (Palumbo *et al.* 1996). The site comprises a complex of more than 100 cells, built around a central block, on the summit of a hill. The predominant pottery associated with the site has been dated to the Medieval period (*i.e.* 12th–15th centuries), although material dating to the early Islamic period (8th–9th centuries) was also evident. It seems likely that the visible remains relate to the Medieval occupation of the site and Wilson suggests that it may have served as a caravanserai for pilgrims. However, the shape of the complex, comprising an ovoid enclosure lined with cells and a central block of at least four rooms, is unusual for a caravanserai and is more reminiscent of a campsite. It may be that the site developed out of the ruins of an early Islamic planned structure, which became the basis for a seasonal, semi-permanent, campsite used by pilgrims on the Hajj. The strategic hill top location together with the defensive outer wall, indicate a need for security, certainly something required by pilgrims on the Hajj. If this can be identified as a Hajj station, it is one of a very few examples of a Medieval Hajj encampment, is of great significance and would repay excavation.

Jize (Figs 9–11 and Plates 23–30) also known as Ziza, or Zizia, is an ancient site with a large number of Roman remains (for a discussion of Roman and early Islamic Zizia, see Appendix 2). The principal feature of the site is a huge Roman reservoir (*c.* 90 × 100 m and more than 6 m deep) from which the name of the site may be derived (*i.e.* Jiz'ah can mean place where a small amount of water is left in a pool or trough (Groom 1983, 131)).

Apart from the reservoir the main feature of the site is a fort, currently used by the Jordanian police, which is evidently of Medieval origin. The oldest part of the fort comprises a large barrel-vaulted chamber (17.5 × 7.2 m) with a smaller cross-vaulted chamber attached to one side. The walls of the fort are more than 2.5 m thick and are made out of large squared limestone blocks (for a full discussion of the fort, see Chapter 9).

al-Lejjun is the site of a legionary fortress, covering an area of 4.6 ha, located next to a small wadi midway between Karak and Qatrana (31.14N 32.53E). The site has been extensively excavated by Thomas Parker (North Carolina State University) who has shown that the site was occupied until the 5th century (Parker 1986; Parker 1987). No remains of Medieval occupation have been reported and it seems unlikely that this is the site mentioned by Ibn Battuta. In any case the position of Lajjun, midway between Karak and the Roman/Ottoman site at Qatrana, make it an unlikely stopping place.

Lahun. It seems more likely that the site of al-Lajjun mentioned by Ibn Battuta should be identified with the site of al-Lahun, recently excavated by De Meulemeester (2008). Lahun is located on the north side of Wadi Mujib (31.27N 35.52E) and comprises a number of settlements of differing dates, from the Early Bronze Age to the Medieval period. The Medieval site is based around a rectilinear courtyard building of the early Islamic period that appears to have been abandoned during the 8th–12th centuries. In the 14th century a mosque with a deep *mihrab* was established and a number of houses were built on a similar alignment (*i.e.* aligned with the *qibla*). The site appears to have been abandoned after the 16th century.

Mahhatat al-Hajj (Lower) (31.27N 35.47E). This rectangular enclosure is also located on the north side of Wadi Mujib. Although the site is of Roman origin, it is likely that it was reused in the Islamic period as a stopping point on the Hajj (*c.f.* Kennedy 2000, 137 for summary and further reading).

Karak is a well known Medieval fortress and town, first fortified in 1142 during the rule of the Crusader King Fulk. During the Mamluk period Karak was the centre of a *Mamlaka* and took a prominent role in the politics of the time when it was used as a base, by the Sultan al-Nasir, in order to secure his power (Milwright 2008). There is plentiful evidence of the Medieval occupation of Karak in the form of large quantities of pottery sherds (unstratified), recently studied by Marcus Milwright (Milwright 2008; Mason and Milwright 1998), as well as the excavations of Robin Brown (Brown 1989) undertaken within the castle and the urban fortifications. Ottoman records from the 16th century indicate that Karak had a market and a khan for Hajj pilgrims, these are likely to date back to the Mamluk period, although this has yet to be confirmed archaeologically.

al-Thaniyya. The pilgrim camp mentioned by Ibn Battuta may be identified with the present day settlement of al-Thaniyya, where Ayyubid–Mamluk pottery was recently recovered during an archaeological survey (see, Brown 1991, site 236; Miller 1991, 91–92). The site is located at the head of a small wadi and forms the intersection of

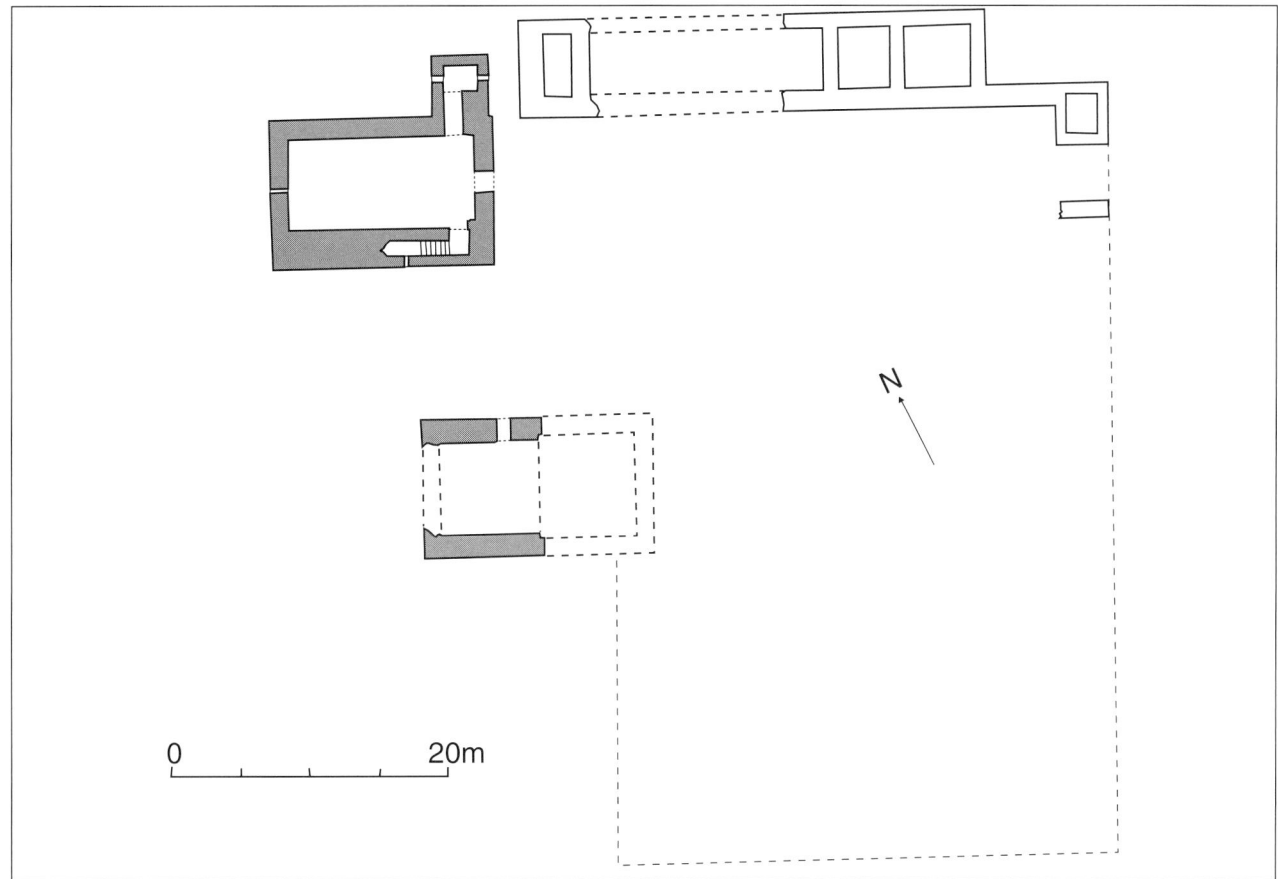

Fig. 2. Plan of Qasr Doshaq, near Shawbak, southern Jordan. Plan after Brünnow and Domaszewski 1905.

the King's Highway and an east–west route which links Qatrana to the Dead Sea.

Shawbak (30.33N 35.36E) is a fortress located on a prominent spur overlooking the Medieval route between Transjordan and Egypt. Although there may have been some settlement at the site before the 12th century, the fortress at the site was established in 1115 by the Crusader King, Baldwin I. The castle remained in Crusader hands until 1189 when it finally surrendered to Salah al-Din. The fortress and the surrounding area were developed under the Ayyubids and Mamluks, though it is apparent that it remained subordinate to its more northerly neighbour at Karak (Bakhit 2008). Although it is not directly mentioned in any Medieval pilgrimage account, its position on the Kings Highway (*Via Nova Traiana*) meant that the Hajj would have passed close to the fortress. In early Ottoman times the fortress played a supportive role to the Hajj forts further east, thus in the mid 16th century (1553–66) it had a garrison of 74 troops (Bakhit 1982, 99 n. 48). Shawbak is also listed as one of the postal stations between Damascus and Cairo, though it seems likely that the actual station may have been located at Doshaq (see below).

Doshaq (Fig. 2 and Plate 1). The enigmatic site of Doshaq lies on a promontory overlooking the Wadi Najal (30.30N 35.37E). The site lies adjacent to the line of the *Via Nova Traiana*, identified by a Roman milestone found nearby, and the remains of the actual road (for the location

on the Roman road system see Graf 1997, 277–79, fig. 4; for the road surface see Brünnow and Domaszewski 1905, 96, fig. 88). It has variously been dated to the Byzantine, Crusader, Saracenic (Medieval Arab) and Ottoman periods. It stands 5 km to the east of Showbak castle and comprises three building blocks set within an enclosure. The site has been discussed by a number of authors including Stuart Gray Hill (1897), Brünnow and Domaszewski (1905), Henry Field (1960) and most recently Alison McQuitty (2001). Gray Hill visited the site in 1896 and described the ruins as 'an early Christian church and a fort with remains of a rampart enclosing both perhaps a place of refuge built by the Crusaders subordinate to Shawbak, but the style of the church seemed Byzantine' (1897, 142). Later in the 1890s the site was visited by Brünnow and Domaszewski who regarded it as a Medieval caravanserai (Karawanserei aus sarazenischer Zeit). They published a plan and a photograph of the complex, together with a brief discussion of the architecture, in volume II of *Die Provinicia Arabia* (1905, II, 96–99). Henry Field's expedition visited Doshaq in May 1928 and gave the following description of the place. 'It proved to be a huge rectangular castle, with sides perhaps 100 × 130 paces. We saw but one small round gate on the south side. Towers were set at intervals, and the outer wall had numerous rooms built along it, as at Qasr al-Azraq. At a later date rooms had also been built in the centre of the courtyard. The whole edifice lay in the most

Plate 1. Doshaq southern Jordan near Shawbak 1898 (courtesy of the University of Princeton).

desolate confusion. It was impossible to either plan the ruin or even imagine its former state. The ruins are those of a fortified castle or rather caravanserai of Arab origin. In the courtyard toward the west there were traces of a small mosque. Nearby lay a birket (33 × 47 × 3.8 m) with stone steps leading down into it' (Field 1960, 83).

Since Field's visit in the 1920s the site has deteriorated considerably and much of the architecture is no longer visible. McQuitty only mentions the site briefly, but makes the important observation that it may be connected with the Hajj route (2001). Detailed examination of the photograph taken by Brünnow and Domaszewski shows the use of chevron mouldings, pointed arches, torus mouldings and drafted masonry, all of which are indicative of Medieval Islamic architecture.

It seems likely that this complex served as both a postal station between Cairo and Damascus and perhaps as one of the stations of the Medieval Hajj. Certainly the position of this site is more accessible than the nearby fortress of Shawbak, given that it is located at a junction of the King's highway and the Hajj route further east.

Ma'an does not figure as a major settlement in pre-Islamic times, though it is known that there was a bishop at the time of the Arab conquest and remains of a Byzantine church have been excavated. During the early Islamic period it is often mentioned as a place of importance connecting Arabia and Palestine and remains of an extensive Umayyad settlement have recently been identified (Genequand 2003). In the 9th century Ibn Khurdhadhibih described Ma'an as a *manzil* on the Hajj route, whilst al-Muqaddasi writing in the 10th century described it as a *manhal* or a *markaz*. During Mamluk times Ma'an was the centre of a *niyaba* and had a busy slave market (Elisséeff 1965, 897). Although no Medieval remains (Ayyubid/Mamluk) have been identified at Ma'an (Genequand 2003) the Ottoman fortress in the

town does appear to incorporate remains from an earlier building which may be Medieval (*i.e.* it incorporates vaults based on the two centre point arch) (for a discussion of Ma'an in the Ottoman period, see Chapter 9).

Conclusion

There has been an assumption from several modern writers that the Medieval Hajj followed the King's Highway via the great Medieval fortresses of Ajlun, Karak and Shawbak (see for example Bakhit 1982). Whilst these fortresses certainly had a role in the Medieval Hajj it appears that the actual stopping places lay outside these fortresses and urban centres, thus at both Karak and Shawbak it seems that sites several miles away were used for the Hajj caravan (*e.g.* al-Thaniyya for Karak and Doshaq for Shawbak). With the notable exception of Bosra the caravan seems to have stopped at centres less well known in Medieval historical sources (*e.g.* Zerka, Ziza, al-Lajjun/Lahun and Ma'an). The implication is that the Hajj was too large and too unwieldy to enter towns and that in any case, this would have caused unnecessary delays.

It is also apparent that the Medieval Hajj diverged from the King's Highway (*Via Nova Traiana*) at some point after Karak in order to follow the route via Tabuk. The most likely route would be to follow the *Via Nova Traiana* as far as Shawbak/Doshaq and then proceed south-east, via Udruh to Ma'an.

It is also worth mentioning that the King's Highway (*Via Nova Traiana*) would have continued in use throughout the Ottoman period, both as an alternative to the main route and as a route for pilgrims from Karak and Palestine across the Dead Sea. It is probably in this context that the small fort at Udruh was built during the Ottoman period.

4. Early Ottoman Arabia and the Syrian Hajj Route

This chapter will discuss the Ottoman presence in Arabia, from the initial conquests in the 16th century to the end of the 18th century when the French invasion of Egypt, followed by the rise of Muhammad Ali Pasha, fundamentally changed the balance of power in the region. In particular, this chapter will set the development of the Syrian Hajj route within the context of wider developments elsewhere in the Arabian Peninsula. The Ottoman experience in each part of Arabia was different, though there are certain trends which are noticeable throughout the region and which can, conveniently, be divided into two main periods, summarized as: Period One, 1515–1700 and Period Two, 1700–1800.

Period One: 1515–1700 – Conquest, Confrontation and Defeat

Before 1515 the Ottomans had no direct connection with Arabia, their knowledge of the region being through either, the accounts of individual pilgrims, such as Şehzade Korkud (al-Tikriti 2005), or through contacts with the Mamluk regime, such as Bayezid's naval alliance in 1510. However, this all changed when the Ottomans defeated the Mamluks at Marj Dabiq in 1516 and subsequently took possession of both Damascus and Cairo (see Chapter 5). For the first time the Ottomans came into direct contact with northern and western Arabia and inherited the ambiguous Mamluk relationship between Turkic rulers and local Arab notables. The first part of Arabia to succumb to Ottoman rule was the Hijaz, which accepted Ottoman suzerainty in 1517 when the Sharif of Mecca, Barakat II, agreed to send his 13 year old son, Abu Nomay, to Constantinople (Bacqué-Grammont and Kroel 1988, 17–18 and 24). Following the occupation of the Hijaz, the Ottomans extended their rule into Yemen, occupying

Aden in 1538 (G. R. Smith 2001, 273). Twelve years later the Ottomans added North Eastern Arabia to their list of territories, when they occupied the al-Hasa oasis. Given their abortive attempt to occupy the straits of Hormuz, it is likely that the Ottomans intended to extend their rule into South Eastern Arabia. The Ottomans claimed that their chief interest in Arabia was the protection of the Holy Cities of Mecca and Medina, although in reality they were much more concerned with the potential financial benefits. The main object of interest in the Peninsula was control of the Indian spice trade, which had been seized from the Mamluks by the Portuguese in the late 15th century. As early as 1538 a truce had been achieved between the Ottomans and the Portuguese establishing respective zones of activity. However, the relationship with the Portuguese remained tense and there were often attempts to alter the status quo, such as Ottoman attempts to capture Bahrain or Hormuz. The Portuguese had superior naval power, though the Ottomans had the advantage of land based forces.

By the middle of the 16th century the Ottoman presence in Arabia was established in three distinct areas, the Hijaz, Yemen and the al-Hasa oasis. The pattern of Ottoman control in each of these areas was complex and often incomplete, though it appears that the most successful Ottoman province was the Hijaz, despite the fact that economically it had considerably less to offer the Ottoman centre in terms of agricultural revenues, or trade. In this chapter it will be suggested that the principle reason for the successful retention of the Hijaz was the Hajj from Damascus and that this was maintained by effective roadside security; detailed in the rest of this volume.

During the 17th century the Ottomans suffered a number of defeats, the most notable of which was their defeat at Vienna in 1683, which was followed by an aggressive counter offensive by the Hapsburg rulers of Austria Hungary (Finkel 2005, 288). On the eastern front the

Ottomans led an intensified campaign against the Saffavids, drawing manpower from other parts of the Empire and in particular from Syria and Arabia. It may well be, that the reduced Portuguese threat in the Indian Ocean and the Gulf meant that the Ottomans attached less emphasis to their Arabian territories. In any case it is noticeable that by the middle of the 17th century they had lost control of two, out of three, of their Arabian provinces.

The Ottoman involvement in Yemen started in 1516, soon after their conquest of Egypt, when an Ottoman force defeated the ruling Tahirids near Zabid. However, a full scale conquest did not take place until 1538, when a large Ottoman expedition, on its way to India, arrived at Karaman island in the Red Sea, capturing Aden in 1538, Ta'iz in 1539 and finally San'a in 1547 (G. R. Smith 2001, 273). Ottoman rule was based on several fortresses and the degree of Ottoman control beyond these strongholds has always been debatable. The Ottomans control of much of Yemen was lost as early as 1566, when the Zaydi Imam Mutahhar expelled the Turkish garrison at San'a. Turkish rule was later re-established, after an expensive campaign led by Koca Sinan Pasha, the Ottoman governor of Egypt (C. K. Smith 2002). A series of rebellions in the early 1600s led to a final Ottoman defeat and withdrawal in 1636 (G. R. Smith 2001, 273). The Ottoman hold on Yemen was always precarious, partly because of its geographical remoteness from Constantinople and partly because many of its inhabitants were Shi'a. Communication to the rest of the Ottoman Empire was maintained through Egypt, via the Red Sea, and through Syria via the Hijaz and the overland pilgrimage routes to Mecca (for a more detailed discussion of the Red Sea area, see Chapter 5).

The Ottoman occupation of al-Hasa was, in theory, less problematic than in Yemen. Although there was a Shi'a presence within the province, there were also large numbers of Sunnis and an apparently peaceful co-existence (Muratada Ibn Alawan cited in Haarman 1979, 248). Unlike Yemen, there was no developed form of political control to rival Ottoman rule – the area had previously been ruled by local tribal chiefs. Like Yemen, al-Hasa was strategically important, as it not only protected the southern approach to Iraq, it also served as a check on the expansion of Saffavid power to the west side of the Arabian/Persian Gulf. In addition, communications within the province were relatively good, with caravan routes running to the coast at al-Qatif, to Basra and Iraq in the north and westwards to Najd and the Hijaz. The province itself was agriculturally rich by Arabian standards and was capable of producing surpluses for the Ottoman Empire. However, the Ottomans were not able to retain control of this area beyond the first half of the 17th century. The reason for this is unclear, although one recent writer has suggested that the Ottomans did not engage with the local population, extorted punitive taxes and relied on large fortresses, rather than establishing a presence in the landscape (Vassiliev 1998, 59–61).

Period Two: 1700–1800 – The Rise of the Wahhabis

By the early 18th century direct Ottoman control in Arabia was limited to the Hijaz, where it was frequently being threatened, both by Bedouin and Wahhabi forces. At this time the Ottoman provinces, peripheral to Arabia, were increasingly ruled by semi-independent rulers such as, Ali Bey in Egypt, Zahir al-'Umar in Palestine and Buyuk Sulaiman Pasha in Iraq. These were effectively independent rulers, who sought legitimacy and titles from the Ottoman Sultan in return for nominal allegiance. Sometimes, the actions of these rulers was in accordance with Ottoman policy and sometimes, in direct opposition, although there was rarely outright opposition to the concept of the Ottoman Empire which would have entailed a rejection of the caliphate, one of the foundations of Sunni Muslim unity. In these circumstances it is not surprising, that the strongest opposition to the Ottoman presence in Arabia came from an area that had never been conquered by the Turks.

Najd comprised a series of settlements based on a complex of oases located on a plateau in the centre of Arabia. Although Najd was outside the area formally conquered by the Ottomans, it was surrounded by territories that had been occupied by the Turks in the 16th century and had considerable trading links with the Empire. To the north-east was the Ottoman province of Basra, to the north-west the province of Damascus, to the west the Hijaz and al-Yaman. The only area with no Ottoman control was the south and south-east comprising the sparsely inhabited, Empty Quarter. As a result of its geographical position most of the inhabitants of Najd would have had some contact with the Ottoman Empire, either through trade or warfare, but the region remained clearly independent. Prior to the 18th century this was an area with little security, where different tribes, or family groups, raided each other's settlements and livestock in order to gain some ascendancy. In the 18th century the Muslim cleric, Abd al-Wahhab, called for a return to fundamental Islamic values, specifically calling for an abandonment of all local ancestral shrines and any religious practices perceived to be innovations since the time of the Prophet Muhammad (Vassiliev 1998, 78). In 1745 Muhammad Ibn Saud, the ruler of al-Diriya, gave refuge to Abd al-Wahhab and began an alliance which was to transform the Arabian Peninsula and lay the foundations of the future Saudi state. The arrangement between Ibn Saud and Abd al-Wahhab enabled the former to continue raids and conquests against neighbouring settlements and tribes, with the added bonus of a religious sanction that elevated his raids to the status of a *jihad*. For Abd al-Wahhab this ensured a sure supply of new followers, who could see the advantages of the new doctrine that ensured a steady supply of food and/or money, as well as increased personal security (Vassiliev 1998, 83–88).

Two groups were particularly at risk from the rising Wahhabi state, these were the Shi'a of eastern Arabia (al-Hasa) and Iraq, and the people of the Hijaz, whose Sunni religious beliefs were closer to those of the Ottoman Turks. In the first wave of their expansion the Wahhabis raided and eventually conquered most of the al-Hasa oasis, destroying ancestral shrines and cutting down sacred trees wherever they found them (Vassiliev 1998, 83–88). From al-Hasa the Wahabis raided deep into Mesopotamia and in 1802 sacked the Shi'a holy shrine at Karbala (Vassiliev 1998, 83–88). The Wahhabis had for some time tried to expand their influence to the Hijaz and as early as 1745 Ibn abd al-Wahhab had sent missionaries to Mecca. During the next half-century relations between the Wahhabis and the Hijaz gradually deteriorated and in 1790 the Sharif of Mecca sent an expedition against Najd (Vassiliev 1998, 83–88). Although the expedition did not succeed the Wahhabis were contained for the next 15 years. In 1805 the Wahhabis finally took control of the Hijaz, taking advantage of the Ottoman defeat in Egypt.

Conclusion

If we compare the Hijaz with the other Ottoman territories in Arabia, one of the main advantages was the existence of a secure, fortified land route linking it to the centre of the Empire. The existence of a secure road for pilgrims also ensured that there was a secure military route, enabling the Ottomans to maintain an active presence in Mecca and the Hijaz in general. Often the Hajj would be combined with a military expedition, as in 1672, when Evliya Çelebi accompanied Husayn Pasha and 8,000 troops to demand redress for the killing of the Ottoman governor of Jedda (Kortepeter 1979, 233).

Although al-Hasa had several caravan routes linking it to Basra in the north and the Hijaz in the west, these routes were not maintained by the Ottomans and there was no protection for those using the routes. Indeed, the Hajj route from al-Hasa to Mecca was closed for most of the Ottoman occupation due to a fear that Shi'a pilgrims would use the road. Anyone using this route was liable to be imprisoned by the governor of al-Hasa (Mandaville 1970, 498). Similarly, although Yemen had long established sea routes linking it to Egypt, the land routes needed to enable the movement of armies were less secure. It is noticeable that Sinan Pasha established Mecca as a secure base for his re-conquest of Yemen and marched his men overland from there to San'a. Although the route between Damascus and Mecca was well fortified, as shown above, the route the route from Mecca to Yemen was less well developed and did not have the fortified posts of the Syrian Hajj route. It is possible that if the Ottomans had extended their fortified road network to other parts of Arabia, they may have retained their Arabian territories and contained the Wahhabi threat. Certainly, when al-Hasa was re-occupied in the 1870s Midhat Pasha recommended the construction of roads with fortified posts (Anscombe 1977, 35).

5. The Ottoman Hajj Route: Motivation and Ideology

As a background to understanding the Ottoman Hajj route in Jordan its is useful to consider the position of the Ottoman Empire, both within the Middle East and further afield in Europe and Asia, during the 16th–18th centuries.

Ottoman rule in Arabia was made possible by two major military victories both of which had considerable ideological significance. The first of these victories was the Ottoman conquest of Constantinople (modern Istanbul) by Sultan Mehmet Fatih in 1453. For the first time in its 800-year history, a Muslim state had taken over the spiritual home of orthodox Christianity and, in the process, had become a major factor in European domestic politics. The prestige accruing from this conquest firmly established the Ottomans as the principal Muslim power worldwide. The second event is the conquest of Egypt and Syria between 1515 and 1517, which also gave the Ottomans control of the Hijaz, including both Mecca and Medina (for a discussion of the Ottomans in Arabia, see Chapter 4). The pre-eminent status of the Ottoman Sultan amongst Muslim rulers was now confirmed; they not only claimed the title of *khalifa*, as successors of the defeated Mamluk regime, they also adopted the role of protectors of the two shrines, adopting the title *khadim al-Harameyn al-Sharifayn* (Esin 1986, 225–26). Neither of these titles was held lightly and it can be seen that the Ottomans did their utmost to be seen as leaders of the Muslim world and defenders of Islam's holiest cities (see, for example, Inscription No. 2 in Chapter 11).

Of course, this new status presented the Ottomans with new responsibilities that had not been encountered when they were a minor Turkish state. Three main challenges arose out of this situation: firstly they were now a global power with global alliances and enemies; secondly they needed to maintain control over the vast territories which they had conquered and; thirdly they needed to provide some sort of religious leadership.

The following discussion will examine how the fortification of the Hajj route, from Damascus to Mecca, relates to each of these issues. However, before discussing these questions it is important to give a brief review of the process and nature of the fortifications (see also Petersen 1989; Petersen 2001).

The Sequence of Fortification (Maps 3, 4 and 5)

Although the Hajj from Cairo to Mecca (*Darb al-Hajj al-Masri*) had been the principal concern of the Mamluks they also supported the Syrian Hajj route, which was accorded almost equal status and had its own *mahmal* ('Ankawi 1974). Whilst the Egyptian overland route had been provided with fortresses and other facilities as early as the 13th century (including the fortress at 'Aqaba; currently under excavation (de Meulemeester and Pringle 2000)) the Syrian route had no forts, with the possible exception of the castles of Zizia (Jize) and Qasr Shebib at Zerka (Petersen 1991) (these forts are described in Chapter 9). Instead, it appears that the Mamluk Hajj caravan from Damascus followed a route largely without facilities, except for those provided at the few settlements on the way (*e.g.* Bosra, Karak and Tabuk) (for a discussion of the Medieval route, see Chapter 3). Within a few years of the conquest (of Syria) the Ottoman Sultan, Selim I, had ordered the construction of fortresses at Sanamayn, Muzayrib and Tell Far'un (Mafraq): all within 60 km of Damascus (these sites are discussed in Chapter 8). By the 1570s the network was extended deep into the Hijaz with forts at Qatrana, 'Unaiza, Ma'an, Dhat al-Hajj, Tabuk, Ukhaydhir, al-'Ula and Hadiyya (Bakhit 1982) (these forts are discussed in detail in Chapters 9 and 10). The forts could only be built by royal decree, although in most cases this was on the recommendation of the provincial governor (Faroqhi

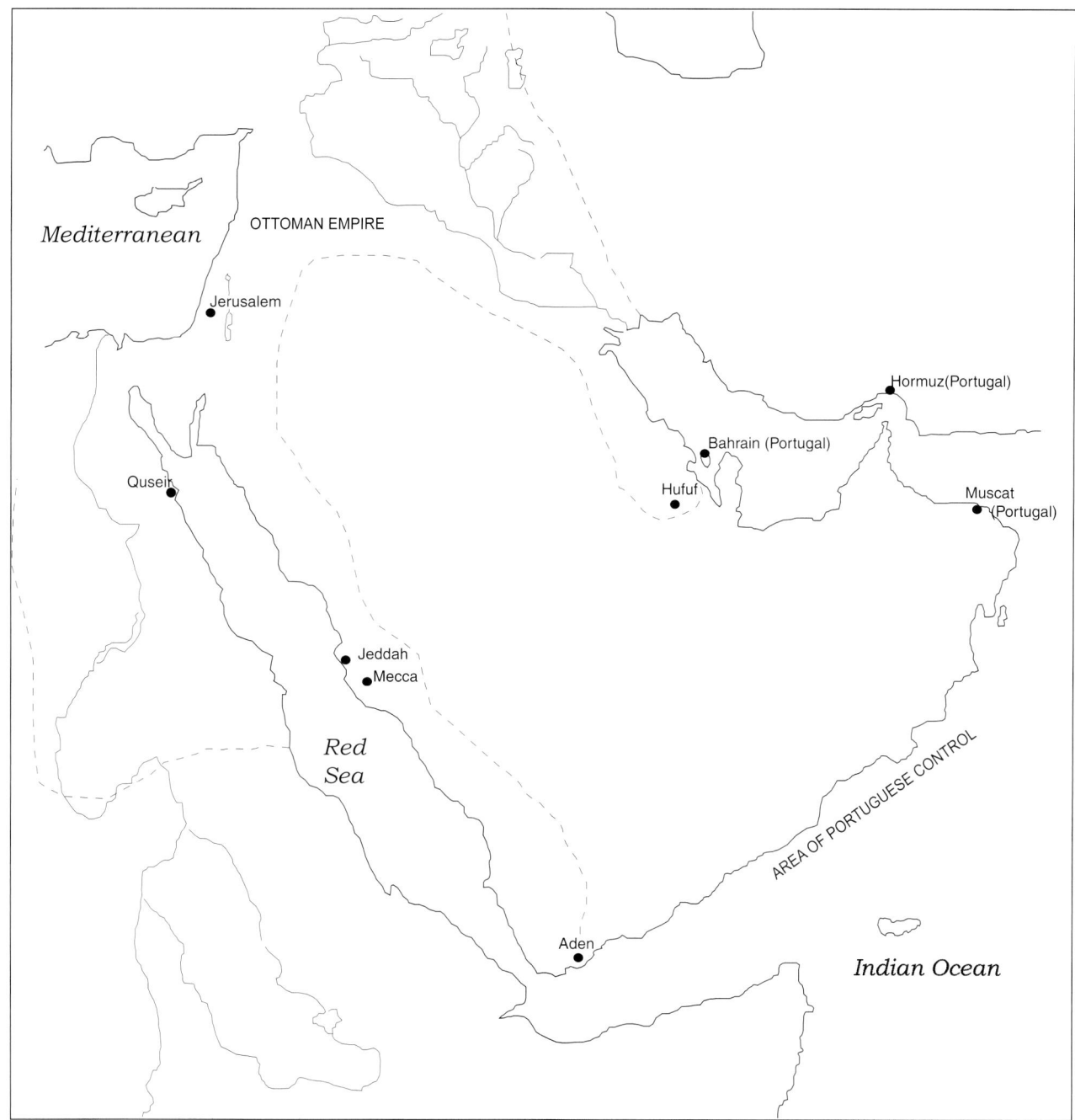

Map 3. Ottoman Arabia.

1994, 72). A limited amount of information survives about the actual construction of the forts, one of the most useful pieces of evidence is the foundation inscription, dated to 1563, above the gateway to the fort at Dhat al-Hajj (for a discussion of the inscriptions see, Chapter 11, Inscription No. 5, and for the fort, see Chapter 10). The remarkable feature of the inscription is that it states that the fort was built within 40 days. Whether this timescale is typical for the construction of one of these forts is not known, though it does indicate the speed that could be achieved when necessary (see also, Heyd 1960, 107–13 which discusses the construction of forts in Palestine).

The design of the Hajj forts differs from previous fortified building types in the region. In particular, the standard Ottoman Hajj fort plan differs from that of Mamluk forts of similar size and function. The main difference is that the Ottoman Hajj forts are built around a central courtyard and that the walls are generally less thick than their Medieval predecessors. Qasr Shebib at Zerka and the fort at Zizia (Jize) provide useful examples of Medieval forts of similar size. In both cases the ground floor comprises a single large vaulted space, with walls more than 2 m thick and access to the upper floors via a staircase built into the thickness of the wall. By contrast,

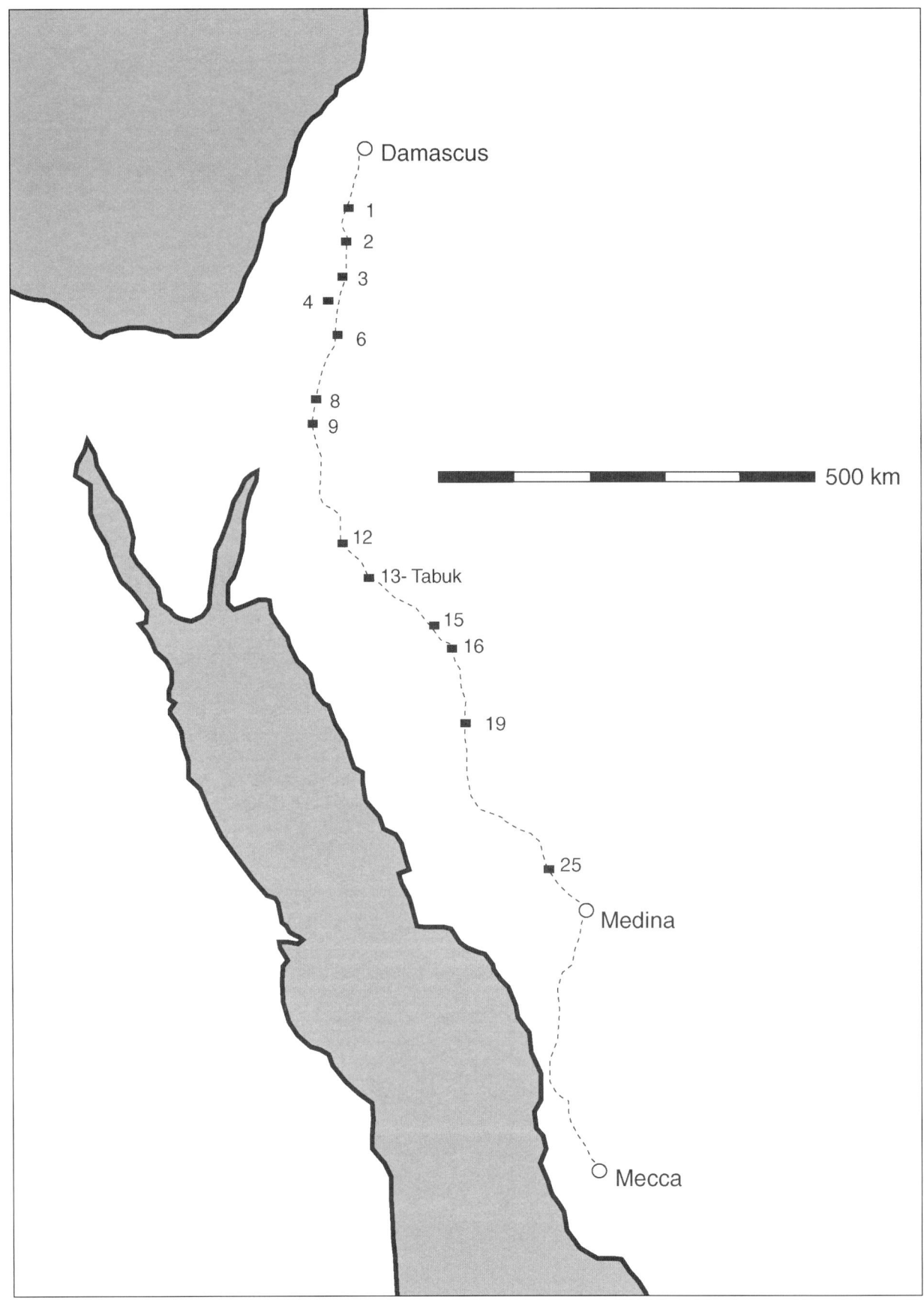

Map 4. Map of Hajj route showing locations of forts in the 16th century. 1) Muzayrib, 2) Mafraq, 3) Zerka (Qasr Shebib), 4) Zizia (Birkat Zizia), 6) Qatrana, 8) 'Unaiza, 9) Ma'an, 12) Dhat al-Hajj, 13) Tabuk, 15) 'Ukhaydhir, 16) Qal'at al- Mu'azzam, 19) al-'Ula, 25) Wadi al-Qura (Biar Naszeif), 26) Hafira.

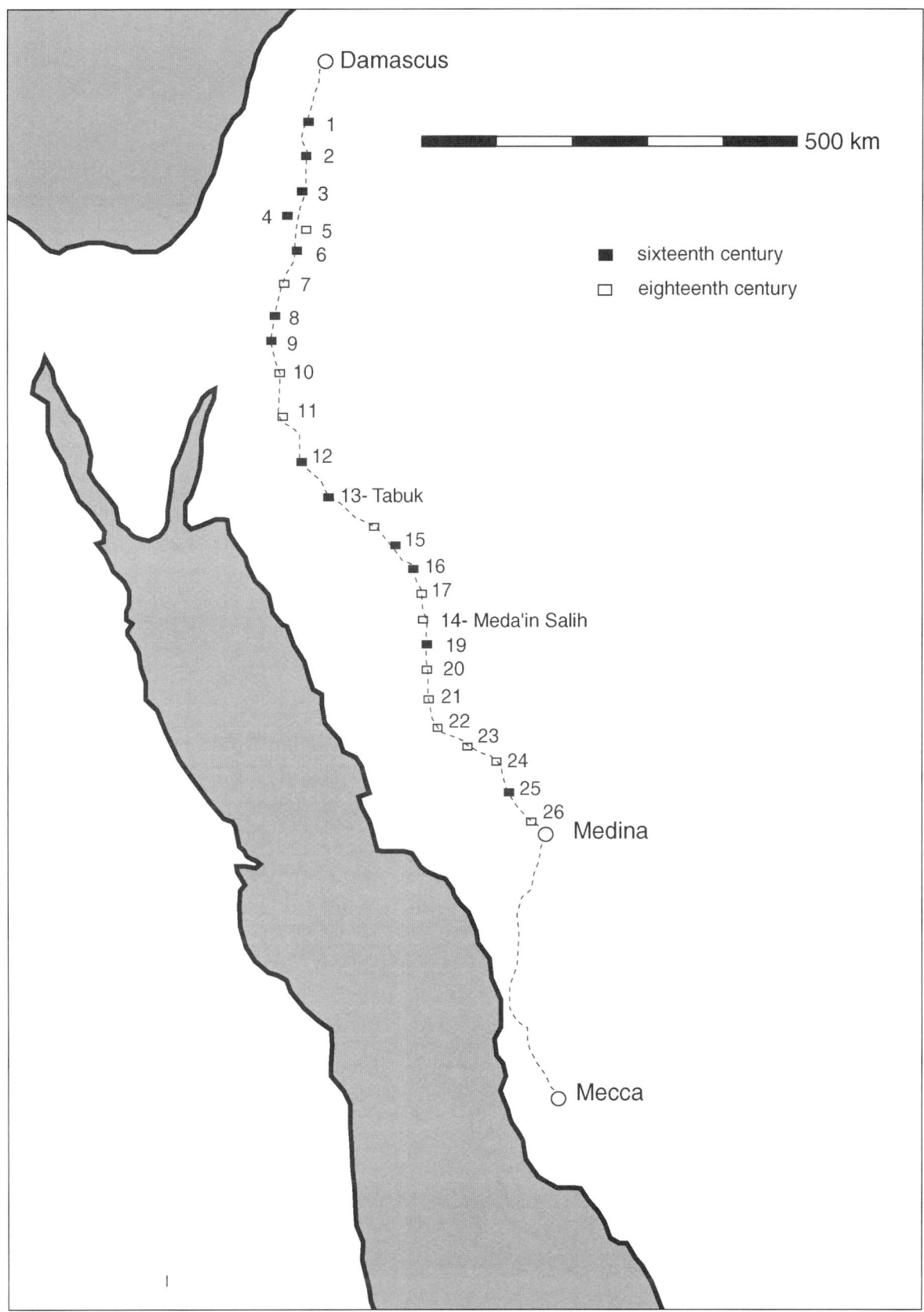

Map 5. Map of Hajj route showing locations of forts in the 18th century. 1) Muzayrib, 2) Mafraq, 3) Zerka (Qasr Shebib), 4) Zizia (Birkat Zizia), 5) Balqa Dab'a, 6) Qatrana, 7) Hasa, 8) 'Unaiza, 9) Ma'an, 10) Fassu'a ('Aqaba al-Hijaziyya), 11) Mudawwara, 12) Dhat al-Hajj, 13) Tabuk, 14) al-Qalandariyya, 15) 'Ukhaydhir, 16) Qal'at al- Mu'azzam, 17) Dar al-Hamra, 18) Mada'in Salih, 19) al-'Ula, 20) Bir al-Ghannam, 21) Zummurud, 22) Sawrah (Bir Jedid, Valide Kuyusu), 23) Hadiyya/Antar, 24) Nakhlatayn (Fahletein, Istabel Antar, Shajwa), 25) Wadi al-Qura (Biar Naszeif), 26) Hafira.

the ground floor of a typical Ottoman Hajj fort comprises a series of small vaulted rooms, built around a square central courtyard, with two open air staircases providing access to the upper floors. This layout has much in common with Medieval khans and caravanserais (*c.f.* Lee, Raso and Hillenbrand 1992), although there is also a more interesting possibility that they were derived from wooden forts used on campaigns in the Balkans (Nicolle and McBride 1983). Each of the Hajj forts measures approximately 20 m per side (min 15 m, max 29 m) with a rectangular central courtyard that generally comprises approximately 20% of the ground floor area of each fort (min 15% and max 36%). Most of the forts are three storeys high (ground floor, first floor and upper floor with parapet), although some, such as Mafraq, were only two storeys high. The forts were built of local materials and were generally plain in appearance with little decoration except that above the gateway (*e.g.* Qatrana with its three balls above the entrance). Although some of the forts were built on earlier sites (mostly Roman), there is little evidence of direct continuity of use/occupation at any of them. Despite their simple appearance, the forts were an unmistakable sign of Ottoman authority and power expressed through the precision and solidity of the masonry. Each of the 16th century forts was located next to a significant water supply, located outside the walls.

The next major phase of fortress construction occurred in the 18th century (Barbir 1980). Forts built during this period include, Qal'at al-Balqa (Dab'a), Qal'at al-Hasa, Qal'at al-Fassu'a ('Aqabat al-Hijaziyya), Qal'at Mudawwara and Medain Saleh. In addition to the construction of the forts, a road and bridge were built at Qal'at al-Hasa and major repairs were carried out at Hadiyya. The architecture of the 18th century forts differs from that of the 16th century buildings. The main difference is that the 18th century buildings have projecting corner turrets with narrow gun slits. There was also an increase in the number of openings in the later forts. Although the 16th century forts also had gun/arrow slits these were less numerous, for example the fort at Ma'an built in 1563, had 16 large splayed gun/arrow slits at first floor level, whereas the fort at Medain Saleh, built in the mid 1700s, had 39 slits at first floor level. The openings not only differ in number, but also in size and shape. In the 16th century forts, many of the openings were tall slits, more than 1 m high, suitable for archers and highly visible from the exterior. Sometimes the tall slits had an enlarged opening at the bottom suitable for cannon (see for example Qatrana Plate 66). In the 18th century forts, the slits were generally smaller (0.5 m tall, or less) and less visible from the exterior. A related observation is that the later forts are even plainer than those of the 16th century, thus there is no carved stone decoration above the doorways similar to that which can be seen at Ma'an and Qatrana.

Anybody who has visited any of these forts can appreciate the massive effort required to build them in remote locations, so far removed from the centres of power. In order to understand the mentality behind the construction of these forts, it is useful to address the three questions raised earlier:

- How do these buildings fit into the Ottoman global policies?
- How do these buildings relate to internal control (stability) of the Empire?
- How do these buildings relate to Ottoman ideas of religious leadership?

Ottoman Global Policy (Map 3)

The Ottomans were relative newcomers to the area of Egypt and the Levant and as such they not only followed many of the policies of their Mamluk predecessors, but also employed many of the same people. For example, the Mamluk governor of Damascus, Janbirdi al-Ghazali, was confirmed in his office by the Ottoman Sultan, Selim I, even though he rebelled a year later (Bakhit 1982, 19). Similarly, the Sharif of Mecca, Barakat II (1495–1524), who had administered the area for the Mamluks, was confirmed in his office by the Ottoman Sultan (Pearson 1995, 84). However, it is clear that the Ottomans had to adapt to the changed conditions following their victory. For example, they will have been aware of the Portuguese (failed) attack on Jedda, which took place in the same year as the Ottoman occupation of Egypt (*i.e.* 1517). They will also have known the Mamluk defeat was largely a result of their unwillingness to adapt to changed circumstances, such as the introduction of firearms (see Ayalon 1956) and the Portuguese presence in the Red Sea and Indian Ocean (Pearson 1995, 81–83). All of these factors will have encouraged the Ottomans to think of the world beyond the Mediterranean. The determination of the Ottoman rulers to fight on a global scale can be seen in 1538, when an Ottoman expedition was sent against the Portuguese in the Indian Ocean. Under the leadership of the Egyptian governor, Sulayman Pasha, a fleet sailed to Gujerat with the aim of 'holding those Indian ports; cutting off the road and blocking [the] way to the sacred cities of Mecca and Medina' (Mughal 1969, 147). The expedition was unsuccessful, largely because Turkish galleys were no match for ocean going Portuguese ships. Another Turkish plan was to dig a canal between the Mediterranean and the Red Sea, so that the Turkish fleets could operate both in the Mediterranean and the Indian Ocean (Farooqi 1989, 156–57). Although neither of these projects succeeded, they do show that the Ottomans had serious global intentions.

How then do the Hajj forts fit into this global strategy? Within this context the Hajj forts can be seen as part of a plan, or process, to secure Arabia from European, specifically Portuguese, attacks (for a more detailed consideration of the Arabian context, see Chapter 4). As with the Hijaz railway, nearly 400 years later (Franzke 2003; Ochsenwald 1980; Peeters 1994, 316–20), the fortification of the pilgrim route had definite military objectives. If we look at Arabia as a whole in the 16th century, it can be seen that it was divided into those areas under Portuguese domination (the coasts of south and south-east Arabia) and the areas of Ottoman control (*e.g.* the Hijaz, Basra and al-Hasa) with the area between controlled by Arab Bedouin tribes who were not, at this time, a military threat to the Ottomans (this situation was to change in the 18th century as will be discussed below). Whilst the Portuguese were obviously more suited to maritime warfare, the Ottomans had the advantage on land, where they were generally welcomed as co-religionists and also had a better knowledge of the territory. This meant that the Red Sea and the Persian/Arabian Gulf were the most likely areas of conflict, as they were accessible to both the Ottomans and the Portuguese.

Within the Persian/Arabian Gulf a stalemate was reached by the middle of the 16th century (see also, Chapter 4). By which time the Portuguese had built a base at Hormuz in 1514 (Castanheda III, cxxxvi cited in Pearson 1995, 96) and the Ottomans had established a base at Hufuf (1552), in the al-Hasa oasis, with a number of outlying forts at al-'Uqayr (1560/1) and al-Qatif (1551) (King 1998, 189, 192–94; Mandaville 1970).

The situation in the Red Sea was more complicated, though it was generally more favourable to the Ottomans. Navigation within the Red Sea was notoriously difficult because of the reefs and the variable wind conditions (for accounts of this see Pearson 1995, 149–51). Against this, the Ottomans had the problem that much of the south part of the African coast of the Red Sea, was outside their control. Also, any Portuguese ships managing to enter the Red Sea would have direct access to Egypt and the cities of Mecca and Medina. In other words, any Portuguese access to the Red Sea would significantly weaken the strategic position of the Ottomans.

The Hajj forts were undoubtedly part of the defence system of the Red Sea coast of Arabia. They provided a secure line of communication directly between the Hijaz, Syria and ultimately Anatolia. This enabled Ottoman troops to move relatively rapidly down along the Red Sea coast to Mecca and Medina and ultimately to Yemen, which the Ottomans occupied in 1538 and finally conquered in 1549 (Hess 1974, 27–29).

To the West, in Africa, the Ottomans built a series of larger forts intended to extend Ottoman power further south, into the area of modern Sudan. Examples should include the fortresses of Qasr Ibrim in Egypt and Qal'at al-Sai in Sudan. Qasr Ibrim is an ancient fortress on the Nile, 220 km south of Aswan, which was rebuilt by the Ottomans in the 1550s. Qal'at al-Sai, is located 650 km south of Aswan and was founded in 1585 (Alexander 1997, 16–20; Alexander 2000). As well as securing the Nile frontier, as argued by John Alexander, it is probable that these forts were intended to provide an Ottoman military presence on the western side of the Red Sea. In addition to the Nile fortresses, the Ottomans also established a fortress and settlement at Quseir in 1571 (Le Quesne 2004, 148), partially in response to a Portuguese attack on the African

Red Sea ports by Don João de Castro in 1541 (Kennedy Cooke 1933).

Whilst the Portuguese appeared to be a significant threat in the first half of the 16th century, by the later part of the same century a status quo had been established and there was even the prospect of a peace treaty between the two powers (Pearson 1995, 88). By the 17th century Portuguese control of the Indian Ocean was being subverted by the English and Dutch. This situation may account for the lack of building activity on the Syrian Hajj route during the 17th century. In any case, by this time Ottoman attention was more focused on south-eastern Europe.

Internal Control (Map 6)

When the Ottomans took control of Syria and Egypt in the early 16th century, they were faced with the problem of establishing their rule over an essentially foreign people. Whilst the Mamluk rulers were also largely non-Arab, they were, at least, more local and their system of government had evolved in Arab lands, using Arabic as the language of government. It was in this context that the Ottomans sought to consolidate their rule through military power in which architecture was a major component. One of the priorities in winning over the support of the local (settled) population was the elimination of the Bedouin threat. Whilst at a high level Ottoman rhetoric was concerned with enemies such as the Portuguese and the Saffavids, in practical terms there was a strong emphasis on controlling the Bedouin. For example, when the Ottomans decided to rebuild Quseir on the Red Sea coast of Egypt, one of their principal concerns was to defend the townspeople from the 'disorders and wickedness of the mischief-making Arabs who many times killed the notables and plundered all their properties'(*Muhimme Defteri* No.12, Document 906 cited in, Le Quesne 2004, 148). If we look at the Ottoman documents relating to Palestine, there is a constant emphasis on controlling the Bedouin and encouraging settled life (see, Heyd 1960, for numerous examples). The massive Ottoman project of rebuilding the walls of Jerusalem was partly a response to the Bedouin threat, as was the construction of fortresses at Ras al-'Ayn (Petersen 1998), Bayt Jibrin (Sharon 1999, 138–39; Heyd 1960, 115), Khan al-Tujjar (Lee, Raso and Hillenbrand 1992), Qal'at Burak (Sharon 1999, 244–46; Hawari, Auld and Hudson 2000) and Jenin (Petersen 1995) (for a discussion of the fortress network in Palestine, see Chapter 7). The construction of the Hajj forts may also be seen as part of this process to control the Bedouin and encourage settled life.

The 16th century Hajj forts were designed for the use of small cannons and bows and arrows (see, for example, Ma'an and Qatrana in, Chapter 9). Although most of the gateways contained hidden machicolations the defences were not particularly sophisticated and were only designed to repel bands of Bedouin who during the 16th century would not have had access to hand held guns.

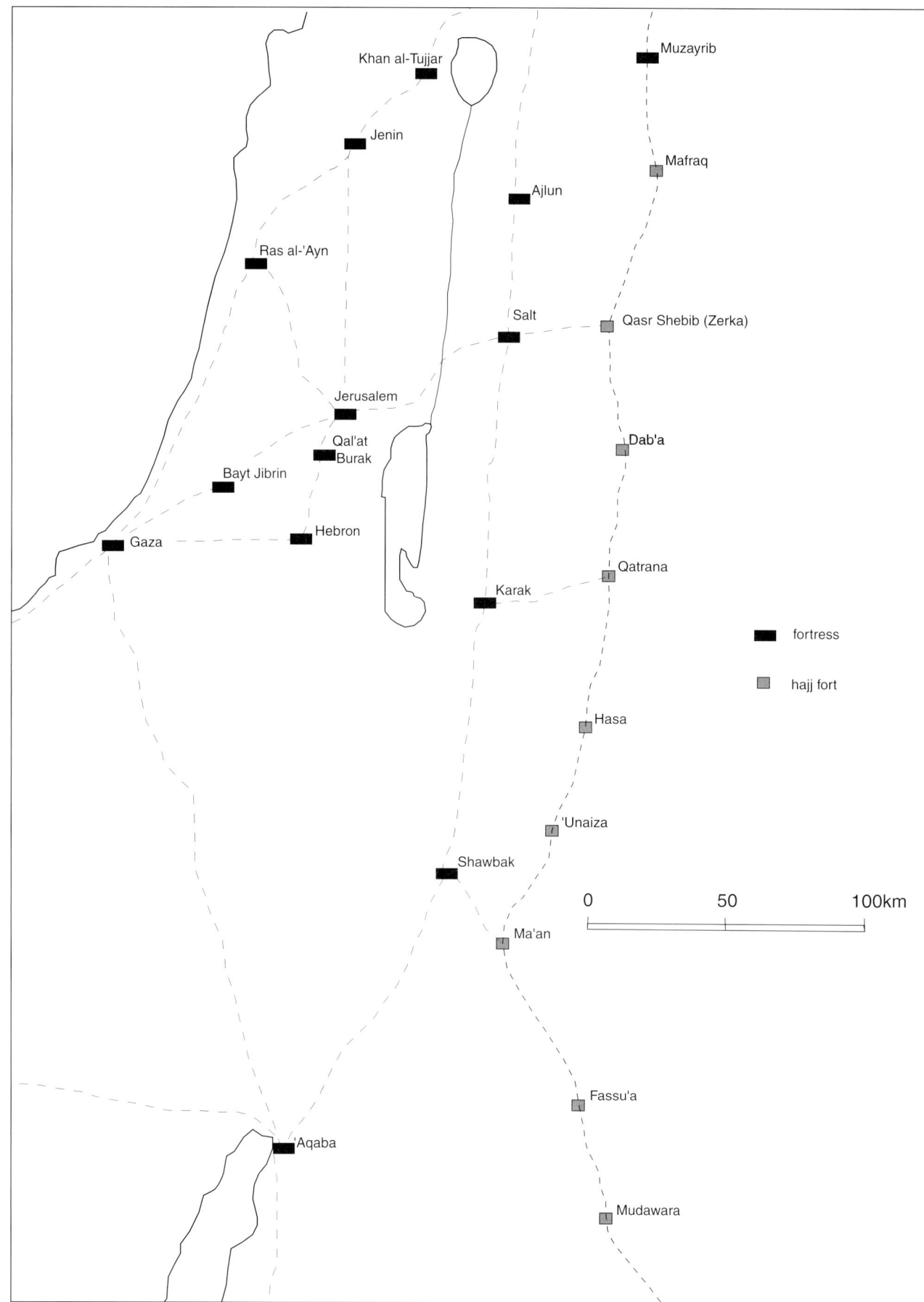

Map 6. Sixteenth century fortress network in Palestine and Trans-Jordan.

Although we have no way of measuring the success of the Hajj forts, or other measures taken against the Bedouin, they appear to have been fairly successful. Certainly the new Ottoman forts in Palestine encouraged a return to settled life in areas that had previously been nomadic territory (Petersen 2005, 41–42; Heyd 1960, 103). However, during the 18th century there was a massive increase in Bedouin attacks on the Hajj caravan, culminating in the attacks of 1757 when the entire Hajj caravan was destroyed by the Banu Sakhr (Rafeq 1966, 213–18; Barbir 1980, 175–76) (see also, Chapter 10, Dhat al-Hajj and al-'Ula). This disaster has been attributed to the failure of the Ottoman rulers to pay the required amount to the Bedouin who lined the route to Mecca (Peeters 1994, 161). It is also possible, that a new influx of Arab tribes, including the Shammar and the 'Anazah, which began in the late 17th century, altered what may already have been a delicate balance at the fringes of the desert (Lewis 1987, 8). This in turn could have been a result of environmental factors such as drought.

However, the successful Bedouin attacks of the 18th century may have been the result of another factor – the acquisition of hand held firearms that could be fired from horseback. In the 16th century the effective range of a hand held firearm was approximately 20 m, during the 18th century the range was considerably extended, by progressive lengthening of the barrel (Elgood 1995, 38). Examination of the 18th century forts in Jordan (Mudawwara, Fassu'a Dab'a and Hasa in Chapter 9) suggests that, whereas the 16th century forts were adapted for the use of small cannon (*e.g. Karathaun*), the 18th century forts were designed for hand held guns. The 18th century forts had projecting corner towers that greatly increased the field of fire and enabled the soldiers inside to protect the corners of the fort.

The acquisition of firearms by the Bedouin was both a technological development and a result of changing patterns of trade. Before the 18th century the Bedouin did not posses guns that could be fired from horseback and consequently were unable to mount a serious attack on a fort, or well defended caravan. During the 16th and 17th centuries it had often been possible to scare off an attack, thus in 1672, the *Amir al-Hajj* (Commander of the Hajj Caravan) only had to get his military band to play, to disperse the would be Bedouin attackers (Peeters 1994, 373, n. 51). The new hand held guns made the Bedouin a much more formidable foe and it is perhaps not surprising that the Wahhabis emerged as a major political force in Central Arabia at the end of this century (see Chapter 4, for a discussion of the rise of the Wahhabis). The mechanism by which the Bedouin obtained weapons is not known in detail, though by the 18th century there were large numbers of private workshops, outside government control, able to produce *tüfneks* (muskets) of a better quality than those produced in Istanbul (Ágoston 2005, 95). The Bedouin were also able to acquire firearms by trade, one source was probably via Zahir al-'Umar, the semi-independent ruler of Galilee, who was (illegally) buying arms from Dutch and French merchants in Acre, Haifa and Sidon, in return for cotton (Edwards *et al.* 1993; Petersen 2000).

Religious Leadership

It is clear that the Ottomans saw themselves as the prime defenders of Islam, this was acknowledged by other Muslim dynasties such as the Mughal rulers of India and the rulers of Acheh in Indonesia (Farooqi 1989, 157–58). The fortification of Jerusalem and the renovation of the Dome of the Rock (*Qubbat al-Sakhra*) with faience tiles was clearly an attempt to show that they were Muslim rulers intent on defending Jerusalem from the Christians (Auld and Hillenbrand (eds) 2000). However, the Hajj was the principal focus of Ottoman religious leadership in the Arab provinces. At the starting point of the Hajj, in Damascus, a magnificent pilgrimage complex, including two mosques, a madrassa and hostel, was built by the famous Ottoman architect Sinan (Goodwin 1978, 256–27). The Ottomans were careful to follow established procedures in the conduct of the Hajj as any deviation from established practice would be regarded as suspicious by the local population. At the other end of the Hajj route, the Ottomans embellished the Holy cities of Mecca and Medina with buildings and gave lavish grants of money to the poor (Esin 1986; Faroqhi 1988).

The fortification of the Hajj route may be seen as part of this process, a method of advertising the Ottoman presence from Damascus to Mecca. However, a survey of the inscriptions on the forts themselves does not indicate a pre-occupation with religious titles, or claims, and simply states the name of the Sultan who ordered the construction, the names of officials who carried out the work and the year the work was completed (for an examination of the inscriptions, see Chapter 11). It is also notable that none of the Ottoman Sultans made the Hajj before the 19th century, whereas at least four of the Mamluk rulers made the journey to Mecca (Burckhardt 1829, 248; 'Ankawi 1974, 154). Of course there may have been practical reasons why the Ottoman Sultans could not have made the Hajj, such as security, health, or the length of the journey, though all of these factors would have operated on other pilgrims. It is, for example, interesting to remember that the king of Mali, Mansa Musa, made the much longer pilgrimage from West Africa in the 14th century (Maqrizi, in, Levtzion and Hopkins 1981, 351). It appears then, that Ottoman support for the Holy Cities was institutional rather than personal, their extensive donations of money and property to the Holy cities was what was expected of them. In this light the Ottoman Hajj forts can be seen as part of a process of increasing the religious status of the Sultans, without them having to make a personal commitment.

Conclusion

What should be clear from this brief discussion is that the Ottoman Hajj forts had a variety of functions, each of which served to increase Ottoman power in the region. The fact that the forts lack any overt religious symbolism, either in terms of decoration or inscriptions, suggests that their primary purpose was the extension of military power in the area. This is not to say that religious considerations were not important, but that they were regarded as coincident to the interests of the state, thus a document dated to 1584 refers to the Haram i Sherif in Mecca as, 'necessary to state and religion' (*Muhimme Defterleri* 12, p. 438 no. 849 cited in Faroqhi 1988, 162). Although the forts were relatively small structures, their significance was increased by the isolation of their locations and the way they fitted into a wider network of fortresses in Palestine and beyond.

6. Travelling on the Darb al-Hajj

Part I: The Hajj Route (Maps 7 and 8)

The contribution of archaeology to the study of pilgrim routes and their landscapes is a relatively recent phenomenon. Important studies include Julie Candy's study of the route to Santiago di Compostella, in north-west Spain, and Wilkinson's study of the landscapes of the Darb Zubayda (Candy 2003; Wilkinson 2003; see also Tate 2007). In her study of the route to Compostella, Candy (2003) adopts a phenomenological approach, focusing on the question of how the landscape shapes the experience of those travelling through it. In particular she is interested in boundaries marking changes in either landscape, or the man-made environment, and how this may have related to individual pilgrims. Wilkinson's (2003, 165–68) work on the Darb Zubayda is more directly related to the physical geography of the Hajj route, focusing, in particular, on geological formations and hydrological features. Elements of both approaches will be used in this chapter in an attempt to gain some insights into how this immense movement of people and beasts, moved through the landscape. In this context it is worth stating that the Hajj route was both a product of its landscapes and had effects on the environments through which it passed.

The Syrian Hajj route can be divided into three major geographical zones, each with its own geological, climatic and human characteristics. These zones were clearly recognized by pilgrims. The northern section, between Damascus and Ma'an, was generally considered as part of Syria, the majority of this part of the route was within a day's journey of an urban centre. The high altitude of this part of the road meant that it was liable to become muddy and very cold during winter, whilst in the summer, although the weather might be hot during the day, the night time temperatures were likely to be much cooler than further south. The central section, from Ma'an to Medain Saleh, was the hardest part of the route as it was remote from urban centres and the climate was likely to be extremely hot and arid during the summer months. The southern section, from Medain Saleh to Medina, was again within reach of settled areas upon which pilgrims could rely for water, shade and provisions, though summer temperatures could be excessive (today temperatures in excess of 50°C are not uncommon). The movement of the Islamic (*Hijri*) year in relation to the Solar year (*i.e.* the year defined by the Gregorian calendar) meant that the Hajj took place during different seasons. When the Hajj fell during the winter, the southern part of the route with its tropical climate would have been preferable to the cold Syrian plateau. However, during a summer Hajj the conditions of the central and southern parts of the route would have been extremely punishing and the northern part of the route would have appeared gentle in comparison.

The best source for information related to the experience of travelling on the Hajj are, of course, the accounts of pilgrims and travellers themselves, which range from dry annotated lists of stops (Burckhardt 1822), to the evocative poetic descriptions of Doughty (1979). There are, as one might expect, some variations in the types of description given depending on whether or not the narrator was Muslim. For example, the Turkish traveller, Evliya Çelebi, took note of Muslim Holy places, mosques and tombs of prominent Muslims, whereas Charles Doughty's account is suffused with references to the Bible and in particular the migration of Jews from Egypt though the Sinai (see, for example, Doughty 1979, 100). It is also notable that earlier descriptions, whether Muslim or Christian, are less likely to convey information about the landscape through which they passed, thus Ludivico di Varthema's early 16th century account contains considerable detail about events on the journey, but makes virtually no reference to the landscape except where it is essential to the narrative.

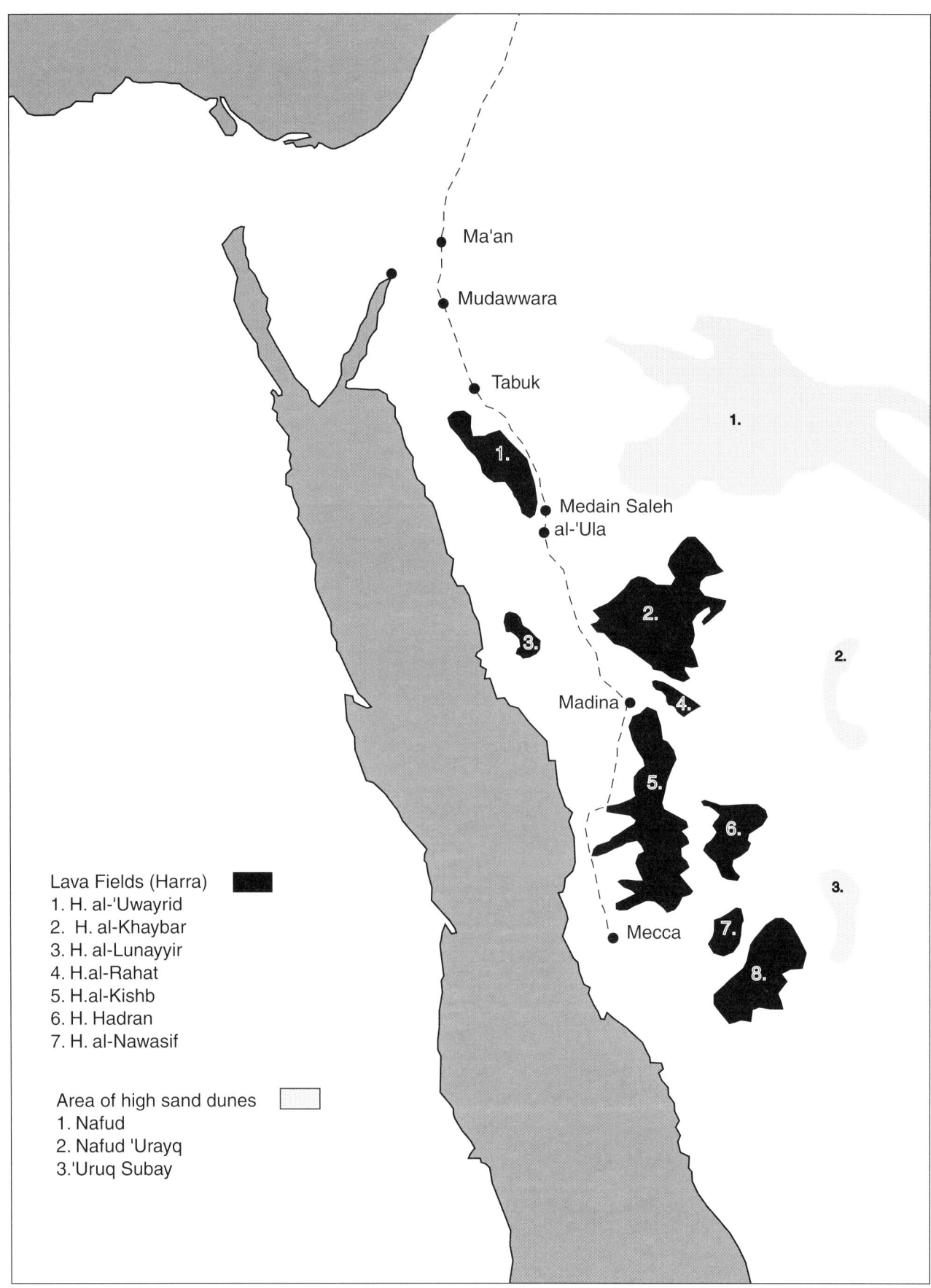

Map 7. Map of Syrian Hajj route with areas of basalt.

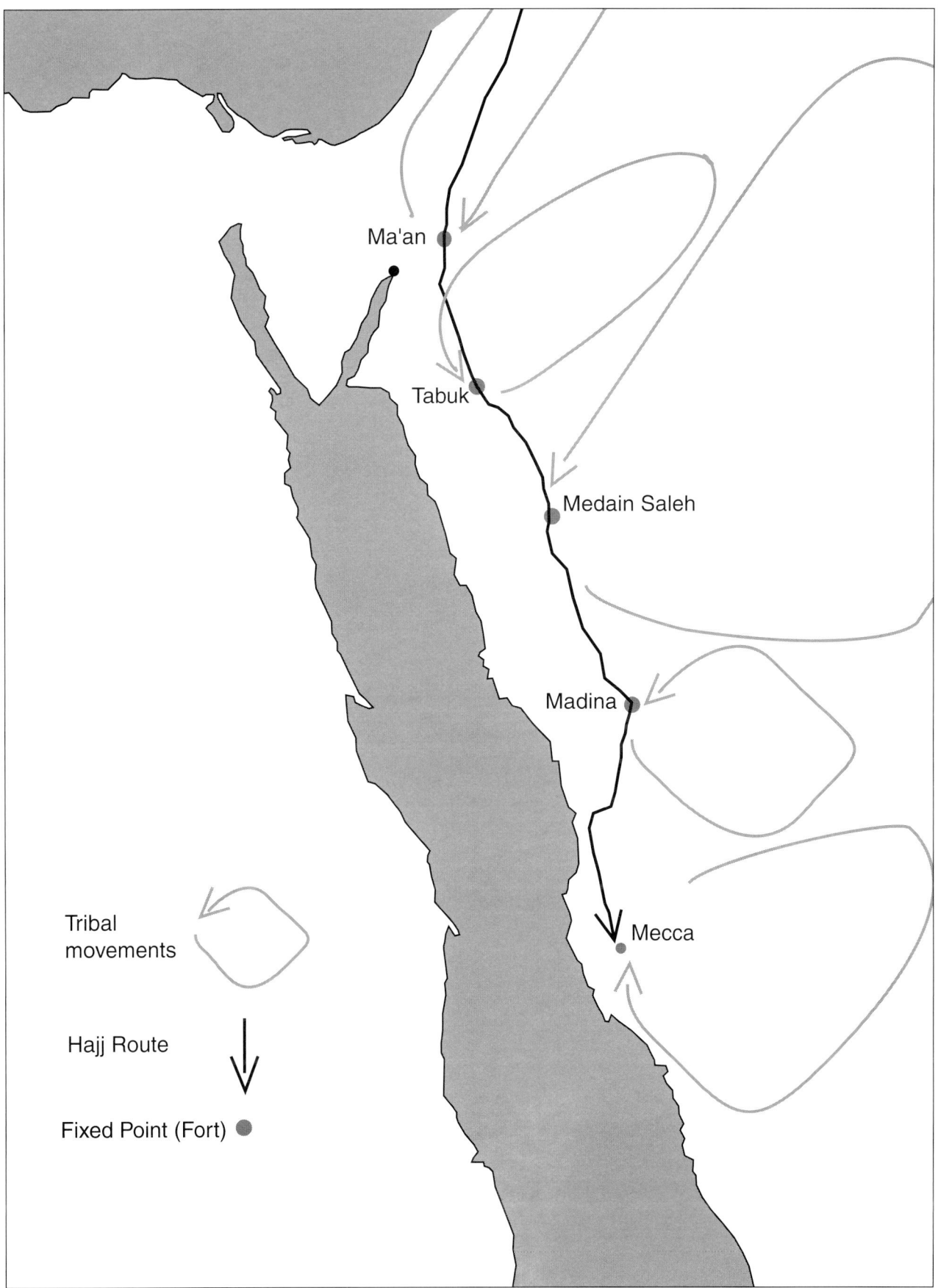

Map 8. Schematic plan of Hajj route to show relationship of forts to tribal migrations.

Ibn Battuta has a little more information on the places passed through, but his interest is primarily in the progress of the caravan. If we move to the 18th century we find that Mehmed Edib contains considerable information on the landscape between stops, for example, he describes 'mountains as black as coal' between Qalandariyya and Ukhaydhir (Bianchi 1825, 132). For Doughty the landscape became a major feature of his account in its own right and he devotes considerable space to visual and geological descriptions of the environment.

The Road Surface

The nature, extent and quality of the road surface of the Hajj route varied considerably, as might be expected from a continuous path stretching a distance of more than 1,000 miles (1,600 km), from Damascus to Mecca. In some places the road was paved and provided with drainage channels (*c.f.* Qal'at al-Hasa in Chapter 9) while in other places the path of the route was only defined by reference to natural features (*c.f.* Doughty 1979, 96 'there is after Maan no appearance of a trodden haj road in the wilderness, all is sea room and our course is held by landmarks').

The road leading out of Damascus formed the core of a north–south linear suburb known as the Maydan. The central road, or Hajj route, was extraordinarily wide for a pre-modern urban road (up to 40 m) and was bordered by shops, bath-houses, mosques and mausolea (Roujon and Vilan 1997; Petersen 2000). Where the Hajj route leaves Damascus it was a broad avenue, described by Burckhardt in 1810 as, 'above one hundred and fifty paces broad which is bordered on each side by a grove of olive trees, and continues in a straight line for upwards of an hour' (Burckhardt 1829). In the 1870s Doughty records the caravan was approximately 100 paces wide when travelling through the plains (Doughty 1979, 100). In the northern part of the route the path was generally visible as an area of trodden earth several hundred metres wide. In 1872 Canon Henry Tristram described the route as follows:

> 'We might have been galloping across a deeply ridged fallow. For about a quarter of a mile in width, every three or four yards was a deep wide rut, all in parallel lines. We were crossing the hadj road. Files of hundreds of camels, slowly following each other in the weary tramp to Makkah, had in the course of ages, worn the hard surface of the desert into these deep furrows' (Tristram 1873).

The route was also visible near Mafraq, thus Grant reported seeing 'a serried multitude of tracks which had been trodden into hard paths by the feet of countless generations of beasts of burden' (Grant 1937, 225). Aerial photographs of the area north of Dab'a, taken by Kennedy in 2003, show the physical remains of the route, visible as a series of ridges either side of a main hollow track way *c.* 4 m wide (Kennedy and Petersen 2004, 14). It would be interesting to compare these marks to those of drovers roads in Britain and America, where similarly large groups of animals

crossed the countryside (for images of the drovers roads, see Godwin and Toulson 1977; for a discussion of drovers roads in Wales and England, see Skeel 1926 and in the USA, see Henlein 1954).

Obviously such trodden earth surfaces became very slippery and muddy during times of rain, or where the route crossed a wadi, as at Wadi al-Hasa. When Mehmed Edib made the Hajj in 1779, he noted that the route in and out of Ma'an was particularly perilous in times of rain and very difficult to traverse (Edib trans. Bianchi 1825, 127). Burckhardt notes that the road south of Muzayrib often became swampy and states that the local villagers had to cover the track in thick layers of straw to enable the Hajj caravan to proceed (Burckhardt 1822, chapter 4, 22). In response to these, sometimes, difficult conditions some areas of the road were paved. Majali and Mas'ad (1987 see esp. 315, figs 2, 3 and 4) have argued that the Mamluks built a number of paved roads in Jordan, giving as an example, the road from Jisr al-Majami' to Umm al-Qutayn, however, there is no evidence of paving on the Medieval Hajj route. Brünnow and Domaszewski (1905, 17) assumed that sections of paved road on the Hajj route were of Roman origin, possibly associated with an assumed *Via Militaris* to the east of the *Via Nova Traiana*. However, Graf (1997) has called into question the existence of a paved *Via Militaris* and makes the point that in Roman North Africa, none of the roads were paved outside the cities.

It seems likely, therefore, that the majority of paved surfaces on the Hajj route were constructed during Ottoman times (*i.e.* after 1516). For example Burckhardt (1829) notes that south of al-Kiswa 'The Hadj route has been paved in several places for the distance of a hundred yards or more, in order to facilitate the passage of the pilgrims in years when the Hadj takes place during the rainy season'. Doughty also noted paved roads in the area north of Muzayrib, thus he wrote 'we came by a beaten way over the wilderness, paved of old at the crossing of winter stream beds for the safe passage of the Haj camels, which have no foothold in sliding ground' (Doughty 1979, 43). Two areas of paved road were discovered within the survey area (Jordan) these were a 3 km stretch across the Wadi al-Hasa and a smaller stretch at Mudawwara (both sites are discussed in Chapter 9). In both cases the road was made of flint cobbles set within kerb-stones. At Hasa the road crosses the floodplain of a wide wadi (Wadi al-Hasa) and includes an arched bridge, as well as numerous drainage channels beneath the road to allow water to flow through without damaging the road. At Mudawwara the paved road is edged with sandstone kerb-stones and passes through an area of shifting sands. There are a few examples of paved surfaces on other Hajj routes, thus al-Thenayian (1999) records a number of places with paving slabs on the Yemeni highland pilgrim route. In general however, paved road surfaces are rare which may simply be a matter of expense, or maintenance, but may also relate to the nature of the terrain and mode of transport. Whereas for wheeled transport paved roads were of great importance, for camels, with the exception of muddy areas, stone paved surfaces were less necessary and may even have been problematic. It is noticeable that for drovers routes in England and Wales unpaved roads were preferred, not only because there were no tolls, but also because the paved surfaces wore down the hooves of the cattle (Skeel 1926).

As well as paved road surfaces there are a number of examples where the natural rock was cut away to form an easy passage for the Hajj caravan, the most notable example is Shak al-Ajuz, which was supposedly cut out at the expense of an elderly female pilgrim who had fallen on the uneven ground surface (Doughty 1979, 121; Bianchi 1825, 134). Similar examples of rock cut roads can be found on the Yemeni (al-Thenayian 1999, 141) and Egyptian pilgrimage routes (Tamari 1982, 517–25). The route could also be made safer in other ways, thus the road between Sanamayn and Muzayrib was protected from flooding by embankments built, at the expense of the Damascus Governor, Aydinili Abdullah Paşa, between 1730 and 1733 (Barbir 1980, 139).

To the south of Ma'an there was no single path, or track, for the Hajj to follow. As the majority of the route was not paved this implies that the route was marked in some other way. Graf (1997, 272) makes reference to the fact that many Roman roads consisted simply of tracks of trodden earth cleared of stones (*viae terrenae*) and it may be that Ma'an marks the change from a single route cleared of stones, to a wide open expanse where 'all is sea room and our course is held by landmarks' (Doughty 1979, 96).

Bridges

In a number of places, particularly on the northern section, the route was provided with bridges to cross the larger wadis. Six bridges were noted within the area of modern Syria (Zebeina, Mefakhar, Kiswa, Khan al-Zayt, Muzayrib and Wadi Um al-Dan) and one in modern Jordan, crossing the Wadi al-Hasa next to the Hajj fort. Most of these bridges were built to serve all forms of traffic and were not specifically built to carry the Hajj route (for a discussion of Medieval bridges in the region, see Petersen 2009). In the 1870s Doughty noted that many of the bridges formerly used by the Hajj caravan were in ruins (Doughty 1979, 43). The bridge at Muzayrib (Plate 2) comprises three arches

Plate 2. Bridge on Hajj route near Muzayrib, built during reign of Mamluk Sultan Baybars in mid-13th century (Creswell Archive EA.CA.5383).

and is paved with black basalt, embedded into the parapet are two white blocks bearing depictions of lions in low relief. Both the design of the bridge and the carved lions, indicate that the bridge was probably built by Baybars as part of the communication route between Damascus and Cairo (see discussion by Creswell 1917/18). The bridge at Wadi Um al-Dan, one hour south of Muzayrib, was built by the Ottoman governor of Acre, Ahmed Jezzar Pasha, specifically for the passage of pilgrims in this otherwise swampy area. In some places the Hajj caravan had to ford through rivers, thus Doughty describes how the caravan simply walked through the shallow waters of the wadi Zerka ('the caravan plashed through the rocky brook, running down towards the Jordan', Doughty 1979, 51). The one bridge specifically built to carry the Hajj caravan is that which crosses the Wadi al-Hasa (Figs 24 and 25), for discussion see Qal'at al-Hasa in Chapter 10.

Roadside Markers

Whilst the exact path of the road may often have been unclear, it is evident that the Hajj caravan used a number of man-made and natural features as a guide to navigation. Unlike the Darb Zubayda, the Syrian Hajj route was not marked with milestones, an exception being the area within the vicinity of Mecca where they were set up on the orders of the Umayyad caliph, Marwan (Musil 1926, 327). There were, however, a number of places where the road was marked with stones, thus Doughty observed a number of small stone cairns marking the way to the road and the bridge crossing the Wadi al-Hasa (Doughty 1979, 65). The road was also marked with stones near Qal'at Fassu'a (see Chapter 9 in this volume) thus, Musil reports a 'tower shaped pile of stones indicating the site of the pilgrimage station' (Musil 1926, 38). The cairn, which is still visible (Plate 115), led Musil to equate this site with Dhat al-Manar, a site described by Yaqut as on the southern borders of Syria. According to Yaqut the name Dat al-Manar referred to the watch tower, where on dark nights a fire was lit to guide the caravan on the right path (Musil 1926, 38 n. 13; Yaqut 1995, vol. 2, 712). Similar watchtowers were built on the Darb Zubayda in Iraq and there are references to their use in pre-Islamic times (al-Rashid and Young 2011).

On the Yemeni Highland Hajj the sides of the road were marked by stones for much of the route, on the Syrian route, however, this appears to have been the exception. For example, near Muzayrib the road was marked out to prevent it being blocked by a temporary market that took place during the Hajj. Schumacher describes the situation as follows:

'To the south of Kul'ah el 'Atikah, on the broad Haj road to Turrah, are to be seen two parallel rows of large stones. Here the market is held, and provisions are sold to the pilgrims during their sojourn at El Mezerib. The tents and the storehouses of the dealers stand behind the stones, and a wide roadway is left between' (Schumacher 1886, 165).

In some places there are reports of white bones of camels being placed by the side of the route to act as markers. For example, Burckhardt states in relation to Tabuk 'if the Hadj arrives at night, the bones of dead camels indicate the way to the castle' (Burckhardt 1822, 659). Elsewhere Burckhardt reports, in relation to the Egyptian Hajj, 'at every twenty yards lay heaps of bones of camels, horses and asses by the side of the road' (Burckhardt 1822, chapter 2). Selim Sawwaf who travelled with the Hajj caravan 30 times between 1875 and 1910 states 'throughout the length of the route, bleached bones and skeletons of camels horses and mules can be found' (Grant 2003, 225). However, Doughty firmly discounts these reports stating 'I saw not anywhere the reported strewn skeletons of camels nor mounds of sand blown on their fallen carcasses. The Arabs are too poor so to lose cattle; but these and the like, are tales rather of an European Orientalism than with much relevance to the common experience' (Doughty 1979, 96). It is difficult to reconcile these various accounts except to observe that Doughty travelled on the Hajj road at a time when it was much diminished and it is possible that by his time markers in the form of camel bones had dispersed. Also, it is possible that Doughty was answering some prevalent travellers' tales that the whole route was strewn with the carcasses of dead animals, which is evidently not true.

Landmarks

Even in places where the route was well marked, either by a trodden surface, or by stones, the leaders of the caravan would have had to know where they were in order to gauge the distance to the next stopping place. Doughty records that the caravan was led by a special guide (*dalil al-Hajj* دليل الحج) who was responsible for navigating the entire route from Muzayrib to Mecca (Doughty 1979, 96). The guide was always a man from Damascus, rather than a Bedouin who were not trusted by the Ottoman authorities. Doughty makes the interesting observation that in consequence, many of the names for landmarks on the route were likely to have been different from those used by the Bedouin and other locals along the route (Doughty 1979, 88). Most of the authors who record their experiences of the Hajj refer to a variety of landmarks along the way. For example, Mehmed Edib mentions a rock between Hadiyya and Nakhlatayn, known as the rock of salutation, which was reported to have greeted the Prophet Muhammad on his journey through the area (Bianchi 1825, 138). Between al-Ukhaydhir and Mu'azzam Doughty notes a curious rock formation which he refers to as 'The hajjies admire upon the east valley side above, a statue like form *ed-dubb* "the bear", whether so made by rude art, or it were a strange mocking herself of mother Nature. It resembles, to my vision, a rhinocerous standing upon legs, and four legs set upon a pedestal. One might guess it had been an idol; I hear from some which had climbed, that the image is natural. The sandstones, in some places of iron durity, in other are seen waste into fantastic forms' (Doughty 1979, 118; see also, al-Faqeer 2009).

Elsewhere Doughty gives several illustrated examples of such rock formations used for navigation by the Bedouin (Doughty 1979, 285). Many of these landmarks had stories associated with them, thus the passage between two sandstone outcrops marking the entrance to the plain of Medain Saleh is known as Mabraq al-Naqa. According to the legends, this was the place a miraculously born female camel was shot by the infidel inhabitants of Hejr (Medain Saleh) (see Chapter 10 for Medain Saleh and references in the Quran *Surras* 7 and 6). The rocks on the sides of this 200 m long passage are covered with a multitude of Arabic and pre-Islamic inscriptions. Jaussen and Savignac (1997, 103–4) noted that many of these inscriptions belonged to pilgrims who felt compelled to record their presence in this place ('Chaque voyager semble avoir tenu á inscrire son nom en passant. Aujourd'hui encore, nombre des pèlerins musulmans continuent la tradition, poussés par un sentiment religieux, car une pieuse légende est attachée á cet endroit').

Part II: The Hajj Caravan

Pilgrims

The numbers of pilgrims using the Syrian Hajj route in any given year is very difficult to calculate, though estimates for the Ottoman period indicate that it fluctuated between 20,000 and 60,000 people (Rafeq 1966, 61; Peeters 1994, 153; Faroqhi 1994, 46). By the late 19th century the number had dwindled to 6,000 (Doughty 1979, 45) and by 1903 there were only 100 pilgrims using the Syrian route (Issawi 1988, 236). Although in theory all Muslims were expected to perform the Hajj, the reality has always been that those with more wealth and resources were more likely to predominate. For example, in the mid 18th century the total cost of the journey for a pilgrim was nearly 200 piasters (Rafeq 1987, 133), half the cost of a Damascus house, or 10 times the income of an imam in the same city (Peeters 1994, 151). It is therefore, not surprising that some people would pay for people to perform the Hajj by proxy, hence the growth of pilgrimage certificates, both for people who went in person and for those who sent a representative (for examples of these certificates see Aksoy and Milstein 2000).

The majority of pilgrims would form groups of between 10 and 20 people, usually friends or relations and engage a *mukawwam* who would provide animals, tents, cooking equipment, as well as servants. However, some pilgrims wishing to avoid the excessive costs would opt to follow the official caravan on foot, or on their own beasts, at considerable danger to themselves (Burckhardt 1822, chapter 4, 21). Another option was to travel with the transport caravan that supplied the main caravan with camels and other supplies. This caravan, known as al-Selma, travelled either one day in front, or one day behind, the main caravan and according to Burckhardt this was the cheapest way of undertaking the journey (Burckhardt 1822, chapter 4, 21).

Death on the Hajj

If any pilgrims died during the Hajj they would usually be buried by the roadside, or at one of the Hajj forts (see, for example, Qal'at Dab'a). However, there was often a fear that the officials of the Hajj would claim all inheritance rights if no immediate relative was present. Thus, a late 16th century document records that 'when a Muslim pilgrim dies, his tent companions are afraid of the fiscal official, the scribe and the *kadi*. In order to avoid harm to the property and honour they do not wash the dead person and do not wrap him/her into a shroud nor do they pray the prayers for the dead'. Instead the deceased person was buried secretly in the communal tent (MD 62, 256, No. 65; Faroqhi 1994, 45). At the other end of the social spectrum were those pilgrims who were sufficiently wealthy, or influential, to pay for their bodies to be conveyed to Mecca after their death. Thus Doughty (1979, 106) records the strange case of a Persian woman who died and was wrapped in the skin of a dead camel and taken to Mecca for burial (an echo of this event appears in literary form in Nakhjavani 2000).

Camels

The camel was the principal mode of transport on the Hajj route, though other animals such as mules, horses and even donkeys were also employed. Generally one person would ride a camel though they could carry two at a time when necessary. Although the camels were well suited to the shifting sands and extremities of heat encountered in Arabia, they were less well suited to the sometimes cold and muddy highlands of Syria and Jordan. Also, camels are not well suited to steep inclines, where their considerable height makes them much less stable than either a horse, or a mule. It is probably for this reason that the inclines of the route were kept so shallow that Doughty was able to remark, that the whole journey could be made by wagons with wheels (Doughty 1979, 100). When descending through narrow passes the Hajj would form a double, or single, file and passengers would dismount and walk beside their mounts. Doughty indicates that the camels were often tethered together and that when proceeding along the Hajj route they were held together in rope lines (Doughty 1979, 107). In addition to carrying people camels could also be used as pack animals, to carry litters and even cannon (see Marsigli, II plate 11, 29, reproduced in Smith 2002, 50, plate 1). Camels could also be eaten when necessary, or even be placed in a line to form a defensive wall, as happened when Ludovico di Varthema was attacked in 1503 (Varthema 1863, 16–19).

The camels for the Syrian Hajj were mostly drawn from Bedouin tribes in the vicinity of Damascus. Other important sources for camels included the Hawran and the region around Nablus. Camels were also supplied from the area of Sukhne near Palmyra. Doughty makes the point that the camels used on the Hajj were larger than the usual Syrian camels and were all strong males. They were fed on balls of boiled pulse 'of which four or five or six are crammed into the great weary beasts' jaws' (Doughty 1979, 105). Varthema mentions a similar form of feed in the early 16th century, indicating a tradition of considerable antiquity (Varthema 1863, 16–19).

The majority of camels were hired privately through the camel masters *mukawwams*. During the Hajj march these dealers, or their agents, would accompany the caravan and were in charge of organizing the marching order, the layout of camp sites and access to the water for the private (non-official) pilgrims. The *mukawwams* generally had a bad reputation, both for the prices they charged and their ferocity in defending their privileged position. For example, pilgrims from the Caucuses brought their own beasts, but they were ill treated by the *mukawwams* who made them march at the rear of the caravan, camp in the worst places and receive their water last. In the 1930s, after the Hijaz railway had made Hajj camels redundant, Christina Grant interviewed a Damascus silk merchant, Selim Sawwaf, who had previously traded as a *mukawwam* between 1875 and 1910. This account gives a good insight into how the trade was conducted:

> 'Camel "owners"….had always been in the habit of buying their camels each year, as cheaply as possible, from the desert Arabs who raised them. Then they hired out these camels at the highest possible price, to prospective *Hajjis* and convoy officials; and sold them at a profit, after their return to Damascus…. In order to take part in contracting for the pilgrims, a single owner or a collective group of camel owners acting as a unit, had to contribute a minimum 'share' of two hundred camels' (Grant 1937, 229).

Burckhardt noted that the high prices charged by the *mukawwams* was partly because they were obliged to provide a replacement mount if a camel died during the journey (Burckhardt 1822, 243–44). An example of how this worked in practice is given by Doughty, whose camel collapsed and died, and was replaced by 'a young black cow-camel, of the Aarab, wild and untaught' (Doughty 1979, 107).

The government also needed camels for the official pilgrims, soldiers and other state functionaries; these were sometimes sourced from the *mukawwams*. The official responsible for buying and hiring camels was known as *mir-i-akhur-i hajj* (Bakhit 1982, 110). However, during the 16th century the Ottoman rulers tried a number of schemes to source camels directly from the Bedouin, thus a decree issued in 1574–75 allowed those tribes supplying camels to the Hajj to display the Ottoman flag. This measure met with limited success as the rivalries set up, led to armed conflict between the tribes (Faroqhi 1994, 49). Another scheme involved creating government owned herds to reduce dependence on the camel brokers. For example, between 1569 and 1571 the Ottoman government brought its own camels and had them raised in Anatolia, where there was more plentiful food supplies (Faroqhi 1994, 48). During this time there was a plan to rebuild the fortress at Bosra where camels could be raised to supply the official Hajj caravan (Bakhit 1982, 98 and 111). In the 1580s the Grand Vizier,

Ibrahim Pasha, established a *waqf* (pious foundation) in Damascus to maintain a permanent supply of camels for the Hajj. Unfortunately the enterprise failed, despite a personal gift of 600 camels from the Vizier, because of the opposition of locals in Damascus (Faroqhi 1994, 49). By the early 18th century the Ottoman government seems to have accepted that they had to deal with the camel brokers, thus a contract dated 1738 is an agreement between the Governor of Damascus and the camel brokers guild, to supply 100 camels to convey the governor's luggage from Muzayrib to Medina (Barbir 1980, 159, n. 156). However, it is likely that the government still tried to maintain control of the *mukawwams*, thus Selim Sawwaf recalls that the government may have once controlled the trade (Grant 1937, 229).

Camel Litters (hawdaj, shuqduf, takht er-Rum)

In addition to the standard method of riding a camel, there were a number of forms of litter, ranging from a simple shade placed over a double saddle, to elaborate contraptions carried by four camels. The litters were mostly used by women, although after the advent of steamships most women used the Red Sea route to Jedda. The litters were generally made and repaired by carpenters in Damascus (Doughty 1979, 41). Three types of litter were used. The simplest was a yoke-like wooden construction with individual seats either side of the hump. The medium sized litter was called a (*shuqduf*), it has been described by Richard Burton as follows:

> 'Thick twigs inserted in the ends and the outer long sides of the framework are bent over the top, bower fashion, to support matting, carpets, any other protection against the sun. These cots have short legs and at a halt may be used as bedsteads' (Burton 1893, 233–34).

The largest type of litter was known as a *takht er-Rum*, or camel coache. These structures were carried between four camels and accompanied by 6 footmen, one for each camel and one either side of the middle. Doughty's description indicates that these were large brightly coloured vehicles with glass windows and ladders and carried by camels covered in brightly coloured fabrics and small mirrors and decorated with ostrich feathers. These litters could also be hired by the day during times of illness, or were sometimes used to carry the dead (Doughty 1979, 105). In addition to camel borne litters there were also mule litters of similar design.

Tents and Camping Grounds

Unlike the route north of Damascus, which was well provided with khans and other forms of accommodation, the Hajj route south of Damascus had no permanent accommodation and all pilgrims were obliged to camp. Although the Hajj forts were not used for accommodation

18th century accounts indicate that tents were sometimes stored in the forts, possibly as spares (Barbir 1980, 141, n. 97). It is not clear what forms of tents were meant, though it is probable that canvas tents were used in preference to the black goat hair tents of the Bedouin. In the 14th century it is possible that Ibn Battuta used Bedouin tents as he relates that his pilgrimage was made in the charge of the 'Ajarima Bedouin, however, by Doughty's time the pilgrims had white canvas tents. A few depictions of Hajj tents appear in miniature paintings, but these are generally too schematic to identify precise types of tent. For example, an illustrated 16th century Ottoman text written in Persian contains several depictions of pilgrim tents, comprising a central pole, with a canopy and four taught guy ropes (Milstein 2001, 302–5 and 329). What seems most likely is that the tents used in the Hajj resembled Turkish military tents, as depicted, for example, in a manuscript of *Nusretname* painted in 1582. The painting shows tents that appear to have a polygonal plan with a pointed roof (Nicolle and McBride 1983, 26). A book produced by the Italian artist Marsigli (1732, II, 15, plate 19) in the 1690s shows a range of rectangular, round and pointed tents, some of which were extravagantly decorated (the plate is reproduced in Smith 2002, plate 4). What is clear from both the literary and pictorial descriptions is that several sizes of tent were used, with specialist tents for dining, preparation of food and sleeping (see, for example, Faroqhi 1994, 43). Within Damascus there was a street with specialist tent makers and repairers (Doughty 1979, 41).

There are several 19th century depictions of the campsites on the Syrian Hajj route, including a large scale engraving showing the pilgrims camped on both sides of the Barada river prior to the commencement of the Hajj (this engraving has been reproduced in a number of publications the most accessible of which is Goodwin 1987, 244). Other illustrations include Doughty's map showing the location of the camp at Ma'an (Doughty 1979, 72) and a typical layout of a campsite produced by Tresse (1937, 229).

The archaeology of nomadism remains a perennial theme in archaeology (see, for example, Barnard and Wendrich (eds) 2008) and there are several archaeological studies of Bedouin encampments within the region (see, for example, Saidel 2008b). The camp sites of pilgrims are likely to be different from those of nomads, both because of the greater density of occupation and because many of the requirements for the camp will have been provided by the Hajj organizers, rather than being sourced directly from the immediate environment. Unfortunately, there is very little published archaeological evidence for the camping grounds used by the Hajj. Part of the problem may be one of identification; the fact that pilgrims only stayed for one or two days at a single site may have meant that the camps made little impact on the landscape. This idea is supported by the archaeological investigation of early modern pilgrimage shrines in Peru, where there was a similar lack of evidence for use, of a site where thousands of pilgrims congregated once a year (see Silverman 1994,

11). This stands in contrast to Bedouin encampments where prolonged and repeated stays at the same site may leave considerable remains (see, for example, the excavation of a 17th–19th century camp site in Qatar, Garlake 1978). It is, however, possible that examination of major stops on the Hajj route, such as Muzayrib or Tabuk, would reveal information about the camping grounds.

In contrast to the archaeological evidence there is considerable written information about the layout and organization of the camp of the Hajj caravan. There was an official (*muhafez al-hajj*) specifically appointed to organize the camping grounds and the location of tents (Tresse 1937, 229). During the 17th century this official had the same status as the deputy amir al-Hajj and was allocated two camels as part of his allowance (Faroqhi 1994, 35–36). Doughty gives a very good description of the camp layout, which is worth quoting in full:

'…little after noon we came in sight of our city of tents, whitened in the sun: from the wady brow I could overlook this Haj encampment, pitched in lower ground, as a military field measured by a camp and great pavilions standing always in the same places; their numbers seemed to me marshal. Their good order has grown up through long generations, the tent rows about two hundred. In each of them with the serving men might be fifteen or twenty persons, many besides are in the smaller tents' (Doughty 1979, 51).

Tresse (1937, 229) gives a schematic layout of the Hajj camp outside one of the forts. At the centre of the camp was the camel park for the official caravan around which were the tents of the pilgrims arranged in three distinct groups, Syrian, Persian and Turkish. The tents of the officials were pitched between the camel park and the fort, whilst the water sellers, merchants and tent carriers were on the far side, away from the fort. The entire camp was ringed with a series of sentries, with unofficial pilgrims and other followers, on the outside. The division of the pilgrims into different groups was maintained once the pilgrims arrived at Mecca and Medina, thus a 16th century miniature painting depicts the camps of the Syrian and Egyptian pilgrims at Ma'ala cemetery, each next to its own water cistern (Milstein 2001, 300 and 328).

7. Ottoman Fortification in Palestine and Transjordan

Palestine was important to the Syrian Hajj route in two different ways, firstly as a Holy Land and secondly, as a source of additional supplies and military support. Fortresses and related infrastructure were important to service both these functions.

To the Muslims Palestine was a holy land, with important religious sites at Jerusalem and Hebron; this meant that pilgrims using the Damascus route would often visit these sacred sites before visiting Mecca. Under the Ottomans this was to become even more common, thus a *firman* dated 1581 (989 AH) ordered the construction of a khan and fortress at 'Uyun al-Tujjar, to protect pilgrims and other travellers (Heyd 1960, 111). Some of these pilgrims could be quite important, for example, in 1572–73 the Ottoman Princess Shah Sultan made the Hajj to Mecca, stopping to visit the holy places of Jerusalem; the visit to Jerusalem was arranged for her by the Governor of Damascus, who gave her a special escort and a privileged position at the head of the caravan (Faroqhi 1994, 129).

In strategic terms the fortresses and infrastructure of Palestine provided additional support to the Syrian Hajj route, supplying both troops and equipment, whilst the Hajj forts themselves provided an eastward extension to the fortress network of Palestine. For example, in addition to its main function of protecting central Palestine, the fortresses at Ras al-'Ayn and Bayt Jibrin were also to supply troops for the Syrian Hajj route (Heyd 1960, 108–9). In this chapter it will be argued that, the network of Ottoman fortifications is the key to understanding the nature of Ottoman rule in the region during the 16th–18th centuries, and that the Hajj forts were an integral part of this network (Map 6). In order to consider the significance of the fortifications it will be necessary to briefly review the situation before the 16th century, then consider the evidence from the 16th–18th centuries (*i.e.* after the Ottoman conquest) and finally to consider the fortifications within the wider context of the Ottoman Empire.

Mamluk Period (see also Chapter 3)

Many of the finest examples of Muslim architecture in Palestine were created during the Mamluk period, such as the buildings surrounding the Haram al-Sharif in Jerusalem, or the Red Mosque in Safed, and the White Mosque in Ramla. However, it is noticeable that the buildings created during this time were primarily religious and there are very few examples of military architecture. Palestine at the end of the 16th century appears to have been a place with very little in the way of military fortification: none of the major cities were enclosed by walls and there were no coastal defences. This was part of a deliberate Mamluk policy intended to prevent the recapture of Palestine by the Crusaders. The idea being, that the Crusaders would not be able to capture any fortifications that could subsequently be used as a base for their re-conquest. Palestine in general and the coast in particular, was regarded as extremely vulnerable in this respect, so not only were the coastal fortifications dismantled but entire towns and cities were destroyed leaving a coastal wasteland. In addition to the destruction of coastal settlements, the Mamluks also introduced nomadic Turcoman tribes into the area to inhibit the return of settled life; large areas of the coastal plain became desolate with salt marshes and grassland replacing the carefully drained agricultural hinterland of the coastal cities. As a counterpart to this negative policy there was an attempt to redevelop internal road systems, as well as reviving some of the cities of the upland region. The revival of the Via Maris, connecting Cairo to Damascus via Palestine, was the most significant investment in the infrastructure of the country – the road was not only provided with bridges, but also with khans and mosques which in some cases (*e.g.* Majdal and Jaljuliyya) became small towns (for examples, see Petersen 2007). Despite this investment there were, with the possible exception of a few towers, very few fortifications of any kind.

Plate 3. Qal'at Ras al-'Ayn, Ottoman fortress (1988).

Early Ottoman Period

Very shortly after the Ottoman conquest of Syria/Palestine, the Ottomans initiated an extensive programme of re-fortification and resettlement. The Ottomans decided to reverse the Mamluk policy of a deserted coastline and unfortified interior for a number of reasons. Firstly, the eastern Mediterranean was no longer under the domination of Christian ships and from the conquest of Cyprus in 1571 Palestine was located within a deep zone of Turkish control. This meant that the coastal plain was no longer the front line between Muslim and Christian forces and could now be re-populated. Secondly, the Ottomans wanted to increase their taxation base, which they could do by promoting the re-settlement of abandoned coastal areas and the improvement of security in the upland areas. Evidence for this new policy can be found in the official Ottoman records, in particular the tax registers and the *firmans* (Imperial decrees). The tax registers (*defters*) indicate a concern for increasing revenue through increased cultivation and population of land (Hütteroth and Abdul Fattah 1977) whilst the Ottoman *firmans* indicate a fear of nomadic (untaxable) Bedouin disrupting settled life and a concern to improve security. In this case the construction of forts was seen as a specific deterrent to Bedouin incursions on settled land. Ottoman fortifications in the region were, therefore, directed primarily against an internal enemy (the Bedouin) rather than an external European invasion.

It is within this context that the rebuilding of the walls of Jerusalem need to be understood (Cohen 1989; van Berchem 1920–23; Wrightman 1993). Although in terms of 16th century European artillery technology, the walls of

Jerusalem may seem backward, they were more than purely symbolic and were clearly intended to keep the Bedouin out of the city. The construction of the walls was intended to be a stimulus to the economy of the city and was part of a bigger programme that included the refurbishment of the city's water supply from Artas (near Bethlehem) and the construction of various charitable institutions within Jerusalem (the most prominent of these was Khasseki Sultan).

None of the Palestinian towns outside Jerusalem were provided with walls, possibly because of the vast expense of such projects, though perhaps also in recognition that the countryside as a whole needed protection and that without this, a walled town would stand isolated. All other examples of Ottoman fortification comprise forts located at strategic locations throughout the country. Each fort is of a remarkably similar design comprising a square or rectangular courtyard, enclosed by high walls, with towers at each corner. Compared with the Medieval castles of the Crusaders and Ayyubids, these forts appear to be lightweight constructions and instead of occupying impregnable natural sites, they are usually located next to roads and are easily accessible.

Qal'at Ras al-'Ayn (Turkish Binar Bashi) (Fig. 3, Plates 3–4)

The site derives its names from its position at the source of the 'Awja river (modern Hebrew, Yarqon) which emerges from a spring directly beneath the fortress. This is an ancient tell site, inhabited since the Early Bronze Age

Plate 4. Qal'at Ras al-'Ayn, Ottoman fortress, detail of south-west tower (1988).

(3,000 BC) and remaining an important town until the 8th century AD, when it was sacked by the Abbasids for siding with the Umayyads (for a summary of the history of the site, see Petersen 1998, 98–101). It appears that the site was uninhabited in 1242 when the Ayyubid prince, al-Malik al-Nasir al-Daud of Kerak, camped next to the springs. In the Mamluk period (1250–1516) some sort of post station, or fort, was established at the site (Harmann 1910, 674–79) though by the 16th century it was probably in ruins.

After the Ottoman conquest in the early 16th century, a fortress was built (or rebuilt) on the top of the Tell. The precise date of the reconstruction is not known, though it had been at least partially built by 1573 when a *firman* records that '…the four walls of the fortress…have been built, but inside them no mosque and houses have been built and the earth has not been removed outside' (Heyd 1960, 107). The work was still not completed in 1576 when Mustafa, commandant of the fortress, reported to the governor of Gaza that the work had still not been completed and that his troops were scattered (Heyd 1960, doc. no. 59, 108, n. 7). At some stage, however, the work was completed (see below Mosque).

The fortress had a large capacity, which in 1579, was listed as 100 horsemen and 30 fortress soldiers, though only 30 troops were actually present at this date (Heyd 1960, doc. no. 60, 108–9). Nearly 100 years later the fortress had

a complement of 54 mounted troops (*beşlüs*) and guards (Heyd 1960, appendix III, 190–91).

The fortress is a massive rectangular enclosure (80 × 100 m) with four corner towers and a gate in the centre of the west side (for an illustration, see Wilson 1881–84, II, 120). Three of the towers have a square ground plan, whilst a fourth tower at the south-west is octagonal.

The Gateway

The gateway is set into the middle of the west wall, facing the spring (Ras al-'Ayn). Unfortunately, the gateway only survives to a height of 1 m above the ground and the exterior face has completely disappeared, though the account of Guerin (1875, 369–70) indicates that it was built of finer stones and in a more careful manner than the other parts of the fortress. Excavations indicate that the gateway had a right angle bend, with a guard chamber and benches either side. The floor was paved with flagstones and it is probable that there were at least two gates: an inner and an outer gateway.

The Walls

The walls stand to their original height (over 10 m) in several places (particularly on the west and south sides)

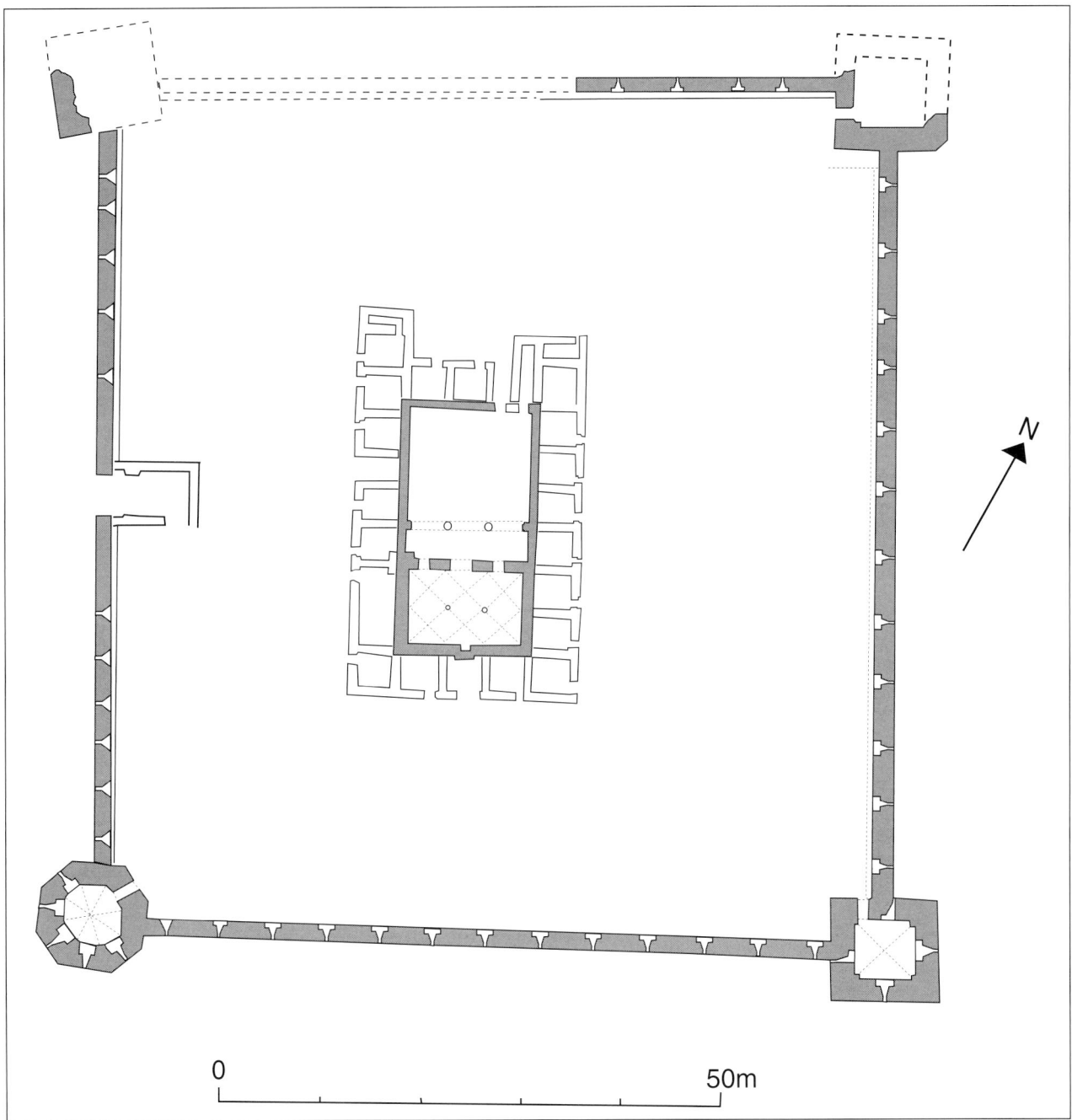

Fig. 3. Plan of Qal'at Ras al-'Ayn, Palestine.

although there are large breaches, particularly on the north side where much of the wall has been destroyed. Where the walls stand to their full height, stepped crenellations are visible, although the majority of these are modern reconstructions. On the exterior of the fortress the lower parts of the walls have a pronounced barter and appear to act as a revetment for an earth platform, or terrace, which forms the ground surface of the courtyard within. The interior face of the fortress wall has two steps that narrow the wall progressively, so that the upper section is only 1.5 m thick, compared with 2.5 m at the level of the courtyard. Each of the steps on the interior act as walkways providing

access to firing points, which, on the upper level are set between crenellations and on the lower level are vaulted niches providing access to loopholes (now mostly robbed out). At either end of the south wall there are traces of steps leading from the parapet to the roofs of the towers. There are traces of rooms built against the wall of the fortress on each side of the courtyard.

The Towers

The south-west tower (Tower 1) has an octagonal plan with alternate short and long sides built on a square base. It is attached to the walls of the fortress on two of the longer sides and has a maximum height of 15 m. The interior comprises two floors, each covered with an octagonal vaulted roof. The lower floor contains 7 vaulted niches with arrow loops, whilst the upper floor only has five. Entrance to the upper floor is from the lower walkway of the west wall and the roof is reached from the parapet walkway on the south wall.

Little remains of the north-west tower (Tower 2) and all that can be said with any certainty is that it had a square plan and contained at least two floors with an exterior access to the upper floor. The north-east tower (Tower 3) is also fragmentary, though it is evident that it was a square two storey building with entrance to the upper floor via an exterior staircase.

The south-west tower (Tower 4) is the best preserved and comprises a vaulted ground floor and a vaulted upper room accessed via an external staircase. There are arrow loops set into vaulted recesses on both the upper and lower floors. Access to the roof was by a staircase leading up from the parapet walkway of the south wall. On the roof of the tower there are traces of a parapet, as well as rainspouts set into the north, east and west sides.

The Mosque

The mosque was located in the centre of the fortress opposite the gateway, though it was removed during excavations that took place between 1972 and 1973. Shimon Dar, the archaeologist who excavated the mosque, noted three architectural phases: i) the prayer hall, ii) the courtyard and iii) a series of 24 small rooms built around the outside. The complex of buildings within the centre of the fortress may be equated with those mentioned in a *firman* dated to August 1573 (26 Rebi' II 981 AH). The *firman* states that the commandant, Mustafa, agreed 'to build, for 2,200 gold pieces, eighty two storied houses (*fevkani ev*), the ground floors of which are to be stables and in the centre a mosque with its minaret' (Heyd 1960, 107).

Summary

A number of features within the design of the fortress indicate that the gateway was the focal point for the defence of the castle. For example, there were no internal staircases within the towers and it is likely that the only access to different levels of the towers and the walls was from the gateway.

The bent entrance is a feature found in Islamic architecture as early as the 8th century, though its use in Ottoman architecture is less common: the only known example from a Hajj fort is at Qatrana.

Qal'at Burak (Fig. 4)

Qal'at Burak is located approximately 10 km to the south of Jerusalem and 3.5 km south of Bethlehem, on the road towards Hebron. The fort is located near the Palestinian village of Artas and immediately next to the fort there are a series of three large cisterns. The two upper pools were probably originally constructed during the Herodian period in the 1st century BC (Abells 1993, 20), whilst the lowest pool was built in 1483 during the reign of the Mamluk Sultan, Qaytbay (r. 1468–95). All three cisterns were renovated during the reign of Sultan Sulayman the Magnificent (1541–68) in the mid-16th century (Salam and Zilberman 1986, 91–106). The pools were supplied by four springs (one of these is located within the fort itself) and provided the main public water source for Jerusalem in the pre-modern period. Water flowed from the cisterns to the Haram al-Sharif in Jerusalem via a series of aqueducts, rock cut channels and ceramic pipes.

The fortress is dated to the 17th century by an inscription above the gate, which states that it was built by the Sultan, Uthman Khan, in the year 1618 (Hawari, Auld and Hudson 2000, 107; Tütüncü 2006, 205–6; see also Chapter 11). However, Evliya Çelebi mistakenly attributed the construction of the fortress to Sultan Murad IV (1623–40), a date followed by Heyd (1960, appendix III, 190–91). Initially the fortress had a garrison of 40–50 soldiers, though by the 19th century this had been reduced to a few guards (Baedecker 1876 [repr. 1973] 147).

The fort has been described and visited by a number of travellers and archaeologists, though the only complete survey of the fortress is that carried out by the British School of Archaeology in Jerusalem during 1995. The published report of this survey (Hawari, Auld and Hudson 2000) forms the basis for the present description, though there is some difference in interpretation. The size and plan of the fort are similar to that of Ras al-'Ayn though on a slightly smaller scale (the internal measurements of the courtyard at Qal'at Burak are 45 × 65 m, compared to Ras al-'Ayn which is 75 × 85 m). Considerably more of the original fabric of the fort survives than at Ras al-'Ayn – of particular importance is the gateway with its inscription and a series of vaulted rooms within the courtyard.

Gatehouse

The gateway comprises a two storey structure built inside the west wall of the fortress. From the outside the gatehouse is marked by a rectangular doorway, set within a tall arched recess containing the foundation inscription, set between two pairs of stylized cypress trees carved in low relief. The upper part of the arched recess is set within a decorative rectangular panel, surmounted with a five-pointed star (Hawari, Auld and Hudson 2000, 104–5, figs 3 and 4). Immediately above the doorway are two small lancet windows. The doorway leads into a square cross-vaulted chamber with a low doorway to the left (north) leading to a vaulted gatehouse, and a large archway to the right leading into the main courtyard. Access to the first floor (upper level) of the gatehouse is via two external staircases, to the west and east, built against the inside of the curtain wall.

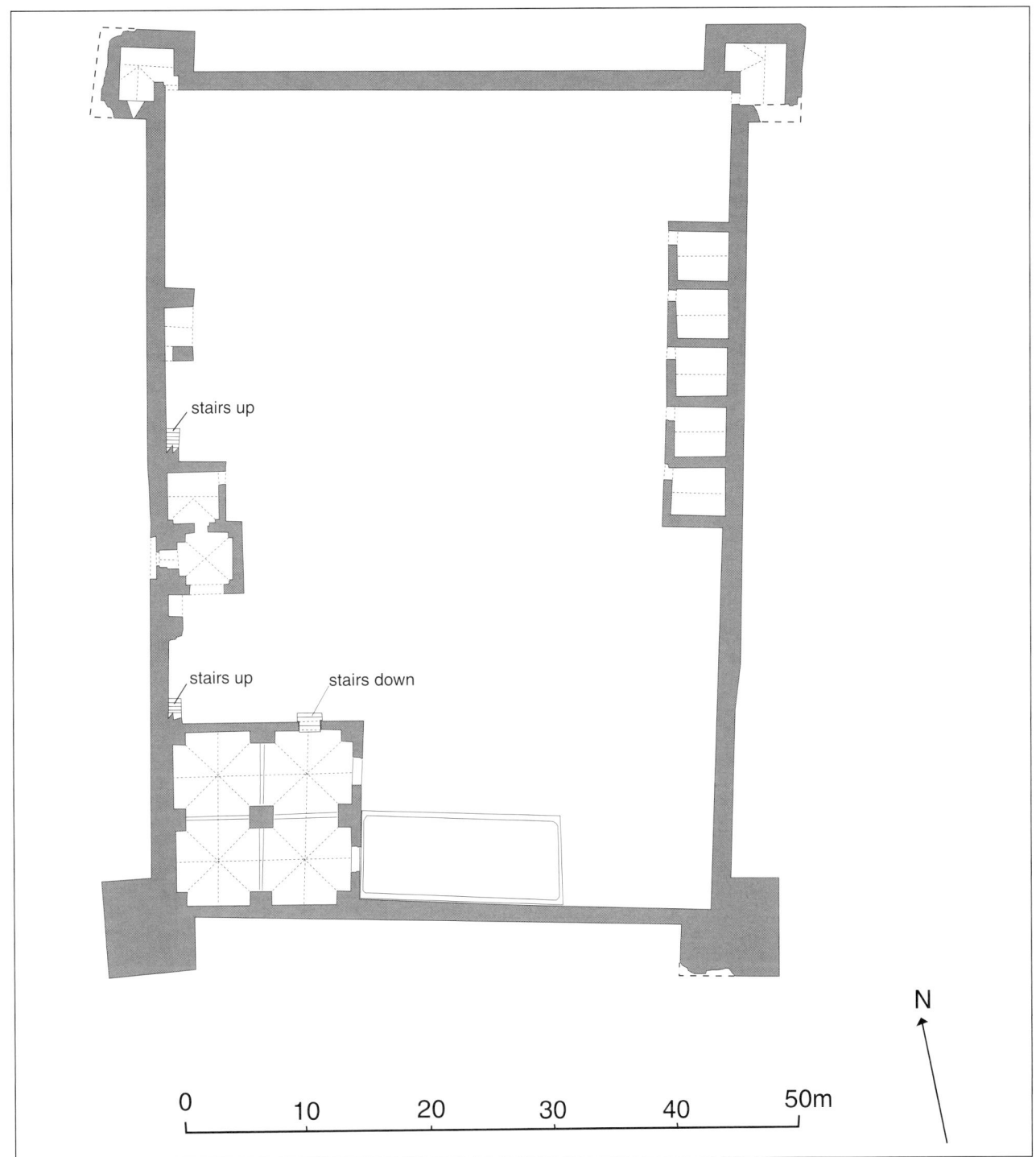

Fig. 4. Plan of Qal'at Burak near Bethlehem. After Hawari et al. 2000.

The upper room has a similar layout to that of the ground floor, with doorways in the east and west sides, above the gateway there are two machicolations opening into the recessed arch of the gateway below. The door on the east side leads onto the flat roof of the guardhouse. From the roof of the guardhouse a small staircase, set into the curtain wall of the fortress, leads up to the parapet walkway and the roof of the gatehouse.

The Walls

Photographs of the fortress from the early part of the 20th century indicate that the walls were crenellated (see, for example, Merrill 1908, opposite p. 353) and that some sections had collapsed. Extensive repairs to the walls were carried out during the 1930s, by a businessman from Bethlehem, who also built a rectangular cistern in the southern part of the courtyard (Hawari, Auld and Hudson 2000, 103). The walls were accessed by two walkways, a middle level walkway at the level of the first floor and an upper level walkway, or parapet, at the level of the crenellations. Both levels were reached via the gatehouse; there was no other communication between the different levels.

Corner Towers

The four corner towers are all, approximately, the same size though the exact design and degree of preservation varies considerably. The two northern towers clasp the corner of the fortress and have 'L' shaped barrel-vaulted rooms on each floor. There is no connection between the upper and lower rooms, with access to the upper rooms via the wall walk.

The south-east corner tower has been both damaged and considerably altered since its original construction, the only thing that can be said with any certainty is that its size was similar to the other towers. However, the south-west corner tower is in a much better condition. The lower part of this tower appears to have been of solid construction and the recent survey of the building (Hawari, Auld and Hudson 2000) found no trace of a chamber at this level. On the upper (first floor) level there is a large square cross-vaulted room with embrasures (arrow slits) in each side. This first floor chamber is entered via a doorway leading from the roof of a large, one storey, vaulted structure which occupies the south-west corner of the fortress (see below for a description and discussion of this structure).

Barracks Block

Approximately in the middle of the east wall of the interior of the fortress there are a series of five barrel-vaulted rooms, each with a doorway opening onto the courtyard and identified as 'Barracks' in the British School report (Hawari, Auld and Hudson 2000, 111–12). Each room contains a number of niches and at least four of the rooms are lit by an opening ('oculus') at the apex of the vault. One of the rooms also contains a fire place with a chimney. The size, design and location of these rooms suggest that they may have functioned as accommodation for the garrison, though significantly, none of the rooms had windows. By analogy with Qal'at Ras al-'Ayn (see above) it is possible that these vaults served as stables and that the accommodation for the garrison was in rooms above. Traces of similar structures built against the inside face of the curtain walls have also been identified in the fortress of Ras al-'Ayn, although they do not survive much above the level of the foundations.

Courtyard structure

Photographs of the fortress taken during the 1940s indicate that there was a long vaulted structure running east–west between the Barracks Block and the Gatehouse (PAM, photos 22.813 and 22.816). If this was part of the Ottoman fortress it would have divided the courtyard in two, with the northern part housing the garrison.

Vaulted Cistern

In the south-west corner of the fortress there is a large, flat roofed structure divided into four cross-vaulted bays, supported by square piers set into the walls and a central square pier. The floor level of the building is considerably lower (at least 1 m) than the rest of the courtyard; the building is entered through a doorway and a set of steps descending to the floor level. The flat roof of the building serves as a terrace and provides access to the vaulted room, which forms the upper part of the south-west corner tower.

The 1995 survey by the British School of Archaeology in Jerusalem identified this building as 'The Stables' (Hawari, Auld and Hudson 2000, 113–15). This attribution was made on the basis of 'worked stone quoins [tethering stones] on all the protruding corners of the interior [which] would have enabled ropes or chains to have been hung at approximately 1.5 m above the ground along all the long sides and around the central pillar' (Hawari, Auld and Hudson 2000, 115). Whilst it is certain that this building was used for the storage of animals in recent times, as indicated by the large quantities of animal dung, it seems less likely that it was originally built as stables. The floor level inside indicates that this building probably functioned as a covered cistern, or pool, collecting water from the spring, as mentioned by Conder and Kitchener (1884, 89). The structure was subsequently reused as an animal shelter after a new cistern was built during the 1930s (Hawari, Auld and Hudson 2000, 103 and 113).

Qal'at Khan al-Tujjar

This site comprises two buildings located either side of the *Via Maris*, 5 km north-east of Jabal al-Tur (Mount Tabor). There is some confusion about the identification and dating of the buildings. The larger of the two stands on the east side of the road and is generally referred to as a khan, whilst that on the west side stands on a small elevation and is referred to as a fort.

The first historical evidence of a fort at this site comes from two Ottoman *firmans* published by Uriel Heyd and dated to October and November 1581 (Heyd 1960, 110–14).

The first *firman* requests that a fortress be built at the site to protect the Muslim pilgrims travelling to Jerusalem and Hebron, as well as the Egyptian merchants using the route. There is some confusion in the documents, as there appears to be another building being constructed at the same time by the Ottoman Grand Vizier, Sinan Pasha. However, what is clear is the necessity for some form of protection at this point, there are indications that the fort(s) were attacked, by Bedouin, while under construction (Heyd 1960, 113–14 n. 18).

The Fort

This is a square structure, standing on a hill 150 m from the larger building. It contains a gateway in the middle of the east side four corner towers and three interval towers on the north, west and south sides. The walls are pierced with a series of gun/arrow slits. Much of the stonework on the exterior walls has been robbed out, though enough remains to indicate that it was faced with *ablaq* or striped masonry of black basalt alternating with light yellow. There are no remains of any structures within the fort, though it is heavily overgrown with bushes and has not been excavated. Evliya Çelebi visited the site in the 1649 and described it as a well preserved, though abandoned, building with sheep and goats grazing inside (Evliya Çelebi trans. Stephan 1934–44, 32–33). From Çelebi's description and the current state of the fortress, it seems likely that it was never finished, with construction shifting to the adjacent khan/fortress.

The Khan

This huge rectangular building (115 m × 166 m) has four round corner towers and is divided into two courtyards. The northern courtyard appears to have been added later and contains the main entrance to the complex. The southern courtyard contains the majority of extant structures and seems to form the core of the original structure. When Evliya Çelebi visited he described a flourishing commercial centre with bathhouses, shops, accommodation for merchants as well as a garrison (Evliya Çelebi trans. Stephan 1934–44, 32–33).

Discussion

The archaeological evidence, together with historical information, indicates that the original building at the site was a khan perhaps dating to the 15th century (*c.f.* Petersen 2001, 200). Later on, under the Ottomans, in the 16th century a fort was built on an adjacent hill. However, during the construction of the fort the caravanserai was also renovated and perhaps a decision was made to combine fortress and caravanserai in one building.

Qal'at Bayt Jibrin

The Ottoman fortress of Bayt Jibrin is built on the remains of an earlier Crusader and possibly Roman fort (see Pringle 1997, 27, no. 34). The fort is square with projecting rectangular corner towers. The only published archaeological evidence for the Ottoman fortress is Guerin's statement (Guérin 1875, 308) that there was a Turkish inscription above the gateway, recording the restoration of the fortress in 958 AH (1551 AD). Unfortunately, this inscription has now been lost, though the date appears to be confirmed by two Ottoman documents published by Uriel Heyd. The first document is a *firman* dated to

1552, which states 'at present the fortress of Jabrin which has already been restored has no arms and no provisions' (Heyd 1960, 115). The second document is also a *firman* issued on the same day stating that 15 of the soldiers who had been transferred from Shawbak to Jabrin had not arrived (Heyd 1960, 116). The fortress evidently had a long-standing relationship with Shawbak and in 1559 a large part of the garrison was re-deployed there. Although the size of the garrison obviously fluctuated, a typical complement of soldiers in the mid-16th century was 40 men (36 *müstafizhan* and 4 *müteferrika*) (Bakhit 1982, 98; *MM* 3723, 51–56). In 1660 the fortress had a garrison of 50 janissaries (Heyd 1960, 190).

Unfortunately, the remains of the fortress do not currently allow a detailed identification of the Ottoman phase. However, it can be said that the size and plan of the fortress roughly corresponds with the fortresses of Ras al-'Ayn and Qal'at Burak.

Qal'at Jenin

In 1564 the caravanserai at Jenin was converted into a fortress on the advice of the governors of Nablus and Lajjun (Heyd 1960, doc. no. 56, 104–5). The fortress had a complement of 40 mounted musketeers and 10 garrison soldiers (Heyd 1960, 104). A similar number of men are reported nearly 100 years later, in 1660, when a report states that it was manned by 37 soldiers (Heyd 1960, 190).

An alternative source for the history of the fort is provided by the account of the Turkish traveller, Evliya Çelebi, who visited Jenin in the mid-17th century (1649–50) and gave the following description:

> 'The governor is its *mutevelli*. A warden with a garrison of three hundred soldiers lives in it. It is a small, yet strong rectangular fortress, situated on a raised terrace, measuring a thousand paces in circumference. Yet is has no ditches. Its two gates face south and north respectively. From within it is fully occupied with guest chambers. In its very centre rises a lovely mosque with a well proportioned minaret covered with a lead roof' (Evliya Çelebi, *Seyhatnâmesi*, 43–45).

Two important facts can be learned from this description. Firstly, the fortress still functioned as a caravanserai (later on he mentions that each resident traveller receives a free loaf of bread and candle). Secondly, the fortress/caravanserai was built around a domed mosque. Today the mosque is the only part of the building to have survived and now forms the centre of the modern town.

Qal'at Hebron

The fortress of Hebron is referred to in a number of Ottoman documents published by Heyd (1960) and Bakhit (1982). Although it is not clear when it was built, it is clear that the fortress was in existence by 1566 at the latest, when it was recorded as having a garrison of 30 troops (Bakhit 1982, 98 n. 9 based on *MM* 3723). In 1576 it was used

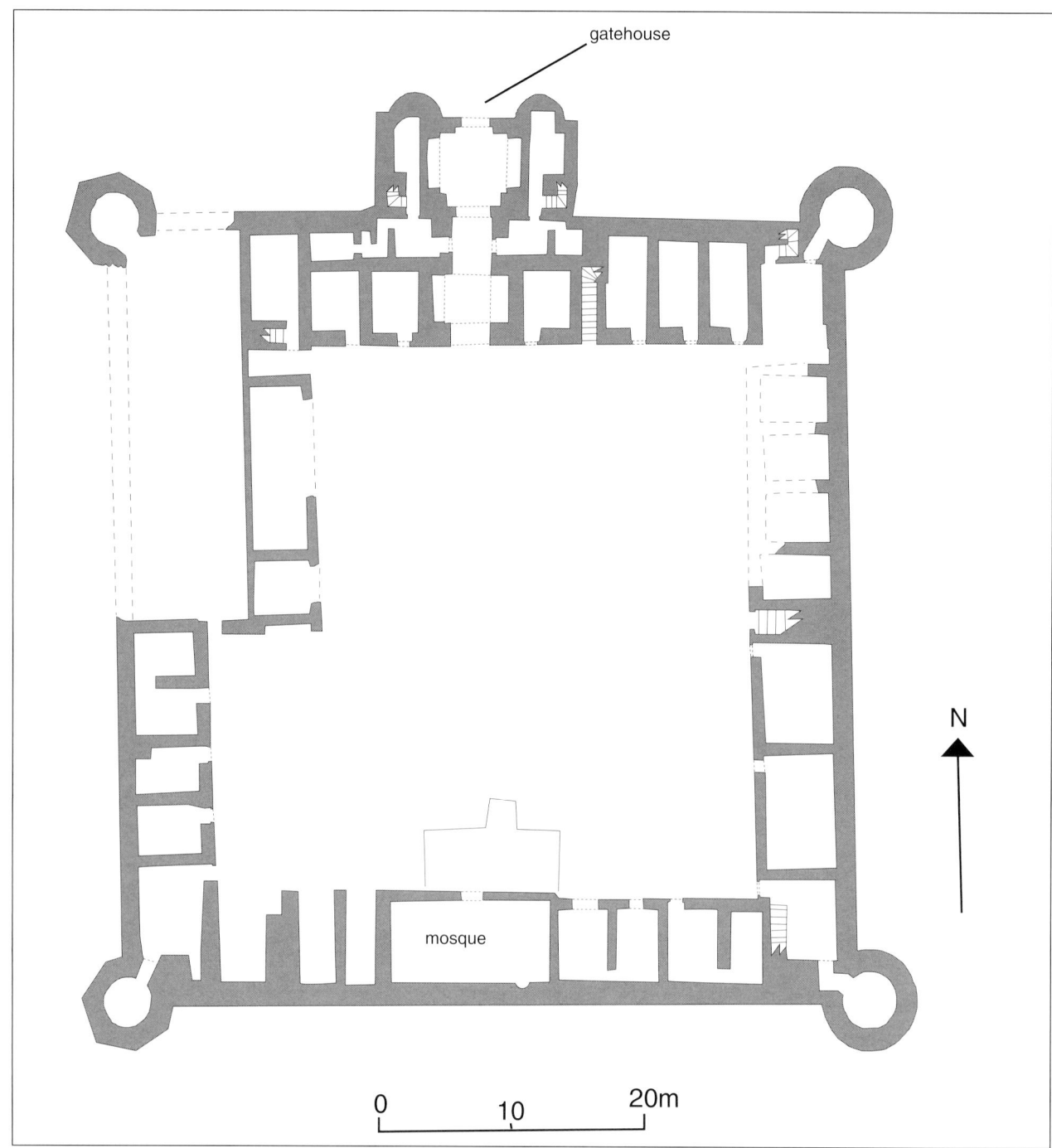

gatehouse

N

0   10   20m

Fig. 5. Plan of Qal'at al-'Aqaba in Jordan, before recent restorations and excavations.

to hold Bedouin hostages as part of a policy of subduing rebellious tribes (Heyd 1960, 98, n. 3). In 1595 an order was given to replace the 6 *zarzuban* of the fortress, as they had become ineffective as a means of deterring rebellious Bedouin (Heyd 1960, 116 n. 5). Unusually, the size of the garrison had increased in the 17th century, so that in 1660 the fortress was listed as having 34 guards (Heyd 1960, 190).

The fortress was located to the west of the centre of Hebron, on the top of a hill in an area known as Rumeidi or Deir al-Arba'in. Although there has been no detailed

archaeological survey of the fortress, there are brief unpublished reports held in the archives of the Department of Antiquities of Palestine, housed in the Rockefeller Museum, Jerusalem: a description of the building is given in an anonymous report, dated 1920. The report notes a 'late Arab fort from three to four hundred years old. Irregular and badly constructed buildings with vaults inside a roughly square enclosure with battlements and embrasures. The masonry is very poor the stones consisting of rubble and mortar.' (PAM – Report on Rumeidi dated 11.11.20).

Another report, also in the Department of Antiquities,

Plate 5. Qal'at al-'Aqaba, interior of courtyard looking north towards entrance (1985).

Plate 6. Qal'at al-'Aqaba, interior looking south-east (1985).

Archives, by S. A. S. Husseini describes the site as follows, 'On a hill at Rumadi W. of Hebron town is a rectangular enclosure built with roughly cut stones, it is entered from the SE corner through a ruined arched door which leads into a small barrel-vaulted passage. Some of the masonry here are fairly large stones and bear bossed drafts. On the SW corner is a square projecting tower. Within the enclosure are remains of ruined vaulted chambers and arches, some are of well cut stones. Along the N. side are a series of large barrel-vaulted chambers, the NE corner of the building is curved. Outside the enclosure and opposite its W corner is a small built and plastered tank.' (PAM – Report by S.

Plate 7. Qal'at al-'Aqaba, south-west tower (1985).

Plate 8. Qal'at al-'Aqaba, gateway exterior, with Hashemite arms above entrance (1985).

Plate 9. Qal'at al-'Aqaba, gateway, exterior detail showing 16th century Ottoman inscription (1985).

Plate 10. Qal'at al-'Aqaba, interior of courtyard west range with south-west tower in background (1985).

Conclusion

There are two point of interest in relation to the Hajj forts, the first concerns the design of the forts in Palestine and the second relates to how they were managed.

Like the Hajj forts, the fortresses in Palestine appear to have had a remarkably uniform design, layout and dimensions. Although there is considerable variation in the size and internal arrangements of theses forts, the similarities are remarkable. Each fort occupies a raised position on a low hill. However, the walls are not built to follow the contours of the hill, as in Medieval fortifications, but follow a rigid rectangular template with four corner towers and a single entrance in the middle of one of the sides. This design suggests a degree of central planning, employing imperial architects to impose a uniform system of fortification on the area. The only example of a building of this type on the Syrian Hajj route, is the fortress at Muzayrib (Fig. 1) built in the early 16th century as a place of assembly at the start of the Hajj (for a discussion of Muzayrib, see Chapter 8). However, a number of Ottoman buildings on the Egyptian Hajj routes are of this type, for example, the fortress/khan at 'Aqaba (Fig. 5 and Plates 5–10) which although of Medieval origin was remodelled

A. S. Husseini dated 15.1.44 based on visits on 21.4.42 and 29.12.43).

Today the site is largely in ruins, though satellite photographs indicate its hilltop location and rectangular shape.

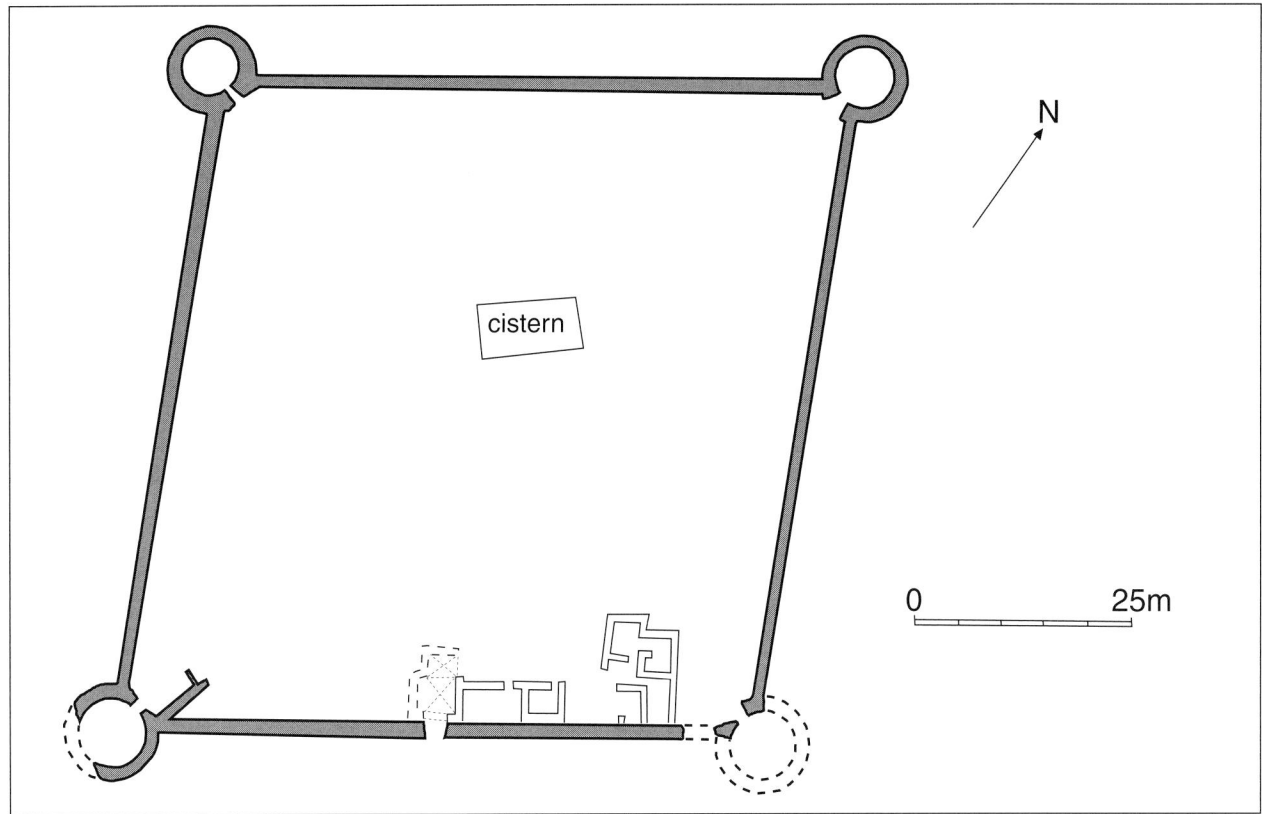

Fig. 6. Plan of Ottoman fortress at Quseir on the Red Sea coast of Egypt. After Le Quesne 2004.

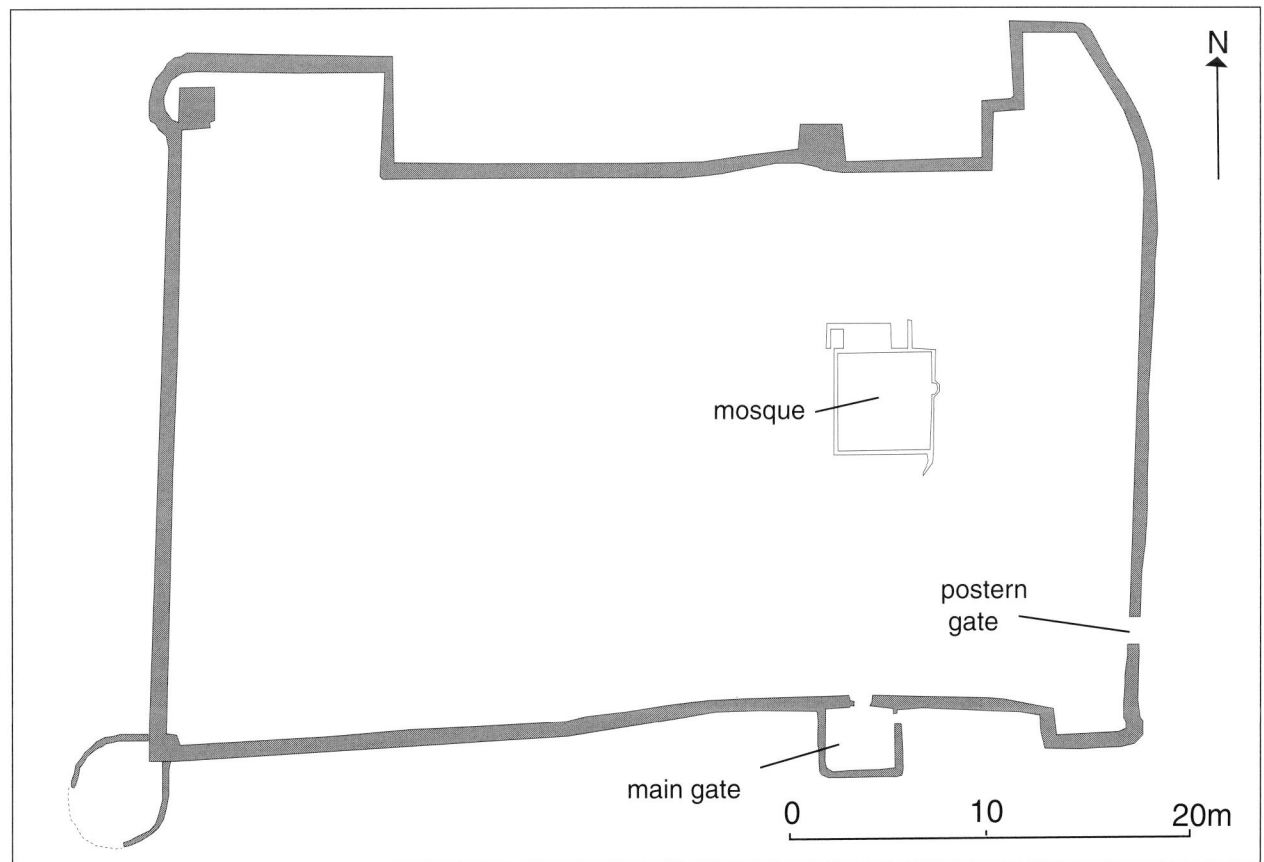

Fig. 7. Plan of Qal'at al-Sai in northern Sudan. After Alexander 1997.

by the Ottomans in the 16th century (*c.f.* De Meulemeester and Pringle 2000; Pringle 2008). Another example on the Hajj route from Cairo is the now destroyed, Qal'at al-Nakhl, in the Sinai, which was enlarged by the Ottomans in the 16th century to form a large, rectangular, enclosure with four corner towers (Tamari 1982, 479). There are also two examples of forts built to this plan where the Middle Egyptian Hajj route crossed the Red Sea – Quseir (Fig. 6) and Qenna (Le Quesne 2004). Examples of this form of fortification can also be found in Sudan at Qasr Ibrim (50 m × 35 m) and Qal'at al-Sai (Fig. 7) where existing fortifications were modified to fit this rectangular format (Alexander 1998). The Ottoman fortress of Kefela, at a strategic position on the Mani peninsula in Greece, is also of this form suggesting that this was an architectural form in use throughout the Ottoman Empire (for a discussion of the fortress of Kefala, see Wagstaff 2009).

The information about how the forts in Palestine were used and garrisoned is mostly derived from imperial *firmans* published by Hyde (1960). These *firmans* show a clear link with the Hajj forts, in that each of the forts in Palestine was linked with a fortress in Jordan providing both troops and equipment. In turn these fortresses in Jordan played a supporting role to the Hajj forts, although there is no explicit statement indicating that they shared either garrisons or equipment. However, what is clear is that the central authorities would have been aware that they were establishing a network of fortifications providing security for the region.

8. The Hajj Route in Syria

This chapter discusses sites on the Hajj route within the boundaries of the modern state of Syria (for an overview of Ottoman Syria, see Petersen 2012). As much of the fieldwork for this book was centred on Jordan, this short introduction provides a regional context for the Syrian Hajj sites.

The Hajj occupied a central place in the life of Ottoman Syria. From the moment of Sultan Selim's conquest of Damascus in 1516, up to the closing years of Ottoman rule in the early 1900s, the finance, accommodation and transport of pilgrims from Syria to Mecca was a major priority (Issawi 1988, 236–39). Barbir has shown the extent to which, in terms of finance, logistics and administration, the whole province of Syria was geared to the Hajj during the 18th century. He observed that although the Syrian provinces participated less and less in imperial wars as time went on, 'an Ottoman 'campaign' involving thousands of troops was conducted each year at pilgrimage time' (Barbir 1980, 111). The cost of the military protection and most of the other expenses of the pilgrimage, were borne by the Syrian provinces of Damascus, Tripoli, Sidon and Aleppo. The Province of Tripoli was responsible for providing the *jarda*, or military caravan, which was sent to meet the returning pilgrims and provide them with necessary provisions. Each year, a few months before the departure of the Hajj caravan, the governor of Damascus made a tour of the Syrian provinces to collect the money required to finance the caravan (Marino 2000, 272–73). However, Syria also benefited financially from the Hajj, both in terms of, selling goods, as well as providing an important influx of exotic goods, which were brought back by pilgrims from Mecca. Items of particular importance coming from Mecca included, coffee, spices, Indian textiles, gems, precious stones and slaves (Estabalet and Pascal 1998, 163). The Hajj also provided a stimulus to the settlement of marginal areas, including areas directly on the route and areas further afield. For example, Bosra and the villages of the Hawran, as well as Sukhne and the region of Palmyra, developed as areas for breeding camels.

The Hajj Route North of Damascus (Table 1)

Damascus was always the official starting point of the Syrian Hajj route, even after the Ottoman conquest in 1517 when many pilgrims would begin their journey in Constantinople. However, the route from Constantinople to Damascus was of considerable importance and was known to contemporaries as 'The Imperial Way' (*Tarik-i Sultani*). It has been identified by Faroqhi as of one of the three major routes of the eastern Ottoman Empire (Faroqhi 1994, 41). Although, in effect, the overland

Plate 11. Sulayman I mosque in Damascus (1554–60) (Tony Grey 1998).

Place Names	Builder	Date	Buildings
Beilan	Selim II	1550	1) vaulted rectangular building 70 × 31 m 2) mosque
Kara Mughurt (Baghras)	Murad IV	1638	1) large courtyard building 161 × 122 m
al-Zanbakiyya		pre 1779	1) khan
Jisr al Shughur		1660–76	1) large vaulted hall with square courtyard
Qal'at Mudiq		late 16th early 17th centuries	1) square courtyard building 40 × 40 m 2) mosque
al-Resten		late 16th early 17th centuries	1) rectangular courtyard 98 × 45 m
Hasye	Sultan Sulayman	1520–66	1) caravanserai comprising, khan (Medieval) fort (Ottoman) khan (Ottoman) 2) mosque
al-Nabk		not before the mid-16th century	1) vaulted rectangular building 65 × 32 m 2) mosque
al-Qataif	Koja Sinan Pasha	1590s	Huge rectangular complex 102 × 155 m comprising 1) rectangular courtyard building (khan) 2) suq (shops) 2) kitchens 3) hammam (bath-house) 4) mosque

Table 1 – Syrian Hajj Caravanserais north of Damascus based on Sauvaget (1937)

Plate 12. Takiyya complex, Damascus, viewed from north (Photograph B_083 courtesy of the Gertrude Bell Archive, University of Newcastle-Upon-Tyne).

Plate 13. Interior of Takiyya complex, Damascus (Photograph B_081 courtesy of the Gertrude Bell Archive, University of Newcastle-Upon-Tyne).

route from Constantinople to Damascus became part of the Hajj route, it continued to be used by other travellers throughout the year and did not have the official supervision

and protection enjoyed by the route south of Damascus. The route between Constantinople and Damascus was recorded by the 18th century traveller, Mehmed Edib

Plate 14. Sinaniyya Mosque (1591 AD), located 300 m south of the citadel in Damascus (Photograph courtesy of Stefan Weber).

Plate 16. Khan Assad Pasha (1751–53 AD), nine-domed khan located in the Suq al Buzuriyya, Damascus (Photograph courtesy of Stefan Weber).

Plate 15. Darwishiyya mosque (1574–75 AD), located 100 m south of the citadel in Damascus (Photograph courtesy of Stefan Weber).

(Bianchi 1825). There were 37 travelling days between Üskudar (the Asian side of Constantinople) and Damascus. An extra 6 rest days on the journey, gives a total time of 43 days from the imperial capital to Damascus. The route cut through the middle of Anatolia, via Iznik (Nicea), Konya and Adana, to Payas, which was the border with Syria. The archaeology and architecture of the stations on the southern part of the route, within modern Syria, has been studied by Sauvaget (1937). The route led from Payas to Antioch and then followed the course of the Orontes River, via Hama and Homs, to Damascus. The Ottoman rulers and their officials provided stops with a range of facilities including, caravanserais, mosques, and, in some cases, bath-houses, shops and kitchens. The most elaborate complex was the khan at al-Kutaifa, which with its vast size, range of facilities and elegant design is a highly sophisticated example of classical Ottoman architecture (Sauvaget 1937; Kiel 2001, 104). This stands in marked contrast to the stations to the south of Damascus, which, with the exception of Muzayrib, simply comprise small forts and reservoirs with no large caravanserais.

The City of Damascus (Plates 11–16)

Whilst the whole of Syria was, in some way, connected to the annual dispatch of the Hajj caravan, the same factors also re-enforced the role of Damascus as regional capital. From the beginning of the Ottoman period an official from Damascus was leader of the Hajj caravan (*amir al-Hajj*), while from the early 18th century, the Caravan was led by the Governor of Damascus in person. The link between Damascus and the Hajj was clearly expressed as soon as Sultan Selim captured Damascus in 1516 and he was addressed by the Qadi al-Farfur as, 'victorious servitor of the two holy cities' (Bakhit 1982, 10). The city obviously benefited from the influx of pilgrims from Anatolia, Iran and Central Asia, both in terms of goods brought and sold, but also in terms of accommodation and food, all of which generated financial activity. In addition to the pilgrims themselves, Damascus was filled with people providing services to the pilgrims from the Syrian provinces, thus in the Maydan there was an area for camel traders from Sukhne, near Palmyra, which also had its own mosque.

The Ottoman conquest of Damascus was marked by a large number of building projects designed to improve the infrastructure and hence the status of the city as a regional capital. Bakhit states that during the 16th century 'Damascus experienced a time of construction and repair. Schools, mosques, convents, bakeries, baths, bridges, markets and carvanserays were either built or repaired. Every class of society and travellers alike benefited from this upsurge' (Bakhit 1982, 115). The majority of these building were religious in nature and none was more significant than the construction of the *takiyya* Sulaymaniyya (Plate 16), the magnificent Hajj complex, built under the orders of Sultan Sulayman between 1554 and 1560, on the site of the Qasr al-Ablaq, originally built by Sultan Baybars in 1264. The complex housed both a Hanafi law school, with its own mosque, as well as a main mosque with shops, soup kitchens, and other facilities for pilgrims. The complex was designed by the imperial architect, Sinan, and characteristically shows a respect for traditional Syrian architecture within Ottoman forms. For example, typical Syrian striped black and white (*ablaq*) masonry is used throughout the complex, including the floor surfaces, whilst the complex is roofed with multiple lead covered hemispherical domes in Ottoman fashion. The most strikingly Ottoman component of the complex is the mosque, which has a large dome resting on a fenestrated circular drum and is flanked by two tall pencil shaped minarets. Adjacent to the *takiyya* a large area (twice the size of the built complex) was enclosed to serve as a camping ground for pilgrims (Goodwin 1987, 255–57). The complex was supported by the revenue from an endowment of 40 Syrian villages (Bakhit 1982, 116; Van Leeuwen 1999, 98).

To the south of Damascus, an area known as the Maydan grew up either side of the Hajj route, stretching for over 5 km. The extraordinary width (more than 40 m in places) of the street, combined with the large number of religious buildings (21 mosques and 17 mausolea), marked the route as an area of particular significance. In addition to the mosques there were at least 6 bath-houses, serving both pilgrims and inhabitants of the quarter. Much of the street front of the Maydan is composed of storehouses, or *baykés*, built to house grain from the Hawran. Each storehouse comprised a rectangular structure, covered with a flat roof supported on a series of transverse arches in the traditional style of the Hawran (Roujon and Vilan 1997; Petersen 2000).

During the 16th century a number of important buildings were erected on the Tariq al-Sultani linking the commercial and administrative centre of Damascus with the Maydan. Notable structures include the complexes built, to the north and south of the citadel in the 1550s and 1560s, by Ahmed Şemsi Pasha and Lala Mustafa Pasha. Other important 16th century foundations include the Murad Pasha mosque complex (1568–70), built on the Maydan and the Sinan Pasha complex built between 1586 and 1588 on the Tariq al-Sultani. These buildings all accentuated the orientation of the Ottoman city towards the Hajj route (Kafescioğlu 1999, 73–74).

The Hajj Route South of Damascus

The route south of Damascus varied over time and depending on circumstances. During the Ottoman period it appears that pilgrims would leave Damascus in their own time, using their own routes, with a rendezvous at Muzayrib where the pilgrimage march would begin in earnest. Between Damascus and Muzayrib a number of significant locations may be noted.

Qubbat al-Hajj

During the Ottoman period the *amir al-Hajj* and the officials of the pilgrimage caravan would spend their first night at a location at the end of the Maydan, on the outskirts of Damascus, known variously as Qubbat al-Hajj, Kasr-ı Küçük Ahmed Paşa (the Palace of little Ahmed Paşa), Ahmed Paşa Turbası (the tomb of Ahmed Pasha), Qubbat Yalbuĝa al-Yahyawi, or Qubbat al-Nasr. This stop was located one hour or 5 km south of the Umayyad mosque and a quarter of an hour south of the southern gate of the Maydan known variously as, Bab 'Allah and Bab al-Mawt (gate of Death). The site was described by Evliya Çelebi (1682) as a magnificent palace located within a beautiful garden and vineyard (Bilge 1979, 216; Evliya Çelebi, *Seyhatnâmesi* IX, 295). It is likely that the majority of structures making up the palace were either tents or wooden pavilions. It is not clear what permanent structures were located at this point, though a white Dome or 'Qubba' and a number of tombs seem to have formed the nucleus of the site. The Qubba seems to originally have been a Mamluk building named after Yalbuĝa al-Yahyawi, governor of Damascus between 1345 and 1347 (Bakhit 1982, 113, n. 135). The Qubba was renovated in 1515 and several times during the Ottoman period, which may account for the change of name. During the 16th century Muhammad ibn Manjik built a palace at the site that was later given to the Governor of Damascus, Küçük Ahmed Paşa, who used it for entertaining prior to the start of the Hajj (Bakhit 1982, 190).

Most authors also refer to a village mosque known as the mosque of the foot (*masjid al-qadm*) that was reputed to be the place where Muhammad dismounted on his journey from Mecca to Damascus (Burckhardt 1822, chapter 2, 2). Both Ibn Kanaan (1663–1740) and Evliya Çelebi (1682) describe a number of festivities at this site and also indicate that the inhabitants of Damascus would accompany the caravan to this spot before returning home (Van Leeuwen 1999, 104–5; Bilge 1979, 216). The caravan commander (*amir al-Hajj*) generally waited at this place for three days, allowing final adjustments in readiness for departure (Bakhit 1982, 113).

Kiswa

This village is located 4 hours (15 km) south of Damascus and was mentioned by Ibn Battuta as the location of the first overnight stop on the Syrian Hajj route (for Kiswa in the Medieval period, see Chapter 3). Evliya Çelebi gives an enthusiastic description of the village, mentioning that it was located within gardens and vineyards tended by a population of 200 families. The village had two Friday mosques, as well as a small mosque (*masjid*), a bath-house and a khan. Evliya was accommodated in a pleasant guest house and dined on chicken, yoghurt and cream (Bilge 1979, 216; Evliya Çelebi, *Seyhatnâmesi* IX, 287). Mehmed Edib (1779) briefly mentions the pleasant location of the village, set amongst trees and running water, but gives no further details (Bianchi 1825, 121). Burckhardt passed through the village in 1810 and stopped for half an hour at a coffee shop by the roadside. He noted that it was a large village with a paved bridge crossing the river and a small khan, or fortified building (Burckhardt 1822, chapter 2, 2). Michael Meinecke made a study of the remains at Kiswa, including the religious complex or *zawiya* built by Manjak al-Yusufi, the governor of Damascus in the 1370s (Meinecke 1992, II, 247 no. 22/47; Meinecke 1996, 46 and plate 15a)

Khan Danun

A quarter of an hour to the south of Kiswa there was a medieval khan completed in 1376; one of the stations on the Mamluk postal route (Sauvaget 1935–45). Like the complex at Kiswa this building was erected by the Governor of Damasucs, Manjak al-Yusufi, though it is actually signed by the architect, or engineer, 'Ali Ibn al Badri (Meinecke 1996, 46 and 53 n. 9). In the Ottoman period it is first mentioned in the late 16th century by the author of *Manazil al-Hajj min al-Sham ila Makka*, who referred to it as Dhay al-Nun (al-Jasir 1969, 184). In 1672 Evliya Çelebi refers to the complex as Tarhani Han, after the soup *tarahan* made of dried curds and flour (*c.f.* Redhouse 1968, 1096), served to returning pilgrims at this site. Çelebi states that there were two small khans, either side of the road, one of which contained 100 soup cauldrons (Evliya Çelebi, *Seyhatnâmesi* IX, 287). By the late 18th century the khan seems to have been deserted and Mehmed Edib observes that it was in a ruinous condition (Bianchi 1825, 121). Burckhardt passed through Khan Danun in 1810 and gives the following succinct description of the site:

> 'This khan, which is now in ruins, was built in the usual style of all the large khans in this country: consisting of an open square, surrounded with arcades, beneath which are small apartments for the accommodation of travellers; the beasts occupy the open square in the centre' (Burckhardt 1822, chapter 2, 3).

Ghabarib

The precise location of the fort is not known, though it seems probable that it should be identified with Ghubaghub (غباغب) a stop on the Hajj route between Danun and Sanamayn mentioned by the 16th century author of *Manazil al-Hajj* (al-Jasir 1969, 184). Burckhardt also mentions 'Ghabarib' three and a half hours to the south of Khan Danun. He noted that the site contains a small ruined fort and a cistern, while nearby there was a small domed shrine called Meziyar Elisha 'to which the Turks resort from a persuasion that the prayers there offered up are peculiarly acceptable to the deity' (Burckhardt 1822, chapter 2, 3). It is possible that this is the same place referred to by Mehmed Edib when he noted a small settlement with a bridge known as Khan Zeit (Bianchi 1825, 121).

Sanamayn

This small ancient town is located approximately 50 km south of Damascus and first appears as a stop on the Hajj route in the 9th century itinerary of al-Harbi (al-Jasir 1969). The place is also mentioned by Ibn Battuta (Ibn Battuta, *Rihala*, 77) who described it as a village when he passed through, on the Hajj, in 1326. Ottoman records indicate that a fort was built here between 1516 and 1520, during the reign of Sultan Selim I (Barbir 1980, 134). Evliya Çelebi notes that Sanamayn (population 2,600) is located on the main road, next to a lake and is built of black stones. To the east of the town, next to the lake, there was a large square fort made of black stones. He also observes that the town has a Friday mosque with minaret, two small mosques, a bath house and a large khan. Although there was no market in the town there were a number of prostitutes who lined up on the roadside (Evliya Çelebi, *Seyhatnâmesi* IX, 287; see also Bilge 1979, 216). Çelebi observed a bridge to the south of the town, which Mehmed Edib dates to the reign of Sultan Selim I (*i.e.* 1516–20). Edib also mentions a fort which he somewhat confusingly refers to as Ghubaghub (غباغب) (Bianchi 1825, 122). Burckhardt noted that the town contained ancient remains and inscriptions but did not examine the place in any detail.

South of Sanamayn authors describe a number of villages including, Zara'a, Lesser Busra, Ketibe, Keskin and Tafs, though the next major stop was Muzayrib.

Muzayrib (Fig. 1)

Most authors agree that the fortress at Muzayrib was built in the early years of Ottoman rule (see, for example, Kiel 2001, 104; Meinecke 1996, 48). However, it is probable that the place had already developed as an alternative stopping point to Bosra in the late Mamluk period (for a discussion of medieval Muzayrib, see Chapter 3). For example, Ludivico di Varthema (1863, 16) stayed at Muzayrib for three days in 1503; during which pilgrims were able to buy whatever they needed, including horses, indicating that there was a large market at the site. There is, however, no mention of a fort, or other building, at the site.

The fortress of Muzayrib first appears in Ottoman official documents in 1563, when it is listed as having a garrison of 51 men (Bakhit 1982, 98). In the same year (971 AH/1563 AD) Muzayrib is mentioned as a stop in the anonymous, *Manazil al-Hajj*, written in 1563 (al-Jasir 1969, 174). Official Ottoman documents indicate that the caravan stopped at Muzayrib for seven days and that there was a large market where camels could be brought and sold. The fortress was used as a centre for financial transactions, thus the governor of Damascus collected taxes from the merchants, whilst the leader of the Hajj (*amir al-Hajj*) used it as a base to distribute payments (*surras*) to the Bedouin chiefs (Bakhit 1982, 113).

The first detailed description of the fortress was written by Evliya Çelebi after seeing it in 1670.

'This castle was built by Hâtem Tay in the time of Hazret-I Ebu Bekir. It is built in the form of a square, situated on a stoney plateau and measures 8,000 paces in circumference. There is a fortress commander and 80 soldiers in the garrison. One of the Ağas of the Pasha sits here with 300 men, as does the kadi of the Hauran. Its Nahiye comprises 270 villages. Inside the castle is a mosque, a small hammam and stores where the treasure of the state as well as the merchants are kept' (Kiel 2001, 104; Evliya Çelebi, *Seyhatnâmesi* IX, 201).

Evliya's account suggests a much larger garrison than the 51 men listed in the 16th century. However, by the mid-18th century (1741–59) Ottoman records indicate that the garrison had contracted to as few as 12 men (Kiel 2001, 104). Mehmed Edib gives little detailed information about the fortress except for the statement that it was built during the reign of Sultan Selim I, thus confirming its 16th century date.

The first European description of the fortress at Muzayrib was by the Swiss traveller Burckhardt, who visited in 1812.

'El Mezareib is the first castle on the Hadj road from Damascus, and was built by the great Sultan Selym, three hundred and eight years ago. It is the usual residence of the Aga of the Haouran…. The garrison of the castle consisted of a dozen Moggrebyns [Moroccans], whose chief a young black, was extremely civil to me. The castle is of a square form, each side being, as well as I can recollect, about one hundred and twenty paces in length. The entrance is through an iron gate, which is regularly shut after sunset. The interior presents nothing but an empty yard enclosed by the castle wall, within which are ranges of warehouses where provisions for the Hadj are deposited; their flat roofs form a platform behind the parapet of the castle wall, where sixteen or eighteen mud huts have been built on top of the warehouses, as habitations for the peasants who cultivate the neighbouring grounds. On the east side two miserable guns are planted. Within the castle there is a small mosque. There are no houses beyond its precincts' (Burckhardt 1822, chapter 4, 19).

Two points are of particular interest in Burkhardt's narrative, firstly, he confirms the attribution of the fort to Sultan Selim and secondly the garrison was still only 12 men strong.

The most detailed description of the fortress is given by Schumacher who visited Muzayrib in the 1880s. This description includes a detailed map of the castle and its immediate surroundings, including, the lake, village and flour mills. It states that the castle was rapidly falling into ruin, although it does mention some recently built mud and stone huts which were used to shelter pilgrims. It is noticeable that there is no mention of a garrison and a recently built set of barracks nearby is described as being in ruins. Schumacher's interests in antiquities enabled him to identify a number of reused Roman and Byzantine masonry fragments, which had been incorporated into the fortress and mosque.

In 1919, in the immediate aftermath of the First World War Muzayrib was visited by K. A. C. Creswell, when he was making a provisional list of historic buildings between Aleppo and Jerusalem. As the description is well written and has not been published before it is worth reproducing in full.

'About a mile to the north of the railway station, and to the north-east of the lake is a khan, about 100 paces square, with a square tower at each angle, and a square tower of the same projection but less width in the centre of each face, except on the north side, where the centre of the façade is occupied by the entrance. The entrance has a pointed arch opening into a cross-vaulted passage, which leads, after two right angled turns into the great courtyard now littered with debris. Vaulted corridors, more or less ruined, run around the sides of the courtyard and the angle and intermediate towers are entered from them.

This building is quite deserted and, although the interior is much ruined, I did not get the impression that the inhabitants of the neighbouring village had pillaged it for stone. This, however is an ever-present danger to be guarded against' (Creswell 1917/18).

Unfortunately Creswell's prediction of stone robbing proved to be true. In 1988 Michael Meinecke described the building as heavily ruined and commissioned a survey of the site by Norbet Hagen and Emad Terkawi (Meinecke 1996, 47, 53 n. 43). Ten years later Machiel Kiel visited the fortress and described it as follows: 'It is utterly ruined and more than two thirds of its masonry has disappeared carried off for modern buildings in the villages nearby' (Kiel 2001, 104).

9. Catalogue of Hajj Forts in Jordan

A total of nine forts in Jordan were surveyed as part of this project (Qal'at Mafraq was destroyed before the survey and access to the area was not possible). Two of these buildings were of Medieval origin (Qasr Shebib, in Zerka, and Jize/Zizia) whilst the rest were built during the period of Ottoman rule, which started in the 16th century. In each case, black and white photographs and plans were made of each fort during the original survey carried out in January 1986. During 2006 each of the forts was re-visited in order to check plans, produce digital photographs and check on the condition of the buildings. Also during the 2006 survey, samples of pottery were taken to complement material retrieved from the excavations at Qal'at 'Unaiza in 2002.

Qal'at Mafraq – (Map 5, No. 2) (Plates 17–20)

(Tal Far'un, el-Ferka, el-Fedhien, Khirbet el-Fedhein, Fudayn, Mizrak, Maaref, Magreb, Mefrak)

Plate 19. Mafraq fort, interior (courtesy of the Israel Antiquities Authority).

Plate 17. Mafraq fort, distant view (courtesy of the Israel Antiquities Authority).

Plate 18. Mafraq fort, exterior with entrance to right. Note entrance with box machicolation above (courtesy of the Israel Antiquities Authority).

Plate 20. Mafraq fort, interior with gateway in centre (courtesy of the Israel Antiquities Authority).

Location: 32.20N 36.12E

Mafraq (Ar. = 'crossroads') is located in northern steppe of Jordan, at the west end of the Hauran (Black Desert), close to the border with Syria. The site lies on a Roman road running south-west from Menara, on the Via Nova to Jerash.

History

There are a considerable number of ancient remains at Mafraq, concentrated at a spring, to the south-west of the Hijaz railway station. Remains include a prehistoric tell, a fort, a Byzantine-Umayyad house and an Abbasid palace (Kennedy 1997, 74–76; Kennedy 2000, 102). The site is first mentioned in the Islamic period, in connection with an Umayyad leader, Saʻid ibn Khalid al-ʻUthmani, who made a bid for the caliphate from his base at al-Fudayn (Ibn ʻAsakir, 53 cited in Northedge *et al.* 1992, 53).

Mafraq is not mentioned in Medieval sources in relation to the Hajj, being first mentioned in the Ottoman period. Soon after the conquest of Syria in 1516, Sultan Selim I (r. 1512–20) ordered the construction of three forts to the south of Damascus, at Sanamayn, Muzayrib and Tall Farʻun (Mafraq) (Barbir 1980 134, n. 68; Kâtip Çelebi (1732/3) *Cihannüma* 538; Sabri, (1888/9) *Mirʼat ʼül-Harameyn*)). Other evidence for the establishment of a fort at Mafraq is provided in the 16th century (971 AH/1563 AD) itinerary of Mustapha Pasha (al-Jasir 1969, 184–85), which mentions Mafraq as a stop between Muzayrib and Qasr Shebib (Zerka).

The first description of the fort is given by Evliya Çelebi who visited it in 1672 (Evliya Çelebi, *Seyhatnâmesi* IX, 292; Bilge 1979, 217). He states that it was a square fort, built in the middle of the desert, by the Bani Hillal. However, at the time of his visit there was no garrison inside, it being occupied by Bedouin who used it as a place to keep sheep and goats. Outside there was a green meadow with large acacia trees and plentiful water. In 1709 the pilgrim, Murtada ibn ʻAlawan, stopped at Mafraq where the pilgrims erected their tents (Murtada b. ʻAli b. ʻAlawan *Rihala* MS fol. 104a). Seventy years later, Mafraq was visited by Mehmed Edib, who noted that it was a dangerous place because of flash floods. According to Edib the name is derived from the fact that, here the returning pilgrims broke free from the caravan and raced back to Damascus (Bianchi 1825, 23; Mehmed Edib 1816/17).

Burckhardt was the first European traveller to mention Mafraq, describing it as 'a castle four hours from Ramtha, where the Pasha keeps a small garrison, under the orders of the Aga, or Obadashi'. Burckhardt notes that the Bedouin of the area use the fort as a storehouse for grain, which they either sell to pilgrims, or keep for the following year (Burckhardt 1822, 657, appendix III). Elsewhere he describes Mafraq as 'a ruined castle situated on the eastern extremity of Djebel Zouueit (1822, chapter 4). When Doughty followed the Hajj caravan from Damascus in 1875

he passed the fort at Mafraq, describing it as ruinous and abandoned (Doughty 1979, 47).

There is little mention of Mafraq by other 19th century travellers and by the 20th century it appears to have been mostly forgotten. In 1932 the Iraq Petroleum Company established one of their principal camps at Mafraq, near the fort (Grant 2003).

The fort was apparently demolished, in 1957, by the Iraqi army, in order to make way for the trans-Arabian pipeline.

Description

Fortunately, photographs of the fort, taken by the Department of Antiquities of Jordan, have survived and are in the Rockefeller Museum in Jerusalem (Plates 17–20). The photographs show that the fort was a square building, located on the brow of a hill and built of large, squared, limestone blocks (21 courses high). The entrance to the fort was an arched opening, set within a panel of dressed stone masonry (possibly *ablaq*). Directly above the arch of the doorway there was a small rectangular recessed panel, probably containing an inscription. Above this, at first floor level, there was a projecting box machicolation. Apart from the area around the entrance, there were no decorative features on the exterior of the fort, though a number of arrow slits/gun ports can be seen at first floor level. The entrance led, via a vaulted *iwan*, into a small central courtyard with a series of rooms at ground floor level. On the upper level (first floor) no rooms are indicated, the only visible features being niches for the gun ports/ arrow slits.

Discussion

References to this fort indicate that it was abandoned by the late 19th century, if not much earlier. It is noticeable that there were only two levels within the fort, whereas most of the other forts have three levels.

Qasr Shebib – (Map 5, No. 3) (Fig. 8, Plates 21–22)

(Zerka, Zarka, Zarqaʻ, Qalʻat al-Zerqa)

Location: 36.07E 32.04N

The fort, today known as Qasr Shebib (قصر شبيب), stands in a prominent position on a spur between two wadis, Wadi Zarqa and its tributary, Wadi Huweijir. It is located in the grounds of the Zarka First Secondary School for Boys and is jointly maintained by the Department of Antiquities and the Ministry of Education.

History

It is probable that the first structure built on this site was

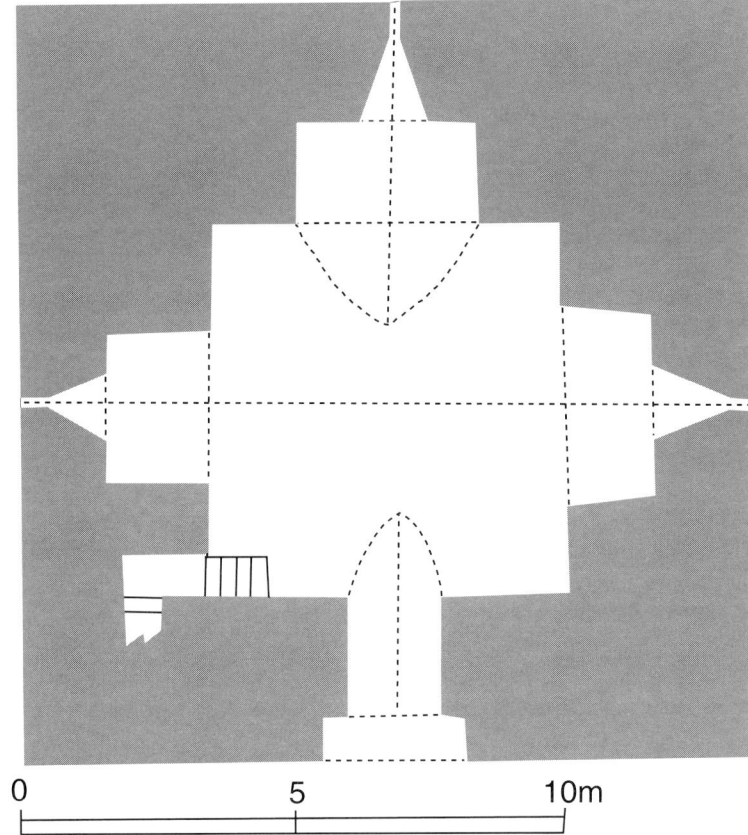

Fig. 8. Ground floor plan of Qasr Shebib at Zerka in northern Jordan.

Plate 22. Qasr Shebib, Zerka, west face of fort (1986).

Plate 21. Qasr Shebib, Zerka, north face with entrance in foreground (1986).

a Roman fort, which is referred to in a Latin inscription dated AD 253/9 embedded into the wall of Qasr Shebib and discovered by the Princeton Expedition in the early 1900s (Butler 1907–49, III, A.2: Inscr. 12; Parker 1986, 34; Kennedy 2000, 86–88, fig. 10.11). The 13th century writer Yaqut (1995, vol. 3, 137) associates the area of Wadi Zarqa with the pre-Islamic Himyarite ruler, Shebib Tubbai, and it seems likely that the name of the fort is also derived from this association. However, the present building, Qasr Shebib, is certainly of Medieval origin, even though not specifically mentioned in Medieval Arabic sources the site was a well-known stopping point for caravans in the

Mamluk period (Bakhit 2008; Majali and Mas'ad 1987, 314). Zarka first appears in Ottoman sources in 1519, in connection with a confrontation between the Ottoman pilgrims and the Mafarija tribe which ended peacefully (Bakhit 1982, 221). The fort, however, is not explicitly mentioned as Qasr Shebib in written sources until 1563 (971 AH), when it appears as the name of a stop in the itinerary of Mustapha Pasha (al-Jasir 1969, 184–85). Peake Pasha, citing an oral source, records that the fort was used as a hiding place in 1611–13 by 'Ali, son of Fakhr al-Din al Ma'ani, when he was being pursued by the Sardiya tribe acting under orders from the al-Hafiz, the governor of Damascus (Peake Pasha 1958, 86). Evliya Çelebi visited the fort in 1672 and described it as a square building, made of fine masonry, built by Nur al-Din al-Shahid. Çelebi also noted that the signature of the architect could be seen on the outside of the building (Evliya Çelebi, *Seyhatnâmesi* IX, 292).

In 1709, Murtada ibn 'Alawan stopped at Zarqa 20 hours after leaving Mafraq and before moving on to Qatrana. He describes it as a dirty and difficult stopping place (خان قطراني), which appeared to be deserted; he does not mention Qasr Shebib or any other form of fort (Murtada b. 'Ali b. 'Alawan Rihala MS fol. 104a). Seventy years later, in 1779, Mehmed Edib arrived at 'Ayn Zarka which he described as an abandoned settlement with flowing water and a fort (Bianchi 1825, 123). In 1812, the fort at Zarqa was used as a base for Ottoman forces engaged in a conflict with the Bani Sakher, who had collected at 'Amman (Burckhardt 1822, 2nd May 1812). Following the Egyptian occupation in the 1820s 'Ayn al-Zarka was inspected by the officers of Muhammad 'Ali Pasha, who noted the large quantities of fresh flowing water in the wadi. The officers also made a note of the fort, which was in a ruinous condition and scheduled for repairs (see Appendix 1). In 1899 the fort was restored by the Ottoman authorities, to protect the area from Bedouin raiders and serve as a nucleus for settlement. In 1903, 36 Chechen families from the Caucusus were settled around the fort (Bakhit 2008).

Burckhardt was the first European to write a description of this site. He describes the Hajj caravan camped at 'Ayn Zarka where the pilgrims 'amuse themselves with hunting wild boars which are found in great numbers on the reedy banks of Wady Zerka'.

Burckhardt's describes the fort as being located in a low wadi and states that it was manned by an 'Aga' from the Ehteim [Beouin] tribe who camp in tents around the fort (Burckhardt 1822, appendix III, 657). In 1875 Doughty also visited Zarka as part of the Hajj caravan, he describes the fort as follows:

> 'a gunshot from the road stands a great old tower, Kellat ez Zerqa. This stronghold in the wilderness is, by tradition from the times before Muhammad; the building is massy and not ruined. This is none of the Hajj forts, and is now seldom a night lodging for nomads and shelter for the Bedouin folds.

Here says the tradition was the residence of an ancient hero Shebib ibn Tubbai' (Doughty 1979, 51).

Later on Doughty connects this fort with a series of watchtowers stretching into the wilderness, including the fortress of al-Lajjun.

Another description of the fort is provided by Selah Merrill (first published in 1881) who refers to the building as, 'Kulat Zarqa'. Merrill's description states that 'there is a fine view from the top of it [the castle] over the Hauran plain and mountains including Salachad'. This description corresponds with the view from the building today, known as Qasr Shebib, although modern buildings partially obscure the view. Merrill actually stayed at the fort and describes how, besides chatting with the people of the castle, he 'went through the nearly endless ceremony of drinking coffee'. He observes that the building is kept in good repair 'as it is needed by the pilgrims to Mecca'. As well as its function as a Hajj station, Merrill notes that the fort was also used by local people – as a place to store grain. He states 'we noticed great quantities of barley and flour stored in boxes and bags. They told us that it belonged to the Bedawin. As no one dare touch it is perfectly safe. This castle is their bank.' The fort was staffed by a keeper and his family, and was occasionally visited by soldiers (Merrill 1883).

Description

The building is a solidly built, square structure, measuring 13.75 m per side, with an entrance in the middle of the north side. The walls are made of large limestone blocks, usually about 0.45 m high and 0.4–1 m long. It is probable that many of the stones were robbed from an earlier Roman structure (*c.f.* Parker 1986, 34). Most of the blocks have rusticated centres within a smooth border, approximately (0.07 m) around the edge. The average height of the fort is 8 m above current ground level. The top of the fort has triangular crenellations on three sides, composed of stone blocks set at an angle of 45° (these appear to be later additions to the original structure). On the south-west and east sides are traces of blocked up arrow slits, 25 cm wide and 1.05 m high. Each arrow slit is situated approximately 0.6 m (*i.e.* one course) above the present ground level.

The North face of the fort is the most interesting, besides containing the entrance it has two small lancet windows, which provide light to the interior staircase. These windows are of a simple construction, formed by a gap/slit between two blocks and arch shape cut into the stone above.

The entrance is composed of a large, pointed, arch recess, 3.4 m high by 1.75 m wide, within which is an arched doorway (2.1 m high × 1.75 m wide) of similar shape to the recess. The larger arch of the recess is built out of two courses of finely cut ashlars. Above the central point of the arch is a single recessed limestone block, which almost certainly once contained an inscription. Between the outer arch and the doorway there is a concealed slot opening, which is 0.15 m wide and 2.75 m long. This opening reaches some 4.5 m upwards, to the same height as the lancet window above the doorway and must have been designed as a concealed machicolation. The doorway (now fitted with a sheet steel door) leads into a large barrel-vaulted chamber. The vault is of a two centre pointed form (similar to that used in the doorway) and runs from east to west, at a maximum height of approximately 6 m above floor level. On the east, west and south sides of the vault there deep recesses within which are set, tall (2.1 m), arrow slits. In the north-east corner is a set of four steps leading to a doorway, which connects with a staircase to the upper floor.

The staircase leads through the thickness of the wall, making a right angle turn leading up, over the entrance. The staircase is illuminated by the two lancet windows visible on the exterior of the north wall. The upper floor of the building is in a ruinous condition, though traces of walls, which may once have comprised rooms, can be seen. Two walls are visible, running from north to south and dividing the floor into three sections; perhaps two rooms and a central courtyard. There are also the remains of an arrow slit on the north side, above the entrance. In any case it is certain that the building was once higher, for the staircase continues upwards, possibly to a second floor, which no longer exists.

Outside the fort there are at least three cisterns, two on the east side and one, 3.5 m from the entrance, on the north side. The entrance to each cistern is the same and consists of a square mouth (0.6 m × 0.6 m) bordered by a bevelled cut stone kerb. It was not possible to determine the depth of any of the cisterns, though all were more than 2 m deep.

Discussion

According to Doughty (1979, 51) the fort derives its name from an ancient warrior, Shebib ibn Tubbai, who is also associated with a wall in southern Jordan. However, most other writers (*e.g.* Parker 1986; Kirkbride 1948) have dated it to the Islamic era. Doughty's attribution of a pre-Islamic date seems to be based on the incorporation of a Latin inscription into the structure and local tradition, rather than a detailed examination of the building.

Several features indicate a Medieval date for the fort; these may be summarized as follows:

1) The cruciform ground plan with wide reveals, tapering to thin arrow loops. Similar designs can be seen in many Ayyubid and Mamluk buildings, for example, the Medieval tower at Safuriyya in Palestine (Petersen 2001, 270) or, the tower near al-Braij in Syria built by Baybars in 1266 (Meinecke 1992, 22, 87).

2) Concealed machicolation above the gateway was a common feature in Islamic buildings from Umayyad times, although concealed machicolations appear to have been primarily a Medieval (11th–16th centuries) innovation.

3) The form of the doorway arch – slightly pointed with two layers of voussoirs. This form of arch can be seen in many Mamluk buildings in the region. See, for example, Buroyne's study of Mamluk doorways in the Old City of Jerusalem (Burgoyne 1971).

4) The arrow loops. Although all of these have been blocked and may have been subject to some alteration, it is evident from the general form (tall slits, with wide reveals set within large casements) that these probably date from before the 16th century.

5) The thickness of the walls. At approximately 3 m thick, the walls of this building, in proportion to its size, clearly indicate a Medieval date.

Whilst on structural grounds it may be fairly safe to ascribe the construction of the building to the Medieval period, any more precise dating must rely on historical information (for a discussion of the Medieval Hajj route, see Chapter 3). It is possible that the Shebib referred to was, Amir Shebib el- 'Uqayli al-Tubbai, who ruled the area of Balqa' between 966 and 968 AD (*c.f.* Kirkbride 1948). However, this date seems too early for the construction of the fort, moreover, there is no particular reason given as to why he should have built it during his two years as governor of the area. However, it is known that during the Mamluk period the Hajj caravan would camp outside Qasr Shebib (Majali and Mas'ad 1987, 314). Another possibility is that the tower was built as a signal station, or fort, during the reign of the Mamluk Sultan Baybars (*i.e.* 1270s) to protect the area from Mongol attacks. Other forts, which might relate to this signalling system, are the fort at Safuriyya in Palestine (Petersen 2001, 270) also on a hilltop location and the fort near al-Braij in Palestine, built by Baybars in 1266 (Meinecke 1992, 22, 87). It is perhaps significant that 'Izz al-Din Aybak 'Abdullah Allawi was put in charge of northern Jordan at this time, with orders to repair the fortresses of al-Rabad and Salt, which may also have formed part of this system (Peake Pasha 1958, 80) (an inscription on the fort at Azraq states that he repaired the fort there as well).

NOTE: I am grateful to the late Professor Meinecke who wrote to me (27.10.92) concerning the tower at al-Braij, pointing out its similarity to Qasr Shebib.

Zizia – (Map 5, No. 4) (Figs 9–11, Plates 23–30)

(Jize, Ziza, Zizya)
Location: 31.42N 35.57E
Zizia is located at an elevation of 681 m on the Madaba Plain, south of Queen 'Ali International Airport and 30 km south of 'Amman. The site comprises a fort, currently used by the Desert Police and a huge rectangular reservoir. Immediately to the east of the site are the Hijaz Railway and Desert Highway and to the west are extensive agricultural lands.

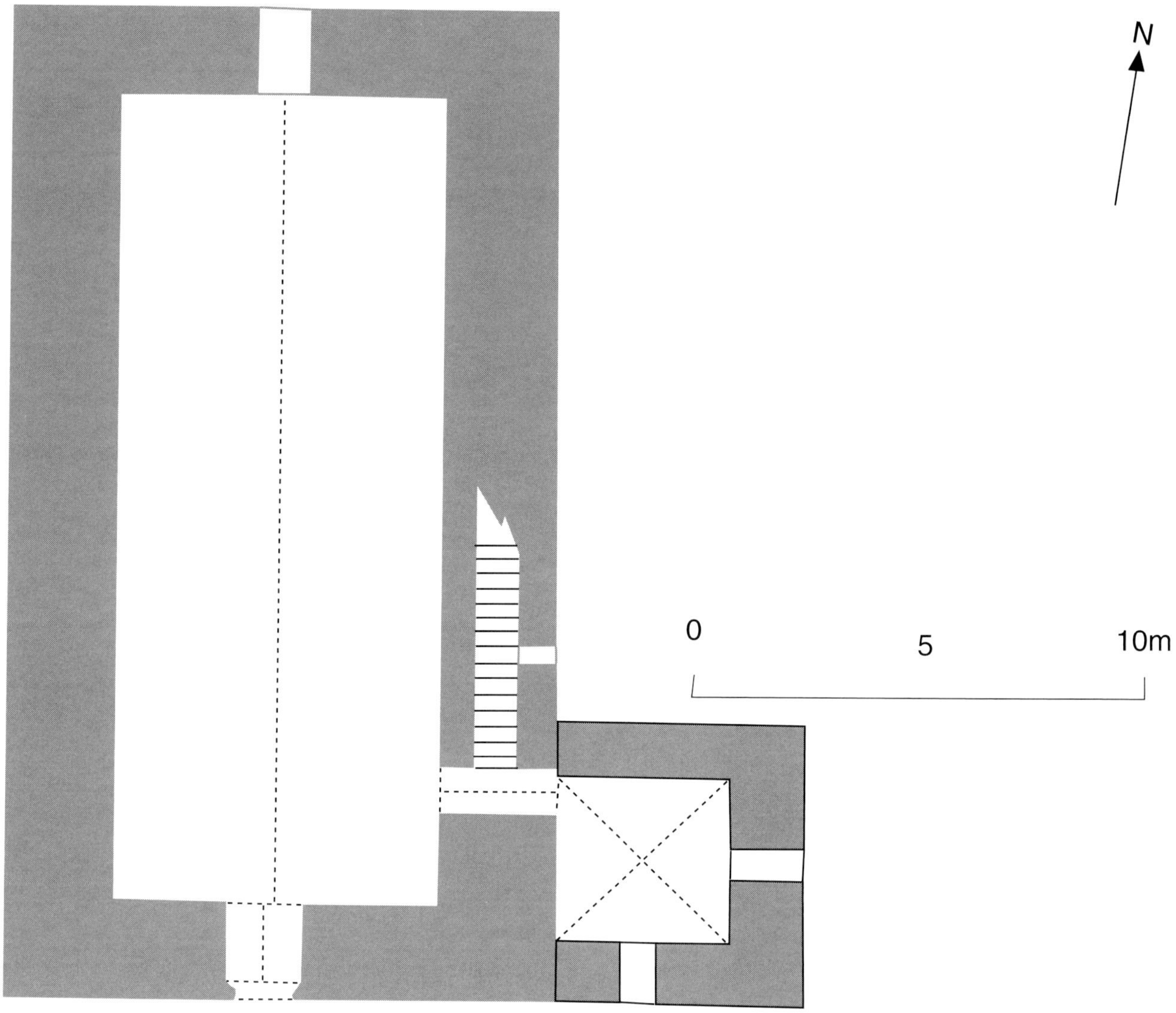

N

0   5   10m

Fig. 9. Ground floor plan of Medieval fort at Zizia in Jordan.

Plate 23. Zizia fort from the south-east (1986).

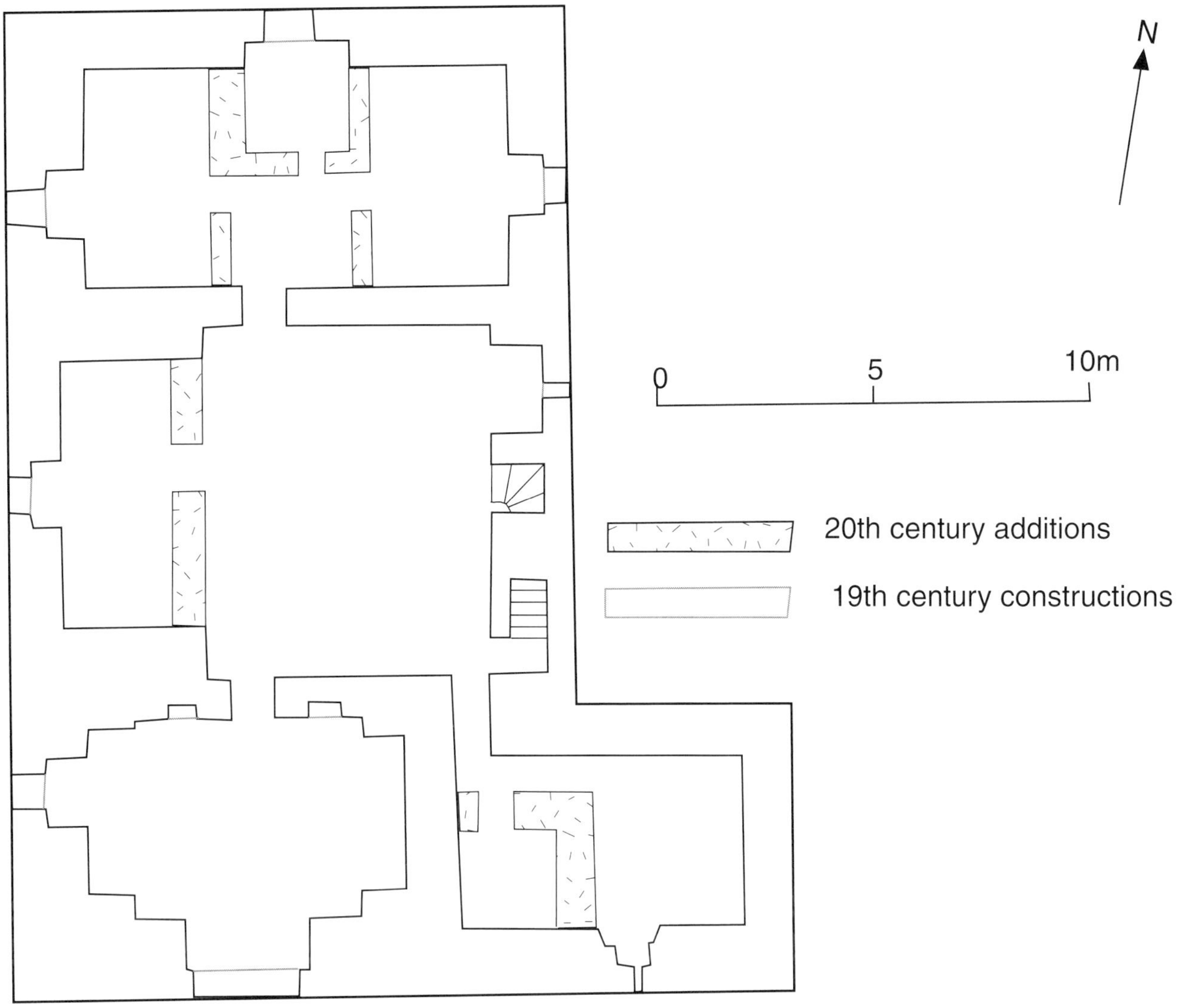

N

0   5   10m

20th century additions

19th century constructions

Fig. 10. First floor plan of Medieval fort at Zizia, in Jordan, with modern additions.

Plate 24. Zizia fort from the east (1986).

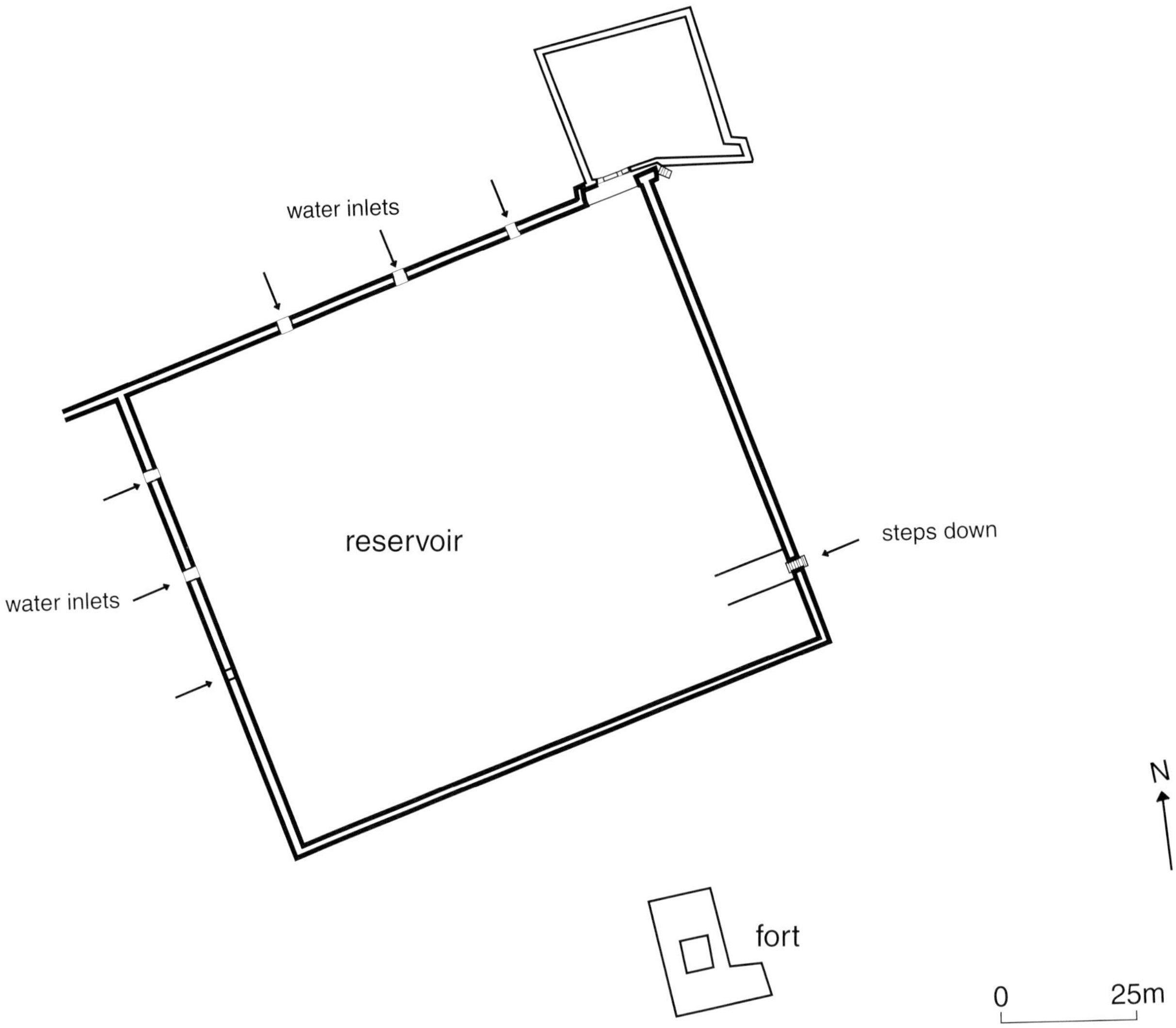

water inlets

reservoir

steps down

water inlets

N

fort

0   25m

Fig. 11. Plan of fort and reservoir at Zizia in Jordan.

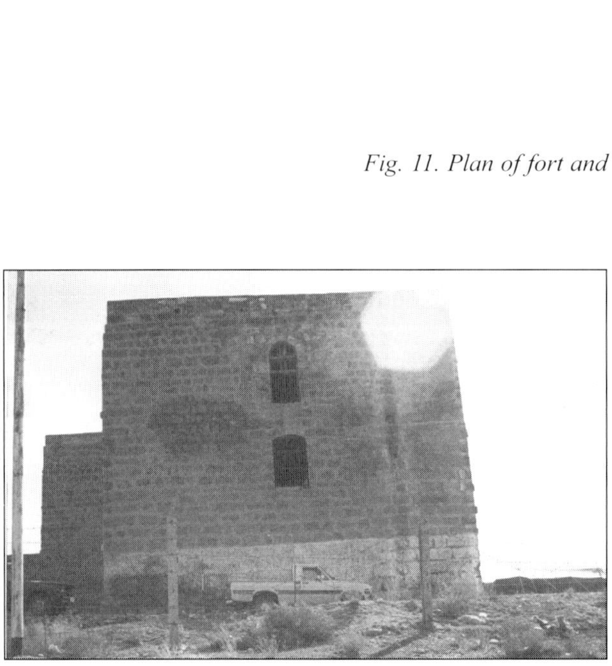

Plate 25. Zizia fort from the north (1986)

History

Zizia is located in an area rich in ancient remains, from the Nabatean era up to the present day. Although extensive Roman ruins were once evident at the site, these have mostly

been obliterated and there is little surviving evidence to date the ruins more precisely. Possibly the earliest literary reference to the site can be found in the declaration of Zeno the martyr, who, in 304 AD, described himself as a nobleman from a fort of Palestine named Zozion. However, this cannot be taken as conclusive evidence that there was a fort at the site, because the text refers to the province of Palestine rather than Arabia (*c.f.* Kennedy 2000, 123). The first undisputed reference to a military presence at the site is in 400 AD, when the *Notitia Dignitatum* describes it as the base of the Dalmatian Ilyrian cavalary (*Notitia Dignitatum* Or 37.7 and 16). Epigraphic evidence, in the form of a Greek inscription built into the wall of the Medieval fort, indicates that a building on the site was repaired in 580 AD.

Although it is likely that the reservoir was in use during the early Islamic period (see discussion below) there is no reference to the site until the early 13th century, when Yaqut (1179–1229) includes it in his geographical dictionary. Zizia is described as a large village on the Hajj route, with a *suq* (market) and a large reservoir (Yaqut,

Plate 28. Zizia, interior of upper floor showing doorways and niches (1986).

Plate 29. Zizia reservoir from fort, showing Desert highway in background (1986).

Plate 26. Zizia fort, interior upper floor showing arches leading to stairs up and down (1986).

Plate 27. Zizia fort, interior upper floor detail of arch and lintel over doorway (1986).

Plate 30. Zizia fort, Desert Police camp (1986).

1995, vol. 3, 123–24). In the 14th century the place is mentioned by both Abu al-Fida' (d.1331) and Ibn Battuta. Abu al-Fida' includes Zizia as one of three named stops between Medina and Hama (Abu al-Fida' 1960, 76–77). Ibn Battuta's caravan stopped for one day at Birka Zizia, in 1326, before proceeding onwards to Karak via al-Lajjun (Ibn Battuta 1958, 159). The first reference to a fort at the site is in 1569, when the Ottoman Sultan ordered the Governor of Damascus to repair the citadel next to the pool at Zizia (Bakhit 1982, 213; *MD* xix, no. 1078, 15 Ramadan, 978, p. 748).

However, after the 16th century Birka Zizia does not appear in itineraries of the Hajj route, suggesting that it had been abandoned in favour of a more easterly stopping point at Qal'at al-Balqa'. However, in *c.* 1611–13 'Ali, son of Fakhr al-Din al-Ma'ani, hid in the fort at Ziziya to escape the Sardiyya tribe, who were pursuing him on the orders of al-Hafiz governor of Damascus, who had already forced his father into exile in Italy (Peake Pasha 1958, 86).

The first European to visit and comment on the site was Canon H. B. Tristram, who visited in the 1870s and described it as 'one of the most important places of Roman Arabia' (Tristram 1873, 197). In particular he noted two buildings, 'which stand in bold relief against the horizon, being on the crest of a ridge, elevated considerably above the depression in which the tank had been excavated'. One of these buildings comprised a large fort, with a parallelogram attached. The fort may be identified with the fort that is still standing and used by the Desert Police. During the stay at Zizia, Tristram's expedition used the fort to house the muleteers and their 40 beasts. He gives the following description:

> 'The first and largest of these building apparently of Saracenic origin, consists of a solidly built fort, 23 yards by 19, with a parallelogram attached, 16 yards by 7. Both were built as it would appear about the same period and with material taken from older edifices… The roof of the lower storey in each building is still perfect, a fine arched vault, but with no aperture for light, except for the door' (Tristram 1874, 187).

The dimensions of the fort described by Tristram coincide exactly with those of the building surveyed in 1986. The attached parallelogram has disappeared entirely, although we do have some idea of how it looked from Tristram's description given below:

> 'The attached parallelogram contains another perfect vaulted chamber, opening only from the great chamber; and the staircase leading to the upper storey, which is entire with the exception of the roof. Semi-circular arches still span it in two places, and it has many loopholes and narrow arched windows. There are also several side chambers entire, and the whole has been fitted for engines of war…another staircase led to the roof and we could walk all round the building on the broad massive roof' (Tristram 1874, 187).

The second building described by Tristram was a large building of which 'only the external walls remain'. Despite the presence of a *mihrab* and Kufic inscriptions, Tristram regarded the building as a Roman temple, later re-used as a fort and then as a mosque. The building also included a highly decorated lintel, which Tristram believed to be late Byzantine or Persian. This lintel has recently been rediscovered, built into the modern mosque at Zizia and convincingly dated to the early Islamic period, suggesting that the whole building was in fact built as an Umayyad mosque (see Denis Genequand's discussion of this lintel in Appendix 2 of this volume).

In 1896 the site was visited by Gray Hill on his way to Petra. This was his second visit and he credited Tristram with its first 'discovery'. Gray Hill was mostly impressed with the reservoir, though he lamented the fact that the water catchment system was no longer in operation, leaving the cistern empty of water (Gray Hill 1897, 37). A more thorough investigation of the ruins at the site was carried out, about the same time, by Brünnow and Domaszewski (1904–9, II, 91–94) although their main focus was on the Roman ruins and cemetery, they identified the large building with a *mihrab* (the second building seen by Tristram) purely as a mosque. A few years later, in the early 1900s, the site was visited by Gertrude Bell, who commented on the large number of ruins. She also commented on the fort, which, though in ruins at the time of her visit, had recently been repaired by Shaykh Soktan of the Bani Sakhr and was 'furnished with a splendour unknown in the desert' (Bell 1908, 35–36). It is tempting to equate Shaykh Soktan with Zattam Ibn Fayiz, Shaykh al-mashaykh of the Bani Sakhr, who made Zizia the centre of the *nahiya* he founded in 1881 (Abu Jaber 1989, 33 and 182 table 10.1). Bell also followed Brünnow and Domaszewski in identifying the building with a *mihrab* as a mosque.

During the First World War the ruins at Zizia were extensively photographed by the German air force, showing the water catchment systems and also the remains of a settlement extending to the south-east (Kennedy 2000, 122–24). During the British Mandate Jiza (Zizia) was established as a base for the Arab Legion and after 1950 (when the new police post was built) it was taken over by the Desert Police.

There has been little archaeological research at Zizia in recent times, though Parker recovered a small number of pottery sherds from the site, including two iron age, one late Roman, 6 early Byzantine and one Mamluk sherd (Parker 1986, 41). More recently Genequand made a survey of early Islamic remains in the vicinity of Zizia (Genequand 2002, 139–40).

Description

The fort at Ziza is solidly built, with the walls of the main building being some 2.5 m thick. The walls are composed of large, square limestone blocks, varying in length between 0.5 m and 1 m and set in courses approximately 0.5 m high. The quoin stones are particularly large, with some measuring over 2 m in length. The finish of the stone varies considerably, with some roughly dressed and some rusticated blocks, indicating that much of the masonry is re-used (Tristram 1874, 187 noted carved depictions of stone crosses and even chariots with horses, on some of the stones). The joins between the blocks had recently been re-pointed in 1986. The outside of the fort displays a number of different window types, varying from narrow slits to triple arched windows. Below is a summary of the types of window on each side of the fort.

South Façade

This side of the fort includes four windows and the doorway (this does not include the more recent structure which butts onto the main building at the eastern end). The doorway itself is fairly simple and consists of a large lintel, above a rectangular opening, 1.3 m wide. Directly above the doorway there is a 1.5 m tall slit, resembling an arrow loop (the position of the window makes it unlikely that it could have served a defensive function). Above the slit there is a triple arched window, surmounted by a single round opening. To the right of the doorway are two simple square/rectangular windows.

East Side

This side of the fort has 6 openings. There are two square/rectangular windows on the first floor level and three slit openings, which may be arrow loops, two on the ground floor and a third on the first floor level. There is also a round window on the first floor, corresponding to the top of the staircase.

North Side

This side, which is the shortest, contains two tall arched windows set one above the other.

West Side

This side has no opening at ground floor level. On the first floor level it has three, evenly spaced, rectangular window openings.

From the outside, at least two, possibly three, phases can be detected. Most of the lower part of the building belongs to the first phase, which is characterized by large blocks set in fairly even courses. The second phase, visible from the outside, is distinguished by lighter coloured blocks set in courses out of alignment with those of the first phase. This second phase is visible around some of the arched windows on the north and south sides of the building. The third phase comprises a line of stone blocks, three courses high, which runs around the top of the building forming a parapet.

The Interior

The interior of the fort consists of two storeys and a flat roof. The main room on the ground floor is a barrel-vaulted chamber, 17.5 m long and 7.2 m wide. The vault has the profile of a two-centre point arch and springs from the walls at a height of approximately 1 m from the current floor level. Apart from the door there are two main openings to the outside from this room, one directly above the door and one directly opposite in the north wall. There is also a doorway recessed into the east side of the vault, giving access to the staircase and an adjacent room. This other room is cross-vaulted and has windows high up in the east and south walls.

The stairs to the first floor run up, through the thickness of the east wall of the building and are illuminated by two windows. The lower window is a small pointed opening tapering from 0.35 m to 0.15 m wide and from 0.6 m to 0.5 m high. The top of the stairs is lit by a circular window (0.4 m diameter).

The fort's floor is, architecturally, more complex than the rest of the building, probably because it has been considerably rebuilt. The first floor consists of four main rooms numbered 1–4 and a central courtyard. Two of the rooms have been sub-divided into smaller units, thus room one consists of four units (1a–d) and room 4 has been divided into two units (4a and 4b).

Access to the first floor is by means of a staircase, which opens onto the first floor courtyard through a pointed arch doorway. Adjacent to this, on the north side, is a wide niche covered with a wide pointed arch, giving access to an arrow slit/gun loop.

The north side of the courtyard has a doorway into the largest room on the first floor (Room 1). The doorway is approximately 1 m wide and comprises a rectangular opening, covered with a lintel set beneath a relieving arch; between the lintel and relieving arch there is a circular opening, presumably providing additional ventilation and light. The lintel is decorated with a rosette – possibly re-used from more ancient ruins. The doorway is further characterized by a bevelled edge and incised line, running all around the door jambs and the lintel. The door itself is made of two wooden leaves, each of which is composed of four panels. Within room 1 there are four small units, formed by the addition of partitions built of modern materials (*c.f.* Khammash 1986, 95). The room as a whole has three windows and a flat roof, built with iron girders, possibly rails from the Hijaz railway. The walls of room 1 are fairly thick, suggesting that it may once have been covered with a vault.

The west side of the first floor courtyard is occupied by room 2. Access to this room is through a modern door with a wooden frame, however, it is clear that originally this was an *iwan*, open to the courtyard, with the roof supported on a wide stone arch which can still be seen. There is a single window looking out to the west.

Room 3, on the south side of the courtyard, is the only room that has not been subdivided and retains its architectural integrity. Like room 1 it is entered through a doorway with a stone lintel, beneath a semi-circular relieving arch – in this case the lintel is decorated with two carved rosettes. The interior of the room is covered with a large cross-vault and in the south wall there is a large triple arched window. In addition there is a smaller window in the west wall and two niches, either side of the door, in the north wall.

Room 4 is the smallest room in the building and is made smaller still by its subdivision into two (4a and 4b). There are two windows in the room, one facing east, the other facing south.

Chronology

From the above description it is obvious that the fort represents several stages of construction. Three main phases are visible. These can be characterized as follows:

First phase: the large vaulted hall on the ground floor and the external walls and staircase on the first floor. Characteristic features of this period are two centre pointed arches and tall arrow loop/slits.

Second phase: the small room on the ground floor and rooms 1, 2 and 3 on the first floor. Characteristic features of this phase are doorways with decorated lintels, surmounted by relieving arches with round ventilation holes in the spandrels. The triple arched window in room 3 also belongs to this phase.

Third phase: the sub-dividing walls in rooms 1, 2 and 4, the wall blocking the archway in the *iwan* (room 2) and the square windows with iron grills. Also part of this phase, are the flat roofs, supported by iron girders, over rooms 1, 2 and 4. Characteristic features of this phase are the use of iron rails from the Hijaz Railway, and wooden doorways and window frames.

Stylistically it would appear that Phase 1 belongs to the Ayyubid–Mamluk period (for a discussion of the Medieval Hajj route, see Chapter 3). The plan of the surviving building with thick walls, long vaulted hall, arrow loops and staircases set into the thickness of the wall, are characteristic of Medieval architecture in the region. It seems likely that the parallelogram, observed by Tristram and partly visible in Gertrude Bell's photograph, was part of this first phase, comprising two large chambers on the ground floor. A building of similar, though larger, plan is that of Khirbat Bir Zayt, north of Ramalla in Palestine (Pringle 1986, 20) where two or three long chambers meet at right angles. It may be suggested that this Medieval fort (or khan) together with the reservoir and the mosque discovered by Tristram (1873, 187), formed part of a pilgrimage complex visited by Ibn Battuta and similar is to that of Bosra (*c.f.* Meinecke 1996, 46; and Chapter 3 in this volume).

Although it is known that the building was repaired some time around 1569 (Bakhit 1982, 213) it has not been possible to identify any 16th century work within the extant structure. The next reference to the fort, records it having been used by the Egyptian troops of Ibrahim Pasha, who wantonly destroyed many of the ancient remains (Tristram 1874, 188; Bell 1908, 36). During Tristram's time the fort seems to have been abandoned and used as an Arab cemetery (Tristram 1873, 188). In the 1880s the fort was again repaired (Bell 1908, 35) this time 'with a splendour unknown in the desert' and it is to this period that the triple arched windows and carved door lintels may be attributed. Such features are typical of 19th century architecture in the region. For example, Ragette (1980, 154, 160 and 162) lists the triple arch, internal niches and circular openings, as characteristic features of 19th century Lebanese architecture. It seems probable that such urban features were incorporated into the houses of prominent families in throne villages in Palestine (Amiry and Tamari 1989, 26). Only a few such building survive in Jordan, examples include, the Abu Jaber farmhouse at al-Yadudeh, the Shurideh family house at Tibneh, the Bisharat family complex at Umm al-Kundom and the mansion at Kufranjeh (Khammash 1986, 92).

Sometime between Gertrude Bell's visit and 1950 (when the new police post was built) more of the building was demolished, leaving the present structure. During the Mandate Period this fort served as a base for the Arab Legion and during this period the rooms of the first floor were sub-divided.

Discussion

The interesting question about Zizia is why was it abandoned as part of the Hajj route in the Ottoman period? The large reservoir and buildings indicate that plentiful facilities were available in the Ottoman period, yet for some reason it was abandoned in favour of a more easterly rote via Qal'at Dab'a. Indeed, the probable removal of a decorated lintel from Zizia to Dab'a (see Appendix 2 in this volume) implies some conscious decision to move away from this ancient site.

Qal'at Dab'a – (Map 5, No. 5) (Figs 12–15, Plates 31–43 and 191–193)

(Qal'at Balqa', Balat, Zir, Kalaat Remeydan)
Location: 31.35N 36.07E
This site is located approximately 1 km due west of Mahattat al-Deb'a, a station on the Hejaz Railway between Jize (Zizia) and Khan al-Zebib. It is situated in a hollow, on the south side of the Wadi al-Khurayim, which runs from east to west towards the Dead Sea. The fort stands at approximately 700 m above sea level, on the eastern edge of the Syrian Desert, on the boundary between steppe and desert. There are also a number of smaller wadis running into the Wadi al-Khurayim at this point, which probably determined the location of the fort.

History

This fort is located to the east of the Medieval Hajj road which passed through Zizia and appears to have been an alternative stopping place established in the Ottoman period. However, the name Balqa' has an ancient significance within Arabic history and at certain times seems to have been a term for the entire region covered by the modern kingdom of Jordan. During the early Islamic and early Medieval periods, Balqa' was an administrative district dependant on the *jund* of Damascus. Generally, however, the term is used to refer to northern Jordan, in particular, those parts centering on the settlements

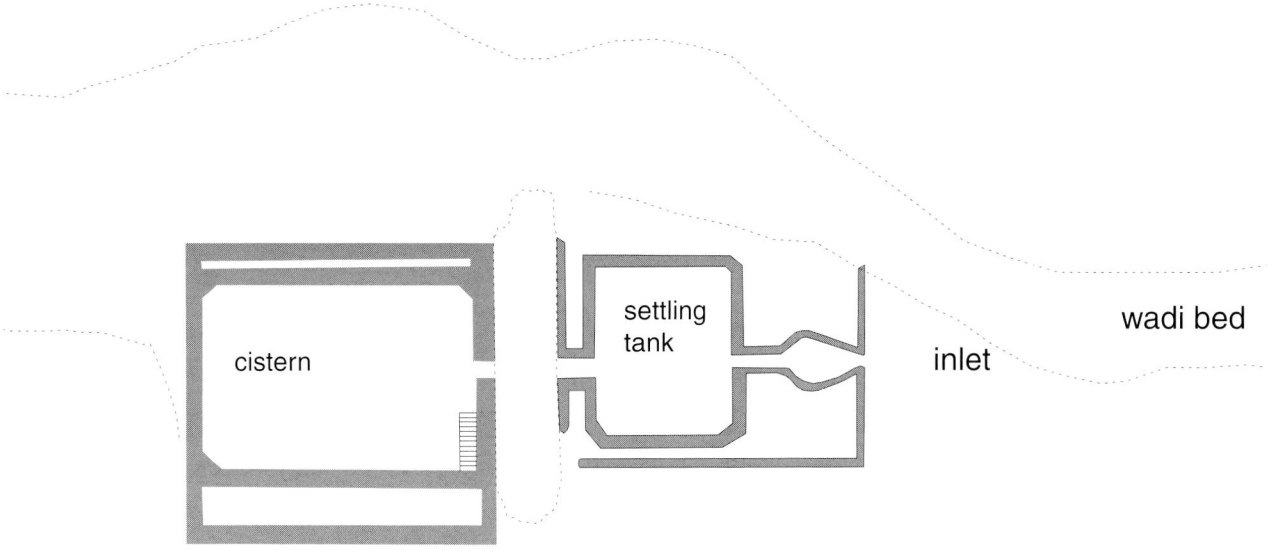

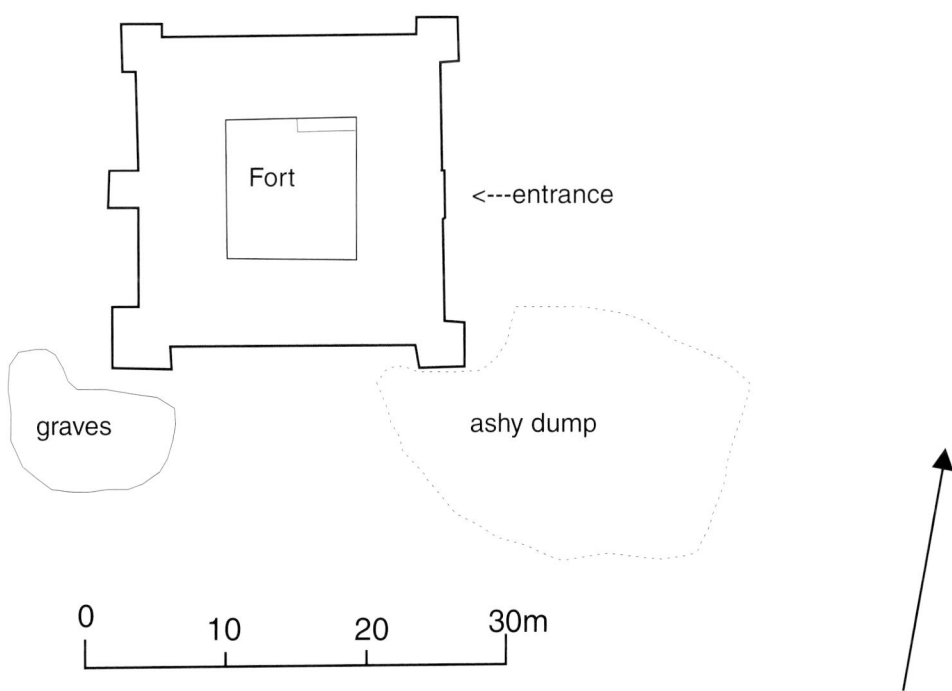

Fig. 12. Plan of fort and cisterns at Qal'at Dab'a in Jordan.

of Hesban, 'Amman and Salt (Sourdel-Thoumine 2008, 997–98). The modern name Qal'at Dab'a is probably a Bedouin name (ضبع dab'a = hyena) referring to the presence of hyenas in the vicinity of the fort.

Possibly the earliest Arabic reference to the site is by al-Baladhuri, who relates a story of how the Muslim general Yazid pursued the Byzantine army as far as a place called Dubiyya (or al-Dabiya?) and proceeded from there into

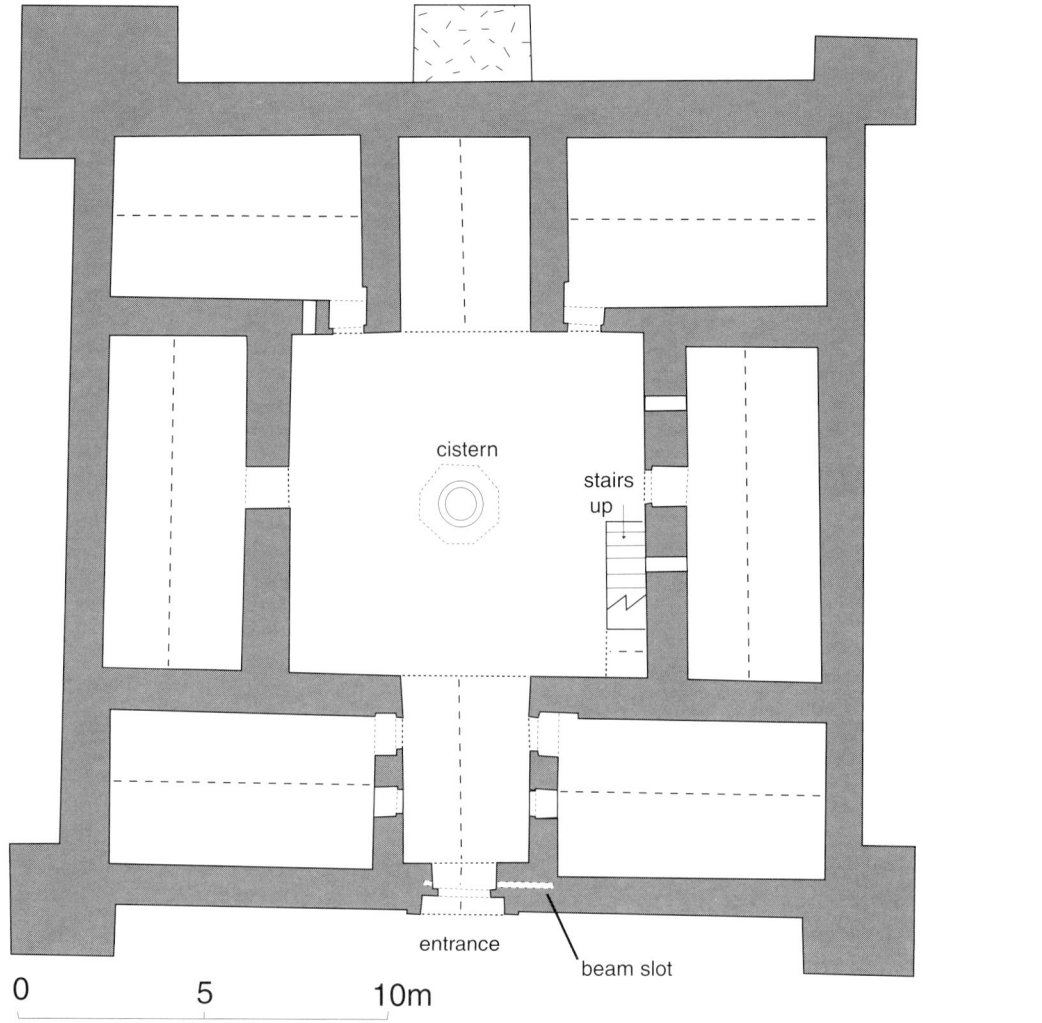

Fig. 13. Ground floor plan of Qal'at Dab'a in Jordan.

Plate 31. Qal'at Dab'a, exterior from West in 1898, by Rudolf-Ernst Brünnow (courtesy of Princeton University).

Plate 32. Qal'at Dab'a, interior of courtyard in 1898, by Rudolf-Ernst Brünnow (courtesy of Princeton University).

Jund al-Urdun (al-Baladhuri, ed. de Goeje, 109). Frenkel (1996, 186) suggests that this story is implausible, basing his views on the assumption that Dubiyya is in the Jordan valley, however, it makes more sense if it is located near the present day Qal'at al-Balqa', where it is know that there was also a Roman military presence (Kennedy 2000, 127).

The 10th century writer, al-Harbi (al-Jasir, 1968, 653), may be referring to this location in his itinerary of the Syrian Hajj route when he mentions Baal'ah, or Balgha,

as a stopping place between Qastal and Ma'an. However, the earliest unambiguous reference to the site is the 16th century (971 AH/1563 AD) itinerary of Mustapha Pasha (al-Jasir 1969, 184–85), which mentions Balqa' as a stop

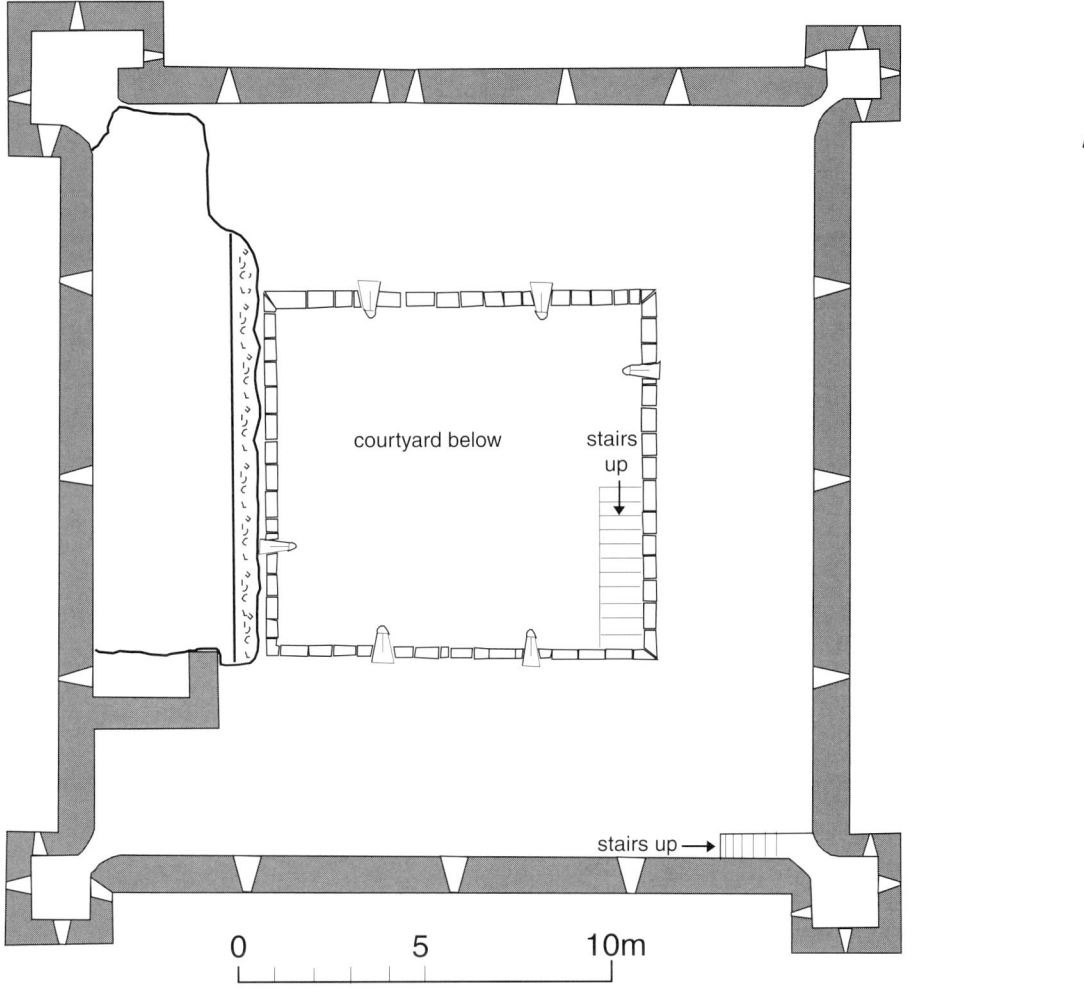

Fig. 14. First floor plan of Qal'at Dab'a in Jordan.

Plate 33. Qal'at Dab'a, interior of courtyard in 1898, by Rudolf-Ernst Brünnow (courtesy of Princeton University).

Plate 34. Qal'at Dab'a, from north-east in 1907, by Jaussen and Savignac (courtesy of the École Biblique).

midway between 'Amman and Qatrana. What is significant about these two early references is that Balqa' appears to be a replacement for Zizia, which is not mentioned in either account.

Evliya Çelebi (Evliya Çelebi, *Seyhatnâmesi* IX, 577; Bilge 1979, 218) mentions a number of sites which carry the name Balqa', one of which is Tabrika which he describes as an uninhabited fort in the desert where many pilgrims were killed. If this is the case, it may imply a deserted Roman fort of which there are many examples in this area (see, Kennedy 2000, 115–27). The first definitive description

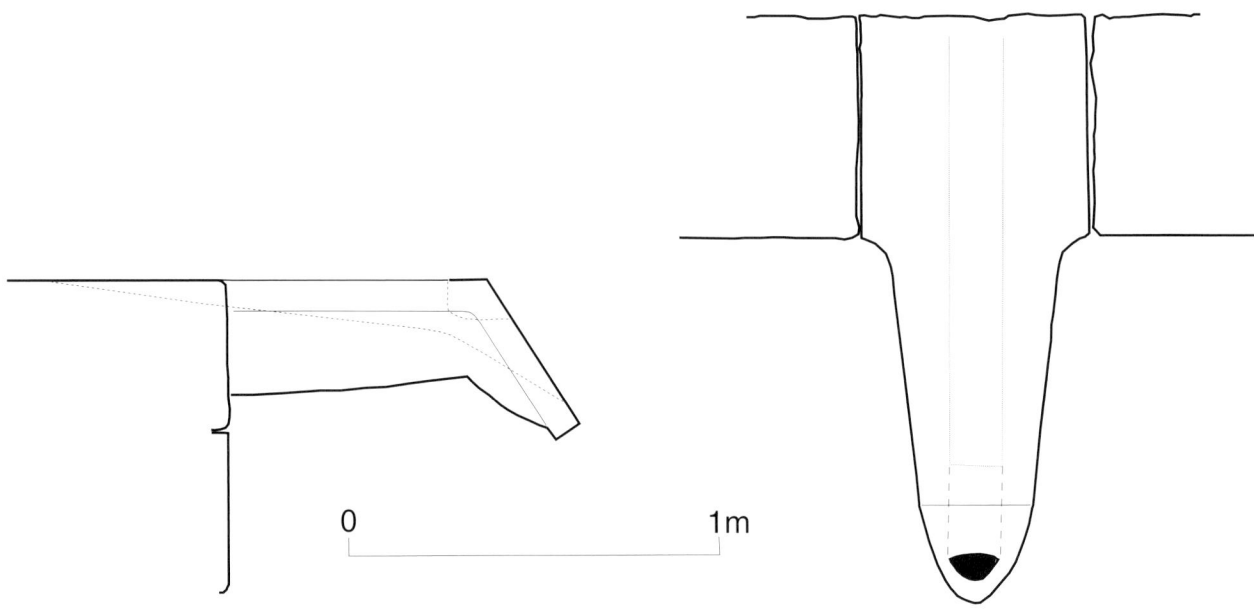

Fig. 15. Detail of rainspout from Qal'at Dab'a in Jordan.

Plate 35. Qal'at Dab'a, from the south in 1907, with graves in foreground, by Jaussen and Savignac (courtesy of the École Biblique).

Plate 38. Qal'at Dab'a, cistern to north of fort (2006).

Plate 36. Qal'at Dab'a, east face with entrance (2006).

Plate 37. Qal'at Dab'a, west face with buttress (2006).

Plate 39. Qal'at Dab'a, gateway interior north side with doorway and paving visible (2006).

Plate 40. Qal'at Dab'a, interior of courtyard with stairs to first floor and arch over the gateway (2006).

Plate 42. Qal'at Dab'a, interior of roofless room on south side of courtyard with remains of curve vault visible to left (2006).

Plate 41. Qal'at Dab'a, interior with roofless room in foreground and gateway visible to left (2006).

Plate 43. Qal'at Dab'a, interior of vaulted room to north of gateway (2006).

of an Ottoman construction is the account of Mehmed Edib (Bianchi 1825, 124–25), in 1779, who states that a fortress and reservoir had been constructed at this place because of the scarcity of water in the area. He points out that water in the wadi flows west towards the Jordan valley and that there is a ruined khan (Khan Uzir) nearby (Khan al-Zebib?). Edib also gives alternative names for the site including, Mashatta, Balata and Zir. At this point the escort from Zerka leaves the caravan.

Qal'at al-Balqa' was visted by the Swiss traveller Burckhardt on a number of occasions in the early 19th century, he gives the following description:

> 'The castle of Belka has a large Birket of rain water. Its commander or Obadashi is always chosen from among the Janissaries of Damascus. It serves the Arabs of the Djebel Belka as a depot for their provisions. To the west of the castle the mountain of Belka terminates. The arabs of Belka live in tents round the castle, and are Felahein or cultivators of the ground' (Burckhardt 1822, appendix III, 657–58).

He also notes that it is one day's journey from Zerka and states that it is called, Kalaat Remeydan by the Bedouin.

The first detailed description of the site is provided by the anonymous author of the, *Report to Muhammad 'Ali Pasha*, in 1825. He observed that the site comprised a square fort and three cisterns. The fort measured 35 cubits per side and was in good condition, apart from one corner which was in danger of collapse and a few of the interior rooms which had already fallen. Within the fort there was a problem with the rainwater cistern, whilst outside there were two reservoirs from which the pilgrims were to drink. The two cisterns were leaking, due to cracks in their sides, although they contained two cubits of water at the time of the inspection. The report also refers to a third cistern outside measuring 50 by 10 cubits per side (for a full translation, see Appendix 1).

Further information about Qal'at Balqa' is provided by Doughty, who visited the site in 1875:

'…at mid-afternoon we passed Khan es-Zeyt where there are arches of an aqueduct. Not much further, after twenty six miles we came to our encampment, in a bottom, beside the recently repaired Kellat al-Belka, being here nearly due east to Jerusalem, beyond the Dead Sea, the land altitude is 2,870 ft' (Doughty 1979, 19).

Twenty-one years in later, in 1896, Balqa' was visited by another Englishman, Gray Hill, who described it as 'a khan for the Haj' and noted that it had stone built pools, full of water (Gray Hill 1897, 39).

The first archaeological investigation of the fort took place two years later, on the 22nd February 1898, when it was surveyed by Brünnow and Domaszewski as part of their study of Roman Arabia. They observed that it was a modern construction, with a large cistern and took photographs of the interior and exterior (Plates 31–33). Most significantly they recorded an Arabic inscription, stating that it was re-built by the Amir al-Hajj 'Uthman Pasha in Dhul Hija 1180 (May 1767). Unfortunately, there is no indication of the location of the inscription, though significantly, it is not mentioned by later visitors to the fort, thereby suggesting that it may have been removed. For example, when the fort was visited by Jaussen and Savignac (Plates 34–35) 7 years later, April 1905, they described it as a very ordinary Hajj fort, with a large reservoir at the side (Jaussen and Savignac 1997).

In May 1928, 10 years after the end of Ottoman rule, Qala'at Balqa' was visited by Henry Field as part of the North Arabian Desert Survey. He described Balqa' as 'a typical and perfect Haj fort', which had been restored in 1767. Field particularly admired, the 'very fine wooden door' at the entrance and the cobbled parapet. The fort was 'owned' by a shaykh of the Bani Sakhr tribe, who was suspicious of Field and his team and would not allow him to copy an (Arabic?) inscription on a limestone block located in the fort. It is possible that this inscription referred to the restoration of the fort in 1767, though it is more likely that Field got the date of 1767 from reading the work of Brünnow and Domaszewski (see above). The guardian of the fort gave them the following information about the history of the fort:

'The fort he said was old work, but had been kept in repair by the Turkish authorities. Sultan Selim had built the birket which lay outside, and it was a place for refreshment on the old pilgrimage road to Mecca. The Sultan Abdul Hamid had set up an inscribed memorial stone at the time of the making of the railway' (Field 1960, 84–85).

Description

Exterior

Lying adjacent to the wadi, the site comprises a square fort and two cisterns. The fort measures about 25 m per side, including the four square corner towers. There appear to be remains of an earlier building on the site, with wall foundations on the north and east sides, whilst the gate contains a re-used lintel, which may be of early Islamic origin. The fort is built on ground sloping down to the north. The entrance to the fort faces east; at each of the four corners are square towers. The two eastern towers are both *c.* 3 m^2 (2.9 m), whilst the south-western tower is the largest and tallest, measuring 4.0 m by 4.2 m. By contrast, the north-west tower is the smallest measuring only 2.5 m^2. In the middle of the west side of the fort there is a large, well built projecting buttress (2.2 m × 2 m and 5 m high) (see Plates 31 and 37). Three of the towers (north-east, north-west and south-west) have rainspouts that project (0.45 m) away from the fort and resemble those inside the fort (see below).

The top of the walls preserve, in two places, the remains of crenellations – on the east side above the gateway and on the west side to the left (north) of the buttress. On the east side each crenellation has a tri-lobed form, composed of two finely dressed limestone blocks placed one top of the other (a large lower rectangular block with rounded corners and an upper half oval shaped block). The area between the crenellations has been filled with small irregular limestone rubble. The crenellations on the west side have a different appearance and composition, here the crenellations are made of large flat limestone blocks, set upright into rubble made of small pieces of limestone, secured with mortar.

All external walls of the fort are pierced by small, simple openings, at a height of about 4 m above ground level, corresponding to the first floor inside. Each of these openings is, in fact, simply a gap in the wall, covered with a lintel stone with a large arch shaped groove over the gap, thus increasing the height of the opening.

Three types of stone are used in the construction of the outer walls, these are:
i)   Finely dressed, square cut stone are used as facing on the gateway and occasionally elsewhere.
ii) Roughly dressed limestone blocks form the basic building material of the fort.
iii) Small lumps of uncut limestone used as a capping for the towers and walls.

Entrance

The entrance occupies the middle of the east wall and is set within a rectangular façade (3.1 m × 4.2 m) of dressed stone, which projects 0.03 m from the rest of the wall face (Plate 36). The top of the façade is surmounted by a narrow cornice ridge, which projects a further 0.05 m from the façade. The entrance itself is set within a shallow (0.50 m) recess covered with a tall pointed arch. The doorway comprises a rectangular opening covered with a re-used lintel (see report on this lintel by Denis Genequand in Appendix 2 of this volume), supported on two cyma recta corbels (this design is repeated on all the doorways inside the fort). On each side of the entrance there is a square block (possibly re-used masonry) with concave sides, which could be used as a small seat or ledge. The gate itself is a heavy wooden construction, pierced with iron studs/nails (this has been stolen since 1986).

Interior

Immediately inside the gateway there are two rectangular stone benches, one on each side. The interior of the gateway comprises a barrel-vaulted *iwan* leading to the central courtyard. On each side of the gateway there is a window and a doorway leading into a large rectangular room. Each room is of identical size (7.0 m × 4.3 m) and covered with a barrel-vault aligned north–south (*i.e.* perpendicular to the entrance vault).

The central courtyard is an approximately square area, paved with rectangular stone slabs. In the centre of the courtyard there is an octagonal plinth (removed since 1986) with a circular hole (0.7 m) in the centre, which opens into a bottled shaped cistern (possibly a well, see, Appendix 1 in this volume). On the south side of the courtyard there is a doorway leading into a rectangular room, originally covered with a barrel-vault (now collapsed). The west side of the courtyard contains three openings, a large central *iwan* and two smaller doorways either side. The *iwan* is covered with a barrel-vault and the floor is raised (0.3 m) above the paving of the courtyard. Each doorway leads into a rectangular room covered with a barrel-vault. Each doorway comprises a large, square limestone lintel supported by two corbels cut in the profile of a *cyma recta* cornice. The north side of the courtyard (Plate 40) contains two features of interest, an external stairway leading to the upper floor and a doorway leading into a long rectangular room of similar size to that on the south side. Unlike the other parts of the fort, this room has a tall flat roof supported by iron girders (from the Hijaz railway?), though the setting for an original barrel-vault can still be seen.

The stairs are made of made of dressed limestone blocks, built around a rubble core. There is a small arched niche beneath the highest part of the stairs (the stairs were destroyed after 1986 and rebuilt in 2004).

There are now no rooms on the first floor, although there are the remains of a building on the southern side, which suggests a rectangular or square room. The surface of the first floor comprises a broad terrace, with flint cobbles laid over limestone rubble and earth. There were originally 8 rainspouts, two per side, projecting from the edge of the terrace into the courtyard (in 1986, seven of the rainspouts were in situ, by 2005 there were none). These rainspouts are of similar design to those projecting from each of the towers (Fig. 15). The exterior walls are pierced with small gun ports set low down (*c.* 0.3 m above the floor level) with occasional (one per side?) openings set higher up. At each corner of the courtyard there is a doorway into one of the towers. Originally each of the towers had a vaulted roof with a second storey, though all the vaults have collapsed. Access to the second storey of the towers was by staircase, only one of which, at the north-east corner, has survived

(this has now disappeared, it was 2.5 m long × 0.7 m wide and 2 m high). On the lower level of each tower there were gun ports, similar to those on the curtain walls.

Reservoirs

In the wadi to the north of the fort there are two rectangular reservoirs (Fig. 12 and Plate 38). The larger of the reservoirs (22.4 m × 21.2 m) is covered with a modern re-enforced concrete roof, though the cistern itself is built of stone blocks and appears to be of a similar date to the fort. On both the south and north sides of the cistern, there is a surface of flint cobbles. At the south-east corner there are a series of steps leading down into the water. At the west end there is an opening, which appears to function as an overflow device, while a similar opening at the east side, appears to function as an inlet. The large reservoir is joined to the smaller cistern by a wide muddy channel (originally stone lined?). The smaller reservoir has a similar shape to the large reservoir and has a set of steps leading down from the north-west corner. On the east side of the smaller cistern there is a leaf-shaped stone lined channel, which appears to have functioned as the inlet from the wadi. Both cisterns are usually full of water and still used by shepherds (observation made in 2005).

Cemetery

To the south of the fort are a large number (*c.* 100) of graves marked with piles of stones (see foreground of Plate 35 and Fig. 12).

Discussion

Both the historical information about the fort and its appearance indicate a complex history, which began well before its restoration in 1767 and continues beyond the survey carried out in 1986.

Probably the most notable aspect of the fort's design are the four solid corner towers, which distinguish it from most of the other Hajj forts. Other Ottoman forts with corner towers include, Muzayrib on the Hajj route, the castle at 'Aqaba and a number of the Ottoman forts in Palestine (*e.g.* Ras al-Ayn, Khan al-Tujjar, Qal'at Burak and Hebron). What distinguishes these buildings from Qal'at Balqa' and the majority of the Hajj forts, is that they are all, at least, four times larger and could be described as fortresses rather than forts. Also, the construction of the towers on the fortresses is different – they have rooms on both the ground floor and the upper floors, whereas, at Balqa', the towers are solid constructions at ground level. The most likely explanation for the unique design of the Balqa' fort is that it has been adapted from an earlier pre-existing structure. The most likely predecessor of the Ottoman fort is a Roman, or late Roman fort, many examples of which can be found in the vicinity of Qal'at

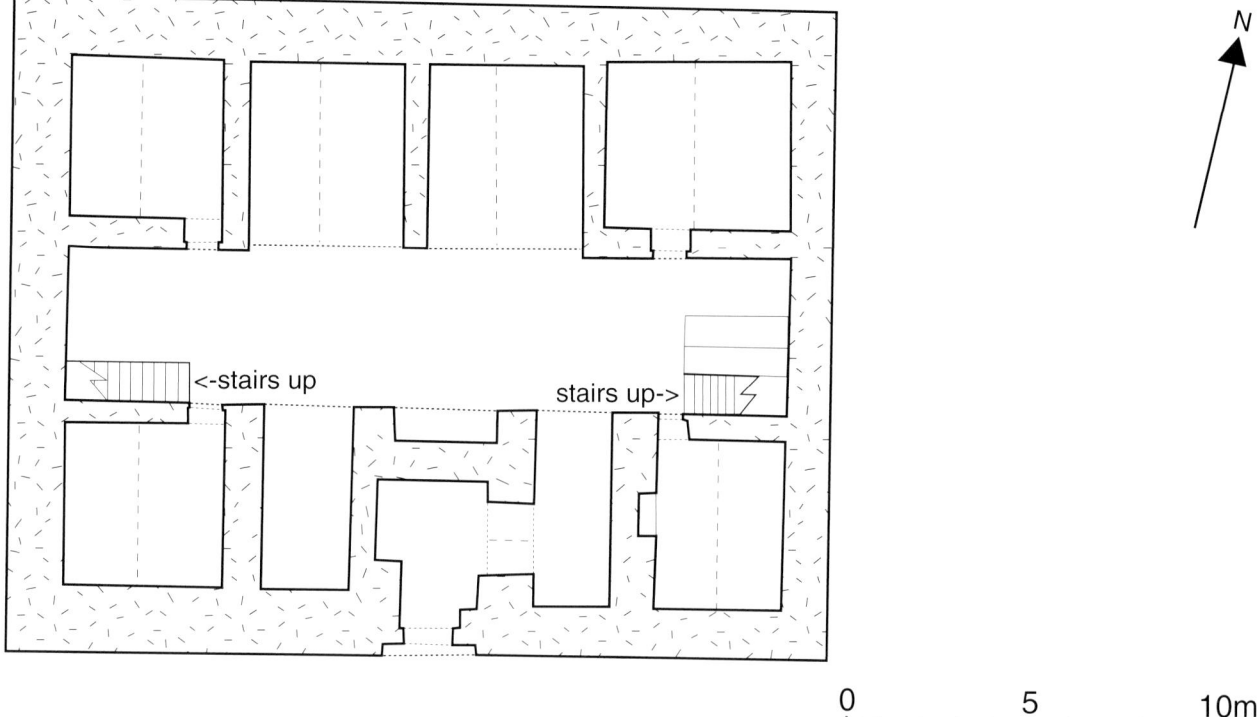

Fig. 16. Ground floor plan of Qal'at Qatrana in Jordan.

Balqa'. Roman forts with similar designs include Quweira and Thuraiyah (Kennedy 2000, 133 and 186–87), though the closest parallels in terms of size and design are the late Roman forts of En Boqeq and Upper Zohar, west of the Dead Sea. In his analysis of Roman military remains in the Madaba plain, Kennedy considers the possibility of a Roman origin for Balqa', but also notes a large ruin, including a tower, 5 km to the north-west, with quantities of Nabatean pottery (Kennedy 2000, 127). He is inclined to identify the latter, rather than Balqa', as a Roman site, though this does not preclude the possibility of Qal'at Balqa' (Dab'a) being a late Roman site.

Another possibility, suggested by the re-used lintel incorporated above the gateway, is that the fort is built on the remains on an early Islamic–Umayyad structure (for a discussion of the lintel, see Appendix 2). However, there is no other evidence of an early Islamic date at the site and the lintel seems much more likely to have originated at Zizia, as suggested by Genequand in Appendix 2.

Reconstructing the later history of the fort is also problematic. If we accept that Balqa' was originally built in the late Roman period, to what date can we assign its re-construction? The most obvious date would be 1767, as recorded in the (now lost) inscription (see Chapter 11 for a discussion of the inscription), however, in view of the historical information given above, it seems likely that it had already been used as a station on the Hajj route earlier in the Ottoman period. If we are to believe the testimony of the guard, as reported by Field, that the cistern was built by Sultan Selim, it seems likely that the fort was rebuilt

some time in the 16th century. However, there is very little architectural evidence for a 16th century refurbishment, with the possible exception of the waterspouts, which resemble those in classical Ottoman architecture of the 16th century, such as the Tekiyya in Damascus. Other features however, such as the corbels supporting the lintels over each doorway, indicate an 18th century date, by analogy with the same features at Qal'at al-Hasa, built, according to an inscription, in 1760. A projecting machicolation, or latrine, visible in the 1898 photographs of Brünnow and Domaszewski (no longer extant) may also have been part of the 18th century reconstruction and is also paralleled by similar features projecting from the exterior walls of al-Hasa, a feature that has subsequently disappeared.

The architectural history of the fort, after the restoration in 1767, is complex and involves integrating information from photographs and historical information, combined with analysis of the structure itself. We know from Doughty that the fort was repaired some time around the 1870s and it is likely that the large projecting solid rectangular buttress on the east wall (and visible in the 1898 photographs of Brünnow and Domaszewski) was added at this time. Reconstruction at the time of Sultan 'Abd al-Hamid, during the construction of the Hijaz railway; parts of the building that date to this period include, the iron roof over the room on the North side of the courtyard and most of the north wall of the fort. At the present time, 2008, a further restoration of the fort is taking place following a general degradation of the structure in the 1980s.

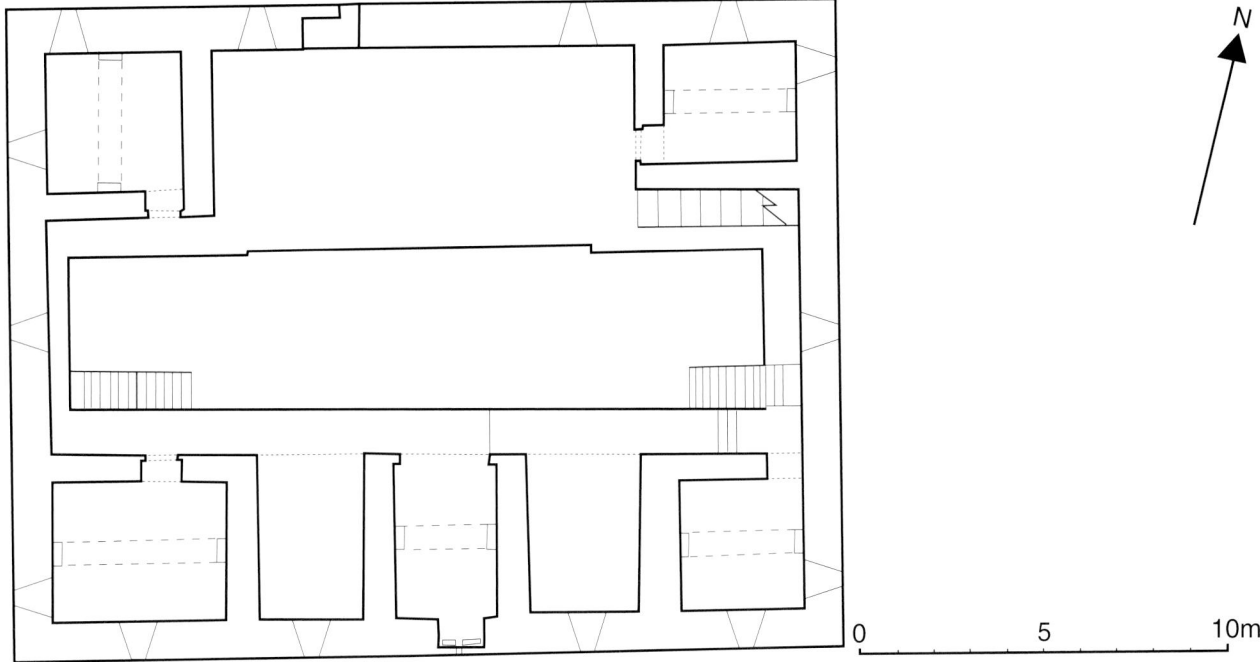

N

0   5   10m

Fig. 17. First floor plan of Qal'at Qatrana in Jordan.

Plate 44. Qal'at Qatrana, fort and cistern from east in 1898, by Rudolf-Ernst Brünnow (courtesy of Princeton University).

Plate 45. Qal'at Qatrana, cistern in 1898, by Rudolf-Ernst Brünnow (courtesy of Princeton University).

Qal'at Qatrana – (Map 5, No. 6) (Figs 16–19, Plates 44–55)

Location: 31.14N 36.03E

The site is located on the west side of the Desert Highway, to the south of the modern settlement of Qatrana and to the west of the Hijaz railway. Immediately to the south of the fort is the wide bed of Wadi Hanifa, which runs south-east to north-west. Recent excavations, during the rebuilding of the desert highway, have made it difficult to determine the exact course of this wadi, though it appears that a smaller wadi joined the Wadi Hanifa at this point. The site stands at an elevation of nearly 800 m above sea level, on the boundary between steppe and desert.

Plate 46. Qal'at Qatrana, south façade with entrance (1986).

History

This is an ancient site, with traces of Nabatean and early Roman occupation, as well as large amounts of Roman period pottery (Koucky 1987, 96–97, site 611). More

specifically, David Graf has suggested that this was the site of a Roman fort on the *Via Militaris* (Graf 1997). There is, however, no evidence for Qatrana having been used during the Medieval period. The earliest mention of a building at the site is in the 1563 (971 AH) itinerary of Mustapha

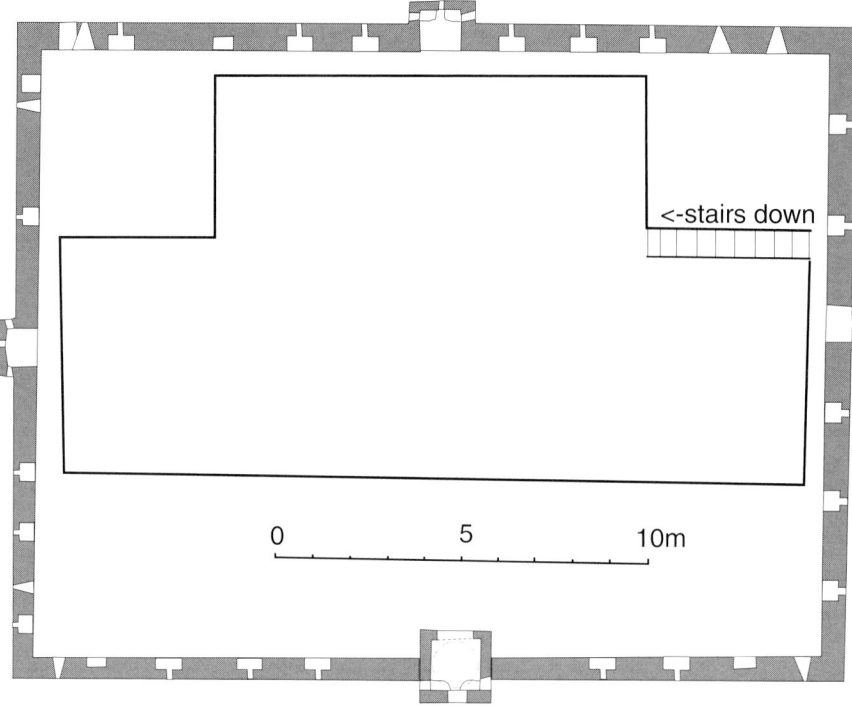

Fig. 18. Upper floor plan of Qal'at Qatrana in Jordan.

Plate 47. Qal'at Qatrana, detail of entrance, note slight horseshoe profile of arch (1986).

Plate 48. Qal'at Qatrana, interior entrance passage with roof of corbelled stone beams (1986).

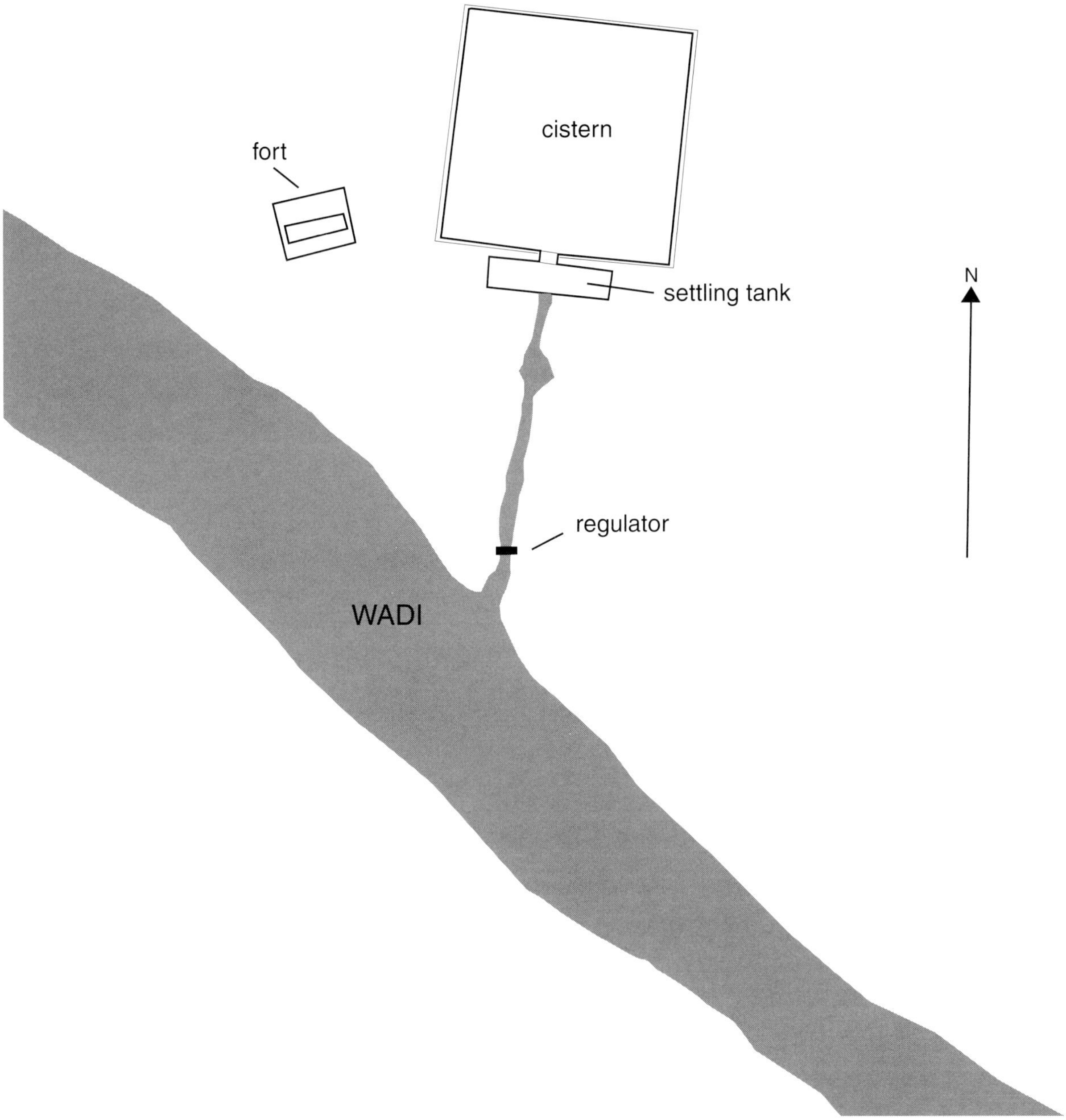

cistern

fort

settling tank

N

regulator

WADI

Fig. 19. Location plan of fort, cistern and wadi at Qal'at Qatrana in Jordan.

Plate 49. Qal'at Qatrana, interior with iwans on north side of courtyard (1986).

Plate 50. Qal'at Qatrana, interior courtyard from upper floor looking west (1986).

Plate 51. Qal'at Qatrana, interior north-east corner (1986).

Plate 53. Qal'at Qatrana, interior looking south towards entrance (1986).

Plate 52. Qal'at Qatrana, interior looking west (1986).

Plate 54. Qal'at Qatrana, water inlet from wadi (1986).

Plate 55. Qal'at Qatrana, settling tank next to large cistern (1986).

Pasha, where it is listed as Khan Qatrani (خان قطراني) (al-Jasir 1969, 184–85). According to al-Ghazzi (d. 1650) (1945–59, vol. ii, 157) and al-Qaramani (d. 1611) (1865, 440) the fort was built on the orders of Sultan Sulayman, in 1559, as part of a building programme which also saw the construction of forts at, Ma'an, Dhat al-Hajj and Tabuk (this date is confirmed by the inscription in the fort at Ma'an).

The fort soon became the focus for political disputes between the Bedouin, the governors of Kerak and the Ottoman central government. Peake Pasha relates an episode that occurred during the later years of the rule of Sultan Sulayman (r. 1520–66). According to oral tribal history the Temiyya tribe rebelled against Ottoman rule and were subsequently defeated by Yusef Nimr of Nablus, on the orders of the governor of Damascus. A new governor was sent to Kerak, though after a short period, he too, declared himself independent of the Ottomans. Sulayman then appointed one of his most trusted senior officials (*pasha*) to deal with the situation. The *pasha* invited the rebellious governor to a conference at Qatrana, where a peace treaty was signed. The *pasha* then went to Constantinople to obtain Sulayman's approval and returned to meet the governor at Qatrana. However, at this second meeting the governor was arrested and sent as a prisoner to Damascus (Peake Pasha 1958, 84–85). This account demonstrates how Qatrana was used as a base for Ottoman authority in an area where tribal rule was still the norm.

The fort is mentioned for the first time in official Ottoman documents dated 1568, during the reign of

Sultan Selim II, when Qansuh b. Musa'da b Muslim b al-Ghazzawi (the Bedouin governor of Kerak-Shawbak 1551 and Ajlun 1564–1568) was accused of several offences. He was arrested by the governor of Damascus and charged with appropriating 15,000 gold pieces intended to pay for the restoration of the Hajj fort and watering place at Qatrana (Bakhit 1982, 213; *MD* vii, no. 2042, 16 Rabi' I, 976, 745).

Just over a century later, in 1672, Qatrana was visited by Evliya Çelebi who states that it was dependent on the fortress of Kerak, in the Sanjak of al-Quds. He describes the fort as follows:

'The fort is in the middle of the desert and is a square building made of small stones (foundations). In the direction of the *qibla* (south) there is a gate. Outside measures three hundred paces but there is no moat. Inside there are seven rooms as well as storerooms and a masjid (mosque). The fort has a commander and seventy troops' (Evliya Çelebi, *Seyhatnâmesi* IX, 294).

The fort appears to have been in the centre of disputes between local forces and the central government. Evliya states that the tribes in the area were in rebellion against Ottoman rule and relates an incident when the Hajj caravan, while in the vicinity of Qatrana, was attacked by 100 Bedouin horsemen. He also notes that the troops in the fort sold goods to the pilgrims for a good profit, but that he personally got provisions much cheaper by going direct to Kerak, two hours to the west (Kortepeter 1979, 236; Bilge 1979, 218; Evliya Çelebi, *Seyhatnâmesi* IX, 264b).

In the early 18th century (1709) the Syrian pilgrim, Murtada ibn 'Alawan, also visited Qatrana which he reached at four in the afternoon, after a journey of 15 hours from Balqa'. He stated that the fort was built within the Wadi Nasur, which had many tributaries. The fort was a high square building, made of white stones with white lime plaster and mortar, whilst the square door was made out of recently cut wood. The water at the site was variable, coming both directly from rain and from watercourses (Murtada b. 'Ali b. 'Alawan MS fol. 105b).

In the mid-18th century it once again became a centre for rebellion against the Ottomans. In 1753 the Bedouin refused to allow the pilgrims safe passage, until they were paid the subsidies and arrears they believed due to them. The Hajj commander reluctantly gave in to the Bedouin and paid them the money. However, the Ottoman government perceived this as a rebellion and had all the tribal leaders executed. This enraged the Bedouin tribes and in 1756 there was a massive attack on the caravan at Qatrana. The Turkish Governor, Abdullah Pasha, had to take refuge in the fort where he stayed for 15 days until the Bedouin had left with their plunder (Peake Pasha 1958, 87).

Twenty-three years later the site was visited by Mehmed Edib, who noted that it was located 16 hours journey from Qal'at Balqa' and contained a reservoir built by Sultan Sulayman. He also mentions that pilgrims could buy supplies at this stop, though he seems to confuse Shawbak with Kerak as the source of these commodities (Bianchi 1825, 125).

Burckhardt visited the site in the early 19th century and describes Kalaat el Katrane as a place with a cistern of rainwater. He also mentions that the commander of the fort makes money selling the pilgrims produce from Kerak (Burckhardt 1822, 658, appendix III). A few years later the fort was inspected by officers of Muhammad 'Ali Pasha (see Appendix 1 in this volume). They provided a detailed report on both the cistern and the fort. The fort is described as a square building (35 × 35 cubits) generally in good condition, although one of the storerooms was damaged and in need of repair. The report also mentions that the residential rooms for the commander of the fort were in need of renovation. The cistern was described as having a huge capacity (2,100 square cubits), with a deflection dam to prevent the accumulation of mud within the cistern. The main action required by the engineers was the repair of the dam. A section of the dam had been destroyed in previous years and the engineers recommended that this be repaired to ensure that the water catchment remained effective.

In the latter part of the 19th century the fort was visited by a number of travellers including, Doughty (1979, 20), Gray Hill (1897, 40) and Brünnow and von Domaszewski (1905, 85). Doughty does little more than mention the fort, but Gray Hill gives an interesting description, based on his visit in 1896, which is worth citing in full:

'We went to see the Khan of Kutraneh. The keeper of it said that his father and grandfather had held the post before him. The Khan does not look very old. There are three small cannon in it, said to have been placed there by Ibrahim Pasha. We bought a sheep and a lamb from some Hajii for the equivalent in Turkish money of 7*s*. At Kutraneh there is a very large and well built reservoir 84 paces square, above it a small one 46 by 8, overflowing into the big one. The earth is embanked round the pools so as to supply water to them. Above the smaller pool a stone wall arrests water descending to a hollow and turns it into the pools; but they contained nothing but mud for want of repair' (Gray Hill 1897, 40).

A few years later Alois Musil visited the fort, describing it as a modern building, next to two large cisterns. Around the sides were earth banks, which Musil thought were designed to deflect water into the cisterns, though it is more likely they resulted from the periodic removal of mud from the interior of the cisterns. Musil also observes that the earth banks had been used as a cemetery in recent times. The most interesting aspect of Musil's account is his discussion with the Algerian commander of the fort; who lived in the fort with his daughter and an old female slave. The commander had once lived in Paris, whilst serving in the French army and talked with Musil in French. The encounter is recorded as follows:

'We were asked in and entered a square, which was surrounded by residential buildings, storage depots and stables. We drew water from a deep well and followed the commander to the first floor, where we found a small passage that connected all the rooms. A stone staircase led to a flat roof, from which our host took us to his small, nearly European furnished place where he served excellent tea' (Musil 1907, 37–40).

In May 1928 the fort was visited by Eric Schroeder of the Field Museum, North Arabian Desert Expedition. Schroeder described it as 'an Arab fortress standing in disrepair nearly a mile from the [Hijaz Railway] station'. He also noted the projecting turrets, which he compared with those of Qasr al-Azraq (Field 1960, 81).

Description

The site comprises a fort, a large reservoir joined to a smaller reservoir and two tunnels which connect to the wadi via sluice gates. There is considerable modern disturbance of the site, which covers an area of approximately 1,000 m².

The Fort

EXTERIOR

The fort is a tall (10 m high), rectangular (22.2 m × 17.35 m) structure, that stands 26 m to the west of the large reservoir and approximately the same distance from the banks of Wadi Hanifa to the south. The south face of the fort, containing the entrance, is built entirely of ashlar limestone blocks (average size 30 cm × 30 cm × 60 cm), whilst the other sides (west, east and north) are built of roughly square limestone blocks, with ashlars only used for the quoins. The top of the wall on each side is crowned with small, dome shaped, crenellations (40 cm × 35 cm high) made of stones covered in plaster.

THE ENTRANCE

The gateway is, approximately, in the middle of the south side and is set within a shallow recess, covered by a horseshoe shaped arch (Plates 46 and 47). Above the recess there are three carved stone balls, two either side of the arch and one above. The doorway itself is covered with a shallow segmental arch, made from three large, stone, blocks. There are two narrow slits, hidden within the arch covering the recess, which form part of a concealed machicolation.

MACHICOLATIONS

Above the gateway there is a second machicolation, in the form of a projecting domed structure resting on three corbels. There are two downward openings between the corbels and a large window opening at the front. There are similar structures in the middle of the other three sides (west, north and east); the fact that they have openings between the corbels suggests that they too were designed to function as machicolations. In addition to the downward openings, each of these structures has three tall arrow/gun slits on each face.

GUN/ARROW SLITS

Two types of opening are visible on the exterior of the fort these are:

Type 1

These slits are nearly a 1 m (4 courses) high and 0.15 m wide, sometimes with a splayed base (0.3 m wide). The most notable feature of these windows/slits is the carved rectangular hood mould, which runs over the top of each opening. The straight slits, Form (a) and those with splayed bases, Form (b), are arranged in a symmetrical pattern where the splayed slits are always in the middle. From this schema it can be seen that the east and west

South	a	b	b	a
East	a	b	a	
North	a	b	b	a
West	a	b	a	

Table 2 – Sequence of openings in the walls of Qatrana Fort

sides only have three slits because of their shorter length. All the windows in the above table occur at exactly the same level (4.5 m above outside level) around the different sides of the fort. There are a few other, shorter, windows with hood moulds and splayed bases on the north and east sides of the fort (there are two slits on each side, one near each corner).

Type 2

The second type of opening is more numerous and located just below the level of the crenellations. These are small openings, sometimes with 'v' shaped heads, which appear to be part of a secondary phase of construction.

INTERIOR

The entrance to Qatrana is at present protected by an elaborately locked iron door. Inside the fort there is a tall rectangular central courtyard and three floors reached by external staircases. Recent restoration (1976) work financed by the Turkish government is very much in evidence in the interior, thus all the walls have been recently plastered, there are steel railings around the courtyard, new brown painted wooden doors to many of the rooms and a few display cases (empty) in some of the rooms.

Entrance to the courtyard is via a bent entrance (Plate 48). The gateway opens into a square room with a flat roof (made from basalt beams or concrete), there is a pointed archway to the right, leading into a small passage, also with a flat roof made of basalt beams (some of these beams have been replaced by re-enforced concrete).

The courtyard is a narrow rectangle (18.6 m east–west × 4.1 m north–south) with a staircase at either end leading up to the first floor (Plates 50 and 52). In the centre of the west side there is a square hole leading into a cistern. Eight rooms, including the entrance passage, lead off from the courtyard at ground level. All the doorways in the fort have the same design, comprising a plain rectangular opening (1.95 m high × 0.8 m wide) covered with a stone lintel.

To the right of the entrance (*i.e.* west) there is a small barrel-vaulted room and to the left (*i.e.* east) there is a narrow *iwan* with a roof made of basalt beams. In the south-west corner there is a square barrel-vaulted room.

On the north side of the courtyard, immediately opposite the entrance, there are two wide *iwans*, each roofed with a barrel-vault and two square barrel-vaulted rooms, one at each corner (Plate 49).

FIRST FLOOR

The first floor comprises seven rooms (five on the south side, two on the north side) linked by a narrow walkway around the courtyard. In each corner there is a square room, roofed with basalt corbels supported by a central transverse arch. The south range comprises two rooms with doorways (one at each corner) and three *iwans*. The central *iwan* also has a roof covered with basalt corbels resting on a transverse arch, whilst the *iwans* either side are roofed with barrel-vaults. Each of the rooms has at least one window/arrow slit with wide reveals. The central *iwan* on the south side gives access to the concealed machicolation above the doorway recess.

UPPER (SECOND) FLOOR

A staircase in the north-east corner gives access to the upper floor (Plate 51). This area contains no rooms; its main function appears to be to provide access to the parapet. On each side there is a box machicolation; each with two downward openings, the machicolation on the south side is distinguished by its dome shaped roof and larger size. Flanking the machicolations there are a series of rectangular niches each containing a gun/arrow slit.

At the west end of the south wall, between the south-west corner and the domed machicolation, there is a small curved wall which rises higher than the crenellations and appears to be some form of enclosed vantage point.

Materials of Construction

Two main types of stone are found in the fort at Qatrana:
1) A buff coloured shelly limestone. This is used, either in the form of ashlars (average size 0.3 m × 0.3 m × 0.6 m) or, as roughly squared blocks (*c.* 0.3 m × 0.3 m × 0.3–0.5 m). The south face of the fort, which is entirely built of ashlars, contains some stones with a smooth wide border and a rough rectangular boss in

the middle. In general the ashlars fit together tightly, whereas the roughly squared blocks have small limestone wedges in the joints.
2) Dark grey basalt beams, with an average length of 2.5 m. These are used for the roofs and for corbels.

Architectural History

At least three phases are visible in the construction of the fort, the latest of which may be attributed to the restoration work carried out by the Department of Antiquities and financed by the government of Turkey in 1976. Parts of the building belonging to this phase include the entire re-plastering of the interior, the reconstruction of the crenellations, the wooden doors and steel railings. In addition to this cosmetic work, there was some structural reconstruction, thus the north-east corner of the fort has been re-built with machine cut blocks of stone. Because of the extensive restoration work it is difficult to see the building phases within the fort.

Apart from this restoration work, a few changes in the design of the building can be detected, thus none of the four machicolations fit well into the sequence of niches and gun/arrow slits on the upper (second floor) level. Also, it is clear that the upper row of gun/arrow slits are secondary and appear to belong to a blocking of the gaps between battlements.

A suggested chronology of building phases is:

1) Original construction, including lower row of windows with crenellations comprising large battlements with gaps in between
2) Box machicolations added (18th century?)
3) Restoration work carried out during the 1970s

The water system

To the east of the fort there are two reservoirs, a large square reservoir and a smaller rectangular basin (Fig. 19, Plates 44 and 55). Both are built of roughly dressed blocks of limestone and basalt.

The large square reservoir (69.5 m per side and 4 m+ deep) has four diagonal slabs in each corner, these may have been intended to strengthen the corners and also to act as markers for the water level (they are set at intervals of 0.7 m). In the south-west corner there are is a broad (2 m wide) set of steps leading down into the bottom of the reservoir.

The rectangular basin (35.5 m × 9.1 m and 3 m+ deep) to the east of the main reservoir is located higher up, with a shallower depth and was clearly intended to act as a settling tank. As in the larger tank, there is a set of steps leading down into the cistern on the west side. The two tanks are connected by a shallow channel (3 m wide and 0.7 m deep), which slopes down into the larger tank.

In the centre of the south side of the smaller cistern there is an opening leading into two parallel vaulted channels.

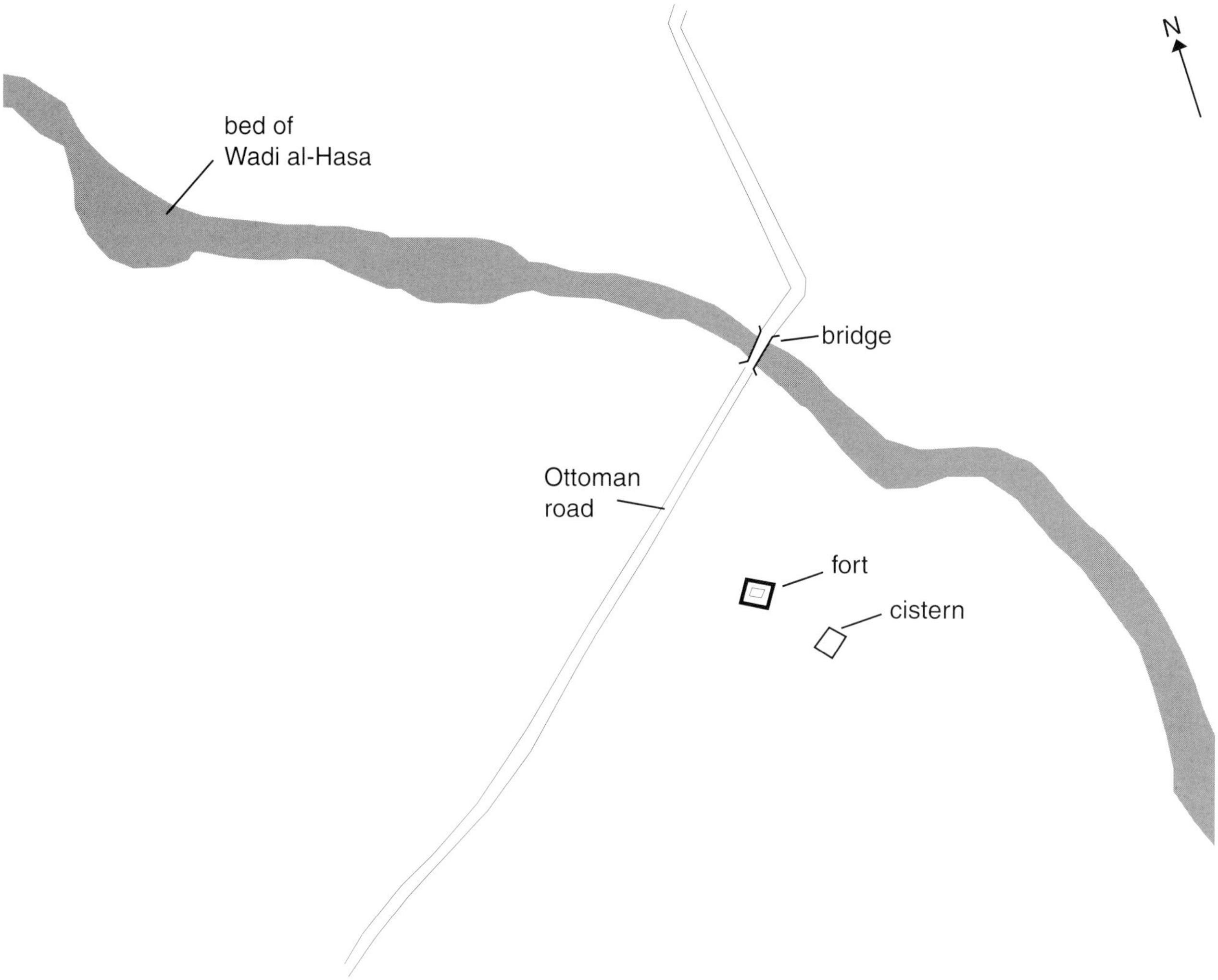

Fig. 20. Location plan of fort, cistern, bridge and wadi at Qal'at al-Hasa in Jordan.

Plate 56. Qal'at al-Hasa, bridge from west in 1898, by Rudolf-Ernst Brünnow (courtesy of Princeton University).

Plate 57. Qal'at al-Hasa, road surface on bridge in 1898, by Rudolf-Ernst Brünnow (courtesy of Princeton University).

The channels run for a distance of 75 m, to a rectangular bridge-like construction (Plate 54).

The bridge-like construction is large (19.6 m long × 2.5 m wide) with a semi-circular arch near the east end. Beneath the arch are the openings of twin-vaulted tunnels separated by a rectangular pier. Between the archway and the entrance to the tunnels there are slots for sluice gates. On either side of the arch are triangular shaped cutwaters, indicating that this structure would have been part of a water catchment system connecting directly to the Wadi Hanifa.

Although the water system has been in use in fairly recent times, it is probable that the two reservoirs, at least, are of earlier construction (Roman or Umayyad) as are the two channels connecting them. The bridge like construction is, however, certainly of more recent construction and may be either, early Ottoman or later.

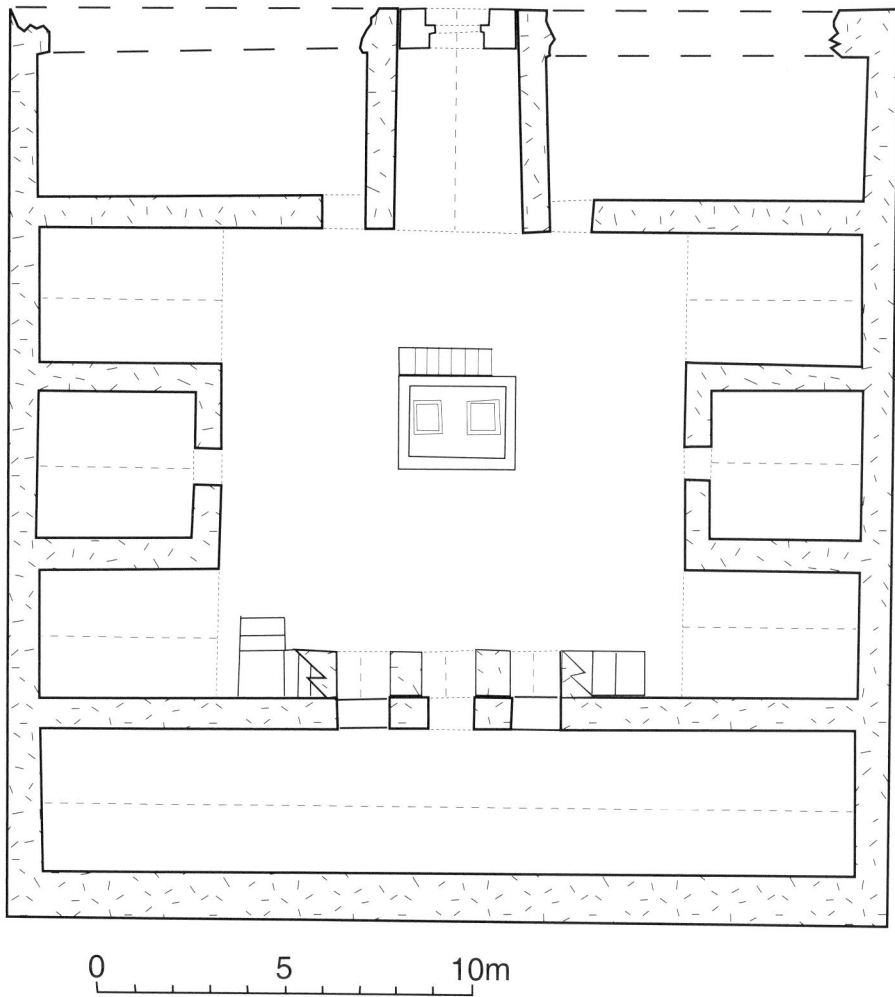

Fig. 21. Ground floor plan of Qal'at al-Hasa in Jordan.

Plate 58. Qal'at al-Hasa, bridge from east in 1898, by Rudolf-Ernst Brünnow (courtesy of Princeton University).

Discussion

From the historical account it can clearly be seen that Qatrana was an important station of the Hajj route and was seen as a place where Bedouin and Ottoman officials could negotiate with each other. The historical accounts also emphasize the relationship with Kerak, both as a source of commodities and as a regional power centre from which the governor of Qatrana could draw extra support. It is also noticeable that several accounts give detailed descriptions

of the fort, in particular, Evliya Çelebi who noted that there were seven living rooms, suggesting that he had been inside the fort; seven rooms are still visible today.

The layout of the fort is similar to that of Ma'an, with rooms on only two sides of the courtyard, rather than on four as is more common in the other later forts. Also the orientation of the building, with the main door facing the *qibla*, is similar to Ma'an and although a prayer room has not been identified in the restored structure, we know, from Evliya Çelebi, that the design included as *masjid* (mosque).

Qal'at al-Hasa – (Map 5, No. 7) (Figs 20–25, Plates 56–79)

(Tabut Korsu, Tabout-Karoussi, Kalaat el Hasa, Kasr el Ahsa)
Location: 30.50N 40.46E
This site is located 5 km north-west of Mahattat al-Hasa on the Hejaz Railway. The site lies on the south bank of the main bed of the Wadi al-Hasa, which flows west from

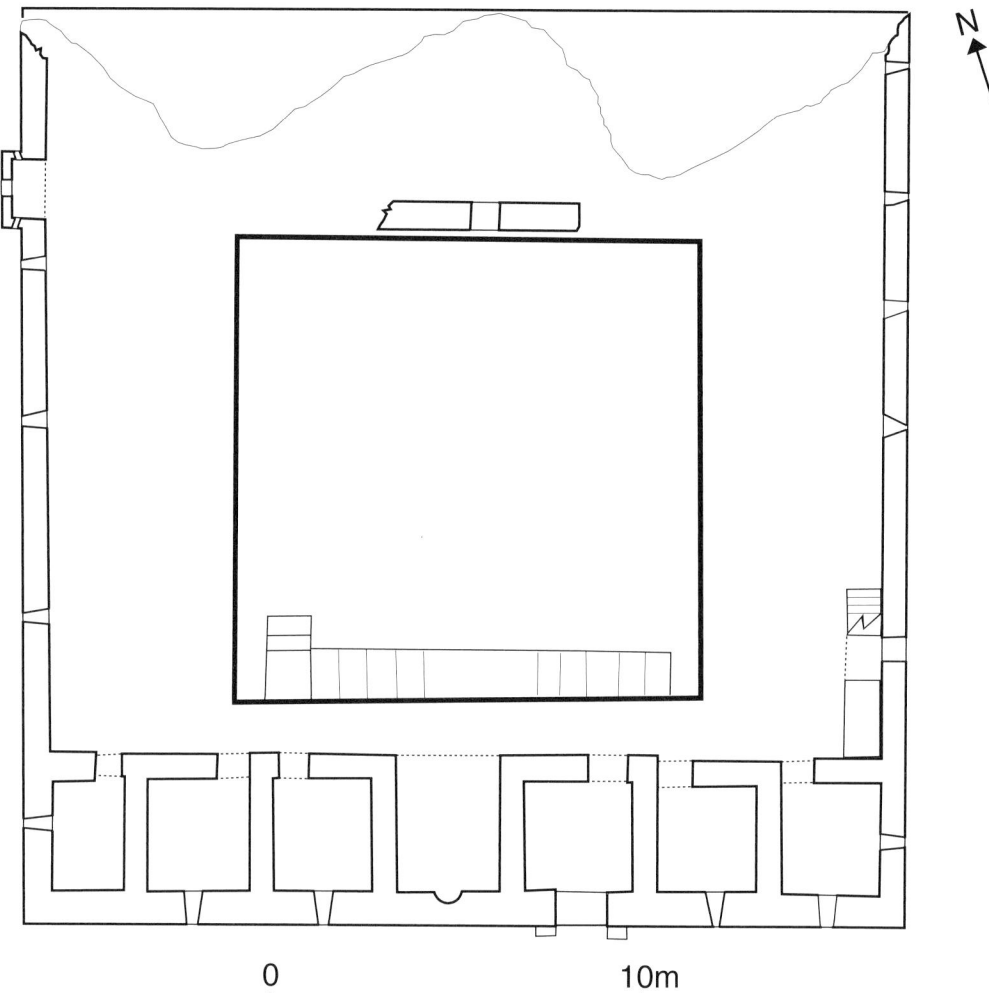

Fig. 22. First floor plan of Qal'at al-Hasa in Jordan.

Plate 59. Qal'at al-Hasa, interior of fort in 1898 looking south, by Rudolf-Ernst Brünnow (courtesy of Princeton University).

Plate 60. Qal'at al-Hasa, interior in 1898 looking north by Rudolf-Ernst Brünnow (courtesy of Princeton University).

here towards the Dead Sea. The immediate environment may be characterized as a broad alluvial plain, intersected by many small wadis, which feed into the main wadi. The site stands as just over 800 m above sea level.

The remains comprise a large square fort (*c.* 24 m per side), a small square reservoir, a section of paved road and a bridge across the Wadi al-Hasa.

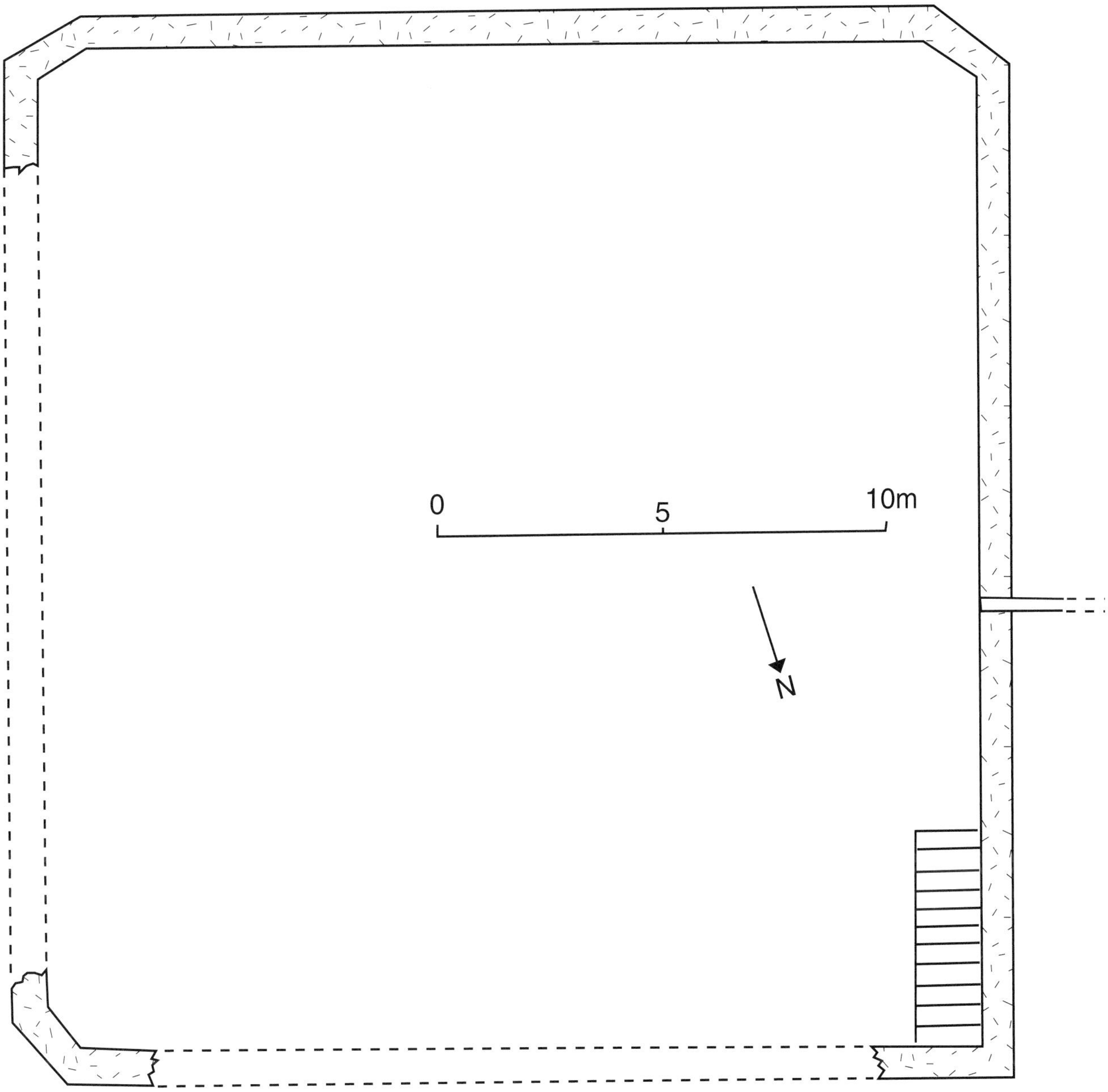

Fig. 23. Plan of cistern at Qal'at al-Hasa in Jordan.

Plate 61. Qal'at al-Hasa, interior looking north-east in 1907, by Jaussen and Savignac (courtesy of the École Biblique).

Plate 62. Qal'at al-Hasa, bridge from west in 1907, by Jaussen and Savignac (courtesy of the École Biblique).

NORTH

Fig. 24. Elevation drawing of bridge over Wadi al-Hasa in Jordan.

5m

0

SOUTH

Plate 63. Qal'at al-Hasa, exterior with entrance and collapsed north wall (1986).

Plate 64. Qal'at al-Hasa, exterior south wall (1986).

Plate 65. Qal'at al-Hasa, exterior east wall (1986).

Plate 66. Qal'at al-Hasa, exterior west wall (1986).

History

This site does not appear to have been part of the Syrian Hajj route before the Ottoman period. Hasa (حسا) is first mentioned as a stop on the pilgrimage route in the itinerary of Mustapha Pasha in 1563 AD (971 AH) (al-Jasir 1969, 184–85). No information is given about the site and it does not appear in Ottoman documents of the 16th century.

NORTH

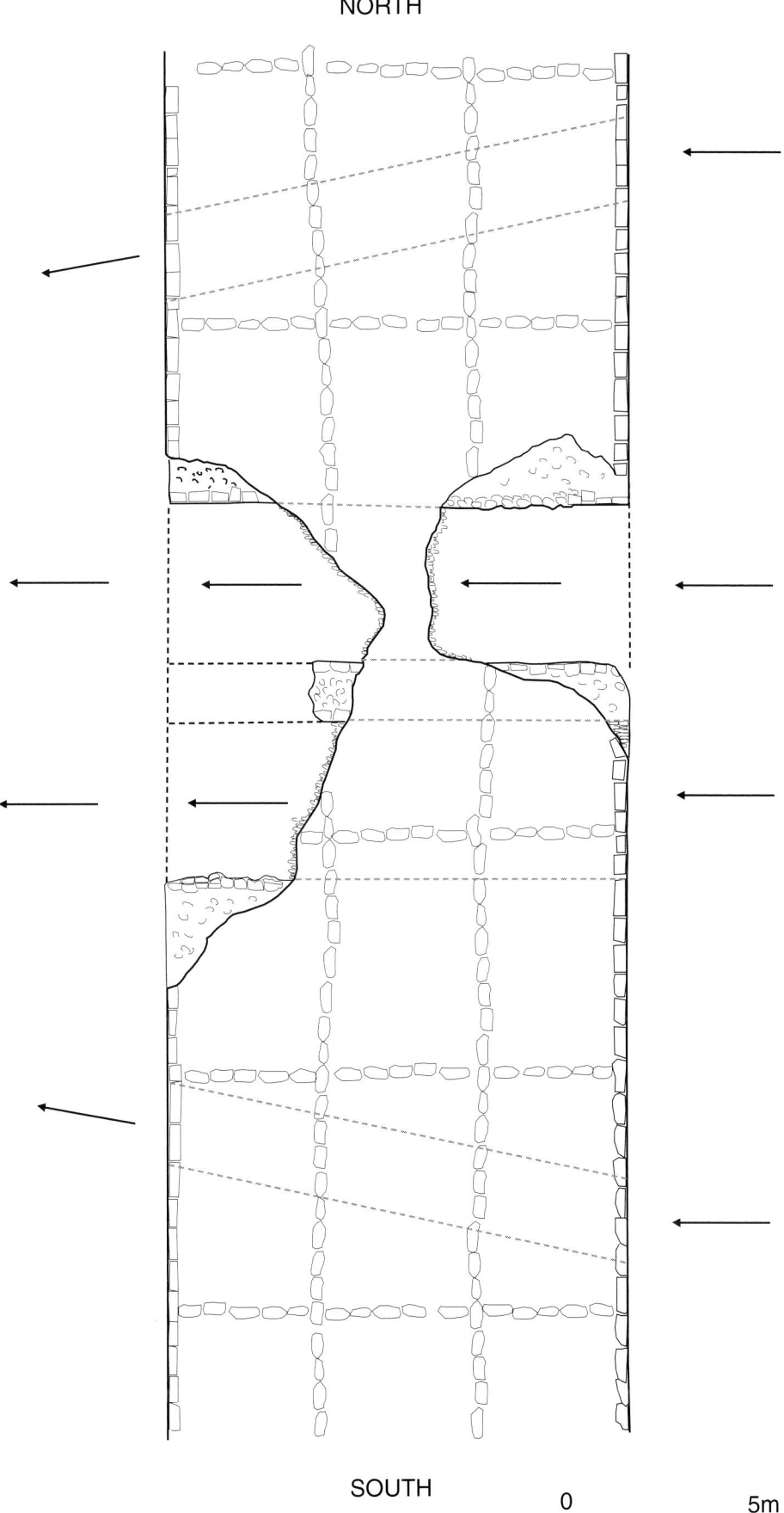

SOUTH

Fig. 25. Plan of bridge over Wadi al-Hasa in Jordan.

Plate 67. Qal'at al-Hasa, interior north wall with remains of upper floor (1986).

Plate 69. Qal'at al-Hasa, exterior with west wall with projecting casement (1986).

Plate 68. Qal'at al-Hasa, exterior with south wall with remains of projecting casement (1986).

Plate 70. Qal'at al-Hasa, interior looking south with mihrab visible in centre of first floor (1986).

However, during his 1672 pilgrimage Evliya Çelebi visited the site of Tabut, located between Qatrana and 'Unaiza in the territory of al-Quds (Jeruslaem), which must be identified with the present site of Hasa (Evliya Çelebi, *Seyhatnâmesi* IX, 587–604; Bilge 1979, 218). Çelebi relates an incident which took place at this site when the caravan was attacked by Bedouin of the Bani Zuhd and al-'Umar tribes. Six of the bedouin were killed, whilst

three others were taken prisoner. The captives informed Husayn Pasha that another attack was planned for the next day, this was avoided by encircling the caravan with troops and producing loud music from the military band after which the Bedouin abandoned their attack (Evliya Çelebi, *Seyhatnâmesi* IX, 581–83; Kortepeter 1979, 236).

In the 18th century Murtada ibn 'Alawan lists Hasa as a stop (*qonaq*) between Qatran (قطران) and 'Anza (عنزة)

Plate 71. Qal'at al-Hasa, detail of mihrab *(1986).*

Plate 73. Qal'at al-Hasa, bridge from west (1986).

Plate 74. Qal'at al-Hasa, bridge, detail of west face of north arch (1986).

Plate 72. Qal'at al-Hasa, door jamb with scroll shaped corbel (1986).

Plate 75. Qal'at al-Hasa, interior looking north (2006).

Plate 76. Qal'at al-Hasa, exterior from north-west (2006).

Plate 77. Qal'at al-Hasa, interior long gallery on south side of courtyard looking west (2006).

Plate 78. Qal'at al-Hasa, bridge from east (2006).

Plate 79. Qal'at al-Hasa, interior courtyard after restoration looking south (2006).

(Murtada b. 'Ali b. 'Alawan MS fol. 104a). Some 30 years later the governor of Damascus, Aydinili Abdullah Pasha, (in office 1730–33) built a bridge across the Wadi al-Hasa to mitigate the effects of flash floods (Barbir 1980, 138). In view of the fact that Aydinili Abdullah Pasha also had a paved road built between Damascus and Qunaytra and strengthened the river banks between Sanamayn and Muzayrib, it is likely that he was also responsible for the paved road leading up to the bridge at Hasa (Barbir 1980, 138, based on Ibn al-Qari, ed. al-Munajjid, 77). In 1779 Hasa was visited by Mehmed Edib, who states that, because, it contained the burial site of Celaleddin Halveti, it was also called Tabut Korsu, or burial grove, (Bianchi 1825, 125–26). Edib states that the bridge is called Lejun and mentions that there was also a fort and cistern at the site. He explains the importance of the bridge, placed at a point where floods were frequently life threatening. Nevertheless, drinking water at the site was scarce. He also mentions another stopping place nearby called Uziyr Sultan, which is infested with robbers.

In the early 19th century (1810–15) the fort was probably visited by Burckhardt during his travels in Syria. Burckhardt refers to the site several times and includes a description, which appears to be based on personal observation, of the site in his appendix on the Hajj route. He notes that the fort is built in the middle of the Wadi al-Hasa and has a well in the middle that draws water by means of a large water wheel. The wadi is said to be dry in the summer, although there are springs nearby which supply water all year round. He also makes the observation that a number of farmers (*fellah*) live around the castle, in small villages, cultivating 'dhourra' [maize] and barley (Burckhardt 1822, 658, appendix III). When passing through Tafila, in August 1812, he noted that the inhabitants sold their produce to the pilgrims at the castle of El Ahsa. This appears to have been a major source of income as he goes on to state that the interruption of the Hajj meant that the livelihood of the inhabitants of Tafila was endangered (Burckhardt 1822, chapter 6).

Fifteen years later the facilities at al-Hasa were inspected on behalf of Muhammad 'Ali Pasha (Appendix 1 in this volume). The report noted that the two corners of the fort (50 cubits square) had been damaged in an earthquake many years before and that repairs carried out in the previous year (1824?) were inadequate. The report also noted that floodwater had swept away a 40 cubit long section of the bridge embankment. As repairs to both fort and embankment were required immediately, an urgent request was sent to the *Hikimadar* who authorized the repairs, which had already been carried out. For the future, the report recommended laying an area of stone paving around the fort, to a radius of 1,500 paces, to complement the paved causeway that already stretched across the bed of the wadi, from the bridge, for a distance of 1,500 cubits (Appendix 1 in this volume).

In the 1860s Christophe Mauss and Henry Sauvaire passed through al-Hasa on their way to Shawbak. They noted the square fort and large adjacent cistern, as well as the bridge of two arches and a portion of paved road. Within the fort, around the central courtyard, was a series of storerooms, as well as living rooms for the garrison (Sauvaire and Mauss 1867, 135–37). They noted that the guards had lived in the area for several generations and had planted a small garden between the fort and the cistern. They stated that the road marked the edge of the desert and was similar to the Roman road at Dhat Ras (Sauvaire and Mauss 1867, 135–37). They also note an inscription on the back wall, of the central room, of the upper floor [the prayer room] dating the construction of the fort to 1760, during the reign of the Ottoman Sultan Mustafa III (1757–73) (Sauvaire and Mauss 1867, 208–9; Brünnow and von Domaszewski 1905, 18).

A decade later (1875) Doughty passed through al-Hasa and recalls 'We came down upon a causey with a little bridge, made for the camels' passage over the slippery loam to our encampment in Wady el-Hasy, which divides the uplands of Moab and Edom'. There is no description of the fort except for the comment that 'the well of stinking water within the kella is ruinous'. He also noted a new cistern built outside the castle (Doughty 1979, 26–27). Twenty years later, in 1896, another Englishman, Gray Hill, visited al-Hasa on his way to Petra, crossing a 'dilapidated old bridge of three arches, and a paved causeway'. He wrote that the fort resembled Qatrana, but was in a ruinous condition stating: 'The north-east corner has given way from the top down, and it looks as if half of the north and east walls would soon fall'. Unlike Doughty he notes that the water in the cistern outside was 'of a very uninviting appearance' compared to the water within the fort, which was 'good drinking water' (Gray Hill 1897, 42).

In the 1890s, Hasa was visited by the German scholars Brünnow and von Domaszewski; in search of Roman antiquities. They describe the fort as modern and half destroyed ('moderne und jezt halb verfallene Kal'a') standing on ground to the south of the wadi bed. They noted the reservoir to the east of the fort, which they described as 'a beautiful, perhaps antique cistern'. They also identified both the road and bridge as Roman, stating: 'At the north-east corner of the northern arch, a column has been built in which is not original, thus the bridge would have been repaired during Roman times; because the RS [Roman

Road] above as well as the use of round arch prove that the structure is undeniably Roman' (Brünnow and von Domaszewski 1905, 30–32).

In 1905 Jaussen and Savignac travelled, one hour and 10 minutes, west from the railway station to the fort at al-Hasa (Jaussen and Savignac 1997, 31–33, inc. 2 photographs). They remarked on the well, where water was available at a depth of 8 or 9 m compared with the railway station, where it was reached at a depth of 30 m. Although they state that the fort is of no archaeological interest ('n'offre qu'un mince intérêt archéologique') they record important details, including the fact that the fort was built during the reign of Sultan Mustapha. Although the interior was in ruins at the time, it was looked after by a guard, appointed by the Shaykh of the Hegaya tribe, who lived there with two members of his family in return for a salary of 25 *megidys* per month. They dispute Brünnow and von Domaszewski's assessment of the bridge as a Roman construction, stating that they believe it to be Arab, even though it may have been built over a Roman predecessor (Jaussen and Savignac 1997, 31–32 n. 1).

In the early 1980s the fort was surveyed as part of the Wadi al-Hasa Archaeological Survey, which surveyed the length of the Wadi, from its origins in the high desert plateau in the East, to the point where it entered the Dead Sea in the West. In addition to the fort (Site 1074), the bridge (Site 1072) and the road (Site 1073) the survey identified the remains of three Ottoman period villages (Sites 1063, 1064, and 1066), as well as a huge enclosure with a diameter of 240 m. It is thought that the enclosure was used by the Hajj caravan, either as a camping ground, or as an area for coralling animals (MacDonald *et al.* 1983, 322 and plate 72 no. 2; MacDonald 1988, chapter 12, 250–80, 'The Islamic Periods' especially, 277–80 and photos 25 [fort] and 26 [bridge]).

Architectural Description

The Fort

EXTERIOR

The fort lies on ground sloping gently down towards the south (Wadi al-Hasa) so that there is a difference of 0.7 m between the north and south sides of the building. None of the walls of the fort survive to their original height, the south side having been nearly completely destroyed (this wall has been partially rebuilt during restoration work carried out in the late 1980s and early 1990s). However, enough remains of the original north wall to show that it was built of well cut ashlars, whilst the other three sides are built of roughly square limestone blocks and occasional blocks of basalt.

Most of the openings in the walls are inconspicuous, comprising narrow slits one course high (0.3 m wide × 0.1 m high) with no decoration.

The west wall is badly damaged, especially at the north

end where the collapse of the north wall has reduced it to 0.5 m above ground level. There are five openings in this wall and a projecting gallery, which also has three openings. The projecting gallery (no longer in existence, destroyed *c.* 1990) is 3.9 m from the north-west corner. The gallery resembles a projecting box machicolation (like those at Qatrana) though there are no downward openings. It is supported on three projecting corbels, each comprised of two basalt beams projecting from the wall of the fort. Most of the rest of the structure is built of ashlar limestone, except for the roof, which is made of basalt and limestone rubble.

On the narrow south and north sides of the gallery there are small slit windows, whilst on the west side there may have been a larger window, though this was damaged and it is difficult to determine the original size (maximum size would have been 1.05 m high and 0.25 m wide).

The south wall of the fort is of similar design to the west, with a series of small slit windows and a projecting gallery located to one side of the centre of the façade. Although most of the projecting gallery has collapsed, leaving a large opening in the wall (2.4 m high × 1.4 m wide), it is clearly of the same design as that on the west side. Apart from this large opening there are 6 other openings, four at first floor level (2.5 m above ground level) and two at second floor level (*c.* 8 m above ground level). The windows at first floor level are similar to those on the west side (0.3 m high × 0.1–0.15 m wide), whilst those on the upper level are larger (0.75 m high × 0.35 m wide). As the wall does not survive to its original height, it is probable that there were other openings of similar size at this height.

The east wall is nearly complete and at the north end appears to stand to its original height, with one crenellation still visible. There is no evidence of a projecting gallery on the east side, although it is possible that there was a projecting gallery higher up (*i.e.* second floor level) which has disappeared. There are six small slit windows in this side, all located at first floor level.

INTERIOR

Ground Floor

Although the entrance façade has disappeared, along with the rest of the south wall of the fort, the vaulted entrance passage has survived. The entrance is located exactly in the middle of the south wall and is covered with a slightly pointed vault made of small flat slabs of limestone, covered in orange/buff coloured plaster.

The entrance leads into a square courtyard (12.5 m per side) paved with limestone slabs. In the middle of the courtyard, in line with the entrance, there is a tall rectangular structure (3.1 m long × 2.5 m wide × 1.9 m high) built over a deep well (minimum 10 m deep). Access to the well is either, through a small doorway on the east side of the structure, or via two holes in the roof. The roof is reached by a set of stairs (0.7 m wide) on the north side, which butt against the rest of the structure (*i.e.* they are not bonded in).

There are 9 rooms arranged around the interior of the courtyard (not including the entrance). The two rooms either side of the entrance, are in a ruinous, unroofed condition. Each room was covered with a barrel-vault aligned east–west. The room to the west of the entrance has the remains of two transverse arches that are not bonded to the main vault and are probably secondary.

On the west side of the courtyard there are two *iwans* (open vaults) either side of a doorway giving access to a small, square, vaulted room. The east range is a mirror image of the west side, with two *iwans*, either side of a central room entered through a doorway.

The south side of the courtyard is dominated by a double set of stairs leading up to the first floor. The stairs rest on a series of three arches, two of which are small recesses (now knocked through), whilst the largest arch in the centre contains a doorway leading into a single, long, vaulted chamber (21.95 m long × 3.73 m wide).

First Floor

The first floor has been very badly ruined so that complete rooms only survive on the southern side of the courtyard, with the exception of one small section of wall, directly over the gateway (see below), containing a large rectangular window (1.20 m high × 0.6 m wide) facing into the courtyard. The interior of the projecting gallery (now destroyed) is set into a recess (1 m deep), covered with an arch made from basalt beams laid edge to edge.

The southern range of the first floor contains six barrel-vaulted rooms, three either side of a central *iwan*. The *iwan* is also roofed with a barrel-vault and contains a plain *mihrab* in the centre of the south wall. An inscription in this room, now lost, recorded the construction of the fort in 1760 (see History above and Chapter 11).

There are no traces of rooms on the east or west sides, although there are projecting corbels that may have supported a parapet walk. In the south-east corner there is a set of stairs leading to the upper floor and the parapet walk.

Although most of the north side of the fort has disappeared, there is evidence for at least one room on the first floor; a small section of wall above the entrance containing a large rectangular window (1.2 m high × 0.6 m wide) facing into the courtyard (see Fig. 30).

Second Floor

The only extant remains of the upper floor are on the south side where two gun slits can be seen. By analogy with other forts it is unlikely that there were rooms on this level, though the flat roofs on the south and north sides would have been connected by a parapet walk (wooden?) supported on stone corbels. There may also have been a projecting gallery, or machicolation, at this level on the east side.

Photographic Evidence and Reconstruction (Plates 59–61)

Two photographs of the interior of the fort, taken less than 10 years apart, give an indication of the rapid disintegration of the building and of subsequent repairs. Comparison of the two photographs also allows us to reconstruct something of the original appearance of the fort, as well as its structural history.

A photograph (Plate 60) taken by Brünnow and Domaszewski in 1898 (1905, 17, fig. 571) shows the interior of the fort, looking north towards the entrance and the north-east corner. The photograph shows the surviving large window above the entrance, with three doors to the right (east) and at least one door to the left (west). It is likely that the range of rooms was symmetrical and that there were also three doors (rooms) to the right (west) of the central window. The photograph also shows that the front (north) wall of the fort was capped with crenellations, with small gun slits at regular intervals. It is also noticeable that the north-east corner of the fort has collapsed, or been destroyed, and the room in the north-east corner is lacking a roof.

Less than 10 years later, Jaussen and Savignac (1997, fig. 34) visited the fort, taking a photograph (Plate 61) from an almost identical position. This photograph shows the existing rectangular windows and two doorways to the right (east). However, in this photograph the corner room has disappeared and the north-east corner and part of the east wall has been rebuilt.

The Reservoir (Fig. 23)

The reservoir is a fairly small structure (20.35 m east–west × 20.3 m north–south) lying 48 m east of the fort. The walls of the reservoir (0.75 m thick) are made of squared limestone blocks and lined with plaster. In the north-west corner there is a set of steps running downwards into the reservoir, along the west wall. Further along, near the top of the west wall there is a small opening, or inlet (0.25 cm wide). The inlet to the reservoir is connected by an underground channel to the fort, where it is fed by the well in the centre of the courtyard. The photograph by Jaussen and Savignac (Plate 61) shows a wooden device (*nourria*) for lifting water out of the well and into the cistern via the subterranean channel.

Road and Bridge (Figs 20, 24 and 25, Plates 56–58 and 73–74)

Hasa is an unusual site on the Darb al-Hajj because it is associated with a stretch of metalled road over 3 km long, which passes to the west of the fort (nearest point 82 m). The road is made of flint and basalt cobbles, set within rectangular panels, edged with squared limestone blocks. The road width varies, but is generally over 10 m wide. In places there are storm drains running diagonally underneath the road.

Approximately 400 m to the north-west of the fort, the road crosses the Wadi al-Hasa via a bridge (30 m long × 12 m wide). The bridge is supported on two large central arches and a smaller arch to the north. The bridge is currently in a ruinous condition and the central pier has fallen. The surface of the bridge is of similar construction to the road, whilst the structure itself is made of rubble and mortar, with an ashlar facing.

The arches are constructed in a similar way to the fort, that is, large flat stones laid face to face. The two large arches have a span of 3.95 m, whilst the smaller arch to the north has a span of 2 m. Whereas the two main arches run perpendicular to the direction of the road, the smaller arch runs diagonally (*c.* 22°) underneath the road. The angle of this arch may suggest that it was designed to drain a tributary wadi.

Discussion

One of the most interesting aspects of the fort at al-Hasa is the extensive evidence for Hajj related structures built in the vicinity, noted by MacDonald (1988) and subsequently destroyed by modern agricultural work. In particular, the large enclosure mentioned above and the series of rectangular stone building complexes, which have been interpreted as structures providing services to the pilgrims. In addition, ash mounds with large quantities of bones and ceramics indicate the presence of a Hajj camp (MacDonald 1988, 280).

The sequence of Ottoman constructions at al-Hasa is quite clear; the bridge was built sometime between 1730 and 1733, followed 30 years later, in 1760, by the construction of the fort. The main question concerning the site of Qal'at al-Hasa is the nature and extent of previous Roman remains on the site. Brünnow and von Domaszewski (1905, 17) were of the opinion that both the road and bridge were Roman constructions, whereas Jaussen and Savignac (1997, 30–32) believe both to have been built during the Islamic period, though with possible Roman predecessors. The similarity of this road to that at Mudawwara, plus the documentary evidence, indicates that both are Ottoman constructions, perhaps utilizing earlier Roman material from the site. Significantly, the Wadi al-Hasa Archaeological Survey, based primarily on ceramic evidence, dates all three features, fort, road and bridge to the Ottoman period (MacDonald 1988).

Qal'at 'Unaiza – (Map 5, No. 8) (Figs 26–30, Plates 80–88) see also Chapters 12, 13 and 14

(Khan 'Unaiza, Anneze, 'Unayza)
Location: 30.29N 35.47E
This site stands on the central Jordan plateau, at a height

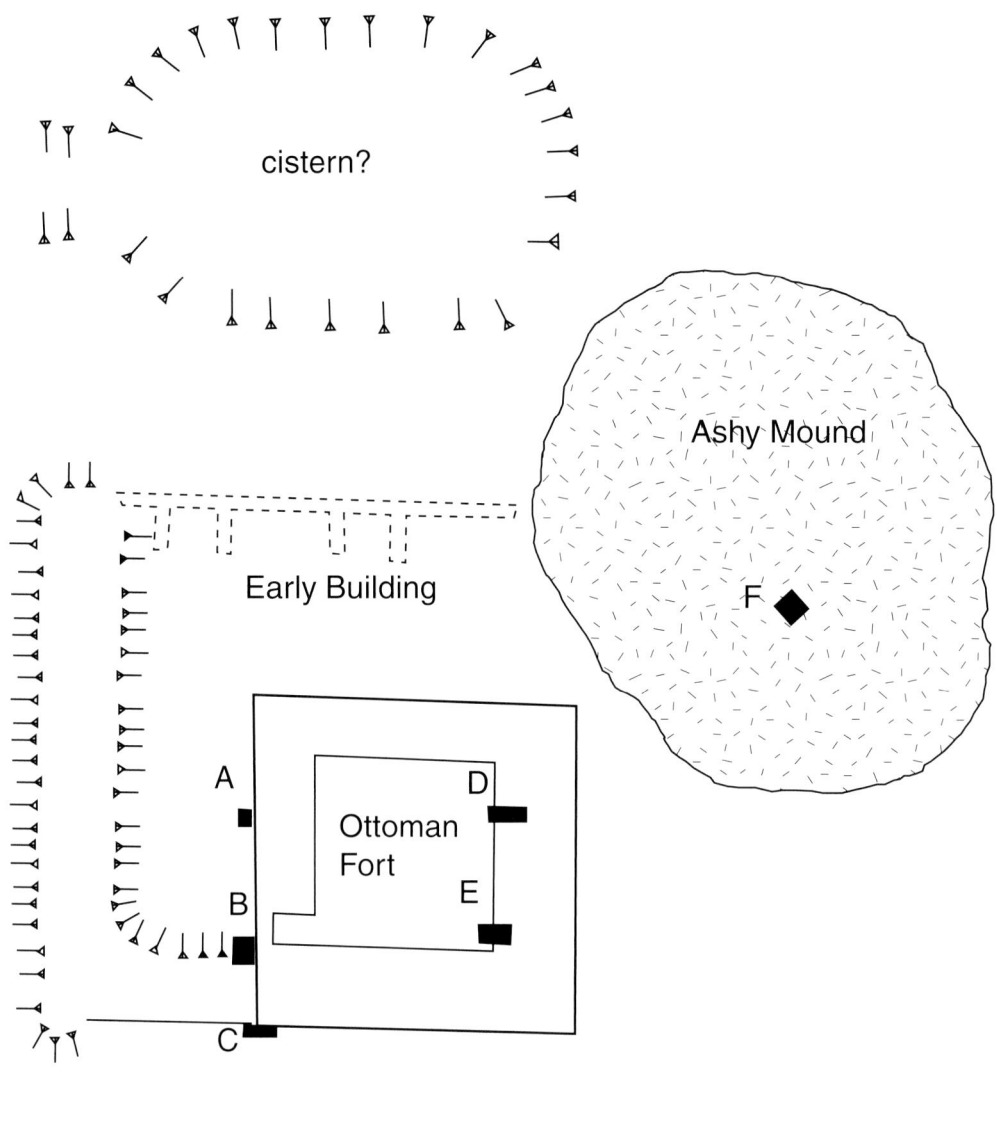

cistern?

Ashy Mound

F

Early Building

A   D

Ottoman Fort

B   E

C

0   20m

Fig. 26. Location plan of Ottoman fort and early building at 'Unaiza in Jordan.

Plate 80. Qal'at 'Unaiza, with entrance from east (1986).

Plate 81. Qal'at 'Unaiza, from west with remains of early building in foreground (1986).

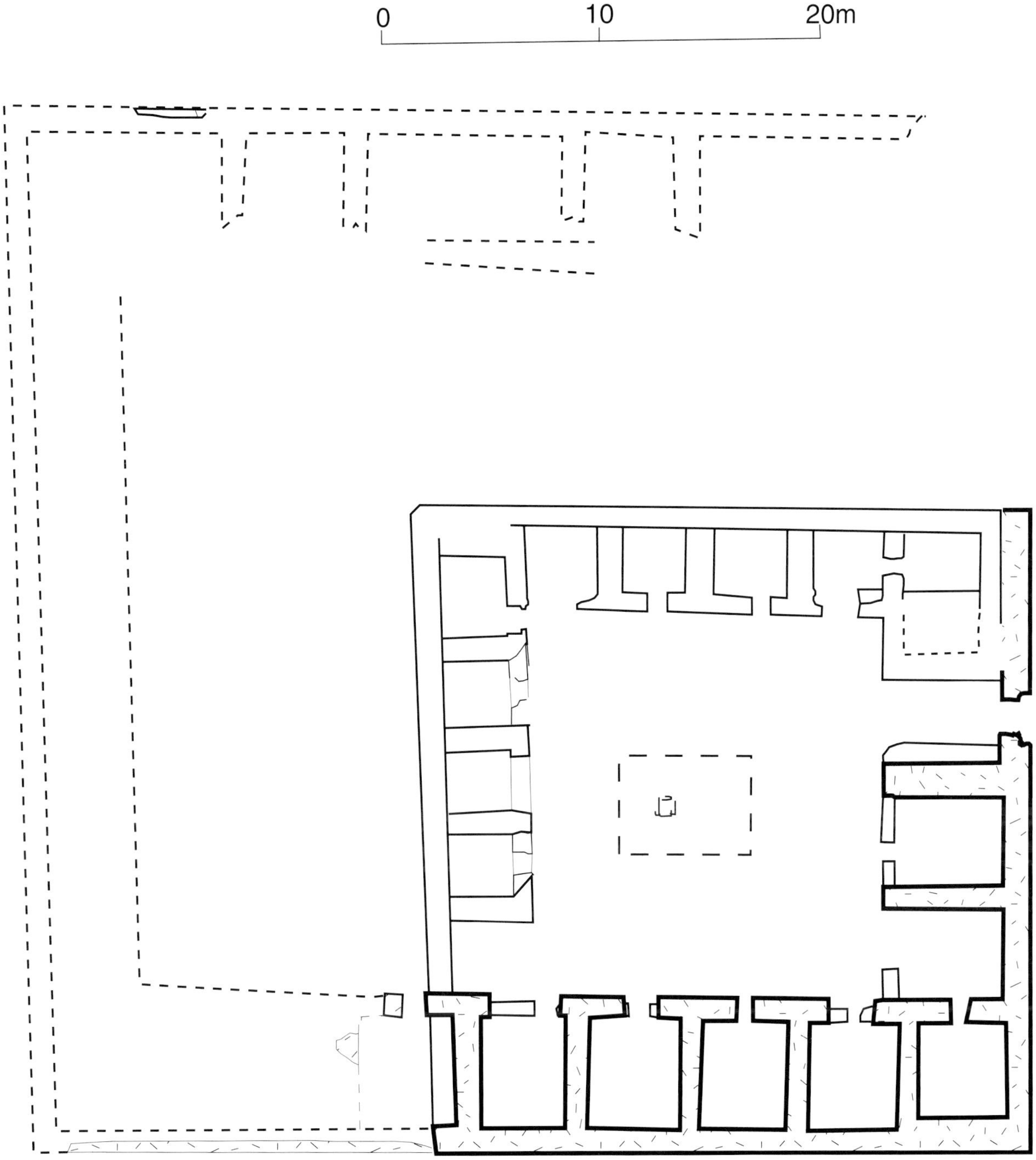

Fig. 27. Plan of Ottoman building in relation to early building at 'Unaiza in Jordan.

Plate 82. Qal'at 'Unaiza, north side (1986).

Plate 83. Qal'at 'Unaiza, south side (1986).

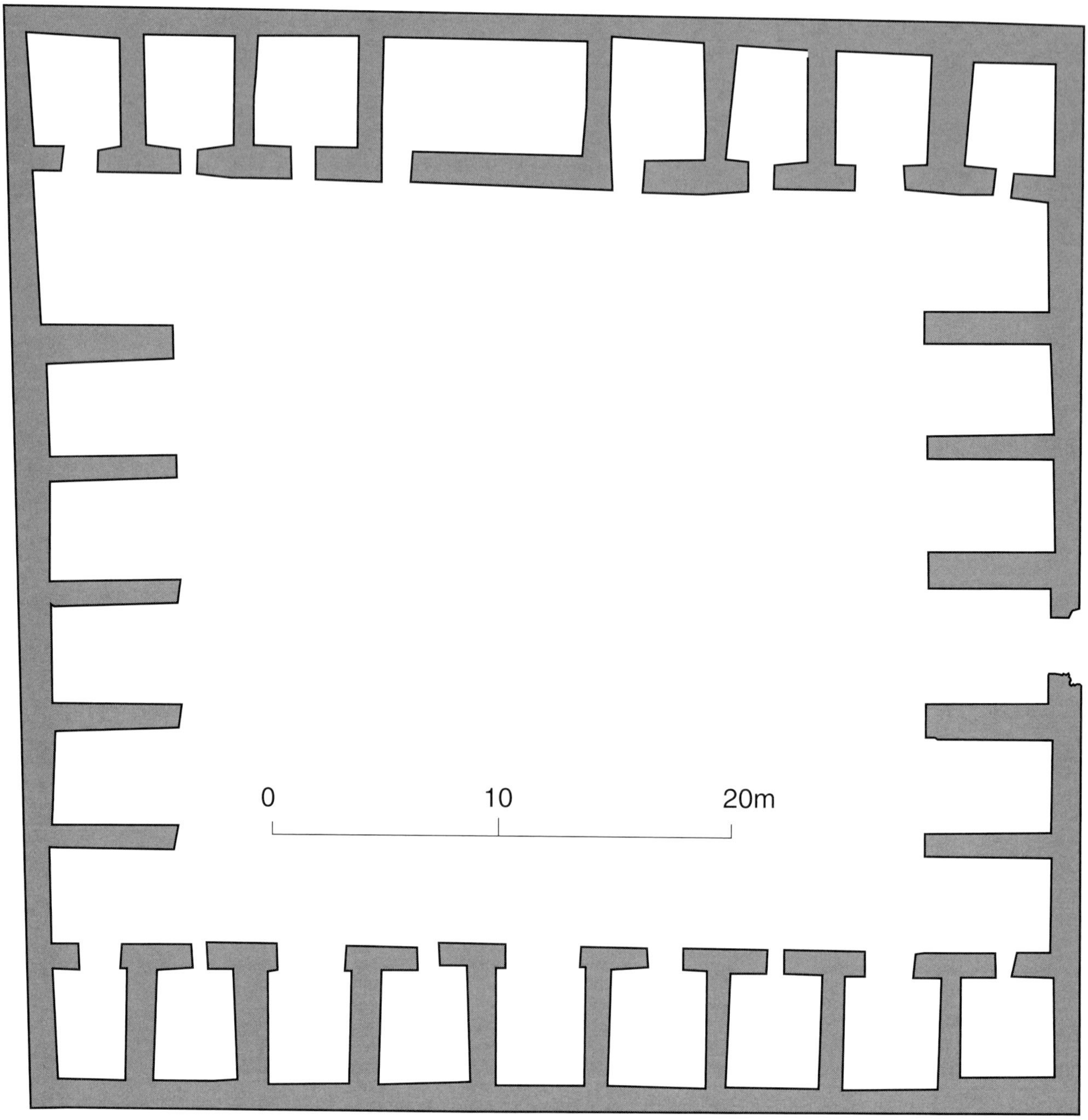

Fig. 28. Reconstruction of early building at 'Unaiza in Jordan.

Plate 84. Qal'at 'Unaiza, detail of projecting opening on exterior of south wall (1986).

Plate 85. Qal'at 'Unaiza, interior with entrance looking east (1986).

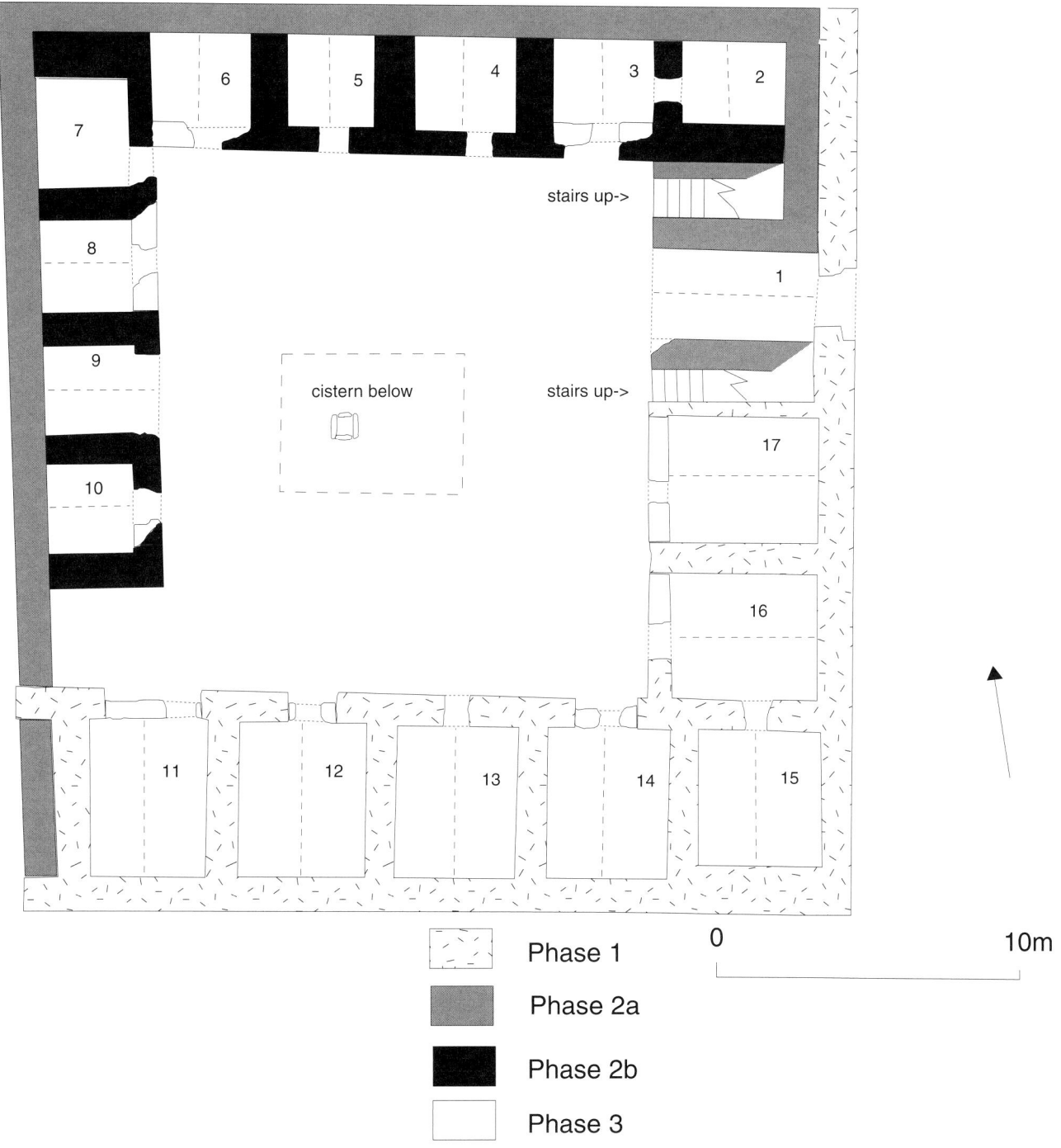

Fig. 29. 'Unaiza, Jordan. Ottoman fort plan of ground floor with phases of construction indicated.

of *c.* 1,000 m above sea level. Four hundred metres to the east is Mahattat 'Unaiza, one of the stations on the Hijaz railway. The Desert Highway runs 300 m to the east of the site. The bed of Wadi Abu Souffan, which runs east towards Qa' al Jafr, can be seen 300 m to the south. The nearest modern settlement is the village of Hashimiyya, located approximately 3 km to the north. The landscape of this area is dominated by Jabal 'Unaiza (1,144 m above sea level), an extinct volcano, located 2 km to the west of the fort, which has covered the surrounding area in a thin layer of basalt.

History

It seems likely that there was a Roman presence at the site, as early as the 2nd century, in the form of a caravanserai that may have been associated with the *Via Militaris* (Findlater 2002, 140–42; see also Chapter 12 in this volume). This early building was almost certainly connected to the nearby fort at Da'ajaniyya (Kennedy 2000, 160–63). There is, however, no evidence of any later occupation at the site until the 16th century.

In 1563 (971 AH) Mustapha Pasha lists the site of

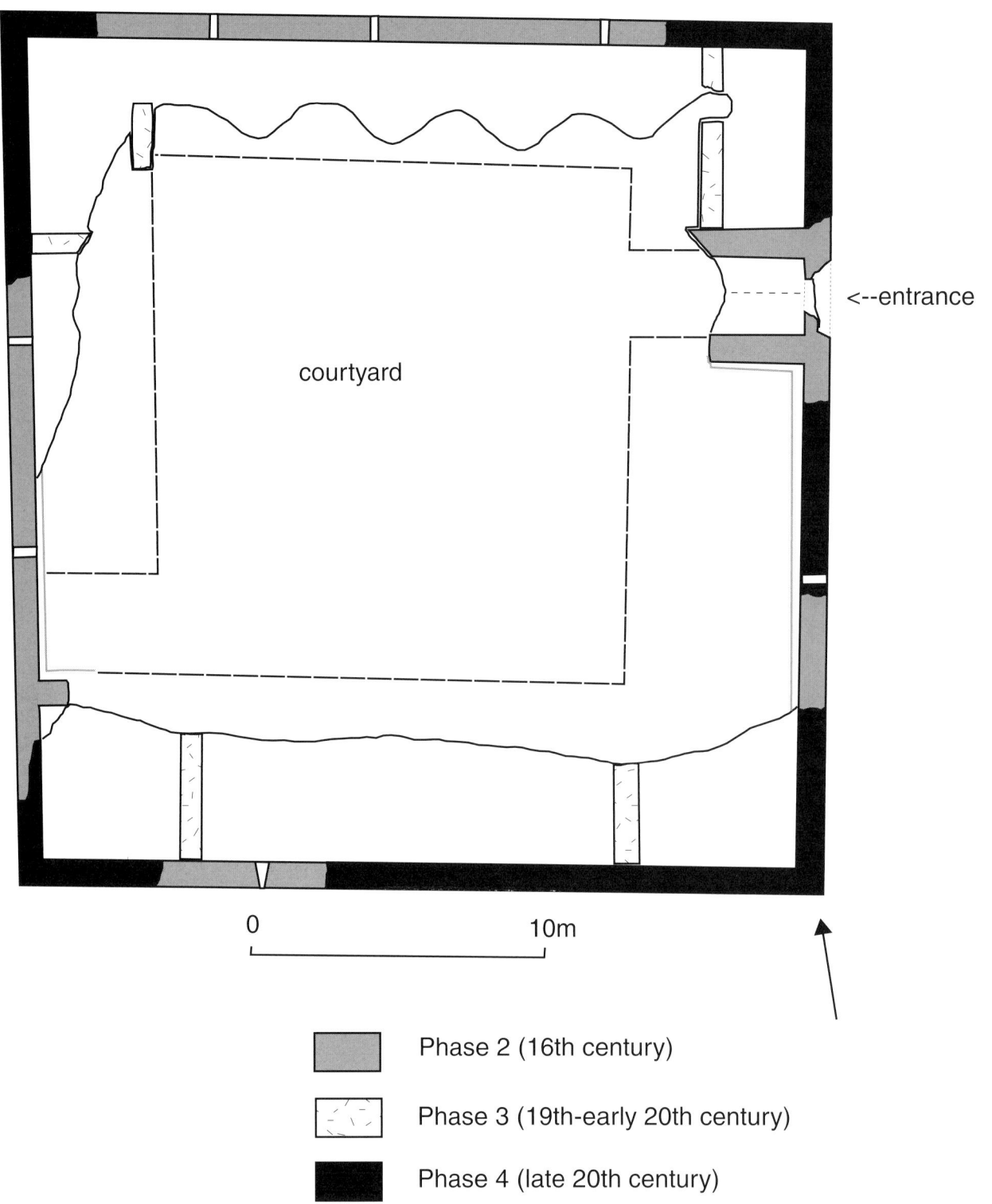

<--entrance

courtyard

0   10m

Phase 2 (16th century)

Phase 3 (19th-early 20th century)

Phase 4 (late 20th century)

Fig. 30. 'Unaiza, Jordan. Ottoman fort plan of first floor with phases indicated.

Khan 'Unaiza (خان عنيزة) between Hasa (حسا) and Ma'an (معان) (al-Jasir 1969, 184–85). It is not clear whether this is the Ottoman fort which still stands, or the remains of the Roman caravanserai which may have been re-used in the first years of Ottoman rule. However, Barbir, following Mehmed Edib, suggests that the fort was built in, or soon after, 1576, by Sulayman Pasha who was also responsible for the construction of a fort at Hadiyya (Barbir 1980, 135; Bianchi 1825, 126). In any case the fort is mentioned by Katip Çelebi (d. 1656) indicating that it was built before the early 17th century, probably during the reign of Murad III (r. 1574–95).

When Evliya Çelebi visited the fort in 1672, he described it as being located in a desolate area with neither villages, nor towns. Unfortunately he gives no description of the fort itself. Whilst at this stop, there was a dispute between Husayn Pasha, the Governor of Damascus and leader of the Hajj Caravan, and the Bedouin of the Wahidat, 'Anayza and Bani Zuhd tribes, over the payment of *sürre* (Trk. Lit. purse = financial subsidy). Several thousand Bedouin were encamped on the nearby mountain (presumably Jabal 'Unaiza) and demanded a payment of 10,000 *kurush*, instead of the 700 offered by the Pasha. One of the Janissaries, a native of Nablus, agreed to negotiate on behalf of the Pasha and stated that if the Bedouin were to receive any payments, they would also have to keep their part of the bargain which included supplying the pilgrims with provisions and water. However, negotiations broke down, with the Bedouin mistrusting the Ottomans, believing that they would be imprisoned if they negotiated in person (Evliya Çelebi, *Seyhatnâmesi* IX, 295; Kortepeter 1979, 237–38; Bilge 1979, 218; Peeters 1994, 373, n. 51).

In 1709, Murtarda ibn 'Alawan arrived at 'Unaiza, carrying water from Hasa because of the heat of the sun. He describes 'Unaiza as a spacious building, larger than expected, well maintained and not in a ruinous condition.

Plate 86. Qal'at 'Unaiza, north side of entrance with plaster decoration visible (1986).

Plate 87. Qal'at 'Unaiza, interior looking west (1986).

Plate 88. Qal'at 'Unaiza, interior looking south (1986).

He states that it was owned by the Bani 'Idha in order to impress people with their power. However, there was no one there to help them with firewood – extremely important in the desert (Murtada b. 'Ali b. 'Alawan MS fol. 104a). The good condition of the fort appears to have been maintained; in 1736–37 minor repairs to 'Unaiza and Hadiyya only cost 600 *kuruş* (Barbir 1980, 139; BA-Cevdet/Askeri 29247).

In 1779 Mehmed Edib visited 'Unaiza which he described as being 18 hours from Hasa, with a fort and reservoir built by Sulayman Pasha – probably the same Sulayman Pasha who built the fort at Hadiyya in 1576. Edib describes this as a difficult place, with very little water, which meant that the escort had to leave the caravan to procure more water sources. Edib also mentions a road leading towards Shobak and its gardens.

In the early 19th century 'Unaiza was inspected by engineers working for Muhammad 'Ali Pasha. They describe the fort as a large square building (50 × 50 cubits) standing next to a cistern of the same size. The interior of the fort, including the gateway and rooms, were described as being in a ruinous condition and this, combined with the fact that it was only half a day's journey to Ma'an, led the inspectors to assert that this stop was not used by pilgrims. However, they indicate the importance of restoring this building as its remote location meant that it would be essential to have water here during a hot summer (Appendix 1 in this volume).

It is possible that Burckhardt visited 'Unaiza at about the same time as Muhammad 'Ali's inspectors, though his cursory description suggests that he had not seen it (Burckhardt 1822, appendix III, 659). Doughty, on the other hand, appears to have visited 'Unaiza at least twice, once in 1874 and again in 1875 when he was on the Hajj. He describes the place as follows:

> '*Kellat Anezy* where is but a cistern for rain water, kept by two lubbers, sons of old Damascene tower guards and of Shobek mothers; but commonly they live at home in their village. My pilgrimage companions would hardly believe me that I had drunk after rain the year before of this birket, they had never found any water there' (Doughty 1979, 68).

Twenty years later, in 1896, Gray Hill visited the fort on his way to Petra after hearing a report that there was water in the cistern. Whilst there he enjoyed, 'the warmth of a great bonfire of scrub gathered by our men' and the view of a fine black mountain [Jabal 'Unaiza] (Gray Hill 1897, 42). The following year, on 19th March 1897, the German scholars Brünnow and von Domaszewski followed the Hajj route north from Ma'an and reached 'Unaiza after a journey of 5 hours and 53 minutes. They described Kal'at 'Aneze as a 'Modernes türkisches Kastell' three minutes to the west of the Hajj route. To the east of the Hajj route they noted a walled cistern filled with water, which may be identical to the cistern within the compound of the railway station (Brünnow and Domaszewski 1905).

In the early 1900s (between 1908 and 1916) a railway station was established to the east of the Ottoman fort. In 1916 it became the terminus of a 36 km branch line leading to Shobek, from where wood was collected to fuel the engines of the Hijaz railway. Between 1922 and 1923 the line was pulled up, though its course is still visible in the modern road (Peake Pasha 1958, 97 and 146 n. 46).

In May 1928 the fort was visited by the North Arabian Desert Expedition, they noted the presence of a ruined fort and two large reservoirs, which were attributed to the work of Sulayman Pasha. Nearby were the black tents of the Howetat, camped either side of the railway line. Outside the fort they found 'an old battered military water flask' which they associated with the campaigns of T. E. Lawrence. Within the fort they noted the cistern and two Turkish shells 'of which only one was exploded' (Field 1960, 82–83).

In 1972 the Jordanian Antiquities Department registered 'Unaiza as an Antiquities Site and made a basic survey of the fort, including a photograph (Anon. 1972). In the late 1990s the fort was included in the Dana Archaeological Survey, which identified the pre-Ottoman building at the site as 'another large classical site on an ancient road that leads to the Ma'an oasis' (Findlater 2002, 140–41 and 148, fig. 2). In 2001 the Ministry of Planning, in co-operation with the Department of Antiquities, began a project to restore and rebuild the fort, both to preserve it as a local heritage site and to provide local employment. Of particular importance was the rebuilding of the entrance and the provision of a new gateway to prevent further damage occurring to the building (Abdel Azzez, Tahani al-Salhi and Ebraheem al-Khreasheh 2002; Department of Antiquities 2004).

Description

Exterior

The site comprises the Ottoman fort and a number of associated walls belonging to an earlier building (Fig. 26). There is also a large depression to the north of the fort, which may originally have been a reservoir. The modernization of the desert highway during the 1980s has altered much of the landscape in the area; few other ancient features are visible.

The Ottoman fort is a roughly square building (27.2 m × 28 m) built of black basalt with white creamy limestone used for the quoins (these have mostly been robbed out and replaced with other stones in the restoration carried out in 2003) and standing to a maximum height of 8.25 m. This is the largest of the Ottoman forts in Jordan and several features indicate that the design of the fort was adapted to a pre-existing structure (see below).

The east side, facing the desert highway, contains the gateway, located north of centre (Plate 80). Unfortunately the sides of the gateway have been robbed of all dressed stone and it is not, therefore, possible to reconstruct its precise original form (between 2003 and 2005 the gateway was reconstructed and a new gate inserted, see Kennedy and Petersen 2004, 13). By analogy with the other forts it is likely that there was some form of machicolation above the entrance.

Much of the south wall was rebuilt in October 2001 on new foundations, which project 0.5 m. from the exterior face of the wall. As recently as 1986 the south wall was mostly complete, with three stepped crenellations visible at the top and a small machicolation projecting from the wall at first floor level (see Petersen 1989, 110, fig. 15 (which is incorrectly described as the north face)). The other notable feature of the south wall is a series of eight rectangular windows, located high up at ground floor level (Plate 83). This is a unique feature, which does not occur at any of the other Hajj forts. There are traces of walls perpendicular to the south wall of the fort, these are probably of Ottoman date (later than the fort) and are made of basalt blocks set in mud mortar.

The west side of the fort overlies and incorporates part of an earlier building (see below). Besides the traces of an earlier building this wall contains few features of any interest, with the exception of two small, square openings visible at first floor level (Plate 81).

The north wall also stands to its full original height in several places, with the remains of, at least, two stepped crenellations still visible (Plate 82). At the east end of the wall there are two projecting corbels below a large rectangular hole. It is probable that these corbels supported a small machicolation, similar to that on the south wall, which has now disappeared.

Interior

GROUND FLOOR

The interior comprises a large central courtyard, with vaulted rooms built around each side. The entrance (Room 1) is located at the north end of the east wall and comprises a large barrel passageway leading directly into the courtyard. The vault is coated with plaster and decorated with a simple motif comprising a band of interlaced semi-circles, below a band of triangles. Unusually there are no benches either side of the entrance passage, though there may have been small seats outside the entrance, as at Qal'at Dab'a/Balqa' (Petersen 1986, plate l2A) and Tabuk (Jaussen and Savignac 1997, 59, fig. 43). The courtyard is larger than at the other Hajj forts and was paved with basalt cobbles, set in lime mortar. Approximately in the centre of the courtyard, there is a vaulted subterranean cistern with a single manhole in the roof (this was in a ruinous condition in 1986, repaired 2003–5). The cistern is fed by a drain/channel running from the south-west corner of the courtyard.

The north range comprises a group of five small vaulted rooms (Rooms 2–6). Room 2 has no direct access to the courtyard and is entered via Room 3. Rooms 4–6 are, more or less, identical square chambers, with a doorway opening onto the courtyard. Unfortunately, the original courtyard façade on the north side has been replaced by a more recent wall, of less skilful construction. However, clearance work carried out in October 2001 exposed the original line of the Ottoman wall, with the positions of the doorways. In one room (Room 7) the original architrave of the doorway is still *in situ* and includes a rectangular recess for the locking mechanism.

The south range (Plate 88) comprises four rooms (Rooms 11–14), each of near identical design, comprising a rectangular area, roofed with a barrel-vault, with two small openings set into the rear (south) wall. Although the rear (external) wall of Rooms 11, 13 and 14 have recently been rebuilt, earlier photographs indicate that the reconstruction is accurate (see, Petersen 1989, 110, fig. 15, which is incorrectly described as the north in the caption). The east range (Plate 85) comprises three rooms (15, 16 and 17), in addition to the vaulted entrance passage described above. Room 15 is reached via a doorway in the side of Room 16 and is shorter than the other vaults on the south and east sides, perhaps to provide additional strength to the corner. Although the vaults of Rooms 16 and 17 have collapsed, it can be seen that they are of similar design and dimensions to those of the south range. The only other features of the east range are two staircases, either side of the entrance vault. Both staircases have deteriorated badly (rebuilt 2003–4), and it is not clear whether they would have been open, or covered with vaults.

FIRST FLOOR

Little remains of the structures on the first floor, partly because the collapse of some of the vaults below has significantly reduced the floor area. The surviving floor surface is similar to that in the courtyard, with small basalt cobbles. The only structure with remains of a roof is the small, vaulted room above the entrance passage. Unfortunately, the west end of the room has been truncated and it is now impossible to tell whether it was originally an open *iwan*, as at Qatrana (Petersen 1989, 102, fig. 3), or was a closed room with a doorway. More importantly, it was not clear whether the access was from one, or both sides. Abutting this room to the north, there are the remains of a north–south wall, which appears to be secondary to the original construction. There are the remains of similar walls in the north-west, south-west, and south-east corners of the fort, perhaps indicating that there was a room in each corner. The thickness of these walls (0.7 m), their relatively clumsy construction and their position in relation to the walls below (*i.e.* not directly above), indicates that they were roofed with wood, mud and plaster, rather than the vaults used elsewhere in the fort. A number of low openings, near floor level, on each side were probably designed for the use of cannon, which would have been mounted on low platforms. It is probable that there was also a wooden gallery above the cobbled surface of the first floor giving access to the upper part of the walls (parapet). Traces of this platform survive in the form of beam sockets and a linear break in the plasterwork, visible on the interior side of the north wall. Evidence of a similar arrangement can be seen at Qal'at al-Hasa, where there are projecting stone corbels and a linear break in the plasterwork (*c.f.* Jaussen and Savignac 1997, 32, fig. 34).

Architectural Phasing

As a result of the architectural survey, a number of observations are possible from which a relative chronology can be defined. First of all, it is notable that the rooms on the north and west differ from those on the south and east according to: a) size, b) method of construction and, c) number of openings.

a)   The east and south rooms are larger (average 5 m × 4 m) than those of the other two sides, which have less than half the floor area (average 2.9 m × 2.9 m).

b)   The vaulting of the south and east sides comprises barrel-vaults springing from the side walls which lean inwards in a smooth curve. The vaults on the north and west sides have a more pointed profile and spring directly from the top of the side walls, which are straight and do not curve inwards to accommodate the vault.

c)   The rooms on the south and east have ventilation slits located near the top of the outside walls, whereas the rooms on the north and west sides have no opening of any kind to the exterior.

These observations form the basis for a relative chronology, the details of which were confirmed by examination of mortar types and physical relationships.

Phase 1 is characterized by the use of blue-grey mortar, vaults springing from incurving walls and walls 1 m thick.

Phase 2a is characterized by grey-white mortar and plaster, built over Phase 1 walls.

Phase 2b is characterized by pointed vaults and white mortar, which overlies phase 1 and 2a structures.

Phase 3 is characterized by roughly coursed, rubble-stone walls, with mud mortar and steel railway sleepers for added strength

Phase 4, the restoration and building project carried out between October 2001 and June 2003, is characterized by hard, pink-white lime mortar and offset concrete foundations on the south side of the fort. Some machine dressed blocks are also used in this phase.

Ottoman Cistern

It is clear from historical accounts that the Ottoman fort stood next to a rain-fed cistern (or cisterns) which would have supplied the needs of the Hajj caravan (Appendix 1 in this volume) (Burckhardt 1882, 661; Doughty 1926, 22; Field 1960, 82–83). By analogy with other forts the reservoir(s) would have been located within 50 m of the fort, however, no definitive location was identified at 'Unaizah.

The most likely location for the cistern is a rectangular depression, aligned east–west, immediately to the north of the remains of the early building. It is evident that the depression is not natural due to the absence of basalt boulders, which elsewhere, cover the landscape. Further support for this theory is provided by the existence of a wide channel (*c.* 2 m wide and 15 m long), which leads into the depression on the west side. It is possible that the stone lining of the cistern was robbed out to provide building stone for the nearby station.

Early Building (Figs 27 and 28)

This is a roughly square enclosure, with a central courtyard and rooms arranged around the sides. Part of the building is visible to the west and north of the Ottoman fort, the rest being incorporated within the fort itself. Parts of the early building integrated within the fort include the eastern end of the south wall, the south-east corner and the southern part of the east wall. It appears that some of the rooms from the early building are preserved, in the Ottoman fort, up to the height of the springing of the vaults (*c.* 2 m above ground level). It also seems likely that the gateway to the Ottoman fort may have formed the entrance to the earlier building, although the vaulted entrance passage is, undoubtedly, of Ottoman construction.

The best preserved parts of the early building, outside the Ottoman fort, are a range of rooms to the west which, although ruinous, form an elongated mound rising nearly 2 m above the surrounding ground level. Although the mound is covered with fallen masonry, the outline of the building is clearly visible and in several places the wall faces are exposed.

On the north side the outline of the building is visible, although the ruins barely rise above the surrounding ground level. Despite this fact, the precise outlines of several rooms can be seen. The only area where there is an absence of remains is in the, presumed, north-east corner. To the west of the early building there are traces of an artificial channel, running east–west and then north–south, connecting to a tributary wadi. The fact that this channel runs directly to the south part, of the west wall, of the early building, indicates that it probably supplied a cistern within the walls (not located).

Discussion

A number of questions present themselves in relation to 'Unaiza, the first concerns the date of construction of the Ottoman fort. Although historical sources indicate that the fort was built in the 16th century the archaeological evidence may indicate a later date. Secondly, the relationship between the Ottoman fort and the earlier Roman building needs clarification, in particular, the date at which the early building was abandoned. Although it is likely that the Roman building was plundered to provide building stones for the Ottoman fort, it is likely that the building of the railway station, in the early 1900s, also employed stones from the ruined Roman building. Unfortunately, there are no photographs of the site before the construction of the railway that give any indication of the condition, of either the fort or the Roman building, prior to the construction of the Hijaz railway. The fact that the site is referred to as Khan 'Uniaza in 1561 (*c.f.* Mustapha Pasha in al-Jasir 1969, 184–85) suggests that the Roman building may have been used as a place for shelter, prior to the building of the fort in 1576.

(For a further discussion of this building see Chapter 12.)

Qal'at Ma'an – (Map 5, No. 9) (Figs 31–34 and Plates 89–97)

Location: 30.11N 35.45E

Ma'an is a district capital, located on the Jordanian plateau, at a height of *c.* 1,000 m, on the border between the desert and cultivated land. The Ottoman fort is located in an urban area, near the modern centre of Ma'an and adjacent to the Wadi Mahatta. The fort has recently been refurbished and is currently used as the local offices of the Department of Antiquities. In addition to the fort itself, associated structures include, a reservoir and a small aqueduct. The area in the immediate vicinity of the fort has recently been landscaped and is now a small park and recreation area. To the south of the fort and along the banks of the Wadi Mahatta, there are a series of semi-dilapidated irrigated palm gardens, enclosed within mud-brick walls and overlooked by small mud-brick towers.

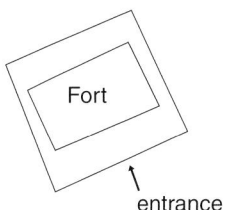

Fig. 31. Ma'an, Jordan. Location plan of fort and cistern.

Plate 89. Qal'at Ma'an, interior of courtyard looking south (1986).

modern entrance

well

<-stairs up

stairs up ->

original entrance

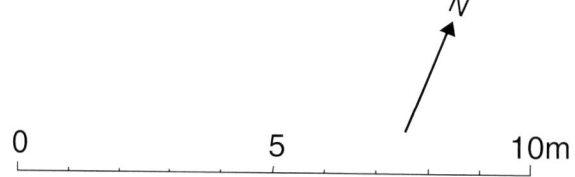

Fig. 32. Ma'an, Jordan. Plan of ground floor of Ottoman fort.

History

The oasis of Ma'an appears to have been an important trading centre before the coming of Islam and in the 1st millennium BC it had a south Arabian colony. There are few direct references to Ma'an during the classical period, probably because at this stage it was overshadowed by the nearby city of Petra (Elisséeff 1965, 897). Archaeological surveys have recovered some diagnostic Roman pottery, but in general this is surpassed by that of later periods (Kennedy

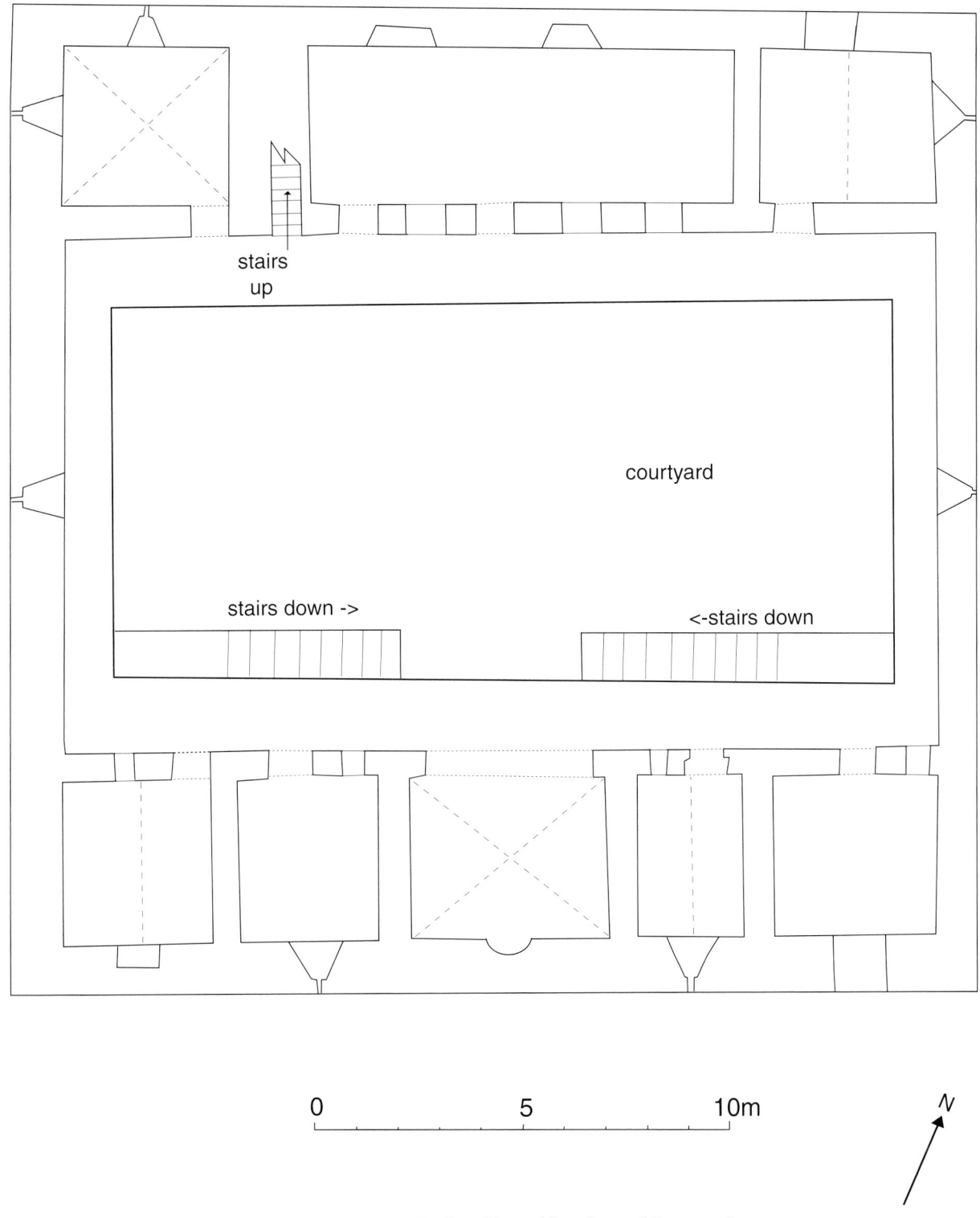

Fig. 33. Ma'an, Jordan. Plan of first floor of Ottoman fort.

1992, 482). However, *Kastron Ammatha* is referred to in the 5th century *Notitia Dignitatum* (ed. Seeck, XXXIV, 33) as the base for a mounted dromedary unit (*Ala Antana dromedariorum*). The town is also mentioned in the Petra Papyri as *Kastron Ammatha* (Gagos and Frösén 1998, 475). Other evidence of a Byzantine presence in Ma'an comes

from early Arabic writers such as al-Bakri, who write that it had a citadel ruled by a governor, Farwa ibn 'Amr, of the south Arabian tribe of Judham. The governor converted to Islam prior to the Muslim conquests and was crucified by the Byzantines as punishment (Musil 1926, 247; Schick 1995, 329–23).

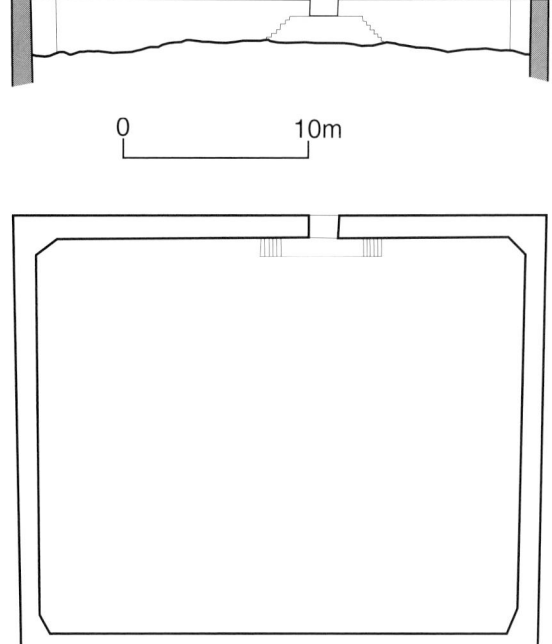

Fig. 34. Ma'an, Jordan. Plan and section of cistern.

Plate 90. Qal'at Ma'an, interior looking north. Note prison bars (1986).

Plate 91. Qal'at Ma'an, detail of decoration above doorway (2006).

Plate 92. Qal'at Ma'an, decoration above doorway (2006).

Plate 93. Qal'at Ma'an, south face with machicolation and original entrance below (2006).

Later on, during the early Islamic period, Ma'an became an important stopping place on the route between Arabia and Syria, thus Muslim soldiers stopped at Ma'an on their way to the battle at Mu'ta. Ibn 'Asakir refers to an Umayyad castle with a green garden (oasis). In the 10th century al-Harbi lists Ma'an as one of the stops between Syria and Mecca (al-Harbi in al-Jasir 1968, 603). Another 10th century writer, al-Maqdisi, refers to Ma'an as one of 6 towns in the Sharah district. In the 11th century al-Istakhri possibly refers to a castle at Ma'an, which he mentions as still being inhabited by the Umayyads and their clients (Schick 1995, 329–30). In addition to the documentary sources, there are significant archaeological remains of the early Islamic period, including a large enclosure, cisterns, an aqueduct and courtyard buildings

Plate 94. Qal'at Ma'an, interior of courtyard looking east (2006).

Plate 96. Qal'at Ma'an, exterior from east (2006).

Plate 95. Qal'at Ma'an, exterior of fort from north (2006).

Plate 97. Qal'at Ma'an, detail of Turkish inscription above entrance (2006).

(for a full description, see Genequand 2003). There are few references to the town in the Medieval period (11th–15th centuries), though in 1326 Ibn Battuta passed through the town, which he described as the last town of Syria (1958, 160) (see Chapter 3 for further references to Ma 'an in the Medieval period).

Ma'an once again became important in the Ottoman period, with the establishment of a fort by Sulayman the Magnificent in 1559 (Bakhit 1982, 98 n. 43 and 223 based on al-Ghazzi, *Kawakib*, vol. ii, 157 and al-Qaramani, *Akhbar*, 440; see also Chapter 11, No. 3 for the foundation inscription). A 16th century description of the Hajj road from Mecca lists Ma'an as one stop after Khan 'Unaiza (Mustapha Pasha in 1563 AD (971 AH); al-Jasir 1969, 184–85). Other sources credit Sulayman with the construction of an aqueduct, as the water within the settlement was not of good quality (Hajji Halfa (*c.* 1732) p. 539, cited in Musil 1926, 247). According to local tradition, as recorded by Peake Pasha, two brothers from Wadi Musa were installed as guardians of the fort. However, due to a quarrel, one of the brothers, Ahmed, returned to Wadi Musa. Several years later Ahmed came back to Ma'an and was able to capture the fort from his brother, Mahmud. However, instead of

leaving Ma'an, Mahmud established his own settlement at a spring nearby. This is given, as an explanation of how Ma'an, came to be divided into two distinct settlements (Peake Pasha 1958, 198).

Unfortunately, there are few contemporary descriptions of Ma'an from the early Ottoman period, though it was visited by Evliya Çelebi in 1672, who states that there was a small square fort, built on a slope, without a moat around it. There were no soldiers at the fort, which was guarded by an iron door. He also noted that the town had three mosques and one bathhouse (Evliya Çelebi, *Seyhatnâmesi* IX, 295–96; Bilge 1979, 218). Ma'an is also included in the itinerary of Murtada ibn 'Alawan in 1709 (Murtada b. 'Ali b. 'Alawan MS fol. 104a). A receipt, dated 1742, shows that the fort was used as a storage depot for barley and indicates that between 1737 and 1742, 78.5 loads of barley were stored there (Barbir 1980, 141, n. 98; TKS-E. 2588/12 and TKS-E. 2588/4). In 1779 Mehmed Edib visited Ma'an after a 12 hour journey from 'Unayza. He noticed two forts, built on hills facing each other, one of which was built by Sulayman the Magnificent. He observed that the town had formerly been called Ma'al and had served as a residence for the Umayyads. The caravan stayed at Ma'an for one day, during which time the caravan attendants and servants were given their wages and tips (*bakshish*). Provisions available included, pomegranates, figs and quinces grown in Ma'an, as well as, oranges and lemons brought from Hebron. Edib also states that the quality of the water within Ma'an was not good and that it was brought, via aqueducts, from springs outside the town. Edib also complains about the quality of the roads leading in and out of the town, stating that they become particularly treacherous during wet weather (Bianchi 1825, 127–28; see also Musil 1926, 248).

The first European description of Ma'an is given by Burckhardt, who visited the town in 1812. He states that the town is divided into two settlements by the Hajj road, the eastern part is called Shamie and the western part is called Ma'an (Burckhardt 1822, appendix III, 658–59). He observes that although the inhabitants grow fruit, they are not able to cultivate wheat and barley and must buy these from other settlements in the area. He gives a vivid description of the commerce of Ma'an during the Hajj:

> 'The inhabitants have scarcely any other means of subsistence than the profits which they gain from the pilgrims in their way to and from Mekka, by buying up all kinds of provisions at Hebron and Ghaza, and selling them with great profit to the weary pilgrims; to whom the gardens and vineyards of Maan are no less agreeable, than the wild herbs collected by the people of Maan are to their camels' (Burckhardt 1822, chapter 6).

In addition to being a centre of commerce Burckhardt also states that Ma'an was a centre for religious scholarship and that the town had a high degree of literacy. He was concerned that the discontinuation of the Hajj, because of hostilities between the Wahabis and Muhammad 'Ali of Egypt, would lead to Ma'an being abandoned as a settlement.

Muhammad 'Ali was certainly concerned about the viability of the Hajj route and a few years later he commissioned a survey of the route, which included a description of Ma'an. The report noted the two settlements built either side of the road and inhabited by settled Bedouin. Although the report mentions a rectangular cistern (35 × 25 cubits) between the two settlements, it does not mention the fort built by Sulayman (Appendix 1 in this volume).

Towards the end of the 19th century Ma'an was visited by a number of European travellers, including Wallin in 1845, Doughty in 1875 and Gray Hill 1896. Wallin states that Ma'an was one of the largest settlements on the Hajj route, with a population of 200 families, divided into seven clans. From this population they were able to produce a force of between 150 and 300 armed men, able to defend the settlement against the Bedouin. Nevertheless, the Bedouin had a good relationship with the town and prefered to obtain their provisions from Ma'an, because the merchants there were willing to extend them credit. However, the mainstay of the town's economy was the Hajj caravan and associated market. Wallin states that Ma'an was entirely dependant

on the four days of each year when the caravan was in the town and during which time it presented 'the aspect of the most stirring and crowded fair in Europe.' (Wallin 1850/1854, 121–24).

Thirty years later Doughty stopped at Ma'an whilst travelling with the Hajj caravan to Medain Saleh. Doughty's account focuses on a physical description of the town and includes a sketch map showing the layout of the two settlements (Ma'an and Shemmia) and the location of the Hajj camp. He states that Ma'an is a *merkez*, or rest station, of the Hajj road where the pilgrims would stay for a number of days. He states that 'Ma'an .... began to be colonized, they say, in the last three centuries; when here, upon an old ruined site, was founded a principal Haj station about the kella, made by Sultan Selim, a benefactor and builder upon the pilgrimage road'. Later on he says that 'the good masonry has been broken up for stones to build the kella (fort)'. In addition to the fort, there was also, at Shemmia, a barracks for a cavalry detachment; this had recently been established, but was soon abandoned. He also noted that there was a warehouse at Ma'an where heavy goods and other possessions, not required on the next part of the journey, could be deposited.

When Gray Hill visited Ma'an in 1896 he was taken 'between mudbrick walls and unfriendly glances, to a large stone house, which is well built apparently out of older materials and recently restored, and is used as a Serai'. From this description it is apparent that this building was probably the barracks for the cavalry detachment, seen by Doughty 21 years earlier.

A few years later, in 1897 and 1898, the ruins of Ma'an were investigated by German scholars, Brünnow and von Domaszewski, in search of Roman antiquities (Brünnow and von Domaszewski 1905, II, 1–6). Their attention focused on the ruins at al Hammam, which were regarded as a Roman military site, though it is now generally accepted that the majority of these ruins belong to the Umayyad period (Kennedy 2000, 174; Genequand 2003). The attention of Jaussen and Savignac was also drawn to the ruins of al-Hammam and a nearby ancient cemetery (Jaussen and Savignac 1997, 34–43). However, they showed less interest in the later remains and it appears that they mistook the late Ottoman barracks at al-Shammia for the Hajj fort (Lawrence 1926, 128 and 129).

Description

The Fort

The fort was still used as a government prison as late as 1983 (see for example Plate 90). During the initial fieldwork campaign, in 1986, the building still retained many modern features from use as a jail. During this time the police retained control of the fort, so access to the interior of the building was very limited. Fortunately its current use as a Department of Antiquities Office meant that we were given full and free access to the building, as well as copies of reports relating to the conservation work carried out since 1986.

EXTERIOR

The fort is nearly an exact square, measuring 23.6 m per side and standing over 9 m high. The current main entrance to the fort is on the north side, through a modern rectangular doorway that has been knocked through the wall of the fort (*i.e.* it was not part of the original design). During the 1986 survey the main entrance was accessed via a modern (concrete block) annex on this side of the fort. The annex comprised a small rectangular courtyard, with a two storey building on the west side and single storey block to the east (this annex was removed after 1994). There was no connection between the annex and the fort, except through the gateway.

In addition to the modern doorway, the north face of the fort has four openings, all located at a height of more than 4 m above ground level (Plate 95). The openings are arranged symmetrically, in the centre, above the modern doorway, there are two long slits (1.29 m or three courses high) with splayed bases. At the west end, near the corner, there is a long straight slit (*i.e.* no splayed base). At the east end of the wall there is a large rectangular window of similar height to the gun/arrow slits, though much wider. In 1986 this window still contained iron bars from its use as a prison, but these have now been removed. It is probable that this window (0.7 m wide × 1.4 m high) is an enlargement of an earlier arrow slit and that the dimensions correspond to the original recess for the arrow slit.

At a higher level, above the arrow slits, there are stone rainspouts, most of which appear to be of fairly modern manufacture. The one exception is a rainspout near the rectangular window, which is partially broken and appears to be older.

The west wall of the fort is very plain and contains only one slit window (1.05 m high × 0.1 m wide) with a splayed base. At the south end of the wall there is, what appears to be, a buttress (2.1 m long) projecting 0.2 m from the main line of the wall. Near the top of the wall are the broken remains of two stone rainspouts and traces of large rectangular crenellations.

The east wall of the fort (Plate 96) is completely blank, except for one plain arrow slit and a stone block, which has a cup carved onto it.

The south wall is the most interesting, as it contains the original 16th century gateway (Plate 93). During the 1986 survey this gateway was blocked with a stone wall. Since the restoration of the fort, in the mid-late 1990s, the doorway has been unblocked and is now used as an additional entrance. The gateway (2.1 m high × 1.4 m wide) is covered with a large dressed stone lintel, with no decoration, though directly above, there are three separate blocks each containing carved decoration in relief (Plates 91–92). The lowest of the blocks contains a concave disc (0.2 m diameter) in the form of a flower, with a central boss

and five overlapping layers of petals. Directly above this there is an inscription, divided into eight cartouches, in four horizontal bands (Plate 97) (see discussion in Chapter 11 in this volume). The third and highest block has the most complex decoration, based on a central motif of a multiple petalled flower, similar to that on the lowest block (Plate 92). This flower is contained within an eight-pointed star, formed from two intersecting squares. On each side of this central decoration are pairs of small, disc shaped motifs, set one above the other. On the right side, a swirled sun wheel sits above a six-pointed flower, while to the left a six-pointed star sits above a sun wheel.

There are four windows, or openings, on the south side of the fort mirroring the arrangement on the north face. On this side it appears that three of the arrow/gun slits have been converted to rectangular windows, leaving only one, to the left (west) of the doorway, which has a splayed base.

Directly above the doorway, at roof height, there is a large projecting machicolation (1.5 m wide, projecting 0.65 m from the face of the wall). The machicolation is supported on three two-tier supports and has a small window/slit in the south face (Plate 93). The machicolation is surmounted by a carved stone representation of the Hashemite coat of arms (*c.f.* Aqaba fort). Also at roof height there are three projecting water-spouts (two to the left and one to the right of the machicolation), which, though damaged, appear to be original.

INTERIOR

The inside of the fort is based around a central rectangular courtyard (7.4 m × 18.5 m). During the 1986 survey there were two modern, one storey blocks/cells, one at either end of the courtyard, which have been removed since 1994 (the beginning of the restoration programme). All of the rooms in the fort are either on the north, or south sides of the courtyard and are symmetrically arranged, with four rooms on each side, set either side of a central *iwan* (Fig. 32). The rooms either side of the entrance, are reached through doorways in the side of the *iwan*, whereas all the other rooms are entered via doorways facing the courtyard. Each of the rooms on the ground floor is covered with a barrel-vault and most have windows facing into the courtyard.

The upper floor is reached via two sets of open staircases, which ascend either side of the (original) entrance *iwan* on the south side (Plate 94). The arrangement of the ground floor is repeated on the first floor, although here modern alterations have altered the original configuration. On the south side of the first floor there are five rooms (Rooms 11–15), three with a rectangular window (11, 12 and 14) and one (14) with an original arrow slit set within a splayed recess. The central room, or *iwan*, is covered with a cross-vault and contains a *mihrab* in the middle of the south wall. The north side of the first floor contains three rooms (16, 17 and 18) two of which (16 and 18) are corner rooms, each with two windows/openings one in each external face. The central room (17) is a long area, covered with a flat (concrete?) roof, with two splayed openings for arrow slits in the north wall. It is likely that this central room is an entirely modern construction and that it was originally open to the sky. At the east end of this room is a set of stairs leading up to the roof. The north and the south ranges are connected by narrow walkways, each of which contains a splayed opening for an arrow slit.

The upper floor of the building comprises a flat roof and there is little trace of machicolations or a parapet.

Reservoir (Fig. 34)

To the south-west of the fort there is a small rectangular reservoir (internally 19.52 × 25.29 m.). Five metres from the south-west corner there is a shallow break (0.8 m wide) in the wall, allowing access to a set of steps leading down into the cistern. The interior of the cistern has recently been restored back to the original stonework, though, unfortunately, this has also removed some of the original plaster lining which would have helped determine its age.

Aqueduct

Some 400 m to the south of the reservoir there is part of a stone built water channel, or aqueduct. The channel runs, for at least 500 m, through a number of private gardens. In a number of places this channel runs underground, forming a *qanat*, with access through square man-holes (0.70 m × 0.70 m) made of dressed limestone blocks. During the 1986 survey four of these holes were discovered, in a line running south to north, adjacent to a bridge over the wadi, built by Italians in 1910. The average distance between holes is between 4.6 m and 7.7 m. At one point the channel crosses a small wadi (drainage channel), which it does by means of a small aqueduct. The aqueduct (0.85 m wide × 7.4 m long) is supported by a single arch (span 4.4 m).

Discussion

Two issues of importance arise in connection with Ma'an, the first is the date of the fort and the second concerns the establishment of the town itself.

Two construction dates are given for the fort – the earliest based on documentary evidence cited by Bakhit, states that it was built in 1559, whilst the inscription above the gate records a date of 1563 (971 AH). Given the huge distances involved, it is likely that the project was initiated in 1559 and completed in 1563. It is notable that Mehmed Edib and several other travellers refer to a second fort on the opposite hill. If this was a construction of the Ottoman government, it is possible, that it was built as a warehouse, to store grain, referred to in 1737–42 (Barbir 1980, 141 n. 98; TKS-E 2588/12 and TKS-E 2588/4).

The second question concerns the date of the foundation of the town. Although it is clear that there was settlement at Ma'an from pre-historic times (Doughty picked up several hand axes from the wadi bed at Ma'an (Doughty 1979, 74–77) there appears to be a gap in occupation between the early Islamic (Umayyad) period and the Ottoman period. During this time it is likely that Petra and Shawbak (Montreal) replaced Ma'an as the major settlements in the area. In this case it seems that the modern settlement of Ma'an is a creation of the Ottoman period and, if one accepts the oral traditions, this was the origin of the two settlements of al-Shammia and Ma'an.

Qal'at Fassu'a – (Map 5, No. 10) (Figs 35–36 and Plates 98–121)

('Aqaba al-Hijazi, 'Aqaba al-Shami, 'Aqaba al-Suwwan, Büyük 'Aqaba, Dhat al-Manar, Fasô'a, Qal'at al-Qasaba)
Location: 29.30N 35.50E
This site is located 2 km west of Mahatta Fassu'a, on the Hijaz railway line. Immediately to the north of the site is Wadi al-Msas, a tributary of the Wadi Abu 'Amid, flowing west to east. The site lies at just over 1,100 m above sea level, at the bottom of a gulley formed by the confluence of the two wadis. The whole area around Fassu'a is a high plateau (Jebal Sherra), intersected by deep, precipitous gullies and, in general, may be characterized as rugged. The ground is, in general, covered by stones of flint and limestone; interspersed with the odd camel thorn bush. Immediately to the south of the site are the abundant remains of a modern gravel quarry. The location of the site is important, as it is the last fort on high ground before the route descends through Batn Ghul to the Arabian Desert.

History

Although the fort at this site is of relatively recent origin, the site appears to have considerable antiquity. The 13th century writer, Yaqut, recalls the site of Dhat al-Manar on the southern border of Syria, where the early Muslim general, Abu 'Ubayda, camped on his way to the conquest of Syria. Yaqut, basing his information on a report by Abu Hudhayfa, states that Abu 'Ubayda entered Syria somewhere to the north of Sorar, which may be identified with modern Mudawwara (Yaqut 1995, vol. 2, 172). On the basis of Yaqut's account, Musil (1926, 38–39, n. 38) states that Dat al-Manar must be located between Mudawwara and Ma'an and is, therefore, likely to be either near, or at, Qal'at al-Fassu'a. Furthermore, Musil points out that the main route from Arabia to Syria would have led from Sorar (Mudawwara) to Ma'an in Syria (Bilad al-Sham) by climbing the escarpment through the narrow pass known as Batn Ghul, the only route suitable for pack animals. On the basis of this information Musil explains that the name, Dhat al-Manar, probably came from a tower, or

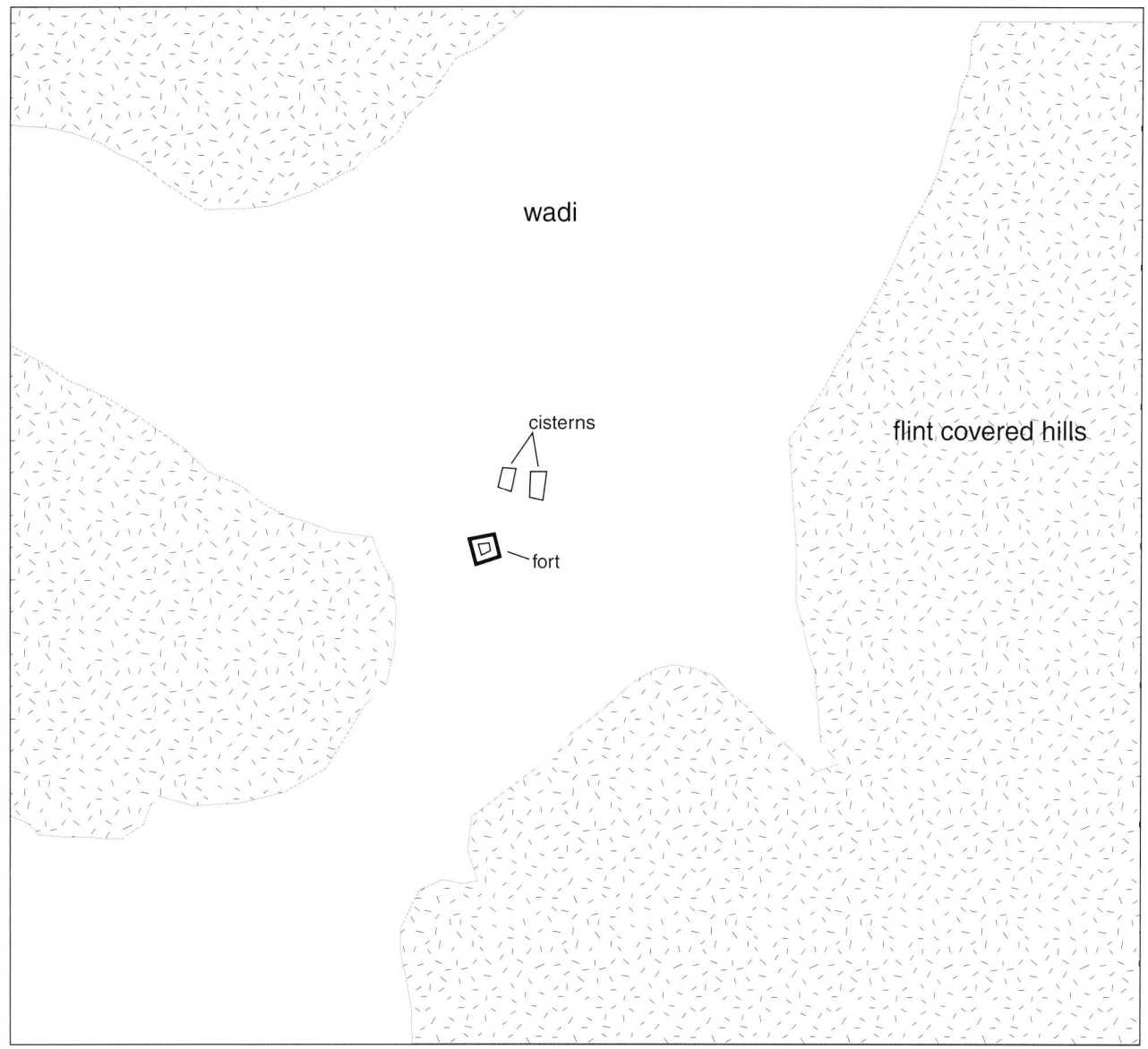

Fig. 35. Fassu'a, Jordan. Location map of fort and cisterns.

signal beacon, at the top of the pass, there to guide the pilgrims and other travellers and giving, as an example, Darb Zubayda which was also provided with watchtowers (Musil 1926, 39; for Darb Zuayda see also Rashid 1980). Al-Harbi, writing in the 10th century (mid 3rd century AH), lists the site of Dhat al-Mathar (ذات المثار) after Ma'an, which is probably an error in writing Dhat al-Manar (al-Harbi in al-Jasir 1968).

During his pilgrimage in 1326, Ibn Battuta (ed. Ramadi, 1958, 78), passed from Ma'an in Syria to 'Aqaba al-Suwwan (the pass of flint), which can certainly be identified with Faussu'a on the basis of the flint strewn ground in this area. In the 16th century (971 AH/1563 AD) itinerary of Mustapha Pasha (al-Jasir 1969, 84–85) the site after Ma'an and Wadi Musa wa Sharra, is referred to as Büyük 'Aqaba (بيوك عقبة), presumably to distinguish it from other smaller passes on the route, rather than 'Aqaba on the Red Sea.

The difficulties of the route in this place are recalled by Evliya Çelebi, who referred to the site simply as 'Aqaba. Çelebi states that it was very difficult to ride the animals at this point, so everyone had to dismount and walk on the stony ground. He also comments that many of the pilgrims were robbed as they passed this point, presumably in the pass leading down towards Mudawarra, 10 hours distant (Evliya Çelebi, *Seyhatnâmesi* IX, 577; Bilge 1979, 218). The Syrian Sufi pilgrim, Murtada ibn 'Alawan, gives a different impression when travelling from Ma'an to the *qonaq* [konak] (قناق) of Zahr al-'Aqaba (ظهر اعقبة) in 1709. He describes it as a pleasant place, with two large trees (Murtada b. 'Ali b. 'Alawan MS fol. 104b).

Up until the mid-18th century there is no indication of a fort at Fassu'a, the first time a fort is mentioned at this site is in the account of Mehmed Edib, who visited in 1779 and observed that a fort and fountain had been built by Osman

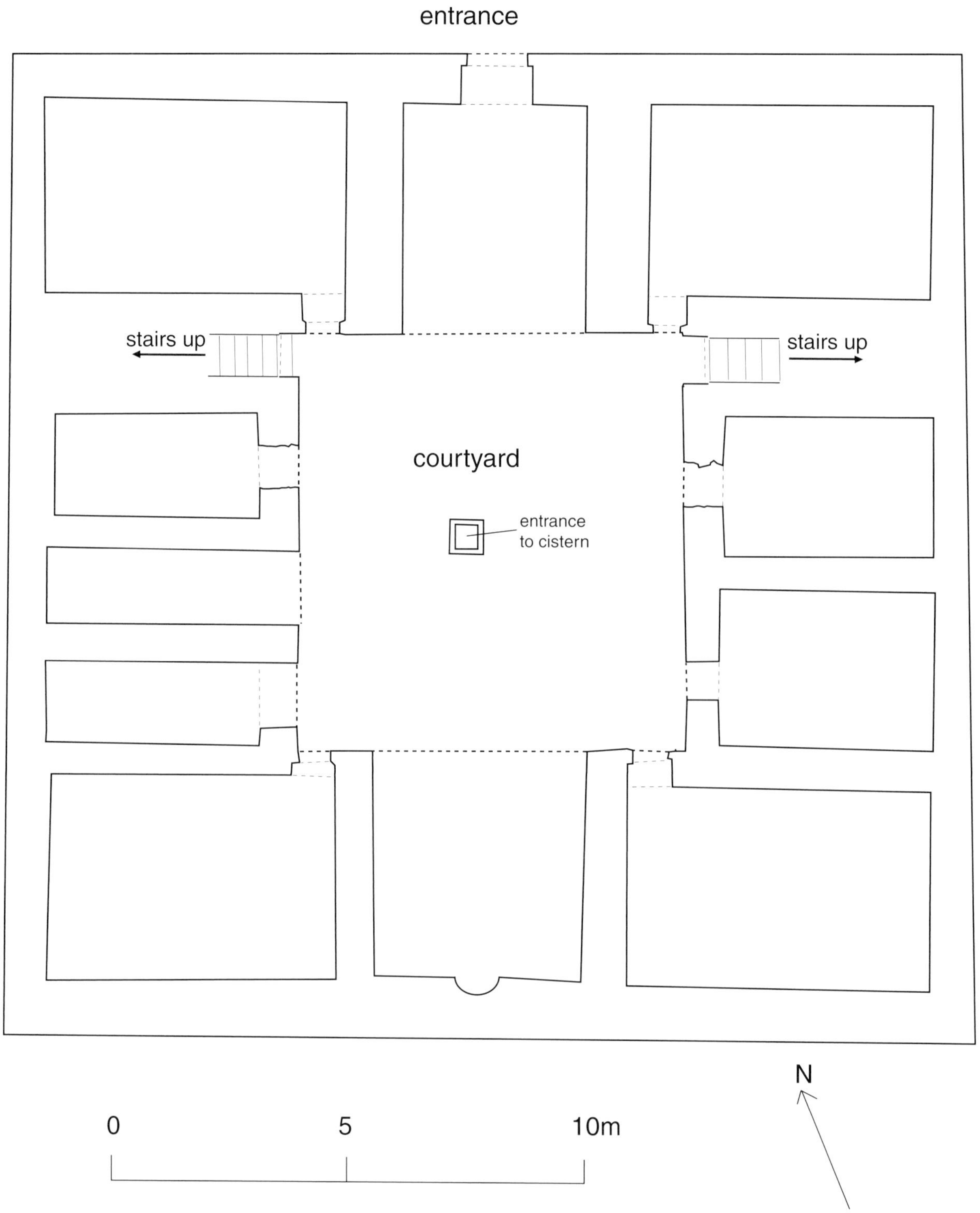

entrance

Fig. 36. Fassu'a, Jordan. Plan of ground floor of Ottoman fort.

Pasha, who is probably to be identified with Gürcü Osman (d.1753) (Ibn al-Qari cited in Barbir 1980, 140, n. 93). Edib observes that the fort is located in a waterless valley strewn with stones and sand, 13 hours south of Ma'an. He also gives a graphic description of the preparation for the descent of the escarpment at this point. The pilgrims get down from their litters and walk down the hill on foot,

whilst the *Amir al-Hajj* sits under a parasol watching their progress and the water carriers distribute sherbert (Bianchi 1825, 128; Musil 1926, 39, n. 33).

It is not clear whether Burckhardt actually visited this fort, although his description of the site suggests that he may be basing his account on an actual visit. Firstly, he observes that the land between Ma'an and Fassu'a could be

Plate 98. Qal'at Fassu'a, north façade with entrance (1986).

Plate 100. Qal'at Fassu'a, entrance (1986).

Plate 99. Qal'at Fassu'a, corner tower detail (1986).

Plate 101. Qal'at Fassu'a, remains of inscription above entrance (1986).

cultivated, but that it was currently 'complete desert on both sides'. Secondly, he states that the fort is under the control of the Howeytat Bedouin who are 'in communication with Cairo' – presumably instead of Damascus. Finally, he gives us another description of the pilgrims' descent of the pass, which takes half an hour, during which time they repeat the following prayer 'May the Almighty God be merciful to them who descend into the belly of the dragon' (Burckhardt 1822, 658–59, appendix III).

In 1825 the fort was visited by Muhamad 'Ali's inspector, who referred to the fort as Qal'at al-Qasba. The inspector notes that the fort (measuring 35 × 35 cubits) is in a ruinous condition, with two of the walls destroyed and indicates that he has written a letter to the shaykhs of Ma'an, asking them to undertake some renovation. He also notes the presence of two cisterns, each measuring 40 × 30 cubits with a depth of 10 cubits. Although both cisterns were in a good condition, they did not collect much water

(Appendix 1 in this volume).

When Doughty passed the same way, 50 years later, he takes little note of this stop, simply observing 'a ruinous kella and cistern are here upon our left hand'. However, he does give an account of how his camel broke loose, as the caravan descended into the pass (*Batn el-Ghröl*), within sight of the *Amir al-Hajj* sitting on a rock under a white parasol (Doughty 1979, 90).

Plate 102. Qal'at Fassu'a, detail of door jamb with beam slot for securing door visible behind (1986).

Plate 103. Qal'at Fassu'a, view of cisterns from within entrance (1986).

Plate 104. Qal'at Fassu'a, interior looking north with gateway below (1986).

Plate 105. Qal'at Fassu'a, interior looking south with prayer room and mihrab *in centre (1986).*

Plate 106. Qal'at Fassu'a, interior looking east (1986).

Plate 107. Qal'at Fassu'a, interior looking west (1986).

In May 1910 the site was visited by Musil, who describes arriving at 'the small ruined fortress of Fasô'a, north of which are situated two artificial rain pools still partly filled with water'. Musil's time at the site was cut short due to the behaviour of his camels, which, very thirsty on arrival, rushed to the cisterns and then ran about searching for pasture until they had eaten everything in sight (Musil 1926, 38–39).

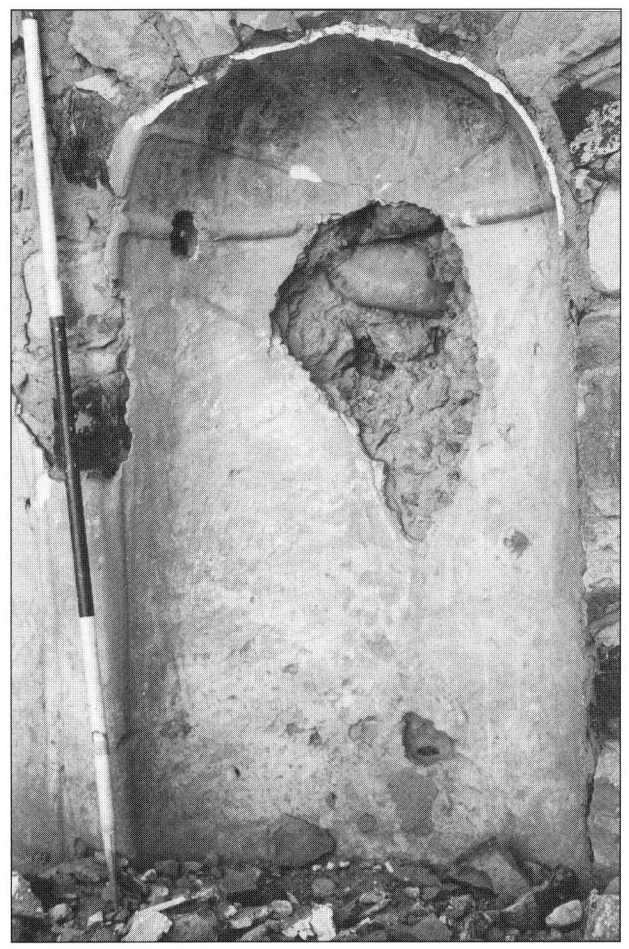

Plate 108. Qal'at Fassu'a, detail of mihrab *on first floor (1986).*

Plate 110. Qal'at Fassu'a, interior west staircase (1986).

Plate 111. Qal'at Fassu'a, fort and cisterns from north (1986).

Plate 109. Qal'at Fassu'a, detail of gun slit (1986).

Plate 112. Qal'at Fassu'a, cisterns outside fort (1986).

Plate 113. Qal'at Fassu'a, detail of cistern (1986).

Plate 114. Qal'at Fassu'a, from east (2006).

Plate 115. Qal'at Fassu'a, from west with location marker in foreground (2006).

Description

This site consists of a fort, two reservoirs and a signal beacon located to the north-west.

The Fort

The fort is roughly square in plan, measuring 20.2 m east–west, by, 20.7 m north–south and standing to an average height of 7.2 m above the surrounding ground level. It is built out of a mixture of slate, flint, basalt and limestone, roughly squared into blocks, the gaps between being filled by small flat pieces of stone. The stone blocks are held together with a lime mortar that shows evidence of repairs in many places. There are no remains of crenellations on any of the walls; instead, the walls are capped with a layer of small stones, mortared together to produce a round ridge, running all around the external walls of the fort.

Plate 116. Qal'at Fassu'a, view from south (2006).

CORNER TOWERS (PLATE 99)

At each of the four corners there is a projecting tower, set at a height of *c.* 5 m above ground level and projecting 30 cm from the face of the wall. All the towers have the same basic design, though with certain variations listed below. Each tower rests on five projecting corbels, two from each side and one projecting from the corner. The corbels are made of basalt and a roughly chipped plate-flint slab, forming a platform upon which the walls of the tower are built.

The dimensions of each tower are listed below:

i)   north-west corner. This is the highest of the towers being 5.5 m above ground level, whilst the tower

itself is 3.2 m tall. The west face measures 1.2 m and includes five openings, set alternately at one and two courses above the base level. The roof of this tower is in the form of a tall honeycomb shape, made of small stones set in mortar.

ii)   south-west corner. This has been very severely damaged, so little of the actual structure remains, although enough survives to give the approximate dimensions. The south face is 1.6 m long, the west side 1.5 m long. Damage to the upper part of this tower looks like intentional removal, rather than collapse, because the supports are still in place and part of the adjoining wall has also been removed.

Plate 117. Qal'at Fassu'a, view from south (2006).

Plate 118. Qal'at Fassu'a, illegal excavation of foundations (2006).

Plate 119. Qal'at Fassu'a, prayer room on ground floor (2006).

Plate 120. Qal'at Fassu'a, wall above entrance after removal of inscription panels (2006).

Plate 121. Qal'at Fassu'a, mihrab *in middle of prayer room on upper floor (2006).*

iii) south-east corner. This tower has also suffered damage and has lost its roof and part of the side-walls. The south face is 1.6 m long and includes two openings, set back, one course, above the platform. The east face is also 1.6 m long and is identical to the south face.

iv) north-east corner tower. This tower is still complete, although it is only 2.2 m high. The east face is 1.2 m long and has 3 windows; all set one course above the platform. The north face is 1.4 m long and is identical to the east face. The roof of this tower is formed by flat stone tiles, leaning, at an angle, against the wall of the fort.

BOX MACHICOLATION (PLATE 114)

Of similar design to these towers is a box machicolation in the middle of the south side of the fort. The structure is set into the wall of the fort at a height of 5 m above ground level and projects 0.4 m from the face of the main wall, resting on corbels similar to those used on the corner towers. The machicolation is 2.2 m high, including the supports and the roof, whilst the face is 1.6 m long and 1.85 m high. The floor of the machicolation is composed of long, flat pieces of plate flint, resembling that of the corner towers, except that there are gaps between the corbels allowing it to function as a machicolation (or latrine?). The side of the machicolation has narrow slits, 0.3 m high and 0.1 m wide, at a height of one course above the base. The south face contains a further three openings of similar size (0.3 m × 0.1 m), two of which are one course above the interior floor level whilst the third is five courses above. Above the level of the openings there is a course of flat stones, laid edgeways to form a relieving arch. As in the corner towers, the machicolations are roofed with heavy stone tiles, laid at an angle to the face of the fort.

There are 14 windows (four on each of the east, west and north sides and two on the south side) set into the outer walls of the fort, at a height *c.* 3.8 m above the outside ground level. These openings are of very simple design, with an average height of 0.7 m and width of 0.1 m. All of the windows are placed symmetrically, being distances of 4 and 6 m apart.

The entrance to the fort is located, more or less, in the middle of the north side (10.3 m from the north-west corner and 9.9 m from the north-east corner). The gateway itself is 1.5 m wide and 2.3 m high and is set within a frame of dressed dark purple sandstone (Plate 117). Above the doorway is a lintel set within a large semi-circular arch, 2.10 m wide and 0.6 m high in the centre. At the corners of the gateway there are corbels with a semi-circular profile (Plate 100).

INSCRIPTION AND MACHICOLATION (PLATES 100–101) (SEE CHAPTER 11, NO. 4)

Directly above the gateway there is a sandstone stone panel (0.8 m high × 1.5 m wide) bearing an inscription (since 1986 this has been removed, its current location is unknown). Above the inscribed panel are two sets of projecting corbels and a large gap in the wall (1.5 m wide, 1.7 m high). It is probable that this was a projecting machicolation, which has now disappeared.

Interior (Ground Floor) (Fig. 35)

The gateway is fairly narrow, only 1.5 m wide at the entrance, but it opens out to 2.05 m on the interior, where it leads into a vaulted entrance passage (3.8 m wide and 4.7 m long). The passageway is roofed with a pointed vault, whilst all the other rooms on the ground floor are covered with barrel-vaults. The entrance passage opens into a central courtyard, which is roughly square (8.8 m × 8.1 m). In the centre of the courtyard there is a square hole, 0.6 m per side, which gives access to a bottle shaped cistern of unknown depth.

The north range of rooms contains three doorways, including the entrance hall, which is in the middle. At the west end of this range there is a doorway (0.9 m wide) with a wooden lintel, which leads into a long room (6.4 m) covered with a vault, running east to west. The doorway at the east end of the north range has exactly the same dimensions and design as that on the west side. There are three rooms opening onto the west side of the courtyard, as well as a staircase to the first floor in the north-west corner. To the south of the staircase there is an entrance (0.9 m wide) covered with a shallow stone arch, leading into a narrow room 4.25 m long and 2.2 m wide. South of this are two more long, narrow rooms, each of identical size and design (*i.e.* 5.35 m long and 1.5 m wide).

The south side of the courtyard leads into three rooms: an *iwan* in the centre – facing the entrance, and two large rooms either side. The *iwan* tapers from 4.5 m at the north open end, to 4.3 m at the south end. In the centre of the south side there is a shallow plastered niche, with a concave hood, set into the wall (this alcove probably functioned as a *mihrab*). The *iwan* vault has a flattened profile at the top, presumably to increase its span. Either side of the *iwan* there are large rectangular rooms (6.2 m × 4.4 m), with vaults, running east–west.

The east side of the courtyard opens onto two rooms, with vaults, running east–west. The room nearest the south-east corner is 4.4 m long and 3.3 m wide, whilst the other room is of the same length, but only 2.9 m wide. In the north-east corner there is a second flight of stairs leading to the upper rooms.

Interior

FIRST FLOOR (FIG. 36)

The first floor is reached by either one of two staircases, facing each other across the courtyard. Each staircase is 1.2 m wide and 4.4 m long and is covered by an arch. The surface of the upper floor is composed of flint cobbles, bordered by dressed limestone blocks. The rooms on the upper floor do not appear to have been vaulted and the remains of wooden roofing beams can be seen in a few places. A photograph of the interior of the fort, taken by Musil, shows the room directly above the entrance covered with a large white dome. The same photograph also shows the room in the north-east corner with a roof of wooden beams, covered with earth and/or plaster (Musil 1926).

The four corner towers are located at different heights above the first floor level and, although the means of access is not clear, it is probable that there were sets of steps (between 0.7 m and 1.3 m high) leading up from the adjacent rooms. The walls of the rooms on this floor are between 0.6 m and 2 m thick.

The remains of five rooms are found on the north side of the first floor. In the centre of the north side is a small, square room (3.05 m per side) filled with rubble to a height of almost 1 m and with a large opening, corresponding to the presumed position of the machicolation, above the entrance. West of this there is a severely damaged room (3.5 m × 3 m) with a window in the north wall and a doorway to the west, leading to another square room (3.5 m per side). This room has narrow openings north and west, as well as a larger window, 0.6 m wide, looking into the courtyard.

The west range contains two shallow rooms located to the south of the stairs. Both of these rooms have walls that have been capped with a layer of small stones set in mortar (*c.f.* exterior wall above), implying that they may not have had permanent roofs.

The south range of rooms is a complex arrangement, centred on a wide arched *iwan* (probably originally covered with a flat roof) with a shallow recessed niche in the centre of the south wall. The niche is lined with plaster and has a scalloped design in the concave hood. Like the niche directly below, this was also probably a prayer room (*masjid*). To the west of the *iwan* there is a complex arrangement of structures, comprising two arched recesses (1.5 m and 1 m high) above which was a rectangular room in the corner, opening into the south-west corner tower and a small square room opening into the machicolation (or latrine). To the east of the *iwan* the arrangement is less complicated, comprising one rectangular and one square room.

The range to the east does not have any standing rooms, although there is rubble, which may indicate the presence of some, now vanished, structures.

The Cisterns (Plates 111–113)

There are two cistern at Fassu‘a, the nearest of which lies 37.5 m from the entrance of the fort. Both reservoirs are of similar size and are laid out parallel to each other, connected by a low wall, 7.5 m long, joining the south ends of both. There is also, in places, a cobbled surface between the two. The eastern reservoir is slightly larger (24 m × 16.8 m) than that to the west (23.6 m × 16 m).

The cisterns are built of semi-dressed sandstone and large blocks of flint, and are plastered internally. The plaster is similar to that used in the fort and also resembles that found on other Ottoman reservoirs (*e.g.* Qal‘at al-Hasa). Where they rise above the ground surface the walls are 0.6–0.65 m wide.

The larger reservoir to the east still contains water and its depth could not be determined beyond 2.1 m. The western reservoir is filled with sand to a height of 0.7 m below the top of the cistern. The design of both reservoirs is similar; each having the corners rounded off with squinches 1.7 m long. The south corner of each reservoir contains steps (1.65 m wide) leading down into the interior. There are inlet holes in the south side of both reservoirs (2 in the east and 3 in the west) as well as 4 (each) on either side of the area separating the two (total 13 inlets). In addition to these small inlets there are large holes in both reservoirs, which, like the inlet holes, appear to be part of the original design.

The small inlets, especially those between the two cisterns were probably intended to catch rainwater directly, whilst the large holes were presumably designed to take water out of the wadis.

Signal Beacon (Manar?) (Plate 115)

Half a kilometre to the west of the fort there is a pile of flint rubble standing to a height of 2 m. Close inspection reveals the remains of rough stone walls, built on a square plan (*c.* 2.9 m per side). In the middle of the east side there is a hole, 0.7 m wide, which gives access to the interior of the structure. To the north-east of this structure, at an angle of 45° and a distance of approximately 750 m there is another structure of similar design. From their high position above the fort, it is assumed that these structures were beacons to guide pilgrims to the fort.

Discussion

From the historical evidence it appears that soon after the fort's construction it fell into disrepair; all the visitors, from 1825 onwards, have referred to it as a ruined structure. There are two features of particular interest in the design of this fort. Firstly, it is notable that there are two prayer rooms (*masajdayn*) one on the first floor, the other on the ground floor. Whilst a prayer room on the first floor is not unusual and to a certain extent to be expected, the presence of a prayer room on the ground floor is unusual. It is unlikely to have been for pilgrims who were kept out of the fort and may simply have served as an extra prayer room, or as a temporary mosque, before the upper floor was built.

The second feature of interest is the complex of structures to the west of the upper prayer room, these may have functioned as a latrine and ablutions area, even, perhaps, a small bath house.

Qal‘at Mudawwara – (Map 5, No. 11) (Figs 37–39, Plates 122–133)

(al-Mudawara, Soragh, Sargh, Sarr, Saru‘,Qal‘at Sorar, Jughayman, Tubaylayat)
Location: 29.20N 36.00E

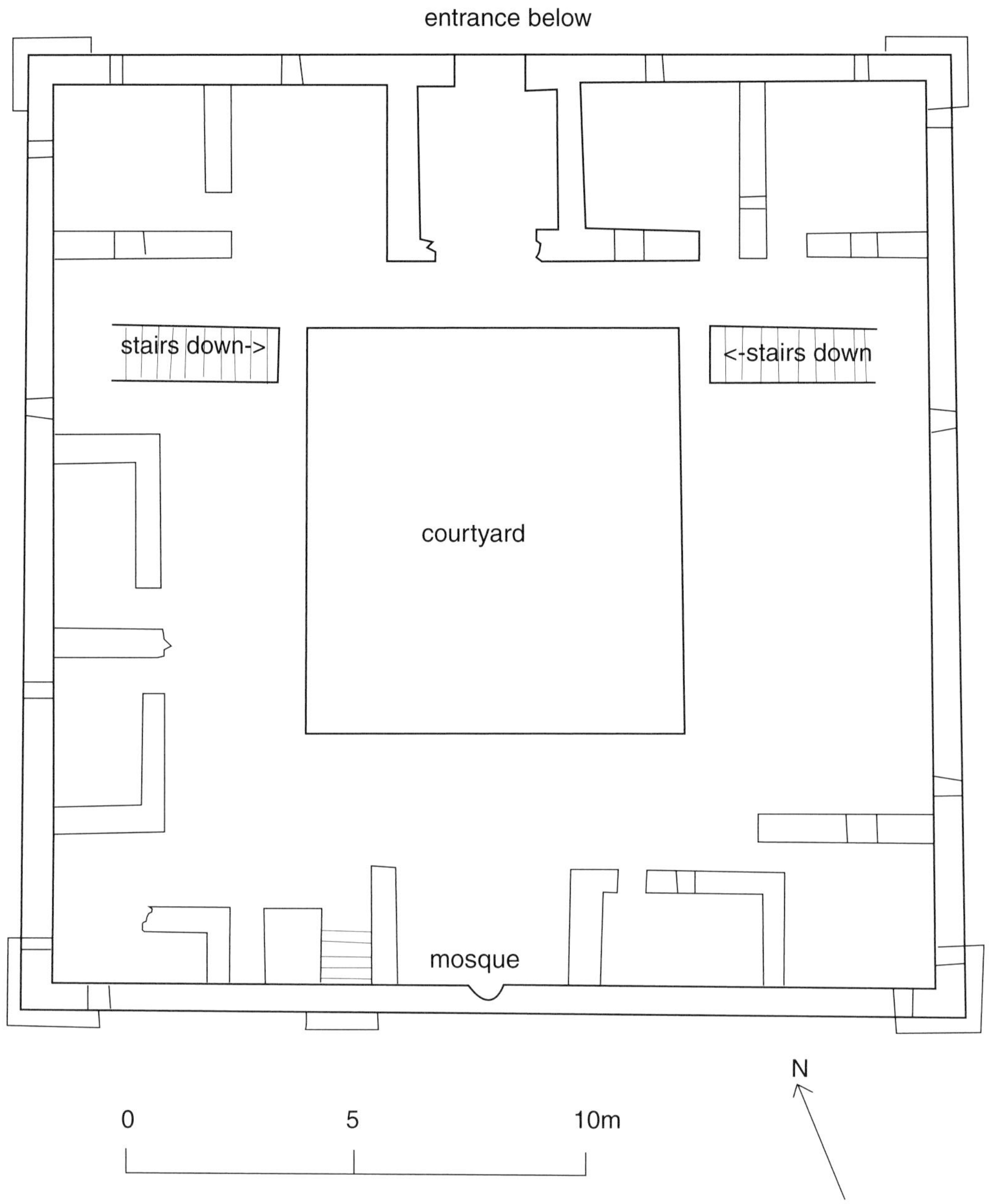

entrance below

stairs down->

<-stairs down

courtyard

mosque

0   5   10m

N

Fig. 37. Fassu'a, Jordan. Plan of first floor of Ottoman fort.

This site is located in a sandy desert at the southernly most point of Jordan, 15 km north of the Saudi border and Halat 'Ammar. Although the area is predominantly flat there are a number of sandstone rock formations in the vicinity of the fort.

History

The site is first mentioned as one of the principal stops on the Syrian Hajj route, in the writings of the 9th century author, Ibn Khurdadhbih, who states that it is between Dhat al-Manazil and Tabuk (Ibn Khurdadhbih 1889, ed. De Goeje 150; see also Musil 1926, 327). The site is also

Plate 122. Qal'at Mudawwara, north side with entrance (1986).

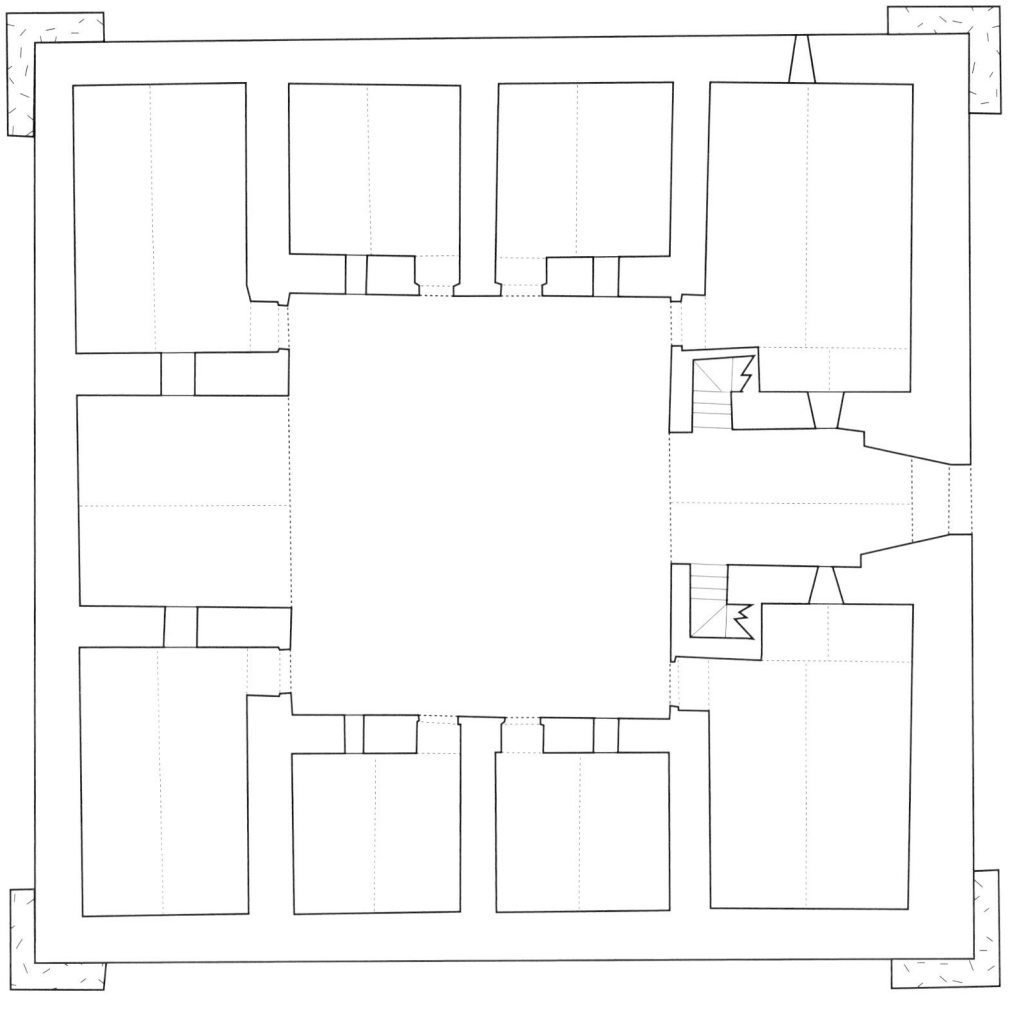

N

Fig. 38. Mudawwara, Jordan. Plan of ground floor of Ottoman fort.

Plate 123. Qal'at Mudawwara, west wall (1986).

Plate 124. Qal'at Mudawwara, south side (1986).

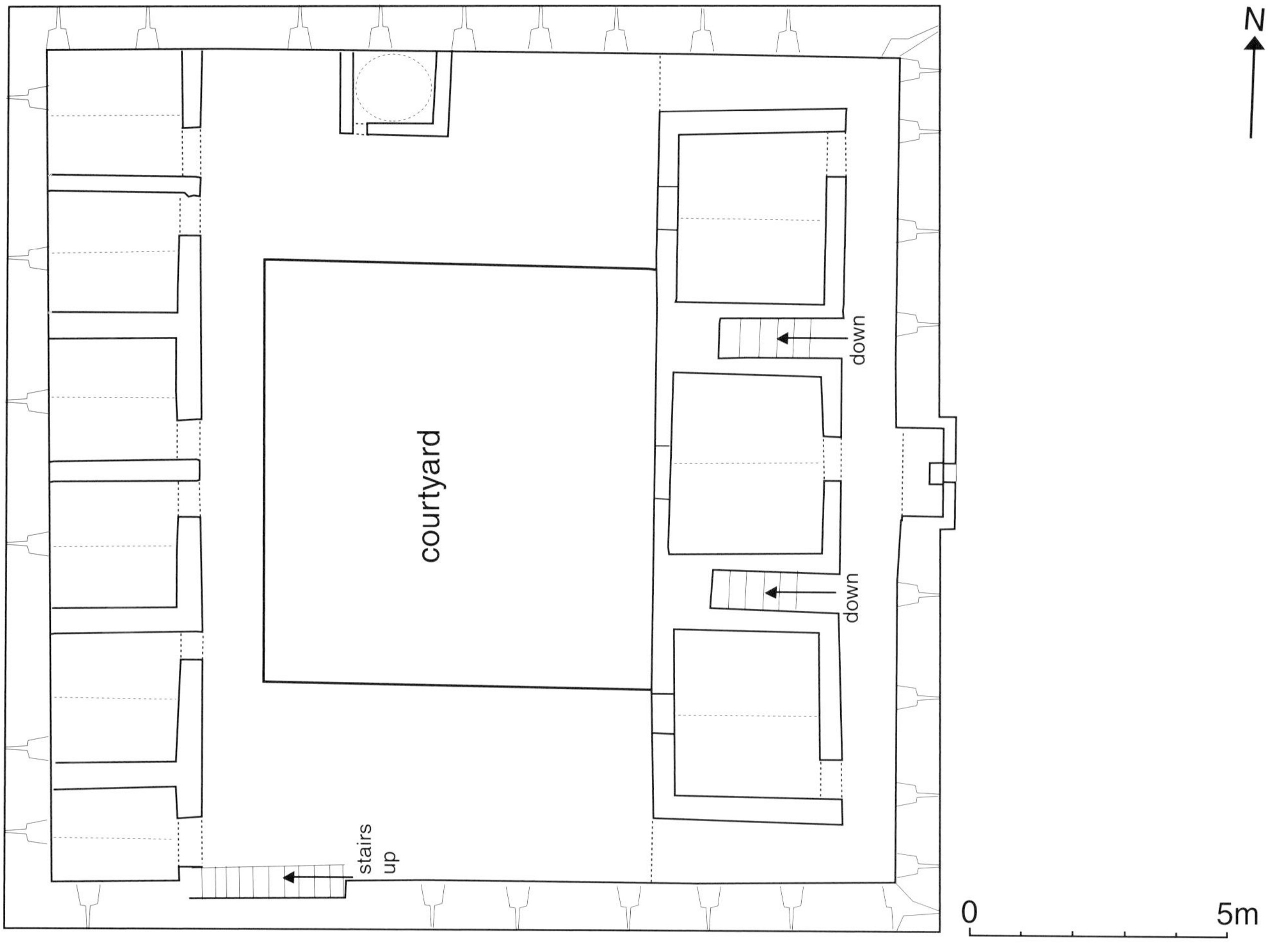

N

Fig. 39. Mudawwara, Jordan. Plan of first floor.

Plate 125. Qal'at Mudawwara, east side (1986).

listed by the 9th century author, al-Harbi, who places Sargh between Mughaysha and Tabuk (al-Harbi in al-Jasir 1969, 653). Other early authors who mention the site are, Ibn Rustah (ed. de Goeje, 183) and Qudamah (ed. de Goeje, 191). However, the site appears to have been by-passed in the 14th century and it is not mentioned by either Ibn Battuta or Abu al-Fida'.

In the 16th century (971 AH/1563 AD) itinerary of Mustapha Pasha, the site is listed as Tubaylayat (طبيليات) though it is incorrectly placed between Halat 'Ammar and

Plate 126. Qal'at Mudawwara, detail of projecting corner tower at north-east corner (1986).

Plate 127. Qal'at Mudawwara, machicolation on north side above entrance (1986).

Plate 129. Qal'at Mudawwara, interior with domed chamber from east (1986).

Plate 130. Qal'at Mudawwara (2006).

Plate 128. Qal'at Mudawwara, interior looking north (1986).

Plate 131. Qal'at Mudawwara, foundations (2006).

Dhat al-Hajj, instead of between Buyuk 'Aqaba [Fassu'a] and Halat 'Ammar (al-Jasir 1969, 184–85). Later on, in 1672, the Turkish traveller, Evliya Çelebi, referred to the site as Kudrat Jugayman. He noted that it contained a castle built out of rock, without any sign of an entrance ('yek pare

bit kaya kal'adir. Ammâ der [ü] dîvârdan alâmet yokdur') (Evliya Çelebi, *Seyhatnâmesi* IX, 296). To the south of the fort there was a well called, 'Asma, after the sister of Sulayman Khan (Bilge, 1979, 218). The name of the site, Kudret Jughayman ('Mighty Jughayman'), probably

Plate 132. Qal'at Mudawwara, east side after collapse (2006).

Plate 133. Qal'at Mudawwara, interior with entrance (2006).

derives from the early 16th century Bedouin chieftan who harassed pilgrims (Bakhit 1982, 20–21 and 221). The rock-cut fort with no door, may be explained by the striking natural rock outcrop located behind the fort (see below discussion). The site is also referred to as Jughayman in the itinerary of Murtada ibn 'Alawan (Murtada b. 'Ali b. 'Alawan MS 105a).

In the 18th century the Governor of Damascus, Aydinili Abdullah Pasha (in office 1730–33), ordered the construction of a fort and two cisterns at al-Mudawwara (Ibn al-Qari 1949, 77 cited in Barbir 1980, 138). Half a century later the fort was visited by Mehmed Edib, who stated that it was built by Abdullah Pasha, at a distance of 15 hours from Zahr al-'Aqaba (Fassu'a). He noted that water was scarce at this site and was only found around the fort. He also makes the observation that the sand around the fort appeared to be impassable, giving the impression of a vast ocean. (Bianchi 1825, 129).

In the early 19th century the site was inspected for *The Report to Muhammad 'Ali Pasha* (Appendix 1 in this volume). The Report referred to the site as Mudawwara and stated that it contained a square fort (50 × 50 cubits) and two cisterns, one small cistern next to the fort and a large rectangular cistern (50 × 30 cubits) at some distance. The Report noted considerable problems with water at this site, including both a low water table and shifting sands filling up the cisterns.

The first European description of the site is given by Doughty, who described it as follows:

'An hour before mid day we ascended three miles through a low girdle of rocky sandstones, which is a train from Hisma, and went down to pitch in the plain before Medowwara where we came to water. The place lies very desolate; the fort is built at a spring, defended by a vault from the Bedouins' hostility' (Doughty 1979, 97).

During the First World War, Mudawwara was the scene of some fierce fighting, in particular, when British and Arab forces attacked the site from 'Aqaba to prevent it being used as a base from which the Turks could attack Palestine (Peake Pasha 1958, 101–2).

Description

The site consists of a Hajj fort, a reservoir and section of stone cobbled road.

Fort

The fort is exactly square, measuring 19 m per side, not including the buttresses that occur at each corner. It is built of dressed sandstone blocks (average dimensions 25–30 cm high and 40–45 cm long) and is located on a sandy ground surface, which slopes gently down from the north to the south. The fort is built directly on the sand, with wide foundations splaying outwards, so the structure is 'floating' on the sand. The walls comprise an inner and outer face and become progressively thinner as they get higher. The east and south walls of the fort are lower than those on the north and west sides which have been built 0.9–2 m higher. The area in the immediate vicinity of the fort has been considerably disturbed in recent years, both from the activities of treasure hunters and recent military use, including barbed wire fencing.

Exterior

EAST FACE (PLATE 122)

The entrance to the fort is in the middle of the east side and comprises a rectangular gateway (1.3 m wide) set beneath a large projecting machicolation (5.7 m high and 2.6 m wide projecting 0.4 m from the face of the fort). The gateway comprises two jambs made of monolithic sandstone blocks (2.3 m × 0.55 m) and a lintel also made of a single sandstone block (though this was cracked in two places). Above the lintel is a series of voussoirs arranged to form a flat relieving arch. Above this there is a rectangular recess, which probably once contained an inscription (in 1986 it contained a small metal panel stating that this was a Desert Police Post – this was no longer in place in 2004). The inscription panel is set within a wide arch, which forms the lower part of the projecting machicolation. On both sides the arch rests on two massive projecting corbels. The springing of the arch on each side is marked with a fine cyma recta molding. A small hole at the apex of the arch functions as the downward opening of the machicolation and a small gun slit also protects the entrance. The upper part of the machicolation contains a wide rectangular opening set beneath a stone, relieving arch, at the top there are two small square openings (Plate 127). Either side of the gateway, at first floor level, there are a series of narrow (0.5 m × 0.1 m) gun slits (5 on each side). At parapet level (second floor) there are a series of wide openings, or gun-ports (0.6 m × 0.45 m) each covered with a flat piece of stone and supporting a continuous series of crenellations.

SOUTH FACE (PLATES 124 AND 132)

There has been some very serious undermining of the fort, under the middle of the south wall, which has led to the collapse of this side of the fort (the collapse occurred some time between 1986 and 2005 though the undermining was already evident in 1986). The south wall was of similar design to the east side, comprising a series of eight gun slits at first floor level and 11 gun-ports at parapet level, capped by a series of crenellations. There is also one, small, rectangular opening (c. 0.3 m × 0.15 m) in the middle of the south side, at ground floor level.

WEST FACE (PLATE 123)

The west face contains a series of six gun slits (each 0.6 m high by 0.1 m wide) at first floor level and a second series of smaller openings at second floor level. At the top of the wall, at parapet level, another wall has been added to increase the height of the fort. This upper section of wall is distinguished by the fact that it is built of rough stone blocks covered in plaster. There are five closely spaced, square, openings at this level, which may have functioned as firing points. At the north end of the wall, near the corner, there is a projecting box-like structure that resembles a machicolation, though it is more likely to be a latrine. At the south end of the wall there is an iron down-pipe dating from the most recent use of the fort in the 20th century and is probably connected to a cess pit (not investigated).

NORTH FACE (PLATE 125)

The north face is similar to the west face; it contains 10 gun slits at first floor level, two at second floor level and one at ground floor level. The west end of the wall is higher, representing a continuation of the later addition to the west wall; this contains three openings.

CORNER TOWERS

1. At the south-west corner, approximately 7 m above ground level, there is a hexagonal tower. It rests on a corbel, on either side of the corner and extends 1.5 m on either face. The upper part of the tower is composed of stones set vertically on end, with tall narrow slits (0.8 m × 0.08 m) between each one. The tower has a flat roof made out of white flat stones.

2. At the south-east corner there is a small turret, set at a height 1.5 m lower than the south-west corner tower (1). The turret extends 1.1 m along both the south and east walls and projects 0.45 m from the face. It rests on three corbels and has three small windows. The roof merges with the wall.

3. The north-east tower is similar to that at the south-east (tower 2).

4. There is no tower at the north-west corner, though there is a projecting box-like structure at the north end of the west side, which probably functioned as a latrine (see description of west side above). This structure (1.3 m wide × 1.2 m high) projects 0.5 m from the face of the wall and rests on two corbels with a narrow slit between.

INTERIOR

The entrance to the fort is protected by a large, modern, iron, gate (removed since 1986) and leads into a tall vaulted passage (4.2 m long × 2.6 m wide × 3 m high). In both the north and the south walls there is a doorway leading into a passageway, leading to the first floor. The entrance chamber leads into a square, central, courtyard paved with stones (now mostly removed).

There are 9 rooms on the ground floor, excluding the entrance passage; all are barrel-vaulted. Directly opposite the entrance there is a large *iwan* that occupies most of the west side of the courtyard. The arrangement of rooms is symmetrical along an axis running, east–west, through the gateway, thus there are four rooms on each side. All the rooms are entered via small doorways (0.7 m wide × 1.5 m high).

The first floor is reached by either one of two staircases (0.8 m wide) ascending from the entrance passage (Plate 133). The plan is identical for both sides, comprising a 90% bend and ascending to a narrow corridor (0.9 m wide) running along the east face of the fort. Three rooms open off this narrow corridor and have windows opening into the courtyard. Access to the rest of the first floor is by means of two open passageways, 4m long and 0.9 m wide. The north side of the first floor is empty, except for an isolated rectangular building (2.6 × 2.1 m) with a domical vault. The west range comprises 6 rooms of identical size (3.6 m × 2.4 m) with flat concrete roofs. The south part of the first floor is empty, except for a set of stairs giving access to the flat roof of the west range. From this flat roof there is access to the north and south-west corner turrets. The

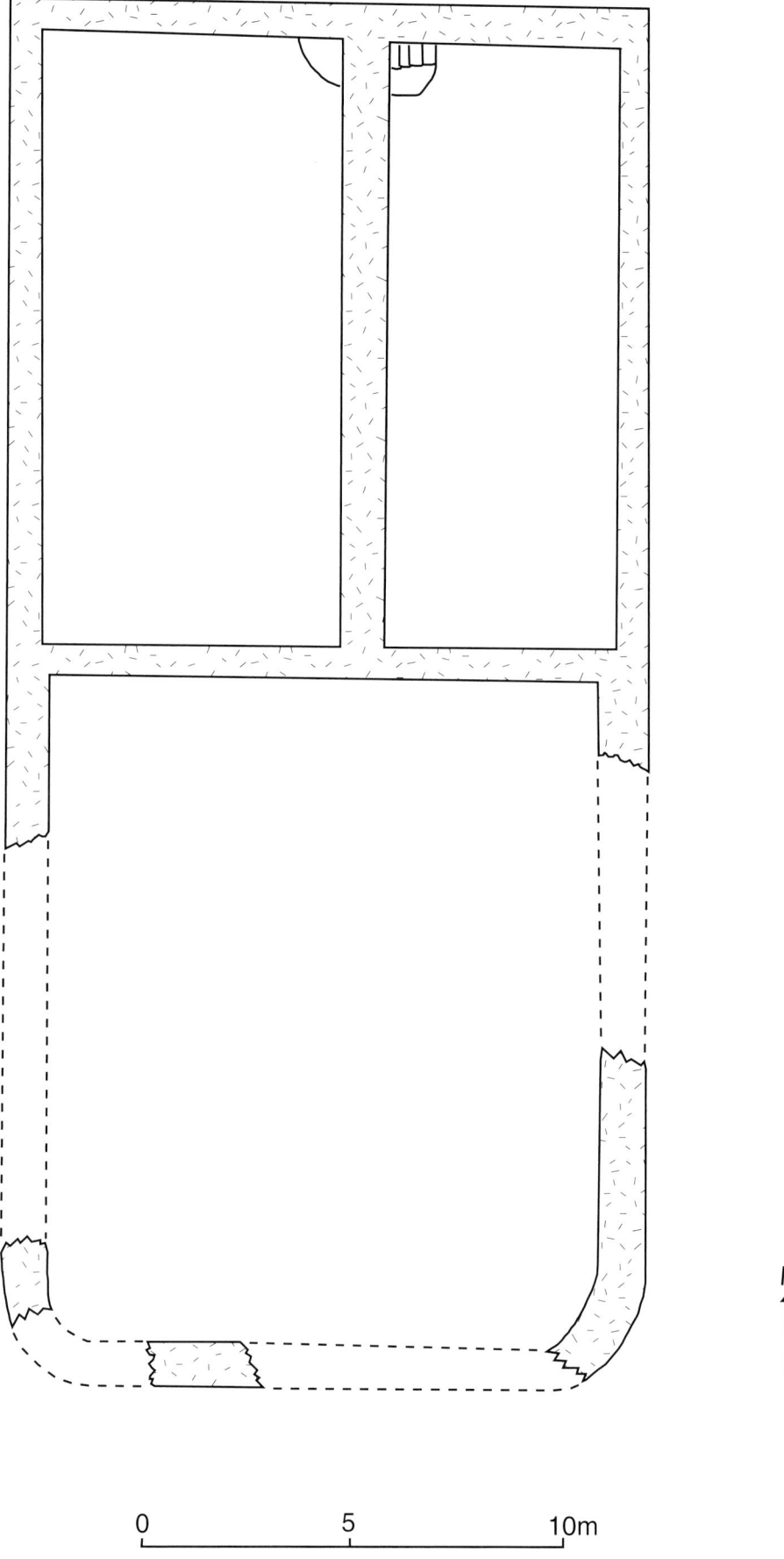

Fig. 40. Plan of cisterns at Mudawarra, Jordan.

south and north-east corner towers may be reached by small staircases at either end of the long corridor.

Architectural Sequence

The architectural sequence is complex, but two major phases can be distinguished. The first phase includes the entire ground floor and probably the east range of rooms on the first floor. The second phase includes the west range of rooms, the upper 1.5 m of the west and north walls and the south-west corner tower. The second phase, based on the use of iron rails in the flat roof of the first floor, probably dates from the early 20th century. The corner buttresses seem to be part of the original design of the fort and are integral to its structure.

Cistern (Fig. 39)

Eighty-two metres to the south of the fort are the remains of a large, rectangular, cistern, with sides measuring 31.8 m north–south and 15 m east–west. The sides of the reservoir are composed of dressed sandstone blocks on the interior face and roughly squared, flint and sandstone blocks in the middle and exterior faces. The width of the walls varies between 1.05 m and 0.75 m. The south-east and south-west corners are right angles, whilst the northern corners have a rounded form.

The interior of the reservoir is divided into three rectangular chambers, which comprise a large (15.1 m × 12.2 m) chamber (I) to the north and two smaller chambers (II, 14 m × 25.3 m and III, 14 m × 7 m). Parts of the walls at the north end have been covered over and can be distinguished as linear humps in the sand. There are two staircases leading into the reservoir, one at the south-east corner of the main chamber and the other in the south-east corner of chamber 3. The reservoirs are full of sand and no measurement of depth was possible.

There is no visible sign of the cistern next to the fort, which is mentioned in the *Report to Muhammad 'Ali Pasha*

(Appendix 1 in this volume) and it is likely that it has been completely covered with sand.

Road

One and a half kilometres to the south-east of Mudawarra are the remains of a cobbled road, stretching for a distance of over 500 m. The road is made of flint cobbles edged with sandstone, with a width of 4–5 m.

Discussion

The name of fort Mudawwara (Ar. = circular) may derive from the Medieval Mamluk term for the large circular tent used by rulers when on campaign (*Encyclopaedia of Islam II*) and implies that this was a camping ground before the construction of the fort in the 18th century. It is likely that Evliya Çelebi's reference to a stone built fort without a door refers to the large, square, rocky outcrop immediately behind the fort, rather than any man-made construction. However, Çelebi's description does provide further evidence that this spot was used as a stopping place, or camping ground, before the construction of the fort. A more detailed survey in the vicinity of the fort could reveal traces of earlier site use and, most importantly, the location of the spring.

All the structural remains at this site appear to date from the 18th century, or later. The cobbled road is similar to that at al-Hasa, which suggests that it is also contemporary with the construction of the fort in the 18th century. The road was probably built to avoid the worst of the shifting sands, which evidently created fear in the minds of some pilgrims (see, Mehmed Edib in History above). The splayed buttresses at the corners are similar to those at Dhat al-Hajj and probably also represent a response to the sandy location.

The fact that the fort continued in use up until the 1950s means that many of the features, visible in other forts, have been replaced or modernized.

10. Catalogue of Forts in Saudi Arabia

This chapter provides a summary of the Hajj forts in Saudi Arabia, from the Jordanian border at Mudawwara to the outskirts of Medina. Although these forts were not surveyed as part of the project, it was thought important to include an account of them, in order to provide a context for the forts recorded in Jordan. The forts north of Medain Saleh were described by, amongst others, Evliya Çelebi, Mehmed Edib, Doughty and Jaussen and Savignac. The account published by Jaussen and Savignac is of particular importance because it includes photographs (1997) taken during their 1907 survey; these photographs are reproduced in this volume. Also of considerable importance are the reports by the Saudi Arabian Antiquities Department, published in *Atlal*, the most comprehensive of which, is the article published by al-Mughannam, al-Helwa and Mursi (1983). The forts between Medina and Mecca are not discussed; though a list can be found in Burckhardt (1822, 660–61) and brief descriptions can be found in Pierard and Legros (1997, 11–16).

Dhat al-Hajj – (Map 5, no. 12) (Plates 134–136)

(Dat Hagg, Dar al-Hagg, Dzat Hadj, That Haj, Hagar, Bijar, Damme, Dimne)
Location: 39.04N 36.10E
Dhat al-Hajj is located 16 km to the south of the modern border with the Kingdom of Jordan.

History

The earliest Arabic reference to Dhat al-Hajj may be by al-Idrisi (1100–66) who states that the settlement of Damma (Dimne) was located to the south of al-Batniyya (Musil 1926, 328; al-Idrissi 1894, 28). However, Musil's identification of Dimne with Dhat al-Hajj is speculative and cannot be relied upon. In the 13th century Yaqut's reference to Dat Haj, as a place between al-Medina and Syria, is more convincing and is the first mention of the site by its present name (Yaqut 1995; Musil 1926, 43 n. 9). A hundred years later, Ibn Battuta also mentions the site stating, 'After two days (from Aqabat al-Sawwan/ Fasoa)

Plate 134. Dhat al-Hajj, interior of fort in 1907, by Jaussen and Savignac (courtesy of the École Biblique).

Plate 135. Dhat al-Hajj fort, from railway station in 1907, by Jaussen and Savignac (courtesy of the École Biblique).

Plate 136. Dhat al-Hajj, from south-west in 1907, by Jaussen and Savignac (courtesy of the École Biblique).

the escort encamped at the halting place of Dat Hagg, where there were two shallow wells with water from below but no building' (Ibn Battuta 1853–58, vol. 1, 254). Abu al-Fida', writing at approximately the same time, describes an incident in 1313, when the Bani Lam Bedouin gathered together at Dat al-Hajj to attack merchants travelling by camel to Tabuk, to trade with pilgrims returning from Mecca. Twenty of the merchants were killed before they were able to gain the upper hand, repulse the Bani Lam and seize 80 of their camels (Musil 1926, 43, n. 14).

A fort was first built at the site, in 1559 AD (976 AH) by Sultan Sulayman: who also established forts at Qatrana, Ma'an and Tabuk in the same year (Bakhit 1982, 98 and 223; al-Ghazzi 1650, vol. ii, 157; al-Qaramani 1611, 440). Evliya Çelebi does not appear to mention Dhat al-Hajj, but, in the place where you would expect to find a description of the site he mentions an otherwise unknown stop, Qal'at Eshme, which has a large fort with 200 rooms built by the caliph Mu'awiyya in 56 AH (Evliya Çelebi, *Seyhatnâmesi* IX, 587–604; Bilge 1979, 218–19). The Ottoman fort of Dhat al-Hajj is described by Nablusi, who travelled on the Hajj in 1694. He describes arriving at the fort, at midnight, where he encountered a group of Syrian soldiers protecting the reservoir. After collecting enough water to last for three days, the caravan departed at four in the afternoon (Musil 1926, 330–31). The Syrian Sufi, Murtada ibn 'Alawan, visited Dhat al-Hajj 15 years later and gives a different view of the castle, which he said had been partially destroyed by the Bedouin. The fort had started to collapse two years earlier, in 1705/6, when the western wall and gateway began to subside, since then the fort had been deserted and left to the Bedouin. Murtada then gives a graphic account, of how the leader of the caravan (*amir al-Hajj*) climbed onto the ruined walls and promised to rebuild the fort once he returned from the pilgrimage (Murtada ibn 'Alawan MS fol. 104b; see also Haarman 1979, 248).

By 1779 the fort appears to have been repaired, as Mehmed Edib makes no mention of it being in a ruinous

state, simply noting that it had been built by, Sultan Sulayman. Edib describes how the reservoir at the site was supplied with water obtained from a well within the fort. He describes the area outside the fort as extremely fertile, with many wild dates growing as a result of the plentiful water. At the time of his visit the fort was under the control of the Bani Selim tribe. The ground outside the fort was covered with gravel (pebbles and flint) (Bianchi 1825, 129; see also Musil 1926, 43, n. 14).

Burckhardt gives a description of Dhat al-Hajj in his appendix, although it is unlikely that he actually visited the site, relying instead on his Bedouin informants. He makes similar remarks to Edib regarding the plentiful water supply at the site, adding that although there are many date palms around the fort, these are all male and therefore, not capable of producing fruit. He also states that Bani Sakhr attacked the Hajj caravan near Dhat al-Hajj in 1757, presumably as part of a co-ordinated campaign which also saw attacks at al-'Ula and elsewhere (Burckhardt 1822, appendix III, 659) (see also, the section on internal control in Chapter 5, which puts this event in context).

In 1825 the water collection system at Dhat al-Hajj was inspected on behalf of Muhammad 'Ali Pasha (Appendix 1 in this volume). The inspector stated that the fort was a square structure, measuring 40 cubits per side and commented that it was in a good state of repair. He noted that there was one cistern (*c.f.* Doughty below) 70 cubits long, 35 cubits wide and 10 cubits deep. At the time of the inspection there was water in the cistern to a depth of 3 cubits. Although the cistern was generally in good condition, the sandy nature of the area meant that it was easily filled up with sand; he recommended, as a solution to this problem, building a wall around the cistern. Water for the cistern was provided by two springs: one inside the fort and one, at some distance from the fort, which flowed through a channel.

Charles Doughty is the first European to give a first-hand description of Dhat al-Hajj. He notes that the fort is 'a good building standing with an orchard of tall palms'. Like Mehmed Edib and Burckhardt he notes the abundance of subterranean water and wild palms in the area. The Bedouin who control the area around the fort are the Robilliat, relations of the Beni Atîeh. Doughty states that there are a number of vaulted cisterns and comments that 'only in the lesser one of them was there stored water for the Hajjaj, by so much is the pilgrimage diminished from its ancient glory' (Doughty 1979, 97).

By the early 20th century Dhat al-Hajj was accessible by the Hijaz railway and was visited by the Dominican priests, Jaussen and Savignac, on their way to Medain Saleh. They state that the fort was in good condition, having been recently restored: standing in the midst of a large date palm plantation, with a large cistern outside the walls. Above the entrance there was an inscription recording the construction of the fort in 971 AH (1563 AD), as well as, a second inscription recording its restoration in 1849 AD: both inscriptions were subsequently published by Moritz (Mortiz 1908, III, fasc. 1, 733) (for a discussion of these inscriptions, see Chapter 11). Within the courtyard of the fort there were 'two or three palms and a few pomegranate trees', in addition to a rock cut well, with a (wooden?) machine installed inside to raise water (Jaussen and Savignac 1997, 54–55).

Five years later, in May 1910, the fort was visited by Alois Musil, who seemed less impressed with the date palm plantation and suggested that it should be possible to plant considerably more given the abundance of water at the site (Musil 1926, 43). In more recent times the fort has been surveyed by the Saudi Department of Antiquities, who noted the presence of a *birka* (cistern) and two buildings associated with the railway line. The report states that the inscription, recording the restoration of the castle, is kept by the Amir of Dhat al-Hajj (al-Mughannam, al-Helwa and Mursi 1983, 51). The fort is also mentioned in the tourist guide of Pierard and Legros, who make the observation that the walls of the cistern are crumbling (1997, 77).

Description

Photographs of the fort taken by Jaussen and Savignac (Plates 134–136), and more recently by Pierard and Legros permit a brief structural description of the exterior of the fort.

Firstly, it is noticeable that the fort stands in a sandy area, where the sand outside the fort appears to be higher than the interior. The fort is built of roughly squared blocks, set into white lime mortar. The doorway is set within a wide, pointed arch recess, set in the middle of one side of the fort. Within the arched recess, directly above the doorway, there is a jagged hole in the 1990s photograph, indicating that the inscription has been removed. The fort has three storeys, a ground floor, a first floor and a crenellated parapet (the crenellations are not visible on the 1990s photo). There are no windows, or openings, on the ground floor level, but at first floor level there are five narrow openings on

each side. Each of the openings is two-courses high, with a pointed arch head cut out from the stone above (*c.f.* Qal'at Balq'a). On the upper floor level there are two rows of openings: the lower row, just above the interior roof height and an upper row with wider openings. At the corner of the fort, next to the entrance, there are two small, box-like, projections that resemble machicolations, though they are more likely to be latrines.

On the two sides of the fort visible in the photograph, there are 6 large buttresses (three on each side) similar to the buttress on the west wall of Qal'at Dab'a (see Chapter 9). The purpose of these buttresses is obviously to stabilize the fort, which has large cracks visible in both the 1905 and 1997 photographs.

Discussion

This is one of the best preserved 16th century forts on the Hajj route and despite several restorations (*c.* 1779, 1849 and *c.* 1900) the fort appears to be close to its original design. It is noticeable that there are no projecting machicolations, or corner towers, other than the obviously modern addition of the box-like latrines on the corner.

It is likely, by analogy with Qal'at Dab'a, repaired in 1870, that the buttresses date to the 1849 restoration of the fort. The other development, noticeable from the various accounts of the fort, is that in earlier times there was more than one cistern, by the 19th century this had been reduced to a single, small cistern.

Tabuk – (Map 5, No. 13) (Figs 40–41, Plates 137–140)

(Thapaua, Asi Hurma, al-Najal al-'Ajiy, 'Ayn Tabuk)
Location: 28.22N 36.32E
The fort at Tabuk stands on a slight elevation, *c.* 1 km south of the Tabuk station of the Hijaz Railway. Today the fort is surrounded by the modern town of Tabuk and is located at

Plate 137. Tabuk, exterior of fort with entrance in 1907, by Jaussen and Savignac (courtesy of the École Biblique).

Fig. 41. Plan of setlement at Tabuk, Saudi Arabia. After Jaussen and Savignac 1997.

Plate 138. Tabuk, exterior, west face with cisterns in 1907, by Jaussen and Savignac (courtesy of the École Biblique).

the junction between the commercial and residential parts of the settlement.

History

In pre-Islamic times Tabuk may be identified with Ptolemy's Thapaua. It was incorporated into the Roman province of Arabia in 106 AD. During the 5th century there was a Byzantine military post in the area, inhabited by the Bani Lakhm, 'Amila and Jdham tribes (Bakhit 2007).

Tabuk is one of the most important and most famous stops on the Syrian Hajj and is mentioned in the *Quran* ('Surat Tawba' IX) in connection with the Prophet Muhammad's expedition *ghazwat al-'usra* in 630 (AD). The expedition was successful and Muhammad received the submission of the towns of 'Ayla (modern 'Aqaba) and 'Adhra (Udruh) in modern Jordan (Ibn Sa'd, ed. Mittoch and Sachau, 165; al-Waqidi, ed. Jones, vol. 3, 989; al-Baladhuri trans. Hitti vol. 1, 92; Bakhit 2007). In the early 8th century (716 AD) the Umayyad caliph, 'Umar ibn 'Abd al-Aziz, built a mosque known as Masjid Tawba, which still survives, though it has been rebuilt many times since, most recently in 1973 (Bakhit 2007).

Tabuk appears early on in the pilgrimage itineraries; it is mentioned by the 9th century writer al-Harbi, as a stop between Sargh and Haditha (al-Harbi in Jasir (ed.) 1968, 653).Yaqut (d. 1225) includes Tabuk in his topographical dictionary and states that Tabuk had a fort with a well, date palms and a wall associated with the Prophet Muhammad (و هو حصن به عين و نخل و حائط ينسب إلى النبي) (Yaqut 1995, vol. 2, 14–15). In the 14th century, Abu al-Fida' (d. 1332), mentions it as one, of only a few, stops on a high-speed journey between Hama and Mecca (Abu al-Fida' 1960, 73). A few years later in 1326, Ibn Battuta visited Tabuk during his first pilgrimage (Hajj) to Mecca and wrote a detailed account of the settlement. He states that the town contained a spring that had been blessed by Muhammad after the famous raid in 630 AD. He relates that when the

Plate 139. Tabuk, interior of fort in 1907, by Jaussen and Savignac (courtesy of the École Biblique).

Plate 140. Tabuk, south-east corner of fort in 1907, by Jaussen and Savignac (courtesy of the École Biblique).

pilgrims reach the outskirts of Tabuk they charge towards it, as if in battle, to recall Muhmmad's conquest of the town. He also describes how the pilgrims camped by the spring for four days, filling huge pools, made of animal skin, in order to provide water for the camels and pilgrims (Ibn Battuta 1958, 160–61). Later, in the Mamluk period, Nasir al-Din Manjik had a permanent pool constructed for the pilgrims (Bakhit 1982, 189).

The site is first mentioned in the Ottoman period, in connection with an attack in 1530, when the Bedouin prevented pilgrims reaching the water at Tabuk by filling the cisterns with cut palm trees (Bakhit 2007). In 1559 Tabuk was one of four places provided with a fort under the orders of Sultan Sulayman (Bakhit 1982, 98; al-Ghazzi vol. ii, 157; al-Qaramani, 440). Four years later, in 1563, a pilgrimage itinerary lists Tabuk as a stop between Qaim al-Basayta and Wadi al-'Athar (Mustapha Pasha in 1563 AD (971 AH) (al-Jasir 1969, 184–85)).

Over a century later, in 1672, the fort was seen by Evliya Çelebi, who referred to the place as Asi Hurma (the wild Date) and stated that it was the halfway point between Damascus and Mecca. Çelebi writes that the fort was originally built in the time of Nureddin eş-Şehid, but that it fell into disrepair and was repaired during the reign of Sultan Mehmed IV. He describes the fort as a rectangular building, standing on a flat, sandy elevation and notes that it was 2,400 paces in circumference (this is either an error, or a reference to the size of the settled area). There was an iron clad gate on the north side, above this was an inscription in glazed tiles stating that the fort was repaired by Nafis Mehmed, chief financial officer of Damascus in 1062 AH (1654 AD), during the reign of Sultan Mehmed IV (r. 1648–87) (see Chapter 11, No. 7). The building accommodated 200 Janissarries, including gunners and armourers, as well as new cannons and an arsenal. Accommodation within the fort included 20 cells (living rooms), a mosque, a small bathhouse and a fountain in the courtyard. Outside the fort there was a large reservoir fed by a spring, as well as 70 or 80 storerooms and a few shops (Evliya Çelebi, *Seyhatnâmesi* IX, 296–97; see also Bilge 1979, 219; Kortepeter 1979, 238).

Twenty-two years later, Abd al-Ghani Nablusi passed through Tabuk on his return from Mecca and camped next to the fort. Within the fort there was an animal powered device, which raised water from the well and, via a channel, fed the large reservoir outside. Nablusi also remarked that returning pilgrims were usually met here by merchants from Damascus, although that did not happen on this occasion (Nablusi cited in Musil 1926, 330–31).

Tabuk was also visited by, Murtada ibn Alawan, during his 1709 pilgrimage. Murtada states that Tabuk is a strong well-organized fort, staffed with the Sultan's troops (قلعة عظيمة البنا و الترتيب و المغني فيها جند من قول السلطان). He comments on the plentiful water resources and states that they carried water from Tabuk to the next stop (al-Ukhaydhir) because his Excellency, the Pasha, believed that water there was scarce (Murtada b. 'Ali b. 'Alawan MS fol. 105a). Seventy years later Tabuk was visited by Mehmed Edib, who, like his fellow Turk, Evliya Çelebi, referred to the place as Asi Khurma. He explains that the name is derived from the wild date palms growing in the vicinity and recalls that it was visited by the Prophet Muhammad during his military campaigns. Reminders of the Prophet's presence included a mosque, recently rebuilt by Umar ibn 'Abd al-'Aziz and the remains of a place where

Muhammad is supposed to have prayed. Edib attributed the construction of the fort to Sultan Sulayman (r. 1520–66). Within the fort there was a large fig tree, beneath which was the well, which supplied water to the reservoir outside. Edib also comments on the cultivation of fruit trees found at the oasis, including fig trees, pomegranates and gourdes. The trees were tended by Arabs who lived in encampments in the vicinity – there were even a few houses (Bianchi 1825, 130–31).

Although it is unlikely that Burckhardt ever visited Tabuk, he does provide a detailed description of the place, probably derived from someone with first hand knowledge. He states that the oasis was inhabited by Arabs who cultivated the soil (*felahein*), producing, aubergines, onions and other vegetables, as well as tending fruit trees. In addition to the cultivated plants were a number of wild herbs, which were collected and sold as camel fodder as far away as Damascus (Burckhardt 1822, appendix III, 659).

Some time around 1825 engineers working for Muhammad 'Ali Pasha visited Tabuk. The short account of the site mentions the fort (40 × 40 cubits) and four rectangular cisterns, as well as a mud-brick village, surrounded by gardens containing fruit trees (Appendix 1 in this volume). Later on during the 19th century, the first European travellers began to visit Tabuk. In 1848 G. A. Wallin explored the settlement and wrote that it comprised 60 houses, in addition to the fort, which had a governor appointed by Damascus (Wallin 1979, 312–20). Twenty-seven years later, in 1875, Doughty visited Tabuk on his way to Medain Saleh; he gives the following account of his arrival, after a march of 26 hours 'We came nodding at eight o 'clock in the morning in sight of Tebuk…that ancient village, built of raw clay, appears of an ochre colour, pleasantly standing before a palm-grove, in a world of weary desert, strewn with sandstone quartz pebbles' (Doughty 1979, 112). The village was occupied by 40 families of the Humeydat tribe who lived under the protection of the fort (*kella*). The commander of the Hajj paid protection money (*surra*) for the fort to the Bani Atieh (Doughty 1979, 112–13). Less than a decade later, in 1884, Charles Huber arrived at Tabuk and described it as totally deserted (Huber 1891).

In the early 20th century Tabuk experienced rapid change; it was chosen to be one of the main stations on the Hijaz railway, with a workshop, hospital and quarantine station. The railway also brought the first archaeological expedition to Tabuk, in the form of the Dominican priests Jaussen and Savignac (1997, 57–70). This expedition provided a thorough documentation of the site, including a map of the settlement, photographs and plans. Their report described both the exterior and interior of the fort, as well as the cisterns noted by other travellers. They also recorded three Arabic inscriptions from the fort, including the glazed ceramic inscription, dated to 1654, above the main entrance, noted earlier by Evliya Çelebi (Jaussen and Savignac 1997, 292–94). Like many of the other Hajj forts, the Tabuk fort had been converted into a telegraph station 10 years before the advent of the railway and new offices for the purpose had been built on the second floor, directly above the entrance (see below for a description of the fort, including the observations of Jaussen and Savignac).

After the collapse of the Ottoman Empire, following the First World War, Tabuk was incorporated into the province of Ma'an, within the newly established Kingdom of the Hijaz. In 1925 the area was annexed by the Saudi King, 'Abd al-Aziz, who installed a governor in the fort (Bakhit 2007). By the 1950s the governors were established in their own, newly built stronghold, known as Qasr al-Sudayri, whilst the old fort was converted for use by the Saudi police (Philby 1957, 217–21). By the 1980s the Police had left. The building was abandoned when visited by King, who provides a detailed description of the interior of the fort (King 1998, 75–78).

Description

The following account is based, primarily, on the descriptions provided by Jaussen and Savignac (1997) and King (1998), as well as observations from photographs (see Plates 137–140 and Figs 40–41).

The Fort

The fort is a square building, measuring 27 m per side, with an entrance in the middle of the north side. It is built of cut stone blocks, many of which have rusticated bosses and drafted margins. The entrance is set within a rectangular panel of fine, dressed masonry. The lower half of the panel is occupied by a tall, arched recess containing the gate, a glazed ceramic inscription lies within the tympanum of the arch. The arch has a slight horseshoe profile and contains a hidden machicolation in the form of two holes, at the apex of the arch (these can be seen in the photograph of Pierard and Legros 1997, 76). The keystone of the arch is decorated with a raised boss, in the form of a rosette; this motif is repeated at the same level on either side, forming a line of three rosettes. Directly above the arch there is a rectangular window. The top of the panel is marked by a plain cornice, which Jaussen and Savignac compare to monuments in Jerusalem (1997, 60, fig. 44). Six arrow/ gun slits are visible at first floor level, with three either side of the entrance façade. The upper part of the wall, at second floor level, does not contain any crenellations, or embrasures, although it does show considerable evidence of having been rebuilt several times. Above this are the two telegraphic offices dating from the early 20th century.

The west, south and east sides all have seven arrow/ gun slits at first floor level, though on the west side, at the north-west corner, there is an additional slit at ground floor level overlooking the reservoirs. Between the time of Jaussen and Savignac's visit and King's visit in the 1980s, a mud-brick corner tower has been added to the south-west corner. In the middle of the south wall there is

a projecting structure, visible both in the early 1900s and in the 1980s, which resembles a box machicolation, although it does not appear to have any openings to the exterior. At the south-east corner there is an additional arrow/gun slit at second floor level.

The interior of the fort is built around a central courtyard, with vaulted rooms on three sides. Directly opposite the entrance on the south side of the courtyard, there is an *iwan*, built in a similar style to the entrance passage, which has been used as a prayer room and has a simple *mihrab* in the south wall (King 1998, 77). Entrance to the first floor is via a set of stairs in the north-west corner, whilst another set of stairs leads up from the first to the second floor. On the first floor, directly above the *iwan* prayer room, there is a second mosque with an inscription, on plaster, giving the name of Sultan 'Abd al-Hamid (Philby 1957, 121). King thinks that this mosque is a recent construction, both on the basis of the inscription and on structural grounds (1998, 78). However, by analogy with other forts it seems likely that there has always been a mosque in this position (*c.f.* for example Ma'an which was also built circa 1559). King also indicates that there was a mosque on the upper floor of the building, with a 'curious…tri-lobed feature in stone directly above the *mihrab*' (1998, 78).

The Reservoirs

To the west of the fort there are three, stone built, ancient tanks (only two now survive) rising above the surrounding ground level. Steps lead down into the interior and there is a subterranean inlet in one of the tanks. Jaussen and Savignac (1997, 61–62) thought that the cisterns were built around existing water sources. This idea is supported by the shape of the cisterns, which have an organic form

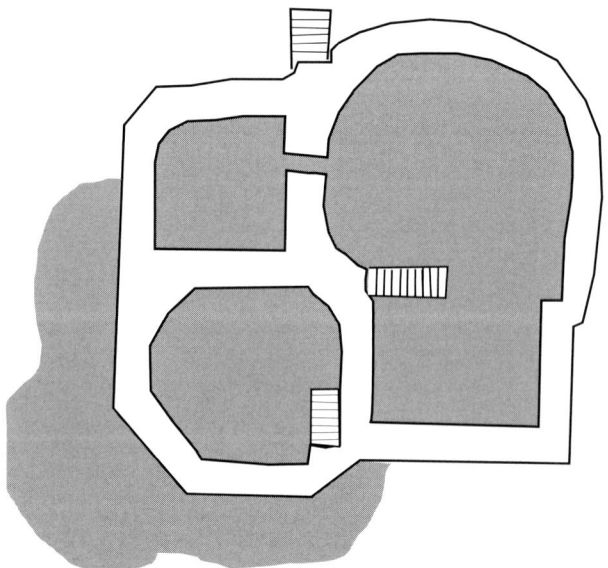

Fig. 42. Plan of cisterns at Tabuk. After Jaussen and Savignac 1997.

rather than the rectangular shape more usual for reservoirs of the Syrian Hajj route. On one of the cisterns there is an inscription dating to the reign of Sultan 'Abd al-Hamid, though it is clear that they are considerably older (Jaussen and Savignac 1997, I, 293–94, no. 3).

Discussion

Most of the writers who have discussed the fort at Tabuk consider it to be considerably older than the 1654 date given in the inscription above the gateway (*e.g.* Evliya Çelebi, Mehmed Edib, King 1998, Jaussen and Savignac 1997). Whilst documentary sources indicate a construction date in the 16th century (Bakhit 1982, 98) the bossed masonry and the mention of a fort by Yaqut, indicate that it could, in fact, be Medieval (*c.f.* van Berchem 1978, 618). Also, the fact that the fort is located on a small tell, suggests that considerably older structures may be found at the site.

Qalandariyya – (Map 5, No. 14)

(Dar al-Maghayr, 'Aqaba Haydar, Maqabrlir, Birka)
Location: 28.15N 37.05E
This site is located between Tabuk and Ukhaydhir, where the Hajj route leaves the plain for the sandstone uplands.

History

Mughayr al-Qalandariyya (مغير القلندرية = caves of the hermits) is first mentioned in the 1563 AD (971 AH) itinerary of Mustapha Pasha, as a stop between Wadi al-'Athar and 'Aqaba al-Ukhaydhir (al-Jasir 1969, 184–85). During his 1672 pilgrimage, Evliya Çelebi, stopped at two places between Tabuk and Menzil-i Akabe ('Aqaba al-Ukhaydhir). Qalandariyya is to be equated with the second of these, which he calls Mekâbir-i Âsafi Berhayâ. Çelebi relates that there was a domed shrine, half an hour from the road and states that it was built from one piece of stone and must, therefore, be the work of the devil. He also explains that the name of the place (Âsafi Berhayâ) comes from, Berhayâ, who was the child of King Solomon's vizier and the Queen of Sheba. He also relates that 5,000 Arabs of the Berhi tribe were massacred at this place – presumably leading to the site being known as, the graveyard (Mekâbir = cemetery Ott.) of the tribe of Berhayâ (Evliya Çelebi, *Seyhatnâmesi* IX, 297). Less than a quarter of a century later, Nablusi, refers to the stop of Morajer Shu'ejb, south of Tabuk, which Musil equates with Zahr al-Hajj and is probably identical with Qalandariyya (Musil 1926, 331). The site is listed in the itinerary of Hajji Khalifa in 1732 (1145 AH), under the name of Morarat al-Kalenderiyye who made the pilgrimage in 1732 (1145 AH) (Musil, 1926, 329).

The Ottoman pilgrim, Mehmed Edib, is the first to mention a fort and a reservoir at the site, which he states

were built by Osman Pasha (to be identified with Gürcü Osman Governor of Damascus 1760–71), who also built forts at Zahr al-'Aqaba (Faussu'a), Nakhlatayn, Dar al-Hamra, Valide Kuyusu and 'Antar (Bianchi 1825, 131; Barbir 1980, 138–39). He states that this site lay at a distance of 13 hours from Tabuk and was short of water, so that, sometimes, water had to be brought to the reservoir by the Hajj escort. A century later Doughty mentions the site of *Dàr el-Múghr* or *el-Kalandary*, which he describes as, a flat place next to mountains inhabited by the Sidenyin Bedu (1979, 115–16).

In the early 20th century, a station of the Hijaz railway was established at this point, complete with a railway fort (*Dar el-Haǧǧ*, Jaussen and Savignac 1997, 71) It seems possible that the fort referred to by Mehmed Edib was used as a quarry for the new buildings associated with the railway line.

Discussion

The fort does not appear to be mentioned after the 18th century (see, for example, Burckhardt 1822, 659; Appendix 1 in this volume – neither of whom included it in their list of stations). Although Doughty mentions the site he makes no reference to a fort, or a cistern. None of the accounts describe the caves, which presumably existed in the vicinity of the site.

al-Ukhaydhir – (Map 5, No. 15) (Fig. 42, Plate 141–142)

(Akhizer, Akhider, Haider, Akhdar, Haydar, Aqabat)
Location: 28.05N 37.09E
This site is located south of Tabuk and Qalandariyya and to the north of Qal'at al-Mu'azzam. It lies in a deep valley, enclosed by steep, rocky slopes, some of which are strewn with black lava. The fort stands in sandy ground at the bottom of the wadi.

History

It is possible that this site is mentioned in the 9th century itinerary of Ibn Khurdadhbih, which lists the site of, al-Muhdata, between Tabuk and al-'Akra (ed. de Goeje 1889, 150). According to Musil, writing in the early 20th century, the site of al-Ukhaydhir was also known as al-Muhdata, although he believed that the place should be identified with al-Mu'azzam (1926, 327). The site is certainly mentioned by Yaqut (d. 1229), who states that Muhammad stopped at this place during his expedition to Tabuk in 630. He also states that a mosque was built on the site where he prayed, which is now in the middle of the wadi bed (Yaqut 1995, vol. 1, 164; see also Jaussen and Savignac 1997, 77).

The first narrative description of the site is written by Ibn

Plate 141. Qal'at al-Ukhaydhir, from north in 1907, by Jaussen and Savignac (courtesy of the École Biblique).

Plate 142. Qal'at al-Ukhaydhir, from south-west in 1907, by Jaussen and Savignac (courtesy of the École Biblique).

Battuta, who states that Wadi al-Ukhaydhir (وادي الأخيضر) is in the middle of the wilderness and compares it to the valley of hell (وادي جهنم). He states that this is because one year the pilgrims became severely ill due to the Samoom wind, which dried up their water supplies. People drank water at a cost of a 1,000 dinars, but both buyers and sellers died. He tells us that this story was inscribed on part of the rock face in the wadi (Ibn Battuta 1981, 78–79; Ibn Battuta 1958, vol. 1, 161).

It appears that a cistern had been built by the early 16th century; a source writing about 1517 states that, there was fighting between the tribes of the area and as a result the pool at al-Ukhaydhir had not been filled with water for the pilgrims (Bakhit 1982, 16; Ibn Tulun, ed. Mustafa 1962, II, 66, 69 and 71). The immediate cause for the construction of a fort at the site was the conduct of Mulhim, one of the chiefs of the Mafarija tribe, who made a series of attacks against the Hajj caravan in 1530. Amongst the deeds perpetrated by Mulhim, was the poisoning of the reservoir at Ukhaydhir with ground colocynth (*hanzal*) (Bakhit 1982, 147). The following year (1531) Sultan Sulayman ordered the construction of a fort at the site. It was stipulated that the fort should be manned with 20 troops, the cost of which was partially to be met by demanding a payment from the pilgrims (Bakhit 1982, 98 and 223; Jaussen and Savignac 1997, 294–96). A few years later, in 1563 (971 AH), Mustapha Pasha lists two sites 'Aqabat al-Ukhaydhir (عقبة الأجيضر) and Birka Hayder (بركة حيدر) either of which may be identified with the present site (al-Jasir 1969, 184–85). However, it seems likely that the former refers to the pass through the wadi, whilst the latter refers to the site chosen for the fort and cistern (*birka*).

Evliya Çelebi visited the fort in 1672, he writes that the place was inhabited by Bedouin of the Haydari (Sufi) sect, who claimed that the fort was built by their founder, 'Ali Haydar al-Karrar, in the year 47 AH. He also states that it was repaired by the Damascus official, Haydar Pasha. It was a strong, square building, located near three water

channels, although it only measured 400 ft in total. He states that the fort had a room for the commander of the Syrian Janissaries. The fort was entered through an ironclad door on the north side and inside there were rooms (places) for 40, or 50 men, as well as 12 long cannons and a mosque (Evliya Çelebi, *Seyhatnâmesi* IX, 297–98; see also trans. in Bilge 1979, 219).

At the end of the 17th century, in 1694, al-Nablusi visited al-Ukhaydhir on his return from Medina. He notes that the well-built fort contained a well of excellent water, said to have been dug by the Prophet al-Khadr (Elijah?). Nablusi also remarks that each year soldiers would come from Damascus, to protect the water cisterns from the Bedouin, who used the water for their animals (Musil 1926, 330–31).

In 1709 Murtada ibn 'Alawan arrived at Ukhaydhir, which they thought was under the protection of Haydar Pasha, though it was, in fact, under the control of the Bani Manjak (Murtada b. 'Ali b. 'Alawan MS fol. 105a). Seventy years later, Mehmed Edib, arrived at Ukhaidhir and wrote a detailed description of the place, stating that it comprised a holy mosque used by the Prophet, a fort with a well and five cisterns outside.

Edib noted a number of religious associations with the site, stating that it was here that Job was covered with insects that were miraculously turned into stones, which were still visible. The site was also called the station of the Prophet Elijah and inside the fort was the tomb of Haydar, also a focus of pilgrimage. The fort was guarded by 20 soldiers, who were responsible for keeping water in the reservoir for the pilgrims. Edib states that the fort was built in 1531 (938AH) by Sultan Sulayman, presumably based on his reading of the inscription which is above the gate to the fort (for a discussion of this point see, van Berchem 1978, 619–22 esp. 621). Edib also gives a vivid description of the setting of the fort, which he describes as surrounded by mountains (Bianchi 1825, 132–31).

Although it is unlikely that Burckhardt ever visited al-

Ukhaydhir, he includes it in his list of stopping places on the Syrian Hajj route and states that 300 years ago (*i.e.* before the Ottoman period) the Hajj followed a different route to the east, which was later known as *Darb al-Sharqi* (the eastern road) (Burckhardt 1822, appendix III, 659). In 1825 the site was inspected by engineers working for Muhmmad 'Ali Pasha, they produced a detailed report on the water resources available there. The report states that the square fort (40 × 40 cubits) is built of stone and in a good state of repair. The report also mentions four cisterns, three of which are in reasonably good repair, while a fourth, large, cistern needed a considerable amount of work before it could be used again (Appendix 1 in this volume).

The first European to have visited Ukhaydhir and left a description was Charles Doughty, who visited in 1875. Like Mehmed Edib before him, Doughty comments on the many religious association of this place, including the shrine of Elijah located within the fort. Doughty also mentions the inscription above the doorway, later published by Jaussen and Savignac (1997, 294–96; see also below), which he compares to a Roman ensign board (see Chapter 11, No. 11). He describes a large cistern outside the fort, divided into three compartments and fed by water from a well within the fort. He also observed some huts next to the fort where a few nomads lived, under the protection of the garrison, in order to harvest 'camel knot-grass'. Whilst camping with the Hajj at this station, Doughty sneaked into the fort to look at some inscriptions carved on the walls, but was discovered by some of the Moorish guards when he entered the shrine of Elijah (Doughty 1979, 116–18).

The first, systematic, archaeological investigation of al-Ukhaydhir, was carried out by Jaussen and Savignac, on April 1st 1907. At the time of their visit the fort was in use as a telegraphic station, with three telegraph operators and two soldiers. In addition to taking photographs of the fort, they produced a plan and a squeeze of the inscription above the doorway, as well as a documentation of the newly built railway bridge across the wadi (Jaussen and Savignac 1997, 74–78 and figs 53–56). In particular, they noted that this was one of the smallest forts on the Darb al-Hajj and that it produced excellent water. They measured the well, which was 2 m in diameter and 10 m deep; they also relate a story that there was a cavern beneath, within which the water flowed like a river ('Au fond existe, parait-il, une grotte dans laquelle, au dire de certaine Arabes, on verrait l'eau couler comme dans une rivierre'). Like Doughty, they mention the Arabs who inhabit the vicinity of the fort, collecting fodder for camels and generally serving the garrison. They also identified the ruins of a small mosque, which they identified as the one mentioned by Yaqut, built to commemorate the place where Muhammad prayed during his expedition to Tabuk in 630 (*c.f.* Yaqut 1995, vol. 1, 164; Jaussen and Savignac 1997, 77). [Although in their text this mosque is described as 4–5 m north of the castle, from the context, it seems more likely that 400–500 m was meant].

Description

The following description is based on the photographs, plans and description of the fort provided by Jaussen and Savignac (1997, 75–78) and others; any interpretation is my own (see, Plates 141–142 and Fig. 42).

The Fort

The fort stands on a flat piece of ground, at the place where the wadi opens out. The fort is three storeys high, built of, at least, 26 courses of dressed stone, with battlements at the top, surmounted by stepped crenellations (merlons). The entrance to the fort is on the north side, although it cannot be approached directly, because it is partially obscured by the walls of one of the five cisterns, which rise approximately 1 m above ground level. Above the doorway there is a panel (1.15 m long × 0.53 m high), containing an inscription detailing the construction of the fort in 1531, during the reign of Sultan Sulayman. Next to this large inscription, a stone has been inserted with a short, 4 line, inscription, also dated to 1531, recording the presence of 100 troops in the fort (for a discussion, see Chapter 11, Nos 11, 12 and 13, as well as, Jaussen and Savignac 1997, 294–96; van Berchem 1978, 619–22). Above the arch of the doorway there is a large, projecting, box machicolation resting on four two-tier corbels. There is one slit, to the east of the gateway, at ground level and two slits either side of the machicolation. At the north-east corner there is a small projecting corner turret.

The west side abuts two of the five basins and contains three slits at ground floor level and two at first floor level. At the level of the parapet (*i.e.* second floor) there are a few small gun slits, just below the level of the crenellations. In addition to these features there are four, square, holes at the north end of the wall, at a level equivalent to the floor of the first level (*i.e. c.* 4 m above ground level). It is also noticeable that the lower parts of the west wall do not appear to be pointed with mortar, in contrast with the upper part of the wall, which is extensively covered in lime mortar. At the south-west corner there is a projecting corner tower, similar to that on the north-east corner. The south wall is similar to the west wall, with slits at first floor and ground floor level. At the level of the parapet, towards the west side of the wall, there is a projecting wooden feature, which evidently functioned as a latrine. At the south-east corner there are remains of a ruined stone structure, which appears to abut the fort.

Although there are no photographs showing the east side of the fort, it is evident from the plan, that a small hut was built next to it, to house a pump for drawing water from the well.

The Cisterns

The cisterns comprise a complex of six stone lined structures, with walls of different thicknesses, rising *c.* 1

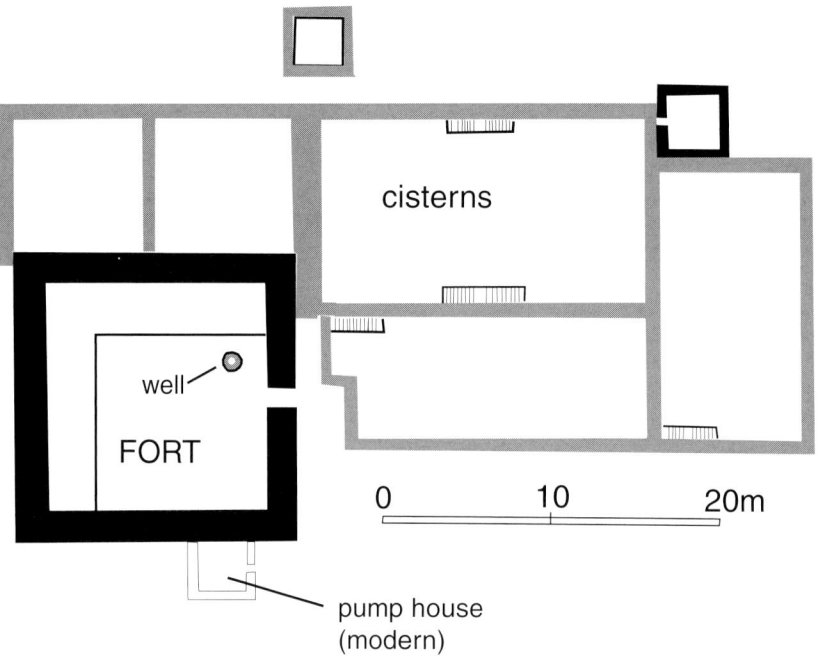

Fig. 43. Plan of fort and cisterns at al-Ukhaydir. After Jaussen and Savignac 1997.

Plate 143. Qal'at al-Mu'azzam, in 1907, by Jaussen and Savignac (courtesy of the École Biblique).

m above ground level. The largest cistern measures 19 m × 10 m and has two sets of steps leading down into the interior. All the cisterns are connected, with the exception of one small tank (3 m × 3 m) lying a few metres west of the others. At the north-west corner of the complex there is a square building, described by Jaussen and Savignac (1997, 77, fig. 55a) as a an ancient room ('chambre ancienne').

This appears to be a small, one room, stone building with a doorway in the south side overlooking the largest cistern.

Discussion

This site is of particular interest because a shrine appears to have been incorporated within the fort. Despite the

1531 date, which is known from the inscriptions above the doorway and the historical sources, it seems likely that the fort incorporates an older construction, particularly when looking at the masonry of the south wall, which has some irregular masonry near the base. The internal arrangement of the fort is also unusual, as rooms are only built against the south and west walls. Certainly the fort would repay further detailed investigation (*c.f.* al-Mughannam, al-Helwa and Mursi 1983, 53, no. 14)

Some attention should also be paid to the name of the site, which is given variously as al-Akhdhar (the Green) and al-'Ukhaydhir (the small green place). The name al-Akhdhar is often linked to the poet Elijah in Middle Eastern tradition and may reflect some ancient association. On the other hand, the name may reflect the greenness of this site, in an area of overwhelming aridity.

Qal'at al-Mu'azzam – (Map 5, No. 16) (Plate 143)

(Vadii-Essed, Qal'at Shirin, Birka al-Mu'azzam, Belkis, al-Muhdata, Qal'at Birkat al-'Adham)
Location: 27.43N 37.27E
Qal'at Mu'azzam is located mid way between Tabuk and Medain Saleh, at an altitude of 967 m. The fort stands next to the confluence of the Wadi Saba and the Wadi al-Dera' and a large mud lake or *qa'* (قاع). It is surrounded by buildings associated with the Hijaz railway including, a small fort, water tower and station.

History

The site of Mu'azzam contains some of the oldest structures built for the Syrian Hajj route. The site may be mentioned as early as the 9th century by Ibn Khordadbeh (820–912), who refers to the site of al-Muhdata south of Tabuk (Musil 1926, 327). However, the earliest clear reference to the site is by Ibn Battuta, who states '[Going on] from there the caravan halts at the pool of al-Mu'azzam, a vast basin, called after al-Malik al-Mu'azzam of the house of Ayyub, in which the rainwater collects in certain years but which is generally dry in others' (Ibn Battuta 1958, vol. 1, 161–62). It is probable that, al-Malik al-Mu'azzam, can be identified with Saladin's nephew, Mu'azzam 'Isa, ruler of Damascus from 1218–27, although it is also possible that it may be Saladin's brother, Turan Shah, who ruled Yemen until 1181.

In the 16th century (971 AH/1563 AD) itinerary of Mustapha Pasha, Birka al-Mu'azzam (بركة المعظم) is mentioned as a stop between Wadi al-Asad and Abu Habib (al-Jasir 1969, 184–85). Birka al-Mu'azzam is also mentioned in connection with an event in 1530 (937AH), when the chief of the Mafarija tribe made a fierce attack on the Hajj caravan at Dhat al-Hajj and then filled the reservoir at Mu'azzam with the corpses of animals to prevent pilgrims drinking the water (Bakhit 1982, 222).

In 1672 Evliya Çelebi visited the site, which he referred to as Qal'at Shirin and Birka al Mu'azzam. He wrote that the facilities at the site were built by the Ayyubid, Turan Shah, son of Malik Shah, in 1250 AD (648 AH) and restored in 1573 (981 AH) during the reign of Sultan Murad, under the orders of Koca Sinan Pasha. He also relates the story of an incident, which took place in 1625 (1035 AH), when the Arabs tricked the garrison with some sweets (*halva*). He states that the fort was built on an elevated position, with four towers and a garrison of 400 men. On the east side there was a gateway, either side of which was an inscription recording the date of construction, the name of the architect was not given (for inscriptions see Chapter 11, Nos 15, 16 and 17, see also Bilge 1979, 220; Evliya Çelebi, *Seyhatnâmesi* IX, 298–29).

Twenty-two years later, Abd al-Ghani Nablusi, visited Qal'at al-Mu'azzam and found it deserted. He states that it had formerly had a garrison of Syrian soldiers, who had been murdered by the Bedouin. In addition to the fort, he noted the presence of a large, square cistern (*birka*), part of which was built of the same material as the fort (Abd al-Ghani Nablusi 1694 AD cited in Musil 1926, 330–31). Murtada ibn 'Alawan visited 15 years later, in 1709, but does not appear to have stopped, perhaps indicating that it was still abandoned (Murtada b. 'Ali b. 'Alawan MS fol. 105b).

Seventy years later the fort was still abandoned according to Mehmed Edib (Bianchi 1825, 133), who noted that the cistern was ruined and incapable of holding water. He also states that the place took its name from the cistern built by Malik al-Mu'azzam in 1204 (600 AH).

The anonymous *Report to Muhammad 'Ali Pasha* (Appendix 1 in this volume), gives the name of the site as, Qal'at Birkat al-'Azzam, and states that the fort is abandoned and the gateway blocked with sand, because the cistern does not contain water. The cistern is described as a square structure, 100 cubits per side and 20 cubits deep. At the time of the inspection it was, at least, half full of mud and was also leaking. In addition to the cistern there was a dam, damaged and in need of repair, which channelled water from the adjacent wadi.

In the 1870s Doughty was clearly impressed by his first site of al-Mu'azzam, writing: 'We came, always ascending in very high country, to our camp, at four in the afternoon, having marched nineteen hours. Here is Birket Moaddam and an abandoned kella, the fairest and greatest in all the road, with the greatest cistern'. However, Doughty also noted that the cistern was ruinous and there was no water to be had at the site (Doughty 1979, 119). The fort was still in a ruinous condition in February 1884, when visited by Charles Huber travelling between Tayma and Tabuk. Huber, who spent the night in the fort, noted that three, out of four, of the domes covering the towers had collapsed (Huber 1891).

Both the fort and the reservoir had been renovated by 1905 when the site was visited by Jaussen and Savignac. On arrival, the Dominican fathers were served with glasses

Plate 144. Dar al-Hamra, in 1907, by Jaussen and Savignac (courtesy of the École Biblique).

of fresh lemonade, made by the resident telegrapher. They described the fort as one of the largest on the Hajj route and also the best built. Above the doorway they noted an inscription stating that it was built in 1031 AH (1621 AD). They describe the interior plan as ordinary, comprising a square courtyard, with storerooms on the ground floor and living quarters on the first floor. They also noted that the façade of the fort was decorated with the skulls of antelopes, bought from local Bedouin. The reservoir was in operation and held water, although it was noted that this was only because of the construction of the railway, as water was very scarce in this area. In addition they noted the large, partly collapsed, deflection dam (Jaussen and Savignac 1997, 87–89 inc. 2 photographs).

In the 1980s the site was included in the Saudi Antiquities Department Survey, which noted that the deflection dam was 500 m long and that there were two wells in addition to the well within the fort (al-Mughannam, al-Helwa and Mursi 1983, 54).

Description

Further to the written description given by Jaussen and Savignac, it is possible to provide additional information based on their photograph of the fort (1997, 87, fig. 58 reproduced as Plate 143 in this volume) and that in the guide of Pierard and Legros (1997, 75–76). Firstly, it is notable that it is built out of bossed masonry, with four round corner towers. There are arrow slits at ground floor level, both in the towers and the curtain walls of the fort. The entrance is set within a shallow arched niche and approached by, at least, three stone steps. Above the entrance there is a large projecting machicolation, resting on five corbels.

Discussion

Jauseen and Savignac assumed that the fort was built

in 1621 (1031 AH), based on the inscription above the entrance. This view is supported by the account of al-Hibri (al-Hibri 1975, 126), who states that the fort was built in the 1620s on the orders of Sultan Osman II. However, van Berchem (1978, 622) believed that the inscription referred to a restoration, rather than the construction of the fort.

Whilst it is clear that the building, in its present form, dates to the 17th century, it is possible, that it is built on the site of, or incorporates some remains from, a 13th century building. The issue will not be settled until a detailed architectural survey of the building has been carried out.

Dar al-Hamra – (Map 5, No. 17) (Plate 144)

(Shaka al-Ajuz, Shaq al-'Ajuz, al-Beraikah)
Location: 27.20N 37.43E
This site is located on a high plain, 3 km to the west of Dar al-Hamra railway station.

History

Although there is no record of a fort at the site before the 18th century, it was clearly a recognized stopping place as early as the 16th century, when Shaq al- 'Ajuz (شق العجوز) is mentioned by Mustapha Pasha as a station between Zalaqat (الزلاقات) and Jabal Tariq (جبل الطارق) (Mustapha Pasha in al-Jasir 1969, 184–85). In 1672 the site was visited by Evliya Çelebi, who states that the name derived from a time when, the caliph 'Ali divided a woman into two parts with his sword (Çelebi trans. Bilge 1979, 219). This site is also mentioned by, Murtada b.'Ali b.'Alawan, who went on the Hajj in 1709 (1120–21 AH) and lists Dar al-Hamra between Qal'at al-Mu'azzam and al-Madain [Saleh] Mabraq al-Naqa (Murtada b. 'Ali b. 'Alawan MS, fol. 105b).

The first description of a fort at the site, is given by Mehmed Edib, who visited the site in 1779. He states that the station is located 18 hours south of Birka al-Mu'azzam and has a number of names including, Maghareh al-Zir, Akhra, Dar al-Hajr, Makbara (the cemetery), Pirinj-Avassi (valley of bronze), Jaltak Salih, Shak al-Ajuz and Dar al-Hamra. Edib states that the fort was built, by order of Osman Pasha, in 1167 AH (1754) and in the following year the site was provided with a reservoir (*birka*). The area around the fort was covered with small stones, which the pilgrims made into cairns. The vicinity of the fort was known by a number of names, including Jabal al-Taf, Jabal al-Nitak, Mezhem and Senoua, although he states that the Arabs generally referred to it as *kuçuk kaya* (Turkish = small rock). On leaving this [elevated] place the pilgrims descended a sandy slope, leading into a narrow passage, known as the place where Salih's camel miraculously appeared; on passing here there was usually a terrible noise of gunfire from the caravan, to mark this legendary spot (Mehmed Edib 1779 in Bianchi 1825, 133–34).

Although Burckhardt mentions Dar al-Hamra in the list

Plate 145. Medain Saleh, exterior in 1907, by Jaussen and Savignac (courtesy of the École Biblique).

of stopping places on the Syrian Hajj, he makes no further comment and it is unlikely that he visited the site (1822 appendix III, 657). The fullest description of Dar al-Hamra is provided by the anonymous author of *The Report to Muhammad 'Ali Pasha*, dated 1825 (Appendix 1 in this volume). The fort (which would have been less than 70 years old at the time of the inspection) is described as a square building, measuring 30 cubits per side. Although, the fort was in an excellent state of preservation, it was not in use due to a shortage of water at this location. The commander of the fort had had the door removed and the entrance filled with sand, to prevent the Bedouin destroying the building and removing its contents. Next to the fort there was large square cistern, measuring 90 cubits per side and 20 cubits deep. Unfortunately, the cistern was full of sand and contained no water. The inspector recommends various measures to improve water catchment at this site, although it is not clear if these were carried out.

Doughty's description of Dar al-Hamra, written 50 years later, gives a similar picture of an abandoned fort. His account also gives a good sense of the emotional impact of arriving at this difficult station:

> 'Before sunset we came to our white tents pitched beside the ruinous kella, without door and commonly abandoned, Dár el-Hamra 'the red house'. Ruddy is the earth and rocks whereof this water-castle is built. High and terrible it showed in the twilight desolation of the world. We are here at nearly 4200 feet. After marching above one hundred miles in forty three hours we were come to the water – water-dregs teeming with worms' (Doughty 1979, 120).

Doughty also notes the different locations in the vicinity of Dar al-Hamra and comments that the passage known

as, Shuk al-'Ajuz, derives its name ('old lady') from a female pilgrim, who gave money to have the roadway made smooth (1979, 121).

On Thursday, 3rd April 1907, Jaussen and Savignac visited Dar al-Hamra on their way to Medain Saleh. They state that the fort had been refurbished for use as a telegraph station, with a garrison of three, or four, soldiers. They note the presence of a tower, outside the north-east corner of the fort, which was joined to the fort by means of a walkway, supported on a high arch. The function of the tower was to enable the garrison to obtain water from the cistern (*birka*), without having to go outside the fort. They also describe a barrage, which was intended to divert water from the wadi, 400 or 500 m away. Unfortunately, there had been no rain in the area for the past three years and the cistern was dry, so the garrison had to obtain water from one of the wells located at a distance of 7, or 8, hours to the south-east (Jaussen and Savignac 1997, 95).

In addition to their comments on the fort, the Dominican fathers also noted the presence of three groups of ruined structures, located to the south of the fort. The first group comprised a group of small, rounded, enclosures built of drystone walls, with a doorway to the east. Facing these structures was a second group of buildings that were generally larger and built of roughly squared stones. The third group, were rectangular structures, or houses, some of which were joined together, whilst others were detached. There were also some drystone enclosures associated with these buildings. This third group also included the remains of a large, rectangular building (10 paces east–west and 11 paces north–south), with a deep concave *mihrab* in the centre of the south wall. The whole complex was interpreted as the remains of an Arab village, or encampment.

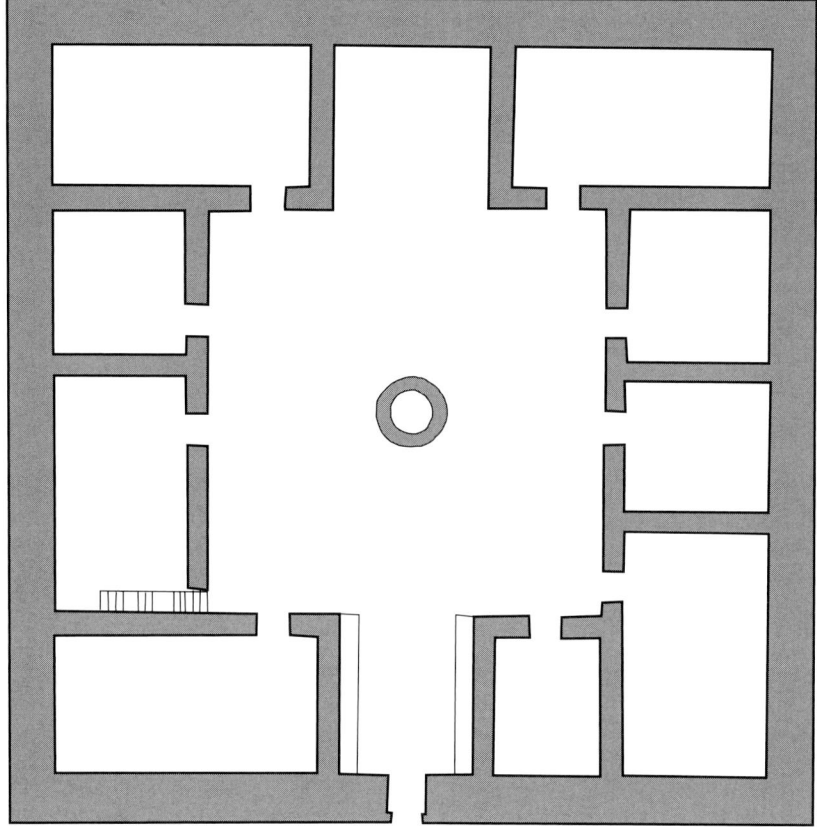

Fig. 44. Plan of ground floor of fort at Medain Saleh. After Jaussen and Savignac 1997.

In the early 1980s the site was surveyed by the Department of Antiquities, who called it, al-Beriakah, to distinguish it from the railway station at Dar al-Hamra, 3 km to the west. It is described as a medium sized site, which includes a partly destroyed *birka* (cistern), a deflection dam and a small, partially destroyed, castle. Pottery at the site was reported to be early Islamic (al-Mughannam, al-Helwa and Mursi 1983, 55).

Architectural Description

It is possible to give a visual description of the fort based on the photograph taken by Jaussen and Savignac (1997, 95, fig. 61). The fort has three storeys, a ground floor, first floor and upper floor, or parapet walk, and is built of (limestone?) blocks in regular courses (min. 27 courses high) with white lime mortar. The south side of the fort, which includes the gateway, appears to be built of finely dressed (ashlar?) masonry, whilst the other sides are built of smaller, squared, blocks. The gateway is set within a tall, shallow, recessed arch, with benches either side. Directly above the gateway there is a box machicolation, resting on four corbels and at both the south-east and south-west corners there are projecting towers of similar design. Four evenly spaced openings are visible (1–2 courses high) at a level corresponding to the base of the upper

floor, or parapet. The tops of the walls are marked by step crenellations and a number of narrow, barely visible slits. Directly above the entrance and the machicolation, there is a domed cupola. It is noticeable that the top part of the south-west corner is missing, however in general, the fort appears to be well maintained.

The external tower mentioned by Jaussen and Savignac is a rectangular structure, joined to the main fort by an enclosed walkway (at parapet level) supported on a wide arch also provided with a box machicolation.

To the south-east of the fort there are traces of two walls meeting at a right angle, this appears to be the corner of an earlier large reservoir, aligned at an oblique angle to the fort.

Discussion

The fort had evidently been repaired between Doughty's visit in 1875 and 1907 when it was converted to a telegraphic station. The external tower was probably added at this time (*i.e.* early 20th century). The other notable feature of the fort is that water appears to have been particularly scarce. The traces of an earlier reservoir, in front of the fort, may relate to pre-Ottoman facilities at the site, whilst the village may also be of Medieval date.

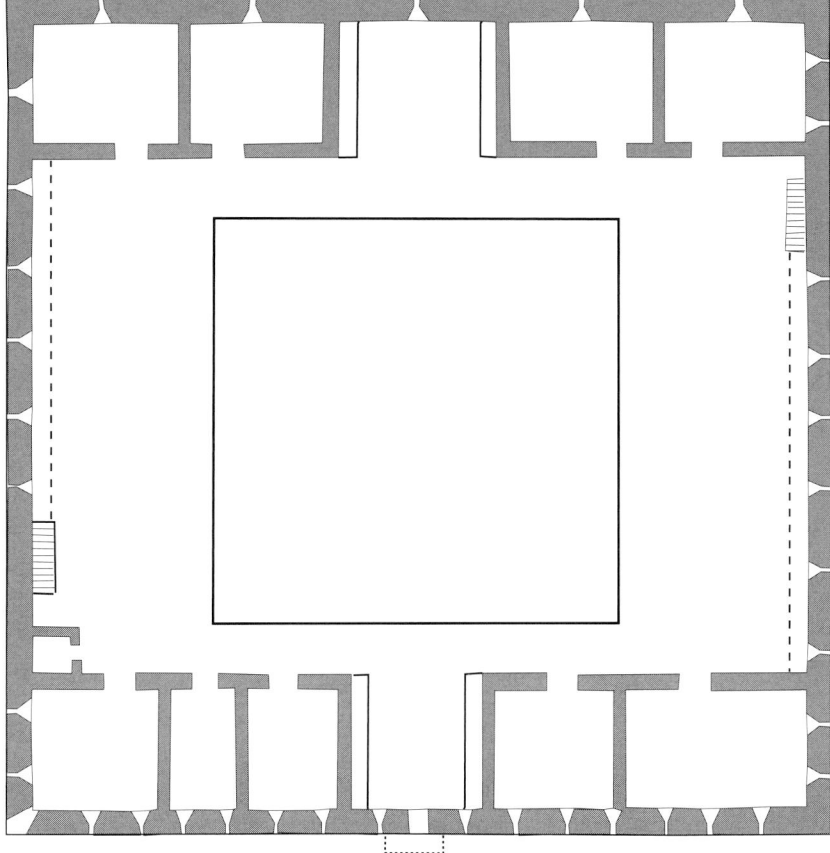

Fig. 45. Plan of first floor at Medain Saleh. After Jaussen and Savignac 1997.

Medain Saleh – (Map 5, No. 18) (Figs 43–45, Plate 145)

(Abyar Salih, Qal'at al-Hijr, Hejr, Medáin Sâlih', Koraï Salih, Hadjer, Aadal)

Location: 26.50 N 37.55E

Medain Saleh is located in a broad, flat, sandy valley to the east of the elevated Harrat al-'Uwayrid. The sides of the valley are sandstone cliffs, which, in various places, have been carved into tomb façades. The fort at Medain Saleh is located next to the Hijaz Railway station and to the north of Jebel Ethlib. The area contains plentiful water from springs and wells, which are surrounded by date palms and other trees.

History

Medain Saleh has a long and detailed history of settlement. In Islamic tradition it is linked with the Prophet Salih, who was one of the ancient Thamud tribe, who lived in the area. The *Quran* (Sura xi, 64–71) relates that Salih preached the doctrine of monotheism to the Thamud and produced a live female camel from a rock, as proof of his beliefs. Instead of believing Salih, the people of Thamud killed the camel and, as punishment, were killed in their houses by a disaster, often interpreted as an earthquake

(*Quran* Sura vii, 77). Pre-Islamic historical texts that refer to the city of Hegra include, Assyrian texts, as well as the writings of Strabo and Pliny. In addition to the historical texts there are hundreds of inscriptions at the site, in a wide variety of pre-Islamic scripts, including Thamudic, Nabatean, Minaean and Lihyanite. The Thamud were probably a tribe of South Arabian origin (South Arabian *hijr* = town) who established themselves at this point on the trade route between Yemen and Syria. Arabic legends locate this as the spot where Hagar and her son Ishmael were buried after being abandoned by Abraham. Remains of the settlement itself are located in the central part of the valley and include the remains of a town wall, building foundations and ceramic sherds. The most notable features of the site are the carved tomb façades, which resemble those of Petra, with which it was linked both by trade and culture.

An Arabic tradition states that Muhammad stopped at the site in (9 AH/631 AD), during a raid on Tabuk, yet he forbade his men from drinking the water from the wells, because the town had been cursed by God (Ibn Battuta 1958, vol. 1, 161–62). Nevertheless, the town continued to be used as a stop on the route between Mecca and Syria, thus in the 9th century (mid-3rd century AH) al-Harbi mentions al-Hijr as a halting place between Juneena and

Wadi al-Qurra. The ancient site appears to have been virtually abandoned by the 10th century, when Istakhri mentions it as a village (Vidal 2008, 365b 'al-Hidjr').

When Ibn Battuta visited the site, in 1326, he made no mention of a town, describing the stop simply as 'the well of al-Hijr'. However, he does give an account of the Muslim traditions surrounding the site, including a description of the bones of the inhabitants lying in their rock hewn houses [tombs], as well as, an ancient mosque and the place where the miraculous camel knelt (Ibn Battuta 1958, vol. 1, 161–62).

Medain Salih is not mentioned in the 16th century description of the Hajj road by Mustapha Pasha (al-Jasir 1969, 184–85). However, Evliya Çelebi, who made the Hajj in 1672, notes that he passed through Abyar Salih where there were the remains of 7 cities. Çelebi also makes the observation that this place marked the border of the *Ka'ba*, presumably a reference to the proximity of the Holy Cities (Evliya Çelebi, *Seyhatnâmesi* IX, 271a; Bilge 1979, 220). The site was also visited by Murtada ibn 'Alawan, who describes al-Madain (المداين) as a *manzil* on the route to Medina (Murtada b. 'Ali b. 'Alawan MS, fol. 106a).

A fort was built at the site, for the first time, in the mid-18th century by Gürcü Osman, on the orders of the Damascus governor, Esat Paşa al-'Azm (Ibn al-Qari *al-Wuzara*, cited in Barbir 1980, 140). The first description of the fort is given by Mehmed Edib, who states that the place contained a fort and a cistern, the cistern being filled from a large well within the fort. He also states that pilgrims stopped at this site for a day and were able to buy a number of provisions, including, lemons, oranges and dates (Bianchi 1825, 134–35).

In 1825 the site was visited by inspectors preparing a report for Muhammad 'Ali Pasha (Appendix 1 in this volume). The inspector reports it to be a square fort (25 × 25 cubits), in a good state of repair, with a large cistern nearby (30 × 30 and 10 cubits deep). Inside the fort there was a well, the water being raised by a device powered by mules. The water from the well would then flow into the cistern by means of a channel, which, at the time of the inspection, had collapsed.

The most detailed description of the fort and associated structures, is given by Charles Doughty, who stayed at the fort for two months in 1875 (Doughty 1979, 125 ff.). He not only describes the architecture of the fort, but also gives a description of daily life in the *kella*, both when the Hajj caravan was present and also in the intervening time. He describes the fort as 70 feet square, with a large well in the centre known as *Bîr en-Nâga*, where the miraculous she camel of Salih is supposed to have drunk. He states that the water was contaminated by water leaking from the adjacent cess pool (Doughty 1979, 133). He describes the foundations of the fort as, made of 'stone without mortar laid upon the weak loamy bottom; the walls above are rude courses of stone laid in clay; the work is only pointed with mortar' (Doughty 1979, 134). He says that the limestone blocks were brought by camel from *Jebel Îss*, two days

away and then burnt to produce lime for the mortar. Outside the fort there was a leaking cistern, 18 × 22 paces and 3 fathoms deep, which was filled with water from the well. Doughty also gives an interesting description of a walled garden outside the fort, cultivated by the commandant of the fort. In addition to the fort garrison, there was a group of Arab nomads permanently pitched outside the fort gate (Doughty 1979, 135).

In April 1907 Jaussen and Savignac visited the site. In addition to providing the most detailed study of the ancient remains, they also made some useful observations on the Ottoman fort. Arriving on 6th April they pitched their tent next to the fort, which was manned by two telegraphers and four guards. Outside there were two black tents, containing several Bedouin women ('d'allure un peu suspecte') and two babies. They described the fort as a square building (20 m × 20 m) built of small, square, blocks, with courses between 0.25 m and 0.3 m in height. Embedded into the walls there were three Minean inscriptions (one in the west wall and two at the south-west corner). They described the well inside the courtyard, powered by mules and soon to be replaced by a pump. Outside, on the east and south sides of the fort there was a garden containing a few pomegranate trees, as well as, 15 date palms of various sizes. There were also, two or three, semi abandoned mud-brick houses built against the north wall of the garden. The rectangular cistern (24 m × 22 m) was located to the south of the fort and had a depth of 4 m (Jaussen and Savignac 1997, 107–10).

Description

It is possible to give an architectural description of the fort from Doughty's written description and drawings, and the photographs and descriptions of Jaussen and Savignac (reproduced here as Plate 145).

The entrance is in the middle of the North side of the fort and directly above this, at first floor level, there is a box machicolation supported by four projecting corbels. On either side of the machicolation there is a single slit (*c.* two courses high) At the north-east corner there is a projecting tower, also supported by corbels. Along the top of the fort, at parapet level, there are a series of slits (two courses high). On the south-west corner there is another projecting tower, located at the level of the parapet (*i.e.* second floor).

Discussion

Because of its location within the precincts of the ancient town of al-Hejr, the Ottoman fort has been recorded by a number of travellers in great detail, however, it is not clear whether the present refurbishment is an accurate representation of the fort in its historical form (see, for example, Pierard and Legros 1997, 77).

One feature of the fort, worth noting, is the relationship between the fort and the cistern. The water to fill the cistern was lifted from a well within the fort, by means of an animal powered device (*saqiya*) and filled the cistern via a subterranean channel. A very similar arrangement can be seen at Qal'at al-Hasa (see this volume, Chapter 9).

al-'Ula – (Map 5, No. 19)

(al-'Ela, El Olla, Aala, El-'Ally, Dedan)
Location: 26.35N 37.55W
Al-'Ula is a small town, located 25 km to the south of Medain Saleh and 45 km north of Abyar Ghannum.

History

In pre-Islamic times the settlement was known as Dedan and large numbers of Dedanite and other pre-Islamic inscriptions have been found in the area (Bosworth 2007; Frenkel, 1996, 180). Recent archaeological surveys of the site have revealed late Byzantine and Umayyad remains, in addition to earlier (Nabatean?) material (Gilmore, al-Hiwah and Resseeni 1982, 10–11, 19, 20).

Tradition states that Muhammad prayed at this place *en route* between Medina and Tabuk. The first mention of the Arabic name of the town is in the work of the 10th century writer, al-Isfahani (al-Jasir 1968, 397), who states that it was called al-'Awali. Ibrahim b. Shuja provides more information, stating that it was a small town with a *qal'a* and an *amir* (Bosworth 2007). al-'Ula is also found in the writings of Abu al-Fida' (d. 1331) (Abu al-Fida' 1960, 73; also cited in Musil 1926, 328) which state that it is one of three main stops on the route between Damascus and Mecca (the others are Birka, Zizia and Medina). At approximately the same time, the famous Moroccan traveller, Ibn Battuta (1958, vol. 1, 161–62), passed through al-'Ula on his first pilgrimage to Mecca. He states that it was a large village, with plentiful water and date palm gardens; he also indicates that it was of considerable importance to the Hajj caravan, which stayed there for four days. During this time the pilgrims were able to wash their clothes, deposit any excess baggage and obtain provisions for the remainder of the journey. Ibn Battuta also states that this was the furthest south that a Christian merchant would be able to travel, as only Muslims were allowed on the route between here and Mecca.

The earliest Ottoman references to al-'Ula are both connected with attacks on the pilgrimage caravan. In 1521 there was an exceptional occurrence, when the villagers of al-'Ula are reported to have attacked the Hajj caravan. In response the villagers were punished and fined – Barbir suggests that the villagers may, in fact, have been Bedouin (1980, 175 and appendix IX, 200). In the 1570s, Sulayman the Magnificent commissioned the construction of a fort at this site, presumably in response to earlier disturbances (Bakhit 1982). In 1632 another attack on the Hajj caravan is reported near al-'Ula, this time by Bedouin armed with muskets. The attackers were repulsed by the use of a cannon, although four pilgrims were killed (al-Hibri 1976, 58; Faroqhi 1994, 67). It is not clear why these attacks

occurred at this place, though it is perhaps significant that commercial caravans were often sent from Damascus to al-'Ula to meet returning pilgrims. For example, in 1567–68, there was an urgent request sent from the commander of the Hajj caravan to send food and camels to al-'Ula (Faroqhi 1944, 44). Also, in 1672, Evliya Çelebi mentions al-'Ula in connection with an arrangement whereby, Bedouin in the region of al-'Ula would provide pilgrims with grain (deposited in the fort?) and in return Bedouin in Muzayrib would receive a payment of grain (Evliya Çelebi, *Seyhatnâmesi* IX, 575, 599; Faroqhi 1994, 43).

The town is also mentioned by other Ottoman travellers, for example, Abd al-Ghani Nablusi (cited in Musil 1926, 330), who stayed there on his way back from Medina in 1694, also, Hajji Khalifa, (*Jihan-numa* (1145 AH) cited in Musil 1926, 329), who visited there some time before 1732 AD. In 1709 the fort was visited by Murtada ibn 'Alawan, who states that there was a plague of locusts in the area, which meant that the pack mules accompanying the Hajj had to be fed with *ma'buk* (camel fodder) made of millet, instead of the usual fresh fodder (Murtada b. 'Ali b. 'Alawan MS fol. 106b; Haarman 1979, 249). Later on in the 18th century, al-'Ula is the location of another Bedouin attack – the worst disaster in the history of the Ottoman Hajj. In 1757 a group of Bedouin, led by chief Qa'dan of the Bani Sakhr, attacked the caravan and killed 20,000 pilgrims (Barbir 1980, 30, 178).

The first detailed description of al-'Ula, is provided by Mehmed Edib (*Menasik* 80–81; Bianchi 1825, 136; Barbir 1980, 135 n. 69) who visited the town during his pilgrimage of 1779. He states that it is located 9 hours from Medain Saleh, lying between two mountains and with plentiful running water. He also observes that the road between here and Abyar Ghanum passes through an area full of Acacia trees. Amongst the produce of al-'Ula he lists, grape vines, dates, citrus fruits (oranges, lemons and limes) melons and cucumbers. Edib is also the first traveller to remark on the fort of al-'Ula, which he indicates was built during the time of Sultan Sulayman [the Magnificent]. The strategic significance of this location is emphasized by the fact that there is a direct, desert route, with 6 stops (including Bosra and Azraq) from here to Damascus. On other occasions, however, al-'Ula is by-passed when the Hajj caravan takes a direct route from Medain Saleh to Zumurrud, known as Sahel al-Matran (Bianchi 1825, 135).

The first European traveller to mention al-'Ula, is Burckhardt (1822, appendix III, 659). Although it is unlikely that Burckhardt visited the town himself, he adds the important information that it comprised about 250 houses and states that the inhabitants are of North African origin. Sixty years later (1875–78), al-'Ula was visited by Charles Doughty whilst staying at the nearby Hajj fort of Medain Saleh. Doughty's description (1979, 180–91) contains a lot of detail about the social structure of the town, as well as information about its history. One of the most interesting parts is his account of the re-foundation of the town by 40 Berber pilgrims:

'Journeying upon the Syrian haj road, with their religious master, from Mecca and Medina, they were pleased with the solitary site, where they found the ruins. The Holy man bade his disciples await him there, whilst he went up to Jerusalem. "How, they answered him, may we endure in this desert place and there is nothing to drink?" Then the saint struck his burdon in the sand, and there welled up a vein of water; it is that luke warm brook which waters their village; also his Jacob's staff put down roots and became a palm tree' (Doughty 1979, 182).

Doughty also made observations about the physical appearance of the town, thus he observed a number of underground water systems (*qanats*), amongst the palm groves, near the entrance to the town (1979, 180; *c.f.* also al-Nasif 1988/1408). The houses were built of stone set in mud mortar, with tamarisk beams used for the ceilings and the roof (Doughty 1979, 184–85). The town had a number of public coffee houses and a mosque (*masjid*), the roof of which served as a platform for the muezzin in the absence of a minaret (Doughty 1979, 182). He also noted that many of the inhabitants had several houses and that most of the people lived on the first floor, because the ground floor rooms were damp (Doughty 1979, 181). It is notable that Doughty makes no mention of a fort, though his chief interest at this point was looking for Nabatean inscriptions.

During the 1980s al-'Ula was investigated by the Saudi Antiquities Department (al-Mughannam, al-Helwa and Mursi 1983, 56), who noted that there was an earlier town lying to the north of the inhabited area (see also, Pierard and Legros 1997, 48, for a view of the old town). The Saudi survey also noted a castle within the ruins of the old town, which included the tomb of Musa ibn Nussair. Sixteen miles south of al-'Ula is the site of al-Mabiyat, which was first excavated in the early 1980s by the Department of Antiquities of Saudi Arabia and which has been identified with the ancient trading town of Wadi al-Qurra (Gilmore, al-Hiwah and Resseeni 1985; Frenkel 1996, 181) and the Medieval settlement of al-Qurhwas ('Abd 'Allahal-Nasif, cited in Bosworth 2007). More recently, in 2006, excavations have been carried out by the Department of Archaeology, King Saud University (Muzhafir 2006). The excavations have recovered ceramic material from the Byzantine and Umayyad periods, up to the 12th century AD (5th century AH). Structures uncovered include houses, as well as a town wall, enclosing an area of 800 m × 800 m. To the north of the early Islamic and Medieval remains, stands a fort known as, Qal'at al Faqeer.

Description

This building, also known as Qal'at al Hafayir, comprises a rectangular courtyard building with four round corner towers. The lower part of the building is made of coursed rubble blocks. The date of this building has yet to be determined pending a detailed structural analysis.

Discussion

It is evident from the historical references and archaeological information that al-'Ula is a town of considerable antiquity, which may have been destroyed and rebuilt several times. One of the more interesting historical references is al-Hanafi's statement, that the town had a *qal'a* as early as the 13th century; it seems likely that this is the ruined building located on the rock outcrop (Jabal Musa bin Nusair) in the middle of the old town of al-'Ula (al-Faqeer 2009, 302–5). The descriptions given by Doughty and Burckhardt indicate that the town was rebuilt, either in the early, or the late, 19th century, by North African settlers. It is possible that this followed the abandonment of the site in the mid-18th century, following the massacre of 20,000 pilgrims by the Bani Sakhr tribe in 1757. The attack took place after two years of drought and was led by the tribal chief, Qa'dan. If this is the case the recovery must have been quite rapid, as Mehmed Edib's description of 1779 indicates a thriving settlement.

Abyar Ghannum/Salih – (Map 5, No. 2)

(Tavamir, Matrân and Khifa el-Zir)
Location: 26.15N 38.15E
There are several references to this site, located between al-'Ula and Qal'at Zumurrud, but they give very little information, either on the nature of the facilities, or, the history of the site. Although the site is marked as a fort on modern maps of Saudi Arabia, there is no modern description of the site and no indication as to the style, date, or condition of the fort and/or its facilities.

Possibly the earliest description of the site as part of the Hajj route, is given by the 14th century traveller, Ibn Battuta (1958, vol. 1, 161–62) who describes a camping ground, one day's journey south of al-'Ula on the Syrian Hajj route. Ibn Battuta gives the name of this site as, Wadi al-'Itas and describes it as 'a place of violent heat', relating a story of how the fatal Samoom wind killed most of the pilgrims at this spot, in the year of the Amir al-Jaliqi. In translating this part of Ibn Battuta's narrative, Gibb identifies Amir al-Jaliq as governor of Gaza, stating, that in 1309 AD (708 AH) the Syrian Hajj was led by his son-in-law, Qutlughtimur al-Nasiri (Ibn Battuta 1958, vol. 1, 163, n. 33). There are, however, no more Medieval references to either the site, or this disaster and it is not certain whether this is the site mentioned in later Ottoman documents as, Abyar Ghanam. However, the location of this site, one day's journey from al-'Ula, matches the 50 km between al-'Ula and Abyar Ghanam.

Evliya Çelebi mentions a fort five hours from al-'Ula, which may perhaps be identified with Abyar Ghanum, although the distance of 50 km between the two would suggest a 10 hour journey. Çelebi states that the fort was located on a sharp rock, in a deep valley and was built by the Fatimid caliph Mu'izz al-Din in 358 AH (Evliya Çelebi,

Seyhatnâmesi IX, 604; Bilge 1979, 220). It is equally possible the Çelebi was referring to another fort, such as the citadel at Khaybar to the north-east of Qal'at Zumurrud (see, for example, Pierard and Legros 1997, 83).

The first official reference to a fort at this site is an order dated, 26th March 1722 (8 Cemaziyelâhir 1132), which stipulates that 300 of the local (Damascus) Jannisaries would share responsibility for garrison duty at Medain Saleh and Abyar Ghanam, on a four year cycle. With this arrangement the combined strength of both garrisons would have been 75 men (Barbir 1980, 148, n. 121–22). More detailed information about the site and fort is found in the writings of the 18th century pilgrim, Mehmed Edib (Barbir 1980, 196–97, appendix VII, n. (c)). Edib states that the site is know by a number of names including, Bir Ghanum, Tavamir, Matrân and Khifa al-Zir. He describes the surroundings as a desert covered with small black stones, next to a vast plain, surrounded with deep gullies. One part of the road leads though a forest of Tamarisk trees, whilst the other part leads through mountains (Bianchi, 1825, 136). He further states that if there is no water at the site it will be brought there by the escort of the Hajj caravan. Finally he states that this is one of the most difficult stations on the entire Hajj route.

The only European writer to mention the site is Burckhardt, who simply lists Biar el-Ghanam as the 21st stop and states that it is a place with many wells of fresh water (Burckhardt 1822, appendix III, 659).

Conclusion

It is possible, that the scarcity of references and the confusion over the identity of this site is a result of the fact that the Hajj took two different routes between Medain Saleh and Zumurrud. One route went via al-'Ula, whilst the other went directly to Zumurrud, using the route known as Sahel al-Matrân (Bianchi 1825, 135), in which case Abyar al-Ghanum would have been by-passed. The date of construction of the fort is unknown, though it was certainly built before 1722 when it is mentioned in official documents (see above) and possibly as early as the 10th century (3rd century AH), if this is, indeed, the same fort as the one mentioned by Evliya Çelebi.

Zumurrud – (Map 5, No. 21)

(Qal'at Zumurrud, Mughyar Zumurrud, Shihab Ahmar)
Location: 26.10N 38.22E
Qal'at Zumurrud is located *c.* 4.5 km west of the Hijaz Railway station of the same name. It stands on flat ground, at the bottom of a narrow wadi and is prone to flash floods.

History

The site is first mentioned in the 16th century (1563/971 AH) account of Mustapha Pasha, where it is referred to as Mughayr al-Zumroud (مغاير الزمد) (1563 (971 AH) (al-Jasir 1969, 184–85). Evliya Çelebi visited Bi'ir-i -Zümürrüd in 1672 and described it as a caravan halt with water, located in the middle of a very harsh stony desert. He states that there was a rocky pass, regarded as very dangerous, until made safe by a brave Turkish soldier (Evliya Çelebi, *Seyhatnâmesi* IX, 303; Bilge 1979, 220). A century later Mehmed Edib visited the site, which contained a fort and a cistern recently repaired by the decree of Mehmed Pasha ('Azm) (Bianchi 1825, 136; Barbir 1980, 196–97).

The first detailed description of the facilities at the site is given in the 1825 *Report to Muhammad 'Ali Pasha* (Appendix 1 in this volume). The report describes the fort as a square, stone building within which there was a mule-powered device, which raised water from a well that was no longer in use. Outside the fort there was a second well, which, according to the engineers, was dependant on rainwater rather than any subterranean source. The *Report* also refers to a square cistern (20 × 20 × 10 cubits), which was completely dry at the time of the inspection. By the 1870s the fort appears to have been abandoned; according to Doughty, who planned to accompany an official expedition to investigate its condition (1979, 204).

In the 1980s the Saudi Department of Antiquities carried out a brief survey of the fort, noting its resemblance to that of Valide Kuyusu (Qal'at al Sawra) (al-Mughannam, al-Helwa and Mursi 1983, 57, no. 30). The site is mentioned by Pierard and Legros who include a photograph of the entrance to the fort (1997, 74–75).

Description

This is a square building, made of roughly squared blocks, set in lime mortar, with dressed limestone blocks used for architectural details. The walls are mostly standing to their full height of three storeys, with stepped crenellations visible at second floor (parapet) level. The gateway is located within a shallow, arched recess in the middle of the west wall. Above the gateway, within the tympanum of the arch, there is a square recess, which almost certainly once contained an inscription. Directly over the entrance there is a box machicolation, with three small slits in the front, resting on four, two-tier, corbels. At the south end of the west face (near the south-west corner) a semi-round tower projects from the façade. The top of this tower is capped with a small dome.

The south wall overlooks the square cistern and has the remains of two projecting towers. The first of these towers is located near the east end of the façade and consists of three projecting corbels and an open arch. The remains of the second projecting tower are located at second floor (parapet) level; the tower appears to have been significantly smaller. The east wall has collapsed through water erosion from the nearby wadi.

Discussion

The fort resembles that at Valide Kuyusu (Qal'at al Sawra) with the exception of the projecting tower, which is a unique feature. Like many of the other forts it requires a full survey.

Valide Kuyusu – (Map 5, No. 22)

(Bir al-Jadid, Qal'at al Sawra, Valide-Capoussi, Sha'ab al Na'im, Bir al-Waalida)
Location: 26.01N 38.34E
This fort is located to the east of the Hijaz railway line, *c.* 2.7 km from the railway station of Bir al-Jedid. It stands on a soft red sandy plain, enclosed by high red volcanic mountains to the west and south.

History

The site may be identified with Sha'ab al-Na'im (شعب النعام = canyon of the ostrich) listed as a stop after Mughayr Zumurud (مغاير الزمد) by Mustapha Pasha in 1563 (971 AH) (al-Jasir 1969, 184–85). The first detailed description of the site appears in the account of Evliya Çelebi, who visited the site in 1672 and refers to it as al- Bi'ir al-Jadid. He discusses how a large well had been built at the site in the previous year (1081 AH/1671 AD) under the patronage of the mother of Sultan Mehmed IV (r. 1648–87). When completed the well was 100 paces (in circumference?) and 40 fathoms deep. However, before the arrival of the Hajj caravan the Arabs had filled the well with stones and brushwood. The Pilgrimage commander Hussein Pasha ordered the soldiers to climb down into the well and remove all the rubbish, which only took one hour. Next to the well a *musalla* (prayer place) with a *mihrab* had been constructed. The place is surrounded on all four sides by very extreme desert. A yellow, putty-like, substance, which doctors were able to use as a laxative, was extracted from the surrounding area. He also states that although the place had a good well for the 70,000 pilgrims, it was in need of cultivation. Near the well Evliya noted a wadi, known as Shu'ayb al-Ni'am, where the prophet Moses looked after the sheep of Shu'ayb. Also nearby was a long grave attributed to the prophet Hud (Evliya Çelebi, *Seyhatnâmesi* IX, 303–4; see also Bilge 1979, 220).

In 1709 Murtada ibn 'Alawan arrived at Sha'ab al Na'im (شعب النعام), which he described as a wadi. Within the wadi there was a place called Bir al-Jadid (البير الجديد), which had a water lifting mechanism (الماء السقية). Seventy years later Mehmed Edib arrived at the place, which he called Valide-Capoussi. He stated that there were many wells at the site and that one was dug under the orders of the mother of Sultan Ahmed I (r. 1603–17). Edib also states that there was a fort and that a reservoir had been built under the orders of Gürcü Osman Pasha (Governor of Damascus 1760–71), who built five other forts on the Syrian Hajj route (Barbir 1980, 139–40; Bianchi 1825, 137).

During the 1820s engineers working for Muhammad 'Ali Pasha inspected the site, which they referred to as Bir al-Walida. They described the fort as a square building (30 cubits per side), well maintained and in a good condition. Within the fort there was a well from which water was drawn using a mule powered device, which provided water to a square cistern (25 × 25 × 10 cubits) outside. In addition there was another well, outside, fed by a spring at the bottom (Appendix 1 in this volume).

In the early 1980s the site was surveyed by the Saudi Antiquities Department, who published a brief description of the fort, which is referred to as Qal'at al-Sawrah (al-Mughannam, al-Helwa and Mursi 1983, 57–58, no. 33). A further description of the site is provided by Pierard and Legros (1997, 74 and 81).

Description

The following description is based primarily on the reports published by al-Mughannam, al-Helwa and Mursi (1983) and Pierard and Legros (1997). The site comprises a fort, a cistern and a well. The well is faced in limestone, has a depth of 15 m and is 8 m wide. The fort is a square building (21 m × 21 m) built around a central, rectangular courtyard (11 m × 10 m). Directly above the entrance, on the north-west side, there is a projecting box machicolation resting on four corbels. On the north-east face there is a projecting tower, similar to the box machicolation overlooking the well. The interior comprises three floors, a ground floor, first floor with accommodation and a parapet on the second floor.

Discussion

It is evident, from the historical accounts above that two different dates are given for the construction of the first well at this site. Evliya Çelebi states that the well was dug under the orders of the mother of Mehmed IV in 1671, whilst Mehmed Edib, writing over 100 years later, ascribes the fort's well to the Mother of Ahmed I, presumably prior to his death in 1617. Without additional information it is not possible to decide which of these accounts is more reliable, though it could be the case that the well was renewed during the reign of Mehmed IV.

Hadiyya – (Map 5, No. 23)

(Hadia, Hadiyah, Hadiyya Eshmesi, Hediye Eshmeler)
Location: 25.31N 38.47E
Qal'at Hadiyah is located in Wadi Khaybar, *c.* mid-way between al-'Ula and Medina and 8 km to the west of Hadiyah railway station. At this point, known locally as al-Waqr, the wadi bed narrows to 500 m as it runs between two rocky outcrops. It's location, near the confluence of several wadis, means that it has plentiful water.

History

The first reference to Hadiyah on the Hajj route, is in the writings of Ibn Battuta, who mentions it as the next stopping place after al-'Ula and the last stop before Medina. He describes it as a camping site with underground water, which is reached by digging through the sand; he complains that the water is brackish (Ibn Battuta 1958, vol. 1, 163; Ibn Battuta, ed. Ramadi, 79). The site is also mentioned in the itinerary provided by Mustaph Pasha in 1563 (971 AH) who locates it between Jabal Ahmar (جبل أحمر) and Mabraq al-Naqa (مبرك الناقة) (Mustapha Pasha in al-Jasir 1969, 184–85). The first time a fort is mentioned at the site is during the rule of Sultan Murad III in 1576 AD (984 AH), when, according to al-Biruni, a citadel and pool were planned at this camping ground (Bakhit 1982, 110, n. 4; MD xxix, no. 224 Dhu'l, 984, pl. 94).

It is not clear whether a fort and cistern was actually built at this time, although this has generally been assumed. However, the pilgrimage account of Evliya Çelebi suggests that either the fort had not been built, or that it had fallen down, or that he was in the wrong place. He states, 'From this station [Bi'r al-Zamurrud] we walked for 17 hours and reached the station of Hadiyya Eshmesi where we saw no building at all. We walked for 15 hours and came to Fahlatayn fort' (Evliya Çelebi, *Seyhatnâmesi* IX, 604; Bilge 1979, 220).

In the 18th century it is clear that the Ottoman authorities believed that there was a fort at Hadiyya, even though it was in a ruinous condition. In 1709 the governor of Damascus, Nasuh Pasha, ordered the repair of the fort of Hadiyya 'to secure a base of operations deep in the Hijaz' (Barbir 1980, 137). The newly repaired fort was to serve as the place where the *cerde*, the 2,000 strong military escort from Damascus, would meet returning pilgrims on their way north. The cost of the enterprise was considerable; a total of 24,122 *kuruş* (15,000 *kuruş* from Aleppo and Damascus in the first year and 9,122 *kuruş* from the poll tax of Damascus in the following year) (Barbir 1980, 137–38 based on official receipts. BA is in Turkish Archive sources).

Seventy years later, the site was visited by Mehmed Edib who gives an interesting account, that, is worth quoting in full:

'Hadiyya Eshmesi, at twelve hours from Valid-Capoussi has a fort built by Sulayman Pasha. The water coming from the wells has a laxative quality it is believed because of the presence of *senna* in the earth because the earth which produces these plants always has a laxative effect. The majority of the people whom the pilgrims come across in this place are either badly dressed or completely naked. There is a fort called Antar built by Osman Pasha. The name Hadiyya (the present) comes from the time of the Prophet's battle against the people of Khaybr after which he came to this place where his comrades gave him presents' (Bianchi 1825, 137).

The significant feature of Edib's description is that he appears to have seen two forts at the same place (this will be discussed further below).

Burckhardt's description of the site, in his appendix, adds the interesting information that the Hajj caravan stopped here for two days, during which time people would make the short (four hour) journey to Khaybar to buy provisions (1822, 659). In 1825 the water sources at the site were inspected on behalf of Muhammad 'Ali Pasha, who describes a small, stone built, fort which had been neglected and allowed to fall into disrepair. Although he states there were no cisterns, he notes that there was plentiful water, which, at the time of the rains, flooded the area around the fort to a depth of one cubit (Appendix 1 in the volume). Doughty (1979, 204) mentions Hadiyya, although he almost certainly did not visit and does not add any information of use.

In the 1980s the site was investigated by the Saudi Antiquities Department, which noted the existence of two forts, one square, the other round, or polygonal (al-Mughannam, al-Helwa and Mursi 1983, 58, site no. 34). In the 1990s both forts were included in a tourist guide to the area (Pierard and Legros 1997, 74 and map, 79). The following description combines information from both sources. The square fort stands within the wadi, whilst the other stands, on a rocky outcrop, 500 m away.

1. Fort in the Wadi

This is a square building, with an entrance (1.3 m wide) on the north side, leading into a rectangular courtyard (12.95 × 12.15 m) from which open a number of rooms on the east and west sides. It is built of black basalt, set in a mortar of sand and mud, and is in a ruinous condition.

2. Fort on rock outcrop

This building stands on an outcrop, 10 m above the wadi. It is built of roughly squared, black basalt blocks, set in a yellow/white gypsum mortar and aligned in even courses. It has a pentagonal shape with towers at each of the angles. There is a low entrance (1.5 m high) on the west side and a well to the east of the fort. Inside there are two levels, with entrances to the towers through low doorways. The towers have two storeys, with a room on each floor, all of which are provided with arrow slits. In addition there is a staircase, leading up to a parapet walk overlooking the wadi.

Discussion

In view of the presence of two forts at this site, it seems likely that these may correspond with the two castles mentioned by Evliya Çelebi. If this is the case, the fort in the wadi is more likely to be the earlier structure, built by Sultan Sulayman, both because of its ruined condition and its shape, which corresponds with other 16th century Hajj forts. The ruined condition of this fort could be explained by its low down location in the wadi, which may have caused it to flood (Appendix 1 in this volume) and eventually be abandoned.

The fort on the rocks is a more likely candidate for the 18th century fort, built to serve as a base for the 2,000 strong *cerde*, sent to escort the pilgrims back to Damascus. The larger size of this building would also explain the considerable costs expended by Nasuh Pasha in the early 1700s. Architecturally, this fort is similar to other Ottoman forts, such as, Rumeli and Anadolu Hisar, guarding the Bosphorus outside Constantinople (Istanbul). Another example may be the Ottoman fort at Tiberias.

Nakhlatayn – (Map 5, No. 24)

(Fahlatayn, Shajwa)
Location: 25.04N 38.59E
This fort is located amongst date palms, in a small oasis, at the northern end of the village of Shajwa. It stands on the bank of a wide wadi, which runs south–north towards Wadi Hamad.

History

One of the earliest historical references to the site is in the 16th century (971 AH/1563 AD) itinerary of Mustapha Pasha (al-Jasir 1970, 184–85), where it is listed as Fahlatayn (الفحلتين) lying between ʿAqaba al-Suwda (العقبة السوداء) and Sad ʿAli (سد علي). The site is also mentioned by Evliya Çelebi, who describes an ancient castle, enclosed by black mountains. Çelebi states that the castle dates from the time of Alexander and was built by a person identified as ʿAntar. However, Çelebi also notes that the castle was deserted ('Ammâ içinde âdemi-zâd yokdur'). He reports that one hour to the east of the ʿAntar fort, there was a place with plentiful water where the pilgrims gathered and were able to wash themselves (Evliya Çelebi, *Seyhatnâmesi* IX, 305). It seems likely that this place may be identified with the site of the later fort. In 1709 the site was visited by the Syrian pilgrim, Murtada ibn ʿAlawan (Murtada b. ʿAli b. ʿAlawan, MS fol. 106b; Haarman 1979). He describes Fahlatayn as a stop (قناق) between Hadiya (هدية) and ʿAqaba al-Suwda (العقبة السوداء).

In 1779, the site was visited by Mehmed Edib, who gives the first description of the Hajj fort and associated facilities soon after they were constructed. He states that the place was surrounded by mountains and recalls the legend of the pre-Islamic ruler, whose castle was located on a hill top nearby. He also indicates that there was a village here, with a well excavated under the orders of Nasuh Pasha, Governor of Damascus from 1708–14. Besides this well the settlement contained seven other wells, which provided sweet water for the pilgrims. The area around the site contained large numbers of trees and the villagers sold citrus fruits to the pilgrims. The fort and associated cistern were built later, under the orders of Gürcü Osman Pasha

(Governor of Damascus 1760–71) who also built forts at Zahr al-ʿAqaba (Faussuʿa), Qalandariyya, Dar al-Hamra, Valide Kuyusu and ʿAntar (Bianchi 1825, 82–83; Barbir 1980, 138–39).

In 1825 the site was inspected by officials – the results were recorded in *The Report to Muhammad ʿAli Pasha* (Appendix 1 in this volume). This document describes the fort as a large, square, building, measuring 40 cubits per side; it was in a good state of repair. Within the fort there was a well from which water was extracted by a mule powered device, which, at the time of the inspection, was not working because one of the mules had been killed and the other had been starved to death (for a complete account of the loss and replacement of the mules, see Appendix 1). Immediately next to the fort there was a rectangular cistern (50 × 35 cubits) and 10 cubits deep. The interior of the cistern had filled up with sand and the engineers recommended cleaning the interior and repairing the plaster lining. The engineers also suggested the construction of a wall around the edges, to reduce the amount of sand accumulating inside. The report also mentions that there was a small town (*medina*) next to the fort, which had its own wells.

There are no records of Europeans visiting the fort, although, it is mentioned by both Burckhardt and Doughty in their descriptions of the Hajj route. Burckhardt wrote that this was the last fort before Medina and also mentioned the presence of apes (probably baboons; see Pierard and Legros 1997, 25–27) 'and what the Arabs call tigers' (probably Arabian leopard) at this place (Burckhardt 1822, appendix III, 660). Both Doughty and Burckhardt mention, Istabel ʿAntar, though Doughty calls this a mountain, rather than an ancient building. Doughty also indicates that the site of the fort is known as Sújwa (Doughty 1979, 204).

The first archaeological investigation of the site took place in the 1980s, when it was surveyed by the Saudi Antiquities Department (al-Mughannam, al-Helwa and Mursi 1983, 60, site no. 38 Shajwa (204/2)). This report states that the fort is a square building (25 m × 25 m) built of black basalt blocks, laid in a mixture of sand and mud, and pointed with white gypsum (lime) plaster. The walls are described as 10 m high and there are four (projecting?) corner towers, each with an entrance covered with a wooden lintel; the fort is also defended by a parapet, with a number of gun/arrow slits. The entrance is set within an arched recess, in the middle of the side of the fort and is set below corbels (originally carrying a machicolation?). A similar corbelled construction (machicolation) is visible on the opposite (west) face of the fort. Above the entrance there is an Arabic inscription, attributing the construction of the fort to Othman Mansour (*c.f.* Mehmed Edib's account above). By the 1990s the fort appears to have suffered some deterioration, thus (Pierard and Legros 1997, 73 and map p. 78) state that three, out of the four, corner towers had fallen. Pierard and Legros (1997) also make the observation that this fort resembles that of Zumurrud.

Discussion

In view of the historical information and location of the site, it seems likely that the village of Shajwa grew up around the fort following its establishment in the mid-18th century. This is one of only a few successful examples, where the establishment of a Hajj fort promoted the development of a permanent settlement – in this case made possible by plentiful water. This may be the reason that the name of the site evolved from Fahlatayn (Ar. = two male beasts), probably a reference to the geological features of Jabal 'Antar, to Nakhlatayn (Ar. = two date palms) indicating a small settlement. The name Shajwa appears to be of more recent origin and probably refers to the village rather than the fort.

Wadi al-Qurra – (Map 5, No. 25)

(Qal'at Abiar al-Nasif, Biar Naszeif, Wadi al-Aqeyq, 'Abyaar Tandheef, Abar Nasief, al-Mililieh)
Location: 24.50N 39.09E
This site is located on the south bank of Wadi Rashad, to the north of the village of Mulayleh. As its name implies ('valley of the villages') this site is located in an area of farmland *c.* 50 km north-west of Medina.

The name Wadi al-Qurra is confusing because it also refers to a series of settlements stretching south from Medain Saleh to Medina (*c.f.* Frenkel 1996, 180). In recent scholarly literature, Wadi al-Qurra has become identified with the ancient trading site of al Mabiyat, near al-'Ula (Gilmore, al-Hiwah, and Resseeni 1985, 109–25; al-Mughannam, al-Helwa and Mursi 1983, 57). However, from the historical source presented below it is evident that, from at least the 18th century, this site was known as Wadi al-Qurra.

History

The site is first mentioned by the 10th century AD (mid-3rd century AH) writer al-Harbi (al-Jasir 1969, 653), who includes it in a list of places on the road from Damascus to Mecca. Harbi locates Wadi al-Qurra to the south of al-Hijr (Medain Saleh) and the north of al-Saqiya.

The site is not mentioned in other Medieval sources on the Hajj, such as Ibn Battuta and Imad al-Din, although this may mean that it was considered as belonging to Medina. In the 16th century, Mustapha Pasha (Mustapha Pasha in al-Jasir 1969, 184–85) lists Wadi 'Aqeeq (وادي العقيق) as four stops south of Fahlatayn (Nakhletayn) and four stops before Medina on the 'Tariq al-Sham ila Makka', indicating that this may be identical to Wadi al-Qurra. In 1672 Evliya Çelebi refers to Wadi al-Qura al-Atiq, suggesting that there may have been ruins, or at least some feeling of antiquity in the area (Evliya Çelebi, *Seyhatnâmesi* IX, 604; Bilge 1979, 220). Çelebi also notes that there were a number of villages in this area and that their agricultural inhabitants were kind to pilgrims; presumably in contrast to the Bedouin.

The first time a fort is mentioned at the site, is in the itinerary of the 18th century pilgrim Mehmed Edib (Bianchi 1825, 139) who visited in 1779. Edib gives a number of names for the site, including, Wadi al-Kareh and Dar al-Koura, he also states that the desert in this location was known as, al-Atik (*c.f.* Wadi al-'Aqeek above). This area was known as the edge of the territory of Medina and was a control point for quarantine in times of plague. Edib describes the environment as a fertile valley, between high mountains, with plentiful water. He further states that this area was the home of the Bani Kalb tribe, until they were dispersed during the rule of the Caliph 'Umar, he observes that the ruins of their buildings are still visible. At the time of his visit the settlement contained, a fort, baths, a mosque and gardens; but they were in a ruinous condition. By tradition, the mosque was once used by the Prophet Muhammad. Within the mosque there was a bone suspended from the roof and on it were written the words, 'Do not eat me for I was poisoned'. On leaving the settlement, Edib noted some irrigated gardens, known as Sakiya Osman (Sakiya is a device for raising water for irrigation).

A number of points are noticeable from Edib's description, firstly, he observes two types of ruins, those that belong to the Bani Kalb and are evidently very old, and those of more recent times, including the baths, mosque and fort. Secondly, the area was considered part of Medina and, as mentioned above, this may have been a reason why it was not included in most pilgrimage itineraries (see above). Lastly, there appears to have been some recent investment in the area by the Ottomans, as indicated by the name, Osman's Well.

Less than 40 years later, Burckhardt (1822, appendix III, 660) mentions the site as the last station before Medina and states that there are a large number of wells, which have to be re-excavated each year due to wind blown sand. Burckhardt does not mention a fort at the site and states emphatically that the last Hajj fort was located at the previous stop, Nakhletein.

The anonymous *Report to Muhammad 'Ali Pasha* (Appendix 1 in this volume), gives the name of the site as 'Abyaar Tandheef (lit. the cleaning wells), presumably referring to the fact that the wells have to be renewed (cleaned) each year. At the time of the inspection, on which this report is based, the location of a number of wells was known, although only one was found to be in working order.

The first archaeological report of the site was made by the Saudi Department of Antiquities (al-Mughannam, al-Helwa and Mursi 1983, 61) in the 1980s and describes a large, square, structure, interpreted as a castle/fort. The report on the site is hard to follow without a plan, though it appears to be built around a large, square, courtyard, with an entrance to the east, a well in the north-west corner and a stairway, leading up to the first floor, in the south-west corner. The fort is built of red granite and black basalt blocks, with mortar and small stones filling the joints. The building is evidently in a ruinous condition, with walls standing to a maximum height of 6 m in some places, but elsewhere only 1 m.

This building is also mentioned in a tourist guidebook (Pierard and Legros 1997, 73); based on a site visit in the 1990s. In this account the maximum height of the walls is 2 m, suggesting that there had been considerable collapse of the structure since the 1980s.

Discussion

This is evidently a site of considerable antiquity, as indicated both by the availability of water and the historical descriptions above. However, what is not clear is whether there was a functioning fort at the site during the Ottoman period. The only author to mention a fort in the Ottoman period is Mehmed Edib and he indicates that it is in ruins. Does this mean that the fort pre-dates the Ottoman period, or that it had been neglected for a period, as with so many of the Ottoman forts on the Hajj route? It is not possible to answer this question without direct examination of the remains, though the ruins described by the Saudi Antiquities team are comparable, in size and design, with many of the Ottoman Hajj forts.

Hafirah – (Map 5, No. 26)

(Djerf, Jerf, Abiar Hamza, Wadi Istaqbal, Dar-i Jurf, Dar-i Veda')

Location: 24.36N 39.22E

This site is the most southerly station of the Syrian Hajj route and is located *c.* 40 km from the centre of Medina and 45 km from Wadi al-Qurra al-Atik.

History

The first time the site is mentioned in itineraries of the Hajj route is in the 16th century, when Abeer Hamza (أبيار حمزة) is listed as the last, but one, place before Medina on the 'Tariq al-Saham ila Makka' of Mustapha Pasha 1563 (971 AH) (al-Jasir 1969, 184–85). In 1672, Evliya Çelebi refers to a *menzil* at Vadi-i Istakbal (he also refers to this as Dar-i Jurf), suggesting that there may have been a khan, or at least a camping ground, at this spot, which he describes as a place full of date palms, acacia and miswak trees, surrounded on four sides by high rocky mountains. Çelebi also notes that it is at this place, that the pilgrims change into their white robes (*ihram*) before entering Medina (Evliya Çelebi, *Seyhatnâmesi* IX, 306a).

However, this site is not mentioned in other itineraries until the 18th century account of Mehmed Edib, based on his pilgrimage in 1779. Edib states that this site, also known as Jurf, is located at a distance of 11 hours from Wadi al-Qurra and contains a fort and wells. Nearby there is a village called Birka (cistern), as well as a place called Sakiyya Sulayman Ibn 'Abd al-Malik. The water wheel [*saqiyya*] channel is fed from a source known as 'Ayn Zerka, which is located in Medina. And there is a field known as Zin, which, by tradition, was particularly recommended for cultivation by the Prophet Muhammad. Edib notes that Jurf is the northern limit of Medina and states that it is here where pilgrims should wash themselves and put on new clothes (*ihram*), as well as asking for forgiveness for all their sins; at this point they are met with joy by the inhabitants of Medina (Bianchi 1825, 139–40).

The site is not mentioned in the early 19th century *Report to Muhammad 'Ali Pasha* (Appendix 1 in this volume). However, the report points out that the distance between Abyar Tandheef (Wadi al-Qurra al-Atiq) and Medina is 20 hours and, as there is no water available in between, they are obliged to carry their supplies from Abyar Tandheef.

The first confirmation for Mehmed Edib's statement concerning a fort at this site, comes from the survey by the Saudi Antiquities Department carried out in the 1980s. The report of this survey noted a square castle (21 m × 21 m) with a gateway (1.7 m wide) leading into a passage (3 m wide) that opens into a large central courtyard (12.3 m × 13.95 m). The walls of the fort stand to a height of 6 m and are built with granite blocks, laid in a mortar of mud and sand. Tamarisk wood was used for beams, whilst hollowed out palm trunks were used for gutters. There was a filled in well next to the fort and two further wells, at a distance of 300 m, to the south-west (al-Mughannam, Helwa and Mursi 1983, 59).

Discussion

It is noticeable that there are few references to this fort, despite the fact that it is mentioned as early as 1779 (Bianchi 1825, 139–40). It is probable that the fort has been missed by many travellers, as indicated by a recent tourist guide book which states: 'The architecture is so simple that many times you may pass by close to this qaal'at without guessing the purpose of this square low building at the edge of the palm grove in the wide bed of the Wadi Hamd' (Pierard and Legros 1997, 3). It is also evident that the construction and design of this building is different from the other Ottoman forts, with the exception of the fort at Wadi al-Qurra al-Atik.

11. Arabic and Turkish Inscriptions on the Darb al-Hajj al-Shami

Mehmet Tütüncü and Andrew Petersen

with a contribution by Gotfried Hagen

This chapter provides a summary of the inscriptions found on, or in association with, the Hajj forts in Jordan and Saudi Arabia. In most cases the readings are by Mehmet Tütüncü; provided on the basis of photographs and squeezes.

Although it is likely that all of the Hajj forts would have had inscriptions detailing when and by whom they were built, as well as any subsequent restoration, or rebuilding, only a few have survived. Thus, a total of 13 inscriptions are known from eight of the Hajj forts, representing less than a third of the probable original number of inscriptions. Of the 13 known inscriptions, one (Qal'at Fassu'a) has disappeared without being read, whilst some of the others have been published to differing extents. Jaussen and Savignac (1997) recorded seven inscriptions; giving the Arabic text, as well as, a French translation. These readings were critically reviewed by van Berchem (1978) and the results incorporated into the readings presented below. Moritz (1908) published two inscriptions from Dhat al-Hajj, as well as a version of the Tabuk inscription, also published by Jaussen and Savignac. Brünnow and Domaszewski published two inscriptions, one relating to Qal'at Dab'a and the other to Qal'at al-Hasa (1905, 76 and 18). The only inscription reported here for the first time relates to the fort at Ma'an and had been overlooked by earlier writers. This important inscription has been transcribed and translated for this volume by Mehmet Tütüncü and Gotfried Hagen.

Ghabbani (1993) published a survey of inscriptions found on both Damascus and Egyptian Hajj routes. This work, written in Arabic, incorporated many pictures and new suggestions for the decipherment of the inscriptions. However, none of the readings can be regarded as definitive because the author lacked knowledge of Ottoman Turkish. The editions below are new and fresh readings by Mehmet Tütüncü, who reviewed and revised (where possible) all the former readings.

Qal'at Dab'a

Four line Arabic inscription transcribed and translated into German by van Berchem and published in Brünnow and Domaszewski (1905, 76).

(Inscription No. 1)
1) Sura 9, 18 (two lines)
2) Restored this blessed place al-Amir al-Hajj the minister
3) Othman Pasha [in the year Dhu'l] Hijje 1180 [1766–67]

The location of this inscription within the fort is not known, though the Quranic verse and the reference to this 'blessed place' indicate that it may have been within a room used as a mosque. It is also possible that this is the inscribed stone found, lying outside the fort, by the North Arabian Desert Expedition (Field 1960, 84–85). In any case the inscription clearly refers to a rebuilding, or renewal of the building and not an original construction.

Qal'at al-Hasa

Arabic verse inscription divided into three lines and six decorative cartouches. The inscribed panels were set into the rear wall of the central room (mosque) on the first floor of the south side of the fort. A transcription and German translation of the inscription together with a photograph of the squeeze, were published by Brünnow and Domaszewski (1905, 18, fig. 1572). The text reads as follows:

(Inscription No. 2)
1) How beautiful temple (worship place) it is dedicated for Allah, For piety has built and set up!
2) by a king with the name Mustafa;

Our Sultan descendant of Ahmad
3) in paradise for him
there will be a splendid house

Although this inscription is not specifically dated, it mentions the name of Sultan Mustafa, which, from the context, appears to be Mustafa III (1757–74). Brünnow and Domaszewski, following Mauss, read the chronogram as 1760. The inscription is interesting because it refers to Sultan Mustafa as a descendant of Ahmad. There is a play with words here: Ahmad is the name of the Father of Sultan Mustafa (Ahmad III who governed between 1703–30), but it is also the name of the Prophet Muhammad. In Arabia there was a deep-rooted belief that the Caliph should be a descendant of the Prophet. It is, therefore, significant that the Ottoman Sultan claims here that he is from the house of the Prophet.

Qal'at Ma'an (Mehmet Tütüncü and Gotfried Hagen) (see Plate 97)

This is the only legible, unpublished, inscription discovered during the course of the 'Darb al-Hajj Survey'. The inscription is expertly carved onto a marble panel and is divided into eight cartouches, in four horizontal bands. This is the earliest Ottoman Turkish inscription in Arabia and one of the earliest in any part of the Ottoman Empire.

(Inscription No. 3)

1. شاه جهاندا هفت اقليمي عثمان اوغلينك

2. ضمير خير ٠٠٠؟.. ٠٠٠امرايلدى رحمان

3. [broken].قباد باشا قوليله عسكر شامه

4. معانده ايلدى بر برج و بركه يابمغنه فرمان

5. (ط.)ريقن (ب)يت معمورك ادوب بحمدالله تعمير

6. اولب حجاجا يدعي زهي خير و زهي احسان

7. بو حقير بنده سى كاتب سكوني ديدى تاريخن

8. معانده يابدى برج بركهء سلطان سليمان

1) The Lord of the world and seven climates the Ottoman's son...
2) the merciful ordered them to do beneficence.
3) (through)... Kubad Pasha his officer in Syria;
4) He ordered to build a fort and a water reservoir in Ma'ân.
5) He repaired – praise to God – the road to the holy site,
6) The pilgrims prayed: what a charity and what a benevolence.
7) humble slave scribe Sükûnî composed its chronogram:
8) Ma'ân Sultan Süleyman built a fort and water reservoir (971)

The last line contains a chronogram, which, when counted, gives exactly the date 971, also written in figures.

Chronogram

معانده	يابدى	برج	بركهء	سلطان	سليمان	
191	150	228	205	27	170	= 971

It is noticeable that although this inscription refers to the Hajj, it is not a particularly religious text, thus there is no Quranic verse. However, the inscription clearly draws attention to the Ottomans as an imperial force and to Sultan Sulayman as the instigator of the fort and water reservoir. Qubbad Pasha, governor of Damascus, was originally from the Ramazanid dynasty of southern Turkey. Another person mentioned in the inscription is the scribe, indicating the high status of this profession.

Qal'at al-Fassu'a (see Plate 101)

(Inscription No. 4)
Directly above the gateway to this fort there is a composite sandstone panel (0.8 m high × 1.5 m wide) bearing an inscription (since 1986 this has been removed and its current location is unknown). The panel comprises a frame, made of seven or eight blocks, with two inscribed blocks in the centre. The inscription is set within a horizontal cartouche 0.8 m long and with each end terminating in a rosette. The bottom of the frame is decorated with a design made of 14 tri-lobed leaves. Above the main cartouche there is a smaller cartouche. Unfortunately, it was not possible to take an impression of the inscription and the photographs are not detailed enough to enable the text to be read. However, there appears to be an *'aya* from the Quran and the name Allah is visible in several places.

Above the inscribed panel there are two sets of projecting corbels and a large gap in the wall (1.5 m wide and 1.7 m high). It is probable that this was a projecting machicolation which has now disappeared.

Dhat al-Hajj

A.) Five line Arabic *naskhi* inscription above the doorway, published without a translation by Moritz (1908, 433). The following translation is based on Moritz's transcription.

(Inscription No. 5)

1. بسم الله الرحمن الرحيم

2. هذا عمل المعلم محمد الا؟؟بر

3. الفقير المعمار بشي الشام سنة

4. أحد وسبعين وتسع مائه في شهر صفر

5. المبارك وكان عمارتها في أربعين يوم

1) In the name of Allah the most merciful.
2) This was made by the famous Muhamad al- Ibar??

3) The humble head of architects from Damascus in the year
4) Nine hundred and seventy one, in the month Safar
5) the blessed and it was built in forty days.

The form of the inscription is remarkable. It is shaped as a *Tabula Ansate*; a square where the five lines of the inscription are incised and at the left and right ends of the square there are 2 triangles, carved with decoration in the form of a fleur-de-lis. Two points of content are of interest, the first concerns the date of construction, the second is the time taken to build the fort. Jaussen and Savignac (1997, 555, n. 1) incorrectly cite this inscription as giving a date of 961 AH, however, the inscription clearly gives the date of construction as, Safar 971 AH, which is equivalent to September/October 1563 AD. This date fits in with the documentary evidence, which gives 1559 as the date when the order for the construction of the fort was given. This is the same year as Qal'at Ma'an, but the Sultan's (Sulayman) name is not mentioned here. Whether the fleur-de-lis is a reference to Sultanic orders, remains a mystery?

The inscription states that the fort was built in 40 days, which is exceptionally fast considering the remote location. The time-scale is comparable with that taken to build the fortress at al-Ukhaydhir, which took somewhere between 40 and 70 days.

B.) Eight line Arabic inscription, published by Moritz without a translation (1908, 433–34). A very similar, if not identical, inscription is now in the National Museum of Saudi Arabia (NMSA Object #896a/b) – recording repairs to a fort in 1849. The nine line inscription is in *naskhi*, on a marble slab (70 cm × 45 cm) the only difference is that this inscription appears to have an extra line between lines 7 and 8.

(Inscription No. 6)

1. تجديد عمارة هذا

2. القلعة وعزال بركتما

3. في عصر مولانا السلطان

4. عبدالمجيد نصره الرب

5. المعين وأيم سعادة أفندي

6. الحاج عثمان باشا وسعادة

7. سردار أمين دركاه عالي

8. السيد أحمد أغا اليوسف

9. كيلار أميني المفخم في محرم سنة ١٢٦٦

1) This building was renewed.
2) The fort and the attached water cistern;
3) During the time of our lord the Sultan
4) 'Abd al-Majid victorious whom Allah granted victory
5) support and days of happiness. The Lord

6) al-Hajj Othman Pasha and and the fortunate
7) Head of the troops of the High Porte (Palace);
8) And Sayeed Ahmed Agha Yussuf
9) The Illustrious head of the depots in Muharram in the year 1266

The date of this inscription is equivalent to November/December 1849. During this period the Ottomans had regained confidence in Arabia. For example, in April 1849 the Ottomans landed troops in Hodeida (Yemen) and also planned to take Najd from the Saudis (Vassiliev 1998, 183). It was within this context that repairs to Dhat al-Hajj were carried out. The inscription contains, beneath the name of the Sultan Abd al-Majid the names of two personalities: Osman Pasha, Commander of the Troops of the Palace (*Serdar Emin Dergahi Ali*) and Ahmed Agha Yusuf, Trustee of Depots (*Kilar Emini*). These individuals were responsible for the safety and food of pilgrims during the time of the Pilgrimage.

Tabuk

A.) This Arabic inscription is unique, because it is written on a series of ceramic tiles, set within a rectangular recessed panel, above the entrance to the fortress at Tabuk.

The inscriptions on the Hajj Route are generally only on stone – this is an exception. This inscription was noticed by Evliya Çelebi in 1672 (see below). A transcription of eight lines, without translation, was published by Moritz in 1908. In 1909 Jaussen and Savignac published their own transcription of the inscription, together with a French translation. However, some aspects of the two transcriptions differed, most notably the number of lines. Thus, in Moritz's transcription there were eight lines, whilst Jaussen and Savignac's version had the same text, but in only seven lines. Comparison of the two transcriptions, with the ceramic panel visible today, indicates that Moritz's transcription was more accurate and that Jaussen and Savignac had squashed four lines into the first three lines of their transcription. This also calls into question another aspect of Jaussen and Savignac's publication, which describes the inscription as painted in red, on ceramic tiles, above the gate of the fortress – 'Inscription arabe du qala'ah de Tebouk, peinte en rouge au dessus de la porte, sur des carreaux de faïence'. Recent photographs of the inscription show an eight line inscription in blue, not red, against a white background, within decorative green cartouches (*c.f.* Pierard and Legros 1997, 76). The discrepancy between the description by Jaussen and Savignac and the inscription as seen today, has led some authors to suggest that the present day ceramic panel is the replacement of an earlier one (*c.f.* King 1998, 77 and 227 n. 166). However, taking into account Moritz's earlier transcription, it seems more likely that Jaussen and Savignac's description was in error, in relation to the colour, as well as the number of lines.

(Inscription No. 7)

١. أمر بتجديد وتعمير هذه القلعة المباركة

٢. حضرة مولانا السلطان ابن السلطان

٣. السلطان محمد خان ابن ال[سلطان] ابراهيم

٤. خان ابن السلطان [احمد خان ابن]

٥. عثمان خلدالله [ملكه الى اخر] الزمان

٦. وتشرف بمبا شره خدمتها العبدالله[فقي]ر

٧. الى الله محمد ابن النا[شف زاده دفتر] جي بدمشق

٨. الشام غفر الله له في سنة أربع وستمين والف 1064

1) Ordered the reconstruction and renewal of this blessed fort
2) Our present lord Sultan son of the Sultan
3) Sultan Mehmed Khan Son of the Sultan Ibrahim
4) Khan Son of the Sultan Ah[med ibn]
5) Othman, may Allah prolong his reign till the end of times
6) and was honoured for his service to him this poor servant
7) to Allah Muhammad ibn al-na[shifzade defter] jiy of Damascus
8) in Syria may Allah pardon him in the year 1064 AH [1654 AD]

The inscription was also noticed by Evliya Çelebi in his famous *Seyahatname*. (Evliya Çelebi, *Seyhatnâmesi* IX, 297). His reading is as follows:

Above the door there is written on tiles a *tarih* (date):
Fî eyyâmi Mevlânâ es-Sultân Mehemmed Hân ibn İbrâhîm
Hân medde zillahu bi-sebebi tamîri Emîn-i Defteri Dimaşk Nâşifzade Mehemmed el Fakîr sene 1062.

The sultan in question is Sultan Mehmed IV who ruled between the years 1648–87.

Evliya notes the year as 1062, but this is not right; we can read from the inscription the year as 1064. Evliya makes the error because the digit 4 is written in a way that resembles a 2.

From Evliya's note we can further restore the destroyed part of the name in line 7 as follows: *Nâşifzade defterci.*

B.) This three line Arabic inscription is engraved on a stone within one of the rooms of the fort. It is not clear whether this inscription was built into the walls, or was a single stone kept within a room of the fort. The following translation is based on the French translation of Jaussen and Savignac (1997, 293, no. 2).

(Inscription No. 8)

١. وقف

٢. هذا بيت الفقرا ال عمر في سنة 1064

٣. لأبنا ال السبيل

1) Waqf [Endowment]
2) this house of the poor was built in 1064
3) for children of the road (travellers)

It is noticeable that the date of this inscription, 1064 AH (1654 AD) is the same as that above the entrance. Jaussen and Savignac thought that this inscription referred to a separate building, or hospice, outside the fort. On the other hand van Berchem (1978, 619) suggested that the fort was, in fact, more of a khan than a fort and that this was the 'house of the poor' referred to in the inscription. From the design of the fort and comparisons with other forts Jaussen and Savignac's idea of a separate hospice seems more plausible.

C.) This eight line inscription was fixed on the *mihrab* of the Mosque of Tabuk. It was mentioned, with a picture (fig. 35), by Shaaban in his Masters Thesis in 1988. Ghabbani published the text in 1993 (Ghabbani 1993, II), 154.

(Inscription No. 9)

١. الفاتحة

٢. أمر بتجديد وتعمير هذه القلعة المباركة

٣. مولانا السلطان عبدالمجيد المجيد خان بن السلطان

٤. محمود خان حلافة عثمان خلدالله

٥. ملكهم وتشرف بمباشر ة عمارتها الحاج ابراهيم

٦. ادهم قبرصلى تحرير افى ٢٢ ذا الحجة

٧. يضباشيها من سنة ١٢٦٠ ه او ضبا شي

٨. أبى عباس الأمباشي

1) Pray the fatiha
2) Ordered the reconstruction and renewal of this blessed fort
3) Our Lord, Sultan Abdelmajid Khan, Son of Sultan
4) Mahmud Khan, Caliph of the Ottomans, may Allah prolong his
5) Reign and was honoured to build this building the Pilgrim (Hajj) Ibrahim
6) Edhem from Cyprus was written in 22 day of Zulhijje
7) By the Subashi in the year 1260 h.
8) by Subashi Abu Abbas el-ombashi

This inscription is remarkable because it gives the name of a person from Cyprus as architect. Ibrahim Edhem Kibrisli (The Cypriot) is not known from other sources.

Another name involved is, Subashi Abu Abbas el-Ombashi, Commander of the Troops, who was skilled enough to write and carve a beautiful calligraphic inscription. The day of completion, 22 Zulhijje 1260 AH, is equivalent to 2nd January 1845 AD. This is the only inscription that gives, exactly, the day the work was completed. An inscription fixed in the mosque's *mihrab* speaks about 'reconstruction and renewal (Tajdid ve tamir) of this blessed fort'.

D.) This six line Arabic and Turkish inscription was made on the wall of the main water reservoir, outside the fort (Jaussen and Savignac 1997, 293–94, no. 3).

(Inscription No. 10)

١. بسـم الله الرحمن الرحيم

٢. ملك البرين والبحرين وخادم الحرمين الشريفين

٣. السلطان الغازى عبدالحميد خان ثانى

٤. افندمز حضرتلرينك عهد همايون عمران

٥. مشحو نلردذه اشبو بركوكر مجددا تعمير ايدلمشدر سنة ١٣١٩

3. Sultân el-gâzí Abdulhamid han-sanî
4. Efendimiz Hazretlerinin ahd, humayun emran
5. meşhunleriz(?)de işbu birke(?)ler müceddeden tamir edilmişlerdir sene 1319

1) In the name of Allah the compassionate, the merciful
2) King of the two earths and the two seas and servant [protector] of the two sanctuaries [Mecca and Medina],
3) Sultan the warrior Abd al-Hamid Khan the second
4) His majesty the Ottoman Sultans orders and instructions
5) these cisterns have been Renewed and restored and filled (with water) in 1319

The date on this inscription, 1319 AH, corresponds to 1901 and would have been fairly new when seen by Jaussen and Savignac. It is noticeable that the inscription refers to repairs to the water reservoirs and does not claim to be a new construction.

al-Ukhaydhir

A.) Arabic inscription located above the gate to the fort. The inscription is contained within a cartouche, 1.15 m long and 0.53 m wide. The last line of the inscription is below the cartouche. The inscription has been removed from its original location.

The following translation is based on the French translation of Jaussen and Savignac (1997, 294, no. 4).

(Inscription No. 11)

١. امر بعمارة هذاالبرج المبارك مولانا السلطان المالك الملك المظفر سليمان خان ابن سليم خان بن عثمان

٢. اعز الله نصره وصار ذالك بنظر امير الامرا الكريم مولانا مصطفى ابلاق باشا المملكة الشامية عظم الله شانه

٣. وكان الواقف على عمارة ذالك الامير طرباى ابن قراجا امير عرب حارثة دام عزه والامير على العمارة المذكور العلائ

٤. على ابن احمد بن طالو والكاتب بها محمد بن على عفا الله عنهما وكان رأيس المعمارية بها المعلم احمد ابن المكاكى

٥. وكان ابتدا العمارة فى العشرين بن شهر شوال سنة ثمان وثلائين وتسعمائة وانتهابها فى شهر الحجة المحرام سنة تاريخه

1) Ordered the construction of this blessed tower (burj) our lord the Sultan, King of kings, the victorious Sulayman Khan ibn Selim Khan ibn Othman.
2) Victorious through the will of Allah. And that has placed the amir of the noble amirs, our Lord Mustapha Ablaq,

pasha of the Province of Damascus, may the Lord magnify his excellence
3) And the supervisor of this construction was the Amir Turabay ibn Aqraja amir of the Arabs Haritah- by whom he is honoured – who worked on this important construction
4) Ali ibn Ahmed bin Talu and the scribe for this Muhammad bin Ali- may Allah forgive them both and the chief architect the learned Ahmed ibn al Makaki
5) And this project started in 20th of Shawwal in the year 938 and was completed in the sacred month of Hajj in the same year.

This important inscription is valuable, not only does it give the date of construction, 938 AH (1531 AD), it also lists the names of those involved in the construction process. Max van Berchem (1978, 149–52) suggested that the hierarchical list of names indicates financial responsibilities for both the Pasha of Damascus and the Amir Turabay. The scribe was probably responsible for noting down expenses and costs, while Ahmed ibn al-Makaki (from Mecca) was in charge of the actual construction. The time-scale, of one to two months, is comparable with that recorded for Dhat al-Hajj (see below) and is remarkably speedy.

B.) This four line inscription was carved into a stone at the side of the main inscription.

The first three lines are in Arabic; the last line is in Turkish.

The following translation is based on the French translation of Jaussen and Savignac (1997, 294, no. 5)

(Inscription No. 12)

١. حضر فى هذه القلعة المنصور

٢. مصطفى صوباشى ومعه مية يك"رى

٣. سنة ثمان وثلائين وتسامئة بوتاريخ

٤. أوقي به دعا أيدنه الله رحمت ايليه

4. Okuyub dua edene Allah rahmet eyleye.

1) Was present within this victorious fort
2) Mustapha Subashi and a hundred soldiers (Yenicheri)
3) in the year 938
4) May Allah have mercy upon them who pray and read (Quran).

This is the same date as the main inscription (1538) and is clearly an indication that, a force of 100 soldiers was required to protect the site, during the construction of the fort (see, van Berchem 1978, 152).

C.) This six line Arabic inscription was carved into a stone at the small entrance of the Fort. The following reading and translation is based on Ghabbani's (1993, II) sketch and picture. Because the stone has eroded, the reading is difficult, with many deficiencies, especially the last line, where the date should be written.

(Inscription No. 13)

١. بسـم الله الرحمن الرحيم والصلوة والسلام علىسيدنا

٢. محمد خاتمالأنبياء والمرسلين وعلى [وصحبه أجمعين]

٣. نصرمن الله وفتح قريب عمر هذاالبرج المبارك [مولانا]

٤. السلطان ابن السلطان الغازى احمد خان بن محمد

٥. خان ابر ابراهيم خان ايدالله ملكه وكان السا

٦. عي فى الخير [ابراهيم باشا] ٠٠٠ عضدالله

[فى سنة]

1) In the name of Allah the compassionate, the merciful. And greetings and blessings to Prophet
2) Muhammed the (seal) last of the Prophets and the right guided and
3) Q 61: 13 'And another (favour will He bestow,) which ye do love, – help from Allah and a speedy victory.' Ordered the construction of this blessed fort Our lord
4) Sultan son of the Sultan the warrior Ahmed Han son of Muhammed Khan
5) Son of the Sultan Ibrahim, may Allah prolong his reign
6) and was honoured for his service to him Ibrahim Pasha
7) in the year ....

The Sultan who ordered the construction of this fort is Sultan Ahmed III, who reigned between 1703–30. This was probably a restoration and not a construction, because, as we have seen, this fort was constructed in 1531 by the orders of Sultan Sulayman.

D.) This inscription was not fixed on the entrance gate, but is in the format of a tombstone placed in front of the fort. This stone is much destroyed and reading many parts of the inscription is impossible. What we have are two photos, Ghabbani (1993, II 161) and Ghabbani (1998, 239). The following reading and translation is based on these pictures.

(Inscription No. 14)
Emir Turkmani Governor of Ajlun

South-western face of the stone (lines broken)

١. هوالمعين

٢. أمر بعمارة ومرمات

٣. هذه [القلعة] والبرك

٤. مولا[نا السلطان]

٥.....

1) On the name of Muin
2) The order to renovate and refurbish
3) this [fort] and cistern is by
4) our lord [Sultan]
5) ....

South-eastern face of the stone:

١. وكان الواقف

٢. على العمارة الأمير موسى ابن محمد

٣. [ابن حسين التركماني] الحاكم بعجلون

٤. [وكان] ابتداء العمارة

٥. ...شهر ذي...

٦.....

1) And the waqf (endowment)
2) of this building by the commander Musa son of Muhammed
3) [] the governor of Aclun
4) And before this Building [...]
5) The month of [...]
6) .....

The only name that is preserved is the name of Musa, son of Muhammed, governor of Ajlun. When, precisely, a governor was undertaking restoration work and endowments, is unknown.

Mu'azzam

There are three inscriptions, all in Turkish (Ottoman), in Qal'at al-Mu'azzam. This Fort was built to guard the water reservoir of Muazzam.

Jaussen and Savignac noted the inscriptions on the façade of Qal'at al-Mu'azzam. It is not clear where each inscription was located, though it appears that one was set above the entrance and one was located within the gateway passage. Although the inscriptions were seen by Jaussen and Savignac, they were, unfortunately, unable to make copies at the time. The published translations are based on copies made by one of the telegraph operators at Muazzam and sent to Jaussen and Savignac at the École Biblique, in Jerusalem. Ghabbani has re-published all the inscriptions, with photos, so we can check the accuracy of the readings. The following readings are based on these photos.

A.) Four line (4 × 2 distiches) Turkish inscription, in verse, written above the entrance gate of the fortress.

(Inscription No. 15)

١. خدايا باعث أولا بو بسايهن   سليمان أغه اير كور مراده

٢. دخي شام حافظى وزير سليمانكه   أنك أرى در خير ايشه مايه

٣. عنايت ايلسون انلارده سلطان   كركدر أو ستلرينه صالح سايه

٤. غريقي رحمت ايده انى يزدان   أو قيوب فا تخة دوره دعاية

1) Hûda'ya ba's ola bu besayan
   Süleymân âğâ er gör murâda
2) Dâhi Şam Muhafızı Vezir Süleymân
   Ki anın ârâdır hayr iyşa (ihsan) mi'ya
3) Inayet eylesun onlarada Sultân
   Gerekdir ustalarına salah saye

4)   Gariki râhmet ede ana yezdân
     Okuyub Fatiha dura du'aya

*1) To the Almighty God this shadowy place (has been built)
and fulfill the wishes of Sulayman Agha,*
*2) The guardian of Damascus, Vizier Sulayman who has
done many good works as to establish the foundations:*
*3) And the Sultan who came to help, for the master (masons)
needed this rescue,*
*4) Let Allah grant them grace in abundance and for whom
one recites the Fatihah and pray for him.*

B.) Inscription on the right wall of the entrance gate.
Turkish inscription with six lines (5 × 2 verses), the last
line contains the signature of the scribe and the year.

(Inscription No. 16)

1. بحق كعبة وحنان ومنان   شهنشا هي جهانه سلطان عثمان

2. منزيل² قلعة يابدي راه حجده¹   معظم بركة سي نامنه عثمان

3. الهي سلطنلره يرقرار ايت   حبيبك حرمتي هم جار ياران

5. ولي فكر ايلر ايكر تاريخي   ديدي هاتيف كمالي خير احسان

6. كتبه يوسف   سنة ١٠٣١

1)   Bîhâk Kâbe ve Henân ve Menân
     Şehinşâhı cihâne Sultân Osmân;
2)   Menzili Ka'le yapdıra hacda
     Muazzam Birkesi nâmına Osmân;
3)   İlahi Sultanlara berkarar et
     Habîbin hürmeti hem car ve yârân;
4)   Veli fikri (ile) dedi? tarihi
     Dedi hatif 'Kemali Hayr Ihsân'
5)   Ketebe Yusuf sene 1031

*1) By the Ka'aba, by the Henan and Menan (names
of Allah); Sultan of the Sultans of the World Sultan
Othman,*
*2) He has built the fortress and resting place of Mu'azzam
and excavated this vast cistern fitting for the name of
Othman,*
*3) May Allah guard the ruler in his majesty by the
intercession of his beloved (prophet) and his neighbours
and family;*
*4) the poor Veli fikri has said its date, the author of this
verse states that the benefaction will be complete.*
5) Written by Scribe Yusuf in 1031

Last line is an *abjad* date which, when calculated, gives
the year 1031 (1621 AD), which is exactly the same date
as that given in numerals.

كمالي خير احسان
130+ 810+101= 1031

C.) Inscription on the left wall of the entrance gate.
Seven line inscription, the first five lines are a Turkish
poem, 5 × 2 verses, while the last two lines contains
the names and signatures of the persons involved in the
renovation.

(Inscription No. 17)

1. مبارك قلعة ديار بولدي حاضر   خسين أغادر اوسته ناظر

2. بياله بر يلوك سر معتمدر   مرادينه ايزه بطان وظاهر

3. محافظ عثمان أغا شيخ مرشيدي   الهي غل غشدن ايله طاهر

4. كه كاتب يوسف ولي وقولكدر   أو لهرلر رحمتك أمركه حاضر

5. بيره دروب دعا أيدن عزيزلر   كوجيه أيمان أيله دنيان اخر

6. امل المعلم علي ابن محمد المعمار باشي بدمشق الشام

7. المعلم قلعة نقولا ابن الياس   نقشه هلال

1)   Mübârek ka'le diyârı buldû huzur
     Hüseyin Ağâdır usta nâzir;
2)   Boyle bir yolun ser-i mu'temeddir
     Muradına ere bâtin ve zâhir;
3)   Muhâfız Osman ağâ şeyh-i mürşiddir
     Ilâhi kıl gışdan eyle tâhir;
4)   Ki kâtib Yusuf veli ve kulundur
     Olurlar rahmetin emrine hazır;
5)   Bura durub du'a eden azîzler
     Göçe iman ile dunyadan âhire;
6)   Amele el ma'alum 'Ali ibn Muhammed el-mi'mar
     bashi bi dimashk el Sham
7)   El ma'lum kal'e Nikola ibn Ilyas nakkas Hilal

*1) This blessed fortress has found the rest, The chief
Huseyin Agha is the master and caretaker.*
*2) He is the head of the protector of this (holy) road. That
Allah will grant both their inner and outer wishes.*
*3) Muhafiz (Quran reciter) Othman Agha, Is the guide of the
Sheikhs, May Allah make clean from all the bad things;*
*4) The writer Yusuf Wali, son is your servant, and is ready
to execute the orders that are given to him.*
*5) The true pilgrims, who pass on this route pray,
let them pass with faith from the this world to the other;*
*6) Made by the famous Ali ibn Muhammed, the head of
architects (master mason) from Damascus of Syria*
*7) By the famous fort builder Nikola (son of Ilyas) and
Nakkase Hilal.*

Comment on Inscriptions 15, 16, 17

Jaussen and Savignac believed that this inscription referred
to the original construction of the fort in 1031 AH (1622
AD). However, van Berchem argues that the inscription
refers to a refurbishment, or rebuilding, of the fort in the
17th century (1978, 622–23). According to Ottoman writer,
Hibri, who made the pilgrimage in 1632 (some 10 years
later) and left us a Pilgrimage route guide: Sultan Osman
II, intended to visit the Kaba and made preparations to do
so, giving orders to build and repair the Hajj route forts
and water reservoirs. The reparation of the Muazzam water
reservoir and the building of the fort, with orders to his
soldiers to guard the fort and water reservoirs, seems to
be a part of his pilgrimage plans (see, Hibri 1975, 126).
But, before Sultan Osman II could realize his plans, he was
murdered by a mutiny of Yenicheri soldiers in 1622. So, we

could assume, with Jaussen and Savignac, that the fort is an Ottoman building. Another fort and water reservoir Osman II had built and repaired, is the famous Solomons Pool (Qal'at Burak) between Hebron and Jerusalem (Tütüncü 2006, 205–6; Hawari, Auld and Hudson 2000; Chapter 7 in this volume).

No.	Name of Building	Location of Inscription	Ottoman Sultan	Foundation or Repair	Language	Date AH / AD	References
1	Dab'a	unknown	Mustafa III	repair	Arabic	1180 AH 1766/67 AD	Brünnow and Domaszewski 1905
2	Hasa	mosque in fort	Mustafa III	foundation ?	Arabic	1174 AH 1760 AD	Brünnow and Domaszewski 1905
3	Ma'an	above gate	Sulayman I	foundation	Turkish	971 AH 1563 AD	Tütüncü and Hagen in this volume
4	Fassu'a	above gate	?	foundation	?	C12th AH? C18th AD?	None
5	Dhat al-Hajj	above gate	Sulayman I	foundation	Arabic	971 AH 1563 AD	Moritz 1908, Jaussen and Savignac 1997
6	Dhat al-Hajj	unknown	Abdul Majid	repair	Arabic	1266 AH 1849 AD	Moritz 1908, Jaussen and Savignac 1997
7	Tabuk	above gate	Mehmed IV	repair	Arabic	1064 AH 1654 AD	Moritz 1908, Jaussen and Savignac 1997
8	Tabuk	unknown	Mehmed IV	foundation	Arabic	1064 AH 1654 AD	Jaussen and Savignac 1997, Van Berchem 1978
9	Tabuk	*mihrab* of the Mosque	Abdul Majid	repair	Arabic	1260 AH 1843 AD	Ghabbani 1993, II
10	Tabuk	wall of the reservoir	Abdul Hamid II	repair	Arabic and Turkish	1319 AH 1901 AD	Jaussen and Savignac 1997
11	al-Ukhaydhir	above gate	Sulayman I	foundation	Arabic	938 AH 1531 AD	Jaussen and Savignac 1997, Van Berchem 1978
12	al-Ukhaydhir	gateway	Sulayman I	foundation	Arabic and Turkish	938 AH 1531 AD	Jaussen and Savignac 1997
13	al-Ukhaydhir	gateway	Ahmed III	repair	Arabic	1115–1143 AH 1703–1730 AD	Ghabbani 1993, II
14	al-Ukhaydhir	front	Unknown	repair	Arabic	Unknown	Ghabbani 1993, II
15	Mu'azzam	gateway	Osman II	foundation	Turkish	1031 AH 1622 AD	Jaussen and Savignac 1997
16	Mu'azzam	gateway	Osman II	foundation	Turkish	1031 AH 1622 AD	Jaussen and Savignac 1997
17	Mu'azzam	gateway	Osman II	foundation	Turkish	1031 AH 1622 AD	Jaussen and Savignac 1997

Table 3 – Hajj fort inscriptions

Only Inscription 16 is dated. The other two are not dated, but are, both in their style and content, surely from the same year, 1031AH/1622 AD. All three inscriptions are related, they are hierarchically composed and mention all the persons responsible for the construction of the fort.

The first Inscription (15) is an ode to the Governor and Commander (*Vizier Suleyman*) of Damascus, who was responsible for the Hajj route.

The second inscription (16) is dedicated to the ruling Sultan of the Ottomans, Sultan Osman II, patron of the fortress. The inscription was written in the last year of his rule, 1622.

The last inscription (17) mentions the names of five persons involved in the construction works and decoration of the fort:

1. *Huseyin Agha* – caretaker
2. *Muhafiz Osman* – a religious person, reciter of the Quran
3. *Katib Yusuf* – probably the same person as in inscription 16

4. *Ali Ibn Muhammed Mimarbashi* – architect from Damascus. It is notable that, as in the case of Tabuk, the mason was from Damascus, a practice that seems to have been common in the Hajj forts.
5. *Nikola son of Ilyas* – caretaker or contractor for the construction of the fort. The name is remarkable because this is the first time that a non-Muslim is mentioned in connection with the construction of the forts.

Notes

1   Ghabbani reads here حجده, which makes no sense, Jaussen reads حجده, which makes it understandable (in pilgrimage). We should read here Hac'da or Hicaz'da (in pilgrimage or in hejaz).

2   Ghabbani reads here نزبيا this should be menzil (resting place).

12. Excavations at Qal'at 'Unaiza

Introduction (Fig. 46, Plates 146–148)

Although the architectural documentation of the fort was the primary objective of the original fieldwork carried out in 1986, it was recognized that it would be useful to excavate at least one of the forts, in order to retrieve information on their material culture and occupation. Practical considerations meant that it was not possible to carry out excavations until 2002, by which time the majority of the

Plate 146. Qal'at 'Unaiza from the Desert Highway with Jabal 'Unaiza behind (2002).

Plate 147. Qal'at 'Unaiza from the north with modern Bedouin cemetery in foreground (2002).

forts had been the subject of conservation and restoration (*e.g.* al-Hasa, Dab'a, Qatrana and Ma'an). The only forts without modern disturbance of the archaeological contexts were, 'Unaiza, Mudawwara, and Fassu'a. Limited funds and practical considerations meant that only one of these sites could be excavated. 'Unaiza was chosen because it appeared to be the only un-restored 16th century building; it was in a ruinous condition, so any excavation would help clarify the architectural history of the building. Furthermore, there were remains immediately outside the fort that could be investigated (for the architecture of 'Unaiza see Chapter 9 and for a discussion of the finds recovered see Chapters 13 and 14).

Six areas, or trenches, were selected for excavation during two weeks in May/June 2002. The trenches were designated A–F. Pierre Brun was responsible for Areas A, D and E, Andrew Petersen was responsible for areas B and F, and Ahmad Shurma was responsible for Area C. All trenches were dug by hand.

Plate 148. Excavations in progress at Qal'at 'Unaiza (2002).

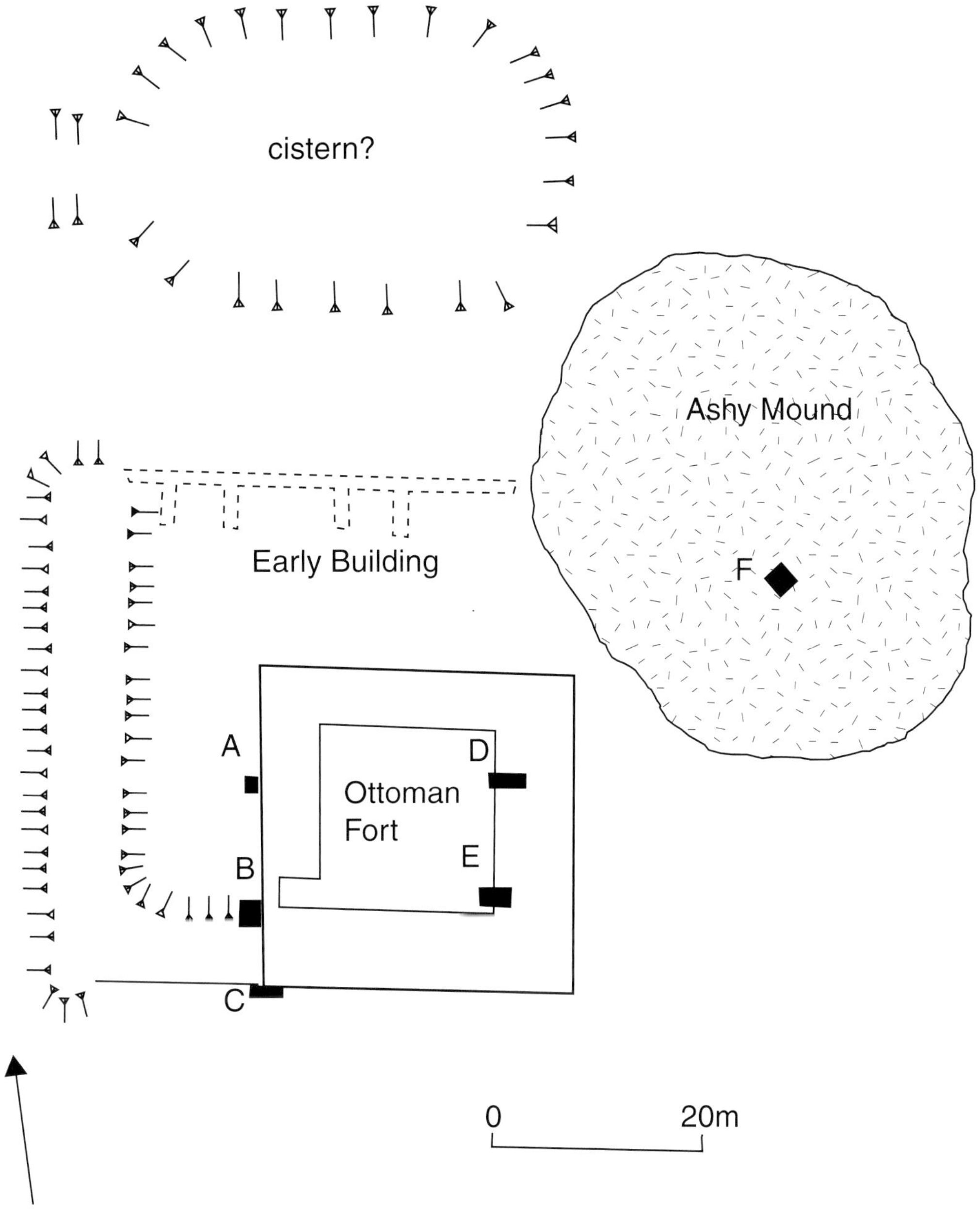

cistern?

Ashy Mound

F

Early Building

A   D

Ottoman
Fort

B   E

C

0   20m

Fig. 46. 'Unaiza site plan showing location of trenches.

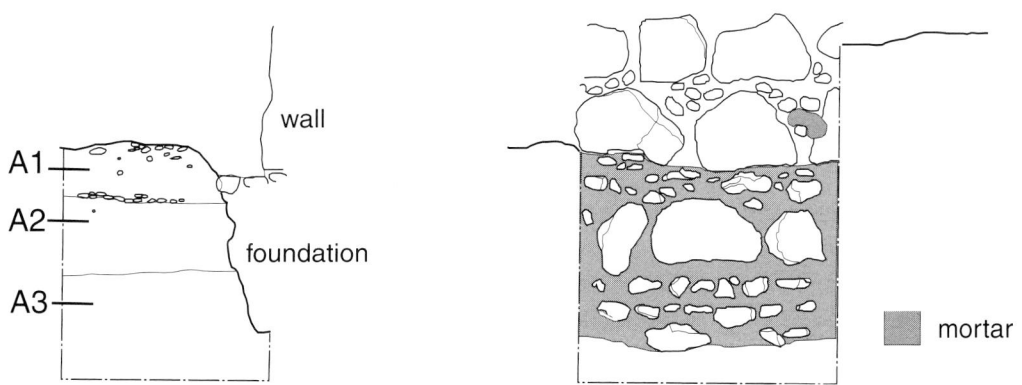

A1

A2

A3

wall

foundation

mortar

Fig. 47. 'Unaiza, Area A, section and elevation.

Plate 149. Excavations at Qal'at 'Unaiza. Trench A (2002).

Plate 150. Excavations at Qal'at 'Unaiza. Trench B (2002).

Plate 151. Excavations at Qal'at 'Unaiza. Trench B showing wall (B2) projecting from wall of Ottoman fort (2002).

Plate 152. Excavations at Qal'at 'Unaiza. Trench B from west (2002).

Trench A (Fig. 47, Plate 149)

Trench A (1 m × 2 m) was dug next to the west wall of the Ottoman fort – which belongs to architectural phase 2 (a). The trench was located 10.8 m south of the restored north-west corner. It was first excavated during the restoration of the fort in October 2001 and expanded during the fieldwork in May/June 2002 (no finds were recovered from this trench).

The 'V' shaped foundation trench for the wall was dug into a red ochre coloured sandy layer, which appeared to be natural. The foundation comprised, from top to bottom, three courses of basalt and limestone blocks (24–30 cm

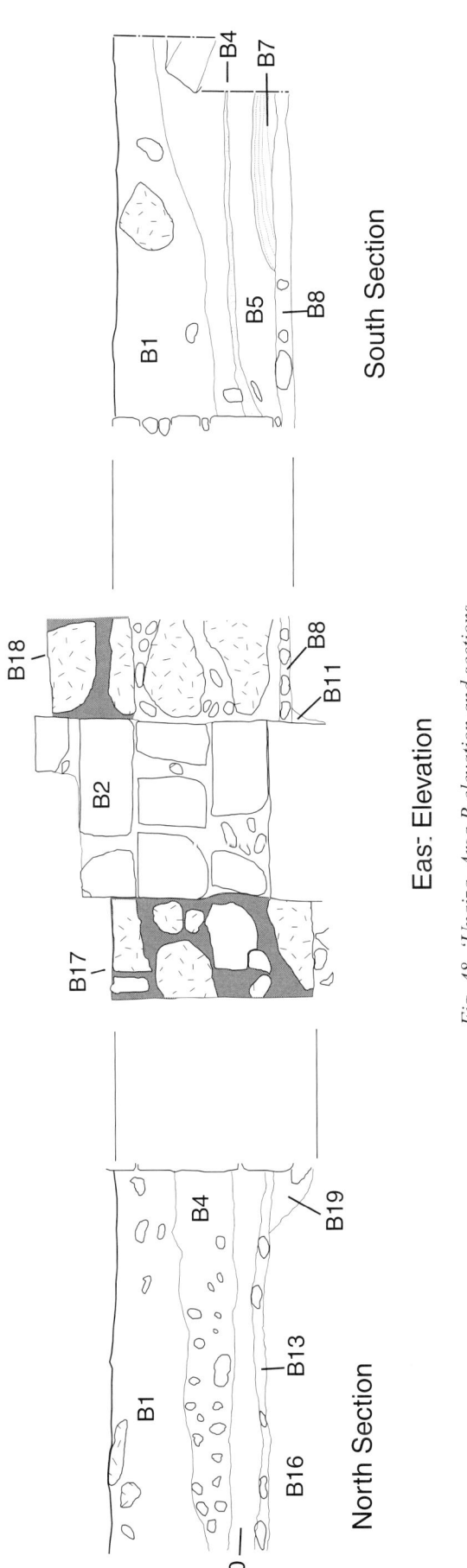

Fig. 48. 'Unaiza, Area B elevation and sections.

Fig. 49. 'Unaiza, Area B plan.

Plate 153. Excavations at Qal'at 'Unaiza. Trench C (2002).

Context	Type	Description	Relationships
B1	top soil	mixed light reddish grey/brown with many stones and patches of blue-grey mortar	overlies B4
B2	wall	wall of roughly squared basalt and limestone blocks projecting from west wall of Ottoman fort	beneath B1
B3	wall	wall aligned east–west (*i.e.* same alignment as B2). Basalt and limestone blocks bedded in blue-grey mortar with limestone grit and charcoal inclusions	beneath B1
B4	deposit	blue-grey mortar	beneath B1 overlies B10
B5	deposit	dark grey ashy layer	beneath B6
B6	deposit	mixed grey orange mortar and ash	beneath B4 overlies B5
B7	deposit	south-west corner of trench to south of B3. Very ashy deposit with traces of severe burning and inclusions of coarse light pink/orange baked mud and vegetal material	beneath B4 overlies B8
B8	surface	uneven hard cobbled surface, made of small irregular shaped basalt stones with mortar	beneath B7 and B5 overlies B12
B9	surface	cobbled surface lying between walls B2 and B3. Probably functioned as a threshold. Basalt stones set in pinkish/orange clay/mortar	beneath B5
B10	deposit	dark grey ashy material, similar to B5	overlies B13
B11	deposit	light grey material which fills rectangular cut B21	overlies B21
B12	deposit	hard compacted red ochre	beneath B8
B13	deposit	hard compacted red ochre with cobble stones	beneath overlies B16
B14	deposit	fill of foundation cut (B19) in north-east corner of trench	beneath B13 overlies B19
B15	deposit	fill of foundation cut of walls B2 and B3. Contains small stones (dia. 3–5 cm) with dark brown ashy material	beneath B13 overlies B20
B16	natural	hard compacted red ochre to north of walls B2 and B3	beneath B13
B17	wall	west wall of Ottoman fort north of B2	
B18	wall	west wall of Ottoman fort to south of B2	
B19	cut	cut for foundation of wall B17	beneath B14
B20	cut		beneath B15
B21	cut		beneath B11

Table 4 –Trench B Contexts

high), a course of basalt blocks (20–26 cm high) and a course of small basalt and limestone blocks (6 cm high). The foundation projects 15–17 cm from the outer face of the west wall and is set in red ochre coloured earth mortar. The same mortar was also used for the rubble core of the wall. A pebble layer, located 10 cm beneath the first course of the wall, was probably from a surface associated with its construction. This was subsequently overlaid by a layer of collapsed masonry.

Trench B (Figs 48 and 49, Plates 150–152, Table 4)

This trench was designed to investigate the earlier wall stump, embedded in the west wall of the fortress. The square trench (2 m × 2 m) was marked out next to the exterior face of the west wall, incorporating the projecting wall (B2) and abutting the walls of the fortress (B17 and B18).

The earliest phase in the trench pre-dated any buildings and comprised a hard compact surface made of red ochre coloured sandy material with small pebbles; the natural ground surface. The first building phase is represented by an east–west wall (B3) projecting from the west wall of the fortress – equivalent to architectural Phase 1. The exterior and interior faces of the wall are built of basalt and limestone blocks, laid in courses and bedded in blue-grey lime mortar, with charcoal inclusions. Between the two faces of the wall, there is a rubble stone core set in yellow ochre coloured clay (B9). The wall stands in a narrow, steep sided, foundation trench (B11 and B15) visible on either side of the wall. The wall (B2/B3) incorporates a doorway (0.9 m wide) with dressed limestone blocks forming the door jambs. No trace of a threshold, or door frames, could be identified, the rubble core formed a cobbled surface. To the south of the wall there was a cobbled surface (B8) which appears to have been contemporary with the doorway and was probably the floor of a room in the early building. To the north of the wall (B2/B3) there was an ashy layer/deposit, lying directly over the natural ground surface (B13), which contained less densely packed cobbles than those of the interior surface (B8). Similar ashy layers

Context	Type	Description	Relationships
C1	deposit	comprising small stone mortar fragments and charcoal	overlies C2
C2	deposit	hard compacted, containing lime and charcoal	beneath C1 and C3
C3	deposit	loosely compacted with lime and ash	beneath C1 overlies C2

Table 5 – Trench C Contexts

Context	Type	Description	Relationships
D1	deposit	multiple layers of organic material (dung). Light compaction, dark brown colour with inclusions of small stones. Variable thickness (3–7 cm)	overlies D2
D2	deposit	layer made of pebbles and plaster, strongly compacted light grey colour	beneath D1 overlies D3
D3	deposit	layer composed of small stones gravel and larger stones (5 cm+)	beneath D2 overlies D4
D4	deposit	collapsed layer, medium brown colour, compacted with inclusions of pebbles, modern plastic and pieces of wood	beneath D3 overlies D5
D5	deposit	medium compacted ashy deposit, dark brown and black	overlies 6
D6	wall	wall (1.07 m wide) made of basalt blocks set in whitish mortar with small stone chips	beneath D5

Table 6 – Trench D Contexts

Plate 154. Excavations at Qal'at 'Unaiza. Trench D (2002).

Plate 155. Excavations at Qal'at 'Unaiza. Trench E (2002).

(B5) overlaid the cobbled surface to the south and the threshold of the doorway. In the south-west corner of the trench there was a very dense concentration of burning (B7), containing much charcoal and ash.

The second building phase was the construction of the wall of the Ottoman fortress – belonging to architectural phase 2a. In the southern part of the trench the fortress wall (B18) was laid directly onto the cobbled surface (B8) on the interior of the room, with a shallow cut through some burnt layers. In the north part of the trench (*i.e.* north of the projecting wall B2), a foundation trench (B19) for the Ottoman wall was dug through the ash layers and hard surface (B13), to a depth of over half a metre. After the construction of the Ottoman fortress, there appears to have been further collapse of the earlier structure, as indicated by masonry rubble (B1) overlying wall B3 and the foundation trench (B19).

Trench C (Plate 153, Table 5)

Trench C (4 m × 0.5 m) was laid out on the exterior of the south-west corner of the fort. At this point the wall of the fort, above ground, is an entirely new construction, dating from the restoration programme of October 2001 (*i.e.* architectural phase 4). The purpose of this trench was to check the relationship between the Ottoman fort and the earlier structure to the west. The excavation exposed the original (*i.e.* phase 1) wall beneath the modern restoration. Two courses of the excavated wall were seen to continue west, beyond the corner of the Ottoman fort and to form the south wall of the early building. The wall was built of medium sized, undressed, basalt stones laid in a blue-grey mortar with charcoal flecks. The gap between the courses was filled with a layer of small stones, set in mortar. The deposits built up against the wall, contained at least three layers (C1, C2 and C3), one of which (C2) appeared to

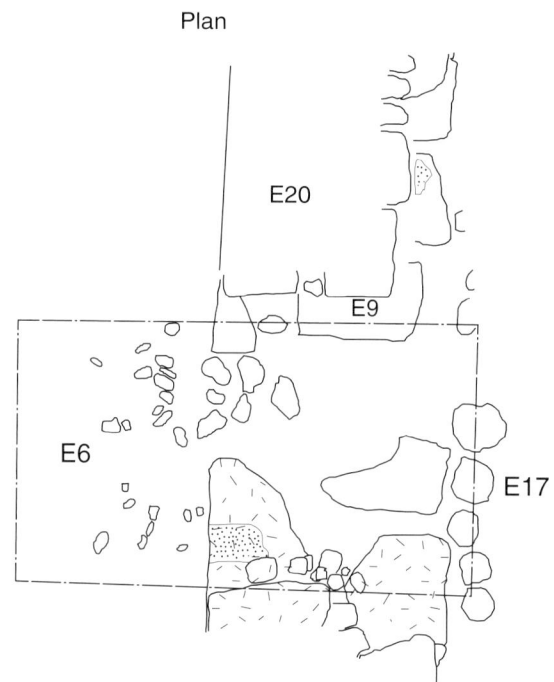

Fig. 50. 'Unaiza, Area E, plan and section.

be a surface, possibly associated with the construction of the Ottoman fort.

Trench D (Plate 154, Table 6)

Trench D was laid out on the south side, of the west end, of the gate passage, adjacent to the newly exposed cobbled surface of the courtyard (Fig. 17). The sounding (1.5 m north–south × 3 m east–west) revealed a succession of very recent trodden surfaces (*i.e.* with modern glass and plastic) overlying an older cobbled surface, which appears to be contemporary with the surface of the courtyard (*i.e.* similar composition and appearance). At the west end of the trench the cobbled surface partially overlies an earlier wall, aligned north–south. The outer and inner faces of the wall were composed of large basalt and limestone blocks.

The core of the wall, between the facings, was made of red ochre coloured earth mortar. It is probable that this wall is part of architectural phase 1.

Trench E (Fig. 50, Plate 155, Table 7)

Trench E was set out at the entrance of Room 16. This was one of only two rooms, not to have been entirely cleared during the recent restoration work at the site and it was hoped that occupation material would be found *in situ*. Five phases were observed in the trench.

Phase One (equivalent to architectural phase 1). During this phase the foundations of a wall (E15 and E13) were built into the natural ground surface. The foundations were made of basalt and limestone blocks. The wall (E9) was 0.92 m wide and comprised outer faces of large basalt

Plate 156. Excavations at Qal'at 'Unaiza. Trench F (2002).

and limestone blocks, with a rubble core set in red ochre coloured clay. The blocks of the inner and outer faces were set in a hard, blue-grey plaster of similar composition to the blue-grey mortar. A well-dressed rectangular limestone block, located in the south part of the trench, may have been the remains of an original doorway that was subsequently removed.

Phase Two (equivalent to architectural phase 2a) comprised a partial rebuilding of the wall using large basalt and limestone blocks, with a rubble core set in red earth. The only difference from the earlier phase is the use of white lime mortar, instead of the blue-grey mortar of the earlier period. The cobbled surface of the courtyard probably also belongs to this phase, although it was not excavated. Lying over and against the structures of this phase, were a succession of trampled surfaces, interspersed with layers of straw and other vegetal material (dung?).

Phase Three. Abandonment of the room is indicated by a series of burnt layers, overlaid by rubble collapse.

Phase Four (equivalent to architectural phase 3) is marked by a re-occupation of the room. Evidence includes the rebuilding of the wall with limestone blocks, with a rubble core set in red ochre earth – no use of white lime mortar. The rebuilt wall is narrower (0.65 m–0.7 m) than the earlier wall and is only roughly coursed. Elsewhere in the fort this phase is associated with the use of metal railway sleepers from the nearby Hijaz railway. Deposits associated with this layer included a series of straw and dung layers.

Phase Five represent the final abandonment of this room with the collapse of the vault (layers E3, E2 and E1).

Trench F (Fig. 51, Plate 156, Table 8)

The aim of Trench F was to recover material associated with the assumed main period of occupation of the fort (*i.e.* 16th–19th centuries). Examination of the area in the vicinity of the fort had revealed large quantities of ceramics and other material on an ashy mound (*c.* dia. 30 m, height 2 m), to the north-east of the entrance to the fort. The

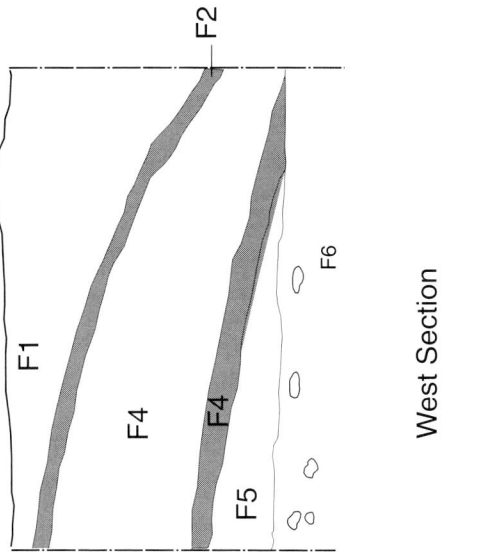

West Section

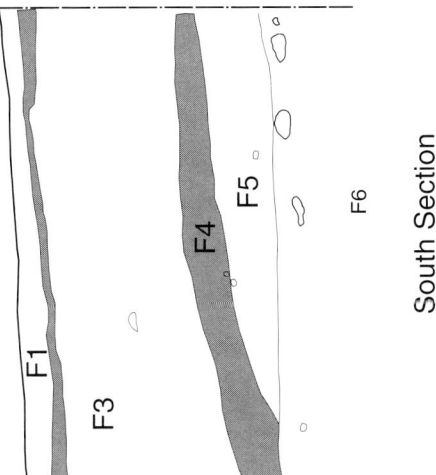

South Section

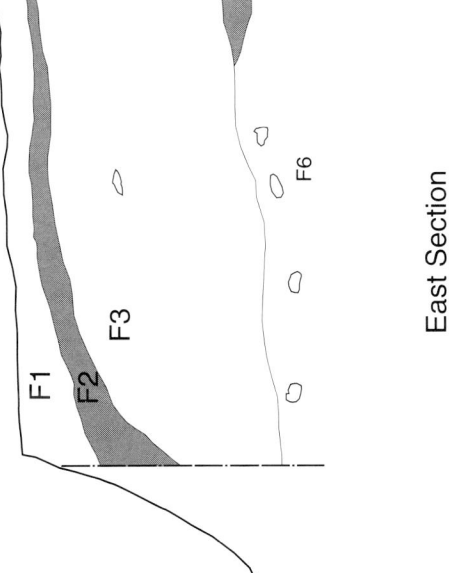

East Section

☐ = dense ashy layer

Fig. 51. 'Unaiza, Area F sections.

Context	Type	Description	Relationships
E1	deposit	rubble layers composed of stones and mixed mortar — represents collapsed layers of first floor and vault of room 16	overlies E2
E2	deposit	organic material (dung). Medium compaction, dark brown colour with inclusions of small stones	beneath E1 overlies E3
E3	deposit	rubble layers composed of stones and mixed mortar with fragments of wood	beneath E2 overlies E4
E4	deposit	organic layer of hay	beneath E3 overlies E5
E5	deposit	organic material (dung). Medium compaction, dark brown colour with inclusions of small stones	beneath E4 overlies E6
E6	deposit	dark grey ashy layer containing cobbles, inclusions of pottery sherds and charcoal pieces	beneath E5 overlies E7
E7	deposit	organic material (dung). Medium compaction, dark brown colour with inclusions of small stones	beneath E6 overlies E8
E8	deposit	ashy deposit with traces of charcoal and small stones medium compaction	beneath E7 overlies E10 and E9
E9	wall	large blocks of basalt and limestone set in blue-grey mortar	beneath E8 overlies
E10	deposit	sequence of mixed ashy and dung layers	beneath E8 overlies E14
E11	deposit	blue-grey mortar on wall E9	beneath E10 overlies E9
E12	deposit	plaster floor surface	beneath E10 overlies E14
E13	fill	small stones	beneath E12 and E9 overlies E15
E14	natural	ochre layer hard compacted.	beneath E12 and E10
E15	cut	foundation trench of wall E9	beneath E13 overlies E14
E16		UNASSIGNED	
E17	deposit	cobbled surface of courtyard	overlies ?

Table 7 – Trench E Contexts

Context	Type	Description	Relationships
F1	deposit	upper surface contains many pebbles and stones with light brownish silt matrix	overlies F2
F2	deposit	soft mixed brown ashy layer with orange and black patches and some vegetal material	beneath F1 overlies F3
F3	deposit	soft brown ashy loam fairly mixed	beneath F2 overlies F4 and F5
F4	deposit	soft orange brown less mixed	beneath F3 overlies F5
F5	deposit	soft orange brown ashy material less mixed with more stones (average length 10 cm)	beneath F4 and F3 overlies F6
F6	Deposit (natural)	hard packed surface with small pebbles. Very flat appears to be surface on which dump is deposited	beneath F5

Table 8 – Trench F Contexts

mound had recently been cut in half by a mechanical digger (bulldozer), with the south-western portion left relatively intact and the northern part flattened and dispersed. The mechanical cut had exposed a long section where the stratigraphy of the mound could be clearly observed. Trench F (2 m × 2 m) was located next to the mechanical cut. During the excavation of the square, the differentiation of the layers became extremely difficult, due to the ashy nature of the deposits and the strong winds prevailing at the time. Therefore, the trench was excavated in artificially determined layers (with depths of 0.05 m, 0.5 m and 0.9 m and 1.3 m), except where there was an obvious difference (*i.e.* F1–3 and F6). At the base of the trench it was found that the mound rested directly on the natural soil – a red ochre coloured, hard, sandy layer.

Finds Summary (see detailed reports in Chapters 13 and 14)

There were very few finds from inside the fort (*i.e.* Trenches D and E), or immediately outside (*i.e.* Trenches A–C). The majority of finds came from Trench F, which appears to be a rubbish tip associated with the Ottoman fort. The finds comprised a wide variety of materials including, ceramics (glazed and unglazed wheelmade pottery, tabun, fritware, porcelain and tobacco pipes), glass (bracelets, beads and vessel fragments), metal (iron and copper alloy), textiles and bone (including worked bone). Environmental samples, including soil samples, charcoal fragments and bone were recovered. Unfortunately the soil samples and bone were lost when the Council for British Research in the Levant's 'Amman office and storage facilities moved in 2003. A total of 6.1 kg of bone was excavated from Trench F (F1, 0.1 kg; F2, 1 kg; F4, 1 kg; and F5, 4 kg) and a brief examination indicated a predominance of sheep and goat (mostly goat) with significant amounts of camel (pers. comm. Alex Wasse, 3/10/02).

Excavation Summary

The excavations confirmed the findings of the architectural survey, in particular, that there were three main phases of construction at the site. The first phase, tentatively dated to the Byzantine–early Islamic period (by analogy with similar structures elsewhere in Jordan, *c.f.* Kennedy 2000, esp. 87, fig. 9.16; 125, fig. 12.9; and 176, fig. 18.3) was identified in Trenches B, C, D and E. The second phase relates to the construction of the Ottoman fort and, on documentary evidence, may be dated to the 16th century (this phase appears in Trenches D and E). The date of the ashy mound (Trench F) has not been precisely determined, though a preliminary assessment suggests that it contains material from the 16th–19th centuries (*i.e.* no 20th century material was identified).

13. Ceramics from Qal'at 'Unaiza and other Hajj Forts in Jordan

Tony Grey and Andrew Petersen

This chapter primarily represents ceramics from the 2002 excavations at Qal'at 'Unaiza. In addition, the chapter includes ceramics collected from Qal'at al-Hasa, Qal'at al-Mudawarra and Qal'at Dab'a during the 2006 survey. Other finds are discussed separately in Chapter 14.

Qal'at al-Unaiza

Qal'at al-Unaiza was built in AD 1576 and used until the early 19th century, with reuse in the early 20th century. Most of the finds are from a, probable, rubbish tip outside the fort and include glazed and unglazed wheelmade pottery, fritware, porcelain, tobacco pipes, glass and other material. The three main phases are: early Byzantine–early Islamic; the 16th century construction phase; the early 20th century reuse phase (Petersen 2003, 65).

Chinese porcelain

Chinese porcelain from the Ottoman period has been published from Acre (Edelstein and Avissar 1997), Damascus Duma (Carswell 1972), Jerusalem Dung Gate (Bahat 1985), Karak (Milwright 1999) and al-Tur, Sinai (Kawatoko 1995; 1996; 1998). Some Chinese imports were made specifically for the Middle Eastern market, including coffee cups, small bowls/cups and larger bowls. A range of 18th century Chinese porcelain was found at Qal'at al-Unaiza, Qal'at al-Hasa and Dab'a forts.

CONTEXT UNAIZA F1 (PLATE 157)

1. Qianlong bowl body sherd in Chinese Imari; dated mid-18th century.
2. Batavian body sherd; dated *c.* 1700 into 18th century.

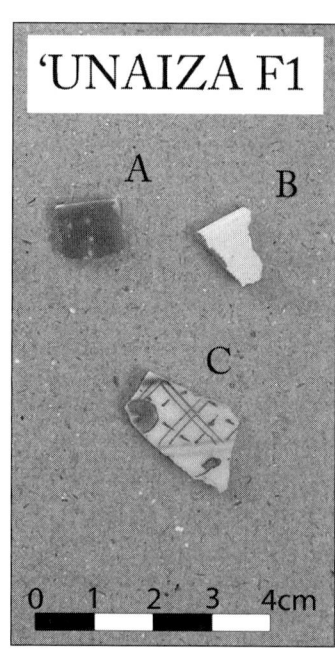

Plate 157. 'Unaiza, F1 ceramics. A = Batavian rim sherd; B = Pearl ware, English?; C = Chinese Imari body sherd.

CONTEXT UNAIZA F2 (PLATE 158)

1. Body sherd of Batavian ware bowl; dated 18th century.
2. Two sherds of Chinese Imari bowl; dated mid-18th century.

CONTEXT UNAIZA F3 (PLATE 159)

1. Body sherd of Chinese Imari; dated 18th century.
2. Blue-on-white glazed ware sherd, with iridescence. Uncertain assignation.

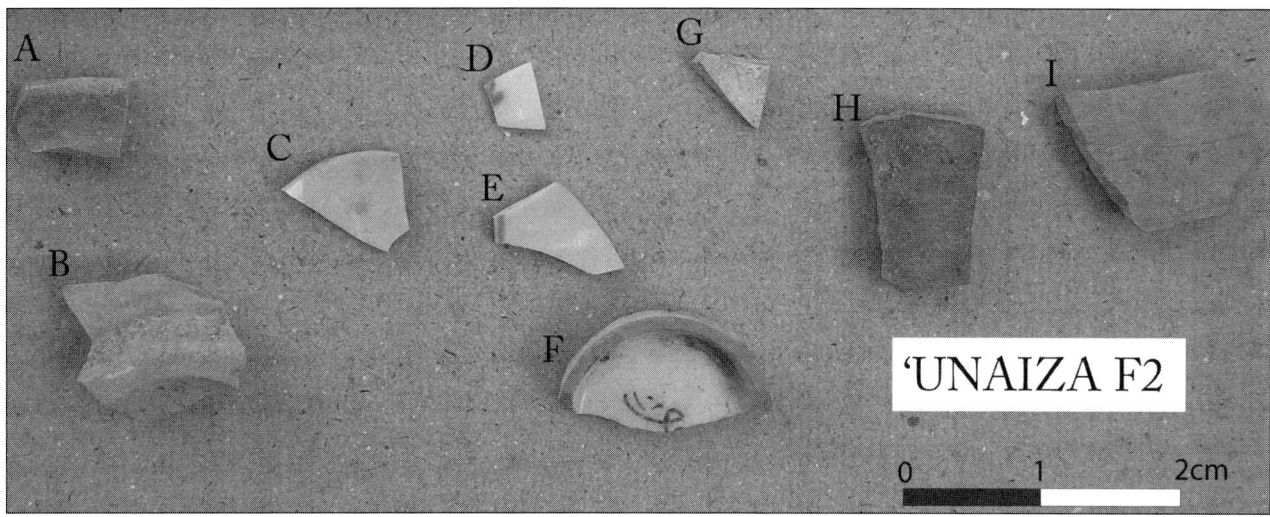

Plate 158. 'Unaiza F2, ceramics. A = rim sherd with green glaze; B = square cut foot ring with patchy green glaze; C = body sherd of Batavian bowl; D–E = body sherds of Chinese Imari bowl; F = ring base of Kutahya frit ware bowl with makers mark; G = buff ware body sherd with transparent glaze; H = body sherd olive green glaze with buff fabric; I = buff ware bowl body sherd with incised line.

Plate 159. 'Unaiza F3. A = body sherd Chinese blue-on-white with irridesence; B = Chinese blue-on-white base of bowl; C = Chinese blue-on-white body sherd; D = Kutahya ware bowl fragment with white glaze over frit body; E–F = Chinese Imari body sherds; G–H = body sherds Chinese blue-on white.

CONTEXT UNAIZA F4 (PLATES 160 AND 161)

1. Base, rim and two body sherds of Chinese cup, with powder blue ground and gilding; dated 18th century (Plate 161).

2. Tiny body sherd of Chinese blue-on-white glazed porcelain. Small, thin coffee cups with blue-on-white, or polychrome decoration, are published from al-Tur (Kawatoko 1995, 10, colour pl. 3:3 and pl. 21:11, pl. 35:10, for 17th–18th century Chinese blue-on-white bowl. Most of the Chinese porcelain from this site is dated 15th–17th century) (Plate 160, F and J).

3. Batavian ware, base sherd of cup, with café-au-lait colour (Plate 160, I).

4. Tiny Chinese celadon sherd (Plate 160, H).

CONTEXT UNAIZA F5 (PLATE 162)

1. Base sherd of Batavian *famile rose* cup, with decorated panels; dated *c.* 1740–60 with a published parallel, dated 17th century, from al-Tur (Kawatoko 1996, 12, pl. 11:8, small 17th century drinking cup) (Plate 162, G).

2. Sherd of Chinese blue-on-white bowl (Plate 162, L).

3. Two sherds of Chinese porcelain cup with powder blue

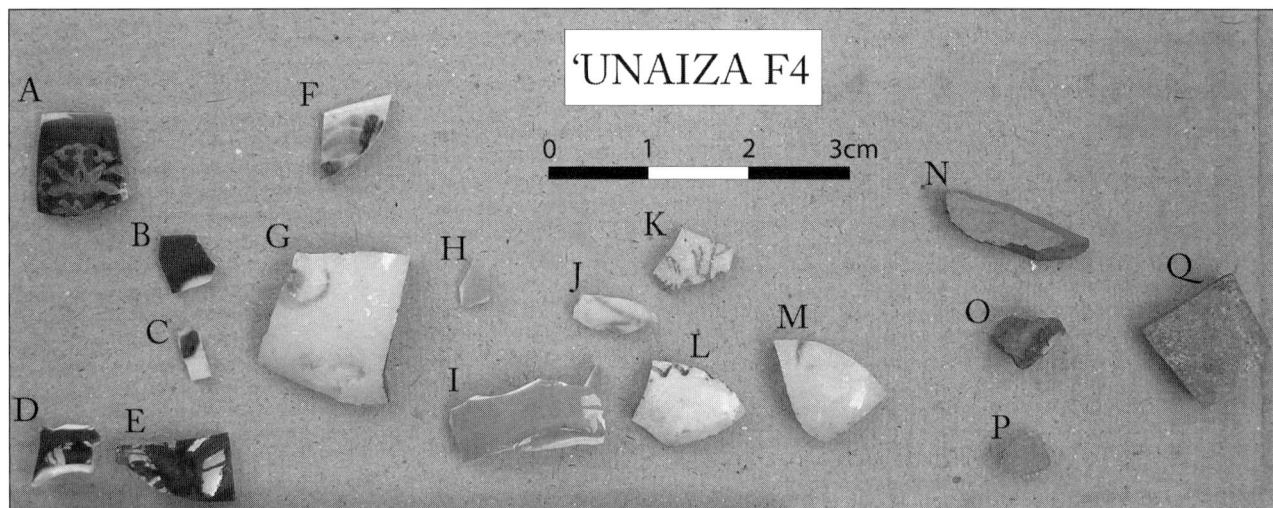

Plate 160. 'Unaiza F4, ceramics. A–E = Chinese cup fragments with powder blue ground and gilding (for detail see Plate 161); F = blue-on-white Chinese porcelain bowl rim sherd; G = Kutahya blue-on-white bowl fragment; H = Chinese celadon sherd; I = Batavian ware base sherd; J = Chinese blue-on-white; K–M = 3 Kutahya ware blue-on-white frit body; N–P three body sherds alkaline blue glaze on red fabric; Q = body sherd of red ware with alkaline green glaze.

Plate 161. 'Unaiza F4. Rim of Chinese cup with powder blue ground and gilding.

ground, gilding and iron brown rim. Thinly potted; dated mid-18th century (Plate 160, I).

CONTEXT UNAIZA B4 (PLATE 163)

1. Rim sherd of bowl in cobalt blue-on-white. Either, provincial Chinese or south-east Asia (possibly Annamese) and probably dated to the late 18th century.

Glazed fritware (Kutahya)

Kutahya and Iznik coffee cups have been excavated at Acre (Muqari 1996; Edelstein and Avissar 1997, pl. III: 4), Jerusalem Citadel (Johns 1950), possibly Jerusalem south side of haram al-Sharif (Ben Dov 1982), al-Tur (Kawatoko 1995; 1996; 1998) and other sites. See, Milwright 2000, 198, fig. 3 for an illustration of an 18th century coffee cup with over-glaze painted decoration, from the Ashmolean Museum: EA C 340. See also published photos and illustrations from al-Tur (Kawatoko 1995, col. pl. 4:5, pl. 34:8; pl. 21:10, pl. 21:8, 9; Kawatoko 1996, 37, pl. 32:6, pl. 32:7; Kawatoko 1996, pl. 39:10, pl. 39:12).

Eighteenth to twentieth century glazed wares were made by Armenian potters, at Canakale and other Turkish sites, as well as at Jerusalem. The 17th and 18th centuries saw the decline of Iznik ware and the rise of inferior and cheaper Kutahya ware, along with Western, Chinese and Japanese imports. Meissen coffee cups, with the crossed swords mark on the base, were made for the Ottoman market (Carswell 1998, 116).

CONTEXT UNAIZA F2 (PLATE 158)

1. Ring base of bowl, with blue-on-white glaze on frit

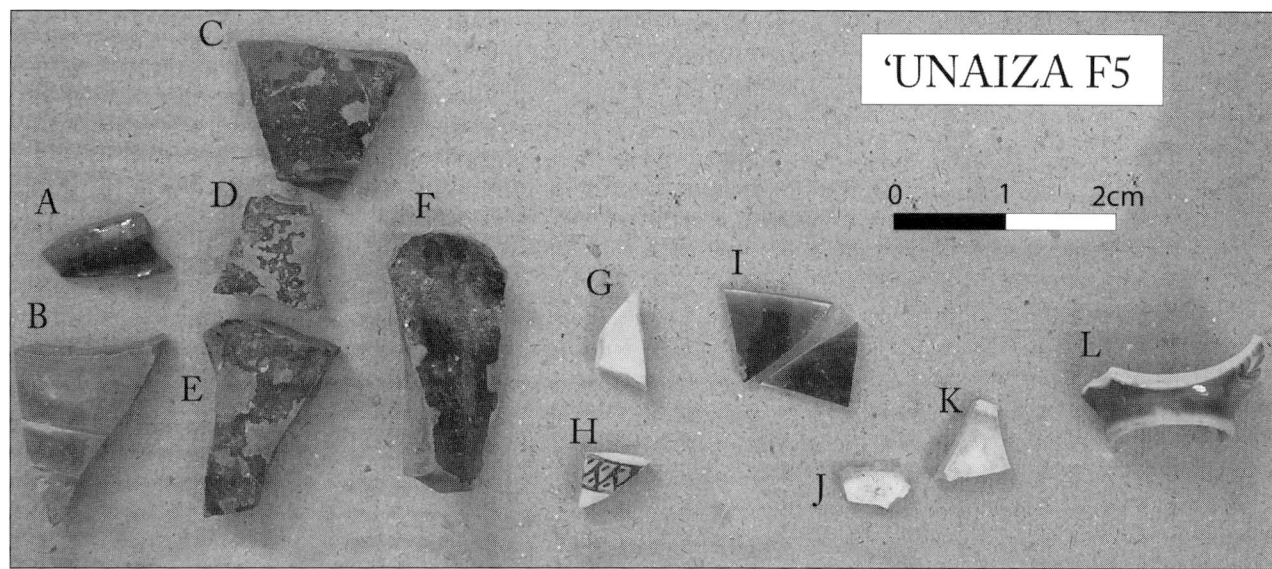

Plate 162. 'Unaiza F5. A = rim sherd dark green glaze on reddish body; B = body sherd of buff ware jug with pale green glaze; C–F laminating red ware with dark green glaze; G = Chinese blue-on-white bowl fragment; H = body sherd Kutahya ware with decorative band; I = rim of Chinese porcelain cup with powder blue ground; J–K two body sherds of Kutahya ware blue-on-white bowl; L= Batavain ware cup base with famille rose design.

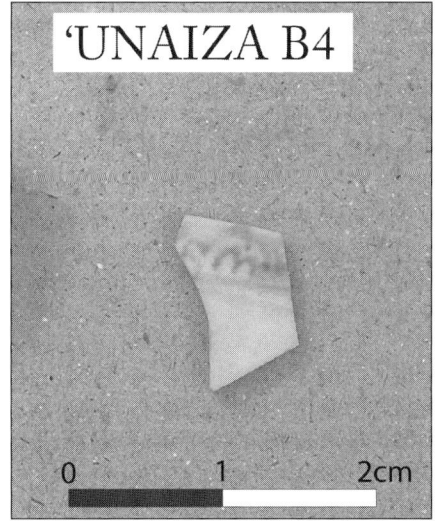

Plate 163. 'Unaiza, B4 ceramics. Rim sherd, Chinese blue-on-white.

body, flower decoration on floor and kiln mark on underside; dated 18th century. For a published parallel from al-Tur, see Kawatoko 1996, pl. 32:7 – for flower pattern and kiln mark (Plate 158, F).

CONTEXT UNAIZA F3

1. Bowl/cup sherd; blue-on-white glaze over frit body.

CONTEXT UNAIZA F4

1. Three cup/bowl sherds, including a rim sherd; blue-on-white glaze on frit body. (Plate 162, H).

2. Body sherds from two cup/bowls; blue-on-white glaze on pink frit body.

3. Sherd of blue-on-white glazed ware over frit body.

CONTEXT UNAIZA F5 (PLATE 162)

1. Body sherd of bowl/cup; glazed ware with blue and black-on-white decorated band with repeating abstract motif, dated 18th century (Plate 162, H).

2. Two sherds of blue-on-white glazed ware; cup/bowl (Plate 162, J–K).

Other glazed ware

CONTEXT UNAIZA F1

1. Tiny rim sherd of bowl resembling English Pearl-ware; dated 19th century (Plate 157, B).

Wheelmade lead-glazed wares

Slipped and unslipped lead-glazed wares have been published from Ti'innik, dated 17th–18th centuries (Ziadeh 1995, 240–42); Jerusalem Citadel (Johns 1950, pl. LXIII: 5–6); Khirbat Zikhrin, dated post-16th century (Milwright 2000, 195); Acre, dated 18th–early 20th centuries (Muqari 1996, 125, fig. 134:3; Edelstein and Avissar 1997, 132–33); Kabrii (Kempinski and Niemeier 1994, 49, figs 22:3, 23:10–15) and Zar'in.

SURFACE FINDS

1. Bowl, or jug, with flat base (8 cm dia.); green glaze

Finewares

Unaiza Trench F

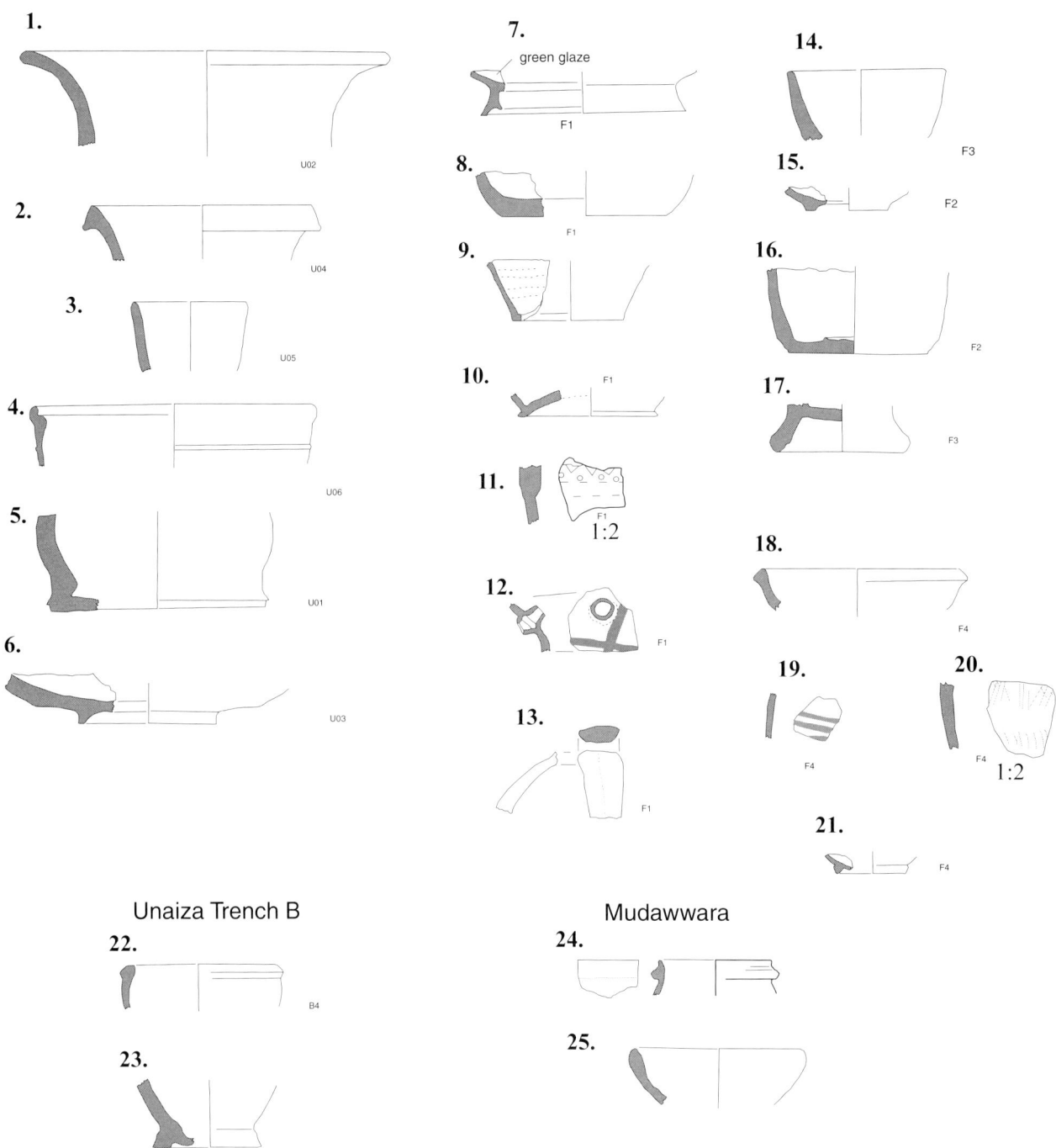

Fig. 52. Fineware ceramics.

over white slip interior and white slip exterior in a hard orange fabric (Fig. 52, no. 5).

2. Possible jug with plain rim and flared neck; greenish glaze over white slip exterior and interior (Fig. 52, no. 1).

3. Bowl ring base; greenish-yellow glaze over white slip interior in a hard fabric (Fig. 52, no. 6).

4. Jar, bowl, or jug neck, with hooked rim; hard, orange, slightly coarse fabric, with dark green glaze on the body (Fig. 52, no. 2).

5. Jug neck with plain rim and a slightly flared neck; hard, orange, slightly coarse fabric, with dark green glaze on the interior body (Fig. 52, no. 3).

Plate 164. 'Unaiza, F1 ceramics. A = foot stand of reduced ware bowl; B = flat base of hand made cooking pot; C = foot stand of large bowl with glaze over white slip; D = foot stand of reduced ware bowl.

CONTEXT UNAIZA F1 (PLATE 164)

1. Foot stand of large bowl; reddish ware with a fairly blistered green slip interior over a white slip. The fabric contains large, round and sub-rounded reddish quartz, occasional black iron and lime. Dating, may be, Mamluk or Ottoman (Fig. 52, no. 7) (Plate 164, C).

CONTEXT UNAIZA F2

1. Rim sherd of possible bowl; pale green glaze over a reddish body (Fig. 52, no. 14).
2. Body sherd; olive green glaze on body exterior, thinner glaze on body of interior on a hard, buff fabric.
3. Body sherd; pale yellow glaze, over a hard, pale buff fabric.
4. Square cut foot rim; buff fabric of a bowl, with patchy green glaze interior (Fig. 52, no. 15).

CONTEXT UNAIZA F4

1. Body sherd of vessel; green glaze interior, on a buff body. The fabric is coarse, soft and silty, with occasional large iron and frequent small quartz, inclusions.

CONTEXT UNAIZA F5

1. Rim sherd of vessel; dark greenish glaze on a reddish body (Fig. 52, no. 18).
2. Three body sherds; laminating red ware, with flaking dark green glaze.

3. Body sherd of possible jug; pale green glaze exterior and thinly applied glaze traces interior.

Other glazed wares

CONTEXT UNAIZA F4

1. Tiny body sherd; thick turquoise-blue, alkaline glaze on fabric containing, occasional irregular iron and small irregular quartz, inclusions.
2. Two body sherds; alkaline, turquoise-blue glaze interior and green glaze exterior.

CONTEXT UNAIZA F

1. Body sherd of possible jug; black manganese glaze exterior, on wheelmade red body.

Wheelmade plain wares

Plain wheelmade pottery is attested from T'innik (dated 16th–early 20th centuries) (Ziadeh 1995, 233–40), Burj al-Ahmar (Pringle 1986, fig. 39), Acre (dated 18th–early 20th centuries) (Muqari 1996, 124–25), Kabris (Kempinski and Niemeier 1994, 49–50, figs 22–23), Tel al-Hasi (Toombs 1985, 106–8) and Zar'in (Grey 1994, 60–61; and forthcoming).

SURFACE FIND

1. Jar rim, with internal groove for lid, seating dia. 10

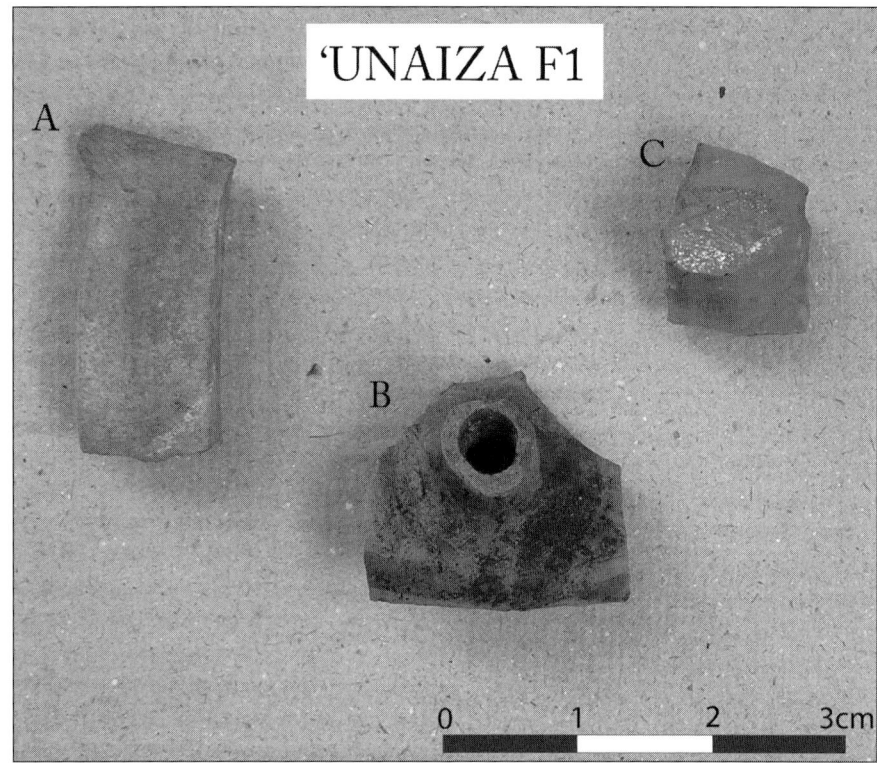

Plate 165. 'Unaiza F1, ceramics. A = jar handle orange/red ware; B = broken tubular spout orange/red ware; C = handle stump orange/red ware.

cm; brittle, burnt orange, fairly coarse ware with a dark grey exterior and some inclusions (Fig. 52, no. 4).

CONTEXT UNAIZA F1 (PLATES 165, 166 AND 167)

1. Broken tubular jug spout, attached to body; reddish ware with reduced black, or sooted, surfaces and traces of purple painted bands on exterior (Fig. 52, no. 12) (Plate 165, B).
2. Various jar body sherds; reddish, or buff, including a jar handle, handle stump and ridged body sherd all of which belong to the Byzantine/early Islamic by period (Fig. 52, no. 13) (Plate 166, B and 165, A).
3. Four body sherds of heavy-duty jars; one buff and three reddish, one with a partly reduced surface, the others lightly ridged. These may be Byzantine/early Islamic by period.
4. Two body sherds of jar with reduced surfaces.
5. Two jar body sherds; reddish ware with cream bloom on exterior.
6. Body sherd of vessel; buff ware, with possible cream bloom on exterior.
7. Body sherd of jar; buff ware with black and ridged exterior. Probably dated to the Byzantine/early Islamic period (Fig. 52, no. 11) (Plate 167).
8. Jar, or cooking pot handle; coarse reddish ware, with fabric containing black iron, rare lime and ill-sorted, irregular quartz of varying size.

9. Jar body sherds; reddish ware with black core and smooth exterior.
10. Four body sherds from heavy-duty jars. One is buff and three reddish. One has a partly reduced smooth exterior surface, while the others are lightly ridged. Possibly Byzantine/early Islamic.
11. Fragment of neck, of possible jug, in buff ware.
12. Fifteen small body sherds of jugs, or jars, including a handle stump; reddish or buff wares. One has a sooted exterior.
13. Foot stand of reduced ware bowl (Fig. 52, no. 10) (Plate 164, A).

CONTEXT UNAIZA F2 (PLATE 168)

1. Base of amphora, or storage jar; buff ware, over fired to a greenish hue, with shrinkage cracks interior and a sooted exterior. The vessel is lightly ridged, hard-fired and very coarse, with inclusions of occasional large irregular iron, up to 3 mm in size, large orange (possibly grog) inclusions up to 1 mm in size and frequent small irregular quartz (Fig. 52, no. 16) (Plate 168, A).
2. Two body sherds; coarse reddish ware (Plate 168, D).
3. Thinly potted, ridged and reduced base/body sherd of a jar. Probably Byzantine or early Islamic (Fig. 52, no. 9).
4. Seven body sherds; buff or cream fabric.

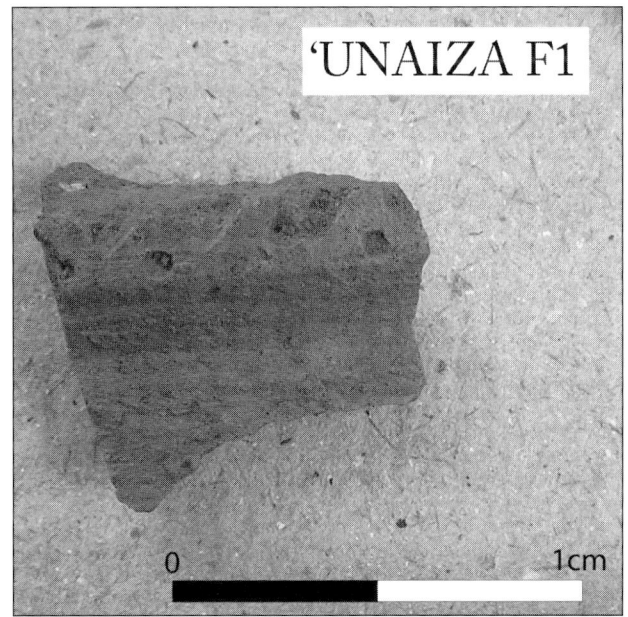

Plate 166. 'Unaiza F1. Various jar body sherds in reduced buff ware.

Plate 167. 'Unaiza F1. Body sherd of jar buff ware with black exterior and ridged decoration (Fig. 52, No. 11).

CONTEXT UNAIZA F3 (PLATE 169)

1. Foot stand in reduced coarse ware, part of possible jug, with burnt interior. The fabric has large black, iron or basalt, inclusions, occasional lime, orange grits and frequent small, ill-sorted, irregular quartz. Probably Ottoman in date (Fig. 52, no. 17).
2. Base of amphora, or storage jar; buff ware, slightly over fired to a greenish hue, in coarse ware with a flat base and ridged exterior. Probably Ottoman in date (similar jar base found at al-Tur, Kawatoko 1998, 67, pl. 38:4).
3. Fourteen jar sherds; reduced-fired coarse ware. Some are ridged, some smooth and all fairly thinly potted. Could be from Byzantine/early Islamic Palestinian bag-shaped jars (7th–9th century AD).
4. Body sherd of possible jug; buff ware with a sharp body ridge exterior.
5. Twelve possible jar body sherds; buff ware, some with exterior brushing/smoothing marks.

Plate 168. 'Unaiza Trench F2. A = base of amphora buff ware; B = body sherd pale yellow glaze on hard buff fabric; C = coarse reddish ware body sherd; D = coarse reddish ware body sherd; E–K = body sherds buff or cream fabric.

CONTEXT UNAIZA *F4*

1. Body sherd; buff ware jar, with red painted bands (Fig. 52, no. 19).
2. Probable neck sherd from a jug; brownish ware with scored cordons. Probably 18th–19th century in date.
3. Body sherd of possible Palestinian bag-shaped jar, with handle stump; reduced grey ware with a ribbed blackish exterior. The fabric is coarse and contains frequent large lime, up to 1 mm in size, smaller lime, small quartz and occasional large iron inclusions. Dated, Byzantine/early Islamic, 7th–9th centuries.
4. Six body sherds; sandy red ware cooking vessels. Three are ridged. The fabric contains occasional large lime and large iron inclusions. These sherds could be dated Nabataean, Roman or Byzantine.
5. Eight assorted body sherds of possible jars; buff, pale orange and reddish wares, with smooth exteriors (Fig. 52, no. 20).
6. Foot ring base of Nabataean bowl/dish; reddish ware with plain glossed surfaces. Probably 1st century AD in date (Fig. 52, no. 21).

CONTEXT UNAIZA *F6*

1. Five body sherds from jars; buff ware, with smooth exterior reduced surface, fairly thinly potted and including a ring handle. Probably Byzantine/early Islamic, 7th–9th century AD.

CONTEXT UNAIZA *B1 (PLATE 170)*

1. Handle tubular.
2. Four fragments of reduced grey ware.
3. Greenish buff ware body sherd.

CONTEXT UNAIZA *B4 (PLATE 171)*

1. Rim of small bowl in reduced ware (Fig. 52, no. 22) (Plate 171, D).
2. Fragment of base of possible jar; buff ware (Fig. 52, no. 23) (Plate 171, A).

CONTEXT UNAIZA *B5*

1. Small thick body sherd; brown-red ware from a heavy-duty jar.

Plate 169. 'Unaiza F3, ceramics. A–L = assorted body sherds in reduced coarse ware; M = base of amphora in buff coarse ware; N–P = coarse ware jar sherds.

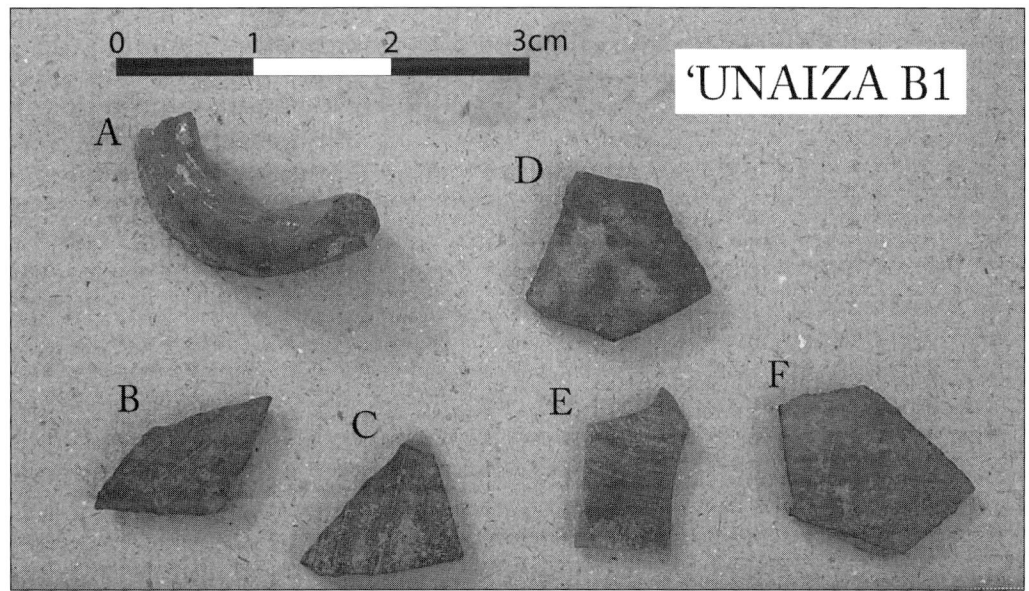

Plate 170. 'Unaiza, B1 ceramics. A = tubular handle; B = buff ware reduced fired body sherd; C = buff ware reduced fired body sherd; D = buff ware reduced fired body sherd; E = buff ware reduced fired body sherd; F = buff ware reduced fired body sherd.

Plate 171. 'Unaiza, B4 ceramics. A = base of buff ware jar; B = wheel made body sherd, reduced ware; C = body sherd, reduced ware; D = rim of possible jar buff ware; E = body sherd reduced ware; F = body sherd reduced ware.

CONTEXT UNAIZA C1 (PLATE 172)

1. Body sherd from a cooking vessel in ridged reddish ware, plus a lid sherd with a red body and reduced exterior surface. Probably Roman to Byzantine in date.

Coarse handmade wares

Handmade wares of the late 19th–early 20th centuries are published from Umm al-Jimal (Parker in de Vries 1998, 215–18) and Zar'in (Grey forthcoming). This low-fired coarse ware, used for cooking vessels and other kitchenware, continues a tradition dating from pre-Ayyubid times to the 20th century. The ware is typically friable with abundant voids and tempered with vegetable chaff and/or quartz, or grog, with limestone (up to 3 mm) inclusions frequently present. Often the surfaces are oxidized to a buff or orange colour, self-slipped and even occasionally burnished, while the core is usually dark grey to black.

This crude, coarse, kitchenware was used alongside glazed, or porcelain, tableware. Large quantities of handmade sherds were retrieved from Qal'at al-Unaiza. Most of these were weighed and discarded. Illustrated sherds are catalogued below.

CONTEXT UNAIZA F1 (PLATE 164)

1. Flat base of large, handmade, cooking pot tempered with chaff and sand, and containing small white shelly inclusions and large lime inclusions, with a reduced interior and reddish exterior, there are brushing/smoothing marks on the interior and some signs of burning. Dated to the Ottoman period (Fig. 52, no. 8) (Plate 164, B).

2. Possible lid; fairly hard-fired ware, with light brown to buff and self-slipped exterior surface, voids and inclusions of limestone and basalt (Fig. 53, no. 13).

CONTEXT UNAIZA F2

1. Rim of possible storage jar (dia. 22 cm); fairly hard-fired ware, with light yellow-brown self-slipped exterior surface, dark grey core and vegetable temper, voids and limestone inclusions (Fig. 53, no.1) (Plate 173).

2. Possible handle: very soft ware, with a buff-grey self-slipped exterior surface with burning, vegetable temper and inclusions of limestone and small molluscs (Fig. 53, no. 7).

3. Body sherd; very soft, friable ware of light buff colour, with coarse vegetable temper and decoration consisting of a band of punched holes (Fig. 53, no. 8).

4. Two body sherds with pitted surfaces, pinkish surfaces and pale grey core.

CONTEXT UNAIZA F3

10 kg of diagnostic and body sherds were weighed and discarded.

1. Rim of possible bowl; friable, chaff-tempered ware with oxidized orange surfaces. Ottoman in date.

2. Five small sherds of quart-tempered cooking pot ware. Ottoman in date.

3. Rim with handle, possibly from a platter or tray; soft, friable ware with light orange-brown, self-slipped

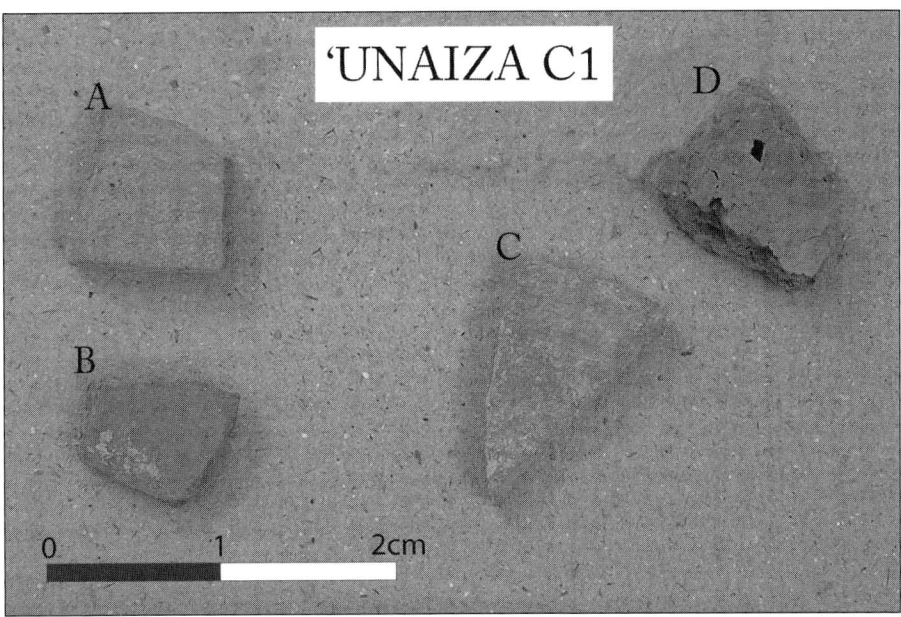

Plate 172. *'Unaiza, C1 ceramics. A = ridged orange/red ware body sherd; B = plain orange/red ware body sherd; C = lid rim sherd orange/red ware; D = coarse ware buff body sherd.*

exterior surface, dark grey-brown core, voids and vegetable temper (Fig. 53, no. 2).

4. Rim of a closed form jar, or cooking pot; self-slipped blackish exterior surface, dark grey core and orange grit inclusions.

5. Lid, or plate; very coarse ware with light brown to dark grey self-slipped exterior surface, grey-brown core, vegetable temper and large limestone inclusions (1–3 mm) (Fig. 53, no. 12).

6. Lid; handmade light buff exterior, with dark grey core and vegetal temper (Fig. 53, no. 11).

7. Possible tray (*c.f.* number 6 above); very coarse ware of light brown-grey colour, with voids and vegetable temper (Fig. 53, no. 10).

8. Thickened and flattened rim of a closed form jar, or cooking pot; light brown-buff ware, with self-slipped exterior surface, vegetable temper and limestone inclusions (1–2 mm) (Fig. 53, no. 14).

9. Handle stump on a body sherd; dark grey fabric with a blackish exterior and grey-brown interior, vegetable temper and limestone inclusions (Fig. 53, no. 6).

CONTEXT UNAIZA F4

4 kg of diagnostic sherds were weighed and discarded. 16 kg of body sherds from both F4 and F5 were weighed and discarded.

1. Eight sherds, including a rim sherd; coarse reddish ware, with grey core and chaff-tempered, plus white shelly inclusions. Ottoman by date.

2. Body sherd.

3. Flat base of a jar, or cooking vessel; reddish-brown ware, with light grey exterior surface, grey-black core, vegetable temper and inclusions of frequent limestone and occasional quartz.

4. Lid; handmade ware, with light buff self-slipped exterior surface, grey-black core, vegetable temper and limestone inclusions. A finger groove is visible on the exterior edge (Fig. 53, no. 9).

5. Rounded rim of a closed form cooking pot, or jar; fairly hard-fired coarse ware, with light orange-grey exterior, light orange-buff interior, voids, vegetable temper and small limestone inclusions (Fig. 53, no. 3).

CONTEXT UNAIZA F5

1.5 kg of diagnostic body sherds were weighed and discarded (see above for F4).

CONTEXT UNAIZA C1 (PLATE 173, D)

1. Coarse buff ware body sherd.

Qal'at Mudawwara (Plates 174 and 175)

Kuthaya glazed ware

1. Rim sherd; blue-on-white lead glazed cup/bowl with cobalt blue, dated mid–late 19th century (Plate 174, B).

2. Tiny body sherd; blue-on-white glaze over a reddish frit body (Plate 174, A).

Lead glazed wheelmade wares

1. Body sherd; reddish ware, with flaking dark green glaze over white slip exterior. The fabric contains, occasional, large red iron-rich inclusions, frequent,

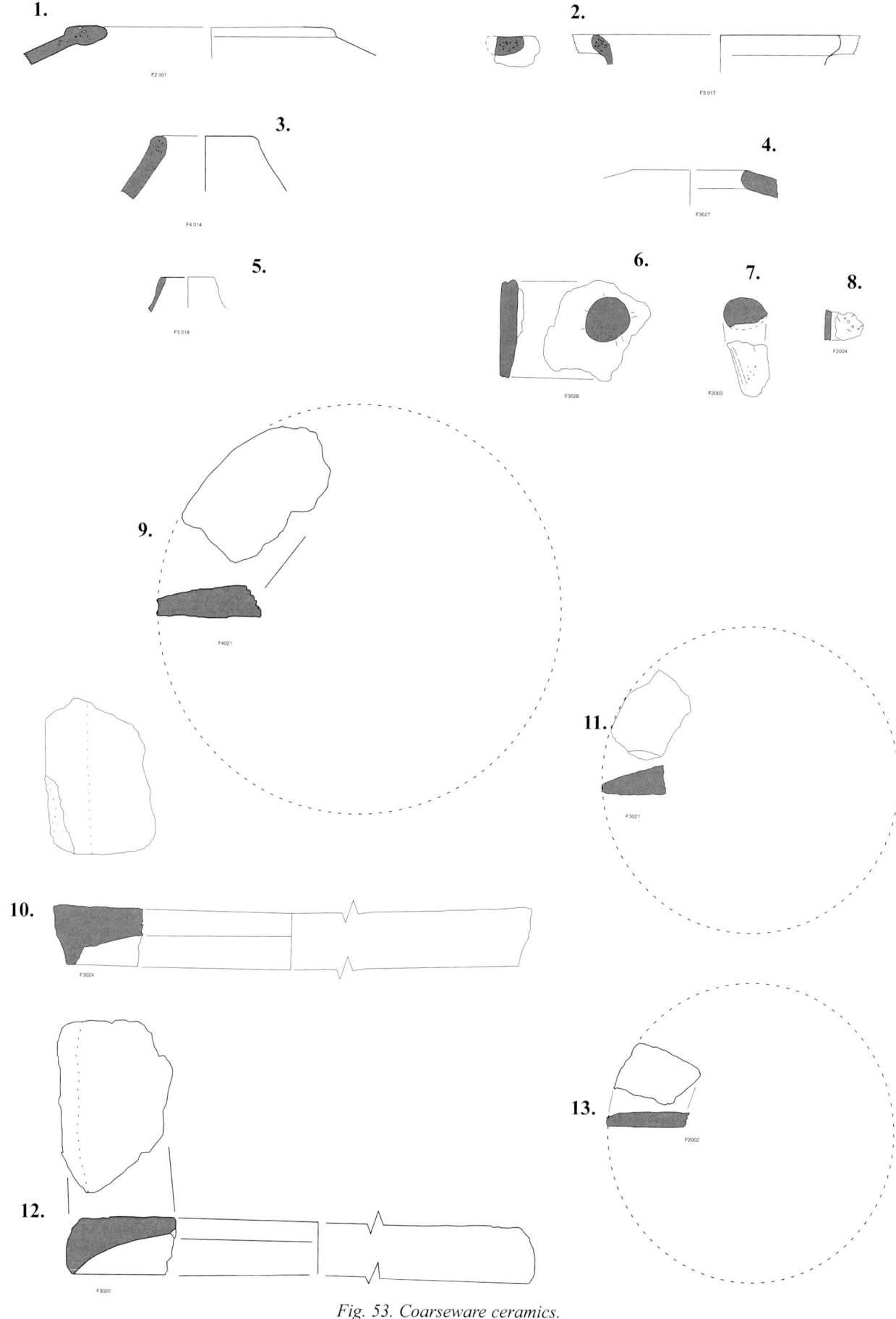

Fig. 53. Coarseware ceramics.

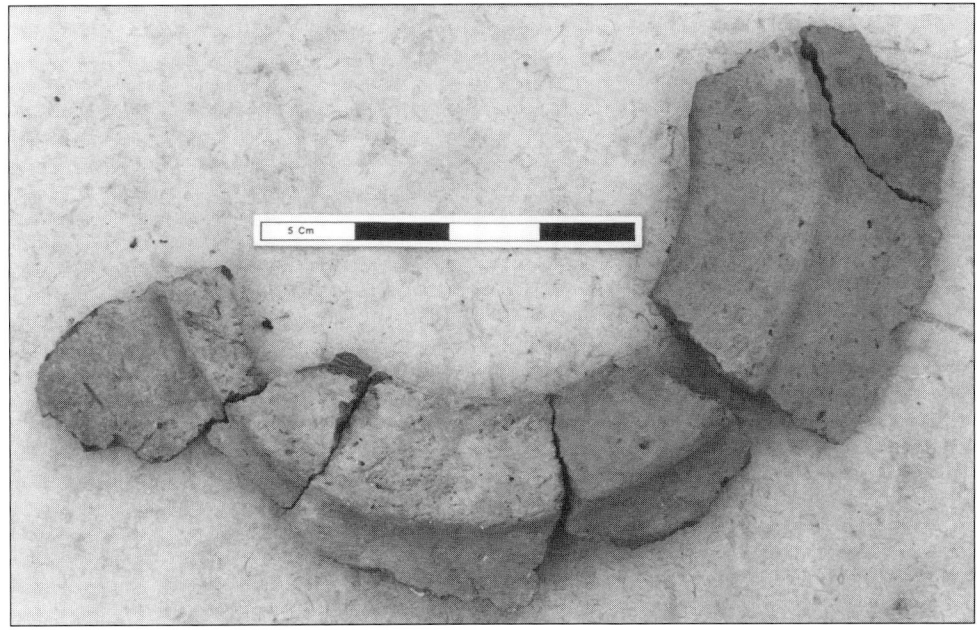

Plate 173. 'Unaiza. Rim of storage Jar from Trench F context 002 (c.f. Fig 53 no. 1).

smaller red and black iron and ill-sorted irregular quartz of varying size.

2. Necked jar with everted rim; pale reddish ware, with a cream exterior and traces of green glaze exterior and interior. The fabric contains occasional platelets and irregular grains of red iron, occasional black iron and small quartz inclusions

Other glazed wares

1. Body sherd; turquoise-blue alkaline glaze, on coarse reddish ware (Plate 174, C).

Wheelmade plain wares (Plate 175)

1. Body sherd of reduced grey ware jar with combed exterior decoration, probably dated early Islamic (Plate 175, K).
2. Rim and body sherd of a bowl; coarse reddish ware with a flat rim, sharp carination at the upper body and an interior groove (Plate 175, E–F).
3. Body sherd of a jar; buff ware over-fired to a greenish hue. The fabric is hard-fired and very coarse, and contains, occasional spherical quartz grains, frequent large angular quartz and occasional black iron, inclusions (Plate 175, H).
4. Four body sherds of jars; fairly thinly potted red ware, with a reduced, blackish, smooth exterior, probably dated Byzantine/early Islamic.
5. Rim of a collared jar; reddish ware. The fabric is coarse and soft, and contains, frequent large angular quartz, frequent red and black iron and occasional large lime, inclusions (Fig. 53, no. 24) (Plate 175, A).

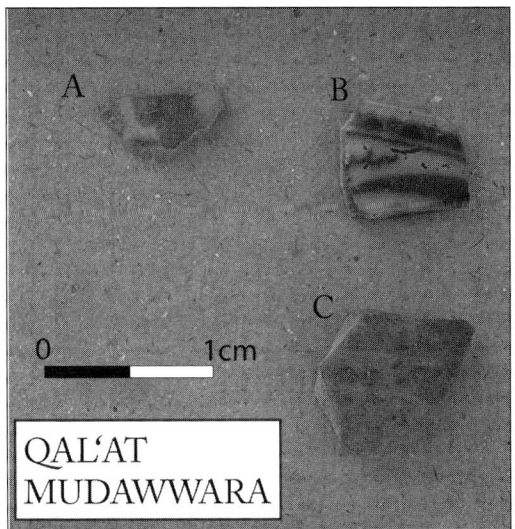

Plate 174. Qal'at Mudawwara. A = blue-on-white Kutahya ware body sherd; B = rim sherd Kutahya blue-on-white; C = alkaline blue-green glaze on reddish fabric.

6. Body sherd of a heavy-duty jar; reddish ware with pitted and lightly grooved exterior. Probably Byzantine/early Islamic (Plate 175, C).
7. Bowl with incurving rim; brownish ware, with a grey core and exterior pitting. The fabric is coarse and hard, with frequent, small lime and occasional black iron, inclusions. Probably Byzantine/early Islamic (Fig. 53, no. 25) (Plate 175, D).
8. Neck base sherd from a jar, or jug; thinly potted reddish ware, with smooth exterior.
9. Body sherd; reddish ware.

Plate 175. Qal'at Mudawwara. A = rim of collared jar in red/orange ware; B = rim sherd of necked jar in pale reddish ware with traces of green glaze; C = body sherd of cooking pot in coarse red ware; D = rim of bowl with incurving rim and traces clear glaze over red ware body; E–F = rim and body sherd of coarse red ware bowl with flat rim; G = fine red-orange ware body sherd; H = body sherd buff ware over fired to green; I–J two body sherds with traces of green painted decoration; K = body sherd reduced grey ware with combed decoration; L = body sherd red fabric with green glaze over white slip.

Coarse handmade wares

Body sherd of cooking pot; pitted reddish exterior with a black core, grog and quartz temper. Probably Ottoman.

Dab'a (Plate 176)

Chinese porcelain

1. Rim sherd of large bowl; blue-on-white. Chinese, made for the Middle Eastern market dated *c.* 1750–1800 AD (Plate 176, C).
2. Body sherd from a cover; blue-on-white.

Lead glazed wheelmade wares (Plate 176, A)

1. Body sherd of vessel; clear lead glaze over reddish body appears as dark brown interior and decayed dark green glaze on exterior. Probably Ottoman.

Other glazed wares (Plate 176, B)

1. Handle stump; alkaline turquoise-blue glaze on reddish ware. Possibly a jug of the Ottoman period, turning iridescent with salts.

Plain wheelmade wares

1. Small body sherd of a jar with a reduced and ridged exterior. Probably Byzantine/early Islamic.
2. Body sherd of a jar; reddish ware with a reduced exterior.
3. Two small body sherds of a jar; reddish ware. Probably Byzantine/early Islamic.

Qal'at al-Hasa (Plates 177 and 178)

Chinese porcelain

1. Bowl/cup rim and body sherd with blue ground, of provincial Chinese origin.
2. Plate/dish; dated 18th century.
3. Bowl/cup ring base; dated 18th century.

Kuthaya ware

1. Footstand base of bowl; blue-on-white glaze on frit body, plus a small body sherd (Plate 176, C).
2. Moulded bowl; blue-on-white glaze, with imitation Meissen mark of crossed swords on underside (parallel from Acre, Edelstein and Avissar 1997, pl. III: 4 and

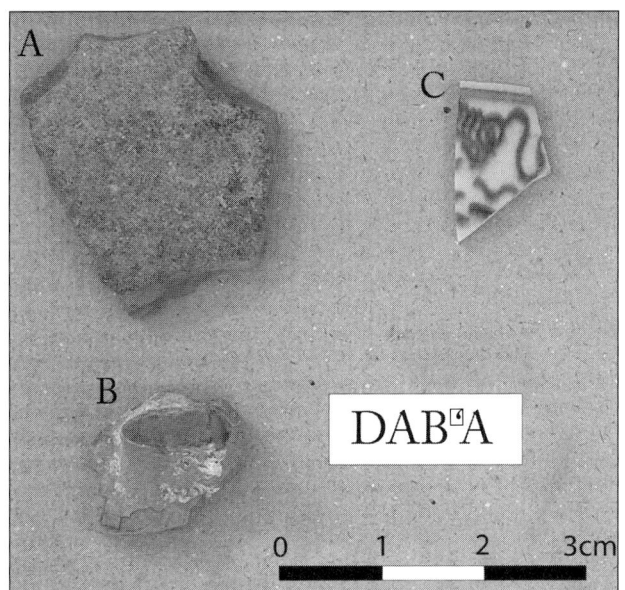

Plate 176. Dab'a. A = Body sherd of green lead glaze on red body; B = handle stem alkaline turquoise glaze; C = rim sherd Chinese blue-on-white.

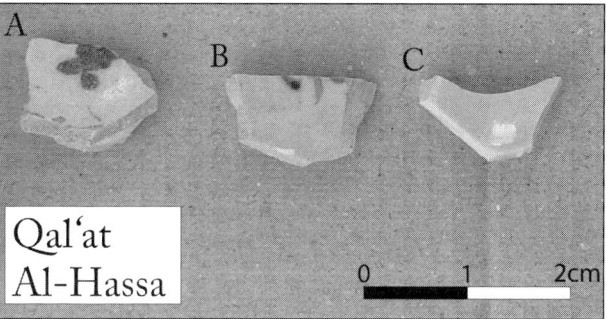

Plate 177. Qal'at al-Hasa. A = foot stand base blue-on-white Kutahya frit body; B = cup base Imari style porcelain southeast Asia; C = moulded ware imitation Meissen.

similar from al-Tur, Kawatoko 1996, pl. 39:12 for Kutuhaya blue-on-white, with imitation Meissen sign or English with combined anchors underside).

3. Bowl/cup; manganese blue glazed decoration.
4. Tiny sherd; white glaze on pink frit body.

Other glazed wares

1. Bowl/cup ring base from south-east Asia (possibly Annam or the Philippines); Imari type decoration on a hard clay body.

Plain wheelmade wares

1. Two jug neck sherds; fine ware with red-brown surfaces and black core, burnished exterior surface. One has rouletted cordons (parallels from Zar'in are Ottoman in date).

Plate 178. Qal'at al-Hasa. A = ring base fragment orange/red ware; B = orange slip painted ware body sherd; C = bowl rim in coarse wheel made buff ware; D = buff ware with incised decoration; E = body sherd with ridges red/orange ware; F = buff ware fragment of jar neck; G = reduced ware body sherd with handle stump; H–J light buff body sherds covered with turquoise alkaline glaze.

14. Finds from Qal'at 'Unaiza and other Ottoman Forts on the Darb al-Hajj

St John Simpson

'The cultural heritage of the Ottoman Empire has traditionally been presented to us through its monuments – mosques, mausoleums, palaces, baths – and its high arts, such as court painting and calligraphy. Our understanding of Ottoman culture has thus come from a world created by and for sultans, viziers and the élite of the Empire' (Faroqhi 2000).

Archaeology offers a powerful tool in countering this view, providing insights into popular culture, what, and how, commodities were produced, moved, used and consumed. Excavations in Istanbul and Beirut provide glimpses into the circulation of material culture in different urban contexts (Hayes 1992; van der Lingen 2003; van der Steen 1997), whereas landscape surveys in rural regions, such as Boeotia, suggest that the landscape was not as empty as some modern commentators have assumed (Vroom 2003). There is growing academic interest in how the borders of the Ottoman Empire operated and to what extent they were frontiers or cross-cultural zones (*e.g.* Rogan 1999). Food historians have begun re-evaluating Court cuisine (Vroom 2006) and analyses of datable classes of Ottoman material culture, such as, Kutahya ware coffee cups and clay tobacco pipes, detail the effects of the introduction, and growing popularity, of coffee drinking and tobacco smoking across the Empire (Vroom 1996; Simpson (ed.) 2011).

Nevertheless, one of the biggest problems still facing the study of everyday Ottoman culture is the comparative lack, of well-quantified assemblages from carefully excavated and closely datable single-period sites. The archaeological study of assemblages from forts along the Darb al-Hajj are, therefore, very important, as they offer a detailed insight into life within a military frontier system, created in the third quarter of the 17th century, incorporated into the Hejaz Railway, but totally abandoned following the Great Arab Revolt and First World War. The following report includes all of the artefact classes, apart from pottery, which is detailed separately by Tony Grey.

Clay pipes

This report is based on 26 clay pipes, 15 of which were recovered from the excavations carried out at Qal'at 'Unaiza in 2002. The remainder are surface finds from three other Hajj forts in Jordan, surveyed by A. D. Petersen in January 2005, namely, Qal'at al-Hasa, Qal'at Dab'a and Qal'at al-Mudawwarra.

The descriptions and illustrations are by the author (Figs 54–56). The terminology used generally follows that established by Robinson (1983) and applied elsewhere to comparable pipes from Ottoman Palestine (Simpson 2000a; 2002; 2008). Each of the pipes was catalogued and drawn at 1:1. Colours were recorded using a Munsell Soil Color Chart (Munsell 1994). In the event of future scientific analysis, samples were taken of the charred dottle present in some of the pipes. Stem length was measured from the shank-end to the centre base of the bowl. The following abbreviations have been used within the catalogue: D = diameter, L = length, W = width, RD = rim diameter, int. = interior, ext. = exterior, g = grammes. Drawing conventions include the use of hatching to designate broken areas, and solid black for bowl/stem interiors and sections.

Qal'at 'Unaiza (Table 9)

Fifteen clay pipe fragments were recovered from excavations in 2002. One of these derived from a secondary rubble context post-dating the construction of the west wall of the fort (Trench B), the remainder came from the sounding excavated near the centre of the large

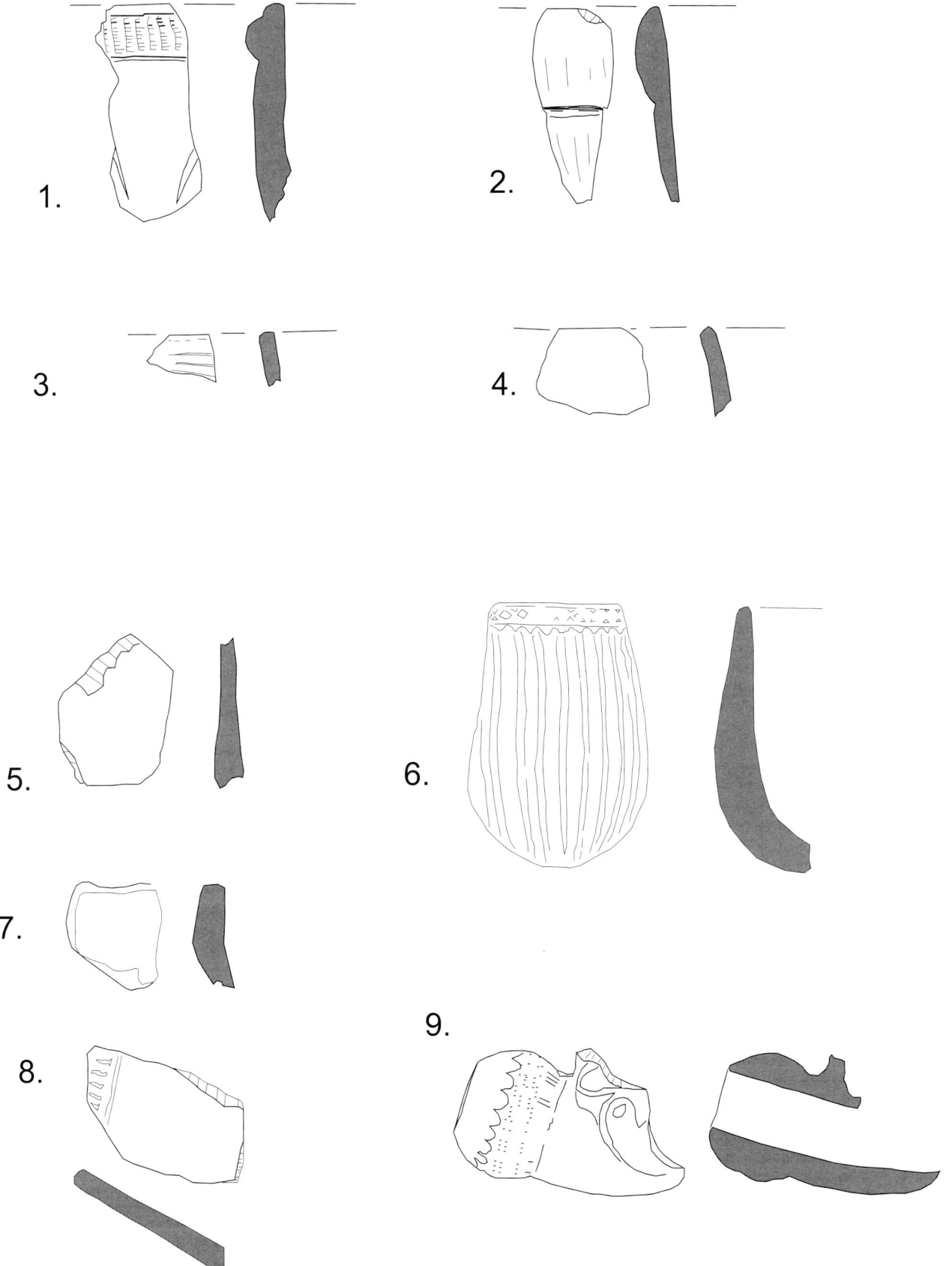

Fig. 54. Tobacco pipes from 'Unaiza F2 and F3.

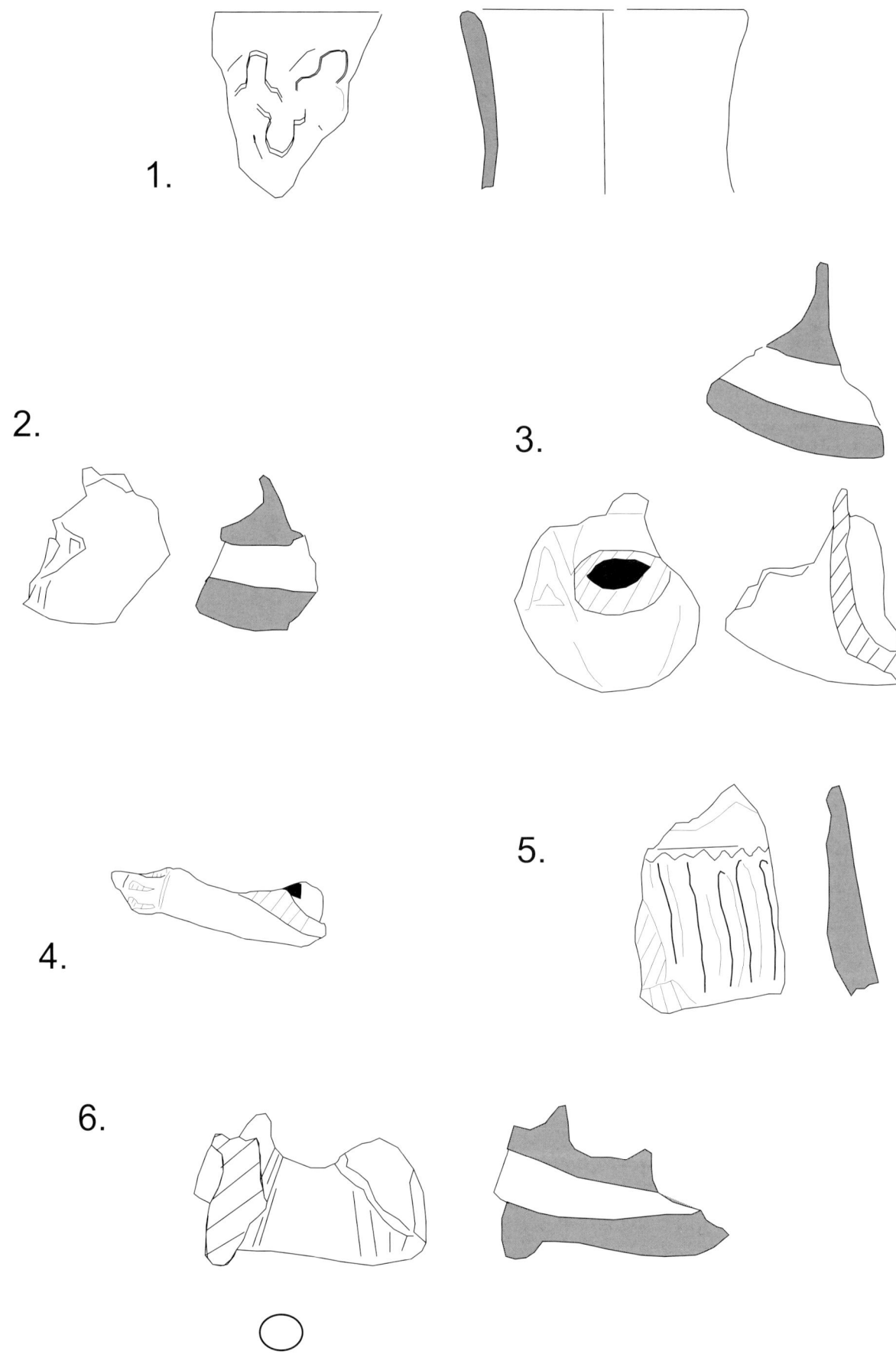

Fig. 55. Tobacco pipes 'Unaiza.

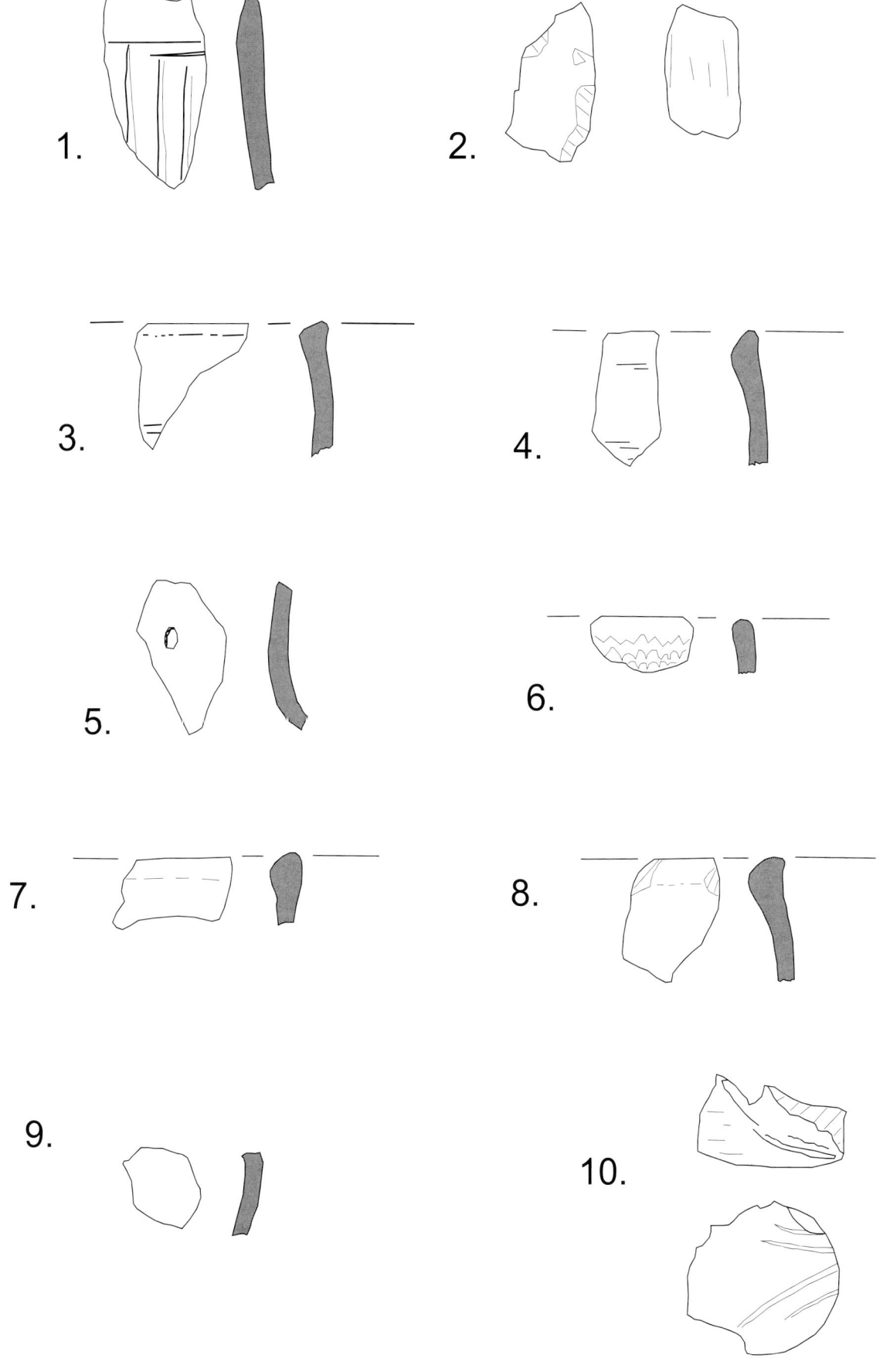

Fig. 56. Tobacco pipes from al-Hasa, Mudawwara and Dab'a.

Cat No.	Description	Wgt (g)	Ctx	Figs
1	Stem; dark grey fabric and slightly mottled weak red burnished slip (10R 4/3); circular bore-hole, D 1.3 cm (shank-end), narrowing to 0.45 cm (bowl/stem junction); gently rounded lower bowl decorated with vertical incised lines; ridged shank-end with notch-rouletted and incised lines below; circular maker's stamp containing indistinct design or inscription, impressed on the underside of the stem, D 0.65 cm; bowl interior blackened with charred dottle adhering; abraded bowl underside.	15.5	B1	
2	Bowl; 1.5 g; brown slightly micaceous fabric and surfaces (7.5YR 5/4); heavily blackened interior with thick crust of charred dottle adhering; unusual fabric.	1.5	F2	54.4
3	Bowl; dark grey fabric and dark dusky red burnished slip; decorated on the exterior immediately below the rim; heavily blackened burnt surfaces.	0.05	F2	54.3
4	Stem; dark grey fabric and reddish brown burnished slip (5YR 4/3); circular bore-hole, D 2.0 cm (shank-end); gently swollen shank-end decorated with a single notch-rouletted line around the stem.	4	F2	54.2
5	Stem; light brown fabric with thick dark grey core and dusky red burnished slip (10YR 3/3); circular bore-hole; stepped shank-end decorated with notch-rouletting; lightly abraded bowl underside.	6	F2	54.1
6	Bowl; dark grey fabric and dusky red burnished slip (10R 3/4); lily bowl; heavily blackened upper interior with charred dottle adhering; secondary charring on the exterior.	3.5	F3	54.5
7	Bowl; dark grey fabric and very dusky red burnished slip (10R 2.5/2); decorated; partially blackened interior with charred dottle adhering.	4.5	F3	54.7
8	Bowl; dark grey fabric and weak red burnished slip (2.5YR 5/2); vertical gadroons alternating plain and decorated with fine lattice pattern.	3	F3	54.8
9	Bowl; RD 3.0 cm dark grey fabric and weak red burnished slip (10R 4/3); decorated with pairs of vertical moulded lines terminating in a row of rounded petals and repeating geometric pattern immediately below the rim; single small dotted circle impression in the centre of the bottom of the bowl, D 0.35 cm; blackened interior with thick crust of charred dottle adhering. Unusual distinctive decoration; *c.f.* similar sherd from F5.	18.5	F3	54.6
10	Stem; dark grey fabric and slightly mottled dusky red (10R 3/3) to weak red (10R 4/3) burnished slip; circular bore-hole, D 1.2 cm (shank-end), narrowing slightly to 1.0 cm (bowl/stem junction); swollen shank-end decorated with lattice pattern with notch-rouletted lines below; partially impressed maker's mark on the right side of the stem; rounded bowl decorated with plain vertical gadroons, with traces of impressed decoration above; bowl/stem junction decorated with a pair of notch-rouletted lines forming a V on the underside of the bowl; traces of mould seam along the bottom of the stem.	18.5	F3	54.9
11	Bowl; dark grey fabric and dusky red burnished slip (10R 3/3); int. RD 4.5 cm; lily bowl decorated with impressed design; blackened interior with charred dottle adhering.	4	F4	55.1
12	Bowl; dark grey fabric and blackened lightly burnished slip, possibly originally dusky red; decorated with pairs of vertical moulded lines terminating in a row of rounded petals; blackened interior with charred dottle adhering; secondary blackening over the exterior. Broadly similar decoration occurs on a pipe bowl from 18th century shipwreck off Sadana island (Ward 2000, 195, fig. 7.6c) and another from Area B at Tell Qaimun (Tel Yoqne'am) (Avissár 2005, 91–92, fig. 4.4, no. 92).	8.5	F5	55.5
13	Bowl/stem junction; dark grey fabric and lightly burnished weak red slip (10R 4/3); circular bore-hole, D 0.6 cm (bowl/stem junction); lower bowl decorated with lattice pattern below two alternating rows of deep wedges with lightly splayed ends; two notch-rouletted lines around the bowl/stem junction, forming a V on the underside; blackened interior with charred dottle adhering.	11.5	F5	55.3
14	Bowl/stem junction; dark grey fabric and dusky red burnished slip (10R 3/2); circular bore-hole, D 0.8 cm (bowl/stem junction); stem decorated with notch-rouletted and incised lines below the break probably corresponding to the beginning of swollen shank-end which subsequently broke away.	8.5	F5	55.2
15	Bowl/stem junction; light yellowish brown fabric and surfaces (10YR 6/4), lightly smoothed; circular bore-hole, D 0.5 cm (bowl/stem junction); shank-end decorated with diagonal short notch-rouletted lines; charred dottle adhering within the lower end of the bore.	6	F5	55.4

Table 9 – Catalogue of Ceramic Smoking Pipes from ʿUnaiza

ashy midden mound outside the fort (Trench F). They weighed a total of 113.55 g and, therefore, represent 58% of the finds assemblage by weight. Most are probably 18th century, although no particularly close parallels have been found. This dating is consistent with the documentary evidence that the fort was constructed in the late 16th century, but largely abandoned by the early 19th century.

Qal'at al-Hasa

Nine fragments were recovered from a surface collection at this fort. They belonged to 7 or more pipes. Most appear to date to the mid/late 19th century.

Cat No.	Description	Wgt (g)	Ctx	Figs
16	Bowl; dark grey fabric and thin light brown (7.5YR 6/4) burnished slip; int. RD 4 cm; bowl decorated immediately below the rim; blackened interior; heavily abraded.	1.0	Surface	56.6
17	Bowl; dark grey fabric and dusky red (10R 3/4) burnished slip; int. RD 3 cm; lily bowl; lightly blackened interior.	1.5	Surface	56.7
18	Bowl; dark grey fabric and dusky red (10R 3/4) burnished slip; int. RD 4 cm; lily bowl; lightly blackened rim interior.	1.5	Surface	56.8
19	Bowl; dark grey fabric and dusky red (10R 3/4) burnished slip; int. RD 3 cm; lily bowl with horizontal lines on the exterior.	1.0	Surface	56.4
20	Bowl; dark grey fabric and reddish brown (5YR 5/4) burnished slip; lily bowl with horizontal lines on the exterior; lightly blackened interior.	1.5	Surface	56.5
21	Bowl; dark grey fabric and dusky red (10R 3/4) burnished slip; lily bowl decorated with impressed oval indent, 0.3 cm high; lightly blackened interior.	1.5	Surface	56.1
22	Stem; light brown fabric (7.5YR 6/4) with thick grey core (7.5YR 6/1) and traces of lightly burnished slip; gently swollen shank-end decorated with pairs of lines incised lengthways with a single row of coarse notch-rouletting impressed near the shank-end; heavily abraded.	3.0	Surface	56.2
23	Stem; dark grey fabric and dusky red burnished slip (10R 3/4).	2.5	Surface	
24	Stem; dark grey fabric and dusky red burnished slip (10R 3/4).	1.5	Surface	

Table 10 – Catalogue of Ceramic Smoking Pipes from Qal'at al-Hasa

Qal'at Dab'a

Cat No.	Description	Wgt (g)	Ctx	Figs
25	Bowl; red fabric and lightly burnished slip (10R 5/6), tip of fine incised line on the interior indicating that the sherd is from close to the bowl/stem junction where the knife has accidentally cut the wall.	0.05	Surface	56.9

Table 11 – Catalogue of Ceramic Smoking Pipes from Qal'at Dab'a

Qal'at al-Mudawwarra

Cat No.	Description	Wgt (g)	Ctx	Plates
26	Bowl; dark grey fabric and slightly mottled dusky red (10R4/3) to light reddish brown (5YR 6/4) burnished slip; two notch-rouletted lines around the lower bowl/stem junction, meeting to form a V on the underside; traces of additional notch-rouletting on the lower bowl; lightly abraded.	5.5	Surface	56.10

Table 12 – Catalogue of Ceramic Smoking Pipes from Qal'at al-Mudawwarra

Discussion

The pipes discussed here were all made of clay and belonged to the so-called Turkish *chibouk*. The general development of these long-stemmed, multi-component, Turkish pipes has been discussed in detail elsewhere (*e.g.* Robinson 1983; Simpson 2008) so will not be repeated here. A growing number of such finds have been published from a wide variety of types of site and archaeological context across the southern Levant, particularly within the past decade. These include a number of village sites, such as, Suba (Belmont) near Jerusalem (Simpson 2000a),

Zir'in (Tel Jezreel) (Simpson 2002), and Mansur al-Aqab, Umm al-Aliq and Beit Khouri (Ramat Hanadiv) on Mount Carmel (Boas 2000a, 222–24; 2000b, 555–59). Small groups from urban contexts have been published from Acre (Akko) (Edelstein and Avissár 1997, 133–35; Stern 1997, 68), Beirut (Bartl 2003; van der Lingen 2003) and Jerusalem (Simpson 2008). Isolated finds from sites such as, Quailibah (Abila) and Hesban, which do not provide any other evidence for substantial occupation, possibly attest the seasonal visits by semi-nomadic tribes, who returned each spring to lightly cultivate the surrounding area and sell the produce to merchant-farmers in the nearest towns. A single pipe found at Khirbet el-Keik, some 20 km west of Jerusalem, was associated with a charcoal oven which was radiocarbon dated to the 16th century (Bacuch 1998). Surveys in the northern Sinai and Negev have provided evidence for pipes from sites that must represent Bedouin encampments (Saidel 2008a). The introduction of smoking into Arabia has been discussed elsewhere by the author (Simpson 2000b). A small number of pipes, which probably belonged to the crews, were found associated with 18th century Red Sea shipwrecks near Sharm el-Sheikh and Sadana island (Ward 2000; Ward and Baram 2006).

Closer to the present study area is the fortress at Karak, which was the administrative centre for the surrounding plateau, although it was only, officially, designated the regional capital in 1895. Several pipes have been published from unstratified deposits, cleared within the standing remains of the Crusader and later castle. These consist of three, 18th century, light grey pipe bowls with rouletted and stamped decoration, a single red-slipped bowl decorated with vertical lines, a cruder bowl fragment (?) and an early 20th century pipe stem, with simple rouletted decoration near the shank end (Milwright 2000, 194, fig. 2.9–14, where slightly earlier dates were estimated). Preliminary archaeological survey reports from Saudi Arabia, refer to the presence of pipes at watchtowers along the southern part of the Hajj route (Zarins *et al.* 1980, pl. 26.17–18), and Le Quesne (2004) has published a selection of the pipes found at the Ottoman fort at Quseir al-Qadim, on the opposite side of the Red Sea. Pipes from other military contexts include those from a fort built by, Dahir al-'Omar, a local ruler of Galilee, at Tell Qaimun (Tel Yoqne'am) (Avissár 2005, 83–93), and a group found at the Turkish citadel of Zabid, in Yemen (Keall 1992).

The pipes discussed here are the first to be published, in detail, from a Turkish military context and they offer a useful insight into the types used along this part of the Ottoman frontier. All of these pipes probably date to the 18th and 19th centuries, although specific parallels are scarce. None are very remarkable and although most are decorated, they do not belong to particularly ornate types and there are no traces of the gilding found on many of those produced at Tophane in Istanbul. Only two definite makers' marks were found, but neither was sufficiently distinct to suggest a workshop origin for these pipes (Table 9, No. 10). These marks are not as common in the southern Levant as they appear to be in Turkey or Greece: although this may be a regional difference, these marks attract disproportionate attention because of the information they offer on place, date and name of the maker; exactly how common they really were remains to be tested through full quantification of excavated assemblages from Istanbul and other urban centres. Nevertheless, there are several other absences from the present assemblage, such as the red-slipped burnished pipes with disc-bases which appear regularly on sites in Palestine and which are represented by a single find from the Wadi Ziqlab in northern Jordan (Simpson 2000a, 163–67,

group VII; 2002, 165–66, group V). This may simply be due to issues of sample size, but the possibility of different circulation patterns cannot be excluded, particularly as this type is also absent from the quantified sample of 59 pipes, from the 2000–3 excavations, carried out at Aqaba Castle by D. Pringle and J. de Meulemeester (Simpson forthcoming). None of the sites yielded fragments of the splash-glazed pipes which occasionally appear at sites in Palestine (*e.g.* Simpson 2000a, 152, group III), nor are there any definite pieces belonging to the, equally distinctive and robust, red-slipped burnished lilies with rouletted shank ends (*c.f.* Simpson 2000a, 157–63, group VI). Splash-glazed pipes have yet to be recognized at any site in Jordan and the author has speculated, elsewhere, that they are an 18th century Palestinian product. The absence of the rouletted lilies is more surprising, as these appear to be ubiquitous at late 19th century and later sites in Palestine, and the type recurs in Syria and Iraq. Finally, it might be added that there are no water pipes: these were also rare among published pipe assemblages from Aqaba, Suba and Zir'in, although they were commoner in Beirut. This distribution reinforces the impression that water pipes were more commonly used in an urban, rather than rural, context. Arguments based on absence are necessarily weak, particularly where the assemblages are small – as in the present case – yet the possibility remains that these small differences reflect a different source of supply.

In this respect, the fundamental point is that these forts are located on a road connecting Syria with the Hejaz, but with relatively poor communication westwards. The annual southward flow of the Hajj caravans from Damascus provided a ready mechanism, by which, Syrian merchants could move goods reliably. The fact that pipes were one such commodity is indicated by Doughty (1926, 246), who refers to how the Bedouin used 'the *sebil*, or earthenware bent tube of the Syrian haj market', in addition to their own, locally made, stone pipe-bowls; several examples of the latter have been excavated at Aqaba Castle (Simpson forthcoming). During the 19th century there was regular commercial caravan traffic between the towns of Palestine and Transjordan, including Nablus and Salt, Hebron and Karak, and Gaza and Ma'an: each of these then served their regional hinterlands; commodities included, dried goods, clothes and hardware, which were exchanged for agricultural products, primarily raisins, raisin syrup, grain, butter, wool, skins and livestock (Rogan 1999, 99). Small portable items were also well suited to being traded by local peddlers and the distances over which items such as, clay pipe bowls, could have been transported should not be under-estimated. Buckingham (1825, 4, 50) describes being guided from Nazareth to Salt, in March 1816, by an individual who dealt 'in every description of goods', and how the bazaar at Salt supplied as far south as Karak. Only four years previously John Lewis Burckhardt (1822, 351, 388) witnessed the highly profitable sale of Arabian ostrich feathers in Damascus, by merchants from Salt who had previously bartered them from Bedouin; and how tobacco was imported to Karak from Jerusalem. Various types of tobacco were traded, but the best varieties were grown in Syria: Burckhardt (1822, 18, 80) refers to the tobacco of Deir al-Ahmar, in the northern Beqa'a valley, as 'the finest in Syria', witnessing extensive cultivation by Druze villagers in the Suweida district of the Hawran.

The question as to who exactly used these pipes is open to question, yet it seems likely, that most use derived from the garrisons of the Hajj forts. These forts were designed to house small year-round garrisons, provide visible evidence of the Ottoman sponsorship of the Hajj and their maintenance of the Holy Places, and act as a line of border control along the desert interface. The garrisons were mostly janissaries drawn from the Damascus region, although, the forts at Ma'an and al-Qatrana were manned by imperial janissaries (Petersen 1995, 304). Within this context of relative isolation for much of the year, it is not surprising to find that these and other garrisons took up smoking. Large numbers of pipes are reported from investigations at the Ottoman Black Sea frontier fortress of Akkerman (Finkel *et al.* 2007, 12), as well as other Ottoman fortresses in Hungary (Haider and Ridovics (eds) 2000, 27, 125–30, 132, col. pl. XXII); others were found during clearance of the citadel moat at Jerusalem in 1982 (Dr. M. Hawari, pers. comm. 1993), perhaps reflecting the fact that 'the southern portion of the ditch is used as a cesspit to receive the drainage of the barracks and its latrines which stand on the edge' (Wilson 1865, 47). During his visit in 1824, George Keppel (1827, 38) describes how the coffee houses in Basra 'were principally filled by Janizaries, who were puffing clouds from their pipes in true Turkish taciturnity'. There is no evidence to prove that smoking was commoner among the military than it was among other parts of the population, yet its popularity in the army was a source of great irritation to the authorities during the attempted suppression of smoking under the reign of Murad IV (r. 1623–40). The 17th century Turkish official and author, Khatib Çelebi (Hajji Khalifah), gives one instance of this in his compendium *The Balance of Truth*:

'When the Sultan was going on expedition against Baghdad, at one halting-place fifteen or twenty leading men of the Army were arrested on a charge of smoking, and were put to death with the severest torture in the imperial presence. Some of the soldiers carried short pipes in their sleeves, some in their pockets, and they found an opportunity to smoke even during their executions. At Istanbul, no end of soldiers used to go into the barracks and smoke in the privies. Even during this rigorous prohibition, the number of smokers exceeded that of non-smokers' (quoted in Kritzeck (ed.) 1964, 372).

Undesirable social and medical side-effects were noted by some authors and religious *fatwas* issued on the grounds that, as tobacco had an intoxicating effect, it was covered under a Qur'anic ban on stimulants, yet prohibitions were rarely successful in the long term. During the reign of Sultan Ibrahim (r. 1640–48), the severest anti-smoking laws were rescinded, followed by a decree in 1646 permitting the consumption of tobacco. By 1680 the Turkish government had realized the huge economic potential offered by a tobacco industry: 10 years later a heavy tax ('duty on tobacco') was introduced on tobacco buyers and sellers in Istanbul, later widened, in March 1697, to cover the ports of Palestine. These moves resulted in one of the largest sources of revenue for the Ottoman government, although it was deeply unpopular among the traders. In the early 1720s, smoking was finally legalized under a counter-*fatwa* entitled *al-Sulh bayna al-ikhwan fi hukm abahat al-dukhkhan* ('Peace Among Friends Concerning the Legalization of Smoking') and issued by the Damascene mufti, al-Shaykh 'Abd al-Ghani al-Nabulsi (1641–1731). Justification was provided on the grounds that 'smoking is like food: if it hurts stop it; if it does not, why not smoke?' The number of pipes found in the archaeological record bear silent testimony to the growing popularity of smoking during the 18th and 19th centuries, although it continued to attract strong disapproval among Wahhabi tribes in Arabia (Simpson 2000b). Clay pipes continued to be made and used throughout much of the Middle East into the 20th century, although against increasing competition from the much cheaper and more convenient cigarettes. By the time of the Great Arab Revolt, those Turkish garrisons remaining in forts along the line of the Hejaz Railway, had probably long since abandoned the pipes of their predecessors in favour of the fag. 'Unaiza had been abandoned even earlier, but T. E. Lawrence (1969, 374) refers to how a Turkish patrol from Qal'at al-Mudawwara passed his men by before taking refuge in, 'the shade of a long culvert, under whose arches a cool draught from the east was gently flowing, and there in comfort they lay on the soft sand, drank water from their bottles, smoked, and at last slept'.

Gaming-piece

A single, carbonized, wooden gaming-piece was found in Trench F. It had been turned on a lathe and simply decorated, with a single incised line near the bottom. This is a simple form, which seems to have changed little between the Roman period and the present day in the Middle East (*c.f.* Contadini 1995, 123–24, figs 34–35). It was intended for use in backgammon, or a similar game, its charred condition perhaps reflecting that it was played

Cat No.	Description	H (cm)	D (cm)	Wgt (g)	Ctx
27	Wooden gaming-piece; carbonized; lathe-turned, flat base, tapering profile, with single incised line around the bottom immediately above the base, upper portion missing.	2.3	2	0.5	F2

Table 13 – Gaming piece from 'Unaiza

with near a campfire, or hearth, being accidentally charred after the game had ended.

Glassware (Table 14)

Only one fragment of glassware was recovered, and that was from Trench F. The sherd was too small to reconstruct the original type, or size, of container, but it had a semi-transparent fabric with light greenish tinge. It may have belonged to the fort, but might alternatively, represent the accidental breakage of an item being transported by caravan along the Hajj route. A larger quantity of glassware, totalling 160 fragments, was recovered from excavations at the Red Sea fort at Quseir, although it was relatively scarce in the pre-Napoleonic phases. The glassware at that site belonged mainly to heavily fragmented oil-lamp linings of light green, light bluish green or, olive green glass, flasks and small containers, and wine and square case-bottles (Le Quesne 2007, 236–40, 242–46). Finally, it might be added that a variety of pink, opaque green, blue and black glass fragments were found in Ottoman and later contexts in the fort at Aqaba, along with clear colourless fabric covered with a thick black weathering layer (Dewulf and Pringle forthcoming).

Glass beads (Table 15)

Four glass beads were recovered from Qal'at 'Unaiza, all from Trench F (Fig. 58) (Plate 179). Each appears to have been furnace-wound. One was clear, colourless, whereas the remainder appeared to share the same opaque bright turquoise blue fabric, although the shapes and sizes of each varied. Beads of the latter colour were the commonest

variety in domestic contexts in the Ottoman and British Mandate village at Suba, near Jerusalem (Grey 2000b, 143–45, fig. 12.4.22); the same colour was common among glass bangles, in Ottoman period Bedouin graves, excavated at Tell el-Hesi (Eakins 1993, 61) and Tel Mevorakh (Stern 1978, 103, pl. 41.21–22).

They are, most likely, to have been produced in a Levantine workshop; the marvered square bead belongs to the so-called 'Hebron bead' tradition. Hebron is attested as a major local centre for glass-working since the 14th century, and, although beads are only attested in travellers' reports and museum acquisitions from the early 19th century onward, it is likely that they were produced as a sideline for a considerably longer period. 'Hebron beads' typically consist of large, but rather crude, monochrome furnace-wound beads (either plain or tooled), smaller light blue glass beads, trailed, spotted or crumb glass beads, single or compound eye beads (intended to reflect the Evil Eye on itself), and pendants representing the hand of Fatima, the daughter of the Prophet Muhammad – representing a direct throwback to the Roman and Late Antique tradition of fist-shaped pendants and hair-pins. There is an even longer tradition of glass bead making at Armanaz, in north Syria (Gaulmier 1936; Meyer 1992, 104). Glass bead makers from Hebron emigrated to set up workshops in western Turkey in the 1880s, travelling between Hebron and Cairo in the late Ottoman period and again in the 1930s (Francis 1999, 78–79; Henein and Gout 1974; Sode 1996; Spaer *et al.* 2001, 146–47, nos 269–80, pl. 22). Traditional glass workshops are also attested from Tripoli, in northern Lebanon, and the Old City in Damascus; the sale of furnace-wound glass beads in Lebanon in recent years has been noted elsewhere by this author (Simpson 1999).

Cat No.	Description	H (cm)	W (cm)	Th (cm)	Wgt (g)	Ctx
28	Body sherd; semi-transparent with light greenish tinge	1.5	1.4	0.2	–	F4

Table 14 – Glassware from 'Unaiza

Cat No.	Description	Form	Beck type	H (cm)	D (cm)	Perf D (cm)	Wgt (g)	Ctx	Figs
29	Glass bead; probably furnace-wound, plain clear colourless with some very fine bubbles	Short circular barrel	I.B.1.b	0.7	0.9	0.3	–	F2	58.7
30	Glass bead; furnace-wound with flattened marvered sides, plain opaque bright turquoise blue	Short square cylinder	IX.B.2.b	1	1.2	0.7	2.5	F2	58.8
31	Glass bead; furnace-wound, plain opaque bright turquoise blue with iron stained bore, flaking	Short circular barrel	I.B.1.b	0.5	0.7	0.1–0.2	–	F4	58.9
32	Glass bead; furnace-wound with flattened marvered sides, plain opaque bright turquoise blue	standard square barrel	IX.C.1.b	0.6	0.6	0.1–0.15	–	F4	58.10

Table 15 – Glass Beads from 'Unaiza

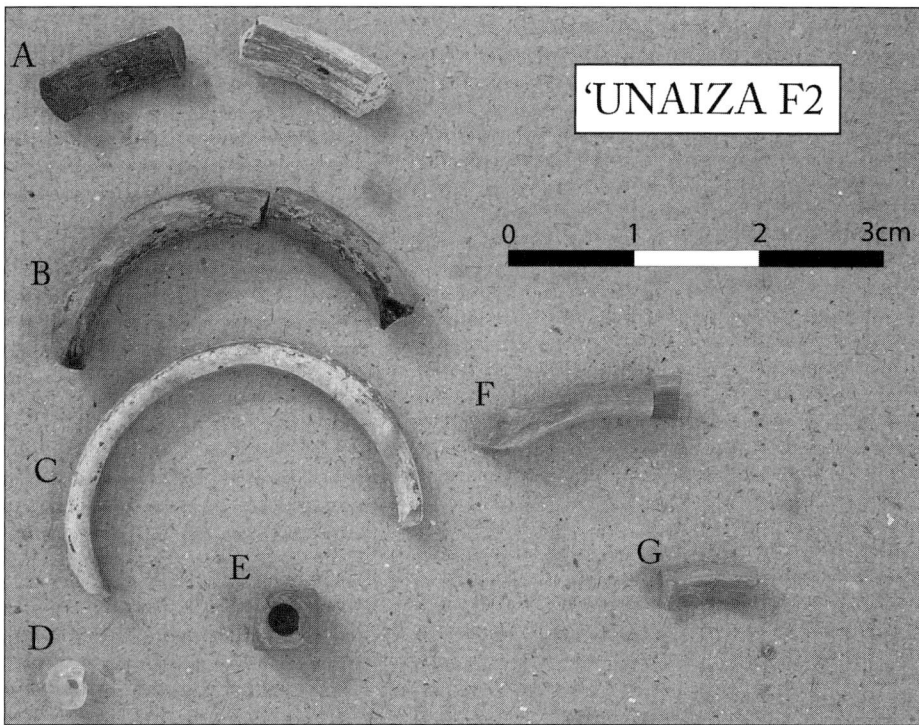

Plate 179. 'Unaiza F2, glass bangles and beads. A = glass bangle in two parts (Table 16, Cat No. 35); B = glass bangle (Table 16, Cat No. 37); C= glass bangle (Table 16, Cat No. 48); D = clear glass bead (Table 15, Cat No. 29); E = square blue glass bead (Table 15, Cat No. 32); F = blue glass bangle (Table 16, Cat No. 42); G = orange glass bangle (Table 16, Cat No. 33).

It is not certain where the beads found at 'Unaiza were made, but it is likely that they arrived at the site together with the glass bangles discussed below.

Glass bangles (Table 16)

Seventeen fragments of different glass bangles were recovered from Qal'at 'Unaiza: one from F1, eight from F2, two from F4 and six from F5 (Plates 179, 180 and 181; Figs 57–58). This is a small group, yet it is one of the first to be documented from a purely Ottoman non-funerary context.

All but two of the present bangles were plain mono-chrome; the exceptions were decorated with simple coloured blobs, which had been marvered smooth with the surface of the bracelet. The commonest colour appeared to be opaque black. All belong to the so-called, seamless type, made by piercing a piece of molten glass with a metal rod and forming a ring through rotation, while expanding the ring with a second rod placed inside, hence the characteristic D-shaped, or flat cross-section and the tool marks and reddish iron staining on the inner surface. One of the present bangles had a flat section, which Spaer (1992, 51) describes as 'common in Ottoman times'. Eight were evenly and strongly pointed, a variety that began in the Mamluk period, the remainder were obliquely pointed, *i.e.* were asymmetric with an off-centre point. This variety is also believed to originate in the Mamluk period; present evidence confirms that both shapes continued into the late Ottoman period.

The inner diameters, where measurable, range between 5 and 8 cm; the smallest may have been worn by children, while the others are consistent with adult use.

Glass bangles were first adopted in the Middle East in the Roman period, but remained relatively rare until the 14th and 15th centuries, when there was an explosion in frequency and variety. The basic chronological development has been outlined by Spaer (1988; 1992): since then there have been a small number of published analyses detailing Mamluk finds from, Tell Abu Sarbut in the Jordan valley (Steiner 1995), the Egyptian Red Sea port of Quseir al-Qadim (Meyer 1992, 90–94, pl. 20), plus Mamluk and later finds from the ports of, Raya and at-Tur, on the Egyptian coast of the Sinai peninsula (Shindo 1996). Within the Persian Gulf they appear in large numbers during the same period, but the majority of those from Kush were made by the, so-called, seamed technique, which differs from that described above, in that, they were simply made by drawing a thick cane of glass and overlapping the ends to form a circle. Francis (1982, 21) reports Indian craftsmen taking about 25 seconds to make such a bracelet and it seems likely that many of these – like the beads found at these Gulf sites – were Indian imports. During this period there were also important centres of manufacture at, Kawd am-Saila, Habil and Zinjibar near Aden, although these products have not been recognized from the northern Red Sea, and they may, therefore, have had a relatively local, or purely Indian Ocean, circulation (Monod 1978; Whitcomb 1988, 201–2, 246–47). Within the southern Levant, Hebron

Cat No.	Description	colour	section	Spaer type	D (cm)	% preserved	Wgt (g)	Ctx	Figs
33	Glass bangle fragment; L 2.0, W 0.9, T 0.6 cm	plain opaque orange	obliquely pointed D-section	A.5.a	6	10%	1.5	F2	
34	Glass bangle fragment; L 1.9, W 0.8, T 0.5 cm	plain semi-transparent dark brown	obliquely pointed D-section	A.5.a			1.0	F2	57.3
35	Glass bangle fragment; containing occasional pin-head sized bubbles, blackened through contact with hot ash; L 3, W 1.1, T 0.7 cm	plain opaque dark	evenly pointed D-section	A.4.a	6	15%	3.0	F2	57.5
36	Glass bangle fragment; L 3, W 1, T 0.7 cm	plain opaque black	evenly pointed D-section	A.4.a	5	17.5%	3.0	F2	57.6
37	Glass bangle fragments (two joining); W 1, T 0.9 cm	plain opaque black	evenly pointed D-section	A.4.a	6	45%	14.5	F2	57.1
38	Glass bangle fragments (two joining); W 0.9, T 0.7 cm	plain opaque black	obliquely pointed D-section	A.5.a	7 – 8	12.5%	3.0	F4	57.9
39	Glass bangle fragment; irregular shape; L 5, W 1, T 0.7 cm	plain opaque black	evenly pointed D-section	A.4.a	5 ?	30%	6.5	F5	58.6
40	Glass bangle fragment; L 4.1, W 1, T 0.8 cm	plain opaque black	obliquely pointed D-section	A.5.a	8	15%	5.0	F5	58.4
41	Glass bangle fragment; L 3, W 1.1, T 0.5 cm	plain opaque black	wide and thin with flat section	A.3	7	12.5%	3.0	F5	58.3
42	Glass bangle fragment; L 4.2, W 1, T 0.7 cm	plain opaque turquoise blue	evenly pointed D-section	A.4.a	8	15%	4.5	F2	57.4
43	Glass bangle fragment; L 1.2, W 0.8, T 0.8 cm	plain opaque turquoise blue	obliquely pointed D-section	A.5.a	?	?	1.5	F5	58.1
44	Glass bangle fragments (flaking); L 1.7, W 1, T 0.8 cm	plain opaque green	evenly pointed D-section	A.4.a	?	?	–	F1	
45	Glass bangle fragment; L 2.5, W 0.9, T 0.6 cm	plain opaque green	obliquely pointed D-section	A.5.a	7	10%	2.5	F2	57.7
46	Glass bangle fragment; L 4.0, W 1.0, T 0.8 cm	plain opaque green	obliquely pointed D-section	A.5.a	7	c. 15%	4.0	F4	57.8
47	Glass bangle fragment; L 1.3, W 0.9, T 0.7 cm	plain opaque green	evenly pointed D-section	A.4.a	?	?	1.0	F5	58.2
48	Glass bangle fragment; W 0.8, T 0.6 cm	opaque green (?) with single yellowish marvered threads running along the point (dorsal edge) and outer edge	obliquely pointed D-section	C	6 (int.) 7.2 (ext.)	50%	8.0	F2	57.2
49	Glass bangle fragment; W 0.6, T 0.5 cm	opaque black with dark brown and matt yellow applied marvered decoration along one edge	evenly pointed D-section	C	6	25%	2.5	F5	58.5

Table 16 – Glass Bangles from ‘Unaiza

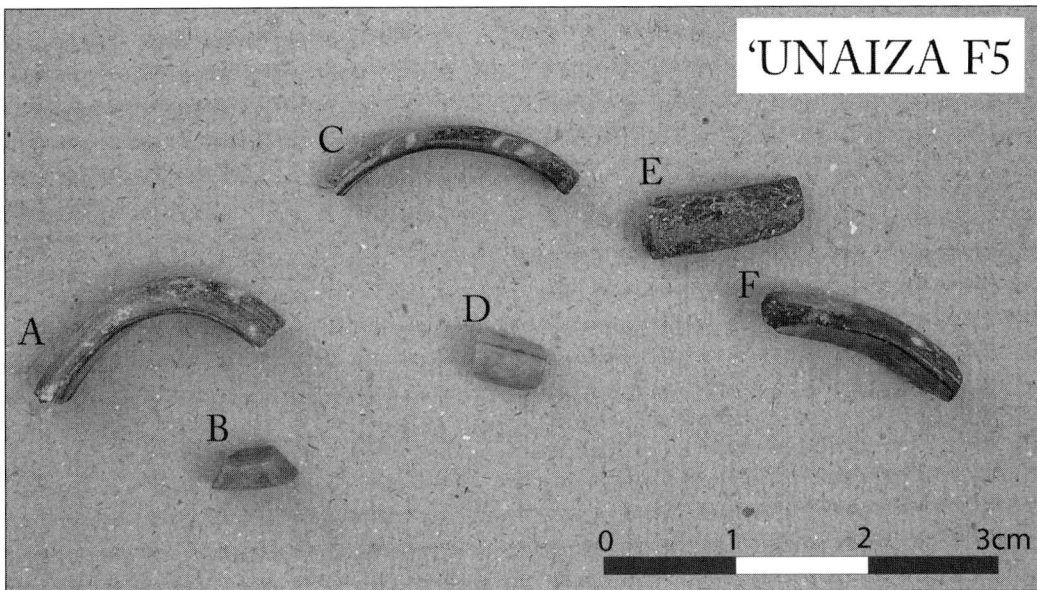

Plate 180. 'Unaiza F5, glass bangles. A = glass bangle black (Table 16, Cat No. 39); B = blue glass bangle (Table 16, Cat No. 43), C = glass bangle, black with marvered decoration (Table 16, Cat No. 49); D = green glass bangle (Table 16, Cat No. 46); E = black glass bangle (Table 16, Cat No. 41); F = black glass bangle (Table 16, Cat No. 40).

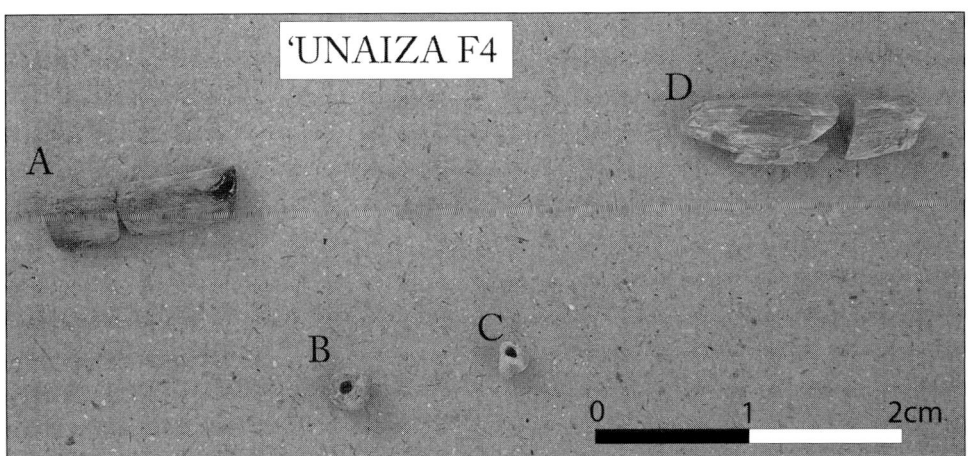

Plate 181. 'Uniaza F4, glass beads and bangles. A = fragment of black glass bangle (Table 16, Cat No. 38); B = glass bead (Table 15, Cat No. 35); C = glass bead (Table 15, Cat No. 31); D = green glass bangle (Table 16, Cat No. 47).

was one centre of production, although, as with the glass beads discussed above, there were probably also workshops in Damascus and other major cities. The first eye-witness account of the Hebron industry was in the 1780s, when the French diplomat C.-F. Volney recorded 'une verrerie fort ancienne, la seule qui existe en Syrie. Il en sort une grande quantité d'anneaux colorés, de bracelets pour les poignets, pour les jambes, pour le bras au-dessus du coude, & diverses autres bagatelles que l'on envoie jusqu' a Constantinople' (Volney 1787, 300).

Securely dated finds of glass bangles are relatively scarce, although a number of seamless and spirally twisted seamed monochrome bracelets, were excavated in the remains of the Ottoman and later, village at Suba (Grey 2000a, 127–30, fig. 10.2.24–40). These finds presumably represent casual discards, following breakage, by women and children living in the village. Six fragments were also found in the Red Sea fort at Quseir, most of which were from 19th or 20th century contexts, although two were from pre-Napoleonic phases: the late examples were translucent blue and three were decorated with added prunts and thus compare closely in style, with examples manufactured in Hebron in the 1860s and 1870s (Le Quesne 2007, 240–41, 246–47, fig. 97). Other excavated finds from post-Medieval graves in Palestine and other parts of the Near East, confirm that they were worn in varying combinations as bracelets on either, or both, arms (sometimes in association with iron and copper alloy bangles), as anklets and possibly attached to head scarves, or woven into the hair: these items should, therefore, be described more accurately as,

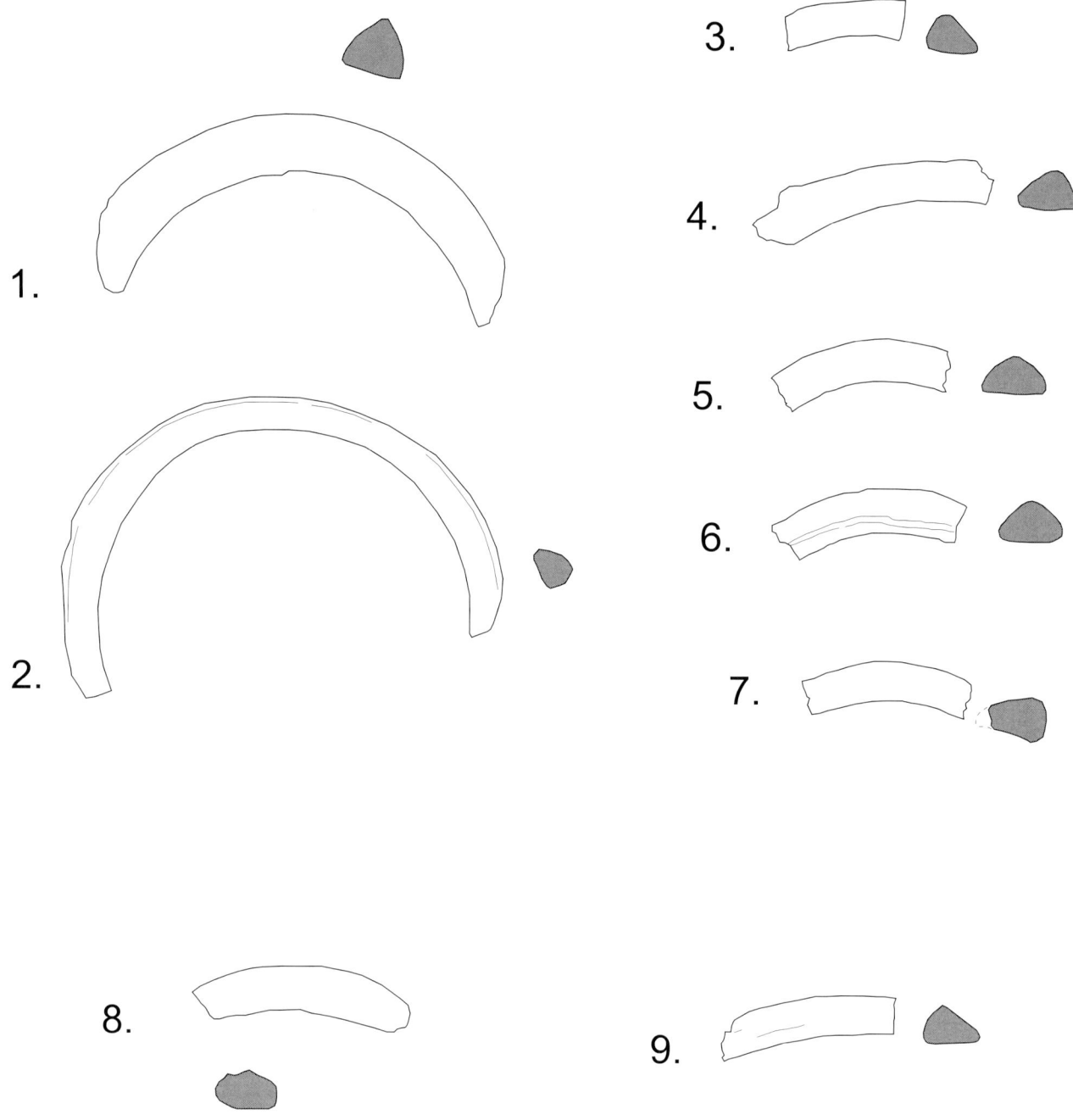

Fig. 57. Glass bangles from 'Unaiza F2 and F4.

bangles, rather than bracelets (Simpson 1995, 246, 251; Steiner 1995, 538). In some other cases they may attest rites of mourning, as fragments found near graves may represent deliberate breakage by female relatives.

The finds from 'Unaiza seem to belong within another category. There is no other evidence to suggest that women, or children, lived in the fort, nor were these items worn by men, least of all by Turkish army garrisons. Given their presence in exclusively ashy midden deposits, in the extramural Area F, it seems most likely that they represent the presence of women, and possibly children, in the vicinity of the fort, either during seasonal markets

of the sort described above, or during temporary halts of the Hajj pilgrim caravans.

Military Equipment (Table 17)

A single lead musket ball, from Trench F, hints at the primarily military function of Qal'at 'Unaiza, although it might not have belonged to a member of the garrison. The Turkish army was initially equipped with muskets until the 1860s, when it began to be re-equipped with rifles, firstly of the Snider and Martini-Henry varieties and then by German and Turkish manufactured Mausers. Local

Fig. 58. Glass bangles and beads.

Bedouin tribes began to be supplied with matchlock and flintlock muskets towards the end of the 16th century: the latter continued to be popular, at least, until the end of the 19th century as they were inexpensive, easy to repair and could be fired immediately (Saidel 2000).

This is not the first time such an item has been recognized from an archaeological context of this period; a small number of related finds have now been reported from archaeological investigations in Israel/Palestine. A 15 mm dia. lead musket ball and a bronze two-piece mould for

Cat No.	Description	D (mm)	Wgt (g)	Ctx	Fig
50	Lead musket ball; cast sphere with traces of casting seam from two-part mould	12	12.5	F2	59.8

Table 17 – Military Equipment from 'Unaiza

Cat No.	Description	D (mm)	Th (mm)	Wgt (g)	Ctx
51	Copper alloy coin	16	1	–	F2
52	Copper alloy coin, single small circular perforation (D 2 mm) near one edge	16	1	–	F3
53	Copper alloy coin	16	1	–	F5

Table 18 – Coins from 'Unaiza

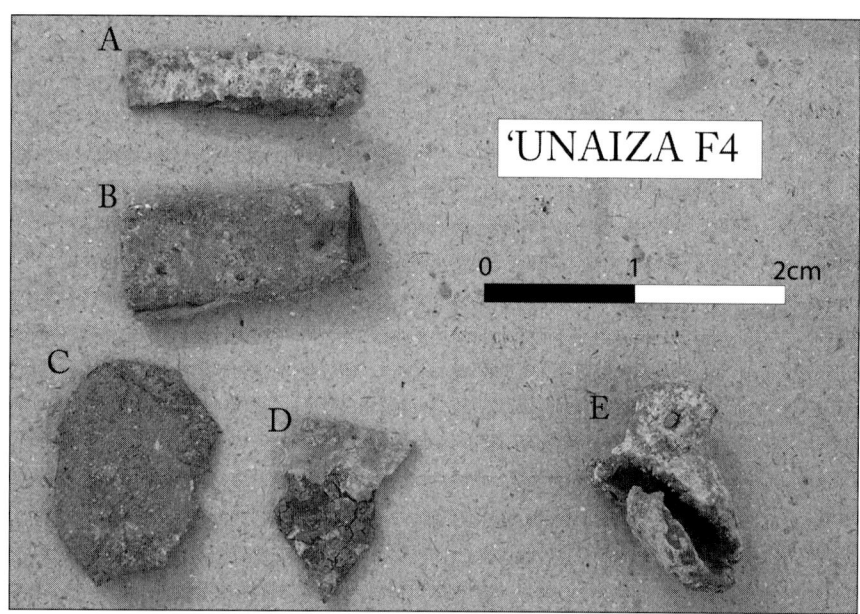

Plate 182 'Unaiza F4, metalwork. A = copper alloy tweezers (Table 20, Cat No. 55); B = copper alloy sheet (Table 20, Cat No. 58); C = copper alloy sheet (Table 20, Cat No. 59); D = copper alloy sheet (Table 20, Cat No. 60); E = copper alloy bell (Table 20, Cat No. 54).

producing shot of the same size, were found at Horvat 'Aqav (Boas 2000a, 224–25, figs 7–8), another such mould, for casting 13 mm dia. shot, was found in a late 18th century context in the Ottoman fort at Quseir, on the Egyptian Red Sea coast; an 18 mm dia. lead ball was also found in a Napoleonic context at Quseir (Hense 2007, 251, 255, fig. 98: 2). Lead musket balls have also been reported from salvage excavations at Khan Minya (Hanot Minnim) (Stepanski 1988, 75), others were found, along with gunflints, belt buckles and other militaria, on the site of the Battle of Nazareth and in a Napoleonic siege-trench surrounding Acre; both events date from the spring of 1799 (Berman 1991; 1997, 98–99). Gun-flints have been found, along with coarse handmade pottery, in stratified deposits inside a rock shelter at Tur Imdai, in south-west Jordan (*c.f.* Saidel 2000, 194–96), while dozens of rifles, including a double-barrelled Winchester, were found at Ras ed-Dabous,

on the outskirts of Jerusalem, in a cave-tomb which had been reused as an equipment store by the Turkish army (Barkay 1986).

Coins and other metalwork (Plates 182, 183 and 184, tables 18 and 19)

Three small copper alloy coins were found (Table 18, Nos 51–53), all from Trench F. They were of identical size and weight and although illegible, probably represent low-denomination Ottoman coins. Similar low-denomination coins were regular occurrences in the Bedouin cemetery at Tell el-Hesi, where it was noted that most had been pounded flat to make them thinner, thus rendering them illegible (Betlyon 1986, 68–69; Eakins 1993, 64). Many of these coins at Hesi had also been perforated, either for stringing as pendants, or threading onto garments, or

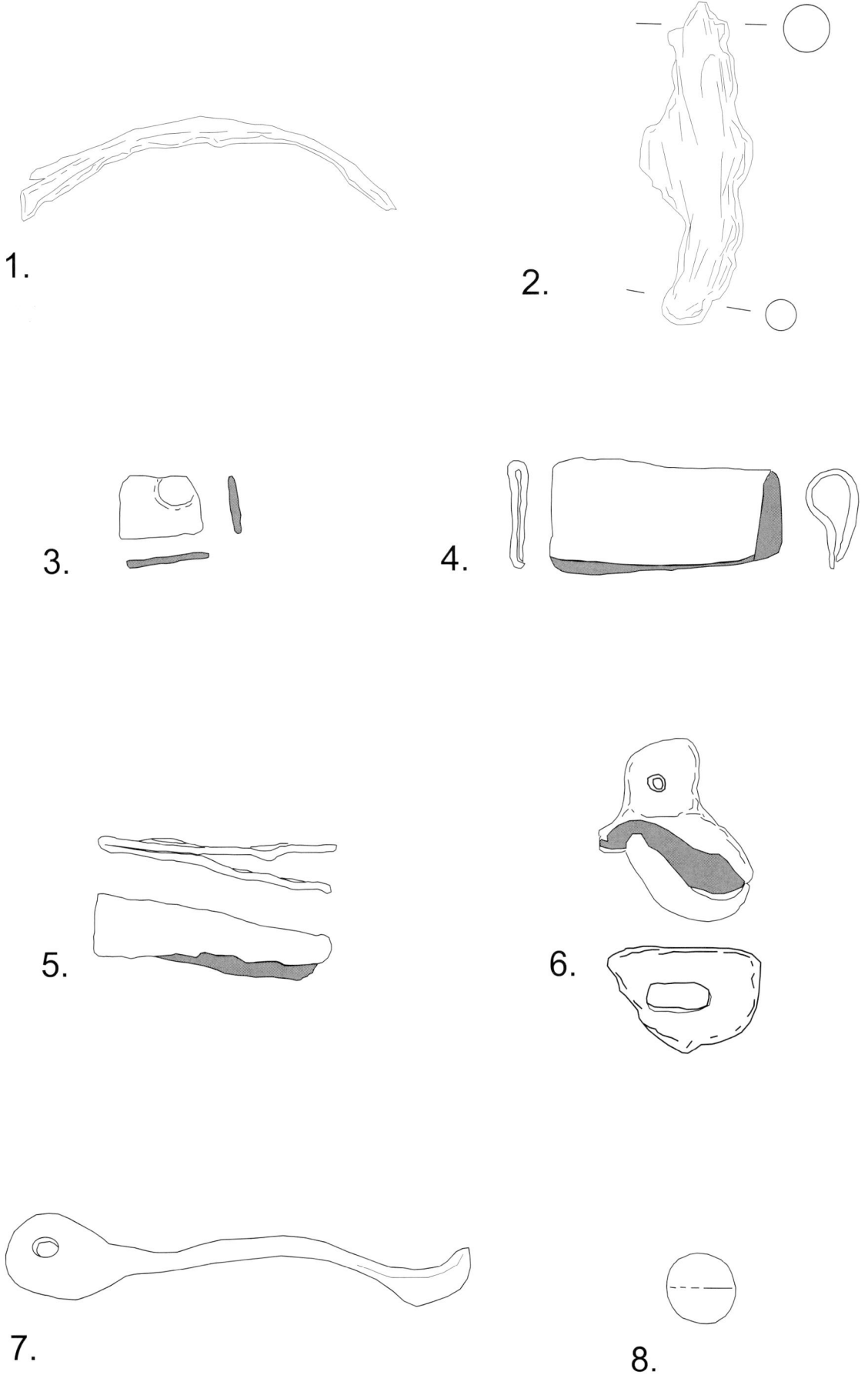

Fig. 59. Metalwork.

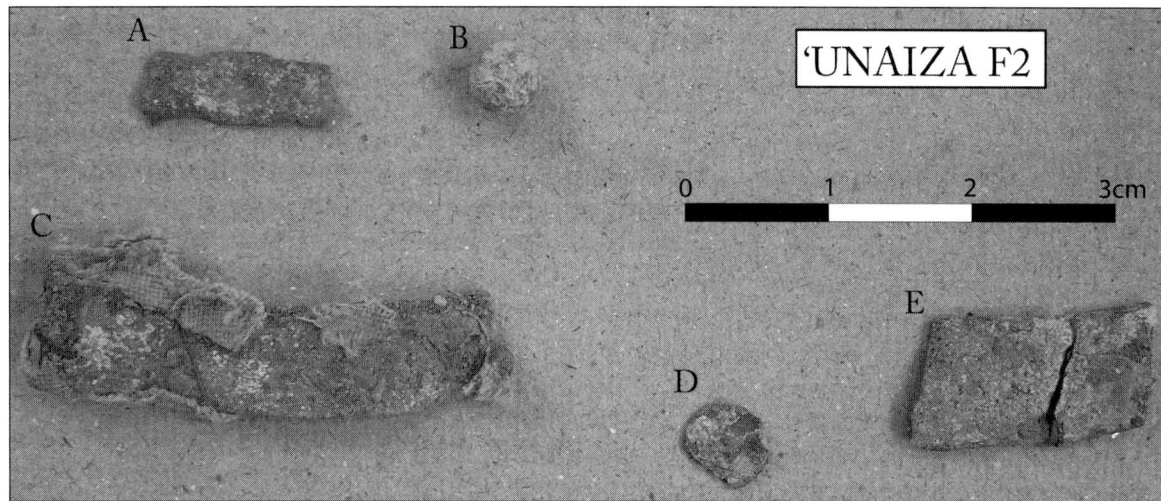

Plate 183. Metalwork from 'Unaiza F2. A = copper alloy sheet fragment (Table 20, Cat No. 62); B = lead musket ball (Table 17, Cat No. 50); C = copper alloy band with attached coarse khaki canvas (Table 17, Cat No. 56); D = copper coin (Table 18, Cat No. 51); E = copper alloy sheet (Table 20, Cat No. 61).

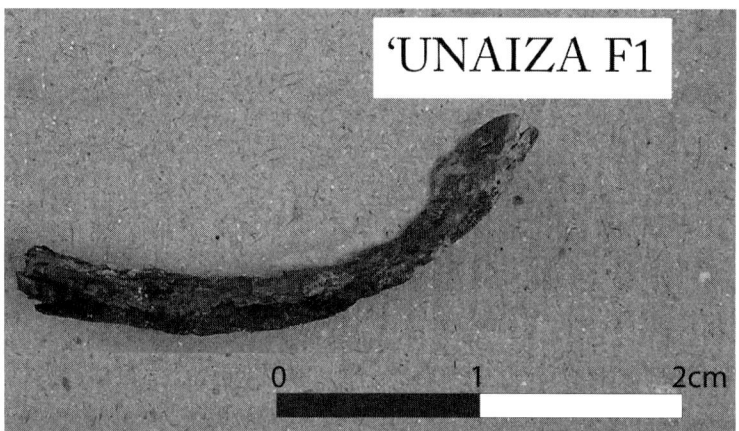

Plate 184. 'Unaiza, F1 metalwork. Iron hoop fragment (Table 20; Cat No. 63).

headdresses; the same applied to one of the coins found at 'Unaiza. As such, they belong to the same category of personal ornament, worn by women and children, as the beads and bangles discussed above.

A total of 15 other pieces of metalwork, weighing 115.5 g, were recovered, again all from Trench F. Nine were copper alloy, the remainder iron (Plates 182, 183, and 184; Fig 59). The only identifiable artefacts were a small cast copper alloy bell (Table 19, No. 54), a simple pair of tweezers (Table 19, No. 55) and two fragmentary iron nails (Table 19, Nos 64–65) (Plate 184). The tweezers were made from springy metal and probably originally had a sliding piece that fitted over both arms, allowing the opening distance of the tweezers to be adjustable. There was also one corroded iron hoop fragment (Table 19, No. 63): although a large number of iron bracelets were present in the contemporary Bedouin cemetery at Tell el-Hesi (Toombs 1985, 104, pl. 81a; Eakins 1993, 62, pls 93–95), this particular fragment appears to have had a more utilitarian function and may originally have been attached to a wooden item.

The remainder of the metal fragments consist of pieces of plain, or decorated, iron or copper alloy sheet, the latter often folded and in one case (Table 19, No. 56) having the well preserved remains of khaki canvas cloth attached. This piece was tentatively identified by Jules Evenhart, finds officer for the Great Arab Revolt Project, as 'some type of crude military webbing or indeed a section of sandbag. The colour of the metal strip ... indicates to me that it is most likely a section of exploded cartridge case and again most likely from a Turkish (Ottoman) Mauser rifle ... perhaps a round exploded in a breech or an incoming shell destroyed some packed ammunition boxes ... most of the sand buried Mauser shell cases we unearthed (at other sites in Jordan associated with the Great Arab Revolt) had this bright green blue crusty patination and many bore adherent plant, wood (ammunition box splinters?) and other organic attachments as can clearly been seen on this example' (email dated 7 May 2008).

Cat No.	Description	H (cm)	W (cm)	Th (cm)	Wgt (g)	Ctx	Figs
54	Copper alloy bell; cast, with perforated suspension loop at the top; semi-complete, partly crushed and missing clapper; its weight suggests it may be a leaded bronze	3.4	3.0	2.3	25.5	F4	59.6
55	Copper alloy tweezers; made by bending over a single piece of thin sheet	4.2	1.0	0.1	–	F4	55.5
56	Copper alloy band with attached coarse weave khaki canvas	8.7	2.5	0.2	27.0	F2	
57	Copper alloy sheet; slight curvature, with dotted circle decoration stamped into outer face	1.6	1.1	0.2	1.5	F1	55.3
58	Copper alloy sheet; folded over, with single small circular hole through one end	1.8	4.3	0.1	10.5	F4	
59	Copper alloy sheet; flat and roughly oval, with some of the edges partly folded over	3.8	2.8	0.1	4.5	F4	
60	Copper alloy sheet fragments (x 2 joining); flat	3.1	4.0	0.1	5.0	F4	
61	Copper alloy sheet fragments (x 2 joining); flat with two parallel edges	5.0	2.4	0.1	9.0	F2	
62	Copper alloy sheet fragment; flat, semi-rectangular with lightly bent over edges	3.6	1.3	0.1	2.0	F2	
63	Iron hoop fragment; D *c.* 9 cm (*c.* 25% preserved)	6.6	0.8	0.5	7.5	F1	
64	Iron nail; shank fragment; square section, broken at both ends	5.5	1.2	1.2	12.5	F3	59.2
65	Iron nail; shank; circular section, broken at the junction with the head, tip bent at 90 degree angle	3.4	0.7	0.7	3.0	F	59.1
66 a-c	Iron sheet fragments (x 3); rectangular, one with identical copper alloy strip adhering to one face	4.7	1.4	0.2	7.5	F	

Table 19 – Metalwork from 'Unaiza

Description	L (cm)	W (cm)	Th (cm)	Wgt (g)	Ctx
Apricot stone	2.6	2	1.4	1.5	F3

Table 20 – Environmental Finds from 'Unaiza

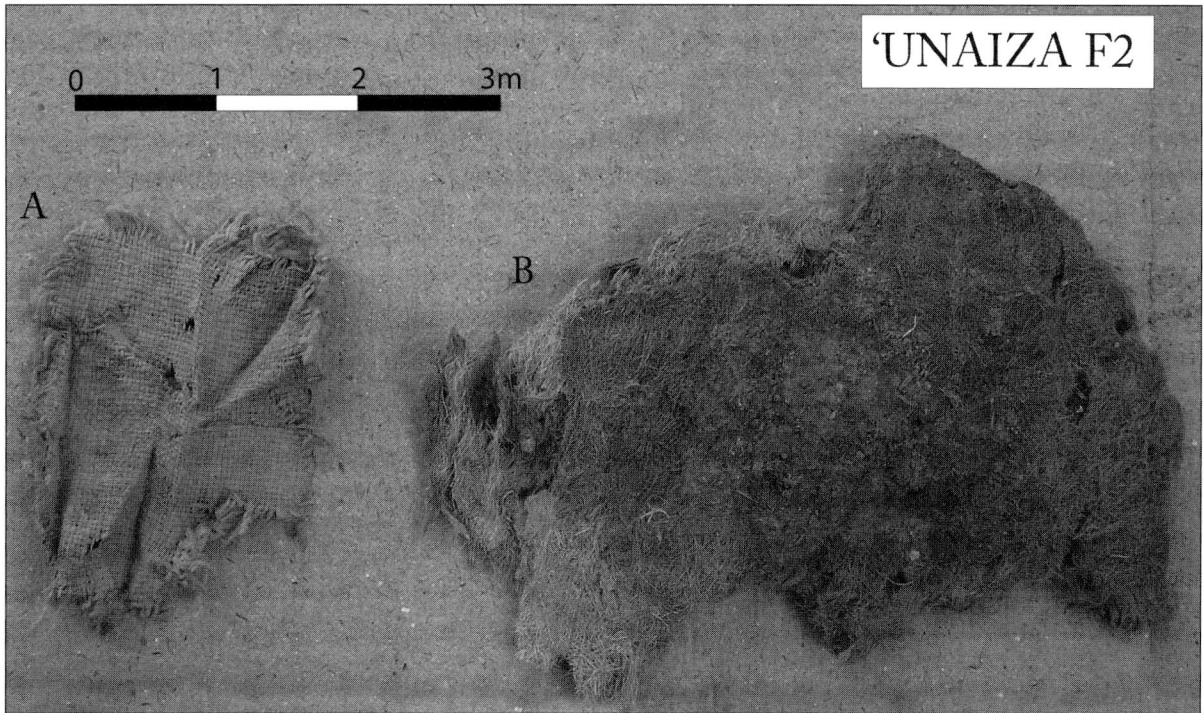

Plate 185. A = Textile probably hemp with traces of red dye, possibly part of storage sack; B = matted piece of fabric made of vegetable fibre, possibly used as padding.

Description	Wgt (g)	Ctx
Charcoal	129.0	B4
Charcoal	4.5	F2

Table 21 – Charcoal fragments from 'Unaiza

Textiles (Andrew Petersen)

Two fragments of textile were recovered from 'Unaiza F1 (Plate 185). A flat, woven, piece of textile, possibly hemp, with traces of red dye or print; possibly part of a storage sack. A matted piece of fabric made of vegetable fibre (grass, hemp, rush, or sisal); possibly used as padding (*çaprak*) for a saddle. Traditionally a *çaprak* is a rectangular pad made of cotton stuffed with pea straw and draped over the camel's hump beneath the saddle frame.

Environmental finds (Tables 20 and 21)

A single apricot stone was recovered from the ashy midden in Area F and represents an imported summer fruit. The extensive orchards surrounding Damascus would have offered the nearest major source of apricot. Apricots were among the cheapest fruits in Damascus during the 18th century, at most times this fruit was no more expensive by weight than bread (Grehan 2007, 111). However, apricot was cultivated on a small scale, along with figs, pomegranates, grapes and cereals, in the immediate environs of Ma'an during the time of Alois Musil's visit in 1910 (Musil 1926, 4). The sale of fruit, both local and imported from Hebron and 'Ula, to pilgrims at various points along the Hajj route, including Ma'an, Tabuk and Medain Saleh, is also noted by Barbir (1980, 165, table 5). Finally, apricot was firmly identified from three contexts dating to the 16th/17th and 18th centuries in the fort at Quseir (Pelling 2007, 279, tables 8–10).

In addition to this fruit stone, a total of 133.5 g of unidentified charcoal was recovered during these investigations. The sale of firewood for transport to Mecca has only been recorded from Ma'an (Barbir 1980, 165, table 5), whereas the production and long-distance transport of charcoal, as the universal fuel source for heating within the Ottoman Empire is well documented. Musil (1926, 126) also refers to the Arab supply of charcoal to the Turkish garrison at al-Hrajbe, on the northern Red Sea coast, in exchange for flour, rice and clothing: the source of the fuel was identified as *sejāl* (acacia), *tarfa* (Tamarisk) and *raza* (a shrub). The latter species was particularly common in the vicinity of Tebūk, whence it was transported by camel as charcoal and thence redistributed by train to forts along the Hejaz railway (Musil 1926, 160, 163).

General Conclusions

The small assemblage of non-ceramic finds from Qal'at

'Unaiza adds to the limited, but gradually growing, body of archaeological data from the Ottoman period. It is the first to be published from a fort on the Hajj route, yet the present analysis suggests that it derives from more than just the garrison within the fort itself.

All of the finds, except for one pipe fragment from Trench B, derived from Trench F, which was excavated in the extramural ashy midden, situated between the fort and the cistern. The size of this midden seems to exceed what would be expected for the size of the garrison of the fort; similar middens have not been noted at other forts along this section of the Hajj route. The finds included some items – namely, glass beads and bangles – which are most likely to have been worn by women and possibly children. As there is no evidence that women and children occupied forts such as 'Unaiza, these presumably either, belonged to Bedouin who visited the site on a temporary basis, or, to members of the caravan who stopped for water and rest near the protection of the fort. The preliminary identification of 'significant amounts of camel' bones from Trench F, as reported by Petersen, Brun and Shurma (2003, 65) supports this hypothesis. During the Hajj season these forts were temporarily surrounded by a huge encampment of pilgrims, who made good use of the adjacent water cisterns. During the rest of the year, at least, some also served as the foci for temporary markets, as they combined secure storage with opportunities for passing traffic. Burckhardt (1822, 510) refers to how the Aqaba fort, 'a square building, with strong walls', contained 'many Arab huts; a market is held there, which is frequented by Hedjaz and Syrian Arabs; and small caravans arrive sometime from Khalyl'. The same author also refers to how the Hajj fort at Muzayrib was stocked with tobacco and other goods (Burckhardt 1822, 242, 388). This process has been particularly documented in the case of forts along the Darb al-Hajj, where the annual pilgrimage to Mecca ensured a ready market; the garrisons were able to purchase items from Bedouin and villagers, and sell them on at greatly inflated prices; in return the guards were able to re-supply the forts (Barbir 1980, 164–67; Petersen 1986, 16–20). This process enabled some soldiers to become relatively wealthy; Burckhardt (1822) refers to one janissary amassing a considerable personal sum after 23 years of service at Nakhlatayn fort.

Further archaeological research is clearly required in order to better understand the context of these forts and how they integrated into the wider economy, but the present results already serve to illustrate the great potential of this approach.

15. Conclusions

Any conclusions regarding the history of the Syrian Hajj route and its facilities must be regarded as provisional. Like the Hajj itself, which is repeated every year at a different time, interpretations and findings in relation to the archaeology and history of the route will be subject to constant re-evaluation. Certainly, more fieldwork is needed, as well as research in Ottoman and Syrian archives, before it will be possible to understand how the Hajj interacted with the societies through which it passed. However, for the present, a number of general points and areas of discussion can be drawn out that are likely to be of value in the long term understanding of this unique, cultural phenomenon. For convenience these observations can be placed into four categories: 1) conclusions relating directly to archaeological survey and excavation; 2) conclusions relating to the architecture, location and function of the Hajj forts; 3) ideas and considerations in relation to the Hajj route as part of national heritage; and 4) directions for further research and conservation.

1) Archaeological Conclusions

It is clear that this book and the archaeological fieldwork on which it is based, does not represent an exhaustive statement on the archaeological remains on the Hajj route. In the first place, this research only discusses the Medieval and Ottoman periods, with occasional reference to the early Islamic period, yet, as Joy McCorriston (2011) has demonstrated, there may be considerable value in investigating the pre-Islamic and even pre-historic roots of Arabian pilgrimage. Also, the book focuses primarily on remains in Jordan and although sites in both Syria and Saudi Arabia are discussed, these were not the subject of fieldwork for this project, and therefore, neither the beginnings, nor the ends, of the route are discussed in the detail they deserve. Even within Jordan the coverage of the Hajj route is partial, because, with the available budget, it was not practical to fieldwalk the entire length of the road. It is certain that there are features, even sites, relating to the period (c. 1000–1900 AD) that have been missed out and which may have relevance to an understanding of how the Hajj functioned. Even at the sites surveyed the fieldwork was not total, thus, there was a concentration on architecture and ceramic finds, which meant that the wider context of the sites was not investigated in depth. In particular, it is noticeable that the camping ground of the pilgrims and escort, have only been tentatively identified at two sites, 'Unaiza and Hasa. In part, this may reflect the fact that the presence of thousands of people, staying for one or two nights, at a particular location may not leave a heavy archaeological imprint (c.f. Silverman 1994, 11). It may also be indicative of the extreme poverty of resources at many of these sites, which meant that any objects, no matter how small or broken, were still valuable enough to be removed. Despite these shortcomings it is clear that the archaeology of the Hajj is a very rich field for investigating the social, religious and economic dimensions of Medieval and Ottoman Muslim society.

It is hoped that in the future it will be possible to carry out more extensive excavations on Hajj related sites. The limited excavations carried out at 'Unaiza, certainly indicate considerable potential for this type of investigation. For example, the ashy mound (Trench F) outside the fort is indicative of extensive fires (probably for cooking food, although also used for heat, to light tobacco pipes and heat coffee pots), which may relate to the pilgrims camping ground. Certainly the presence of considerable quantities of sheep/goat bones amongst the ashes, suggests the large-scale consumption of meat, probably sourced locally (although camel was also present, it was in very small quantities). It is interesting that the material culture recovered from the excavations at 'Unaiza and samples retrieved from other sites, predominantly date to the 18th or 19th centuries – in other words, material which can be dated to the 16th or 17th centuries is comparatively rare. This suggests that over time there was a gradual increase of material items used by, or required by, pilgrims and their escort.

If we look at the range of material recovered both from 'Unaiza and other sites, it is clear that a wide range of material is present, ranging from, glazed ceramics, to a single apricot stone. Within this huge array of material, ceramic vessels accounted for, by far, the largest category, followed by ceramics pipes. The ceramics were predominantly wheelmade and were generally small fragments with no complete vessels recovered. The most telling aspect of the ceramic assemblage was the preponderance of glazed wares, including lead glazed earthenware, Kutahya fritware and Chinese porcelain. This indicates the far-reaching trade networks to which the Hajj route was connected, with Chinese imports via the Red Sea and Ottoman wares from Anatolia. A general scheme for phasing the presence of these wares indicates that lead glazed earthenware was gradually replaced by fritwares and Chinese porcelain. The Chinese porcelain is predominantly dated to the 18th century, becoming increasingly significant into the 19th century. Both the Kutahya fritware and the Chinese porcelain fragments are derived from small bowls, or cups, probably used for coffee. Although coffee had been consumed in Yemen and Ethiopia prior to the 16th century, the export and consumption of coffee beyond the region only appears to have started after the Ottoman conquest in 1547. From this date the spread of coffee consumption appears to have been fairly rapid, thus, in 1554 the first coffee house was opened in Constantinople and coffee soon became established as a major commodity within the Ottoman Empire (Hattox 1985). Many pilgrims purchased coffee whilst on the Hijaz and made substantial profits by selling it once they had returned home (Faroqhi 1994, 170). It is interesting that the ceramic tobacco pipes, also appear to date predominantly from the 18th century and later, suggesting a culture of coffee consumption with smoking tobacco (*c.f.* Grehan 2007, esp. 1365 fig. 2).

2) Architecture, Location and Meaning

The design of the Hajj forts is remarkably simple and in many ways the buildings do not appear to be significant pieces of architecture. Certainly, their small size and lack of ornamentation indicates that they were built as functional units, rather than statements of dynastic glory. Even the inscriptions, which have been recorded above some of the gateways, are generally modest, both in content and style, when compared with inscriptions on earlier Mamluk fortifications (see, for example, the gateway of the fort at 'Aqaba in Glidden 1952). However, the stark appearance of the buildings should not be taken as an indication of,

either a deficiency in the design, or, the symbolic value of these buildings. In terms of design it should be noted that the forts were constructed during the heyday of Ottoman architecture. It is worth remembering that the official starting place of the Hajj in Damascus was the pilgrimage complex known as the Tekiyya, designed by the most famous of Ottoman architects, Mimar Sinan. Although the Tekiyya is acknowledged as a masterpiece of Ottoman architecture, it is also small in scale and modest in terms of its decoration. Like the Hajj forts, the Tekiyya was, essentially, a functional building with both its location and design chosen to serve the needs of the pilgrims. Similarly, the Hajj forts were built to house small garrisons, with appropriate space inside for storerooms, accommodation for troops and a variety of gun-ports and arrow loops to control the area outside (see Chapter 5 for a discussion of the development of the military capability of the forts).

Probably the best way to appreciate the symbolic value of the Hajj forts, is to look at them in their geographical context – like the forts of the Roman frontier in Jordan, or Scotland, there is a remarkable consistency of design and construction, even in the most remote of locations. All of the forts are built of coursed stone – usually with dressed stone used for the main façade – with the gateways set in a recess, beneath a projecting machicolation. The speed and efficiency of the construction was evidently a source of some pride, as recorded in the inscriptions above the gateways of the forts at Dhat al-Hajj and al-Ukhaydhir. None of this will have been lost on the pilgrims travelling along the Hajj road, or on the Bedouin, in whose territory the forts were built. To the pilgrims the forts will have been the reassuring presence of an all powerful Empire, whilst to the Bedouin they represented a military reality.

The Ottoman concern for the efficient running of the Hajj is also evident in the specifics of the route chosen. The Mamluk Hajj route, through Jordan, generally followed that of the Roman Via Nova Traina, or King's Highway, via Karak, whereas the Ottomans adopted the more easterly route, currently known as the Desert Highway. Oral tradition in Jordan (Peake Pasha 1958) attributes this change to the daughter of Sultan Sulayman, who complained of bandits and steep slopes on deep wadis on the King's Highway (for a discussion of the origins of the Via Nova Traiana see Borstad 2008). The new Ottoman route, known as Tariq al-Bint, was much less precipitous and more suitable for the larger numbers of pilgrims using the route. Incidentally, the adoption of the new route meant that after leaving Damascus pilgrims would not see another town, or city, until they reached Medina; this would have made the pilgrims, both easy to control and minimized the risk of confrontation with inhabitants of settled areas.

When considering the role of the forts along the Hajj road, it is clear that they fulfilled multiple functions based on their identity as symbols of Ottoman authority. One clear role for the forts was the protection of water resources along the route, thereby reducing the risks to the efficient functioning of the Hajj caravan (*c.f.* Faroqhi

1994, 71). The forts also had a role as part of a distribution and supply system for the Hajj caravan, thus important provisions, such as camel fodder and grain, as well as military equipment, could be kept in sealed storerooms. The forts would also have functioned as police posts, both for the Hajj caravan and for the locality in which each fort was located (it is, for example, notable that the fort at Ma'an remained a police station into the 1970s). Collectively the forts may also be seen as part of a border, or frontier system; within Arabia (*i.e.* south of Ma'an) the line of forts were outposts of nominal Ottoman authority, whilst to the north (between Damascus and Ma'an) they formed part of a network of fortifications controlling access to, and within, the settled zones either side of the Jordan river (see Chapter 5). One of the most important functions of the forts, often overlooked, is their role as centres for mediating the relationship between the Ottoman state and the Bedouin tribes. Specifically, each fort could be used as a place for distributing payments to the local tribes to ensure the safe passage of the Hajj caravan. For example, Doughty describes how the fort at Tabuk was used for making *sürre* payments to the Bani Atieh (1979, 112–13). In addition to payments, the forts could be used for diplomatic exchanges, thus, in the 16th century Qatrana was used for peace negotiations between the Temiyya tribe and the Ottoman State (Peake Pasha 1958, 84–85). From the Bedouin perspective the forts were seen as locations for contact with the central government, in much the same way as buildings at al-Risha functioned as a permanent address for the local Arab tribes (Lancaster 1990). For the Bedouin, the forts were a fixed point in the landscape that would have influenced their seasonal migrations (Map 8). The balance of these various functions may have changed over time, though the survival of the forts, long after the disappearance of the Hajj caravans, is an enduring testament to the strength of Ottoman rule.

3) The Hajj Route as Heritage

One of the most interesting aspects of studying the archaeology of the Hajj is that it is a living tradition. Although the Hajj has been transformed by modern modes of transport, which has meant that the majority of pilgrims now travel by air, the concept of the journey is still an essential part of the Hajj experience. It is also worth pointing out that the overland Hajj caravan has only recently passed out of living memory. A report, from as late as 1903, records the departure of the caravan from Damascus, even though, by that time, the majority of pilgrims went by sea, which was not only less arduous, but considerably cheaper (Issawi 1988, 237). Even today a few pilgrims take the overland route, travelling by car from Turkey, Syria, or Jordan and following the ancient Hajj route. This route is still the major trade route between Turkey and Saudi Arabia and truck drivers can be seen stopping at Turkish restaurants in Qatrana and elsewhere.

The Turkish interest in the heritage of this route is strong and as early as 1976 the Turkish government paid for the restoration of the Ottoman fort at Qatrana. Since then there has been a steady, but growing, interest in the heritage of this Hajj road in Jordan. For example, in 1986 the fort at Dab'a was included as the destination of a, one day, British Airways Concorde trip from London to 'Amman. More recently, in 2001, the Friends of Archaeology organized an event involving the re-enactment of the Hajj using Jordanian school children and others. The focus of the event was, again, the Ottoman fort at Qatrana where aspects of the traditional Hajj were recalled through food, costumes, stories and songs. In addition, there was a market where children were introduced to real Uzbek and Kazakh pilgrims returning from the Hajj (Bajali nd). More recently there has been an initiative to conserve, rebuild and reuse some of the other Hajj forts in Jordan. For example, following survey and excavations at 'Unaiza in 2002 (Petersen, Brun and Shurma 2003) the fort was cleared of rubble, consolidated and partially rebuilt using plans derived from the excavations. The fort is now protected from casual vandalism by a new wooden door. More recently the 16th century fort at Ma'an has been converted from its former use, as a prison, into a regional antiquities office.

Despite the growing interest in the Hajj forts, a scarcity of funds and a growing population means that many of the sites are increasingly under threat from vandalism and treasure hunters. For example, the inscription above the gateway at the 18th century fort at 'Aqaba Hijazi (Fassu'a) was stolen some time between the initial survey in 1986 and a subsequent visit in 2002. The most endangered of the surviving Hajj forts is Mudawwara, which, despite its remote location, has been the subject of continuing vandalism, including undermining of the foundations. Today, with only three sides still standing, Mudawwara stands on the verge of complete collapse.

4) Directions for Research and Conservation

One of the aims of this book is to stimulate interest in the Hajj forts as a heritage resource and to prompt the establishment of a programme for their long term survival. Whilst physical reconstruction of the fabric of some of the forts is useful, it is essential that they are also put to some appropriate use. The fort at Ma'an is perhaps the best example of adaptive reuse of these buildings, though it is a model that cannot be adapted for all cases. What is needed is a management plan, covering all the buildings, which treats them as component parts of a national and international network of major significance. Individual forts may not appear to be of major architectural, or historical significance, yet collectively, they form one of the most important monuments to Islamic culture. Ideally, the forts in Jordan could become part of an international World Heritage site, which also incorporates the forts, khans and carvanserais in Turkey, Syria and Saudi Arabia.

Plate 186. Udruh, Ottoman period fort with entrance (1986).

Plate 188. Udruh, Ottoman period fort rear (1986).

Plate 187. Udruh, Ottoman period fort detail of box machicolation above entrance (1986).

Plate 189. Udruh, Ottoman period fort interior with gun slots (1986).

Plate 190. Udruh, Ottoman period fort first floor interior (1986).

The designation of the Syrian Hajj route as a World Heritage site would enable the co-ordination of academic research in the participating countries and lead to a much better understanding of the mechanisms underlying the Hajj. Examples include, a thorough study of the ceramics and other finds associated with the Hajj route, which would allow studies of trade, commerce and the movement of people. Both tobacco (in the form of smoking pipes)

and coffee (represented by coffee cups and bowls) are commodities of particular interest because they are both stimulants and are easily transported over long distances. Tobacco represents an introduction from the New World that became established as a crop in the Middle East, whilst coffee (with origins in Arabia and Ethiopia) became and remains, one of the highest value traded commodities in the world. The Hajj must certainly have been one of the major mechanisms by which these commodities became established throughout the modern (post 1500 AD) world.

A study of the wider environment of the route could provide information about the impact of large numbers of people moving through the landscape and how local people interacted with this annual event. In particular it would be useful to know how the Hajj stimulated local economies and how it affected the balance between agriculture and pastoral nomadism. More detailed investigation of the architecture and construction of the forts might indicate the extent to which they were centrally planned and their effect on local architecture For example, the 16th century fort at Ma'an may well have served as a model for the nearby Ottoman period fort at Udruh (Plates 186–190), which is of similar size and design and even has a box machicolation over the gateway. It is not certain when and by whom the fort at Udruh was built, though it is almost certainly from the Ottoman period and was probably built by a local leader, rather than the Ottoman authorities.

Finally, a programme of research and preservation of the monuments of the Hajj route is an ideal opportunity to present the best aspects of Muslim civilization in terms of organization, endurance and faith. Just as in the early 1900s, the construction of the Hijaz railway by public subscription demonstrated international solidarity and a commitment to progress, so the conservation of the more ancient remains will indicate a renewed awareness of a common heritage.

Appendix 1. Report Presented to His Highness Muhammad Ali Pasha, Viceroy of Egypt, 1828

By an anonymous Officer of Engineering in the Viceroyal Egyptian Army

Translated by Dr. Michael V. Diboll

Introduction

This is a report concerning the necessary repairs and water coursing of the cisterns and streams that exist by the waystations and alighting-points situated on the road between Damascus in Syria and the Noble city of Mecca, the maintenance of which has been made possible in accordance with the wishes of His Eminence the Pasha; [this report] has been collated in compliance with his commands.

Regarding the water existing at the waystation of *Al Muzaib*, this arises from a lake into which gather five to 10 springs; the water here is very plentiful, and there is no restriction of water supply here, so that every part of the lake defies description.

Al Ramthah

This waystation is four hours from *Al Muzaib*. A quarter-of-an-hour further on is a square cistern made of stone. This is in the middle of a *wadi*. This cistern does not need a lot of restoration, as it is of modern construction. [But there is a small problem,] close to the cistern is an opening carved from the rock to form another cistern. This safeguards the water, [and is designed so that] during heavy rain dust and mud does not fill up the two cisterns. Rain has not fallen very heavily this year, so that the two cisterns are now filled with dust. This dust quickly absorbs whatever water does flow into them. Now, this waystation is only four hours from *Al Muzaib*, and is surrounded by small villages. By using local labour it might be possible to clear the cisterns of mud and dust, uncover the bottom of the cisterns, and remove any easily repaired blockage. But if this cannot be done, we've carried water with us from *Al Muzaib* to *Ain Al Zarqa'*, in view of the water shortage here.

Ain Al Zaqra'

This waystation is about 24 hours further on from *Al Muzaib*. It has plenty of water since the *Ain Al Zaqra'* river drains through it. The waters are very sweet, and numerous plants grow around it, including *Zuqaam* trees. This waystation is situated between two mountains, and contains an old fort which is on the verge of collapse. An order for its restoration has been raised from his Highness the *Hikimdar*.

Al Balqa'

About 14 hours further down the road from *Ain Al Zarqa'* stands a fort named *Al Balqa'*. This fort is square-shaped and is built from stone along all four sides to a length of 35 architectural cubits. The fort is well constructed, but one or two of the rooms erected inside the building have been completely razed, and the remainder are also in need of restoration. One of the four corners of the fort is on the point of collapse and urgently needs rebuilding.

As ordered, a well has been dug inside the building in order to help preserve drinking water. The water supply for this well comes from the vicinity of a cistern situated outside the fort. It is said that the bottom of the well is broken, since the water drains away into the soil.

Clearly, this well is vital to the life of this district, but its condition demands that repairs be made to the bottom of the well. Thus, two cisterns have been built outside of the fort in order to supply the Hajj pilgrims [*Hujjaaj*] with drinking water. However, the bottoms of these cisterns are cracked, so that the rainwater that collects in them seeps away into the earth.

These two cisterns have been passed by many times, and it is clear that they have to be cleaned. During our inspections of these cisterns they have been shown to contain a depth of about two cubits of water. We returned and measured the water when the rain had been falling heavily, and it filled both cisterns to the brim. But now both cisterns contain less than three cubits of water, and this is traceable to the fissures at the bottom of the cisterns.

In summary, these cisterns should not require too much restoration, since their basic structure is sound. If the mud which has accumulated in the cisterns is cleared away, and repairs to the two cisterns are completed properly so that water no longer runs away into the ground, there should be no difficulties regarding the water supply at this waystation, and the *Hujjaaj* can be supplied with water for up to two years.

There is also another cistern here, 50 architectural cubits long by 10 wide and 5 deep. This cistern is oblong in shape and there are no cracks or fissures in its structure. However, this cistern does need to be purified of mud.

To summarize, the order calls for a skilled itemization of the repairs to the fort, and for repairs, restoration of the cisterns and the removal of the mud to be undertaken so that water could be provided for the *Hujjaaj*, as well as other visitors, to ensure their comfort and well-being.

al-Qatrana

This name derives from a fort situated on the road about 12 hours from *Al Balqa'*. The fort is square-shaped, and each wall is built to a length of 35 architectural cubits. There are no cracks or fissues in the structure, except for one which is inside the fort, situated in the storeroom. This room is delapidated, and must be repaired, as must the rooms in which the Governor resides, for those are also in need of renovation. The stone needed for these repairs is plentiful; all that is required is that the necessary manpower is recruited.

Outside of the fort is a very large cistern, built 100 architectural cubits square, with a capacity of 2,100 square cubits. The cistern's construction is sound. However, mud has collected in it and this must be cleared; the cistern also needs to be relined. According to the Governor of the fort, the water level of this cistern has receded only by about two hands over a period of a month, this is because of a large lake situated nearby which replenishes the cistern. After we returned to this waystation and measured the water level, it had decreased by only one hand; and in spite the fact that this cistern had supplied a great deal of water to the *Hujjaaj* and their animals, a large amount of water remains in the cistern. If, therefore, the relining of this cistern is carried out properly, it should be able to supply enough water to satisfy all needs for about two years.

A section of the flood drain that flows into this cistern runs parallel to one side of the cistern, and a stone dam or embankment 300 architectural cubits long has been erected, and two wells have been dug one behind the other along the watercourse. In this way the mud which is carried by the floodwaters will not flow into the cistern, therefore the water is kept pure. When the floods first come down the watercourse, they drain into the first well. When this is full they then flow into the second well, and in this way the floodwater is purified before it enters the cistern.

However, it seems that some of the floods which flowed through this watercourse in previous years were very severe, so much so that they damaged a section of the afore-mentioned dam about 20 architectural cubits long, tearing down the dam wall. Since the section of the dam destroyed during previous rainy seasons is situated alongside the edge of the cistern, floodwater now flows out of the dam, and thus much water is wasted and the cistern does not fill to its full capacity.

There is a real danger that if work on the damaged section of the dam does not commence withing a suitable timeframe, and if – may God preserve us – we once more experience severe floods, then what remains of the dam will surely be swept away. If the dam is destroyed the cistern will become useless, and this will cause great distress to the *Hujjaaj*. Should the *Hujjaaj* have to return from Hajj during summertime, they would therefore be compelled to carry water or scavenge for it over a journey of some 30–40 hours. Clearly, then, the dam must be repaired urgently, in order to prevent the *Hujjaaj* from having to face such a horrible prospect.

al-Hasa

This name is derived from a fort which is situated 15 hours further on from *al-Qatrana*. The fort is built of stone, and is square-shaped, each side measuring 50 architectural cubits. Two of the four corners of the fort have been damaged by an earthquake that occurred many years ago, and are on the point of collapse. It should be emphasized that the refacing of the walls of the fort that took place last year has not proved to be an effective repair; moreover, if the work required to properly fix the two corners is delayed any further, they will collapse, and repairing them to their original condition will demand a very great expenditure of effort.

A well has been dug to supply water to the cistern which is situated inside the fort, opposite the place earmarked for the erection of another fort in this location. An irrigation device has been built over this well, but this is also delapidated and is on the point of collapse. At its centre is a circular mule-track; and two stone pillars are situated at either side of the well, these concentrate the water supply to the watercourses which branch off from the device. Without doubt, repairing this device will be useful in restoring the cistern to proper use.

Outside of the fort is another cistern, this is square-shaped, each side measuring 40 architectural cubits; it is 20 cubits deep, and is fed by the irrigation device situated inside the fort. This cistern is of sound construction, and is situated in the vicinity of a great wadi, into which flow floodwaters during the rainy season. During the flood season, crossing this wadi is utterly impossible. Thus, a large bridge spanning the wadi was commissioned.

However, very severe floods destroyed an approximately 40 architectural cubit section of the levees flanking the bridge. This damage had to be repaired, since it would hinder the passage of the *Hujjaaj* over the wadi, there being no other way to cross during the torrential flood that flows through the wadi during the rainy season.

Permission for these repairs was sought from the Office of His Highness the *Hikimdar*. The labour and administration required to undertake this work was despatched, and the work needed to repair and renovate the fort was undertaken. However, there is a road which extends from in front of the fort and which consolidates the bridge at each side. This conveys the *Hujjaaj* some 1,500 cubits over some very fine dust which resembles flour in its whiteness and powderiness. It is clear that when the *Hujjaaj* try to cross this bridge during the rainy season they will be confronted by manifold difficulties and be seriously inconvenienced. We have heard from the residents of Al Hayra that a few years ago a number of *Hujjaaj* approached this area of land during the rains, and were not able to cross the bridge without encountering extreme difficulties: they were put to the test by receiving many injuries to themselves and to their camels; although this piece of land is not more than 1,500 cubits long, it took the *Hujjaaj* an entire day to cross over it!

It should be noted that previously the rainfall has been so strong as to render the *Hujjaaj*'s passage over this piece of land nigh-on impossible, since when rain falls heavily on the layer of soft, powdery sand, the camels sink deep into the sand, up to the level of the cameleer. If the area around this fort is paved to a radius of 1,500 paces in order to protect the *Hujjaaj* from such calamities, this would indeed be a good, charitable work, the tongues of the *Hujjaaj* would be filled with sweet supplications; the materials needed for this project are plentiful and at-hand, and hewn stone in a nearby place, and other materials needed can be bought up from the waystation of *Ma'an.*

Dhahr al-'Unaiza

This is the name of a fort situated a little over 10 hours from *Qal'at al-Hasa*; this building is square-shaped, and is built of stone to a length of 50 architectural cubits on each side. Both the entrance and the rooms within the fort have all collapsed, as has the rest of the superstructure. As a result, the Governor of the fort no longer resides there. Notwithstanding the various investigations that have been undertaken into its condition, this fort has remained in the same dilapidated condition for a very long time indeed.

There exists at a distance of about a cannon's shot away from the fort a square cistern built to a length of 50 architectural cubits on each side, and the water is about three architectural cubits deep; but the cistern is filled to about half its depth with submerged muddy sediment. Moreover, the cistern is corroded from the inside, so that rainwater flowing into it soon disappears.

I assume that this place, that is to say the fort, is not used as one of the waystations on the Hajj road, and that instead wayfarers continue on to *Ma'an*; thus, to-date there has not yet been any enumeration of the repairs needed for its restoration. However, the repairs to this fort should not be neglected. For if it should so happen that the return of the *Hujjaaj* take place during summertime, their need for water would become very severe indeed; and abandoning this fort on account of its current, dilapidated condition will lead to the site becoming desolate and almost entirely devoid of water.

Ma'an

This is the name of a waystation situated at a distance of about 10 hours from *Dhahr al-'Unaiza*, which is built over two depressions in the ground. There are two small settlements situated here, one facing the other, built from kiln-fired brick of a fort-like construction. This waystation was originally populated by settled Bedouin, and here several varieties of pomegranate, quince, and figs are grown. Situated in the vicinity of these two settlements, in the midst of a wadi, are a number of small springs; likewise, in the second settlement a number of wells are to be found. Situated between the two settlements is a cistern 35 cubits long by 25 wide, and 15 cubits deep. Water is fed to this cistern by wells situated in some elevated land; thus, praise be to God, there is no restriction whatsoever in the water supply to this waystation.

Qal'at al-Fassu'a

This fort is some 15 hours further on from *Ma'an,* and is situated a considerable distance from the road. It is built from stone and is square-shaped, each side measuring 35 architectural cubits. In view of the fact that two sides of the fort have been razed, we have written to the elders of *Ma'an* with respect to raising the minimum manpower needed to undertake the necessary repairs; the fort's superstructure is also in need of renovation. Situated beside this fort are two cisterns; both measure 40 architectural cubits long, 30 wide, and are 10 cubits deep. However, it is said that neither cistern contained any water at all throughout the previous year, although in this blessèd year water has accumulated to a depth of a cubit-and-a-half. Despite of this, upon our return, we found no amount of water there; and, since the *Tajreek* had settled in this region, and had extracted from the cistern whatever water remained.

Neither of these two cisterns needs much renovation, except with respect to the mud which has settled around their inclines. Since this sediment restricts the flow of water into the cisterns, it has been requested that the cisterns be cleansed of mud; this should be easily accomplished, if it is possible to requisition the labour needed to undertake this operation from *Ma'an.*

Qal'at al-Mudawwara

This fort is situated about 14 hours further down the road from *Qal'at Al 'Aqaba*. It is built of stone, and is square-shaped, measuring 50 architectural cubits on each side. Neither fort requires a great deal of repair.

Facing *Qal'at al-Mudawwara* is a rectangular cistern measuring 50 by 30 architectural cubits. Inside this cistern are a number of small springs, and the cistern is also fed with water by a man-made channel which connects it to another cistern, situated by the second side of the fort.

This cistern is also oblong in shape, measuring 40 architectural cubits long by 25 cubits wide and 15 cubits deep. When we arrived here we found it to contain three cubits of water. The area surrounding the cistern containing the springs is surrounded by sand. When the winds blow they carry sand to the cistern and block the springs within it and reduce the water supply to the cistern. Thus, upon our return to this waystation we were somewhat distressed because there was insufficient water in the second cistern. This was because the sand had settled in the bottom of the cistern and had covered the springs, thereby reducing the water supply.

We commissioned the drainage engineers that had been bought with us along with the renovators in the restoration of a cistern at *Medain Saleh* with the examination of this cistern, and they reported the following: that the 400 pace channel connecting the two cisterns had collapsed; that this was preventing the flow of water from the first cistern to the second; that it was in need of restoration and repair along its entire length; and that using four teams of drainage engineers, 10 plasterers, and 50 labourers it might be possible to complete the repairs within one month.

To summarize, since our return to this waystation we have suffered badly from the restricted water available here. Undoubtedly, the solution to this problem is as follows: the commissioning the repairs and renovations needed within a suitable timeframe; detailing the drainage engineers needed for this work from Syria, and having the rest send down to us from *Ma'an;* ordering the construction of a one-cubit high barrier wall around the cistern, in order to prevent the wind from carrying sand into it.

Qal'at Dhat al-Hajj

This is the name of a fort situated 14 hours further on from *Qal'at al-Mudawwara*. The fort is built of stone and is square-shaped, measuring 40 architectural cubits on each side. This fort does not require a great deal of repair or renovation.

Situated outside of the fort is an oblong-shaped cistern measuring 70 architectural cubits, by 35, and 10 cubits deep; upon our arrival here it contained three cubits of water.

The cistern is of functional construction, and does not require repair or restoration. However, the sand surrounding the waystation is carried up by the wind, and deposited within the cistern, filling it to half its depth. Accordingly, it has been ordered that the cistern be cleared of sand. Moreover, if a wall were to be raised around this cistern to prevent the deposition of sand, the supply of water would become plentiful. This is because water does not collect in this cistern because of rainfall; rather, the water flows from two springs. One of these arises from the rim of a depression, situated about half an hour's journey from the fort. Its waters flow through a channel until they drain into the cistern; however, the water which this spring provides is not plentiful. The other spring arises from a place situated inside the fort, and empties into the cistern like the other one; but this spring does not provide a great deal of water either.

If the water is able to flow into the cistern by a better method, the water supply to the cistern should become more plentiful. Sand has accumulated and has filled the cistern to half its depth, and this accumulation of sand extends practically to the fort where the water supply originates. The water descends from the fort through a channel until it connects with the cistern, where it is confronted by the sand which half-fills the cistern, thereby inhibiting the flow of water from outside.

If the cistern, and the channel that drains into it are cleared of sand, and a wall is raised to a height of one cubit around the cistern to prevent further deposition of sand, then the water supply to this cistern will become much more plentiful, and the matter of supplying to the *Hujjaaj* will be made easy.

Qal'at al-Tabuk

This fort is situated 24 hours further on from *Faraa' Al Hajj*,[1] and is sometimes called *Al Najal Al 'Aajiy*.[2] The fort is square-shaped, measuring 40 architectural cubits on each side.

In the vicinity of the fort is a small village built of sun-brick, and facing this are four oblong cisterns, each measuring 20 architectural cubits long by 10 wide; a spring arises from one of these cisterns, and the overflow from this pool feeds the other two with water.

Vineyards and gardens surround the fort, lemon trees and date palms grow in the midst of the fort, along with fig trees, pomegranate, apricots, and plum trees, whilst okra and aubergines are grown in the gardens; these gardens are irrigated by water from the three cisterns, and, praise be to God, water is freely available here.

Qal'at al-Ukhaydhir

This is a fort situated 18 hours further on from *Qal'at al-Tabuk*. It is built of stone, and is square-shaped, measuring 40 architectural cubits on each side; it is of sound construction, and does not require a great deal of restoration.

In bygone days a well was built inside the fort, over

a spring; this well is 24 fathoms deep, and is plentifully supplied with water, so that the presence of travellers settling here makes no impact upon the depth of water in the well for several days. The waters of this well are sweet, but we have heard from those living at this fort that the waters drain out of the well, and that during their stay at this fort they have felt the water draining away.

A circular irrigation device turned by three mules has been erected over this well, but these mules were lost over the past few months, and as a consequence the cistern near the fort has not been filling up. We wrote to His Excellency Sharif Pasha regarding the purchase of more mules, and these were sent to the Governor of the fort. The swift dispatch of these mules by special detachment has meant that upon our return to this fort we no longer experienced any shortage of water.

Outside of the fort is a rectangular cistern measuring 30 architectural cubits long, by 10 wide and 10 deep, and is now well supplied with water because of the purchase of the mules. Two other cisterns are also situated here. These are both oblong in shape, and both measure 35 architectural cubits long, by 20 wide and 10 deep. Both of these cisterns are full; however, a considerable quantity of sand has accumulated in them, and there is no doubt that they must be cleared out.

These two cisterns have filled up on account of the fact that the entire fort and cistern complex is situated in a very sandy area, enclosed by mountains on both sides. These form a strait in which sand builds up, and is then picked up by the winds and deposited in the cisterns. A wall one cubit high has been erected around the cisterns in order to prevent the deposition of sand within them. However, sections of this wall have become dilapidated and are in need of repair. If this wall is left at its present height, the need to dredge the cisterns of the sand which accumulates in them will continue. The cleaning out of the cisterns was undertaken and completed about two years ago, and the sand was removed and deposited outside of them. However, the winds have filled the cisterns once more, to the extent that there is no longer room in them to fit a single seed! This means that a renewed and increased effort is now needed in order to once more clear the cisterns of sand.

Clearly, it is incumbent upon us to as soon as possible give serious thought to the matter of the low wall protecting the cisterns, and to delegate one of the labour overseers to look at it. This would surely raise from the lips of our Muslim brethren the *Hujjaaj* a flow of sweet supplications, particularly because water has not reached the large cistern for some two years now – through God's inscrutable wisdom – and has been completely empty of water for the past year. Thus, we conserved what water we had with us until we reached the oasis which is named *Ghadir* or *Jinniyya Al Kaa'in*,[3] some 30 hours further on from the fort, where we were able to make use of the copious amount of rainwater that had accumulated in the pool. Had water not been available here, we would have been severely put to the test by having to travel all the way to *Medain Saleh*,

using only the water we had bought with us, a journey of some 60 hours from *Qal'at al-Ukhaydhir.*

Since the return from Hajj will fall during the summertime, when one's need for water is very great indeed, it is likely that the water existing at the three pools at *Qal'at al-Ukhaydhir* will prove insufficient for purpose. There is, however, a fourth cistern near to the fort, other than the three already mentioned. This cistern is 35 architectural cubits long, by 15 wide and 10 deep. However, this cistern is very dilapidated, and is in need of extensive repair.

Qal'at Birkat al-'Adham [Qal'at al-Mu'azzam]

This fort is situated 17 hours further down the road from *Qal'at al-Ukhaydhir*. It is square-shaped, measuring 40 architectural cubits on each side, and is not in need of a great deal of restoration. The Governor of the fort had undertaken to have the fort's entrance blocked with sand, fearing that Bedouin raiders would evict him from the fort. However, the lack of water available at this fort has led to it being unoccupied. It is to be understood from the word of the Governor that in previous years he had purchased *Bughaziyya*-type long-necked water-skins, but this solution to the water storage problems here proved to be inadequate, and now the Governor resides in *Qal'at al-Ukhaydhir*. Clearly, if whatever is impeding the flow of water is left unfixed, surely this fort will waste away until it becomes utterly useless.

Situated outside of the fort is a large cistern measuring 100 architectural cubits square and connected to the fort. This cistern has filled up to over half its depth with mud; it is thought to be about 20 cubits deep, the depth from its brim to the accumulated mud being 10 cubits. The exterior of the structure is sound and free from fissures. However, without doubt the cistern must be excavated and cleared of mud until the bottom of the structure is reached, and any fissures found therein repaired, since according to what the Governor has said, there are some fissures existing at the bottom of the cistern. If this cistern is cleared of mud, repaired, then filled with water, it will – with God's care – satisfy the water requirements of the *Hujjaaj* for several years to come. In years gone by the Hajj community residing at the fort had attempted to clean out the cistern, but they encountered thickly accumulated mud caked around the sides of the cistern. Without doubt, this accumulation of mud within the cistern and around its sides must be removed, and the facing stones within the cistern reset; then, when heavy rain falls, water will once more flow into the cistern and be retained there.

However, the damming wall that has been erected at either side of the main watercourse is damaged over a length of some 200 architectural cubits, and this too restricts the flow of water. Therefore, repairs to the dam have also been commissioned.

Dar al-Hamra

The fort *Dar al-Hamra* is situated 16 hours further down the road from *Birkat al-'Adham*. This fort is of excellent stone construction, and is square-shaped, measuring 30 architectural cubits on each side. However, because of the water shortage – for some years now rainwater has not reached the cistern situated near the fort – the Governor of this fort now resides at *Medain Saleh*, and has had the entrance blocked with sand, to prevent the fort being looted by Bedouin. The door at the fort's entrance could probably be re-installed into its correct place without too much difficulty, and it does not require much by way of repair.

Connecting to the fort is a square-shaped water cistern measuring 90 architectural cubits on each side, and approximately 20 cubits deep. It is of sturdy construction; however, sand has settled in it to about half its depth, and has also accumulated around one of its corners to the height of the wall; this has collapsed, and its débris has accumulated in the cistern. Without a doubt, this rubble and the accumulated sand must be taken out of the cistern, and any loose-hanging or dilapidated stonework must be repaired. One of the previous Hajj Emirs had attempted to undertake this work, a fitting response to the earnest supplications of the *Hujjaaj* who have trod this road praying that the cistern be cleared of sand that had accumulated within it. However, what he did not realize at that time was that it was the sand that had accumulated *around* the cistern that was the cause of the blockage preventing the flow of water into it – but now curses arise in place of sweet supplications! This is because he and subsequent Hajj Emirs should have had the sand excavated and deposited a long way away from the watercourse, if necessary liberating some of authorized fund held in order to facilitate the transportation of the sand to a far away place; his successors should also have done likewise. Instead, the sand emptied from the pool has been thrown over the watercourse so that it has become a dam blocking the flow of floodwater into the cistern, so that no matter whether the rain falls hard of falls lightly, it never reaches the pool. Without doubt it is essential to remove both the sand that has accumulated inside the cistern and that which has accumulated within it, and also to repair the damaged sides of the pool.

God in His wisdom has willed that no rain has fallen in the vicinity of *Birkat al-'Adham* or in the vicinity of this pool for some years now. But should He will that the rains once more return to these places, the cisterns situated there will be unable to make good use of this rainfall. For if the rain should pour down heavily in this location, useful amounts of water should flow in abundance, since the cistern is situated in a narrow strait between two mountains; this area, and the road between *Qal'at al-Ukhaydhir* and *Medain Saleh*, are both lined with mountains and rocky outcrops, and the road here is not well-ordered and maintained. Should the return of the *Hujjaj* fall during the hot season when the sun blazes as if it were white-hot, and the water supply at both here and at *Birkat al-'Adham* were anything less then plentiful, then they would find themselves in very dire straits indeed, would suffer painfully, and be put to very great expense.

It happened that upon our return the weather here was very humid, so that the water we had bought with us was sufficient for our utility.

Medain Saleh

The fort *Medain Saleh* is situated 20 hours further down the road to Mecca from *Qal'at Dar al-Hamra*. It is built of stone and is square-shaped, measuring 25 architectural cubits on each side. It does not require a great deal of restoration.

Inside the fort is a spring, and built over this is an irrigation device turned by mules. This feeds a cistern situated outside of the fort with water. However, the channel connecting the fort with the cistern has collapsed; accordingly, a drainage engineer has been assigned to the detachment undertaking the repairs.

Restoration of the irrigations device depends on having at least two mules to turn it; however, one has died, and the other is not at present fit for work. From our investigations it has become clear that the *Oda Bash* and his entourage have sold the barley which was especially assigned as fodder to these mules, and this has led to their emaciation. The mules at this waystation would not have got into this sorry condition where it not for the fact that they have been starved, and the *Oda Bash* has not been able to find any way to deny this.

They make the excuse that they obtained *matériel*, livestock and foodstuffs from Syria, but that for a year they have had to stay here without supply. The army had previously assumed responsibility for their welfare in the accustomed manner, but now, when supplies reach the forts, the army was no longer present to supervise the distribution of supplies, so that these supplies have been transported from one fort to another by means of certain Bedouin – whose origins are unclear – and thus a large quantity of these supplies has been lost *en route*.

In view of the fact that the forts are situated in the desert wilderness, and that it is very difficult to buy anything out here, it is perhaps not surprising that supplies run short in this way, and that therefore *matériel*, livestock and foodstuffs have been lost in this way.

Accordingly, it appears that the *Oda Bash* is probably telling the truth in this matter; indeed, it is apparent that we ourselves have also had to resort to such measures. If the Government were to supervise staged transport between the forts, and provide for the safety and well being of the teamsters working on these transports, this would put an end to what is being said, and what the *Oda Bash* say, about the difficulties here.

With respect to the shortfalls in *matériel* and livestock and making good these losses, a mule has been purchased to take the place of the mule that was sold, and this has been left at the fort; as for the emaciated mule, this has been given to the *Oda Bash* in exchange for a strong one, on the condition that the sick mule is made well. If this mule is not returned in good condition the strong one will be kept, so that there will be two good mules at the fort as there were before.

We have noticed outside the fort and connecting to it, a square-shaped water cistern measuring 30 architectural cubits on each side, and 10 cubits deep; this cistern is fed by water via the mule-driven irrigation device described above. Further, situated around the cistern are 7 wells of which the *Hujjaaj* can make use. Accordingly, there is no restriction here at all with respect to the water supply at this waystation – praise be to God! No other building whatsoever, other than the fort, can be seen in the vicinity of this waystation, the nearest being the settlement *Al Maali*. So the natives of this village transport to the fort at *Medain Saleh* lemons, limes, tangerines, *beljiq* dates, and other foodstuffs typical of this area, in order to sell these to the *Hujjaaj*.

Bi'r al-Zumurrud

The fort of *Bi'r al-Zumurrud* is situated 30 hours further on from *Medain Saleh*. It is square-shaped and built of stone. Inside it is a well, and water is raised from this by means of a mule-powered device. However, God in his wisdom has willed that it has only been possible to extract water from this well for some two years. Since then the fort has became useless and the *Hujjaaj* have avoided this waystation. We have found that the bottom of this well consists of stone, from wherein the water emerges. However, since the stones have been displaced, the water now returns from whence it flows. From what we understand, one of the Hajj Emirs sought to bring from Syria some fine pieces of stone, but the stone shattered so that it was of no use, and so the spring no longer produces any useful amount of water. So one of the foremost drainage engineers commissioned the excavation of this well, and from what I understand this well no longer supplies any water because the ground that surrounds it is very sandy, and this sand absorbs any rain water which seeps around the well or dribbles into the deep bottom of the well.

Situated in the vicinity of the fort there is another well, dug in the midst of the sands. Water has collected in this well, perhaps because it has been dug deeply, and is situated outside of the fort, for the water from the well situated inside the fort seems to have seeped into this well. Thus, one of the drainage experts has commissioned the erection of an irrigation device over the well situated outside the fort, and the erection of a wall around the well.

The truth regarding this fort is that the water which drains away during the rainy season should be feeding the cistern, and if the situation is left as it is, any water that might have collected in the well will continue to seep deep into the depths of the sand. If this is allowed to continue, this fort will become nothing more than a Bedouin habitation, for the simple reason that however severe the heat of the sun, there will be no water available here, and therefore there will be nobody left here to protect the fort and its environs. Consequently, it is of the utmost importance that the problem of the water supply at this fort is given urgent treatment, since the water we have found at the next waystation, *Al Bi'r Al Jadeed* (to be discussed below), does not seem to live up to the promised expectations of well-watered lushness. Therefore, there is no doubt that a well-renowned expert in drainage and irrigation must be appointed to oversee the work needed to increase the supply of water at both *Bi'r al-Zumurrud* and *Al Bi'r Al Jadeed*. Unless this is done this road will not flourish, the *Hujjaaj* will withhold their sweet supplications.

There is a square-shaped cistern in the vicinity of this fort, measuring 20 architectural cubits on each side, and 10 deep; but it does not hold a single drop of water. Unquestionably, it must undergo renovation. The Governor of this fort resides at *Medain Saleh*.

Bi'r al-Waalida [Valide Kuyusu]

This fort is sometimes named after *Bi'r al-Waalida*, and sometimes after *Al Bi'r Al Jadeed*, it is situated 8 hours further down the road from *Bi'r al-Zumurrud*. It is built of stone and is square-shaped, measuring 30 architectural cubits on each side. It is not in need of a great deal of repair. Inside the fort is a well, 28 hands deep; over this stands a mule-driven irrigation device.

Adjoining the fort, on the outside, is a square-shaped water cistern measuring 25 architectural cubits on each side, and ten cubits deep. It is fed with water from the above-mentioned well; inside the cistern there are no fissures that would require it to be relined.

Linked to the fort from the outside there is another well, five architectural cubits across, and 24 hands deep. It is understood that this well does not contain a spring; instead, it is fed by rainwater which soaks through the ground and then seeps into where the well is bored. It is reasonable to assume that when the rain falls well, water will collect in the well filling it up to the brim, thereby fulfilling the requirements of the *Hujjaaj*. However, God – in His Wisdom – has seen to it that the water in the well inside the fort has seeped away, so that if the rainfall is slight, the well inside the fort will be drained to the bottom, and whatever water is in the external well will also drain away so that the well will be empty and the water will be lost. If the irrigation device standing over the internal well is turned, the water inside it peters out and eventually stops, and the rotation of the device has to be halted for a few hours while the water in the well is replenished; thus, we did suffer somewhat from lack of water upon our return to this waystation.

al-Hadiyya

This waystation is situated at a journey of some 20 hours further on from *Bi'r al-Waalida* on a fissure on the earth, and around each side there are four depressions. There is a small stone-built fort built here, this has been in a ruinous condition for some years now, and one of its corners has collapsed. There are no water cisterns here, and in view of its lack of functionality, this fort has been neglected and allowed to fall into disrepair. Since this waystation is situated in a sandy area, the rainy season floods drain into there earth here, and from what I have discovered emerges around the fort to a depth of over a cubit. This floodwater is plentiful at the edges for the mountains, from where it flows toward the waystation; but here the water becomes thick as a result of the foreign matter and desert dust that accumulates in it.

al-Nakhlatayn

Qal'at al-Nakhlatayn, also called *Qal'at al-Sajwa* or *al-Sajiyya*, is situated 20 hours further on down the road from *al-Hadiyya* waystation. It is built of stone and measures 40 architectural cubits on each side.

Inside the fort is a spring, over which a well has been constructed, and over this is a mule-driven irrigation device that extracts water from the well; two mules were assigned to turn this device. However, the Bedouin who were supposed to be serving the fort killed one, and ate the fodder that was reserved for the other, so that the poor beast starved to death. They then beat up the governor of the fort, because he did not have enough money in the fort's treasury to pay their allowances. The Governor of Al Medina sent one mule up to this fort so that its irrigation device would not fall idle, but this mule proved insufficient for the purpose. Last year the servants of the fort dispatched out of their allowance – the allowance money for this year – as compensation in the form of the price of the mule they had killed, so that they may continue to reside at the fort and execute their required duties honestly and in security. They also purchased another mule to replace the one that starved, this cost them 850 H, and this they submitted to the *Oda Bash* in charge of this fort.

This fort does not require much by way of restoration. Adjoining the fort is an oblong water cistern measuring 50 architectural cubits long, 35 cubits wide, and 10 deep. However, this cistern is situated in a very sandy area, so that the winds carry sand into it. This sand has filled the cistern up to half its depth, necessitating that it be cleaned of sand, and a wall one cubit high erected around the cistern to keep out any further sand from collecting in it. If this is not done, the situation will demand that the cistern be dug out every year. Likewise, the material lining the inside of the pool has been eaten away, and this needs to be fully renovated.

There is a conveniently placed well serving the local *medina*, and in addition to this there are three other wells nearby, in addition to the one in the fort.

'Abyaar Tandheef

The waystation of *'Abyaar Tandheef* is situated about 13 hours further down the road from that of *al-Nakhlatayn*. There is no fort here, but a number of wells have been dug in the sandy soil of the area; it seems likely, however, that the rainy season floods which flow through here seep away quickly into the soil. There is just one hole dug, measuring only one cubit, that purifies the water that flows through it, although this is well supplied with water.

Medina (Al Medina, The City Illuminated by the Light of God the Exulted Until the Day of the Resurrection)

This city – peace and prayers be on her most illustrious inhabitant – is 20 hours further on from *Diaar Nadheef*. No water whatsoever is available on the way, so travellers are obliged to carry whatever water they need from *Bayaar Nafheef*.

'Abyaar Ali

This waystation is situated at a journey of just two hours from *Al Baladat Al Tayyiba*. This area is pleasantly wooded, and the water supply here is plentiful.

Al Shuhada'

This waystation is situated at a journey of 14 hours further on from *Biyaar Ali*. Work is now underway to dig new wells here, on account of the fact that there are at present no wells situated on the road to this waystation. So far, workers have dug to a depth of 25 architectural cubits; however, it is expected that the water at this new well will be more pure if they dig down a further five cubits, since from what we have heard the water here is better purified at a depth of 30 cubits. Water does currently exist at this site, but this is situated at least an hour further south down the road. Thus, the *Hujjaaj* are currently experiencing considerable difficulty in obtaining water here. However, this situation can be remedied if the following measures are undertaken: due effort is expended in completing the excavation of the wells currently under construction; a mule-driven irrigation device is constructed over the new well; a square-shaped wall is built to enclose the vicinity of the well measuring 50 architectural cubits on each side, by 10 cubits high; and lastly a tower is constructed at the side of the wall from which a watchman can guard the well and the irrigation equipment. All this is to be done for the comfort and ease of the *Hujjaaj*.

Between this waystation and *Al Jadeed* is the well called Dhaat Al 'Ilm; unfortunately, the waters of this well are insufficient for the requirements of the *Hujjaaj*, so they are obliged to carry the water they require from *Biyaar Ali* all the way to *Al Jadeed*.

Notes

1   'The Tributaries of the Hajj' – possibly the place where Hajj routes conjoin for the final part of the journey through the Hijaz?

2   'The Ivory Progeny', or possibly 'Ivory Couch Grass', if /najal/ is read as /najeel/.

3   'Ghadir' can mean 'pool', 'stream', 'creek', or 'brook'; given the desert context I have translated this as 'oasis'. 'Jinniyyat' meand 'a female jinn or demon'. While this is possible, I think this is most likely a typographical error for 'Jinnat', 'Garden', which would fit better with the choice of names for the site: 'Ghadir *or* Jinnat Al Kaa'in': 'The Living Oasis' or 'The Living Garden'.

Appendix 2. The Early Islamic Lintel from Qal'at al-Dab'a

Denis Genequand

Introduction

The lintel of the gateway at Qal'at al-Dab'a is a monolith, bearing a very carefully carved decoration. It is a reused element, which raises two questions, quite apart from its artistic value: its date and its provenance. A detailed analysis of the ornamental style allows it to be assigned an early Islamic date, going back to the Umayyad period. A discussion of the possible origin of the lintel allows for the possibility that it came from Zizia, some 14 km to the north-west of Qal'at al-Dab'a. Zizia was a stop on the *Darb al-Hajj* and, before that, had been an important late Antique and early Islamic settlement. The recent discovery, in Zizia, of a fragment of a carved lintel displaying some similarities to the one at Qal'at al-Dab'a, reinforces this hypothesis regarding its origin.

The Lintel

The lintel is a rectangular monolith, slightly larger than the gate (Plates 191 and 192). Only one of its faces is carved; the others, as far as it is possible to observe, are finely dressed. The piece is made of soft, yellow limestone of local origin. This kind of limestone was widely used for carved decorations during the Roman, Byzantine and Umayyad periods in central Jordan. The carved decoration is separated horizontally in two different fields, an upper and a lower one. The first also frames the latter's sides, following a model frequently seen in door frames. It is highly probable that, on the original building, the ornament extended onto the door jambs.

Both fields are separated by a simple torus without ornament. The lower field comprises foliated scrolls; with flowers alternating with large leaves and oblique acanthus leaves terminating both ends of the field. Their oblique position is likely to mark the transition to a vertical field that was on the jamb. The foliated scrolls include four flowers of similar type, but unevenly preserved, and five leaves of three different types. The flowers have eight petals (four and four superimposed) around a central pistil

Plate 191. The lintel over the gateway of Qal'at al-Dab'a (Photo: Denis Genequand).

Plate 192. Dab'a Lintel. Detail of the right part of the lintel (Photo: Denis Genequand).

with a little hole in the middle. Leaves on the left part of the lintel are in a lateral position turned right, while those on the right of the lintel are in a frontal position turned left, with a little palmette in the middle. The central medallion is poorly preserved, but seems to bear two, smaller, tri-lobed leaves with crossing stems, turned respectively left and right.

The upper field is, itself, divided into two sub-fields by a little torus. The main one comprises a regular frieze of palmettes in a vertical position; the stems are divided in two, joining each palmette together with its neighbours. Therefore, each palmette grows out of a double stem. They comprise seven lobes: a small rounded one in the centre and six pointed ones on the sides (three on each side). The upper sub-field, poorly preserved, is a repetitive strip of small vegetal, or rounded (?) elements separated by a wavy line; it is reminiscent of a degenerated *rais-de-coeur* (lesbian kymation), or a very simplified strip of ovolos. The transition to the vertical field, here partly preserved and with similar motives, is also marked by large oblique acanthus leaves.

The moulding of the lintel is not very pronounced. Viewed in profile, the upper field is a regular ogee moulding (*talon droit*), whose relief is not very high. Down the torus, the lower field is marked by a little recess and the strip is flat.

Stylistic comparison and date

From a stylistic point of view, it is clear that this carved decoration is derived from the classical Graeco-Roman tradition, but it is, nevertheless, closely related to a whole series of ornaments found on Umayyad period buildings. Among these, one should especially mention the stone and stucco carved decorations from the Umayyad palaces such as, Qasr al-Tuba, Qasr al-Mshatta, Khirbat al-Mafjar and Qasr al-Hayr al-Gharbi, or, the Golden and Double Gates of the Haram al-Sharif in Jerusalem, which present very fine carvings and similar elements. To a lesser extent the 'Amman Citadel, Qastal and Qasr al-Muwaqqar should also be mentioned, because they present contemporary carved decorations, but the quality of the workmanship is not as good and the motives in low relief differ much more from the classical tradition. It should be noted that all these sites are situated in the area around 'Amman, in modern Jordan, with the exception of, Jerusalem, Khirbat al-Mafjar in the Jordan Valley and Qasr al-Hayr al-Gharbi in Syria. All of them present extensive stone carved decoration, except Khirbat al-Mafjar where stone and stucco are used and Qasr al-Hayr al-Gharbi where stucco is largely predominant. Finally, all of them date back to the very late 7th and first half of the 8th centuries AD.

Of course, when looking at the decoration of the lintel, one should also think about late Antique sculpture. Parallels for the different elements could also be found quite easily on 6th and 7th century AD monuments. But it will be argued, based on what is known about the regional context

in the Balqa' area between the 6th and 8th centuries AD, that an early Islamic date is much more likely.

One element indicating a rather late date is the relative flatness of the lintel and the very simple form of the profile. The moulding is not very pronounced; something much more pronounced would be expected for an Antique or late Antique carving of such quality. A good comparison is found at Qasr al-Tuba where both carved lintels (rooms B and B') are completely flat (Jaussen and Savignac 1997, pls X, XI and XVII). This unfinished structure is dated to the late Umayyad period and could have been a palace commissioned by al-Walid b. Yazid, before he was assassinated in 744 AD (al-Tabari, *Ta'rikh*, II, 1743, 1795).

The palmette strip of the upper field is a motive frequently found in both Antique and early Islamic sculpture. Nevertheless, one of the closest parallels is found on the entablature of the façade at Qasr al-Mshatta, another late Umayyad structure (Creswell 1969, I.2, fig. 456, strip h). The palmettes from Qasr al-Mshatta also have seven lobes and are connected by their stems; they only differ in having a much longer and wider central lobe than that seen at Qal'at al-Dab'a. At Qastal, another Umayyad castle, situated near Qasr al-Mshatta and only 5 km north of Zizia, a capital related to the mosque displays a similar row of seven lobed palmettes (Brünnow and Domaszewski 1905, 102, fig. 685); in this case they are not joined by their stem. At Qasr al-Hayr al-Gharbi, dated to the beginning of the reign of Hisham b. 'Abd al-Malik, a stucco frieze from the façade of the entrance structure presents a row of five lobed palmettes, similarly organized, but separated by smaller and higher ones (Schlumberger 1986, pl. 62c). At Qal'at al-Dab'a, the strip of the upper sub-field is too poorly understood to be compared.

Foliated, or vine, scrolls are also very frequent in both Antique and early Islamic sculpture. Flowers with eight petals occur frequently on the stucco decoration at Qasr al-Hayr al-Gharbi; for example on several strips on the entrance structure, where they also alternate with different kinds of leaves, or, on the parapet of the central courtyard (Schlumberger 1986, pl. 65a and b, 69a (last panel). Leaves in a frontal, or lateral position, also appear on the strips from Qasr al-Hayr al-Gharbi (Schlumberger 1986, pl. 65a and b).

Oblique acanthus leaves, separating horizontal and vertical fields, are less well documented in a similar position on early Islamic carved lintels. They appear, nevertheless, in a different way, on the upper acanthus leaf strip of the Double Gate at Jerusalem, now generally accepted as an Umayyad construction (Rosen-Ayalon 1989, 40, ill. 23). Some oblique acanthus leaves also appear on the façade at Qasr al-Mshatta, for example, at the junction of a horizontal and oblique cornice on triangle A (Brünnow and Domaszewski 1905, 150, fig. 734). On the other hand, there are many transitional oblique palmettes of carved stucco at Qasr al-Hayr al-Gharbi (Schlumberger 1986). On lintels, however, oblique acanthus leaves are extremely frequent, during the Byzantine period, in the limestone massive of northern Syria, where there are numerous examples dated to the 5th and 6th centuries AD (Naccache 1992, pl. XX.2 (Babisqa), CXIV.1 (Qalbloza), CXXXVII.2 (Baqirra), CLVIII.2 (Dayr Turmanin), CLXXVI.2 (Kafr Kila)).

In the context of the Balqa' region, motives that fully cover the support and are repetitive, are more likely to be early Islamic, than late Antique, as clearly shown by sculpture in the different Umayyad castles, such as Qasr al-Mshatta, Qasr al-Tuba, or Qastal.

Origin of the lintel: early Islamic Zizia

If an Umayyad date now seems quite sure, the provenance of the lintel still needs to be found. There is no early Islamic occupation at Qal'at al-Dab'a. This means that the piece necessarily comes from another site. The closest Umayyad site is Khan al-Zabib, situated only some 10.5 km to the south (Bujard and Genequand 2001). It was partly excavated recently and did not provide consistent carved architectural decorations. Only one piece, with a different style, was found in a secondary position (Bujard 1997, 368, fig. 30). At the end of the 19th century Tristram reported and illustrated more carved decorations, but they were rather sparse and with a very different style (Tristram 1874, 171–74, figs 13–14). Brünnow and Domaszewski's good photographs of the monuments confirm that decorations were very sparse and that most of the lintels were undecorated (Brünnow and Domaszewski 1905, 76–82, figs 657 and 660). So, it is unlikely that the lintel originated from Khan al-Zabib. At a greater distance are sites such as Qasr al-Tuba, Qasr al-Mshatta and Qastal, already mentioned in relation to the sculpture and rich in carved decorations. But, given the architectural data at hand, it is unlikely that the lintel originates from one of them. Also in the same area, is the Umayyad site of Umm al-Walid, where, despite large-scale excavations, no early Islamic carved element, other than simple capitals has been found (Bujard and Genequand 2001). This is also the case for many Byzantine sites in the area (such as, Umm al-Rasas, Jumail, or Nitl) that kept a strong occupation during the early Islamic period, or, indeed, other sites further away. Carved decoration at these sites is found mainly on church capitals and on church and house lintels, where it consists simply of crosses; only the decoration on liturgical furniture is more developed (Piccirillo and Alliata 1994, 290–317; Sodini 2003). Nevertheless, it never takes the form and development presented by the Qal'at al-Dab'a lintel. By comparison with northern Syria, or some major cities such as Jerusalem, Byzantine carved decoration in the Balqa' region is very poor and sparse, even in cities such as Madaba, 'Amman/Philadelphia, or Jarash/Gerasa. The carved lintel from Qal'at al-Dab'a makes no real sense in a late Antique regional setting. This fact reinforces the possibility of an Umayyad date, and, given the quality of the piece, the necessity to find a likely origin.

For various reasons, the only site where a provenance seems possible, given the present state of research, is Zizia (Ziza in the textual sources). During the Ottoman period, Zizia was an ancient stopover on the *Darb al-Hajj*, but it has a much more ancient history, going back to Roman times. During the Nabataean–early Roman period, there was in Zizia a temple dedicated to Zeus-Baalphogor, built by a certain Demas, son of Hillel/Ellen from 'Amman, as attested by a bilingual Nabatean and Greek inscription (Gatier 1986, 180–81, n° 154). A Doric capital found during the renovation of the mosque is another witness from this period (Genequand 2002, 140). During the late Roman period, Zizia (*Ziza*) was an important garrison, where, according to the *Notitia Dignitatum*, the *Equites Dalmatae Illyriciani* were stationed around AD 400 (*Notitia Dignitatum*, Or. 37. 16). No trace of the fort is preserved, but a very large, open-air cistern (*birka*) is still visible along the main road in the modern village. It is perhaps related to the military settlement in Zizia. A Christian officer from the garrison at Zizia, called Zeno, and his servant Zena, are said to have been decapitated in Philadelphia/'Amman during Diocletian's persecution (Piccirillo 2002, 371). In the Byzantine period, another inscription, dated AD 580, records the reconstruction, under the *dux* Flavius Paulus, of an unknown building by an *archontos* Peter, probably a local chief and a local leading citizen called Christogonos (Gatier 1986, 182–83, n° 155). A 6th century (AD 560) north-apsed church was also excavated recently (Piccirillo 2002) and late 19th century descriptions attest to the site's extension during late Antiquity, as well as the presence of several ruined churches (Tristram 1874, 182–90; Brünnow and Domaszewski 1905, 90–94). When Parker surveyed Zizia during the late 1970s, he reported only a handful of sherds from the Iron Age II, Roman, Byzantine and Mamluk periods (Parker 1986, 41).

Like many other sites in the area, Zizia kept its importance during the early Islamic period. It was one of the very first places in the area to be captured by Muslim armies at the time of the conquest, by an army led by 'Ubayd Allah (Al-Azdi, *Ta'rikh futuh al-Sham*, 29). Later on, al-Walid b. Yazid, who is also likely to be the builder of nearby Qasr al-Mshatta, resided in Zizia and is said to have built there a staging-post on the pilgrims' road, where returning pilgrims and their riding animals were supposed to be fed for a period of three days (al-Tabari, *Ta'rikh*, II, 1754). Under the Abbasid caliph, al-Ma'mun, at the time of Sa'id b. Khalid al-Faddayni's revolt, Zizia, along with a possible stronghold, was devastated by the troops of Yahya b. Salih, sent against the rebels (Ibn 'Asakir, *Ta'rikh madinat dimashq*, vol. 21, 56–57; Yakut, *Mu'jam al-buldan*, III, 854; Cobb 2001, 63).

The presence of an Umayyad construction in Zizia, whether a *qasr*, or a caravanserai, or both, seems quite clear from al-Tabari's text, but nothing has survived. Nevertheless, Tristram's and Brünnow and Domaszewski's descriptions suggest that it was still visible when they visited the ruins, in 1872 and 1897 respectively (Tristram 1874, 182–90; Brünnow and Domaszewski 1905, 90–94).

Both describe two forts, one being the Mamluk–Ottoman *Hajj* fort, which is still visible, the other one, a square, or rectangular enclosure. Tristram provides the following description of the latter: 'Near the western end (of the ruins) is a fine Saracenic building, quite perfect up to Ibrahim Pasha's time. The gateway still remains, with its richly carved façade. There are several semi-circular niches in the walls, and fragments of Cuphic inscriptions appear in many places on the courses' (Tristram 1874, 190). He also provides a drawing of part of it, while the Germans have a photograph with a similar view (Tristram 1873, 188, fig. 18; Brünnow and Domaszewski 1905, 91, fig. 672). To the north-west of this structure was a mosque that Tristram interpreted, first, as a castle or temple: 'The other castle, to the east of this, is apparently of the Roman age, and has been reduced to a ruinous state by the troops of Ibrahim Pasha. The external walls alone remain, with a conspicuous inner niche, alcoved in the south face. It looks like an old temple utilized, first as a fort, and then as a mosque. In it is a beautifully carved lintel, of very rich late Byzantine, or perhaps Persian work; and other sculptured stones are built in, as well as some fragments of Cuphic inscriptions' (Tristram 1874, 189). Brünnow and Domaszewski specify that the 'Cuphic inscriptions' are only Bedouin tribal marks and provide a good photograph of the *mihrab* (Brünnow and Domaszewski 1905, 92, fig. 673).

The short description, by Tristram, of a carved door lintel, makes it very likely that the structure is, at least in part, early Islamic. On the one hand, scholars at the beginning of the 20th century frequently described the Umayyad works at Qasr al-Mshatta, Kharana, or elsewhere, as Persian or Persianizing works. On the other hand, it has been shown above, that the late Antiquity did not produce this kind of carved element in the regional context of Zizia. It would make sense to see a mosque and a residence or caravanserai, of early Islamic date in these two structures. It is not impossible that the latter was also the Illyrian

horsemen's late Roman fort, which was modified during the Umayyad period.

During a recent survey, a fragment of a carved lintel, displaying some similarities to the one from Qal'at al-Dab'a, was discovered in Zizia (Plate 193) (Genequand 2002, 139–40). It is nowadays, in a secondary position, in the eastern half of the northern façade of the mosque, in the ancient part of the village of Zizia, to the south-east of the modern town. The fragment is incorporated into the masonry at a height of about 4 m. Of course, the motives are not the same, but there are several similarities, given the regional context, that are striking. The lintel is divided horizontally into two fields, separated by a torus. These two fields extend onto the door jambs. The moulding is not very pronounced. The upper field is a frieze of acanthus leaves, with a slightly larger one, in an oblique position at the corner in order to assure the transition to the vertical register. A smaller sub-field, almost completely destroyed, extends onto the top and side of the upper field. The lower field is a foliated scroll with vine leaves. Some parallels can be found, individually, for both motives at Qasr al-Mshatta. Despite the poorly preserved state of the piece and its almost inaccessible position, there are enough elements to consider it as having exactly the same composition as the lintel from Qal'at al-Dab'a. It only differs in the respective motives of the two fields: acanthus leaves, instead of palmettes; scrolls with only leaves, instead of flowers and leaves; and no oblique acanthus leaves on the lower field. The probability that the two lintels originate from the same structure is, therefore, quite high and since one of them has been found in Zizia itself, it strongly reinforces the proposed origin for the Qal'at al-Dab'a lintel.

Conclusion

This short study has allowed an early Islamic–Umayyad date, to be assigned to the carved lintel reused over the gateway of the Ottoman fort of Qal'at al-Dab'a and to propose a possible origin for it. If the proposed date seems quite sure, the proposed origin rests on a hypothesis based on comparison with another carved fragment, on textual sources and on ancient descriptions all concerning Zizia. It is a likely proposal that seems quite reasonable given the actual state of research in the area. It sheds some light on what was probably an important early Islamic site, that is now largely lost to archaeological research. Of course, chance, like the recent discovery of a 6th century church, will perhaps reveal more elements about Zizia in the future and will allow confirmation, or contradiction, of what has been proposed here. Nevertheless, the Umayyad date of the lintel of Qal'at al-Dab'a will remain and testifies once more to the vitality and importance of the Balqa' area during this period – an area chosen by the Umayyad Caliphs and élites to build many of their residences.

Plate 193. Fragment of a carved lintel from Zizia (Photo: Denis Genequand).

Bibliography

General

Abells, Z. (1993) *Jerusalem's Water Supply.* Asher Arbit: Jerusalem.

Abu Jaber, R.S. (1989) *Pioneers Over the Jordan; Frontier Settlement in Jordan, 1850–1914.* I.B. Tauris & Co. Ltd: London.

Adams, W.Y. (1973) J. L. Burckhardt, Ethnographer. *Ethnohistory* 20, No. 3, 213–28.

Ágoston, G. (2005) *Guns for the Sultan; Military Power and the Weapons Industry in the Ottoman Empire.* Cambridge University Press: Cambridge.

Aksoy, Ş. and Milstein, R. (2000) A collection of thirteenth-century illustrated Hajj certificates. Pp. 73–134 in İ.C. Schick (ed.), *M. Uğur Derman. 65th Birthday Festschrift.* Sabancı Üniversitesi: Istanbul.

Alexander, J. (1997) Qalat Sai, the most southerly Ottoman fortress in Africa. *Sudan and Nubia* (The Sudan Archaeological Research Society Bulletin) 1, 16–20.

Alexander, J. (1998) The forgotten Ottoman garrisons of the Nile Valley. In A. Temimi (ed.), *Architectures des demeures, inscriptions funéraires et dynamique de restauration.* Fondation pour la Recherche Scientifique et l'Information Zaghouan, Août 1998. Tunisia.

Alexander, J. (2000) The archaeology and history of the Ottoman frontier in the Middle Nile Valley 910–1233 AH/1504–1820 AD. *Adumatu* 1, 47–61.

Amiry, S. and Tamari, V. (1989) *The Palestinian Village House.* British Museum Press: London.

Andre-Salvani, B., Demange, F., Juvin, C. and al-Ghabban, A. (eds) (2010) *Roads of Arabia: Archaeology and History of the Kingdom of Saudi Arabia.* The Louvre/Somogy Editions d'Art: Paris.

'Ankawi, A. (1974) The pilgrimage to Mecca in Mamluk times. Pp. 116–70 in R.B. Serjeant and B.L. Bidwell (eds), *Arabian Studies* I. Hurst and Company: London.

al-Ansary, A.R., Abdalla, A.M., Mortel, R.T. and al-Sakkar, S. (eds) (1979) *Studies in the History of Arabia Vol. 1: Sources for the History of Arabia.* Proceedings of the First International Symposium on Studies in the History of Arabia, 23–28 April 1977, sponsored by the Department of History, Faculty of Arts, University of Riyad, Saudi Arabia. Part 2. Riyad University: Riyadh.

Anscombe, F.A. (1997) *The Ottoman Gulf: the Creation of Kuwait, Saudi Arabia and Qatar.* Columbia University Press: New York.

Auld, S. and Hillenbrand, R. (eds) (2000) *Ottoman Jerusalem, the Living City.* World of Islam Festival Trust and Scorpion Books: London.

Avissár, M. (2005) *Tel Yoqne'am. Excavations on the Acropolis.* IAA Reports, No. 25. The Israel Antiquities Authority: Jerusalem.

Ayalon, D. (1956) *Gunpowder and Firearms in the Mamluk Kingdom: A Challenge to a Mediaeval Society.* Frank Cass and Co Ltd: London (2nd edition London 1978).

Bacqué-Grammont, J.-L. and Kroel, A. (1988) *Mamlouks, Ottomans et Portugais en Mer Rouge. L'affaire de Djedda en 1517.* Institut français d'archéologie orientale: Cairo.

Bacuch, U. (1998) Charcoal Installation. *Excavations and Surveys in Israel* 17, 116.

Baedeker, K. (1876) *Palestine and Syria: handbook for travellers.* Fritz Baedeker: Leipzig and London.

Bajali, N. (n.d.) The revival of the Damascene pilgrim caravan: a student activity.

Bakhit, M.A. (1982) *The Ottoman Province of Damascus in the Sixteenth Century.* Librairie du Liban: Beirut.

Bakhit, M.A. (2007) Tabuk. *Encyclopaedia of Islam*, 2nd edn, vol. 10, 50, col. 2.

Bakhit, M.A. (2008) al-Shawbak. *Encyclopaedia of Islam*, 2nd edn, vol. 9, 373, col. 1.

Bangert, S. (2010) The archaeology of pilgrimage: Abu Mina and beyond. In D. Gwynn and S. Bangert (eds), *Religious Diversity in Late Antiquity.* Brill: Leiden.

Barbir, K.K. (1980) *Ottoman Rule in Damascus 1708–1758.* Princeton University Press: Princeton.

Barkay, G. (1986) *Ketef Hinnom. A Treasure Facing Jerusalem's Walls.* Exhibition catalogue 274. Israel Museum: Jerusalem.

Barnard, H. and Wendrich, W. (eds) (2008) *The Archaeology*

of Mobility: Old World and New World Nomadism. Cotsen Advanced Seminars 4, Cotsen Insitute of Archaeology. UCLA: Los Angeles.

Bartl, K. (2003) Clay Pipes from Ottoman Beirut. *BAAL [Bulletin d'Archéologie et d'Architecture Libanaises]* 7, 321–40.

Bell, G. (1908) *Syria the Desert and the Sown.* William Heinemann: London.

Ben-Dov, M. (1982) *The Dig at the Temple Mount.* Keter: Jerusalem (Hebrew).

Berman, A. (1991) Bonaparte's Campaign in Galilee, Survey. *Excavations and Surveys in Israel 1991* 10, 167.

Betlyon, J.W. (1986) Coins excavated between 1970 and 1983 at Tell el-Hesi. *Palestine Exploration Quarterly,* 66–69.

Bianchi, M. (1825) *Itinéraire de Constantinople à la Mecque.* Recueil des Voyages et des Memoires publies par la Societe de Geographic: Paris.

Bilge, M. (1979) Arabia in the work of Awliya Chalaby (The XVIIth century Turkish Muslim Traveller). Pp. 213–27 in al-Ansary *et al.* 1979.

Boas, A.J. (2000a) Medieval and post-medieval finds [from Horvat 'Aqav]. Pp. 211–25 in Y. Hirschfeld *et al., Ramat Hanadiv Excavations. Final Report of the 1984–1998 Seasons.* The Israel Exploration Society: Jerusalem.

Boas, A.J. (2000b) Pottery and small finds from the Late Ottoman village and the Early Zionist settlement [at Horvat 'Eleq]. Pp. 547–80 in Y. Hirschfeld *et al., Ramat Hanadiv Excavations. Final Report of the 1984–1998 Seasons.* The Israel Exploration Society: Jeruslaem.

Borstad, K. (2008) History from geography: the initial route of the Via Nova Taiana in Jordan. *Levant* 40:1, 55–70.

Bosworth, C.E. (2007) al-'Ula. *Encyclopaedia of Islam,* 2nd edn, vol. 10, 800.

Bowerstock, G.W. (1981) *Roman Arabia.* Harvard University Press: Cambridge, MA and London.

Breen, C., Forsythe, W., Smith, L. and Mallinson, M. (2011) Excavations at the Medieval Red Sea Port of Suakin. *Azania* 26, No. 2, 205–20.

Broadhurst, R.J.C. (1952) *The Travels of Ibn Jubayr.* Cape: London (reprinted Goodword books 2001).

Brown, R. (1989) Excavations in the fourteenth-century Mamluk Palace at Kerak. *Annual of the Department of Antiquities of Jordan* 33, 287–304.

Brown, R. (1991) Ceramics from the Kerak Plateau. Pp. 232–46 in Miller 1991.

Brünnow, R.E. and Domaszewski, A. v. (1905) *Die Provincia Arabia.* Karl J. Tubner: Strassbourg.

Buckingham, J.S. (1825) *Travels among the Arab tribes inhabiting the countries east of Syria and Palestine, including a journey from Nazareth to the mountains beyond the Dead Sea, and from thence through the plains of the Hauran to Bozra, Damascus, Tripoly, Lebanon, Baalbeck, and by the valley of the Orontes to Seleucia, Antioch, and Aleppo.* Longman, Hurst, Rees, Orme, Brown, & Green: London.

Bujard, J. (1997) Umm al-Walîd et Khân az-Zabîb, cinq qusûr omeyyades et leur mosquées revisités. *Annual of the Department of Antiquities of Jordan* 41, 351–74.

Bujard, J. and Geneqaund, D. (2001) Umm al-Walid et Khan az-Zabib, deux établissements omeyyades en limite du déserrt jordanien. Pp. 189–218 in B. Geyer (ed.), *Conquête de la steppe et appropriation des terres sur les marges arides du Croissant fertile.* (TMO 36). Maison de L'Orient Méditerranéen: Lyon.

Burckhardt, J.L. (1819) *Travels in Nubia.* John Murray: London.

Burckhardt, J.L. (1822) *Travels in Syria and the Holy Land.* John Murray: London (reprinted 1983 AMS Press New York).

Burckhardt, J.L. (1829) *Travels in Arabia.* Henry Colburn: London.

Burckhardt, J.L. (1830) *Arabic Proverbs, or the Manners and Customs of the Modern Egyptians.* Henry Colburn: London.

Burckhardt, J.L. (1831) *Notes on the Bedouins and the Wahabys.* Henry Colbourn and Richard Bentley: London.

Burgoyne, M. (1971) Some Mameluke doorways in the Old City of Jerusalem. *Levant* 3, 1–30.

Butler, H.C. (1907–49) *Syria: Publications of the Princeton University Archaeological Expeditions to Syria in 1904–5 and 9.* Brill: Leiden.

Candy, J. (2003) Landscape and perception. The Medieval Pilgrimage to Santiago de Compostella from an archaeological perspective. *eSharp.* Issue No. 2.

Carswell, J. (1972) China and the Near East: the recent discovery of Chinese porcelain in Syria. Pp. 20–25 in W. Watson (ed.), *The Westward Influence of the Chinese Arts from 14th to 18th century.* Percival David Foundation Colloques on Art and Archaeology in Asia 3: London.

Carswell, J. (1998) *Iznik Pottery.* British Museum: London.

Cohen, A. (1989) The walls of Jerusalem. Pp. 466–77 in C.E. Bosworth *et al.* (eds), *The Islamic World from Classical to Modern Times. Essays in Honour of Bernard Lewis.* Darwin Press: Princeton.

Conder, C.R. and Kitchener, H.H. (1884) *Survey of Western Palestine.* Vol. 3. Palestine Exploration Fund: London.

Contadini, A. (1995) Islamic ivory chess pieces, draughtsmen and dice. Pp. 111–54 in J. Allan (ed.), *Oxford Studies in Islamic Art X: Islamic Art in the Ashmolean Museum, Part One.* Oxford University Press: Oxford.

Creswell, K.A.C. (1969) *Early Muslim Architecture: Umayyads, Early Abbasids and Tulunids.* 2 vols. (3 Parts). Oxford University Press: Oxford.

al-Dayel, K. and al-Helwa, S. (1978) Preliminary report on the second phase of the Darb Zubayda reconnaissance 1397/1977. *Atlal* 2, 51–64.

De Meulemeester, J. (2008) Rural settlement from the Byzantine to the Mamluk times at Lehun (District of Madaba, Jordan). Pp. 159–68 in K. D'Hulster and J. Van Steenbergen (eds), *Continuity and Change in the Realms of Islam; Studies in Honour of Urbain Vermeulen.* Orientalia Lovaniensa Analecta 171. Peeters: Leuven.

De Meulemeester, J. and Pringle, R.D. (2000) *The Aqaba Castle Project Report.* Ministiere de la Region Wallone: Cardiff-Namur.

Dewulf, J. and Pringle, D. (forthcoming) Glass. *Excavations at 'Aqaba Castle. Archaeological Excavations and Survey 2000–2003.*

Doughty, C.M. (1926) *Travels in Arabia Deserta.* Jonathan Cape Ltd & The Medici Society: London (reprint; two volumes in one).

Doughty, C.M. (1979) *Travels in Arabia Deserta.* Vol. 1 (2 vols). Clarendon Press: Cambridge (first published in 1888 and reprinted by Dover Books 1979).

Eakins, J.K. (1993) *Tell el-Hesi. The Muslim Cemetery in Fields V and VI/IX (Stratum II).* The Joint Archaeological Expedition to Tell el-Hesi, vol. 5. Eisenbrauns: Winona Lake.

Edelstein, G. and Avissar, M. (1997) A sounding in Old Acre.

'Atiqot 31, *Excavation Reports and Historical Studies*, 129–36.

Edwards, C., Livingstone, K., Boyd, D. and Petersen, A. (1993) Dayr Hanna: an eighteenth century fortified village in Galilee. *Levant* 25, 63–92.

Elgood, R. (1995) *Firearms of the Islamic World in the Tareq Rajeb Museum, Kuwait.* I.B. Tauris: London.

Elisséeff, N. (1965) Ma'an. *Encyclopaedia of Islam*, 2nd edn, vol. 5, 897–98.

Elisséeff, N. and el-Hakim, R. (1981) *Mission Soudano Française dans la Province de la Mer Rouge (Soudan).* Maison de l'Orient Méditerranéen: Lyon.

Esin, E. (1986) The renovations effected, in the Ka'bah mosque, by the Ottoman Sultan Selim II (H.974–82/1566–74). Pp. 225–32 in A. Temimi (ed.), *La vie économique des provinces arabes et leurs sources documentaries à l'époque ottoman.* Tome III. Publications du Centre d'Etudes et de Recherches Ottomanes, Morisques, de Documentation et d'Information: Zaghouan.

Estabalet, C. and Pascual, J.-P. (1998) *L'ultime voyage pour La Mekke. Les inventraires après décès des pèlerins morts à Damas vers 1700.* Institut français de Damas: Damascus.

al-Faqeer, B.A. (2009) *Nature and Antiquities in al-'Ula Province/ Saudi Arabia.* Badr Bin Adel al-Faqeer: Riyadh.

Farès-Drappeau, S. (2004) RR. PP. A. Jaussen et R. Savignac – Mission archéologique en Arabie. Pp. 325–30 in *Revue des mondes musulmans et de la Méditerranée* [en ligne], n°89–90 – *Figures mythiques des mondes musulmans*, juillet 2000. http://remmm.revues.org/document2681.html

Farooqi, N.R. (1989) *Mughal Ottoman Relations (A Study of Political and Diplomatic Relations between Mughal India and the Ottoman Empire 1556–1748).* Idarah-i Adabiyat-i Delli: Delhi.

Faroqhi, S. (1988) Ottoman documents concerning the Hajj during the sixteenth and seventeenth centuries. Pp. 151–63 in A. Temimi (ed.) *La vie sociale dans les provinces arabes à l'époque ottoman.* Tome III. Publications du Centre d'Etudes et de Recherches Ottomanes, Morisques, de Documentation et d'Information: Zaghouan

Faroqhi, S. (1994) *Pilgrims and Sultans; The Hajj under the Ottomans 1517–1683.* I.B. Tauris: London.

Faroqhi, S. (2000) *Subjects of the Sultan. Culture and Daily Life in the Ottoman Empire.* I.B. Tauris: London/New York.

Ficalho, C. de (1898) *Viagens de Pedro de Covilham.* A.M. Pereira: Lisbon.

Field, H. with contributions by E. Andrav, D. Garod and E. Schroeder (1960) *North Arabian Desert Archaeological Survey, 1925–50.* Papers of the Peabody Museum of Archaeology and Ethnology, Harvard University, Vol. 45, No. 2: Cambridge MA.

Findlater, G. (2002) Limes Arabicus, via militaris and resources control in southern Jordan. Pp. 137–49 in P. Freeman, J. Bennet, Z.T. Fiema and B. Hoffman (eds), *Limes XVIII: Proceedings of the XVIIIth International Congress of Roman Frontier Studies held in 'Amman Jordan (September 2000).* Vol.1. BAR International Series 1084(I): Oxford.

Finkel, C. (2005) *Osman's Dream: The History of the Ottoman Empire.* John Murray: London.

Finkel, C., Bilyayeva, S., Haddlesey, R., Mathieu, J. and Ostapchuk, V. (2007) Historical-archaeological investigation of Akkerman fortress, Ukraine 2007. *Anatolian Archaeology* 13, 11–14.

Foote, R.M. (1999) Frescoes and carved ivory from the Abbasid family homestead at Humeima. *Journal of Roman Archaeology* 12, 423–28.

Francis Jnr., P. (1982) *Glass Beads of India.* The World of Beads Monograph Series 7. Lapis Route Books: Lake Placid.

Francis Jnr., P. (1999) *Beads of the World.* Schiffer: Atglen PA.

Franzke, J. (2003) *Bagdad- und Hedjazbahn: Deutsche Eisenbahngeschichte im Vorderen Orient.* DB Museum: Nürnberg.

Frenkel, Y. (1996) Roads and stations in southern Bilâd al-Shâm in the 7th–8th centuries. *Aram* 8, 1 and 2, 177–88.

Gagos, T. and Frösén, J. (1998) Petra Papyri. *ADAJ* 42, 473–81.

Garlake, P. (1978) An encampment of the seventeenth to nineteenth centuries on Ras Abruk, Site 5. Pp. 164–71 in B. de Cardi (ed.), *Qatar Archaeological Report, Excavations 1973.* Qatar National Museum and Oxford University Press: London.

Gatier, P.-L. (1986) *Inscriptions de la Jordanie.* T. 2, Région centrale (Amman – Hesban – Madaba – Main – Dhiban). IGLS XXI (BAH, T. CXIV). Geuthner: Paris.

Gaulmier, J. (1936) Note sur la fabrication du verre a Armanaz. *Bulletin d'Etudes Orientales (Institut Français de Damas)* 6, 53–59, pls VIII–IX.

Genequand, D. (2002) Projet 'Implantations umayyades de Syrie et de Jordanie' Rapport sur une campagne de prospection et reconniassance (2001). *SLSA-Jahresbericht* 2001, 131–61.

Genequand, D. (2003) Ma'an, an early Islamic settlement in southern Jordan: preliminary report on a survey in 2002. *Annual of the Department of Antiquities of Jordan* 47, 25–35.

Ghabbani, A. (1993, I) *Northwestern Saudi Arabia, Part I, Studies in the History and Archaeology.* Riad (Arabic).

Ghabbani, A. (1993, II) *Northwestern Saudi Arabia, Part II, Islamic Archaeology of North Western Saudi Arabia. An Introduction.* Riad (Arabic).

Ghabbani, A. (1998) *Ottoman inscriptions on the monuments in Northwestern Saudi Arabia situated on the Syrian and Egyptian (Pilgrimage) route.* Pp. 201–42. Actes du IIéme Congres du Corpus d'Archeologie Ottomane dans le Monde sur: Architecture des demeures, Inscriptions funéraires et dynamique de restauration, Zaghouan. Archeologie Ottomane II: Zaghouan.

Gibb, H.A.R. (ed.) (1958) *Travels of Ibn Battuta.* Vol. 1. Hakluyt Society, Cambridge University Press: Cambridge.

Gilmore, M., al-Hiwah, S. and Resseeni, I. (1982) Preliminary report on the northwestern and northern regions survey. *Atlal* 6, 10–11, 19 and 20.

Glidden, H.W. (1952) The Mamluk origin of the fortified Khan at al-'Aqabah, Jordan. Pp. 116–18 in G.C. Miles (ed.), *Archaeologica Orientalia: In Memoriam Ernst Herzfeld.* Augustin: New York.

Glueck, N. (1951) Explorations in Eastern Palestine, IV. *Annual of the American Schools of Oriental Research*, Nos 25–28. ASOR: New Haven.

Godwin, F. and Toulson, S. (1977) *The Drovers Roads of Wales.* Wildwood House: London.

Goodwin, G. (1978) The Tekke of Süleyman I Damascus. *Palestine Exploration Quaterly* 110, 127–30.

Goodwin, G. (1987) *A History of Ottoman Architecture.* Thames and Hudson: London.

Graf, D. (1997) The *Via Militaris* in Arabia. *DOP* 51, 271–81.

Grant, C.P. (1937) *The Syrian Desert; Caravans, Travel and Exploration*. Kegan Paul: London, New York, Bahrain (reprinted 2003).

Gray Hill, S. (1897) A Journey to Petra, 1896. *PEQ* 35–44.

Grehan, J. (2007) *Everyday Life and Consumer Culture in 18th-century Damascus*. University of Washington Press: Seattle/London.

Grey, A. (1994) Pottery of the later periods from Tell Jezreel: an interim report. *Levant* 26, 51–62.

Grey, A. (2000a) The glass. Pp. 127–30 in R.P. Harper and D. Pringle, *et al.*, *Belmont Castle. The Excavation of a Crusader Stronghold in the Kingdom of Jerusalem*. Oxford University Press on behalf of the Council for British Research in the Levant: Oxford.

Grey, A. (2000b) Miscellaneous objects of stone, bone and terracotta. Pp. 139–45 in R.P. Harper and D. Pringle, *et al.*, *Belmont Castle. The Excavation of a Crusader Stronghold in the Kingdom of Jerusalem*. Oxford University Press on behalf of the Council for British Research in the Levant: Oxford.

Grey, A. (forthcoming) Classical to Ottoman Period Pottery from Zarin. In C. Whiting and B. Finlayson (eds), *Excavations at Tel Jezreel 1990–1996*. CBRL Monographs in Archaeology. Oxbow: Oxford.

Groom, N.St. (1981) *Frankincense and Myrrh*. Longman: London.

Groom, N.St. (1983) *A Dictionary of Arabic Topography and Place Names: transliterated Arabic-English dictionary with an Arabic glossary of topographical words and place names*. Longman: London.

Guérin, M.V. (1875) *Description géographique, historique et archéologique de la Palestine. Vols 1–2 Judée*. Société Géographique: Paris.

Guthrie, S. (1995) *Arab Life in the Middle Ages: an Illustrated Study*. Saqi Books: London.

Haarmann, U. (1979) Murtada b. Ali b. 'Alawan's journey through Arabia in 1121/1709. Pp. 247–51 in al-Ansary *et al.* 1979.

Haider, E. and Ridovics, A. (eds) (2000) *The History of the Hungarian pipemakers' craft. Hungarian history through the pipemakers' art*. Hungarian National Museum & the Balatoni Museum: Budapest.

Harff, A. von (1946) *The Pilgrimage of Arnold von Harff, Knight...in the years 1496–99*. Ed. and trans. M. Letts. Hakluyt Society: London.

Hartmann, R. (1910) Die Straße von Damascus nach Kairo. *Zeitschrift der Deuthschen Morgenlandischen Gesellschaft* 64, 665–702.

Hattox, R. (1985) *Coffee and coffeehouses: the origins of a social beverage in the Medieval Near East*. University of Washington Press: Seattle and London.

Hawari, M., Auld, H. and Hudson, J. (2000) Qalat al-Burak. A fort of the Ottoman Period South of Bethlehem. *Levant* 32, 101–20.

Hayes, J.W. (1992) *Excavations at Saraçhane in Istanbul. Vol. 2. The Pottery*. Princeton University Press: Princeton.

Henein, N.H. and Gout, J.-F. (1974) *Le Verre Soufflé en Egypte*. L'Institut français d'archéologie orientale: Cairo.

Henlein, P.C. (1954) Cattle driving from the Ohio Country, 1800–1850. *Agricultural History* 28 No. 2, 83–95.

Hense, M. (2007) Metal Finds. Pp. 248–56 in Le Quesne 2007.

Hess, A.C. (1974) Piri Reis and the Ottoman Response to the Voyages of Discovery. *Terrae Incognitae* 6, 19–37.

Heyd, U. (1960) *Ottoman Documents on Palestine*. Oxford University Press: Oxford.

Hogarth, D. (1905) *The Penetration of Arabia; a Record of Western Knowledge Concerning the Arabian Peninsula* pub. Alston Rivers: London.

Hogarth, D. (1929) *The Life of Charles M. Doughty*. Garden City: New York.

Huber, C. (1891) *Journal d'un Voyage en Arabie (1883–4)*. Publie par la Société Asiatique et la Société de Géographie. Imprimerie National: Paris

Hütteroth, W. and Abdulfattah, K. (1977) *Historical Geography of Palestine, Transjordan and southern Syria in the late 16th century*. Frakische Geographische: Erlangen.

Insoll, T. (1999) *The Archaeology of Islam*. Blackwell: Oxford.

Insoll, T. (2001) *Archaeology and World Religion*. Routledge: London.

Insoll, T. (2007) *Lines: a Brief History*. Routledge: London.

Issawi, C. (1988) *The Fertile Crescent 1800–1914; A Documentary History*. Oxford University Press: Oxford.

al-Jasir, H. (1969) *Fi shamal gharb al-Jazira*. Dar al-Yamama: Riyadh.

Jaussen, R.R. and Savignac, P.P. (1922 [1997]) *Mission Archéologique en Arabie (Mars-Mai 1907) de Jérusalem au Hedjaz Médain-Saleh*. Vol. 1 (3 vols). Ernst Leroux: Paris [New Edition Institute Français d'Archéologie Orientale Le Caire 1997].

Johns, J. (1950) The Citadel of Jerusalem: a summary of work since 1934. *QDAP* 14, 121–90, pls 18–28.

Jomier, J.J. (1953) *Le Mahmal et la caravane égyptinne des pelerins de la Mekke*. Institute française d'archéologie orinetale: Cairo.

Kafescioğlu, C. (1999) 'In the image of Rūm': Ottoman architectural patronage in sixteenth century Aleppo and Damascus. *Muqarnas* 16, 70–96.

Kawatoko, M. (1995) *Al-Tur, a Port City Site on the Sinai Peninsula: the 11th Expedition in 1994 (a Summary Report)*. The Committee for Egyptian Islamic Archaeology, the Middle Eastern Culture Center: Japan.

Kawatoko, M. (1996) *Al-Tur, a Port City Site on the Sinai Peninsula: the 12th Expedition in 1995 (a Summary Report)*. The Committee for Egyptian Islamic Archaeology, the Middle Eastern Culture Center: Japan.

Kawatoko, M. (1998) *Al-Tur, a Port City Site on the Sinai Peninsula: the 13th Expedition in 1996 (a Summary Report)*. The Committee for Egyptian Islamic Archaeology, the Middle Eastern Culture Center: Japan.

Keall, E.J. (1992) Smokers' pipes and the fine pottery tradition of Hays. *Proceedings of the Seminar for Arabian Studies* 22, 29–39.

Kempinski, A. and Niemeier, W. (1994) *Excavations at Kabri, Preliminary Report of the 1992–1993 Seasons, 7–8*. Tel Aviv.

Kennedy, D. (1992) The Roman frontiers in Arabia (Jordanian Sector). *Journal of Roman Archaeology* 5, 473–89.

Kennedy, D. (1997) Roman roads and routes in north-east Jordan. *Levant* 29, 71–93.

Kennedy, D. (2000) *The Roman Army in Jordan*. Council for British Research in the Levant, British Academy: London.

Kennedy, D. and Petersen, A.D. (2004) Guardians of the Pilgrims Wells; Damascus to 'Aqaba. *Saudi Aramco World* 55 No. 1, 12–19.

Kennedy Cooke, B. (1933) The Red Sea Coast in 1540. *Sudan Notes and Records* 16, 151–59.

Keppel, G. (1827) *Personal narrative of a journey from India to England in the year 1824.* Henry Colburn: London.

Khammash, A. (1986) *Notes on the Village Architecture of Jordan.* University Art Museum, University of Southwestern Louisiana: Louisiana.

Kiel, M. (2001) The Caravanseray and Civic Centre of Defterdar Murad Çelebi in Ma'arrat an-Nu'man and the Külliye of Yemen Fatih Sinan Pasha in Sa'sa. Pp. 103–11 in N. Akin, A. Batur and S. Batur (eds), *7 Centuries of Ottoman Architecture 'A Supra National Heritage'.* Papers presented to the international congress which took place at Istanbul Teknik University Taşkişla Campus on 25/26/27 November 1999. Published for Istanbul Chamber of Architects Metropolitan Istanbul Branch by Yem Yayin: Istanbul.

King, G. (1998) *The Traditional Architecture of Saudi Arabia.* I.B. Taurus: London.

Kirkbride, A. (1948) Shebib's Wall in Transjordan. *Antiquity* 22 No. 87, September 1948, 151–54.

Knudstad, J. (1977) The Darb Zubayda Project: 1396/1976. *Atlal* 1, 41–68.

Kondorosy, S. (2007) Cseréppipák az Esztergomi Várból [Clay pipes from Esztergom Castle]. *Communicationes Archaeologicae Hungariae* 305–30.

Kondorosy, S. (2008) A szegedi vár pipái I [The pipes of Szeged Castle]. *Néprajzi Tanulmányok, Studia Ethnographica* [Szeged] 6, 331–64.

Kortepeter, C.M. (1979) A source for the history of Ottoman-Hijaz relations: the Seyahatname of Awliya Chaalaby and the Rebellion of Sharif Sa'ad b. Zayd in the years 1671–1672/1081–1082. Pp. 229–46 in al-Ansary *et al.* 1979.

Koucky, F. (1987) Survey of the *Limes* zone. Pp. 41–105 in Parker 1987.

Kritzeck, J. (ed.) (1964) *Anthology of Islamic Literature. From the rise of Islam to modern times.* Pelican Books: London (reprint).

Lancaster, W. and Lancaster, F. (1990) Modern ar-Risha: A Permanent Address. Pp. 67–70 in S. Helms, *Early Islamic Architecture of the Desert.* Edinburgh University Press: Edinburgh.

Lawrence, T.E. (1926) *Revolt in the Desert.* Garden City: New York.

Lawrence, T.E. (1969) *Seven Pillars of Wisdom.* Penguin Modern Classics: Harmondsworth.

Lawrie, W. (2005) The coverings of the two Holy Mosques. *Canvas: Art and Culture from the Middle East and the Arab World*, vol. 1, issue 5, 110–12 and 127.

Lee, M., Raso, C. and Hillenbrand, R. (1992) Mamluk caravanserai in Galilee. *Levant* 24, 55–94.

Leiser, G. Lav. (1977) The Crusader raid in the Red Sea in 587/1182–3. *Journal of the Maerican Research Centre in Egypt*, 14, 87–100.

Le Quesne, C. (2004) Quseir Fort and the archaeology of the Hajj. Pp. 145–56 in D. Kennet and S. Simpson (eds), *Trade and Travel in the Red Sea Region; Proceedings of the Red Sea Project I.* Society for Arabian Studies Monographs No. 2. BAR International Series 1269: Oxford.

Le Quesne, C. (2007) *Quseir. An Ottoman and Napoleonic fortress on the Red Sea coast of Egypt.* American Research Center in Egypt, Conservation Series 2. American University in Cairo: Cairo.

Levtzion, N. and Hopkins, J.F.P. (1981) *Corpus of Early Arabic Sources for West African History.* Fontes Historiae Africanae: Series Arabica IV. Cambridge University Press: Cambridge.

Lewis, N. (1987) *Nomads and Settlers in Syria and Jordan, 1800–1980.* Cambridge University Press: Cambridge.

MacDonald, B., Rollefson, G.O., Banning, E.B., Byrd, B.F. and D'Annibale, C. (1983) Wadi al-Hasa Survey. *Annual of the Department of Antiquites of Jordan*, 322 and pl. 72 no. 2.

McCorriston, J. (2011) *Pilgrimage and Household in the Ancient Near East.* Cambridge University Press: Cambridge.

McQuitty, A. (2001) The Ottoman Period. Pp. 561–93 in B. MacDonald, R. Adams and P. Bienkowski (eds), *The Archaeology of Jordan.* Sheffield Academic Press: Sheffield.

Majali, R. and Mas'ad, A.-R. (1987) Trade and trade routes in Jordan in the Mamluke era (AD 1250–1516). Pp. 311–16 in A. Hadidi (ed.), *Studies in the History and Archaeology of Jordan* III. Department of Antiquities: Amman.

Mandaville, J.P. (1970) The Ottoman Province of al-Hasa in the sixteenth and seventeenth centuries. *Journal of the American Oriental Society* 90, 486–513.

Marsigli, L.F. (1732) *Stato Militare dell' Imperio Ottomano.* 2 vols. The Hague.

Mason, R. and Milwright, M. (1998) Petrography of Middle Islamic Pottery at Karak. *Levant* 30, 175–94.

Mazhfar, H. (2006) Al-Mabiya: the forgotten city. *Al-Sharq al-Awsat* 03.05.2006.

Mehmed Edib ibn Mehmed Derviş (1825) *Menasik-I hacc-i şerif.* Istanbul, AH 1232'1816–1817. Translated by M. Bianchi. *Itinéraire de Constantinople à la Mecque.* Paris.

Meinecke, M. (1992) *Die Mamlukische Architektur in Ägypten und Syrien (648/1250 bis 923/1517).* I–II. Verlag J.J. Augustin: Glückstadt.

Meinecke, M. (1996) *Patterns of Stylistic Changes in Islamic Architecture; local traditions versus migrating artists.* New York University Press: New York.

Merril, S. (1883) *East of the Jordan: a Report of Travel and Observation in Countries of Moab, Gilead and Bashan.* Darf: London (reprinted 1986).

Merril, S. (1908) *Ancient Jerusalem.* Flemming Revel: New York.

Meyer, C. (1992) *Glass from Quseir al-Qadim and the Indian Ocean trade.* The Oriental Institute of the University of Chicago; Studies in Ancient Oriental Civilization No. 53: Chicago.

Miller, J. M. (ed.) (1991) *Archaeological Survey of the Kerak Plateau.* American Schools of Oriental Research 1. Scholars Press: Atlanta, Georgia.

Milstein, R. (2001) Kitab Shawq Nama, an illustrated tour of Holy Arabia. *Jerusalem Studies of Arabic and Islam* 25, 275–345.

Milwright, M. (1999) Trade and Patronage in Middle Islamic Jordan. The Ceramics of Karak Castle. Unpublished PhD thesis, 2 vols. Oxford University.

Milwright, M. (2000) Pottery of Bilad al-Sham in the Ottoman Period: a review of the published archaeological evidence. *Levant* 32, 189–208.

Milwright, M. (2008) *The Fortress of the Raven: Karak in the*

Middle Islamic Period (1100–1600). Islamic History and Civilization. Studies and Texts 72. E.J. Brill: Leiden.

Minorsky, V. (1958) *The Chester Beatty Library: a catalogue of the Turkish manuscripts and miniatures*. Hodges Figgis and Co.: Dublin.

Miquel, A. (2008) Ibn Battuta. *Encyclopaedia of Islam*, 2nd edn, vol. 3, 735–36.

Monod, T. (1978) Sur un site a bracelets de verre des environs d'Aden. *Raydan* 1, 111–24.

Morgan, C. and al-Helwa, S. (1981) Preliminary report on the fifth phase of the Darb Zubayda reconnaissance 1400–1980. *Atlal* 5, 85–108.

Moritz, B. (1908) Ausflüge in der Arabia Petraea. *Mélange de la Faculté Orientale de Beyrouth* 3, 387–436.

Mughal, M.Y. (1969) The expedition of Suleyman Pasha al-Khadim to India (1538). *Journal of the Regional Cultural Institute, Tehran* 2, 146–51.

al-Mughannam, A., al-Helwa, S. and Mursi, J. (1983) Catalogue of stations on the Egyptian (coastal) and Syrian (inland) pilgrim routes. 1403 AH, 1983 AD. Part II. Feneral Survey Reports. *Atlal* 7, 42–75.

Munsell (1994) *Munsell Soil Color Charts*. Rev. edn Macbeth Division of Kollmorgen, New Windsor: NewYork.

Muqari, A. (1996) 'Akko, the Old City. *Excavations and Surveys in Israel* 15, 124–25.

Musil, A. (1907) *Kuesjr 'Amra*. 2 vols. Kaiserliche Akademie der Wissenschaften: Vienna.

Musil, A. (1926) *The Northern Heğâz*. American Geographical Society, Oriental Explorations and Studies, No. 1: New York.

Naccache, A. (1992) *Le décor des églises de village d'Antiochène du IVe au VIIe siècle*. 2 vols (BAH, T. CXLIV). Geuthner: Paris.

Nakhjavani, B. (2000) *The Saddlebag*. Bloomsbury: London.

al-Nasif, 'A.A. (1988/1408) *Al-'Ula. An historical and archaeological survey with special reference to its irrigation system*. King Saud University: Riyadh.

Nicolle, D. and McBride, A. (1983) *Armies of the Ottoman Turks; 1300–1774*. Men at Arms 140. Osprey Books: Oxford.

Northedge, A. *et al.* (1992) *Studies on Roman and Islamic 'Amman*. Vol. 1, History, Site and Architecture. British Academy Monographs in Archaeology. Oxford University Press: Oxford.

Ochsenwald, W. (1980) *The Hijaz Railroad*. University Press of Virginia: Charlottesville.

Oleson, J.P. (2001) King, Emperor, Priest, and Caliph: cultural change at Hawara (Ancient al-Humayma) in the first millennium AD. Pp. 569–80 in *Studies in the History and Archaeology of Jordan* VII. Department of Antiquities: Amman.

Oleson, J.P., Foote, R., 'Amr, K., Reeves, B., de Bruijn, E. and Schick, R. (1999) Preliminary report of the al-Humayma Excavation Project, 1995, 1996, 1998. *Annual of the Department of Antiquities of Jordan* 43, 411–50.

Palumbo, G., Munzi, M., Collins, S., Hourani, F., Peruzzetto, A. and Wilson, M.D. (1996) The Wadi az-Zarqa/Wadi al-Dulayl Excavations and Survey Project. Report on the October–November 1993 fieldwork season. *Annual of the Department of Antiquities of Jordan* 40, 375–427.

Parker, S.T. (1986) *Romans and Saracens: a history of the Arabian Frontier*. ASOR Dissertation Series 6. Eisenbrauns: Winnona IN.

Parker, S.T. (ed.) (1987) *The Roman Frontier in Central Jordan: Interim Report on the Limes Arabicus Project, 1980–1985*. 2 vols. BAR International Series 340: Oxford.

Parker, S.T. (1998) The later Castellum. Pp. 215–18 in B. de Vries, *Umm al-Jimal: a frontier town and its landscape in northern Jordan*.

Paul, A. (1955) Aidhab: a medieval Red Sea port. *Sudan Notes and Records* 36, 64–70.

Peacock, A.C.S. (ed.) (2009) *The Frontiers of the Ottoman World*. Proceedings of the British Academy 156. Oxford University Press: Oxford.

Peake Pasha, F. (1958) *A History of Jordan and its Tribes*. Coral Gables: Miami.

Pearson, M.N. (1995) *Pilgrimage to Mecca: the Indian Experience 1500–1800*. Markus Wiener Publishers: Princeton.

Peeters, F.E. (1994) *The Hajj: the Muslim Pilgrimage to Mecca and the Holy Places*. Princeton University Press: Princeton.

Pelling, R. (2007) Plant Remains. Pp. 270–85 in Le Quesne 2007.

Petersen, A.D. (1986) Early Ottoman Forts on the Hajj Route in Jordan. Unpublished M.Phil. thesis. Oxford University.

Petersen, A.D. (1989) Early Ottoman Forts on the Darb al-Hajj. *Levant* 21, 97–118.

Petersen, A.D. (1991) Two forts on the Medieval Hajj route in Jordan. *ADAJ* 35, 347–59.

Petersen, A.D. (1994) The archaeology of the Syrian and Iraqi Hajj routes. *World Archaeology*, 47–56.

Petersen, A.D. (1995) The fortification of the Pilgrimage Route during the first three centuries of Ottoman Rule (1516–1757). Pp. 299–305 in K. 'Amr, F. Zayadine and M. Zaghoul (eds), *Studies in the Archaeology of Jordan*, vol. 5. Department of Antiquities: Amman.

Petersen, A.D. with Appendix by T. Padgett (1998) Qal'at Ras al-'Ayn: a sixteenth century Ottoman Fortress. *Levant* 30, 97–112.

Petersen, A.D. (1999) The Archaeology of Muslim Pilgrimage and Shrines in Palestine. Pp. 116–27 in T. Insoll (ed.), *Case Studies in Archaeology and World Religion*. BAR International Series 755: Oxford.

Petersen, A.D. (2000) Review of *Le Midan*, Roujon *et al*. *Palestine Exploration Quarterly*, 85–86.

Petersen, A.D. (2001) Ottoman Hajj Forts. Pp. 685–91 in B. MacDonald, R. Adams and P. Bienkowski (eds), *The Archaeology of Jordan*. Sheffield Academic Press: Sheffield.

Petersen, A.D. (2003) Excavating a sixteenth century Turkish fortress in southern Jordan. *CBRL Newsletter*, 15–16.

Petersen, A.D. (2005) *The Archaeology of Towns in Muslim Palestine*. BAR International Series 1381. Archaeopress: Oxford.

Petersen, A.D. (2007) Mamluk new towns in Palestine. Pp. 497–510 in U. Vermeulen and K. D'Hulster (eds), *Egypt and Syria in the Fatimid, Ayyubid and Mamluk Eras*. V. Orientalia Lovaniensa Analecta 171. Peeters: Leuven.

Petersen, A.D. (2008a) The Medieval Hajj Route Through Syria and Jordan. In K. D'Hustler and A. van Tongerloo (eds), *Festschrift Professor Urban Vermeulen; Fatimid, Ayyubid and Mamluk Studies*. Peeters: Leuven.

Petersen, A.D. (2008b) The Ottoman Hajj route in Jordan: motivation and ideology. Pp. 31–50 in *Bulletin d'études orientales Supplément* 57 (March), *Le pouvoir lâge des sultanats dans le Bilad al-Sham*. Proceedings of a seminar held at IFPO–ACOR, Amman, 15–16 mai 2005.

Petersen, A.D. (2008c) The Turkish Conquest of Arabia. In Peacock 2009.

Petersen, A.D. (2009) Medieval bridges of Palestine. Pp. 289–302 in U. Vermeulen and K. D'Hulster (eds), *Egypt and Syria in the Fatimid, Ayyubid and Mamluk Eras*. VI. Orientalia Lovaniensa Analecta, Peeters: Leuven.

Petersen, A.D. (2011) Islam. Chapter 60 in T. Insoll (ed.), *The Oxford Handbook of the Archaeology of Ritual and Religion*. Oxford University Press: Oxford.

Petersen, A.D. (2012) Ottoman Syria. In J. Tubb (ed.), *Syria: Birthplace of Culture*. Stacey International: London.

Petersen, A.D., Brun, P. and Shurma, A. (2003) Excavations and Survey at Qal'at 'Unaiza in Jordan. *Levant* 35.

Piccirillo, M. (2002) La chiesa del vescovo Giovanni a Zizia. *Liber Annuus* 52, 367–84.

Pierard, P. and Legros, P. (1997) *Off Road in the Hejaz*. Arabian Heritage Guides, Motivate Publishing: London, Dubai, Abu Dhabi.

Philby, H.St.J. (1957) *The Land of Midian*. Ernest Beim: London.

Pringle, R.D. (1986) *The Red Tower (al-Burj al-Ahmar) Settlement in the Plain of Sharon at the Time of the Crusaders and Mamluks*. British School of Archaeology in Jerusalem: London.

Pringle, R.D. (1987) The planning of some pilgrimage churches in Crusader Palestine. *World Archaeology* 18.3, 341–62.

Pringle, R.D. (1997) *Secular Buildings in the Crusader Kingdom of Jeruslaem. An Archaeological Gazetteer*. Cambridge University Press: Cambridge.

Pringle, R.D. (2008) The Castle of al-'Aqaba in the Ottoman Period. In Peacock 2009.

Rafeq, A.K. (1966) *The Province of Damascus, 1723–1783*. Khayats: Beirut.

Rafeq, A.K. (1976) The law-court registers of Damascus, with special reference to craft corporations during the first half of the eighteenth century. In J. Berque and D. Chevalier (eds), *Les Arabes par leurs archives (VIEe–XXe siècles)*. CNRS: Paris.

Rafeq, A.K. (1987) New light on the transportation of the Damascene pilgrimage during the Ottoman period. Pp. 127–36 in R. Olson (ed.), *A Festshrift in Honor of Wadie Jweideh*. Amana Books: Brattleboro.

Ragette, F. (1980) *Architecture in Lebanon: the Lebanese house during the 18th to 19th centuries*. Caravan Books: New York.

al-Rashid, S. (1978) Darb Zubayda in the Abbasid period: Historical and archaeological aspects. *Proceedings of the Seminar for Arabian Studies* 8, 33–45.

al-Rashid, S. (1979) Ancient water tanks on the Haj Route from Iraq to Mecca and their parallels in other Arab Countries. *Atlal* 3, 55–62.

al-Rashid, S. (1980) *Darb Zubayda. The Pilgrim Road from Kufa to Mecca*. Riyadh University Press: Riyadh.

al-Rashid, S. (1986) *al-Rabadhah: Portrait of early Islamic civilization in Saudi Arabia*. King Saud University Press: Riyadh.

al-Rashid, S. and Young, M.J.L. (2011) Darb Zubayda. *Encyclopaedia of Islam*, 2nd edn, vol. 12, 198.

Redhouse, J. (1968) *Turkish/Ottoman-English Dictionary*. Revised and supplemented by editorial committee. Redhouse Yayinevi: İstanbul.

Renan, E. (1891) *Documents Épigraphique recueillis dans la Nord del'Arabie par M. Doughty*. Imprimerie Nationale: Paris.

Robinson, R.C.W. (1983) Clay tobacco pipes from the Kerameikos. *Mitteilungen des Deutschen Archäologischen Instituts (Athenische Abteilung)* 98, 265–85, pls 52–56.

Rogan, E.L. (1999) *Frontiers of the State in the Late Ottoman Empire. Transjordan, 1850–1921*. Cambridge University Press: Cambridge.

Rosen-Ayalon, M. (1989) *Early Islamic Monuments of al-Haram al-Sharif*. Institute of Archaeology of the Hebrew University of Jerusalem (Qedem 28): Jerusalem.

Roujon, Y. and Vilan, L., with Filicoteaux, V. and Guignard, M. (1997) *Le Midan: Actualité d'une Faubourg Ancien de Damas*. Institut Français de Damas, CEAA Ville Orientales: Damascus.

Saidel, B. (2000) Matchlocks, flintlocks, and saltpetre: the chronological implications for the use of matchlock muskets among Ottoman-period bedouin in the Southern Levant. *International Journal of Historical Archaeology* 4/3, 191–216.

Saidel, B. (2008a) Smoking out Ottoman sites in northern Sinai, Egypt: the use of clay tobacco pipes for identifying the nature of settlements in the Ottoman period. *Palestine Exploration Quarterly* 140, 559–69.

Saidel, B. (2008b) The Bedouin tent: an ethno-archaeological portal to antiquity or a modern construct? Pp. 465–86 in Barnard and Wendrich 2008.

Salam, O. and Zilberman, Y. (1986) Jerusalem water supply in the sixteenth and seventeenth century. *Cathedra* 41, 91–106.

Sauvaget, J. (1935–45) Un relais de Barîd mamelouk. Pp. 41–48 in *Mélanges Gaudefroy-Demombynes*. Institut français d'archéologie orientale: Cairo.

Sauvaget, J. (1937) Les caravanserais Syriens du Hadjdj de Constantinople. *Ars Islamica* 4, 98–121.

Scham, S. (2006) History and anthropology of tribes and tribalism in Jordan. *Near Eastern Archaeology* 69:1, 29.

Schick, R. (1995) *The Christian Communities of Palestine from Byzantine to Islamic Rule. A Historical and Archaeological Study*. Darwin Press: Princeton.

Schlumberger, D. (1986) *Qasr el-Heir el-Gharbi*. Geuthner: Paris.

Schumacher, G. (1886) *Across the Jordan: being an exploration and survey of part of Hauran and Jaulan* (with additions by L. Oliphant and G. Le Strange). Richard Bentley and Son: London.

Shaaban, T.M. (1988) Suudi Arabistanin Kuzyinde bulunan Osmanlı dönemine ait Kaleler ve Camiler, Ankara 1988, 297s. Ankara Universitesi, Social Sciences Institute.

Sharon, M. (1999) *Corpus Insriptonum Arabicarum Palaestinae (CIAP)*. Vol. 2. Brill: Leiden, Boston, Köln.

Shindo, Y. (1996) Islamic glass bracelets found in the Red Sea region. Pp. 269–76 in *Annales du 13e Congres de l'Association Internationale pour l'Histoire du Verre (Pays-Bas, 28 août–1 septembre 1995)*. AIHV: Lochem, Netherlands.

Shyrock, A. (1995) Popular genealogical nationalism in Jordan. *Comparative Studies in Society and History* 37, No. 2.

Silverman, H. (1994) The Archaeological Identification of an ancient Peruvian pilgrimage centre. *World Archaeology* 26.1, 1–18.

Simpson, St.J. (1995) Death and burial in the Late Islamic Near East: some insights from archaeology and ethnography, Pp. 240–51 in S. Campbell and A. Green (eds), *The Archaeology of Death in the Ancient Near East*. Oxbow: Oxford.

Simpson, St.J. (1999) Modern glass melon beads from Syria and Lebanon. *Bead Study Trust Newsletter* 34 (winter), 3.

Simpson, St.J. (2000a) The clay pipes. Pp. 147–257 in R.P. Harper and D. Pringle, *et al.*, *Belmont Castle. The Excavation of a Crusader Stronghold in the Kingdom of Jerusalem*. Oxford University Press on behalf of the Council for British Research in the Levant: Oxford.

Simpson, St.J. (2000b) Vice or Virtue? Early Reactions to the Spread of Tobacco in Arabia. *Bulletin of the Society for Arabian Studies* 5, 14–18.

Simpson, St.J. (2002) Ottoman Pipes from Zir'in (Tell Jezreel). *Levant* 34, 159–72.

Simpson, St.J. (2008) Late Ottoman pipes from Jerusalem. Pp. 443–46 in K. Prag (ed.), *Excavations by K.M. Kenyon in Jerusalem 1961–1967*. Vol. V. Levant Supplementary Series. Oxbow: Oxford.

Simpson, St.J. (ed.) (2011) *Turkish delight: studies in Late Ottoman and related clay pipe traditions*. Archaeopress: Oxford.

Simpson, St.J. (forthcoming) The smokers' pipes. In D. Pringle and J. de Meulemeester (eds), *Excavations at 'Aqaba Castle*.

Skeel, C. (1926) The cattle trade between Wales and England from the fifteenth to the nineteenth centuries. Pp. 135–58 in *Transactions of the Royal Historical Society*, 4th Series, vol. 9.

Smith, C.K. (2002) Kawkaban, the key to Sinan Pasha's campaign in the Yemen (March 1569–March 1571). *Proceedings of the Seminar for Arabian Studies* 32, 287–94.

Smith, G.R. (2001) al-Yaman, 3. History. *Encyclopaedia of Islam*, 2nd edn, vol. 11, 271–74.

Sode, T. (1996) *Anatolske Glasperler*. Forlage Thott: Copenhagen.

Sourdel-Thoumine, J. (2008) al-Balka. *Encyclopaedia of Islam*, 2nd edn, vol. 9, 97.

Spaer, M. (1992) The Islamic bracelets of Palestine. *Journal of Glass Studies* 34, 44–62.

Spaer, M. *et al.* (2001) *Ancient Glass in the Israel Museum. Beads and Other Small Objects*. The Israel Museum: Jerusalem.

Steiner, M. (1995) Glass Bracelets from Tall Abu Sarbut. *Studies in the History and Archaeology of Jordan* 5, 537–39.

Stern, E. (1978) *Excavations at Tel Mevorakh (1973–1976). Part One: From the Iron Age to the Roman Period*. Qedem 9. The Hebrew University of Jerusalem: Jerusalem.

Stern, E. (1997) Excavation of the Courthouse Site at 'Akko: The Pottery of the Crusader and Ottoman Periods. *'Atiqot* 31, 35–70.

Stopford, J. (1994) Some approaches to the archaeology of pilgrimage. *World Archaeology* 26.1, 52–72.

Tamari, S. (1982) *Darb al-Hajj in Sinai; an Historical-Archaeological Study*. Serie VIII, vol. XXV, fasc. 4. Academia Nazionale dei Lincei: Rome.

Tate, R. (2007) Landscape of pilgrimage: the Hajj and the Sinai: pilgrimage in the Middle Islamic Period (*c.* AD 1000–1400/ AH 390–800). Paper presented at remembering landscapes conference, Columbia University, New York, NY. April 14, 2007.

Tezcan, H. (1966) *al-Astaar al-Haramayn*. Istanbul.

al-Thenayian, M.A.R. (1999/2000) *An Archaeological Study of the Yemeni Highland Pilgrim Route Between Sana and Mecca*. Deputy Ministry of Antiquities and Museums: Riyadh.

al-Tikriti, N. (2005) The Hajj as justifiable self-exile: Şehzade Korkud's Wasīlat al-ahbāb (915–916/1509–1510). *Al-Masaq: Islam & the Medieval Mediterranean*, vol. 17, issue 1, 125, 22.

Tomka, G. (2005) Cserép pipafejek az ónodi vár ásatásaiból. *Herman Ottó Múzeum Évkönyve* [Miskolc] 44, 607–26.

Toombs, L.E. (1985) *Tell el-Hesi. Modern military trenching and Muslim Cemetery in Field I, Strata I–II*. The Joint Archaeological Expedition to Tell el-Hesi, Vol. 2. Wilfrid Laurier University Press: Waterloo, Ontario.

Tresse, R. (1937) *Le Pélierinage Syrien aux Villes Saintes de l'Islam*. Impremerie Chaumette: Paris.

Tristram, H.B. (1873) *The land of Moab. Travels and discoveries on the East side of the Dead Sea and the Jordan*. Harper and Brothers: New York.

Tristram, H.B. (1874) *The land of Moab. Travels and Discoveries on the East Side of the Dead Sea and the Jordan*. John Murray: London.

Turner, V. and Turner, E. (1978) *Image and Pilgrimage in Christian Culture*. Columbia University Press: New York.

Tütüncü, M. (2006) *Turkish Jerusalem (1516–1917) (Ottoman Inscriptions from Jerusalem and Other Palestinian Cities)*. SOTA: Haarlem.

Van Berchem, M. (1920–23) *Matériaux pour un corpus inscriptonum arabicorum Part II; Syrie du Sud-II, Jérusalem Ville*. Institut français d'archéologie orientale: Cairo.

Van Berchem, M. (1978) Sur la route des villes saintes. Pp. 615–28 in *Opera Minora*. Slatkine: Geneva.

Van der Lingen, B. (2003) Smoking in the Ottoman empire and an introduction to the clay tobacco pipes from the Beirut Souks excavations. *Berytus* 47, 129–42.

Van der Steen, E.J. (1997) What happened to Arabic geometric pottery in Beirut? *Aram Periodical* 9, 121–27.

Van Leeuwen, R. (1999) *Waqfs and Urban Structures; The case of Ottoman Damascus*. Brill: Leiden.

Varthema, L. (1863) *The Travels of Ludico di Varthema in Egypt, Syria, Arabia Deserta and Arabia Felix, in Persia, Ethiopia and India, AD 1503 to 1508*. Trans. W. Jones, ed. G.P. Badger. Hakluyt Society: London.

Varthema, L. di (1928) *The Itinerary of Ludovico di Varthema of Bologna 1502–8*. Ed. Sir Richard Temple. Hakluyt Society: London.

Vassiliev, A. (1998) *The History of Saudi Arabia*. Saqi Books: London.

Vidal, F.S. (2008) al-Hidjr. *Encyclopaedia of Islam*, 2nd edn, vol. 3, 365b.

Volney, C.-F. (1787) *Voyage en Syrie et en Egypte pendant les années 1783, 1784 et 1785*. Volland et Desenne: Paris.

Vroom, J. (1996) Coffee and archaeology: A note on a Kütahya Ware find in Boeotia, Greece. *Pharos* 4, 5–19.

Vroom, J. (2003) *After Antiquity. Ceramics and Society in the Aegean from the 7th to the 20th century AC. A Case Study from Boeotia, Central Greece*. University of Leiden: Leiden.

Vroom, J. (2006) Lunch at the Topkapi Palace: The archaeology of the table during Ottoman times. Pp. 143–61 in M. Carroll, D. Hadley and H. Willmott (eds), *Consuming Passions:*

Dining from Antiquity to the Eighteenth Century. Alan Sutton: Stroud.

Wagstaff, M. (2009) Evliya Çelebi, the Mani and the Fortress of Kefela. In Peacock 2009.

Wallin, G.A. (1850/1854) [1979] Narrative of a journey from Cairo to Medina and Mecca, by Suez, Araba, Tawila, Al-Jauf, Jubbe Hail Nejd in 1845. *Journal of the Royal Geographical Society* 24 (1854), 114–207; Notes taken during a journey through part of Northern Arabia in 1848. *Journal of the Royal Geographical Society* 20 (1850), 114–207, 293–344. Reprinted in 1928 with new prefaces as *Travels in Arabia (1845 and 1848)*. Falcon-Oleander: London and New York.

Walmsley, A. (2007) *Early Islamic Syria; an Archaeological Assessment*. Duckworth Debates in Archaeology. Duckworth: London.

Ward, C. (2000) The Sadana Island Shipwreck. A mid-eighteenth Century Treasure Trove. Pp. 185–202 in U. Baram and L. Carroll (eds), *A Historical Archaeology of the Ottoman Empire: Breaking New Ground*. Kluwer Academic/Plenum Publishers: New York.

Ward, C. and Baram, U. (2006) Global markets, local practice: Ottoman-period clay pipes and smoking paraphernalia from the Red Sea Shipwreck at Sadana Island, Egypt. *International Journal of Historical Archaeology* 10/2 (June), 135–58.

Whitcomb, D. (1988) Islamic archaeology in Aden and the Hadhramaut. Pp. 176–263 in D.T. Potts (ed.), *Araby the Blest*. Carsten Niebhur Institute: Copenhagen.

Wilkinson, T.J. (2003) *Archaeological Landscapes of the Near East*. University of Arizona: Tuscon.

Wilson, C.W. (1865) *Ordnance Survey of Jerusalem*. Ariel: Jerusalem (reprint 1980).

Wilson, C.W. (1881–84) *Picturesque Palestine Sinai and Egypt*. 4 vols. S. Virtue: London.

al-Wohaibi, A. (1973) *The Northern Hijaz in the writings of the Arab geographers 800–1150*. Al-Risalah Publishers: Beirut. [1969 PhD, SOAS, London]

Wright, J.K. (1927) Northern Arabia: The explorations of Alois Musil. *Geographical Review* 17, 177–206.

Wrightman, G.J. (1993) *The Walls of Jerusalem from the Conquest from the Canaanites to the Mamluks*. Mediterranean Archaeology Supplement 4: Sydney.

Zarins, J., Whalen, N., Ibrahim, M., al-Jawad Mursi, A. and Khan, M. (1980) Comprehensive archaeological survey program. Preliminary report on the central and southwestern provinces survey: 1979. *Atlal* 4, 9–36, pls 1–33.

Ziadeh, G. (1995) Ottoman ceramics from Ti'innik, Palestine. *Levant* 27, 209–45.

Pre-Islamic Sources

Nottitia Dignatatum. Ed. O. Seeck. Weidmann, Berlin (1876). Reprinted Frankfurt 1962.

Arabic and Turkish Primary Sources

Abu al Fida' (d. 1332) *al-Mukhtasar fi akhbar al-bashar*. Cairo 1960.

al-Baladhuri, *Futuh al-Buldan*. Ed. M.J. de Goeje. Leiden 1866.

Evliya Çelebi (1996) *Seyahatnâmesi*. 10 vols. Yapi Kredi Yayinlari Ltd. Şti: Beyoğlu, İstanbul.

Evliya Çelebi, trans. H. Stephan (1934–44) Evliya Tschelebi's Travels in Palestine (1648–1650), with note by L.A. Mayer, *QDAP* 4, 103–8, 154–64; 5, 69–73; 84137–156; 9, 81–104. Facsimile edn in one volume with new pagination and index. Ariel Press: Jerusalem 1980.

al-Ghazzi, Najm al-Din Muhammad (d. 1061/1650) *al-Kawakib al-Sa'ira bi a'yan al-ma'a al-'ashira*. Ed. J. Jabbur. 3 vols. Beirut 1945–59.

al-Harbi, *Kitab al-Mamasik wa amakin, Turuq al-Hajj wa ma 'din al-Jazira*. Ed. al Jasir. Riyadh 1968.

al-Hibri, 'Abd al-Rahman (1975) Menasik-i mesalik I. Ed. S. Ilgürel. *Tarih Enstitüsü Dergesi* 6, 112–18.

Ibn Battuta (1958) *The Travels of Ibn Battuta, AD 1325–1354*. Trans. with revisions and notes by H.A.R. Gibb. Vol. 1. Hakluyt Society, Cambridge University Press: Cambridge.

Ibn Battuta *Voyages*. Ed. and trans. C. Defrémery and B.R. Sanguinetti. 4 vols. Paris 1853–58.

Ibn Battuta (1981) *Rihala Ibn Battuta*. Ed. J. al-Din Ramadi. Dar al Kitab: Beirut.

Ibn Jubayr (1949–51) *Ibn Jobair. Voyages*. Trans. and annotated by M. Gaudefroy-Demomboynes. 2 vols. Paul Geuthner: Paris

Ibn Khurdadhbih (d. 893–894) *Kitab al-Masalik wa- 'l-Mamalik* [*The Book of Routes and Provinces*]. Ed. M.J. de Goeje. Leiden 1889.

Ibn Rustah, Abu 'Ali Ahmad b. 'Umar, *Kitab al-A 'laq al Nafisah*. Ed. M.J. de Goeje. Leiden 1891–92.

Ibn Sa'd, *Kitab al-Tabaqat al-Kabir*. Ed. E. Mittoch and E. Sachau. 2 vols. Leiden 1904–7.

Ibn Tulun, Shams al-Din Muhammad b. 'Ali (d. 953/1546) *Mufakahat al-khillan fi hawadith al-zaman*. Ed. M. Mustafa. 2 vols. Cairo 1962–64. Extracts from it ed. R. Hartmann, 'Das Tubinger Fragment der chronik des Ibn Tulun', schriften der Konigsberger Geselschaft, 3 Jahr, Heft 2, Berlin 1926, pp. 118–70.

Ibn al-Qari, Raslan 'al-Wuzara' al-ladhim hakamu Dimashq', *Wulat Dimshaq fi ahd al- 'Uthmani*. Ed. S. al-Din al-Munajjid. Damascus 1949.

al-Idrissi (1154) *Nuzhat al-Mushtaq*. Ed. and trans. R.A. Brandel, *Om och ur arabiske geografen Idrisi*. Akademisk afhandling. Uppsala 1894.

Kâtip Çelebi (Mustafa ibn 'Abd Allah, Hajji Khalifa), *Cihannüma*. Istanbul AH 1145/1732–33.

Mehmed Edib ibn Mehmed Derviş, *Menasik-i hacc-i şerif* . Constantinople AH 1232/ 1816–17.

al-Qaramani al-Dimashqi, Ahmad b. Yusef b. Ahmad (d. 1019/1611) *Akhbar al-duwal wa athar al-uwal*. Ed. M. Amin b. Ahmad al-Baghdadi. Baghdad 1282/1865.

Qudamah, b. Ja'far al-Baghdadi, *Nubdhah min Kitab al-kharaj wa san'at al-Kitabah*. Ed. M.J. de Goeje. Leiden 1967.

al-Tabarî, Abû Ja'far Muhammad b. Jarîr, *Ta'rîkh al-rusul wa-l-mulûk*. Ed. M.J. de Goeje *et al*. Brill: Leiden 1879–1901.

Sabri, Eyyüb, *Mir'at 'ül-Harameyn*. Vol. 3. Istanbul AH 1306/1888–89.

al-Waqidi, *Kitab al-Maghazi*. Ed. M. Jones. London 1912.

Yaqut, ibn Abdullah al-Hamawi al-Rumi al-Baghdadi (1995) *Mu'jam al-Buldan* (1179–1229). 6 vols. Dar al-Sader: Beirut.

Arabic Manuscript Sources

Anon, *Report to Muhammad 'Ali Pasha*. Transcription R. Abu Jaber. Amman, Jordan (location of original unknown).

Murtada b. Ali b. 'Alawan, *Rihala* [Untitled] Berlin (Ahlwardt No. 6137 = Wetzsten II no. 1860, fol. 102a–115b).

Turkish Archival Sources

MD = Mühimme Defteri

TKS-E = Topkapi Saray Arşivi Evrak (Topkapi Palace Archives, loose documents)

BA-Cevdet/Askeri = Collection of loose documents, military affairs subdivision, Başbakanlik Arşivi, Istanbul

Mühimme Defteri, vols i–ivc, years 961–1052/1553–1643, Başbakanlik Arşivi, Istanbul

Modern Archives

Abdel Azzez, M., al-Salhi, T. and al-Khreasheh, E. (2002) 'Restoration and Maintenance of Unizeh Castle Project 2002'. Unpublished Report, Archives of Department of Antiquities, 'Amman, Hashemite Kingdom of Jordan.

Creswell, K.A.C. (1917/18) Manuscript describing monuments in occupied enemy territory (Syria, Lebanon, Jordan and Palestine) currently held in Mandate Archives of Rockefeller Museum, Jerusalem.

Department of Antiquities of Jordan (2004) Press release relating to restoration work at Qal'at 'Unaiza [ARABIC] (April–July 2004).

PAM (Palestine Antiquities Museum). Archives of the Department of Antiquities during the British Mandate in Palestine 1918–48.

Index

Abbasids 9, 40, 58
Abd al-Hamid II (Ottoman Sultan r. 1876–1909) 74, 76
Abd al-Majid (Ottoman Sultan r. 1839–69) 158, 159
abjad 161
ablaq 54, 58
Abu al-Fida' 65, 134
'Abyaar Tandheef see Wadi al-Qurra
'Abyar 'Ali 221
'Abyar Ghannum 148–49
'Abyar Salih see Medain Saleh
Acheh 27
Acre 177, 188, 195
Adana 53
Aden 18, 199
'Adhra see Udruh
Africa 2–3, 6, 25, 27
African Association of London 6
Ahmed I (Ottoman Sultan r. 1603–7) 150
Ahmed III (Ottoman Sultan r. 1703–30) 160
Aidhab see 'Aydhab
'Ajlun 12, 160
Akkerman fortress Ukraine 197
Aleppo 8, 10
Alexandria 6
amir al-Hajj 10, 26, 27, 37, 53, 54, 55, 74, 114, 115, 131
'Amman 7, 69, 211
Anatolia 35, 53
animals 34–36, 93, 112, 113, 138, 141
Antioch 53

'Aqaba 2, 9, 12, 46–48, 113, 196, 198
'Aqaba Hijazi see Fassu'a
'Aqabat 'Ayla see 'Aqaba
Artas 42
'Aydhab 2, 5, 9
Aydinili Abdullah Pasha (Governor of Damascus 1730–33) 33, 92, 126
'Ayla see 'Aqaba
Ayyubids 12–16, 39, 40, 141

Baghdad 9–10, 197
Baghras 53
Bahrain 17
al-Bakri 107
Balkans 24
Balqa see Dab'a
bangles 199–202
Bani Hillal 58
Banu Hudhayl 5
Banu Sakhr 27, 66, 74, 147
Barakat II sharif of Mecca 17
Barakat Trust Oxford xii
Basra 18, 19, 197
Batavian 174–76
bathhouses 12, 13, 32, 52, 53, 54, 109, 135, 153,
Baybars 9, 10
Bayezid II (Ottoman Sultan r. 1481–1512) 17
Bayt Jibrin 25, 38, 45
beads 198–99
Bedouin 25–27, 34, 35, 44, 90, 115, 131, 147, 196, 211
Beilan 52

Beirut 195
Bell, Gertrude 66, 68
Berbers 147
Bethlehem 42, 43
Bianchi 5–6
Bi'r al Waalida see Valide Kuyusu
Bi'r al-Zumurrud see Zumurrud
birka see cisterns
Birka al-Mu'azzam see Mu'azzam
Birkat al-'Adham see Mu'azzam
Boeotia 190
Bosra 7, 9, 10–12, 12–13, 20
bridges 33, 84, 87, 89, 91–95, 112
British Institute at 'Amman for Archaeology and History (BIAAH) 1
British School of Archaeology in Jerusalem 42
Brünnow, R. E. 7, 16, 32, 74, 93, 95
Burckhardt, J. L. 6, 55, 73, 92, 110, 196
Byzantine 9, 15, 58, 180, 181, 186, 187

Cairo 15, 50, 115, 198
camels 32, 35–36
canal 24
Candia (Crete) 5
çaprak 208
caravanserais 1, 3, 12, 14, 15, 16, 24, 45, 52–53, 99, 100
CBRL (Council for British Research in the Levant) 173
ceramics 174–89
chibouk see pipes

Chinese porcelain see porcelain
cisterns 44, 47, 49, 64, 69, 75, 79,
    83–84, 87, 95, 96, 104, 105, 108,
    112, 113, 121, 128, 129, 131,
    136–37, 139–40, 142, 149, 159,
    165, 214–22
coffee 190, 197, 210
coins 204, 206
Constantinople 5, 17, 18, 20, 52
Creswell 56
Cyprus 39, 158

Dab'a 7, 24, 68–76, 155, 162, 188,
    195, 214–15
Damascus 15, 27, 29, 32, 34, 35,
    51–54, 58, 60, 65, 66, 68, 73, 76,
    80, 81, 92, 101, 115, 126
Dar al-Hamra 142–43
Darb Zubayda 1–2, 3, 9, 29, 33,
    113
death 35, 75
Dhahir al-'Umar see Zahir al-
    'Umar
Dhar al-'Unaiza see 'Unaiza
Dhat al-Hajj 20, 27, 130–32, 156–
    57, 162, 217
Domaszewski, A. von 7, 16, 32,
    74, 93, 95
Dome of the Rock (Jerusalem) 27
Doshaq 15–16
Doughty, C. 6–7, 29–32, 60, 73–74,
    93, 102, 110, 115, 126, 131–32,
    135
Dutch 25

École Biblique et Archéologique
    Française 7, 160
Egypt 2–3, 19, 24
Elijah 138–39
environmental finds 208
Equites Dalmatae Illyriciani 64
Ethiopia 212
Evliya Çelebi 5, 29, 45, 55, 58,
    60, 71, 81, 90, 101, 109, 113,
    125–26, 135, 137, 138

Fassu'a 24, 112–21, 156, 162, 216
Field, H. 15–16, 74, 82
firearms 22, 27, 206
firmans 25, 40, 42, 44, 50
Flavius Paulus 225
food 190
al-Fudayn see Mafraq

Gaza 40
Ghabarib 55
ghadir 218, 222

glass 198–202
glass bangles 199–202
glass beads 198–99
Gray Hill, S. 66, 81, 102, 110
Great Arab Revolt Project 206
Gujerat 24

Hadiyya 20, 34, 100, 150–52, 221
Hafira 154
Hama 12, 53, 134
Hammam al-Manjak 13
al-Harbi 14, 70, 108, 113, 124,
    134
Harun al-Rashid (Abbasid caliph r.
    706–809) 9
Hasa (Jordan) 7, 24, 85–95, 156,
    162, 188–89, 195, 215–16
al-Hasa (Saudi Arabia) 17–19, 25
Hasye 52
Hawran 35, 197
Hebron 45–48, 198, 201
Hejaz Railway 24, 67, 85
Hesban 12, 69, 195
Hijaz 17, 18, 19
Homs 53
Hormuz 17, 25
Horvat 'Aqav 204
Howetat Bedouin 115
Humeima 9
Hungary 17, 197
Husayn Pasha 5, 19, 90, 101

Ibn Battuta 4–5, 10–12, 32, 68, 113,
    130–31, 134, 137–38
Ibn Fahd 10
Ibn Jubayr 4, 9
Ibn Juzayy 4
Ibn Khurdhadhibih 16, 122, 137
Ibn Saud, Muhammad 18
Ibn Taghribirdi 10
Ibrahim Ottoman Sultan (r. 1640–
    48) 197
al-Idrissi 12, 130
Imari porcelain 174–75, 189
India 3, 6, 199
Indian Ocean 24, 199
inscriptions 66, 109, 120, 135,
    155–63
Iran 3, 4, 53
Iraq 18, 33
al-Istakhri 108
Istanbul see Constantinople
Iznik 176

janissaries 45, 73, 101, 138, 161,
    197
jarda 51

Jaussen, A. 7, 74, 93, 110, 132,
    135
Java 6
Jedda 4, 5, 6, 10, 19, 24, 36
Jenin 25, 45
Jerusalem 5, 25, 27, 38, 39, 42, 44,
    46, 56, 58, 61, 136, 148, 160,
    162, 176, 177, 179, 195, 196,
    197, 198, 204, 224
Jisr al-Shughur 52
Jiza see Zizia
Jordan 57–129

Ka'ba 5, 146
Kara Mughurt see Baghras
Karak 4, 9, 10, 14, 15, 20, 196,
    197
Karbala 19
Kefala 50
al-Khadr see Elijah
Khan Danun 12, 55
khans 36, 45, 53, 54
Khan al-Tujjar 25, 38, 44–45
Khan al-Zebib 9, 10, 68, 73, 225
Khirbat al-Mafjar 224
Khirbat Makhloul 14
Kings Highway 15, 16
Kiswa 54
Kiswah (covering of Ka'ba) 10
Konya 53
Kufa 2
Kutahya (ceramics) 76–77, 185,
    188–89

Lahun 12, 14
Landmarks 34
Lawrence, T. E. 7, 197
al-Lejjun 12, 14
Ludivico di Varthema 29

Ma'an 7, 10, 16, 20, 24, 29, 36, 105–
    12, 156, 162, 197, 213, 216
machicolation 25, 58, 61, 76, 82,
    94, 103, 108, 111, 112, 120, 121,
    126–27, 132, 136, 139, 142, 143,
    146, 149, 150, 152
Madaba 61
Mafraq 57–58
mahmal 10, 20
Mamluks 9–16, 20, 24, 27
Ma'mun (Abbasid caliph r. 813–33)
    225
Mansa Musa 27
al-Maqdisi 108
Marj Dabiq 17
Mashatta 7, 9, 11, 73, 224
Mausser rifle 22, 206

Maydan (Damascus) 32, 54

Mecca 2, 4, 5, 12, 13, 20, 24–25, 27–28, 32, 33–35, 37, 51, 54, 60, 74, 108–9, 130, 131, 134, 145, 147, 159, 208

Medain Saleh 6, 7, 24, 29, 34, 145–47, 219–20

Medina 2, 4, 5, 9, 10, 12, 20, 25, 27, 29, 36, 37, 65, 130, 138, 146, 147–48, 150, 151, 152, 153, 154

Mehmed II (Ottoman Sultan r. 1444–46 and 1451–81) 20

Mehmed IV (Ottoman Sultan r. 1648–87) 135, 150

Mehmed Edib 5–6, 32, 34, 52, 56, 73, 81, 100, 102, 109–10, 113–14, 131–32, 135, 137, 138, 139, 141, 142, 146, 147, 148, 149, 150, 151, 152, 153, 154

Merril, S. 60

Mesissen 176, 188, 189

metalwork 204–7

Midhat Pasha 19

Mongols 9

Mshatta see Mashatta

Mu'azzam 34, 141–42, 160–61, 162, 218

Mu'azzam 'Isa (Ayyubid Sultan r. 1218–27) 13

Mudawwara 12, 24, 121–29, 185–88, 195, 197, 211, 217

Mughals 27, 32

Muhammad (Prophet) 10, 13, 134–35, 154

Muhammad Ali Pasha (r. 1805–48) 73, 102, 92–93, 115, 126, 131, 135, 214

mukawwams 34, 35–36

Murad III (Ottoman Sultan r. 1574–95) 100

Murad IV (Ottoman Sultan r. 1623–24) 42, 150, 197

Murtada b. 'Ali b. 'Alawan 5, 81, 90, 101–2, 109, 113, 131, 135, 138

Musil, A. 7, 81, 116

Mustafa III Ottoman Sultan (r. 1757–74) 162

Mustapha Pasha 5, 70, 88, 99–100, 124–25

Muzayrib 12, 13–14, 32, 33, 48, 55–56

Nabateans 6, 7, 9, 77, 182

al-Nabk 53

Nablus 35, 101

Al-Nablusi, 'Abd al-Gahni (1641–1731) 131, 135, 197

Najaf 3

Najd 18

Nakhlatayn 34, 152–53, 208, 221

Nazareth 196

Nikola ibn Ilyas 161

oral history 8

Osman II (Ottoman Sultan r. 1618–22) 142, 161–62

Ottomans 20–28, 39–40, 48–50

Palestine 27–28, 38–50

Palmyra 35

Payas 53

Peake Pasha 8, 80, 109

Petra 6, 7, 66, 106

Photographs 7, 95

pipes (tobacco) 190–97, 209

porcelain 174–76, 188

Portuguese 21, 24–25

pottery 174–89, 210

Qalandariyya 32, 137–41

Qal'at Balqa see Dab'a

Qal'at Birkat al-'Adham see Mu'azzam

Qal'at Burak 25, 42–44, 162

Qal'at Dab'a see Dab'a

Qal'at Dhat al-Hajj see Dhat al-Hajj

Qal'at Fassu'a see Fassu'a

Qal'at al-Hasa see Hasa

Qal'at Ma'an see Ma'an

Qal'at Mu'azzam see Mu'azzam

Qal'at Mudawwara see Mudawwara

Qal'at Mudiq 52

Qal'at al-Nakhl 50

Qal'at Qatrana see Qatrana

Qal'at Ras al-'Ayn see Ras al-'Ayn

Qal'at Sai 25, 49–50

Qal'at Tabuk see Tabuk

Qal'at al-Ukhaydhir see Ukhaydhir

Qal'at 'Unaiza see 'Unaiza

Qal'at Zumurrud see Zumurrud

Qasr al-Ablaq 53

Qasr al-Hayr al-Gharbi 224

Qasr Ibrim 25

Qasr Mshatta (see Mashatta)

Qasr Shebib 14, 20, 58–61

Qasr al-Tuba 224

Qastal 9, 14, 224

al-Qataif (Syria) 52

al-Qatif (Saudi Arabia) 18, 25

Qatrana 7, 20, 24, 77–85, 215

Qenna 50

Qianlong 175

Qubbat al-Hajj 54

Quran 10, 34

Qusayr 'Amra 7

Quseir 2, 25, 49–50, 198, 199

Quseir al-Qadim 199

al-Rabadah 2

Ramtha 58, 214

Ras al-'Ayn 25, 38–42

Red Sea 3, 24, 25, 113, 196, 199

al-Resten 52

roads 29–34, 95

Saffavids 18–25

Safuriyya 61

Sahara 3

Salah al-Din 15

Saldin see Salah al-Din

Salt 12, 61, 69, 196

San'a 2, 18

Sanamayn 10, 33, 55

Santiago di Compostella 3, 29

Saudi Arabia 1–2, 130–54

Savignac, R. 7, 74, 93, 110, 132, 135

Sawra see Valide Kuyusu

Selim I (Ottoman Sultan r. 1512–20) 20, 51, 53, 55, 56, 58, 76

Selim II (Ottoman Sultan r. 1566–74) 81, 110

Shajwa see Nakhlatayn

Shaq al-'Ajuz see Dar al-Hamra

Shawbak 4, 9, 15, 81, 93

Shi'a 3, 18, 19

Sidon 27

Sinai 2, 196, 199

Sinan (Ottoman architect) 27, 210

Sinan Pasha (Grand Vizier) 44

smoking see tobacco

Sorar see Mudawwara

Sri Lanka 6

stables 44

Suakin 3

Suba 195

Sudan 3, 25

Suknhe 35

Sulayman I (Ottoman Sultan r. 1520–66) 80, 81, 109, 131, 135, 138, 147, 156, 157, 159

Sulayman Pasha 24, 100, 102

Sulayman the Magnificent see Sulayman I

sürre 55, 211

Syria 51–56, 211

Tabuk 12, 20, 132–37, 157–59, 162, 217
Tafila 92
Takiyya see Tekiyya
Tariq al-Bint 210
Tayma 141
Tekiyya 52, 76, 210
Tell el-Hesi 179, 204, 206
Tell Qaimun see Yoqne'am
tents 36–37
textiles 208
al-Thaniyya 12, 14–15
Ti'innik 177
tobacco 195–97
Tophane 196
Trajan 9
Triploi (Lebanon) 198
Tristram, H. 32, 66
tüfneks (muskets) 27
al-Tur 175, 177, 181, 199

Udruh 16, 134, 212–13
Ukhaydhir 20, 32, 34, 159–60, 162, 217–18
al-'Ula 20, 27, 147–48
'Umar ibn'Abd al-Aziz (Umayyad caliph r. 717–20) 134, 153
Umayyads 40, 58, 61, 108, 109, 223–26
'Unaiza 20, 95–105, 164–73, 174–85, 190–94, 216
al-'Uqayr 25

Valide Kuyusu 150, 220
di Varthema see Ludivico di Varthema
Via Maris 38, 44
Via Militaris 32, 77, 99
Via Nova Traiana 32
Volney, C. F. 201

Wadi Hanifa 77
Wadi al-Hasa 32, 33, 86, 93, 95

Wadi Mujib 14
Wadi Musa 109
Wadi al-Qurra 153–54, 221
Wadi Ziqlab 196
Wahhabis 18–19, 197

Yaqut al-Hamawi 33, 59, 64, 112, 130, 134, 137
Yemen 2, 17–19, 25, 32–33
yenicheri see janissaries
Yoqne'am 196

Zabid 18, 196
Zahir al-'Umar 18, 27, 196
Zanbakiyya 52
Zar'in see Zir'in
Zarka see Zerka
Zerka 14, 21, 58–61, 214
Zir'in 189, 195, 196
Zizia 12, 14, 20, 21, 61–68, 223, 225–26
Zumurrud 149–50, 220